Becoming a Teacher

fifth edition

Forrest W. Parkay
Washington State University

Beverly Hardcastle Stanford
Azusa Pacific University

Allyn and Bacon

Boston ■ London ■ Toronto ■ Sydney ■ Tokyo ■ Singapore

This book is dedicated to our students—their spirit continually renews us and inspires confidence in the future of teaching in America

Vice President, Editor-in-Chief	Paul A. Smith
Executive Editor and Publisher	Stephen D. Dragin
Senior Developmental Editor	Linda Bieze
Series Editorial Assistant	Barbara Strickland
Senior Marketing Manager	Brad Parkins
Marketing Manager	Rick Muhr
Marketing Assistant	Kim Friberg
Editorial Production Administrator	Rosalie Briand
Editorial Production Service and Photo Research	Helane M. Prottas/Posh Pictures
Composition Buyer	Linda Cox
Manufacturing Buyer	Megan Cochran
Cover Administrator	Linda Knowles
Text Designer	Debbie Schneck/Schneck-DePippo Graphics
Electronic Composition	Dayle Silverman/Silver Graphics

Copyright © 2001, 1998 by Allyn & Bacon
A Pearson Education Company
Needham Heights, MA 02494

Internet: www.abacon.com

Library of Congress Cataloging-in-Publication Data

Parkay, Forrest W.
    Becoming a teacher / Forrest W. Parkay, Beverly Hardcastle Stanford.—5th ed.
      p. cm.
    Includes bibliographical references (p.) and indexes.
    ISBN 0-205-31686-7
      1. Teaching—Vocational guidance. 2. Education—Study and Teaching—United States.
  3. Teachers—United States—Attitudes. 4. Teaching—Computer network resources.
  I. Stanford, Beverly Hardcastle, 1938- II. Title.

LB1775 .P28 2000
371.1'0023'73—dc21

                        00-021334

Printed in the United States of America
10 9 8 7 6 5 4 3 2 1   03 02 01 00

Photo credits begin on p. 622, which constitutes a continuation of the copyright page.

Contents

Part Two

Influences on the Professional Lives of Teachers 78

Dear Mentor 78

3 Ideas and Events That Have Shaped Education in the United States 80

6   Ethical and Legal Issues in Education in the United States   200

14 Education Issues for the Twenty-First Century 544

Preface

We hope that you share our belief that teaching is the world's most important profession. To facilitate your students' journey toward becoming professional teachers, the fifth edition of *Becoming a Teacher* emphasizes the concept of mentoring. For example, the **"Dear Mentor"** feature that opens each part provides practical advice from highly accomplished teachers for meeting the complex challenges of teaching. This popular feature presents the responses of experienced mentor teachers to questions and concerns raised by preservice teachers much like the students who will be using this book. In their responses, the mentors, including award-winning teachers and Teachers of the Year, provide practical and wise advice.

Throughout the fifth edition of *Becoming a Teacher,* we highlight **teacher leadership,** since today's teachers are assuming diverse leadership roles beyond the classroom. For instance, in Chapter 12, **"Teachers as Educational Leaders,"** readers learn about the exciting new leadership roles that await teachers.

New Features of the Fifth Edition

An entirely new chapter, **"Teaching with Technology"** (Chapter 11), provides an up-to-date overview of how educational technologies are influencing schools and the profession of teaching. This chapter describes how teachers are using computer-assisted instruction (CAI); microcomputer-based laboratories (MBL); newsgroups, chat-rooms, and research assignments on the Internet; home-school communication systems; and high-quality hypermedia simulations. Also, each chapter has a new feature, **"Technology Highlights,"** that illustrates how educational technology is related to chapter content.

"Where Do You Stand?" and **"Case to Consider,"** two more new chapter features, give opportunities to reflect on the realities of teaching and on controversial trends and issues that have aroused public opinion and attracted media attention. Among the issues addressed in these features are violence in schools, vouchers and school choice, character education, psychological assessments of teaching candidates, school uniforms, and increased standardized testing.

Organization of the Book

The text has been extensively revised, based on feedback from students and instructors. To allow for expanded coverage of critical trends and issues in education, we have organized the book into four parts: "Part One: The Teaching Profession," "Part Two: Influences on the Professional Lives of Teachers," "Part Three: The Art of Teaching," and "Part Four: Your Teaching Future."

Chapters 1 and 2, which make up Part One, are on the theme of teachers and teaching. After reading these chapters students will be better able to determine whether teaching is a good career choice for them. Among the topics we address are why people choose to teach, the challenges and realities of teaching, the knowledge and skills needed to become a teacher, and how to establish mentoring relationships.

Chapters 3–6 in Part Two take up the foundations of education, which every professional teacher needs to know. These foundational areas include the philosophical, historical, social, cultural, political, financial, and legal dimensions of U.S. education. Philosophical and historical foundations are treated in a new chapter, **"Ideas and Events That Have Shaped Education in the United States"** (Chapter 3).

Chapters 7–11, which make up Part Three, examine student characteristics and the worlds of the classroom and the school. Here, readers learn about characteristics of students at different stages of development, students as learners, the dynamics of classroom life, the curricula that are taught in schools, and teaching with technology.

Finally, in Part Four, Chapters 12–14 discuss issues and trends that will impact each student's quest to become an effective teacher, especially the expanding leadership role of teachers, planning for a successful first year of teaching, international education in a changing world, and the teacher's role in shaping the future of education.

Additional Features and Learning Aids

Included in *Becoming a Teacher* are many additional features we believe will help prepare students for rewarding futures as professional teachers. To guide study, **"Focus Questions"** at the beginning of each chapter reflect the questions posed in the main headings of the text. **Opening scenarios** present decision-making or problem-solving situations to reflect upon and resolve. These situations are referred to again in the chapter and give readers an opportunity to apply new learning in specific problem-solving contexts.

To inspire preservice teachers with the experiences of outstanding teachers, a **"Keepers of the Dream"** feature in each odd-numbered chapter profiles an individual in education whose philosophies and professional contributions reflect a commitment to touching others' lives through teaching. A **"Professional Reflection"** feature in each chapter gives readers an opportunity to reflect on their beliefs and values and on the issues teachers face. This feature is designed to give practice in the applied reflective inquiry that should characterize every teacher's professional life.

In addition, the book includes in its chapter-ending material a **"Teacher's Database"** feature with **online activities** for using the vast resources of the World Wide Web and the Internet to facilitate professional growth. Cyberspace has transformed teaching and learning in many schools and classrooms; and advanced telecommunications will continue to change the way teachers teach and assess students' learning.

This edition of *Becoming a Teacher* continues the popular **"Professional Portfolio"** feature that will enable preservice teachers to document their growth and accomplishments over time. Each chapter includes guidelines for creating a portfolio entry that readers can actually use when they begin teaching; in addition, students may wish to use selected portfolio entries during the process of applying for a first teaching position.

As a further study aid, **"Key Terms and Concepts"** are boldfaced in the text and listed with page cross-references at the ends of chapters. An expanded **"Glossary"** at the end of the book helps readers quickly locate the definitions of key terms and concepts and the text pages on which they appear.

Other end-of-chapter learning aids in this edition include a concise **"Summary"** and suggested **"Applications and Activities."** Applications and activities include journal-writing opportunities in **"Teacher's Journal"** and field experiences in **"Observations and Interviews."** In "Teacher's Journal," we continue a feature that has proved useful and popular with instructors who ask students to keep a teacher's journal to encourage active reflection as they learn about teaching. The short, optional journal-writing activities are based on the "writing-to-learn" and "writing-across-the-curriculum" concepts.

A **Teacher's Resource Guide,** appendices for 12 of 14 chapters, located on the book's Companion Website (http://www.abacon.com/parkay), provides a rich and varied array of materials, sources, strategies, contacts, and data that beginning teachers can rely on for support. These materials—from a checklist for evaluating a school's effectiveness at integrating technology into the teaching-learning process to sample questions to ask during a job interview—will prove extremely valuable in preparing for, and beginning, a first teaching position. Other student resources on the Companion Website include **learning objectives, web links, message boards, chat rooms,** and an **online study guide.**

New with this edition, the **Interactive Companion website,** a restricted-access website available only to students who purchase the text new, offers a case study, audio and video clips, activities, weblinks, key term and concept checks, and a practice test with answer feedback for each chapter of the text.

Supplements for the Instructor

To help you get the most out of using *Becoming a Teacher* with your students, we have provided a number of useful supplements:

- **Instructor's Resource Manual** in which, for each chapter of the text, a Chapter-at-a-Glance organizer correlates chapter outlines, learning objectives, and teaching supplements; an Annotated Lecture Outline provides examples, discussion questions, and student activities; suggestions for additional readings and media extend chapter learning; and handout masters provide additional lecture support materials.
- A **Test Bank** of more than 1,000 questions, including multiple choice items, true/false items, essay questions, case studies, and authentic assessments, plus text page references and answer feedback.
- **Computerized Testing Program,** an integrated suite of testing and assessment tools for Windows and Macintosh platforms.

- Allyn & Bacon Interactive Video for *Becoming a Teacher,* Fifth Edition, featuring news reports from around the country on topics covered in the text.
- Allyn & Bacon Transparencies for Foundations of Education and Introduction to Teaching, a set of one hundred acetate transparencies related to topics in the text.
- Allyn & Bacon Digital Media Archive for Education, a CD-ROM containing PowerPoint lectures, images, video clips, and weblinks arranged topically to import into your own lectures and classroom presentations.

Acknowledgments

Many members of the Allyn and Bacon team provided expert guidance and support during the preparation of the fifth edition of *Becoming a Teacher.* Clearly, Linda Bieze, our developmental editor, heads the list. From suggestions for revision, feedback on draft manuscripts, and skillful coordination of the revision process, from beginning to end, to coordination of the book's supplements, Linda's hard work is deeply appreciated. In addition, the authors benefited from excellent suggestions made by Steve Dragin, Executive Editor and Publisher. His extensive understanding of textbook publishing enriched the fifth edition immeasurably.

The authors extend a very special thanks to Paul A. Smith, Vice President and Editor-in-Chief; Brad Parkins and Richard Muhr, Marketing Managers; Kim Friberg, Marketing Assistant; Helane Prottas, Production Coordinator and Photo and Fine Art Researcher; Rosalie Briand, Production Editor; and Sallie Steele, Indexer, all of whom were steadfast in their support of the fifth edition.

The authors extend a special thanks to the late Jon Walther and to Christi Gilchrist, Research Assistant at Washington State University's Assessment and Evaluation Center. Jon and Christie prepared an outstanding set of Practice Tests for the Interactive Companion Website. Additional thanks go to Steven Million of Winthrop University for writing the Test Bank and test items for the online study guide, plus developing the new technology-based assessment component of the Test Bank. Finally, thanks go to mutindi ndunda and Diane Cudahy of College of Charleston for preparing the Instructor's Resource Manual and Handout Masters for this edition.

We are also grateful to the many people throughout the United States who have used the previous edition and provided suggestions and materials for this edition, including our students. We also wish to thank the following reviewers, who provided concise, helpful suggestions during the developmental stages of this book: Satnam Singh Bhugra, Lansing Community College; C. Lynn Davis, Plymouth State College; Ellen Eckman, Marquette University; Virden Evans, Florida A&M University; Frank Orlando, Rowan University; Lawrence H. Simon, Elon College; and Charles W. Smith, Ohio University.

Forrest W. Parkay appreciates the support of his family, friends, and colleagues during the intensive, months-long revision process. In particular, Judy N. Mitchell, Dean of the College of Education at Washington State University; Dennis Warner, Associate Dean; Donald B. Reed, Chair of the Department of Educational Leadership and Counseling Psychology; and the faculty, teaching assistants, and research assistants in the Department of Educational Leadership and Counseling Psychology gave him much-appreciated encouragement and support. In addition, the following colleagues provided Dr. Parkay with ideas, resources, and suggestions for this edition—Steve Casmar, Cindy Kaag, Merrill M. Oaks, Margaret Paden, Barbara Paulson, Nils Peterson, and Chris Sodorff, all of Washington State University; Robert Leahy, Stetson University; Ralph Karst, Northeastern Louisiana University; Satnam Singh Bhugra, Lansing Community College; Lyn Middleton, University of Wollongong, Australia; Liping Liu, Brevard College; Norma Bailey, Central Michigan University, and Soren Wheeler, American Association for the Advancement of Science. And, for demonstrating the power of professional inquiry, he owes a profound debt to a great teacher, mentor, and friend, Herbert A. Thelen, Professor Emeritus, University of Chicago.

Finally, the personal support Dr. Parkay received from his family was invaluable. During the revision process, the moments he spent with his daughters Anna, Catherine, and Rebecca were very special and brought much-needed balance back into his life. To Arlene, his wife, friend, and helper, he gives a deep thanks. She was always there to provide the support that made the fifth edition possible. Moreover, she made many valuable contributions to the project, not the least of which was obtaining and keeping track of letters of permission. Since the first edition of *Becoming a Teacher* was published in 1990, Arlene's encouragement, patience, and understanding have been remarkable.

Beverly Hardcastle Stanford thanks the many individuals who provided inspiration and assistance in the preparation of the fifth edition of this textbook.

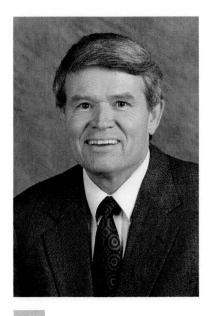

Forrest W. Parkay

Beverly Hardcastle Stanford

Dr. Stanford also appreciates the participation of Azusa Pacific University students who wrote the "Dear Mentor" letters, J. Casey Medlock, Elizabeth Acevedo, Darryl Hampton, and Sara Waltmire. She is grateful to school counselor DonnaLee Brown for writing the case study entitled "Help! Tell Me about This Kid!" She values the inspiration provided by the Keepers of the Dream, 1999 State Teachers of the Year, Peter White of New York and Mary L. Peacher of Oklahoma, and California administrator Marcia McVey. And she recognizes the fine contributions made by the expert teachers who wrote responses to the Dear Mentor letters; Andy Baumgartner, 1999 National Teacher of the Year; Diana Crim, Utah State Teacher of the Year; Joe Bacewicz, Connecticut Teacher of the Year; and Janice James, Kentucky Teacher of the Year.

At Azusa Pacific University, the encouragement and support of President Richard Felix and Provost Patricia Anderson enable faculty to dream about and toil on projects such as this. Stanford is also grateful to Dean Alice Watkins for her ongoing practical and spiritual support. She appreciates her colleagues' sharing of insights on issues addressed in the text and gives special thanks to John Anderson, Nancy Brashear, Dave Harmeyer, Roger Harrell, Dennis Jacobsen, Ruth Kidd, Maria Pacino, Joe Rocha and Lillian Wehmeyer. She pays tribute to her colleagues who teach creatively with this book: Nancy Brashear, Paul Flores, Dennis Jacobsen, and Mimi Zamary.

Finally, Dr. Stanford thanks her students, from those beginning to teach to those leading schools as administrators. She continues to learn from and with them. Her greatest thanks in this endeavor go to her husband, Dick, for his ongoing support and enthusiasm for the project, from the days of the first edition to the present.

Forrest W. Parkay
Beverly Hardcastle Stanford

part one

The Teaching Profession

dear mentor

On Determining Whether Teaching Is the Right Profession for You

Dear Mentor,

As a new college graduate, I am searching for the right profession. Others have encouraged me to teach because I work well with children, but how might I truly know whether teaching is the right profession for me? I definitely desire to be a teacher, yet will my first year be the determining factor?

Sincerely,

J. Casey Medlock

Dear Casey,

As a twenty-three year veteran teacher, I am always excited to share my experiences with those who are considering my profession for themselves. You are wise to ask whether teaching is right for you, but more important, you should ask whether you are right for teaching! An ability to work with students is certainly the most important characteristic of the teaching persona but many others are also important. Some other questions you might ask are

- Do I enjoy the company of children enough to spend most of my day with them?
- Do I have a limitless supply of energy?
- Do I possess a great deal of patience and perseverance?
- Do I enjoy learning and am I able to be a model of life-long learning for my students?
- Am I willing to learn from my students and use what they teach me to improve my ability as a teacher?
- Am I a person of strong convictions who can demonstrate those convictions in every aspect of my life?
- Can I focus on what is important and positive in my work while some around me seem to focus on negativism and dissension?
- Am I willing to be a strong advocate for the teaching profession, who is unwilling to accept the status quo and is prepared to fight to strengthen the profession, despite difficult odds?
- Can I always make the needs of my students the central reason for all that I do in teaching?

In response to your second question, whether your first year will be the determining factor in your success, the answer is both yes and no. I believe that the first year of any new experience has the potential to be a "make or break" year. This is one reason why I have chosen to teach kindergarten. Some children, like my son, find their kindergarten year such an abysmal experience that teachers and parents are never able to readjust their thinking and excite them about school. I have, therefore, made it my goal to ensure an enjoyable, productive kindergarten year for all of my students. What was true for my son in kindergarten seems also to be true for many new teachers—the first year sets the pattern for the rest. Furthermore, in education, the least experienced teachers have traditionally been placed in the most difficult situations. For some, this baptism by fire ignites a tenacity and strength that catapults them into "legendary teacher" status. But for too many, it either turns them away from teaching altogether or disillusions them, making them apathetic, ineffective teachers. I would say that if a teacher survives the first year and can look back with any feelings of accomplishment and a desire to return and try again, then he or she has potential to do well in the field. I doubt that you will find any teacher who believes his or her first year of teaching was the best. Becoming a good teacher is definitely a combination of innate ability, excellent preparation, an abundance of "on the job training," and stubborn persistence.

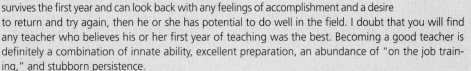

In a society that too often equates success with wealth and recognition, it is sometimes difficult for teachers to see themselves as successful, since they usually do not earn six figures and receive little acclaim for a job whose importance and responsibilities exceed those of almost all other professions. Those teachers who consider themselves successful have learned early in their careers to identify and celebrate their accomplishments! Helping one child is a reward in itself; helping many children is a measurement of great prosperity!

My twenty-three years of teaching have contained many peaks, plateaus, and valleys. But when I look into the faces of my students, I have never doubted the importance of my work. To teach is to impact directly the entire course of human destiny. It is an awesome responsibility, an incredible challenge, and a limitless opportunity for satisfaction and reward.

Sincerely,
Andy Baumgartner
1999 National Teacher of the Year

1

Teaching: Your Chosen Profession

1. Why do you want to teach?

2. What are the challenges of teaching?

3. What is teaching really like?

4. What does society expect of teachers?

5. How do good teachers view their work?

Your first interview for a job as a teacher is today, and you can hardly believe that it was only two years ago that you began to take courses to become a teacher. Several questions about your readiness for teaching occupy your mind while you walk from the faculty parking lot toward the school, which was just selected by the local newspaper as a "blue ribbon" school for its use of technology. "Am I ready? Do I have what it takes to become a good teacher? Can I handle the stress? Do I have sufficient skills to use educational technology in my classroom?"

Approaching the main entrance, you look at the dozens of students playing on the open field next to the building. Their joyful, exuberant sounds this warm late-August morning remind you of your own school days. Some children are moving constantly, running in tight circles and zig-zags as they yell and motion to friends who are also on the move. Others stand near the entrance in groups of two or three, talking and milling about as they wait for the bell signaling the start of the first day of school.

At the bottom of the long stairs leading up to a row of green metal doors, you overhear the conversation of three students.

"It's a great movie. What time should we meet?" the taller of two girls asks. Before her friends can respond, she adds, "My aunt's going to pick me up at four o'clock, so I should be home by four-thirty."

"Let's meet at five o'clock," the other girl says. "I can be ready by then."

"Si, pero no creo que pueda hacerlo para las cinco," the boy says. "Tengo que llevar a mi hermanita a la clinica. ¿Podermos hacerlo después?"

"Bueno, pero no muy tarde," the tall girl says, switching effortlessly to Spanish. "Tenemos que reunirnos con los otros chicos."

"Si, además no quiero perder el comienzo de la película," says the other girl.

Reaching the top of the stairs, you open a door and walk through the vestibule out into a brightly lit hallway. The main office is directly in front of you. To the right of the office door is a bulletin board proclaiming in large red block letters, "Welcome back, students!" Beneath that greeting, in smaller black letters, is another message: "It's going to be a great year!"

Inside the office, you approach the counter on which sits a plastic sign that says "Welcome" in five languages: English, Spanish, Swahili, Chinese, and Russian. You introduce yourself to the school's head secretary. He remains seated behind a gray steel desk covered with loose papers.

"I have an appointment with Ms. Wojtkowski," you inform him. "It's about a replacement for Mr. Medina."

"Good. She's expecting you. Why don't you have a seat over there?" He motions for you to sit on the couch across from the teachers' mailboxes. "She's working with some teachers on setting up a meeting of our Site-Based Council. She ought to be finished in just a few minutes."

While waiting for Ms. Wojtkowski, you think about questions you might be asked. Why did you choose to become a teacher? What is your philosophy of education? How would you use technology in your classroom? What is your approach to classroom management? How would you meet the needs of students from different cultural and linguistic backgrounds? How would you set up a program in your major teaching area? How would you involve parents in the classroom? What are your strengths? Why should the district hire you?

Reflecting on these questions, you admit they are actually quite difficult. Your answers, you realize, could determine whether or not you get the job.

Though predictable, the interview questions just posed are surprisingly challenging. Why did you decide to become a teacher? How will you meet the needs of all students? What do you have to offer students? The answers to these and similar questions depend on the personality and experiences of the person responding. However, they are questions that professional teachers recognize as important and worthy of careful consideration.

The primary purpose of this book is to orient you to the world of education and to help you begin to formulate answers to such questions. In addition, this book will help you answer your own questions about the career you have chosen. What is teaching really like? What are the trends and issues in the profession? What problems can you expect to encounter in the classroom? What kind of rewards do teachers experience?

We begin this book by asking you to examine why you want to become a teacher because we believe that "good teachers select themselves" (Carmichael 1981, 113). They know why they want to teach and what subjects and ages they want to teach. They are active in the choosing process, aware of the options, informed about the attractions and obstacles in the field, and anxious to make their contributions to the profession.

Why Do You Want to Teach?

People are drawn to teaching for many reasons. For some, the desire to teach emerges early and is nurtured by positive experiences with teachers during the formative years of childhood. For others, teaching is seen as a way of making a significant contribution to the world and experiencing the joy of helping others grow and develop. And for others, life as a teacher is attractive because it is exciting, varied, and stimulating.

Desire to Work with Children and Young People

Figure 1.1, based on a national survey of more than 1,300 teachers, shows that most teachers say they began teaching because they wanted to work with young people. Though the conditions under which teachers work may be challenging, their salaries modest, and segments of their communities unsupportive, most teach simply because they care about students.

The day-to-day interactions between teachers and students build strong bonds. Daily contact also enables teachers to become familiar with the personal as well as the academic needs of their students, and this concern for students' welfare and growth outweighs the difficulties and frustrations of teaching. Like the following teachers, they know they can make a difference in students' lives:

> When I was struggling as a kid, one of my teachers was really there for me. She listened to me and supported me when nobody else believed in me. I want to pay her back by helping others like me (Zehm and Kottler 1993, 35).

> [Students] need someone to recognize their uniqueness and specialness and respect it and nurture it (Hansen 1995, 132).

Others, no doubt, love students because they appreciate the unique qualities of youth. They enjoy the liveliness, curiosity, freshness, openness, and trust of young children or the abilities, wit, spirit, independence, and idealism of adolescents. Like the following teacher, they want to be connected to their students: ". . . I now know that I teach so I can be involved in my students' lives, in their real life stories" (Henry et al. 1995, 69).

Teachers also derive significant rewards from meeting the needs of diverse learners. While students from the United States' more than one hundred racial and ethnic

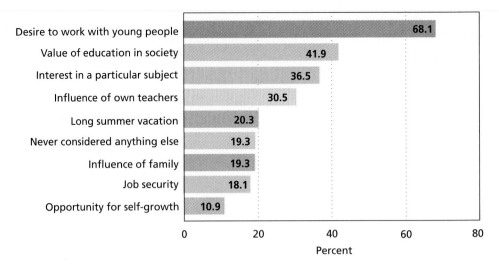

Figure 1.1

Why do teachers teach? Based on a survey of a nationally representative sample of 1,325 public school teachers who responded to a survey mailed in March 1996.
Source: NEA Research, "Status of the American Public School Teacher, 1995–96: Highlights." http://www.nea.org/neatoday/9709/status.html. Derived from National Education Association, *Status of the American Public School Teacher 1995–96.* Washington, DC: NEA, 1997. (© 1997 NEA, All rights reserved.)

groups and students with special needs are increasing in number, effective teachers recognize that their classrooms are enriched by the varied backgrounds of students. To enable you to experience the satisfaction of helping all students learn, significant portions of this book are devoted to **student variability** (differences among students in regard to their developmental needs, interests, abilities, and disabilities) and **student diversity** (differences among students in regard to gender, race, ethnicity, culture, and socioeconomic status). An appreciation for such diversity, then, will help you to experience the rewards that come from enabling each student to make his or her unique contribution to classroom life.

The opportunity to work with young people, whatever their stage of development and whatever their life circumstances, is a key reason people are drawn to teaching and remain in the profession.

Love of Teaching

The *Metropolitan Life Survey of the American Teacher, 1984–1995: Old Problems, New Challenges* includes the following observation: ". . . teachers overwhelmingly agree with the statement, 'I love to teach.' This is true for teachers in urban as well as suburban and rural schools" (Louis Harris and Associates 1995). The survey, based on a nationally representative sample of 1,011 public school teachers interviewed in 1995, goes on to report that teachers express a great deal more personal satisfaction with teaching than they did in 1984, and they are more likely to say they would recommend teaching as a profession. Why do teachers find teaching so satisfying? What does it mean to *love* teaching?

Love of Subject   Some teachers who expressed a love of teaching may have meant that they love teaching in their discipline. The opportunity to continually learn more in one's profession and to share that knowledge with students is a definite attraction. Most of us can recall teachers who were so excited about their subjects that they were surprised when students were not equally enthusiastic. The affinity of such teachers toward their subjects was so great that we tended to see the two as inseparable—for instance, "Ms. Gilbert the French teacher" or "Mr. Montgomery the math teacher." Though other factors may draw teachers to their work, a love of subject is clearly one of them.

Love of the Teaching Life   For those teachers who always enjoyed school, it is often the life of a teacher that has appeal—to be in an environment that encourages a high regard for education and the life of the mind, and to have daily opportunities to see students become excited about learning. Albert Einstein, for example, regretted that he did not devote his career to the teaching life:

> Believe it or not, one of my deepest regrets [is that I didn't teach]. I regret this because I would have liked to have had more contact with children. There has always been something about the innocence and freshness of young children that appeals to me and brings me great enjoyment to be with them. And they are so open to knowledge. I have never really found it difficult to explain basic laws of nature to children. When you reach them at their level, you can read in their eyes their genuine interest and appreciation (quoted in Bucky, 1992, 99).

Love of the Teaching–Learning Process   To love teaching can also mean to love the act of teaching and the learning that can follow. Many teachers, like the following high school special education teacher, focus on the process rather than on the subject or even the students: "I enjoy what I do. . . . I've been teaching long enough that when the fun stops . . . I'll get out. But it hasn't stopped yet, after thirty-four years. Every day is different. Every day is interesting" (Godar 1990, 244). Persons with this orientation are attracted by the live, spontaneous aspects of teaching and are invigorated by the need to think on their feet and to capitalize on teachable moments when they occur. "[T]hey possess a variety of schemata for seeing what is important, [and they] have a broad repertoire of moves with which to quickly and gracefully act on the situation that they see" (Eisner 1998, 200).

Influence of Teachers

It seems reasonable to assume that the process of becoming a teacher begins early in life. In fact, a Metropolitan Life Survey of 1,002 graduates who began teaching in a public school in 1990–91 reported that 52 percent decided to become teachers before college (Louis Harris and Associates 1990). Although it is not true that some people are born teachers, their early life experiences often encourage them to move in that direction. A teacher's influence during the formative years may have been the catalyst. In most cases, the adults who have the greatest influence on children—beyond their parents or guardians—are their teachers. For example, two University of Chicago researchers reported that 58 percent of the teenagers they interviewed said one or more teachers influenced them to become the kind of people they are (Csikszentmihalyi and McCormack 1986, 414–419).

Evidence also suggests that those who become teachers were often more influenced by their teachers as people than as subject-matter experts. "It is the human dimen-

where
do you
stand?

Should psychological assessments be used to identify students who should not become teachers?

Candidates for teacher-education programs are required to jump over a number of hurdles to be accepted into the programs that lead to a state teaching credential, the ticket to public school teaching in the U.S. State, college, and program directors hope the hurdles will eliminate individuals who could harm students personally, physically, or academically. To address safety and health concerns, programs call for candidates to submit fingerprints so their criminal histories can be checked and to present evidence that they are free of tuberculosis. In addition, candidates are required to have (1) passed a test of their basic skills in reading, writing, and mathematics; (2) passed a course or test on the U.S. Constitution; (3) passed a preliminary course in child, adolescent, or human development; (4) mastered the subject(s) they plan to teach; and (5) earned a bachelor's degree from an accredited college or university.

Most programs also include an admission interview with one or more directors, professors, or advisors, who help determine whether candidates are likely to become good teachers. In most programs this interview is the sole means of screening out mentally unhealthy people. Should formal psychological assessments be used to further assist in the screening process? Would using such tests lead to lawsuits against the colleges and universities that conduct them? Can a psychological instrument measure who is likely to be a good or poor teacher?

Psychological assessments should be used to identify students who should not become teachers.

With our increasing knowledge about how the brain develops and its responsiveness to stimuli in the environment, especially for the young, we realize the power teachers have to impact students' cognitive and emotional development for good or ill. Teachers who appear threatening to students can impact their learning as well as their sense of emotional well-being. A teacher who has problems with authority, a quick temper, insensitivity to the

feelings of others, or poorly defined personal boundaries can be a menace to children and youth. Psychological assessments should be used to screen out teacher-education candidates with these characteristics.

Just as extra psychological screening is needed for pilots and air traffic controllers, so too is it needed for people who work with the minds of our children and youth. In all three groups, if the individuals in positions of power fail to live up to their responsibilities or make mistakes, the consequences can be serious. The substitute teacher who exposed himself to a class of second graders, the physical education teacher who had sexual relations with students, and the fifth grade teacher who regularly ridiculed and humiliated students in class should not have been permitted to teach in the first place. Psychological assessments of them would have revealed their mental health problems and prevented them from entering the profession.

Psychological assessments should not be used to disqualify students who want to become teachers.

Psychological assessments should not be used to disqualify prospective teachers because they could screen out potentially superb teachers and could admit others likely to fail in a classroom. How can an assessment measure something that years of education research have failed to determine, the ingredients of a good teacher? If psychological assessments are used, will teachers begin to look alike, measured against a narrowly defined profile? How can instruments measure the rich array of personalities that motivate students to learn and love learning?

Psychological assessments are costly in terms of both money and personnel time. For example, one test being used in a teacher-education program in California requires that three evaluators participate in the interviews of candidates. These evaluators must undergo extensive and expensive training before they can join an assessment interview team. Not many colleges and universities can afford such a time- and cost-intensive approach.

The legalities of screening out candidates on the basis of a psychological assessment is another obvious concern. Could teacher education institutions be sued by people who believe they were denied admission to their programs on false grounds?

An assessment instrument or process is not able to measure the psychological dimension that encompasses what today's teachers need: "interpersonal skills, willingness to confront and deal with social and cultural complexity, self-awareness and disposition toward reflection, cosmopolitanism, and a well-developed social conscience" (Griffin 1999, 10). An interview process similar to that proposed by Martin Haberman is more likely to get us closer to the mark. In attempting to predict the best candidates for teaching successfully in urban schools, Haberman (1996) proposes asking questions that address classroom situations and test character traits such as perseverance, resourcefulness, and ability to tolerate ambiguities. For instance, candidates are asked what they would do if a student didn't turn in his or her homework. Then they are asked, "What if that didn't work?" After a reply, again, "What if that didn't work either?" Such an approach is more likely to identify who should not be in a classroom than a psychological assessment.

Where do you stand on this issue?

1. What support can you give for your position?

2. How would you measure up in the homework question exercise?

3. What other situational and character-trait testing questions can you suggest to someone wanting to use Haberman's evaluation approach?

4. What legal challenges might be raised about psychological assessments for teacher candidates? What ethical challenges might be raised?

Recommended Sources

Griffin, G. A. (1999). Changes in teacher education: looking to the future. In G. A. Griffin (Ed). *The education of teachers: ninety-eighth yearbook of the National Society for the Study of Education.* Chicago: The University of Chicago Press.

Haberman, M. (1996). Selecting and preparing urban teachers. In J. Sikula (Ed.). *Handbook of research on teacher education: a project of the Association of Teacher Educators* (2nd ed.). New York: Macmillan.

Jensen, E. (1998). *Teaching with the brain in mind.* Alexandria, VA: Association for Supervision and Curriculum Development.

sion that gives all teachers . . . their power as professional influencers" (Zehm and Kottler 1993, 2). Behind the decision to become a teacher is often the inspirational memory of earlier teachers to whom one continues to feel connected in a way that goes beyond the subjects they taught.

Desire to Serve

Many choose to teach because they want to serve others; they want the results of their labor to extend beyond themselves and their families. Some decide to select another major or leave teaching in order to earn more money elsewhere, only to return to teaching, confiding that they found the other major or work lacking in meaning or significance. Being involved in a service profession is their draw to the field.

For many teachers, the decision to serve through teaching was influenced by their experiences as volunteers. Nearly half of the teachers surveyed by the New York City School Volunteer Program, for example, reported that they had served as volunteers in an educational setting before deciding to become a teacher, and 70 percent of these teachers reported that this experience contributed to their decision to become a teacher (Educational Testing Service 1995). As one New York teacher said, "I always wanted to be a teacher, and all of my volunteer experiences contributed to this career choice" (p. 8).

The desire to serve others and give something back to society is a key attraction of the **Teach for America** program developed in 1989 by Wendy Kopp as an outgrowth of her senior thesis at Princeton University. Teach for America volunteers, recent graduates from some of America's best colleges and universities, are assigned to teach for a minimum of two years in urban and rural school districts with severe shortages of science, math, and language arts teachers. Volunteers complete five weeks of intensive training at the Teach for America Institute in Houston. After two years of teaching, being monitored by state and school authorities, and taking professional development courses, Teach for America teachers can earn regular certification. Upon completion of their two-year assignment, volunteers then return to their chosen careers in other fields, though more than half remain in education as teachers, principals, and educational administrators (Teach for America 1999).

Explore more deeply your reasons for becoming a teacher. The following Professional Reflection feature focuses on several characteristics that may indicate your probable satisfaction with teaching as a career.

 **Professional Reflection**   **Assessing your reasons for choosing to teach**

For each of the following characteristics, indicate on a scale from 1 to 5 the extent to which it applies to you.

	Very applicable			Not at all applicable	
1. Love of learning	1	2	3	4	5
2. Success as a student	1	2	3	4	5
3. Good sense of humor	1	2	3	4	5
4. Positive attitudes toward students	1	2	3	4	5
5. Tolerance toward others	1	2	3	4	5
6. Patience	1	2	3	4	5
7. Good verbal and writing skills	1	2	3	4	5
8. Appreciation for the arts	1	2	3	4	
9. Experiences working with children (camp, church, tutoring, etc.)	1	2	3	4	5
10. Other teachers in family	1	2	3	4	5
11. Encouragement from family to enter teaching	1	2	3	4	5
12. Desire to serve	1	2	3	4	5

Total score _____

Now that you have completed the self-assessment, calculate your total score; the highest score = 60, the lowest = 12. Interpret the results of your self-assessment with caution. A high score does not necessarily mean that you will be dissatisfied as a teacher, nor does a low score mean that you will be highly satisfied.

Practical Benefits of Teaching

Not to be overlooked as attractions to teaching are its practical benefits. Teachers' hours and vacations are widely recognized as benefits. Though the number of hours most teachers devote to their work goes far beyond the number of hours they actually spend at school, their schedules do afford them a measure of flexibility not found in other professions. For example, teachers with school-age children can often be at home when their children are not in school, and nearly all teachers, regardless of their years of experience, receive the same generous vacation time: holiday breaks and a long summer vacation. On the other hand, with the continued growth of year-round schools—2,800 schools in forty-one states were on year-round schedules in 1997–98—many teachers have three or four "mini vacations" throughout the year and welcome the flexibility of being able to take vacations during off-peak seasons (National Association for Year-Round Education 1999).

Salaries and Benefits   Although intangible rewards represent a significant attraction to teaching, teachers are demanding that the public acknowledge the value and professional standing of teaching by supporting higher salaries. As a result, teacher earnings have increased steadily since the 1980s—for example, the average salaries (in 1997 constant dollars) of all teachers in 1980–81 was $32,711 (National Center for Education Statistics 1999); for 1998–99, the average was $40,582 (National Education Association 1999). In 1996–97, 40 school districts serving the nation's 100 largest cities had maximum salaries exceeding $50,000; Yonkers had the highest maximum salary ($74,854) followed by Jersey City ($73,175), Rochester ($68,863), Pittsburgh ($62,200), and Anchorage ($60,775) (American Federation of Teachers 1998). Table 1.1 shows a state-by-state ranking of salaries for public school teachers for 1998–99.

Though the general consensus is still that teachers are underpaid, teacher salaries are becoming more competitive with other occupations; in fact, salaries are becoming one of the attractions for the profession. For example, based on the fact that 884 teachers were paid more than $70,000 during 1997–98 in New Jersey, John Challenger, a job placement specialist and CEO, predicted that New Jersey would see its first $100,000 teacher before the next millennium. According to Challenger, occupations typically stereotyped as moderate-to-low paying will experience a "windfall" in the twenty-first century. As private businesses invest in public schools to help develop tomorrow's skilled workforce, teachers will be "able to contract their skills and wares to the highest corporate bidder, yet remain on the payroll at their school" (United Press International 1998).

When we are comparing teacher salaries state-by-state, it is important to remember that higher salaries are frequently linked to a higher **cost of living,** a more experienced teaching force, and a more desirable location. For example, the National Center for Education Statistics found a $23,000 difference between the highest and lowest average state teachers' salaries in 1995; after using a regional cost-of-living index, however, the difference narrowed to about $14,000 (National Center for Education Statistics 1995). Another study by economists at North Carolina State University found that New Hampshire, which ranked twenty-fifth among states in actual salaries for 1995, jumped

Table 1.1

Average salaries of public school teachers, 1998–99

	State	Average Salary		State	Average Salary
1	Connecticut	51,584	27	Vermont	36,800
2	New Jersey	51,193*	28	Tennessee	36,500
3	New York	49,437*	29	North Carolina	36,098
4	Pennsylvania	48,457	30	Florida	35,196
5	Michigan	48,207*	31	Alabama	35,820
6	District of Columbia	47,150*	32	Kentucky	35,526
7	Alaska	46,845	33	Texas	35,041
8	Rhode Island	45,650	34	Arizona	35,025*
9	Illinois	45,569	35	Iowa	34,927
10	California	45,400*	36	Maine	34,906
11	Massachusetts	45,075*	37	Missouri	34,746
12	Delaware	43,164	38	South Carolina	34,506
13	Oregon	42,833	39	West Virginia	34,244
14	Maryland	42,526	40	Idaho	34,063
15	Indiana	41,163	41	Wyoming	33,500
16	Wisconsin	40,657	42	Utah	32,950*
17	U.S. and D.C.	40,582*	43	Nebraska	32,880
18	Hawaii	40,377	44	Louisiana	32,510
19	Georgia	39,675	45	New Mexico	32,398
20	Minnesota	39,458	46	Arkansas	32,350*
21	Nevada	38,883	47	Montana	31,356
22	Washington	38,692	48	Oklahoma	31,149*
23	Colorado	38,025*	49	Mississippi	29,530
24	Virginia	37,475*	50	North Dakota	28,976
25	Kansas	37,405	51	South Dakota	28,552
26	New Hampshire	37,405			

*estimated

Source: National Education Association, *Rankings & Estimates: Rankings of the States 1999 and Estimates of School Statistics 2000.* Washington, DC: National Education Association, 1999, p. 64.

to ninth in the ranking adjusted for cost of living, while Indiana dropped from sixteenth to thirty-eighth (*Education Week,* January 10, 1996a, 16).

Teachers' salaries are typically determined by years of experience and advanced training as evidenced by graduate credit hours or advanced degrees. Additional duties, such as coaching an athletic team, producing the yearbook and school newspaper, sponsoring clubs, or directing the band, bring extra pay for many teachers. Most districts offer at least limited summer employment for teachers who wish to teach summer school or develop curriculum materials. Additionally, about one-fourth of the nation's two million public school teachers **"moonlight"** (i.e., hold a second job) to increase their earnings.

Teachers also receive various **fringe benefits,** such as medical insurance and retirement plans, which are usually given in addition to base salary. These benefits vary from district to district and are determined during collective bargaining sessions. When considering a school district for your first position, carefully examine the fringe benefits package as well as the salary schedule and opportunities for extra pay.

Job Security and Status Compared to workers in other sectors of U.S. society who experienced increasing layoffs during the first half of the 1990s, teachers enjoyed a higher level of job security during the same period. Technological advances, corporate mergers and breakups, and a need to cut costs to remain competitive in a global economy led to huge layoffs in the early 1990s. Not surprisingly, 77 percent of teachers surveyed in 1995 rated job security as better in teaching than in other occupations they had considered (Louis Harris and Associates 1995). In addition, the widespread practice of **tenure** (job security granted to teachers after satisfactory performance for a specified period, usually two to five years) contributes to job security for teachers.

As a result of what researchers call a demographic "echo" of the baby boom, America's school-age population in 2002 is expected to be double what it was in 1986. This enrollment increase, plus the fact that about one-third of teachers are 50 years of age or older and nearing retirement, means many job opportunities for teachers in the near future (American Federation of Teachers 1999b). A 1998 *Education Week* article, "New Teachers Are Hot Commodity," reported that schools would need to hire two million new teachers during the next decade and that competition for teachers was leading some school districts to offer bonuses, housing assistance, and higher starting salaries. For example, the Baltimore school system raised starting salaries by $3,000 and offered teachers an incentive package that included on-the-job mentoring, $5,000 toward closing costs on a home, and $1,200 for relocation expenses (Bradley 1998).

Perhaps the most accurate view of the status accorded teachers comes from the teachers themselves. In 1984, 47 percent of the 1,981 teachers responding to *The Metropolitan Life Survey of the American Teacher* agreed with the statement, "As a teacher, I feel respected in today's society." According to the 1995 survey of 1,011 teachers, the number of teachers agreeing with the statement had increased to 53 percent (Louis Harris and Associates 1995, 16). In addition, it should be noted that teachers, as members of the "professional middle class," are accorded status "based on education, rather than on the ownership of capital or property" (Ehrenreich 1989, 12). As a result, "many teachers and school administrators now are thought to be of a more elite social class than the majority of the population in the United States" (Parker and Shapiro 1993, 42).

Job Opportunities for Teachers from Diverse Groups During the first part of the twenty-first century, there will be exceptional job opportunities for teachers from diverse racial and ethnic backgrounds and for teachers with disabilities. Clearly, students from diverse racial, ethnic, and cultural backgrounds and students with disabilities benefit from having role models with whom they can easily identify. In addition, teachers from diverse groups and teachers with disabilities may have, in some instances, an enhanced understanding of student diversity and student variability that they can share with other teachers.

Data released in 1998 by the National Center for Education Statistics indicated the following percentages for enrollment in public elementary through secondary schools: 70.4 percent white, 16.1 percent African American, 9.9 percent Hispanic, 2.8 percent Asian or Pacific Islander, and 0.9 percent Native American/Native Alaskan. When contrasted with the diverse mosaic of student enrollments, the backgrounds of today's teachers reveal less diversity, a situation that has been labeled a "crisis" (King 1993). A 1997 survey by Recruiting New Teachers, Inc., found that 92 percent of the largest urban districts reported an immediate need for teachers from minority races and ethnic groups, and *Education Week* reported that only 20 percent of undergraduate teacher education students were minority-group members in 1998.

Table 1.2 shows the actual numbers of teachers in public and private schools by race and ethnicity. These data provide the basis for calculating the respective percentages of public and private school teachers from minority groups: African American, 7.4 percent in public schools and 3.1 percent in private schools; Hispanic, 4.2 percent and 3.2 percent; Asian American/Pacific Islander, 1.0 percent and 1.4 percent; and Native

Table 1.2

Teachers in public and private elementary and secondary schools, by gender and race/ethnicity, 1993–94

Selected Characteristics	Total*	Percent of Teachers, by Highest Degree Earned		
		No Degree	Associate	Bachelor's
1	2	3	4	5
Public Schools				
Total	**2,561,294**	**0.6**	**0.2**	**52.0**
Men	694,098	1.3	0.4	45.2
Women	1,867,195	0.3	0.1	54.1
Race/ethnicity				
White	2,216,605	0.5	0.1	51.8
Black	188,371	0.5	0.2	48.4
Hispanic	108,744	0.9	0.5	62.8
Asian or Pacific Islander	27,510	0.9	0.4	49.3
American Indian or Alaskan	20,064	0.8	0.3	54.9
Private Schools				
Total	**378,365**	**5.2**	**1.5**	**59.0**
Men	93,130	4.4	0.9	47.3
Women	285,235	5.4	1.7	62.8
Race/ethnicity				
White	347,811	4.8	1.3	59.4
Black	11,664	8.3	3.7	55.8
Hispanic	12,221	11.1	4.9	57.4
Asian or Pacific Islander	5,167	6.8	0.9	46.1
American Indian or Alaskan	1,502	3.4	6.0	49.4

*Data are based upon a sample survey and may not be strictly comparable with data reported elsewhere. Note: Excludes prekindergarten teachers. Data are based on a head count of all teachers rather than on the number of full-time-equivalent teachers reported on other tables. Details may not add to totals because of survey item nonresponse and rounding.

American 0.8 percent and 0.4 percent. Furthermore, the percentage of teachers from minority groups is declining, perhaps as a result of increased opportunities in other professional fields for people from diverse backgrounds.

Research indicates that people with disabilities can be effective educators (Anderson, Keller, and Karp 1998; Karp and Keller 1998). "They hold positions in a variety of educational professions, such as all types of teaching, counseling, administration, and speech therapy, and have a variety of disabilities, such as learning disabilities, physical disabilities, visual impairments, deafness and hearing loss, medical conditions, and brain injuries" (Keller, Anderson, and Karp 1998, 8).

The percentage of children with disabilities receiving special education in public

Table 1.2

(Continued)

Percent of Teachers, by Highest Degree Earned			Percent of Teachers, by Years of Full-Time Teaching Experience			
Master's	**Education Specialist**	**Doctor's**	**Less Than 3**	**3 to 9**	**10 to 20**	**Over 20**
6	*7*	*8*	*9*	*10*	*11*	*12*
Public Schools						
42.0	**4.6**	**0.7**	**9.7**	**25.5**	**35.0**	**29.8**
45.7	5.1	1.3	8.9	21.6	29.9	39.6
40.6	4.4	0.5	10.0	26.9	37.0	26.1
42.5	4.4	0.7	9.4	25.5	35.1	30.0
44.6	5.4	0.9	8.5	20.8	35.5	35.2
29.8	4.6	1.4	16.7	32.1	34.1	17.1
34.7	13.1	1.7	14.9	29.7	29.2	26.2
39.1	4.3	0.6	11.3	27.6	34.5	26.6
Private Schools						
29.8	**2.9**	**1.7**	**20.9**	**33.9**	**29.6**	**15.6**
40.6	2.6	4.3	21.7	28.2	28.7	21.4
26.3	3.0	0.8	20.6	35.8	29.9	13.7
30.2	2.6	1.6	20.4	33.6	30.0	16.0
26.4	4.8	1.0	26.9	34.9	27.9	10.3
19.9	4.4	2.3	25.5	41.8	21.6	11.1
36.8	5.7	3.6	26.1	34.6	26.6	12.7
16.1	25.1	(2)	29.1	42.8	17.9	9.9

Source: Excerpted from *Digest of Education Statistics 1998.* Washington,DC: National Center for Education statistics, 1999, p. 78.

preK–12 schools is approximately 10 percent (Hardman, Drew, and Egan 1999), and the current critical need for special education teachers is expected to continue well into the twenty-first century. Nevertheless, there is an apparent lack of information on the number of educators with disabilities—a situation that leads Keller, Anderson, and Karp (1998, 8) to suggest that our need to "approach the question of how many educators have disabilities so tentatively and circumspectly is perhaps telling."

What Are the Challenges of Teaching?

Like all professions, teaching has undesirable or difficult aspects. As one high school social studies teacher put it: "Teaching is not terrible. It's great. I love it. It just feels terrible sometimes" (Henry et al. 1995, 119).

Prospective teachers need to consider the problems as well as the pleasures they are likely to encounter. You need to be informed about what to expect if you are to make the most of your professional preparation program. With greater awareness of the realities of teaching, you can more purposefully and meaningfully (1) reflect on and refine your personal philosophy of education, (2) acquire teaching strategies and leadership techniques, and (3) develop a knowledge base of research and theory to guide your actions. In this manner, you can become a true professional—free to savor the joys and satisfactions of teaching and confident of your ability to deal with its frustrations and challenges. Table 1.3 shows that teachers must deal with a variety of problems in the schools.

Classroom Management and Increasing School Violence

For three of the five years from 1994 to 1998, the public ranked lack of discipline as the most important problem facing the schools in the annual Gallup Polls of the Public's Attitudes toward the Public Schools. For the other two years, the public ranked fighting, violence, and gangs as the most important. Not surprisingly, discipline and increased crime and violence among youth are strong concerns for education majors. Before teachers can teach they must manage their classrooms effectively. Even when parents and the school community are supportive and problems are relatively minor, dealing with discipline can be a disturbing, emotionally draining aspect of teaching. Moreover, the last few years of the 1990s were marked by frequent reports of random, horrific violence in and around schools. Thirty-six percent of parents in 1998 feared for their oldest child's safety while at school; in 1977, only 25 percent of parents had such fears (Rose and Gallup 1998). Several communities previously immune to such tragedies were thrust into the national spotlight as a result of violent incidents: Littleton, Colorado; Paducah, Kentucky; Moses Lake, Washington; Springfield, Oregon; and Jonesboro, Arkansas, to name a few. Though such acts of violence in schools are rare, the possibility of experiencing such events can cause additional job-related stress for teachers.

In addition, many schools have high **teacher–student ratios,** which can make classroom management more difficult. Feeling the press of overcrowding and valiantly resisting the realization that they cannot meet the needs of all their students, teachers may try to work faster and longer to give their students the best possible education. All too often, however, they learn to put off, overlook, or otherwise attend inadequately

Table 1.3

Teacher's perceptions of the frequency of discipline problems

About how often do each of the problems listed occur at the school where you teach?

Most of the Time/Fairly Often

	All Teachers			Elementary Teachers			High School Teachers		
	1997	**1989**	**1984**	**1997**	**1989**	**1984**	**1997**	**1989**	**1984**
	%	%	%	%	%	%	%	%	%
Schoolwork/homework assignments not completed	71	79	76	68	76	73	78	85	80
Behavior that disrupts class	58	87	47	65	60	48	45	50	47
Talking back to, disobeying teachers	50	45	43	54	45	42	43	44	43
Truancy/being absent from school	41	45	47	35	32	29	57	67	62
Sloppy or inappropriate dress	40	45	37	36	43	33	51	49	41
Cheating on tests	27	45	40	19	33	29	47	64	51
Stealing money or personal property belonging to other students, teachers, or staff	21	21	32	21	26	25	25	40	39
Vandalizing school property	20	25	29	18	20	22	25	34	35
Skipping classes	18	29	35	9	18	16	41	59	57
Using drugs at school	15	14	17	5	5	6	39	30	29
Theft of school property	14	15	23	13	13	18	15	19	29
Selling drugs at school	9	14	13	3	1	4	26	32	24
Racial fights	6	6	4	5	5	3	6	9	5
Carrying of knives, firearms, or other weapons at school	5	4	8	3	3	5	7	8	10
Drinking alcoholic beverages at school	4	6	10	1	1	2	10	14	17
Sexual activity at school	4	6	8	1	1	3	8	13	12
Taking money or property by force, using weapons or threats	2	2	2	2	2	2	2	2	2
Physical attacks on teachers or staff	2	2	1	2	2	1	2	2	1

Note: Figures add to more than 100 percent because of multiple answers.

Source: From Carol A. Langdon, "The Fourth Phi Delta Kappa Poll of Teachers' Attitudes toward the Public Schools," *Phi Delta Kappan,* November 1997, p. 213. Used by permission of the author and publisher. Copyright 1997, Phi Delta Kappa.

to many students each day. The problem of high teacher–student ratios becomes even more acute when complicated by the high **student-mobility rates** in many schools. In such situations, teachers have trouble not only in meeting students' needs but also in recognizing students and remembering their names! As you will see, developing a leadership plan, a learning environment, and communication skills will help you face the challenges of classroom management.

Social Problems That Impact Students

Many social problems affect the lives and learning of many children and youth, such as substance abuse, teen pregnancy, homelessness, poverty, family distress, child abuse and neglect, violence and crime, suicide, and health problems such as HIV/AIDS and fetal alcohol syndrome. The social problems that place students at risk of school failure are not always easy to detect. Students' low productivity, learning difficulties, and attitude problems demand teacher attention; yet teachers may be unaware of the source of those difficulties. Even when teachers do recognize the source of a problem, they may lack the resources or expertise to offer help. Teachers feel frustrated by the wasted potential they observe in their students. In addition, when the public calls for schools to curb or correct social problems, that expectation can increase the stress teachers experience.

Need for Family and Community Support

Support from parents and the community can make a significant difference in the teacher's effectiveness in the classroom. Increasingly, there has been a realization that school, parents, and community must work together so that children and youth develop to their maximum potential academically, socially, emotionally, and physically. For example, 53 percent of the student leaders who attended the 1999 United States Senate Youth Program said "parental support" was the biggest factor in their success at high school (William Randolph Hearst Foundation 1999). Parents who talk with their children, help with homework, read to them, monitor their television viewing, and attend meetings of the Parent Teacher Organization (PTO) and school open houses can enhance their children's ability to succeed in school (Henry 1996; Moore 1992; Fuligni and Stevenson 1995). Similarly, communities can support schools by providing essential social, vocational, recreational, and health support services to students and their families. While teachers in suburban and rural schools believe that parental and community support has increased since 1984 (see Figure 1.2), teachers in inner-city schools have seen an alarming decrease in support. Also, among teachers who seriously considered leaving teaching in 1995, "lack of respect/support from parents" was identified by 14 percent as a major factor (Louis Harris and Associates 1995, 60).

A low rate of parental participation in their children's schooling is reflected in the 1994 Gallup Poll of the Public's Attitudes toward the Public Schools, which reported that less than 50 percent of the parents of public school students attended a PTA (Parent-Teacher Association) meeting dur-

Figure 1.2

Percentage of teachers who believe parental support is "excellent" or "good," 1984, 1995, and 1998

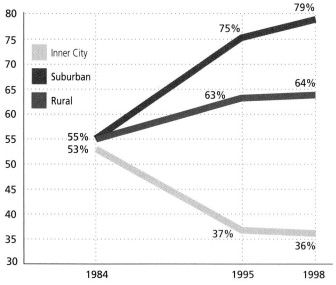

Source: The Metropolitan Life Survey of the American Teacher, 1984–1995: Old Problems, New Challenges. New York: Louis Harris and Associates, 1995, p. 20; and The Metropolitan Life Survey of the American Teacher, 1998: Building Family–School Partnerships: Views of Teachers and Students. New York: Louis Harris and Associates, 1998, p. 12.

ing the academic year, and in the 1995 poll, which reported that only 38 percent of parents attended a school board meeting during the past school year. Nevertheless, the 1997 poll revealed that 69 percent of the public would be willing to work as an unpaid volunteer in local schools—a significant increase compared to 1992, when 59 percent indicated their willingness to volunteer.

Long Working Hours and Job Stress

The official working hours for teachers are attractive, but the real working hours are another matter. Not built into contracts are the after-hours or extra assignments found at all levels of teaching—from recess duty and parent conferences to high school club sponsorships and coaching. Also not obvious are the hours of preparation that occur before and after school—frequently late into the night and over the weekend. Over 90 percent of teachers work more than forty hours per week, with the largest percentage working more than 55 hours per week (Louis Harris and Associates 1995).

The need to complete copious amounts of paperwork, including record keeping, may be the most burdensome of the teacher's nonteaching tasks. On average, teachers spend ten hours per week on school-related responsibilities not directly related to teaching (Louis Harris and Associates 1995, 68). Other nonteaching tasks include supervising student behavior on the playground, at extracurricular events, and in the halls, study halls, and lunchrooms; attending faculty meetings, parent conferences, and open houses; and taking tickets or selling at concessions for athletic events. Individually, such assignments and responsibilities may be enjoyable; too many of them at once, however, become a burden and consume the teacher's valuable time.

In addition to long working hours, factors such as students' lack of interest, conflicts with administrators, public criticism, overcrowded classrooms, lack of resources, and isolation from other adults cause some teachers to experience high levels of stress. Unchecked, acute levels of stress can lead to job dissatisfaction, emotional and physical exhaustion, and an inability to cope effectively—all classic symptoms of teacher **burnout**. To cope with stress and avoid burnout, teachers report that activities in seven areas are beneficial: social support, physical fitness, intellectual stimulation, entertainment, personal hobbies, self-management, and supportive attitudes (Gmelch and Parkay 1995, 46–65).

Gaining Professional Empowerment

In an interview with journalist Bill Moyers, noted Harvard educator Sara Lawrence Lightfoot eloquently describes why teachers desire **professional empowerment:**

> [Teachers are] saying, "I haven't had the opportunity to participate fully in this enterprise." Some teachers are speaking about the politics of teachers' voice. They're saying, "We want more control over our lives in this school." Some of them are making an even more subtle point—they're talking about voice as knowledge. "We know things about this enterprise that researchers and policy makers can never know. We have engaged in this intimate experience, and we have things to tell you if you'd only learn how to ask, and if you'd only learn how to listen" (Moyers 1989, 161).

Although some teachers may experience frustration in their efforts to gain professional empowerment, efforts to empower teachers and to "professionalize" teaching are leading to unprecedented opportunities for today's teachers to extend their leader-

Will I be prepared to teach in a digital age?

One of the challenges of teaching in the twenty-first century will be to keep abreast of new technologies that can enhance students' learning. Therefore, it will be important throughout your teacher-education program to evaluate your ability to use newly emerging technology. Most colleges and universities offer a wide range of courses and training in the use of technology. To make a self-assessment of your current level of technological literacy, compare your skills with those highlighted in the following case illustration of a teacher-education student at Valley City State University, North Dakota, where all students are required to use a notebook computer.

> Before going to class I access my e-mail to read responses from two instructors regarding clarification of assignments, four messages from fellow students, and a message from my mom who lives on the opposite side of the state. I make revisions for my part of our cooperative learning group's PowerPoint presentation for a class later in the week. I am scheduled for three classes today.
>
> I try to get to all my classes five minutes early to plug in my notebook computer and to get organized. All our classrooms have power sources and are linked directly to the Internet. The instructor uses a teaching station set up in the front of the classroom so he can project information on a 54-inch television screen.
>
> I use my laptop in my first class to take notes from the PowerPoint presentation the professor is giving. I'm creating a web page for this class, and later this week I'll videotape myself teaching a mathematics lesson. Then I'll digitize the video clip and link it to my mathematics web page.
>
> In my next class, the students are working in cooperative learning groups using the WWW to find information for a research project.
>
> I'm working on a portfolio project in my language arts class, and the other students and I are in the process of scanning pictures into our PowerPoint presentations. We have all had the opportunity to develop electronic portfolios this semester and we are getting ready to complete them so that we can turn them into a CD-ROM. We will present our portfolio projects to the rest of the class during finals week. Each of us has been compiling digitized video of lessons taught, various scanned pictures, and other pertinent information that will help us to demonstrate what we have learned in the class this past semester.

Source: National Council for Accreditation of Teacher Education, "A Day in the Life of a Current Teacher Education Student," in *Technology and the New Professional Teacher: Preparing for the 21st Century Classroom.* Washington, DC, 1998.

ship roles beyond the classroom. In fact, "teachers in the U.S. today are developing leadership skills to a degree not needed in the past . . . the continuing professional development of teaching as a profession requires that teachers exercise greater leadership at the school level and beyond" (Parkay et al. 1999, 20–21).

What Is Teaching Really Like?

In this section we examine six basic **realities of teaching** that illustrate why teaching is so demanding and why it can be so exciting, rewarding, and uplifting. And when we say that teaching is demanding, we mean more than the fact that Mr. Smith's third-period plane geometry students just can't seem to learn how to compute the area of a triangle; or that Ms. Ellis's sixth-grade composition class can't remember whether to use *there* or *their;* or even that 35 percent of teachers in 1995 reported they were "under great stress" almost every day or several days a week (Louis Harris and Associates 1995, 55). Although there are many frustrating, stressful events with which teachers must cope, the difficulty of teaching goes much further, or deeper, than these examples suggest.

Reality 1: The Unpredictability of Outcomes

The outcomes of teaching, even in the best of circumstances, are neither predictable nor consistent. Any teacher, beginner or veteran, can give countless examples of how the outcomes of teaching are often unpredictable and inconsistent. Life in most classrooms usually proceeds on a fairly even keel—with teachers able to predict, fairly accurately, how their students will respond to lessons. Adherence to the best laid lesson plans, however, may be accompanied by students' blank stares, yawns of boredom, hostile acting out, or expressions of befuddlement. On the other hand, lack of preparation on the teacher's part does not necessarily rule out the possibility of a thoroughly exciting class discussion, a real breakthrough in understanding for an individual student or the entire class, or simply a good, fast-paced review of previously learned material. In short, teachers are often surprised at students' reactions to classroom activities.

Students' Responses   Contrary to the popular notion that teaching consists entirely of specific competencies or observable behaviors that have predetermined effects on students, the reactions of students to any given activity cannot be guaranteed. Furthermore, teachers, unlike other professionals, cannot control all the results of their efforts.

One example of the unpredictability of teaching is given in a teacher intern's description of setting up an independent reading program in his middle-school classroom. Here we see how careful room arrangement and organization of materials do not ensure desired outcomes and how a teacher learned to adjust to one reality of teaching.

> I wanted everything looking perfect. For two more hours, I placed this here and stuffed that in there. . . . There were stacks of brand-new books sitting on three odd shelves and a metal display rack. . . . I coded the books and arranged them neatly on the shelves. I displayed their glossy covers as if the room was a B. Dalton store.

A few weeks after setting up the reading program, however, this teacher observes that

> The orderly environment I thought I had conceived was fraught with complications. For example, the back rows of the classroom were inaccessible regions from which paper and pencil pieces were hurled at vulnerable victims, and there were zones where, apparently, no teacher's voice could be heard. . . . The books . . . remained in chaos. Novels turned up behind shelves, on the sidewalks outside, and in the trash can. And still, at least once a week, I dutifully arranged them

until I was satisfied. But something was happening. It was taking less and less for me to be satisfied. . . . [I] loosened up (Henry et al. 1995, 73–76).

Contrary to the preceding example, unpredictability in the classroom is not always bad. Another teacher intern describes her unexpected success at setting up a writing workshop at an urban middle school with a large population of at-risk students. One day she began by telling her students that

"We're going to be starting something new these six weeks. . . . We will be transforming this classroom into a writing workshop." What was I trying to do here? They're not writers. . . . Raymond stared down at *Where's Waldo.* Michael was engrossed in an elaborate pencil drum solo. Edwina powdered her nose and under her eyes.

"Listen to me, you guys," I said, trying not to lose it before we even started. "We're starting something completely different, something you never get a chance to do in your other classes."

A few heads turned to face me. Veronica slugged Edwina, and Edwina slid her compact into her back pocket.

"What, Miss... chew gum?"

In spite of her initial reservations, this teacher made the following observations the next day—the first day of the writing workshop.

Today, it's all clicking.

"Aw, man, I told you I don't understand that part. Why does that guy in your story. . . Chris. . . say that it's too early to rob the store?" David pleads. "It doesn't make sense."

Raymond tips his desk forward and smiles. "It's too early because they want to wait until the store's almost closed."

"Well, then, you've got to say that. Right, Miss?"

I lean against the door frame and try not to laugh. I listen to the conversations

In what ways must this classroom teacher face the reality of unpredictable outcomes? What are five other basic realities that all teachers face in their work?

around me. Yes, they're loud and they're talking and they're laughing. But they're learning. My students are involved in their writing, I say to myself and shake my head (Henry et al. 1995, 54–55).

Philip Jackson describes the unpredictability of teaching in his well-known book *Life in Classrooms:* "[As] typically conducted, teaching is an opportunistic process. . . . Neither teacher nor students can predict with any certainty exactly what will happen next. Plans are forever going awry and unexpected opportunities for the attainment of educational goals are constantly emerging" (Jackson 1990, 166).

Results in the Future   Teachers strive to effect changes in their students for the future as well as for the here and now. In *Life in Classrooms,* Jackson labels this the preparatory aspect of teaching. In addition to having students perform better on next Monday's unit exam or on a criterion-referenced test mandated by the state, teachers expect students to apply their newly acquired skills and knowledge at some indeterminate, usually distant, point in the future.

Just as months or years may pass before the results of teaching become clear, teachers may wait a long time before receiving positive feedback from students. The following comment by a kindergarten teacher illustrates the delayed satisfaction that can characterize teaching:

> About a month ago I had a 22-year-old boy knock on the door. He said, "Miss R?" I said, "Yes." He is now in England, an architect; he's married and has a little girl. I thought, "This is not happening to me. I had you in kindergarten." If you teach high school and a kid comes back and he's married in two or three years, that's expected, but 16 years or 18 years—first year in kindergarten. It's rewarding. . . be it one year, or ten years down the road. . . . There are daily satisfactions—"She got it!"—that's a reward in itself, but I think it's a little bit down the road that you get your satisfaction (Cohn and Kottkamp 1993, 42–43).

Reality 2: The Difficulty of Assessing Students' Learning

It is difficult to assess what students learn as a result of being taught. The ultimate purpose of teaching is to lead the student to a greater understanding of the things and ideas of this world. But, as even the most casual appraisal of human nature will confirm, it is very difficult, perhaps impossible, to determine precisely what another human being does or does not understand. Although the aims or intentions of teaching may be specified with exacting detail, one of the realities of teaching, as the following junior high school teacher points out, is that some of what students learn may be indeterminate and beyond direct measurement:

> There is no clear end result. . . . That frustrates me. I want so badly for my joy [of teaching] to be neatly tied up so that I can look at it admiringly. . . . I want so badly to *see* my successes—I don't know, give me certificates or badges or jelly beans. Then I can stack them up, count them, and rate myself as a teacher (Henry et al. 1995, 68–69).

In spite of state-by-state efforts to institute standardized tests of basic skills and thereby hold teachers accountable, the conventional wisdom among teachers is that they are often uncertain about just what their students learn. We have miles of computer printouts with test data, but very little knowledge of what lies behind a child's written response, little understanding of how the child experiences the curriculum. As one

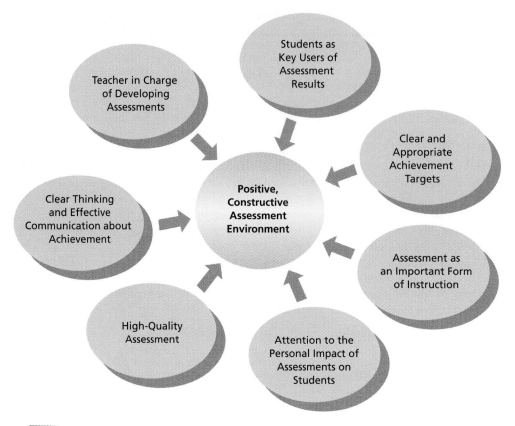

Figure 1.3

The principles of sound assessment: a critical blend
Source: Adapted from Richard J. Stiggins, *Student-Centered Classroom Assessment,* 2nd ed. Upper Saddle River, NJ: Merrill, 1997, p. 10.

educational researcher concludes: "The inaccessibility of data is similar both in science and in learning. We cannot directly 'see' subatomic particles, nor can we 'see' the inner-workings of the mind and emotions of the child. Both are inferential: both are subject to human interpretation" (Costa 1984, 202).

On the one hand, then, teachers must recognize their limited ability to determine what students actually learn; on the other, they must continuously work to become aware of the latest approaches to assessing students' learning. Figure 1.3 presents a set of guiding principles for teachers to follow in developing a student-centered approach to classroom assessment.

Reality 3: The Need for Teacher–Student Partnership

The teacher's ability to influence student behavior is actually quite limited. The very fact that we refer to the teaching–learning process indicates the extent to which classroom events are "jointly produced" (Doyle 1986, 395) and depend upon a teacher–student partnership. According to Arthur Combs (1979, 234–35) in a book aptly titled *Myths in Education: Beliefs That Hinder Progress and Their Alternatives:*

A teacher's influence on all but the simplest, most primitive forms of student behavior, even in that teacher's own classroom, cannot be clearly established. The older children get, the less teachers can influence even those few, primitive forms of behavior. The attempt to hold teachers responsible for what students do is, for all practical purposes, well nigh impossible.

At best, a teacher tries to influence students so that they make internal decisions to behave in the desired manner—whether it be reading the first chapter of *The Pearl* by Friday or solving ten addition problems during a mathematics lesson. Teaching is a uniquely demanding profession, therefore, because the work of teachers is evaluated not in terms of what teachers do but in terms of their ability "to help the students become more effective as learners," to "become active seekers after new development" (Joyce and Weil 2000, 408, 399). This reality underscores the need for a partnership between teacher and learners, including learners who are culturally diverse.

Reality 4: The Impact of Teachers' Attitudes

With the role of teacher also comes the power to influence others by example. Educational psychologist Anita E. Woolfolk (1998, 223) states that "teachers serve as models for a vast range of behaviors, from pronouncing vocabulary words to reacting to the seizure of an epileptic student, to being enthusiastic about learning." Clearly, students learn much by imitation, and teachers are models for students. In the primary grades, teachers are idolized by their young students. At the high school level, teachers have the potential to inspire students' emulation and establish the classroom tone by modeling expected attitudes and behaviors.

In *The Tact of Teaching: The Meaning of Pedagogical Thoughtfulness*, Max van Manen (1991, 167) states the importance of teachers' attitudes toward students:

> An educator needs to believe in children. Specifically he or she needs to believe in the possibilities and goodness of the particular children for whom he or she has responsibility. My belief in a child strengthens that child—provided of course that the child experiences my trust as something real and as something positive.

A high school social studies teacher expresses the same idea in this manner: "[The] relationship between teachers and students is becoming one of the most important aspects of teaching. [In] a world of broken homes and violence, the encouragement of their teachers may be the only thing students can hold onto that makes them feel good about themselves" (Henry et al. 1995, 127).

Teachers also model attitudes toward the subjects they teach and show students through their example that learning is an ongoing, life-enriching process that does not end with diplomas and graduations. Their example confirms the timeless message of Sir Rabindranath Tagore that is inscribed above the doorway of a public building in India: "A teacher can never truly teach unless he is still learning himself. A lamp can never light another lamp unless it continues to burn its own flame."

Reality 5: The Drama and Immediacy of Teaching

Interactive teaching is characterized by events that are rapid-changing, multidimensional, and irregular. We have already discussed how the outcomes of teaching are unpredictable and inconsistent. Yet the challenges of teaching go beyond this. The face-to-

How do teacher's attitudes affect students' learning? In what ways are teachers significant role models for students?

face interactions teachers have with students—what Jackson (1990, 152) has termed **interactive teaching**—are themselves rapid-changing, multidimensional, and irregular. "Day in and day out, teachers spend much of their lives 'on stage' before audiences that are not always receptive . . . teachers must orchestrate a daunting array of interpersonal interactions and build a cohesive, positive climate for learning" (Gmelch and Parkay 1995, 47).

When teachers are in the **preactive teaching** stages of their work—preparing to teach or reflecting on previous teaching—they can afford to be consistently deliberate and rational. Planning for lessons, grading papers, reflecting on the misbehavior of a student—such activities are usually done alone and lack the immediacy and sense of urgency that characterize interactive teaching. While actually working with students, however, you must be able to think on your feet and respond appropriately to complex, ever-changing situations. You must be flexible and ready to deal with the unexpected. During a discussion, for example, you must operate on at least two levels. On one level, you respond appropriately to students' comments, monitor other students for signs of confusion or comprehension, formulate the next comment or question, and be alert for signs of misbehavior. On another level, you ensure that participation is evenly distributed among students, evaluate the content and quality of students' contributions, keep the discussion focused and moving ahead, and emphasize major content areas.

During interactive teaching, the awareness that you are responsible for the forward movement of the group never lets up. Teachers are the only professionals who practice their craft almost exclusively under the direct, continuous gaze of up to thirty or forty clients. Jackson (1990, 119) sums up the experience: "The *immediacy* of classroom events is something that anyone who has ever been in charge of a roomful of students can never forget."

Reality 6: The Uniqueness of the Teaching Experience

Teaching involves a unique mode of being between teacher and student—a mode of being that can be experienced but not fully defined or described. On your journey to become a teacher, you will gradually develop your capacity to listen to students and to convey an authentic sense of concern for their learning. Unfortunately, there is no precise, easy-to-follow formula for demonstrating this to students. You will have to take into account your personality and special gifts to discover your own best way for showing this concern.

One reason it is difficult to describe teaching is that an important domain of teaching, **teachers' thought processes,** including professional reflection, cannot be

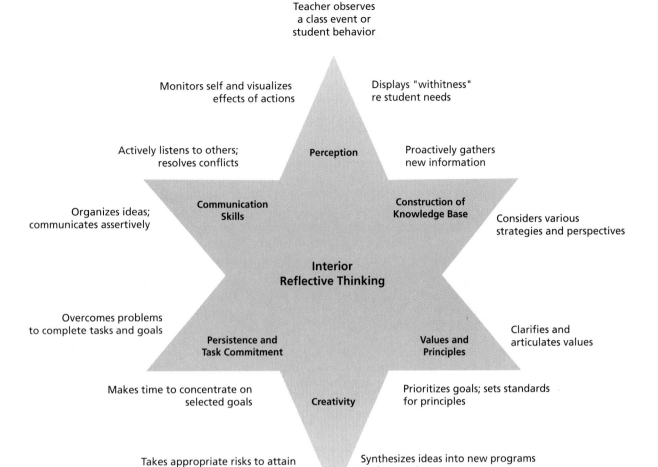

Teacher observes
a class event or
student behavior

Monitors self and visualizes
effects of actions

Displays "withitness"
re student needs

Actively listens to others;
resolves conflicts

Perception

Proactively gathers
new information

Organizes ideas;
communicates assertively

**Communication
Skills**

**Construction of
Knowledge Base**

Considers various
strategies and perspectives

**Interior
Reflective Thinking**

Overcomes problems
to complete tasks and goals

**Persistence and
Task Commitment**

**Values and
Principles**

Clarifies and
articulates values

Makes time to concentrate on
selected goals

Creativity

Prioritizes goals; sets standards
for principles

Takes appropriate risks to attain
high-priority goals

Synthesizes ideas into new programs
and strategies

**Exterior
Reflective Action**

Figure 1.4

A model of reflective action in teaching
Source: Judy W. Eby, *Reflective Planning, Teaching, and Evaluation: K–12,* 2nd ed. Upper Saddle River, NJ:
Merrill, 1996, p. 14. © 1996. Reprinted by permission of Prentice-Hall, Inc., Upper Saddle River, NJ.

observed directly. Figure 1.4 shows how the unobservable domain of the teacher's "interior reflective thinking" interacts with and is influenced by the observable domain of the teacher's "exterior reflective action." Teachers' thought processes include their theories and beliefs about students and how they learn, their plans for teaching, and the decisions they make while teaching. Thought processes and actions can be constrained by the physical setting of the classroom or external factors such as the curriculum, the principal, or the community. On the other hand, teachers' thought processes and actions may be influenced by unique opportunities, such as the chance to engage in curriculum reform or school governance. The model also illustrates a further complexity of teaching—namely, that the relationships between teacher behavior, student behavior, and student achievement are reciprocal. What teachers do is influenced not only by their thought processes before, during, and after teaching but also by student behavior and student achievement. This complexity contributes to the uniqueness of the teaching experience.

What Does Society Expect of Teachers?

The prevailing view within our society is that teachers are public servants accountable to the people. As a result, society has high expectations of teachers—some would say too high. Entrusted with our nation's most precious resource, its children and youth, today's teachers are expected to have advanced knowledge and skills and high academic and ethical standards. Although promoting students' academic progress has always been their primary responsibility, teachers are also expected to further students' social, emotional, and moral development and to safeguard students' health and well-being. Increasingly, the public calls on teachers and schools to address social problems and risk factors that affect student success.

The Public Trust

Teaching is subject to a high degree of public scrutiny and control. The level of trust that the public extends to teachers as professionals varies greatly. The public appears to have great confidence in the work that teachers do. Because of its faith in the teaching profession, the public invests teachers with considerable power over its children. For the most part, parents willingly allow their children to be influenced by teachers and expect their children to obey and respect teachers. However, the public trust increases and decreases in response to social and political changes that lead to waves of educational reform.

In the 1970s, for example, teachers were portrayed as incompetent, unprofessional, unintelligent, and generally unable to live up to the public's expectations. Calls for higher standards and minimum competency testing were an expression of diminished public trust. Further professionalization of teaching has been the response. During the 1980s, the image of teachers was battered by ominous sounding commission reports, a negative press, and public outcries for better schools. National reports, such as *A Nation at Risk,* declared that U.S. education was shockingly inadequate, if not a failure.

In the 1990s, however, deliberate efforts were made to restore dignity to the profession of teaching. To highlight the important work of teachers, public and commercial television stations aired programs with titles such as "Learning in America: Schools That Work," "America's Toughest Assignment: Solving the Education Crisis," "The Truth about Teachers," "Why Do These Kids Love School?", "Liberating America's Schools," and "America's Education Revolution: A Report from the Front." The Learning Channel began to air *Teacher TV,* a news-style program that explores education trends and issues and features teachers, schools, and communities around the country. Many national corporations initiated award programs to recognize excellence among teachers. Disney Studios, for example, initiated Disney's American Teacher Awards in 1991. As a tribute to countless outstanding teachers, a major media campaign to recruit new teachers in the early 1990s was formed around the slogan, "Be a Teacher. Be a Hero." Table 1.4 shows how people rated their public schools in selected years between 1983, just after the release of *A Nation at Risk,* and 1999.

Table 1.4

Ratings given the local public schools (in percent)

	1999	1998	1995	1993	1991	1989	1987	1985	1983
A & B	49	46	41	47	42	43	43	43	31
A	11	10	8	10	10	8	12	9	6
B	38	36	33	37	32	35	31	34	25
C	31	31	37	31	33	33	30	30	32
D	9	9	12	11	10	11	9	10	13
Fail	5	5	5	4	5	4	4	4	7
Don't know	6	9	5	7	10	9	14	13	17

Source: Alec M. Gallup, Lowell C. Rose, and Stanley M. Elan, "The 24th Annual Gallup Poll of the Public's Attitudes toward the Public Schools," *Phi Delta Kappan,* September 1992, p. 32; Stanley M. Elam and Lowell C. Rose, "The 27th Annual Phi Delta Kappa/Gallup Poll of the Public's Attitudes toward the Public Schools," *Phi Delta Kappan,* September 1995, p. 42; and Lowell C. Rose and Alec M. Gallup, "The 30th Annual Phi Delta Kappa/Gallup Poll of the Public's Attitudes toward the Public Schools," *Phi Delta Kappan,* September 1999, p. 45.

Teacher Competency and Effectiveness

Society believes that competent, effective teachers are important keys to a strong system of education. Accordingly, teachers are expected to be proficient in the use of instructional strategies, curriculum materials, advanced educational technologies, and classroom management techniques. They are also expected to have a thorough understanding of the developmental levels of their students and a solid grasp of the content they teach. To maintain and extend this high level of skill, teachers are expected to be informed of exemplary practices and to demonstrate a desire for professional development.

Teacher competency and effectiveness includes the responsibility to help all learners succeed. Though today's students come from a diverse array of backgrounds, society expects teachers to hold strong beliefs about the potential for all children. Regardless of their students' ethnicity, language, gender, socioeconomic status, family backgrounds and living conditions, abilities, or disabilities, teachers have a responsibility to ensure that all students develop to their fullest potential. To accomplish this, teachers are expected to have a repertoire of instructional strategies and resources to create meaningful learning experiences that promote students' growth and development.

Teacher Accountability

Teachers must "be mindful of the social ethic—their public duties and obligations—embodied in the practice of teaching . . ." (Hansen 1995, 143). Society agrees that teachers are primarily responsible for promoting students' learning, though it is not always in agreement about what students should learn. In any case, society expects teachers to understand how factors such as student backgrounds, attitudes, and learning styles can affect achievement; and it expects that teachers will create safe and effective learning environments. Society also believes that teachers and schools should be accountable for equalizing educational opportunity and maintaining high professional standards.

Teacher accountability also means meeting high standards of conduct. Teachers are no longer required to sign statements such as the following, taken from a 1927 contract: "I promise to sleep at least eight hours a night, to eat carefully, and to take every precaution to keep in the best of health and spirits, in order that I may be better able to render efficient service to my pupils" (Waller 1932, 43). Nevertheless, society does expect teachers to hold high standards of professional ethics and personal morality and to model behaviors that match those standards.

How Do Good Teachers View Their Work?

Teachers' overall satisfaction with their careers has increased steadily since 1981 (National Education Association 1997). Figure 1.5 shows that 62.6 percent of all teachers say they "certainly" or "probably would" become a teacher again—a proportion that compares favorably to the level of satisfaction reported by members of other professions.

Good teachers derive greatest satisfaction when they are effective in promoting students' learning—when they "make a difference" in students' lives. When you recall your most effective teachers, you probably think of particular individuals, not idealizations of the teacher's many roles. What good teachers do can be described in terms of five **modes of teaching,** which are more general and significant than a discussion of roles. You may recognize these modes in your observations of teachers and in the writings of gifted teachers when they reflect on their work. You may even acknowledge these modes of teaching as deeper reasons for becoming a teacher.

A Way of Being

In becoming a teacher, you take on the role and let it become a part of you. Increasingly, the learning of facts can be achieved easily with good books, good TV, CD-ROMs, and access to the Internet. What cannot be done in these ways is teaching styles of life, teaching what it means to be, to grow, to become actualized, to become complete. The only way a teacher can teach these qualities is to possess them. "They become living examples for their students, showing that what they say is important enough for them to apply to their own lives. They are attractive models who advertise, by their very being, that learning does produce wondrous results" (Zehm and Kottler 1993, 16).

A Creative Endeavor

Teaching is a creative endeavor in which teachers are continually shaping and reshaping lessons, events, and the experiences of their students. In *The Call to Teach*, David Hansen (1995, 13) describes the creative dimensions of teaching this way: "In metaphorical terms,

Figure 1.5

Percentage of teachers who would choose teaching again

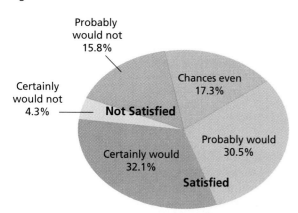

teaching is. . . more than carrying brick, mortar, and shovel. Rather, it implies being the architect of one's classroom world."

With careful attention to the details of classroom life, effective teachers artistically develop educative relationships with their students; they "read" the myriad events that emerge while teaching and respond appropriately. One high school teacher, identified as highly successful by her principal, reported: "I have to grab the kids that don't want to do math at all and somehow make them want to do this work. I'm not sure how I do it, but kids just want to do well in my class. For some mysterious reason, and I don't care why, they really want to do well."

What are the modes of teaching that define the essence of good teaching and distinguish gifted teachers? Which mode of teaching might this photo represent?

A Live Performance

Teaching is a live performance with each class period, each day, containing the unpredictable. Further, teachers are engaged in live dialogues with their classes and individual students. The experience of teaching is thus an intense, attention-demanding endeavor—an interactive one that provides minute-to-minute challenges.

Some teachers embrace the live performance aspect of teaching more than others, believing that within it lies true learning. They recognize that teaching ". . . is full of surprises; classroom lessons that lead to unexpected questions and insights; lessons that fail despite elaborate planning; spur-of-the-moment activities that work beautifully and that may change the direction of a course; students who grow and learn; students who seem to regress or grow distant" (Hansen 1995, 12).

A Form of Empowerment

Power is the dimension of teaching most immediately evident to the new teacher. It is recognized in the first-grader's awed "Teacher, is this good?" on through the high school senior's "How much will this paper count?" Customarily, teachers get respect, at least initially; the deference derives from their power to enhance or diminish their students' academic status and welfare.

Even in the most democratic classrooms, teachers have more influence than students because they are responsible for what happens when students are with them, establishing the goals, selecting the methods, setting the pace, evaluating the progress, and deciding whether students should pass or fail. How you use this power is critical. As

Caroline Bitterwolf

National Board Certified Teacher

> "*I was amazed at what I found.*"

Caroline Bitterwolf remembers sitting at her typewriter, completing her application for national certification, with a fellow teacher helping her assemble the final materials. They just made the 9:00 A.M. deadline. At least 100 hours of preparation preceded that moment, and, according to Bitterwolf, she could not have done it without the support of family, friends, her school colleagues, students, and their parents. Later, with the rigorous evaluation behind her, she would become the first Idaho teacher and one of the first 81 (of 289) national candidates to be certified by the National Board for Professional Teaching Standards (NBPTS).

Bitterwolf's telephone inquiry to the NBPTS in Detroit marked what she describes as "the beginning of a wonderful relationship." The staff's friendliness encouraged her, but when the Board's directions and standards arrived, she found them daunting. "I'll never do it. The expectations are so high. No way I'll measure up," she thought, and she put the box of information on a back shelf.

She tried to forget the box but couldn't. So she began working through the materials, and discovered that nothing was required that she was not already doing. The directions guided the seventh-grade study skills teacher to constantly reflect on and write about what she was doing, why, and how it fit her students. She also needed to document her practices with lesson plans, videotapes of her teaching, and written analyses. The time-consuming effort proved to be of real value. "I was amazed at what I found. Who I was, why I was teaching, what my goals were—it consolidated everything for me."

For the final phase of the review, the Moscow, Idaho, teacher traveled to the Vancouver, Washington, assessment center where she participated in two 12-hour days of activities, developing curriculum, evaluating materials, responding to videos of others teaching, writing essays, and being interviewed. She regards the overall application and assessment process as "the best professional development activity I have ever experienced."

Bitterwolf's involvement in national certification did not stop with her achieving national certification. She also participated in a video promoting the national standards and was elected to the National Board for Professional Teaching Standards.

That she came so far she attributes to the wonderful teachers she knew and met along the way. In addition to the teachers in her family and in her own schooling experience, Bitterwolf gives credit to a woman she regards as her professional mentor, Sally Borghart, "a four-foot ten-inch English lady who wore wedgies," who helped her teach ninth grade inner city remedial reading in Annapolis, Maryland. It was the only job Bitterwolf was able to get—a teaching assistantship through CETA (Comprehensive Employment Training Act). The transition from a southern church preschool to the tough vocabulary of inner city youths caused the young teacher to spend most of the first semester in tears. "But Sally had a way with these young adults and through her I learned, really learned, how to communicate with my students—to empathize with them. She literally taught me how to diagnose student problems and set up programs to meet their individual needs, how to set up thematic units. She was way ahead of her time."

For a teacher who moved from "no way, I'll never measure up" to being a nationally certified teacher and member of the National Board for Professional Teaching Standards, Bitterwolf's words of advice for teachers fit well: "Constantly strive to keep learning. . . do not be afraid to try new things," and be active in your profession so that we "can be the best we can be."

you know, students at any level can be humiliated by teachers who misuse their power or convey negative expectations to students. A student teacher in a fifth-grade class comments on the impact negative expectations can have on students:

> They [students] can sense how a teacher feels, especially how she feels about them personally. Students often find themselves locked into a role that they have played for so long they don't know how to get out of it. Students deserve the right to have an education. They should not have to worry about what negative comments their teachers are saying about them (Rand and Shelton-Colangelo 1999, 107).

An Opportunity to Serve

To become a teacher is to serve others professionally—students, the school, the community, and the country, depending on how broad the perspective is. Most who come to teaching do so for altruistic reasons. The altruistic dimension of teaching is at the heart of the motivation to teach. The paycheck, the public regard, and the vacations have little holding power compared to the opportunity to serve. As the authors of *On Being a Teacher* observe:

> Very few people go into education in the first place to become rich or famous. On some level, every teacher gets a special thrill out of helping others. . . . [The] teachers who flourish, those who are loved by their students and revered by their colleagues, are those who feel tremendous dedication and concern for others—not just because they are paid to do so, but because it is their nature and their ethical responsibility (Zehm and Kottler 1993, 8–9).

Whatever form the altruistic rewards of teaching take, they ennoble the profession and remind teachers of the human significance of their work.

As Keepers of the Dream

Many of our country's most talented youth and dedicated veterans in the teaching field retain the desire to teach. In part, the desire endures because teachers have been positively influenced by one or more teachers of their own, who enriched, redirected, or significantly changed their lives. The desire also endures because teachers recognize the many joys and rewards the profession offers.

Reflecting on dedicated teachers and their contributions to our lives, we are guided to teaching for the benefit it brings to others. In doing so, we become keepers of a part of the American dream—the belief that education can improve the quality of life. That dream, more powerful than all our images of teachers, is alive throughout the country in classrooms where outstanding teachers work. This textbook acknowledges these teachers in selected chapters in a special feature called *Keepers of the Dream*.

SUMMARY

Why Do You Want to Teach?

- An important reason for becoming a teacher is a desire to work with children and young people.
- Other reasons include a passion for teaching based on a love of subject, the teach-

ing life, or the teaching–learning process; the influence of teachers in one's past; and a desire to serve others and society.

■ Practical benefits of teaching include on-the-job hours at school, vacations, increasing salaries and benefits, job security, and a feeling of respect in society.

■ In contrast to the diversity of student enrollments, the backgrounds of today's teachers are less diverse; thus teachers from diverse racial and ethnic backgrounds and teachers with disabilities will experience exceptional job opportunities for the foreseeable future.

What Are the Challenges of Teaching?

■ Working conditions for teachers can be difficult and stressful; however, for most teachers satisfactions outweigh dissatisfactions.

■ Though problems in schools vary according to size of community, location, and other factors, teachers in most schools face five challenges: classroom management, social problems that impact students, need for family and community support, long working hours and job stress, and need for professional empowerment.

■ Maintaining discipline and avoiding school-based violence are major concerns among preservice teachers.

■ Social problems that impact the lives of many children and youth include substance abuse, teen pregnancies, homelessness, poverty, family distress, child abuse, violence and crime, suicide, and health problems such as HIV/AIDS and fetal alcohol syndrome.

■ Since the 1980s, teachers in suburban and rural schools have seen a steady increase in essential support from families and communities, while teachers in urban schools have seen an alarming decrease.

■ Though hours in the teacher's work day may appear attractive, over 90 percent of teachers work more than forty hours per week and spend an average ten hours per week on work not directly related to teaching assignments.

■ Though job-related factors cause some teachers to experience high levels of stress, stress-reduction activities can help teachers cope and avoid burnout.

■ As a consequence of nationwide efforts to improve schools, teachers are assuming new leadership roles and experiencing higher levels of professional empowerment.

What Is Teaching Really Like?

■ The outcomes of teaching, even in the best of circumstances, are neither predictable nor consistent.

■ It is difficult to assess what students learn as a result of being taught.

■ The teacher's ability to influence student behavior is actually quite limited.

■ With the role of teacher also comes the power to influence others by example.

■ Interactive teaching is characterized by events that are rapid-changing, multidimensional, and irregular.

- Teaching involves a unique mode of being between teacher and student—a mode of being that can be experienced but not fully defined or described.

What Does Society Expect of Teachers?

- Society has high expectations of the teachers to whom it entrusts its children and youth.
- The public's image of teachers and its attitudes toward schools have improved since the 1980s.
- Society expects teachers to be competent and effective, and it holds teachers accountable for student achievement, for helping all learners succeed, and for maintaining high standards of conduct.

How Do Good Teachers View Their Work?

- Teachers' overall satisfaction has increased significantly since the 1980s.
- Helping students learn and making a difference in students' lives provide teachers with their greatest satisfaction.
- The essence of good teaching can be described in terms of modes of teaching illustrating what good teachers do.
- Five modes of teaching are teaching as a way of being, a creative endeavor, a live performance, a form of empowerment, and an opportunity to serve.

KEY TERMS AND CONCEPTS

burnout, 19
cost of living, 11
fringe benefits, 13
interactive teaching, 26
modes of teaching, 30
moonlight, 12
A Nation at Risk, 28

preactive teaching, 26
professional
   empowerment, 19
professional portfolio, 37
realities of teaching, 21
student diversity, 6
student-mobility rates, 7

student variability, 6
Teach for America, 10
teacher accountability, 30
teacher–student ratios, 16
teachers' thought
   processes, 26
tenure, 13

APPLICATIONS AND ACTIVITIES

Teacher's Journal

1. Consider your reasons for deciding to become a teacher. How do they compare with those described in this chapter?
2. Describe a former teacher who has had a positive influence on your decision to teach. In what ways would you like to become like that teacher?
3. What is your impression of the public's image of teachers in your state or community today? What factors might be contributing to the kind of attention or lack of attention teachers are receiving?

4. Think about a time when a teacher truly motivated you to learn. What did that teacher do to motivate you? Do you believe other students in the class had the same reaction to this teacher? Why or why not?
5. Recall and describe specific experiences you had with teachers in elementary school, middle school or junior high school, or high school. Were you ever made uncomfortable because of a teacher's power over you? Were you ever ridiculed or diminished by a teacher? Or have you experienced the opposite—being elevated by a teacher's regard for you?

Teacher's Database

1. Make a list of recent portrayals of teachers in the movies, television, and other media. Analyze the portrayals in terms of the type of teacher image they present—positive, neutral, or negative.
2. Clip articles in a major newspaper that relate to one of the focus questions in this chapter. Analyze the clippings as sources of information and examples you can use to develop an answer to that question.
3. On the World Wide Web, visit the home page of Allyn and Bacon Textbooks in Education. From there you will find many resources specifically designed to help you get the most out of *Becoming a Teacher,* succeed in the course you are taking, and advance your career planning. Features include general and text-specific databases, opportunities to communicate directly with other students and faculty using *Becoming a Teacher,* and invitations to contribute your essay, portfolio idea, or written case for possible publication. Download all the information you need to participate fully in the on-line programs that have been developed for your course.
4. While you are on the Web, use your favorite search engine and search for information by key words or topics such as: teacher burnout, cost of living, moonlighting, Teach for America, accountability, teacher–student ratios, and tenure.

Observations and Interviews

1. As a collaborative project with classmates, visit a local school and interview teachers to learn about their perceptions of the rewards and challenges of teaching. Share your findings with other groups in your class.
2. Arrange to observe a teacher's class. During your observation, note evidence of the five modes of teaching discussed in this chapter. Ask your instructor for handout master 1.1, "Observing Modes of Teaching," which has been developed for this activity.
3. Ask your instructor to arrange group interviews between students in your class and students at the local elementary, middle, junior, and senior high schools. At each interview session, ask the students what characterizes good and not so good teachers. Also, ask the students what advice they would give to beginning teachers.
4. During an observation of a teacher's class, note evidence of the six realities of teaching discussed in this chapter. How many realities are evident during your observation? Which reality is most prevalent? Least prevalent? To help you record your observations, ask your instructor for handout master 1.2, "Observing Realities of Teaching."
5. Visit a first-year teacher (possibly a graduate from your institution) and ask about his or her first impressions of becoming a teacher. What aspects of teaching were difficult? Which easy? What surprises did this first-year teacher encounter? How would this person have prepared differently?

Professional Portfolio

To help you in your journey toward becoming a teacher, each chapter in this textbook includes suggestions for developing your **professional portfolio,** a collection of evidence documenting your growth and development while learning to become a teacher. At the end of this course you will be well on your way toward a portfolio that documents your knowledge, skills, and attitudes for teaching and contains valuable resources for your first teaching position.

For your first portfolio entry, expand on Teacher's Journal entry #1, which asks you to consider your reasons for becoming a teacher. In your entry (or videotaped version), identify the rewards of teaching for you. Identify the satisfactions. Also, describe the aspects of teaching that you will find challenging.

2

Learning to Teach

Teaching ultimately requires judgment, improvisation, and conversation about means and ends. Human qualities, expert knowledge and skill, and professional commitment together compose excellence in this craft.

—National Board for
Professional Teaching Standards

focus questions

1. What essential knowledge do you need to teach?

2. What are five ways of viewing the teacher knowledge base?

3. How do reforms in teacher education affect you?

4. What can you learn from observing in classrooms?

5. How can you gain practical experience for becoming a teacher?

6. How can you develop your teaching portfolio?

7. How can you benefit from mentoring relationships?

8. What opportunities for continuing professional development will you have?

The room was filled with the chatter of writing workshop. Nat puzzled over two crayons in his hand, one of them blue: "Mrs. Hankins, ain't you had you a blue bicycle when you was a little-girl-teacher?" Nat had a way of naming me for what I was: always a teacher—or was it always a little girl? I answered Nat's present question, remembering my past blue bicycle and a childhood story about it that I had shared with the children recently.

Perhaps it was one of those "tell-me-about-when-you-were-little" moments that brought writing memoirs to the forefront of my teaching journal. Perhaps it was the need to make some sense of the cacophonous days with my three special students, Nat, Loretta, and Rodney, who had all been damaged in utero by crack cocaine or alcohol. The original impetus for these writings is lost to me now, but, as Lucy Calkins (1991, 169) says, writing memoirs "has everything to do with rendering the ordinariness of our lives so that it becomes significant." The past seemed to wrap itself around my present-day questions, and as the number of memoirs grew, my journal became a place for uncovering the significant. . . .

I wrote up a study of Nat, Loretta, and Rodney's journey through kindergarten and presented parts of the study at a conference. After the presentation, I wrote the following reflection in my journal:

So, I keep this journal. It was easier when no one else knew or cared that I wrote. It's a teaching journal. It's a personal journal. It's a research journal. It's both a personal and teaching journal because John Dewey first and Lucy Calkins later taught me to reflect on my day and my life in the same breath. It's both a teaching and research journal because I no longer believe that teaching can be separated from research. (Perhaps it CAN be but it shouldn't be.) The question is . . . I guess . . . Can it be both personal and research journal? That's what people really want me to defend. But how can I tell people what my heart and head do together in my classroom? (journal entry, April)

I wrote at nap time, while waiting for faculty meetings to begin, during the last ten minutes before turning out the light each night, and on the backs of church bulletins or napkins in restaurants. I had never heard of field notes at the time. I read recently a definition of ethnographic field notes as "the systematic ways of writing what one observes and learns while participating in the daily rounds of the lives of others" (Emerson, Fretz, and Shaw 1995, 18). As the year progressed, I fell into a system of sorts as I recorded the "lives of others." My journal served, then, as the field notes of a teacher. Mine were records of what Emerson et al. (1995) call "headnotes"—mental notes—"hard notes"—direct observations—and "heartnotes"—my feelings and reflections. . . .

When I began seriously listening to my life, my teaching life, I also began to listen to my students' lives at a different level. . . . I became more tolerant of those who were different from me. When I began to stop and examine the flashes of memory that jolted me, I became a more patient teacher. I more often saw the students and their parents as people; people walking in and out of pain, in and out of joy, in and out of socially constructed prisons (Hankins 1998, 81, 83, 93).*

In the preceding excerpt from her article in the *Harvard Educational Review,* Karen Hale Hankins, a first-grade teacher at Whit Davis Elementary School in Athens, Georgia, describes how reflective journal writing enabled her to see significant connections between her personal history and her present experiences in the classroom. By purposely examining her "mental notes," "direct observations," and "feelings and reflections," Hankins learned how to "reach and teach" the students with whom she once felt she had little in common. Her ability to reflect upon her experiences in the classroom and her appreciation for the interconnectedness of teaching and research are the hallmarks of a professional teacher. Furthermore, her reflections are reminders that teaching is a complex act—one that requires thoughtfulness, insight into the motivations of others, and good judgment.

What Essential
Knowledge Do You Need to Teach?

Students preparing to become teachers must have three kinds of knowledge before they can manage effectively the complexities of teaching: knowledge of self and students, knowledge of subject, and knowledge of educational theory and research. It is to this essential knowledge that we now turn.

Self-Knowledge

Effective teachers are aware of themselves and sensitive to the needs of their students. Although it is evident that teachers should understand their students as fully and deeply as possible, it is less evident that this understanding depends on their level of self-knowledge. If teachers are knowledgeable about their needs (and, most important, able to take care of those needs), they are better able to help their students. As Arthur Jersild (1955, 3), one of the first educators to focus attention on the connection between the teacher's personal insight and professional effectiveness, pointed out, a teacher's self-understanding and self-acceptance are prerequisites for helping students to know and accept themselves.

Teachers' self-evaluations often are influenced by emotions that teachers may experience when they teach, such as anxiety or loneliness. Promoting anxiety are the realities of teaching outlined in Chapter 1. For example, three conditions that cloud teachers' efforts are (1) the interminable nature of teaching (i.e., their work is never completed), (2) the intangible and often unpredictable characteristics of teaching results, and (3) the inability to attribute learning results to specific teachers' instruction. Unlike architects, lawyers, and doctors, teachers can never stand back and admire their work. If a student does well, that success rightfully belongs to the student.

Teachers thus need to develop the ability to tolerate ambiguities and to reduce their anxieties about being observably effective. Without this ability, a teacher "can feel that one is 'wrong,' 'missing something,' a 'bad fit' with students and with teaching itself. One can feel that one's circumstances are unfair, that one is giving but not receiving. One can feel helpless, not knowing what to do, not even knowing how to get the frustration out of mind let alone how to resolve it in practice" (Hansen 1995, 60).

Teachers can also experience loneliness or psychological isolation, since most of their time is spent interacting with children and youth, not adults. Though increased opportunities for professional collaboration and networking are reducing teacher isolation, teachers are behind classroom doors most of the day, immersed in the complexities of teaching and trying to meet the diverse needs of their students. Most teachers would welcome more interaction with their colleagues, especially time to observe one another. Without opportunities to receive feedback from one's peers, teachers are deprived of an important catalyst for professional growth. As Elliot Eisner puts it: "The result of professional isolation is the difficulty that teachers encounter in learning what they themselves do in their own classrooms when they teach. [How] can a teacher learn that he or she is talking too much, not providing sufficient time for student reflection, raising low-order questions, or is simply boring students? Teachers unaware of such features of their own performance are in no position to change them" (1998, 160–61). Additionally, by observing how a colleague responds to the challenges of teaching, the observer has an opportunity to reflect on his or her approaches to meeting those same challenges. For example, a fourth-grade teacher came to the following insight as a result of observing his teaching partner: "Being a teacher is so much more than an extensive repertoire of strategies and techniques. [To] be a teacher is to find a way to live within an environment filled with dilemmas" (Hole 1998, 419).

Knowledge of Students

Knowledge of students is also important. Student characteristics such as their aptitudes, talents, learning styles, stage of development, and their readiness to learn new material are among the essential knowledge teachers must have. The importance of this knowledge is evident in comments made by an intern at a middle school: "To teach a kid well you have to know a kid well. . . . teaching middle school takes a special breed of teachers who understand the unique abilities and inabilities . . . [of] those undergoing their own metamorphosis into teenagers" (Henry et al. 1995, 124–25). Teachers gain this kind of knowledge through study, observation, and constant interaction. Without considerable understanding of children and youth, teachers' efforts to help students learn and grow can be inappropriate and, in some cases, counterproductive. Teachers' expectations of students directly affect student achievement. The following Professional Reflection activity is designed to guide you in reflecting on opportunities you have already had to acquire knowledge about learners.

 **Professional Reflection**   **Inventorying your knowledge of children and youth**

To be accepted into a teacher preparation program, you may be required by your college or university to have prior experiences working with children and youth. For admission to Washington State University's teacher education program, for example, students must have 80 hours of supervised work (paid or volunteer) in a "teaching" capacity with persons age four through adult. The knowledge of children and youth acquired through such experiences provides an excellent foundation upon which to begin your preparation for becoming a teacher.

Use the following outline to inventory your experiences working with children and youth. Your experiences might include working with service clubs such as Girl Scouts or Boy Scouts, 4-H, Campfire, and youth groups; volunteering at a child care center; coaching a sport as part of a parks and recreation program; or tutoring young children in reading or mathematics.

After completing your inventory, reflect on your experiences. During which experiences were you functioning, at least partially, in the role of "teacher"? For example, did you have to demonstrate the skills involved in a particular sport? As a member of a club in high school, did you explain club activities to new members or to parents? While holding a leadership position in a group, were you expected to function as a "role model" to other members of the group?

Setting	Activity	Participants' Age and Sex	Your Role	Date
Example:				
Summer sports program	Taught swimming	Coed, ages 6–8	Camp counselor	Summer 2000
1.				
2.				
3.				

Knowledge of Subject

With the title of *teacher* comes an assumption of knowledge. Those outside the field of education expect a teacher to be a ready reference for all sorts of information. Clearly, teachers who have extensive knowledge of their subjects are better equipped to help their students learn. However, knowledge of subject matter does not translate into an understanding of *how* to share that knowledge with students —a point illustrated in a case study conducted by a team of researchers at the National Center for Research on Teacher Learning. The case focused on "Mary," an undergraduate literature major enrolled in a teacher education program at a major university. By any standards, Mary was a subject-matter expert—she was valedictorian of a large, urban high school; had straight A's in the literature courses she had taken; and had a sophisticated understanding of literature, especially poetry. The case study revealed that Mary had little understanding of classroom activities that would show her students *how* to read with sophistication and concluded that "some prospective teachers may come to teacher education unaware of how they have learned the processes they use and that render them expert. Unaided by their disciplines in locating the underpinnings of their expertise, these skilled, talented, and desirable recruits may easily become, ironically, those who can *do* but who cannot *teach*" (Holt-Reynolds 1999, 43).

Extensive knowledge of subject matter, as the National Board for Professional Teaching Standards (1994, 19–20) puts it, "entails more than being able to recite lists of dates, multiplication tables, or rules of grammar. [Accomplished] teachers possess what is sometimes called **'pedagogical content knowledge.'** Such understanding is the joint product of wisdom about teaching, learning, students and content. It includes knowledge of the most appropriate ways to present the subject matter to students through analogies, metaphors, experiments, demonstrations and illustrations."

Knowledge of Methods for Applying Educational Theory and Research

Theories about learners and learning guide the decision making of professional teachers. Not only do such teachers know that a certain strategy works, but they also know *why* it works. Because they recognize the importance of theories, they have at their disposal a greater range of options for problem solving than teachers who have not

Which type of knowledge do teachers need more— subject-matter knowledge or professional knowledge?

I f you know your subject well, can you teach it well? If you know how to teach well, can you teach anything? Which of the two forms of knowledge is more important for teachers—subject-matter knowledge or professional knowledge?

At one time, individuals preparing to become teachers majored in elementary or secondary education. After publication of *A Nation at Risk,* described later, many states prohibited such majors and required instead that students preparing to teach major in an academic subject or, in the case of those preparing to teach at the elementary level, in multiple academic subjects. Today, that shift in requirements is being reconsidered. Some educators see the need to return to an emphasis on pedagogy, stressing the importance of teaching skills and knowledge about learning, brain research, and communication. Others are still emphatic that it is more important that teachers be well-educated individuals who have an in-depth knowledge of the subjects that they teach. Where do you stand on this issue?

Subject-matter knowledge is most needed.

Satisfaction with the quality of the education that teachers in the United States were providing was at a disturbingly low point in 1983 when the National Commission on Excellence in Education published its report *A Nation at Risk.* The report alarmed the American public by stating that "if an unfriendly foreign power had attempted to impose on America the mediocre educational performance that exists today, we might well have viewed it as an act of war (National Commission on Excellence in Education 1983). Teachers became the scapegoats for the problem. Critics said that teachers might be able to teach well, but they had nothing to teach and were uneducated themselves. Around the country, state-wide testing programs were implemented to screen out teachers who were inadequately prepared in the basic reading, writing, and mathematics skills and in the subject matter they taught. In some states, students in teacher preparation programs

were not allowed to student teach until they had passed state tests on their subject-matter expertise.

In addition to the argument that teachers need to be prepared with subject-matter knowledge in order to meet students' curricular needs is the recognition that teachers model to their students what an educated person is. For all teachers, but especially those at the elementary school level, what they teach most is themselves, who they are. Day in and day out, they show students their values, beliefs, and knowledge, even as they teach the subject matter they are required to teach. The illustrations they offer, the language they use, and the perspectives they take draw on their personal knowledge base.

Marva Collins, the Chicago teacher who stretched the minds of inner-city children with the writings of Aristotle and Shakespeare, was successful in her teaching in large measure because of who she was and what she knew. Her knowledge of history, economics, and literature, especially poetry, enriched the learning of her elementary school children. Similarly, Jaime Escalante attracted national attention and became the subject of a popular film, *Stand and Deliver,* because of his success teaching his economically stressed Latino students to perform impressively well on the Scholastic Achievement Test in calculus. Most who followed his story would agree that his effectiveness was more attributable to his personal spirit, his in-depth knowledge of mathematics, and his understanding of history and culture than to his knowledge of pedagogy per se.

Subject-matter expertise is thus more important for teachers because they must offer students much more than limited, superficial information about increasingly complex topics and because they should model to students what an educated person is.

Professional knowledge is most needed.

Today, some education scholars support returning to a greater emphasis on professional knowledge. They base their position on research results such as these:

■ Many studies have found positive relationships between education coursework and teacher performance in the classrooms. These relationships are stronger and more consistent than those between subject matter knowledge and teacher performance (Darling-Hammond, Wise, and Klein 1995, 24).

- States are beginning to require that students in teacher preparation programs pass tests of pedagogical skills. In California, candidates for certification in elementary education must pass a test assessing their skills in the teaching of reading, and in Maryland, all teachers seeking certification must pass four reading methods courses (Sosniak 1999, 185–204).

The premise of these efforts is that subject-matter knowledge alone is not enough. To paraphrase author Walker Percy's observation, "Some people get all A's and flunk life," in education, some people get all A's and flunk teaching. Academic knowledge does not translate automatically to teaching effectiveness. That fact can be illustrated by the teachers who drop out of Teach for America, an ambitious program that attempts to bring the United States' best minds, graduates from the nation's most respected universities, to the country's neediest students in urban and rural communities. Some in the program find that their desire to serve, their expertise in their discipline, and five to eight weeks of intensive training are not enough to survive in a classroom.

Proponents of greater professional knowledge for teachers observe that teaching has become an increasingly complex and challenging endeavor. Students in today's classrooms are more diverse in cultural backgrounds, educational needs, and communication and learning styles. As Linda Darling-Hammond (1999, 222–223) observes:

In a typical classroom of 25 students, today's teacher will serve at least four or five students with specific educational needs that require professional expertise previously reserved to a few specialists . . . [and] will need considerable knowledge to develop curriculum and teaching strategies that address the wide range of learning approaches, experiences, and prior levels of knowledge the other students bring with them, and an understanding of how to work within a wide range of family and community contexts.

Professional knowledge is thus more important for teachers because simply knowing a subject well does not guarantee being able to transmit it well, especially in light of the diverse and complex needs of students in today's classrooms.

Where do you stand on this issue?

1. What arguments can you give to defend your position?

2. What compromise position would be feasible and effective?

3. How can students best learn each type of knowledge?

4. What other questions are raised within each position—for instance, how specific should subject matter knowledge be? Should one know all of "science" or only "biology"?

5. Which type of professional knowledge is most needed for new teachers and which would be more useful later in a teacher's career?

Recommended Sources

Darling-Hammond, L., Wise, A. E., and Klein, S. P. (1995). *A license to teach: Building a profession for 21st-century schools.* Boulder:Westview Press.

Darling-Hammond, L. (1999). Educating teachers for the next century: Rethinking practice and policy. In *The education of teachers: Ninety-eighth yearbook of the National Society for the Study of Education,* Part 1. Chicago: University of Chicago Press.

National Commission on Excellence in Education. (1983). *A nation at risk: The imperative for educational reform.* (Washington, DC: Government Printing Office.)

Sosniak, L. A. (1999). Professional and subject matter knowledge for teacher education. In G. A. Griffin (Ed.). *the education of teachers: ninety-eighth yearbook of the National Society for the Study of Education,* Part 1. Chicago: University of Chicago Press.

What kinds of basic knowledge and skills do teachers need to do their jobs well? How will you acquire and develop knowledge and skills in these areas?

developed their repertoire of theories. Your ultimate goal as a professional is to apply theoretical knowledge to the practical problems of teaching.

To illustrate the usefulness of research on students' learning, we present six teaching strategies that Barak Rosenshine (1995, 267) recommends, based on his and others' research on cognitive processing, studies of teachers whose students have higher achievement gains than students of other teachers, and research on cognitive strategies.

1. Present new material in small steps so that the working memory does not become overloaded.
2. Help students develop an organization for the new material.
3. Guide student practice by (a) supporting students during initial practice and (b) providing for extensive student processing.
4. When teaching higher level tasks, support students by providing them with cognitive strategies.
5. Help students to use cognitive strategies by providing them with procedural prompts (e.g., questions students ask themselves while learning new material— "who," "what," "why," "when," etc.) and modeling the use of procedural prompts.
6. Provide for extensive student practice.

Research on students' learning is not intended to set forth, in cookbook fashion, exactly what teachers should do to increase students' learning. Instead, it may be helpful to think of educational research as providing teachers with rules of thumb to guide their practice. For example, Rosenshine, Meister, and Chapman (1996, 198) point out that, in spite of extensive research on the effectiveness of procedural prompts, "at the present time, developing procedural prompts appears to be an art. [It] is difficult to derive any prescriptions on how to develop effective procedural prompts for cognitive strategies in reading, writing, and subject matter domains." Finally, noted educational psychologist Lee Cronbach (quoted in Eisner, 1998, 112) may have put it best when he said "[educational research] is to help practitioners use their heads."

What Are Five Ways of Viewing the Teacher Knowledge Base?

Just as people hold different expectations for schools and teachers, there are different views on the knowledge and abilities teachers need to teach well. The complexities of teaching make it difficult to describe in exact detail the **knowledge base** on which teaching as a profession rests. This difficulty results, in part, because there is no universally accepted definition of what good teaching is. Educational researchers are still learning

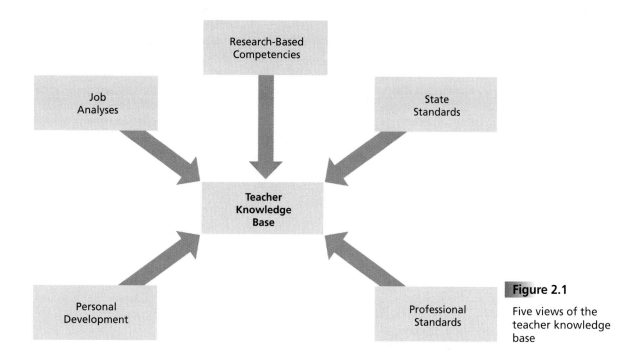

Figure 2.1

Five views of the teacher knowledge base

what good teachers know and *how* they use that knowledge. Five widespread views of teachers' knowledge and abilities are portrayed in Figure 2.1.

A Personal Development View

One view of what teachers need to know and be able to do places primary emphasis on who the teacher is as a person. According to this view, teachers should be concerned with developing themselves as persons so that they may learn to use themselves more effectively. The importance of personal development is described as follows by the authors of *On Being a Teacher*: ". . . teachers who appear in charge of their own lives, who radiate power, tranquility, and grace in their actions, are going to command attention and respect. People will follow them anywhere. . . . What we are saying is that you have not only the option, but also the imperative, to develop the personal dimensions of your functioning, as well as your professional skills" (Zehm and Kottler 1993, 15).

What this approach requires, then, is that teachers continually develop their powers of observation and reflection so that they can most effectively respond to the needs of students. Teaching becomes an authentic, growth-oriented encounter between teacher and students. An important dimension of this **personal development view** is the teacher's need for self-knowledge, particularly in regard to oneself as a learner.

Research-Based Competencies

Since the late 1980s, several states and a few large cities have developed their own lists of **research-based competencies** that beginning teachers must demonstrate. These competencies are derived from educational research that has identified what effective teachers do. Typically, the states have developed *behavioral indicators* for each competency, which trained observers from universities and school districts use to determine to what extent teachers actually exhibit the target behaviors in the classroom.

The Florida Performance Measurement System (FPMS) was the first research-based performance system to be implemented on a statewide basis. Beginning teachers in Florida must now demonstrate behaviors in six domains: planning, management of student conduct, instructional organization and development, presentation of subject matter, verbal and nonverbal communication, and testing (student preparation, administration, and feedback). Appendix 2.1 presents the Summative Observation Instrument for the FPMS and the "effective" and "ineffective" behavioral indicators for four of those domains.

State Standards

In addition to sets of research-based competencies for evaluating practicing teachers, several states have developed performance-based standards for what new teachers should know and be able to do. Known as **outcome-based** or **performance-based teacher education,** the new approach is based on several assumptions:

- Outcomes are demonstrations of learning rather than a list of teaching specializations, college courses completed, or concepts studied.
- Outcomes are performances that reflect the richness and complexity of the teacher's role in today's classrooms—not discrete, single behaviors.
- Demonstrations of learning must occur in authentic settings—that is, settings similar to those within which the teacher will teach.
- Outcomes are culminating demonstrations of what beginning teachers do in real classrooms.

Typically, outcome-based standards are developed with input from teachers, teacher educators, state department of education personnel, and various professional associations. To illustrate state standards for teacher preparation, we present standards from Kentucky in Appendix 2.2.

A Job-Analysis Approach

Another view of what teachers need to know and be able to do is based on the job analyses that some school districts conduct. Typically, a **job analysis** begins with a review of existing job descriptions and then proceeds to interviews with those currently assigned to the job and their supervisors regarding the activities and responsibilities associated with the job. These data are then analyzed to identify the dimensions of the job. Finally, interview questions based on the dimensions are developed and used by district personnel responsible for hiring.

To illustrate the job-analysis view of the knowledge, skills, and attitudes needed by teachers, we present the thirteen dimensions used for selecting "star" urban teachers. By comparing the behaviors and beliefs of outstanding urban teachers with those of quitters and failures, Martin Haberman (1995, 779–80) and his colleagues at the University of Wisconsin, Milwaukee, identified thirteen characteristics of successful teachers of low-income urban students. These characteristics, identified by principals, supervisors, other teachers, parents, and the teachers themselves, include the following:

technology

highlights

What technology related knowledge and skills do teachers need?

Today, thousands of teachers and students routinely use desktop and laptop computers with built-in modems, faxes, and CD-ROM players; camcorders; optical scanners; speech and music synthesizers; laser printers; digital cameras; and LCD projection panels. In addition, they use sophisticated software for e-mail, word processing, desktop publishing, presentation graphics, spreadsheets, databases, and multimedia applications.

To prepare teachers to use these new technologies, many teacher education programs and state departments of education have developed technology competency guidelines for classroom teachers. For example, Colorado teachers are now required to have technology skills in three areas: basic computer/technology operations and concepts, personal and professional use of technology, and integration of technology into a standards-based curriculum. The following competencies are included in the Colorado guidelines. How many of these competencies do you possess, and what steps can you take to acquire those you do not have?

1. Media Communications and Integration
- Set up and operate video media [e.g., videotape recorders, laser disk players and digital video disk (DVD)]
- Connect video output devices and other presentation systems to computers and video sources for large-screen display
- Use painting, drawing, and authoring tools
- Plan, create and use linear and nonlinear multimedia presentations
- Use imaging devices such as scanners, digital cameras, and/or video cameras with computer systems and software

2. Telecommunications
- Connect to the Internet or an online service

- Use Internet search engines
- Use a web browser to access and use resources on Internet and World Wide Web (WWW)
- Download and print resources from the WWW
- Use URL management tools (e.g., "bookmarks" and/or "favorite sites")
- Telnet to a remote computer on the Internet
- Connect to, and use resources from, the Access Colorado Library and Information Network (ACLIN) and the CDE web site
- Use electronic mail (compose, send, retrieve, read, reply to sender, reply to all and forward)
- Attach files to e-mail messages
- Retrieve and use attachments (e.g., view, read, save and print)
- Configure and use specialized e-mail lists relevant to professional information needs
- Create and use group addresses for electronic mail
- Collaborate with peers through available tools (e.g., e-mail, web sites, threaded and other on-line discussions)

Source: Adapted from *Colorado Technology Competency Guidelines for Classroom Teachers and School Library Media Specialists,* Educational Telecommunications Unit, Colorado Department of Education, January 1999.

- *Persistence*
- *Protecting learners and learning*—Star teachers see protecting and enhancing students' involvement in learning activities as their highest priority. . . .
- *Application of generalizations*—[Stars are] able to take principles and concepts from a variety of sources (i.e., courses, workshops, books, and research) and translate them into practice.

What Are Five Ways of Viewing the Teacher Knowledge Base?   **49**

- *Approach to students "at-risk"*—Star teachers believe that, regardless of the life conditions their students face, they as teachers bear a primary responsibility for sparking their students' desire to learn.
- *Professional versus personal orientation to students*—[Stars] use such terms as *caring, respect,* and *concern,* and they enjoy the love and affection of students when it occurs naturally. But they do not regard it as a prerequisite for learning.
- *Burnout: its causes and cures*—[Star teachers] recognize that even good teachers will eventually burn out if they are subjected to constant stress, so they learn how to protect themselves. . . .
- *Fallibility*—[Stars] can accept their own mistakes.

The remaining six dimensions are *organizational ability, physical/emotional stamina, teaching style* modeled on coaching, *explanation of success* based on students' effort rather than ability, *rapport* with students, and *readiness* to believe that education will provide students with the best chance of "making it" in American society.

Professional Views

Various professional associations have outlined what teachers should know and be able to do. The **National Board for Professional Teaching Standards (NBPTS),** established in 1987 as an outgrowth of the Carnegie Forum report *A Nation Prepared: Teachers for the 21st Century,* has developed the following five general standards on which voluntary national teacher certification will be based; specific standards are also being developed in more than thirty certification areas.

- Teachers are committed to students and their learning.
- Teachers know the subjects they teach and how to teach those subjects to students.
- Teachers are responsible for managing and monitoring student learning.
- Teachers think systematically about their practice and learn from experience.
- Teachers are members of learning communities (National Board for Professional Teaching Standards 1994, 13–14).

By the end of 1999, the NBPTS had set the national standard for excellence in teaching, and almost 2,000 teachers held Board certification. The goal of the NBPTS is to have 100,000 Board certified teachers by 2006.

Standards proposed by the **Interstate New Teacher Assessment and Support Consortium (INTASC),** also established in 1987, reflect a trend toward performance-based or outcome-based assessment of essential knowledge and abilities for teachers. In other words, such standards describe what teachers should know and be able to do rather than list courses that teachers need in order to receive a license to teach. To enhance collaboration among states for the initial licensing of teachers, INTASC proposed in early 1993 ten principles that are compatible with the standards proposed by the NBPTS (see Appendix 2.3). Specific statements for essential "knowledge," "dispositions," and "performances" were also developed for each principle.

In light of the five differing views of what teachers ought to know and be able to do, it seems clear that becoming a teacher is complex and demanding. We believe that effective teachers use five kinds of knowledge and skills to meet the challenges of the profession. As Figure 2.2 shows, effective teachers are guided by **reflection** and a **problem-solving orientation.** On the basis of reflection and problem solving, they use knowledge of self and students (including cultural differences), knowledge of subject matter, and knowledge of educational theory and research to create optimum conditions.

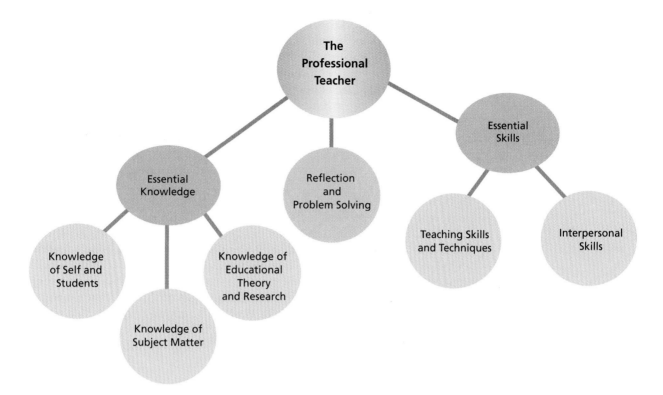

Figure 2.2

Essential knowledge
and skills for the
professional teacher

How Do Reforms in Teacher Education Affect You?

Since the publication in 1983 of *A Nation at Risk: The Imperative for Educational Reform,* the United States has experienced an unprecedented push for reform in education. During that time, numerous commissions were established and scores of reports were written outlining what should be done to improve America's schools. Most of these reports called for changes in the education of teachers. In fact, the preparation program you are now involved in probably has been influenced by this **educational reform movement.** Calls for reform in teacher education have emphasized increased academic preparation, an expanded role for schools, and a national board for teacher certification.

Increased Academic Preparation

One call for the reform of teacher education was made by the **Holmes Group,** named after Henry W. Holmes, dean of the Harvard Graduate School of Education during the 1920s. The Holmes Group was initially made up of ninety-six major universities. In *Tomorrow's Teachers,* a 1986 report written by thirteen deans of education and one college president, the Holmes Group recommended that all teachers have a bachelor's degree in an academic field and a master's degree in education. Although the Holmes Group viewed additional academic preparation as a means of enhancing the professional status of teachers, critics maintained that students' education would be delayed and be more expensive, with no assurance that students who spent five years obtaining a teaching certificate would be paid more.

The Holmes Group held an action summit in 1993 to develop a comprehensive plan for redesigning the schools of education at Holmes Group member institutions. The plan outlined steps for creating Tomorrow's School of Education (TSE)—an institution that has put into practice the Holmes Group agenda for the reform of teacher education. In early 1995, the Holmes Group released the TSE plan, which recommended that teacher educators become more involved with schools and that students move through a five-year program in cohorts. The report also urged colleges of education to establish **professional development schools** (PDSs) that are linked to colleges or universities and operate on the same principle as teaching hospitals. Students act as intern teachers, and college faculty and school staff develop new teaching methods and collaborate on educational research projects.

In 1996, after a decade of what it described as "uneven progress" in the reform of teacher education and a realization that "the reform of professional education is so complicated and difficult that it has not yielded to any one reform group's efforts to improve it," the Holmes Group joined with other professional organizations—including the National Board for Professional Teaching Standards, the National Education Association, and the American Federation of teachers—to create the **Holmes Partnership.** The Holmes Partnership adopted six principal goals: high quality professional preparation; simultaneous renewal (of public K–12 schools and pre- and in-service education); equity, diversity, and cultural competence; scholarly inquiry and programs of research; faculty development; and policy initiation (Holmes Partnership 1999).

Expanded Role for Schools

Based on his study of teacher education programs around the country, noted educator John Goodlad set forth his plan for the simultaneous renewal of schools and teacher preparation programs in his 1994 book, *Educational Renewal: Better Teachers, Better Schools.* To improve teacher preparation, Goodlad recommended the creation of Centers of Pedagogy that would operate according to a specific set of principles. These centers would take the place of current teacher education departments, and they would be staffed by a team of teacher educators, liberal arts professors, and educators from local schools. In addition, Goodlad recommended that school districts and universities create jointly operated partner schools. Selected teachers at the partner school would divide their time between teaching students at the school and supervising beginning teachers. Partner schools would thus become centers for the renewal of education as well as laboratory schools for the professional development of beginning teachers.

National Certification

The National Board for Professional Teaching Standards (NBPTS) was created to issue certificates to teachers who meet the Board's high standards. The NBPTS is governed by a sixty-three member board of directors, the majority of whom are active classroom teachers. In 1995, five nationally certified teachers were elected to the board.

The NBPTS encourages school districts and states to pay its certification fee ($2,000 for 1998–99) on behalf of teachers who seek board certification. Candidates first submit portfolios documenting their performance over several months; then they complete a series of exercises at an assessment center. Examples of NBPTS portfolio activities and assessment center activities for the early childhood/generalist and early adolescence/English language arts are presented in Appendix 2.4 and in "NBPTS Assessment Center Activities on this book's web site.

State Standards Boards

To regulate and improve the professional practice of teachers, administrators, and other education personnel, states have established **professional standards boards.** In some states, standards boards have the authority to implement standards; in others, they serve in an advisory capacity to educational policymakers. In Washington state, for example, the Washington Advisory Board for Professional Teaching Standards recently made a recommendation to the State Board of Education calling for a three-level teacher certification system. Candidates, on completion of an approved program, would receive a Residency Certificate. With demonstration of successful teaching and a recommendation from the employing school district, a candidate then would be eligible for a renewable, five-year Professional Certificate. Finally, persons who hold national certification from the National Board for Professional Teaching Standards or who hold a combination of advanced degrees, experience, and proficiency in performance-based standards would be eligible for the optional Professional Career Certificate.

In the wake of national reports such as *What Matters Most: Teaching for America's Future* (National Commission on Teaching and America's Future 1996) and *Quality Counts 2000: Who Should Teach? (Education Week* 2000), which highlighted the common practice of teachers teaching "out-of-field," professional standards boards in many states have launched extensive reviews of their teacher certification standards. Also, some standards boards have addressed whether education students' subject matter preparation should continue to be separate from professional preparation and whether alternative routes to certification such as school district-controlled internship programs should be encouraged.

What Can You Learn from Observing in Classrooms?

Classroom observations are a vital element of many **field experiences.** Students report that these experiences aid them greatly in making a final decision about entering the teaching field. Most become more enthusiastic about teaching and more motivated to learn the needed skills; a few decide that teaching is not for them. Recognizing the value of observations, many teacher education programs are increasing the amount of field experiences and placing such fieldwork earlier in students' programs. For example, at Washington State University (WSU), students preparing to become elementary teachers complete one week of classroom observations as part of their first education course. Later in their program, WSU students participate in "Schools First!", a three-week, full-day practicum (or field experience) at a school. In addition, as part of a required methods course, the WSU program is piloting an "advanced" practicum that spans eight weeks and requires several hours of classroom observation each week.

Technology and Classroom Observations

Currently, many universities and school districts are cooperating on the use of two-way interactive compressed video technology to enable preservice teachers on campus to observe live coverage in school classrooms off campus. Compressed video can be transmitted over existing telephone lines or the Internet in a relatively inexpensive, unob-

Ruth's Dilemma

This case recounts a dilemma typical for many who decide to enter the teaching field. Ruth, who works in the same department as one of the authors, will have made her decision by the time this text is in print.

Ruth knew it was time to begin the process to become a teacher. She wondered what had influenced her decision most—her love of English literature, her youngest son's graduation from high school, or the fact that she was surrounded daily by people teaching or taking education classes. As secretary to the School of Education's associate dean, she oversaw the details of class schedules, textbook orders, room assignments, program evaluations, faculty teaching loads, and students' petitions, all to help smooth the way for others to become teachers. Now she had decided to enter the field herself.

She had applied to the program, outlined a plan, and sought her dean's permission to proceed. The former school superintendent was sincere in his encouragement. Certainly she could leave the office early on Tuesdays to attend classes. And what level did she plan to teach? High school or elementary? Ruth wasn't sure.

The question remained even after she had made several elementary and high school classroom observations in her Introduction to Teaching class. The answer wasn't as clear for Ruth as it seemed to be for many of her classmates. Like many of them, she had wanted to be a teacher for as long as she could remember, but unlike them, she had given up the idea because she was unable to gain the needed financial support until she learned that staff could participate in the university's degree completion program. Also, like a number of her classmates, a teacher had inspired her—her high school English teacher had made the subject come alive for her.

By the end of this course, she would have to choose between preparing to teach at the secondary or elementary school level, and her dilemma remained. She loved English literature. Whenever she talked about the books she had read, she felt that words were inadequate for capturing the experience. With other students in class, she thought out loud about the problem: "In high school you have so many students. How could

trusive, and time-efficient way. **Distance learning**—the use of technology such as video transmissions that enables students to receive instruction at multiple, often remote sites—now enables teacher education programs to use the power of models for learning how to teach. For example, distance learning enables students at Texas A & M University and the University of Memphis to observe inner-city classrooms and afterwards to discuss their observations with the teachers. One of the designers of the interactive video program at Memphis comments on its benefits: "Previously everyone visited different schools and saw very different things. [This] shared clinical experience will lead to a more focused discussion of teaching methods" (University of Memphis 1994/95, 2).

you possibly get to know 120, 150, or more students? It's just not possible. Just think about it. Over a hundred! You couldn't get to know all of them and not many very well. How much of an impact could I have on their lives?"

"In elementary school, it's different," she continued. "You really can get to know the children well. You would be with them every day, all day, all school year. And there wouldn't be that many, maybe twenty-five or thirty. Even less in some places—only eighteen or twenty-one in a class. You'd even know their families. And you certainly could have an impact on their lives. But then the curriculum isn't that interesting. I would miss teaching literature."

Ruth knew that at the end of her first education course she would have to decide between the two. The classes in the remainder of her program were focused on either elementary or secondary teaching, and she could not do both.

Questions

1. Should Ruth become a high school English teacher or teach children at the elementary level? On what basis should she make her decision?

2. Is teaching a generic skill or art that can be applied to any level, or does it require distinctive skills geared to the students' ages and educational needs?

3. What factors other than teaching skills need to be considered when making this decision? Do the two levels draw upon different personality strengths? Is there a greater demand for teachers at one level than at the other? How do salaries and benefits compare for the two levels?

4. How do motivations to teach vary with the stage of life in which the decision to become a teacher is made?

5. What research activities might help someone decide whether to teach at the elementary or the secondary level?

Focused Observations

Observations are more meaningful when they are focused and conducted with clear purposes. Observers may focus on the students, the teacher, the interactions between the two, the structure of the lesson, or the setting. More specifically, for example, observers may note differences between the ways boys and girls or members of different ethnic groups communicate and behave in the classroom. They may note student interests and ability levels, study student responses to a particular teaching strategy, or analyze the question and response patterns in a class discussion.

Observations may also be guided by sets of questions related to specific areas. For

Intrinsic Motivation	Extrinsic Motivation
What things seem to interest students at this age?	How do teachers show their approval to students?
Which activities and assignments seem to give them a sense of pride?	What phrases do teachers use in their praise?
When do they seem to be confused? bored? frustrated?	What types of rewards do teachers give (e.g., grades, points, tangible rewards)?
What topics do they talk about with enthusiasm?	What reward programs do you notice (e.g., points accumulated toward free time)?
In class discussions, when are they most alert and participating most actively?	What warnings do teachers give?
What seems to please, amuse, entertain, or excite them?	What punishments are given to students?
What do they joke about? What do they find humorous?	How do teachers arouse concern in their students?
	How do students motivate other students?
What do they report as being their favorite subjects? favorite assignments?	What forms of peer pressure do you observe?
What do they report as being their least favorite subjects and assignments?	How do teachers promote enthusiasm for an assignment?
How do they respond to personalized lessons (e.g., using their names in exercises)?	How do teachers promote class spirit?
How do they respond to activity-oriented lessons (e.g.,fieldwork, project periods)?	How do teachers catch their students' interest in the first few minutes of a lesson?
How do they respond to assignments calling for presentations to groups outside the classroom (e.g., parents, another class, the chamber of commerce)?	Which type of question draws more answers—recall or open-ended?
	How do teachers involve quiet students in class discussions?
How do they respond to being given a choice in assignments?	How do teachers involve inactive students in their work?
	In what ways do teachers give recognition to srudents' accomplishments?

Figure 2.3

Guiding questions for observing motivation

instance, since beginning teachers are frequently frustrated by their lack of success in interesting their students in learning, asking questions specifically related to motivation can make an observation more meaningful and instructive. Figure 2.3 presents a helpful set of focused questions on motivation. Similar questions can be generated for other focus areas such as classroom management, student involvement, questioning skills, evaluation, and teacher–student rapport.

Observation Instruments

A wide range of methods can be used to conduct classroom observations, ranging from informal, qualitative descriptions to formal, quantitative checklists. With reform efforts to improve education in the United States has come the development of instruments to facilitate the evaluation of teacher performance, a task now widely required of school administrators. Students preparing to teach can benefit by using these evaluative instruments in their observations. An example is the "Formative Observation of Effective Teaching Practices Instrument," on this book's web site.

weblink

How Can You Gain Practical Experience for Becoming a Teacher?

A primary aim of teacher education programs is to give students opportunities to experience, to the extent possible, the real world of the teacher. Through field experiences and carefully structured experiential activities, preservice teachers are given limited exposure to various aspects of teaching. Observing, tutoring, instructing small groups, analyzing video cases, operating instructional media, performing student teaching, and completing various noninstructional tasks are among the most common experiential activities.

Classroom Experiences

Because of the need to provide opportunities to put theory into practice before student teaching, many teacher education programs enable students to participate in microteaching, teaching simulations, analyses of video cases, field-based practica and clinical experiences, and classroom aide programs.

Microteaching Introduced in the 1960s, **microteaching** was received enthusiastically and remains a popular practice. The process calls for students to teach brief, single-concept lessons to a small group of students (five to ten) while concurrently practicing a specific teaching skill, such as positive reinforcement. Often the microteaching is videotaped for later study.

As originally developed, microteaching includes the following six steps.

1. Identify a specific teaching skill to learn about and practice.
2. Read about the skill in one of several pamphlets.
3. Observe a master teacher demonstrate the skill in a short movie or on videotape.
4. Prepare a three- to five-minute lesson to demonstrate the skill.
5. Teach the lesson, which is videotaped, to a small group of peers.
6. Critique, along with the instructor and student peers, the videotaped lesson.

Simulations As an element of teacher training, **teaching simulations** provide opportunities for vicarious practice of a wide range of teaching skills. In simulations, students analyze teaching situations that are presented in writing, on audiotape, in short films, or on videotape. Typically, students are given background information about a hypothetical school or classroom and the pupils they must prepare to teach. After this orientation, students role-play the student teacher or the teacher who is confronted with the problem situation. Following the simulation, participants discuss the appropriateness of solutions and work to increase their problem-solving skills and their understanding of the teacher's multifaceted role as a decision maker.

With recent advances in computer technology, some teacher education programs now use computer-based simulations that enable students to hone their classroom planning and decision-making skills. Students at Nova Southwestern University in Florida, for example, learn to diagnose learning disabilities among children and youth by analyzing computer-simulated cases (Brown 1994). In addition, continuing progress in the development of virtual reality technology suggests that preservice teachers soon will be able to practice their skills with computer-simulated students who "learn" by interacting with humans (VanLehn et al. 1994; Sigalit and VanLehn 1995).

Video Cases   Teacher education students who view, analyze, and then write about video cases have an additional opportunity to appreciate the ambiguities and complexities of real-life classrooms, to learn that "there are no clear-cut, simple answers to the complex issues teachers face" (Wasserman 1994, 606). Viewing authentic video cases enables students to see how "teaching tradeoffs and dilemmas emerge in the video 'text' as do the strategies teachers use, the frustrations they experience, the brilliant and less-brilliant decisions they make" (Grant, Richard, and Parkay 1996, 5).

Practica   A **practicum** is a short-term field-based experience (usually about two weeks long) that allows teacher education students to spend time observing and assisting in classrooms. Though practica vary in length and purpose, students are often able to begin instructional work with individuals or small groups. For example, a cooperating teacher may allow a practicum student to tutor a small group of students, read a story to the whole class, conduct a spelling lesson, monitor recess, help students with their homework, or teach students a song or game.

Classroom Aides   Serving as a teacher's aide is another popular means of providing field experience before student teaching. A teacher aide's role depends primarily on the unique needs of the school and its students. Generally, aides work under the supervision of a certified teacher and perform duties that support the teacher's instruction. Assisting teachers in classrooms familiarizes college students with class schedules, record-keeping procedures, and students' performance levels, and provides ample opportunity for observations. In exchange, the classroom teacher receives much needed assistance.

Student Teaching

The most extensive and memorable field experience in teacher preparation programs is the period of student teaching. As *The Student Teacher's Handbook* points out, student teaching "is the only time in a teaching career that one is an apprentice under the close guidance of an experienced mentor" (Schwebel et al. 1996, 4). States require students to have a five-week to semester-long student teaching experience in the schools before certifying them as teachers. The nature of student teaching varies considerably among teacher education programs. Typically, a student is assigned to a cooperating (or master) teacher in the school, and a university supervisor makes periodic visits to observe the student teacher. Some programs even pay student teachers during the student teaching experience.

Student teaching is a time of responsibility. As one student teacher put it, "I don't want to mess up [my students'] education!" It is also an opportunity for growth, a chance to master critical skills. According to data gathered from 902 teacher education institutions in the United States, about 60 percent of the student teacher's time is actually spent teaching (Johnson and Yates 1982). The remaining time is devoted to observing and participating in classroom activities. The amount of time one actually spends teaching, however, is not as important as one's willingness to reflect carefully on the student teaching experience. Two excellent ways to promote reflection during student teaching are journal writing and maintaining a reflective teaching log.

Student Teacher Journal Writing   Many supervisors require student teachers to keep a journal of their classroom experiences so that they can engage in reflective teaching and begin the process of criticizing and guiding themselves. The following two entries—the first written by a student teacher in a fourth-grade classroom, the second by a student teacher in a high school English class—illustrate how journal writing can help student teachers develop strategies for dealing with the realities of teaching.

> Today I taught a lesson on the geography of the Northeast, and the kids seemed so bored. I called on individuals to read the social studies text, and then I explained it. Some of them really struggled with the text. Mr. H. said I was spoon-feeding them too much. So tomorrow I am going to put them into groups and let them answer questions together rather than give them the answers. This ought to involve the students in the learning a bit more and enable some of the better readers to help out those who have difficulty, without the whole class watching. I feel bad when I see those glazed looks on their faces. I need to learn how to be more interesting (Pitton 1998, 120).

> I had good feedback on small groups in their responses to questions on *Of Mice and Men*. They were to find a paragraph that might indicate theme and find two examples of foreshadowing. We found five!

> The short story unit was awful during fourth hour. The kids just didn't respond. I quickly revamped my approach for the next hour. Fifth hour did seem to go better. (Mostly though, I think it was just that I was more prepared, having had one class to try things out.) I can see how experience really helps. Now that I've tried the story "The Tiger or the Lady," I would use the same material, but I would know HOW to use it more effectively! (Pitton 1998, 143).

Relatively unstructured, open-ended journals, such as the ones from which these entries were selected, provide student teachers with a medium for subjectively exploring the student teaching experience.

Reflective Teaching Logs   To promote the practice of reflecting more analytically, some supervisors ask their student teachers to use a more directed and structured form of journal keeping, the **reflective teaching log.** In this form a student lists and briefly describes the daily sequence of activities, selects a single episode to expand on, analyzes the reason for selecting it and what was learned from it, and considers the possible future application of that knowledge.

To illustrate the reflective teaching approach to keeping a log, we share here a partial entry for one episode that was recounted and critiqued by a college student tutoring a student in Spanish. The entry is of particular interest because it provides us with a glimpse of a college student's first experience with a pupil's difficulty in understanding subject matter.

Log #1: February 14, 1991 (10:00–10:30am)

Sequence of Events: Worked with Richy on his Spanish

Episode: Because I wasn't sure of Richy's level, I asked him a few questions to see what he knew. His homework exercises involved work like reflexives, irregular verbs, and vocabulary. But when he and I started reviewing, he didn't remember the very basics of conjugation. He said, "I know this stuff, I just need review." We reviewed the conjugation of regular verbs. I set up a chart of *ar, er* and *ir* end-

What strategies can you use to make your student teaching experience truly valuable to you in becoming a teacher? In what sense will you remain a student teacher throughout your career?

ings and had him fill in the correct forms. He kept saying, "I just don't remember," or "Oh yeah, I knew that." His facial expressions reflected concentration and perhaps frustration. At times, he would just stare at the page until I gave him a hint. His forehead was scrunched up and he fidgeted a bit with his hands and legs. After working on the regular endings, he wanted to get a drink. I told him to go ahead. . . .

Analysis: I guess that I was just shocked at how little Richy knew. What we went over was the most simple form of Spanish grammar and in a way he was acting as if he had no idea what we were doing. I was surprised, like I said, but only on the inside. I just helped him along, showing him why the concepts made sense. I had no idea how we were going to do his homework assignments since they were considerably more difficult . . . (Posner 1993, 116–117).

Though student teaching will be the capstone experience of your teacher education program, the experience should be regarded as an *initial* rather than a terminal learning opportunity—your first chance to engage in reflection and self-evaluation for a prolonged period.

Gaining Experiences in Multicultural Settings

The enrollment in schools in the United States of students from diverse cultural backgrounds will continue to increase dramatically during the twenty-first century. As this trend continues, it is vitally important that those entering the teaching profession achieve an understanding of children's differing backgrounds. For example, students in Washington State University's teacher education program must document how they have met the following "administrative code" for teacher certification: "All candidates for teacher certification must demonstrate in their field experience their ability to work effectively with students of various backgrounds including (1) students from racial and or ethnic populations other than the candidate's, and (2) students with exceptional needs (i.e., those with handicapping conditions and the highly capable)."

As a teacher you can be assured that you will teach students from backgrounds that differ from your own—including students from the more than 100 racial and ethnic groups in the United States and students who are poor, gifted, or have disabilities. You will have the challenge of reaching out to all students and teaching them that they are persons of worth and can learn. You will also be confronted with the difficult challenge of being sensitive to differences among students while at the same time treating all equally and fairly. To prepare for these realities of teaching, you should make every effort to gain experiences in multicultural settings.

Induction and Internship Programs

In response to widespread efforts to improve education, many states and local school districts, often in collaboration with colleges and universities, have begun teacher induction and/or internship programs. Among the programs that have received national attention are the Florida Beginning Teacher Program, the California Mentor Teacher Program, the Virginia Beginning Teacher Assistance Program, and the Kentucky Beginning Teacher Internship Program.

Induction programs provide beginning teachers with continued assistance at least during the first year. **Internship programs** also provide participants with support, but they are usually designed primarily to provide training for those who have not gone through a teacher education program. In some instances, however, the terms *induction* and *internship* are used interchangeably.

Most induction and internship programs serve a variety of purposes:

1. To improve teaching performance
2. To increase the retention of promising beginning teachers during the induction years
3. To promote the personal and professional well-being of beginning teachers by improving teachers' attitudes toward themselves and the profession
4. To satisfy mandated requirements related to induction and certification
5. To transmit the culture of the system to beginning teachers (Huling-Austin 1990, 539).

To accomplish these purposes, induction programs offer resources such as workshops based on teacher-identified needs, observations by and follow-up conferences with individuals not in a supervisory role, support from mentor (or buddy) teachers, and support group meetings for beginning teachers.

School-Based Teacher Education

A new model of teacher preparation that provides students with extensive practical field experiences is known as **school-based teacher education.** In most instances, school-based programs are designed for students who have received a bachelor's degree and then wish to obtain teacher certification. Two examples are the school-based teacher education programs in Texas and the Teachers for Chicago Program.

Since 1985, completion of a school-based program has been one path to teacher certification in Texas. Candidates complete a year-long paid internship at a school, during which they undertake intensive practical study of teaching. Interns are mentored by the supervisor of the district's teacher education program, the district's curriculum specialist, the principal, the assistant principal, and, in some cases, a university supervisor. Area universities deliver courses specifically designed for the interns. At the end of the year, interns take district- and/or state-adopted tests of content and pedagogy to become eligible for standard certification.

To select, train, and retain effective teachers for Chicago's schools, a group of schools, the Chicago Teachers Union, deans of education at area universities, and the Golden Apple Foundation for Excellence in Teaching created the Teachers for Chicago Program. Candidates, selected through a rigorous interview process, enroll in a graduate education program at one of nine area colleges and universities. After a summer of coursework, they begin a two-year paid internship under the guidance of a mentor teacher. Interns fill vacant teacher positions in the schools and are responsible for the academic progress of their students. On completion of the program, interns have earned a master's degree and have met state certification requirements.

Substitute Teaching

On completion of a teacher education program and prior to securing a full-time teaching assignment, many students choose to gain additional practical experience in classrooms by **substitute teaching.** Others, unable to locate full-time positions, decide to substitute, knowing that many districts prefer to hire from their pool of substitutes when full-time positions become available. Substitute teachers replace regular teachers who are absent due to illness, family responsibilities, personal reasons, or professional workshops and conferences.

Each day, thousands of substitutes are employed in schools across the United States. For example, during one school year at the fifteen high schools in a large urban district, the total number of absences for 1,200 regular teachers equaled 14,229 days. Mul-

Advantages and Disadvantages of Substitute Teaching

Advantages
- Gain experience without all the nightly work and preparation
- Compare and contrast different schools and their environments
- Be better prepared for interviews by meeting administrators and teachers
- Teach and learn a variety of material
- Get to know people—network
- See job postings and hear about possible vacancies
- Gain confidence in your abilities to teach
- Practice classroom management techniques
- Learn about school and district politics—get the "inside scoop"
- Choose which days to work—flexible schedule

Disadvantages
- Pay is not as good as full-time teaching
- No benefits such as medical coverage, retirement plans or sick days
- Lack of organized representation to improve wages or working conditions
- May receive a cool reception in some schools
- Must adapt quickly to different school philosophies
- Lack of continuity—may be teaching whole language one day; phonetics the next

Figure 2.4

Advantages and disadvantages of substitute teaching
Source: John F. Snyder, "The Alternative of Substitute Teaching." In *1999 Job Search Handbook for Educators.* Evanston, IL: American Association for Employment in Education, p. 38.

tiplying this figure by five (the number of classes per day for most high school teachers) yields 71,145 class periods taught by substitutes that year (St. Michel 1995).

Qualifications for substitutes vary from state to state and district to district. An area with a critical need for subs will often relax its requirements to provide classroom coverage. In many districts, it is possible to substitute teach without regular certification. Some districts have less stringent qualifications for short-term, day-to-day substitutes and more stringent ones for long-term, full-time ones. In many districts, the application process for substitutes is the same as that for full-time applicants; in others, the process may be somewhat briefer. Often, substitutes are not limited to working in their area of certification; however, schools try to avoid making out-of-field assignments. If you decide to substitute teach, contact the schools in your area to learn about the qualifications and procedures for hiring substitutes.

In spite of the significant role substitutes play in the day-to-day operation of schools, ". . . research tells us that they receive very little support, no specialized training, and are rarely evaluated. . . . In short, the substitute will be expected to show up to each class on time, maintain order, take roll, carry out the lesson, and leave a note for the regular teacher about the classes and events of the day without support, encouragement, or acknowledgement" (St. Michel 1995, 6–7). While working conditions such as these are certainly challenging, substitute teaching can be a rewarding, professionally fulfilling experience. Figure 2.4 presents several advantages and disadvantages of substitute teaching.

How Can You Develop Your Teaching Portfolio?

Now that you have begun your journey toward becoming a teacher, you should acquire the habit of assessing your growth in knowledge, skills, and attitudes. Toward this end, you may wish to collect the results of your reflections and self-assessment in a **professional portfolio.** A professional portfolio is a collection of work that documents an individual's accomplishments in an area of professional practice. An artist's portfolio, for example, might consist of a résumé, sketches, paintings, slides and photographs of exhibits, critiques of the artist's work, awards, and other documentation of achievement. Recently, new approaches to teacher evaluation have included the professional portfolio. The National Board for Professional Teaching Standards, for example, uses "portfolios [and] other evidence of performance prepared by the candidate" (National Board for Professional Teaching Standards 1994, 55) as one way of assessing whether teachers have met the high standards for Board certification. Teacher education programs at several universities now use portfolios as one means of assessing the competencies of candidates for teacher certification. Also, many school districts are beginning to ask applicants to submit portfolios that document their effectiveness as teachers.

Portfolio Contents

What will your portfolio contain? Written materials might include the following: lesson plans and curriculum materials, reflections on your development as a teacher, journal entries, writing assignments made by your instructor, sample tests you have prepared, critiques of textbooks, evaluations of students' work at the level for which you are preparing to teach, sample letters to parents, and a résumé. Nonprint materials might include video- and audiotapes featuring you in simulated teaching and role-playing activities, audiovisual materials (transparencies, charts, or other teaching aids), photographs of bulletin boards, charts depicting room arrangements for cooperative learning or other instructional strategies, sample grade book, certificates of membership in professional organizations, and awards.

Your portfolio should represent your *best work* and give you an opportunity to become an advocate of *who you are* as a teacher. Because a primary purpose of the professional portfolio is to stimulate reflection and dialogue, you may wish to discuss what entries to make in your portfolio with your instructor or other teacher education students. In addition, the following questions from *How to Develop a Professional*

What questions might you ask a mentor teacher about developing your professional portfolio?

Portfolio: A Manual for Teachers (Campbell et al. 1996) can help you select appropriate portfolio contents:

> Would I be proud to have my future employer and peer group see this? Is this an example of what my future professional work might look like? Does this represent what I stand for as a professional educator? If not, what can I revise or rearrange so that it represents my best efforts? (p. 5).

Using a Portfolio

In addition to providing teacher education programs with a way to assess their effectiveness, portfolios can be used by students for a variety of purposes. Campbell et al. (1996, 7–8) suggest that a portfolio may be used as

1. A way to establish a record of quantitative and qualitative performance and growth over time.
2. A tool for reflection and goal setting as well as a way to present evidence of your ability to solve problems and achieve goals.
3. A way to synthesize many separate experiences; in other words, a way to get the "big picture".
4. A vehicle for you to use to collaborate with professors and advisors in individualizing instruction.
5. A vehicle for demonstrating knowledge and skills gained through out-of-class experiences, such as volunteer experiences.
6. A way to share control and responsibility for your own learning.
7. An alternative assessment measure within the professional education program.
8. A potential preparation for national, regional, and state accreditation.
9. An interview tool in the professional hiring process.
10. An expanded résumé to be used as an introduction during the student teaching experience.

How Can You Benefit from Mentoring Relationships?

When asked "What would have been most helpful in preparing you to be a teacher?" a majority of respondents to the 1991 Metropolitan Life Survey of the American Teacher said, "a skilled, experienced teacher assigned to provide [me] with advice and assistance" (Louis Harris and Associates 1991, 15). Like the following first-year suburban high school teacher, the teachers surveyed realized the value of a mentor: "I wish I had one [a mentor] here. . . . There are days that go by and I don't think I learn anything about my teaching, and that's too bad. I wish I had someone" (Dollase 1992, 138).

In reflecting on how a mentor contributed to his professional growth, Forrest Parkay defined **mentoring** as

> . . . an intensive, one-to-one form of teaching in which the wise and experienced mentor inducts the aspiring protégé [one who is mentored] into a particular, usually professional, way of life. . . . [T]he protégé learns from the mentor not only the objective, manifest content of professional knowledge and skills but also a subjective, nondiscursive appreciation for *how* and *when* to employ these learnings in the arena of professional practice. In short, the mentor helps the protégé to "learn the ropes," to become socialized into the profession (Parkay 1988, 196).

Table 2.1

Problem-solving approaches used by a mentor

Prescription giving	Remedy given by the mentor with a rationale, examples, alternatives, parameters of use, or rules
Personal storytelling	The mentor gives an example of his or her own classroom experiences to set a context for the prescription
Rehearsal	Verbal practice or rehearsal by the mentor and novice teacher of a strategy to be implemented in the classroom the next day, together with problem anticipation and troubleshooting
Role-playing	Playing and reversal of roles by the mentor and novice teacher reflecting problem situations or concerns of the novice teacher; both teacher and student roles are played
Modeling	Verbalization by the mentor of a teaching strategy or interaction technique with demonstration
Oral blueprinting	Oral planning by the novice teacher with critique and refinement by the mentor
Replay	Reconstruction of the day's events by the novice teacher with probing and clarifying questions and feedback from the mentor

Source: J. A. Ponticel and S. J. Zepeda. "Making Sense of Teaching and Learning: A Case Study of Mentor and Beginning Teacher Problem Solving," in D. J. McIntyre and D. M. Byrd, eds., *Preparing Tomorrow's Teachers: The Field Experience: Teacher Education Yearbook IV.* Thousand Oaks, CA: Corwin Press, p.127. Copyright © 1996 by Corwin Press. Reprinted by permission of Corwin Press, Inc.

An urban middle school intern's description of how his mentor helped him develop effective classroom management techniques exemplifies "learning the ropes": "'You've got to develop your own sense of personal power,' [my mentor] kept saying. 'It's not something I can teach you. I can show you what to do. I can model it. But I don't know, it's just something that's got to come from within you'" (Henry et al. 1995, 114).

Those who have become highly accomplished teachers frequently point out the importance of mentors in their preparation for teaching. A mentor can provide moral support, guidance, and feedback to students at various stages of professional preparation. In addition, a mentor can model for the protégé an analytical approach to solving problems in the classroom. Table 2.1 shows several problem-solving approaches a mentor can demonstrate to a novice teacher.

What Opportunities for Continuing Professional Development Will You Have?

Professional development is a life-long process; any teacher, at any stage of development, has room for improvement. Many school systems and universities have programs in place for the continuing professional development of teachers. Indeed, teachers are members of a profession that provides them with a " . . . continuous opportunity to grow, learn, and become more expert in their work" (Lieberman 1990, viii).

Self-Assessment for Professional Growth

Self-assessment is a necessary first step in pursuing opportunities for professional growth. A teacher comments on the importance of self-assessment after being certified by the National Board for Professional Teaching Standards: "Serious reflection and self-examination [were necessary] as I gauge[d] my skills and knowledge against objective, peer-developed, national standards in specific teaching areas" (National Board for Professional Teaching Standards 1995, 13).

Several questions can help you make appropriate choices as a teacher: In which areas am I already competent? In which areas do I need further development? How will I acquire the knowledge and skills I need? How will I apply new knowledge and practice new skills? Answers to such questions will lead you to a variety of sources for professional growth: teacher workshops, teacher centers, professional development schools, the opportunity to supervise and mentor student teachers, and graduate programs. Figure 2.5 illustrates the relationship of these professional development experiences to your teacher education program.

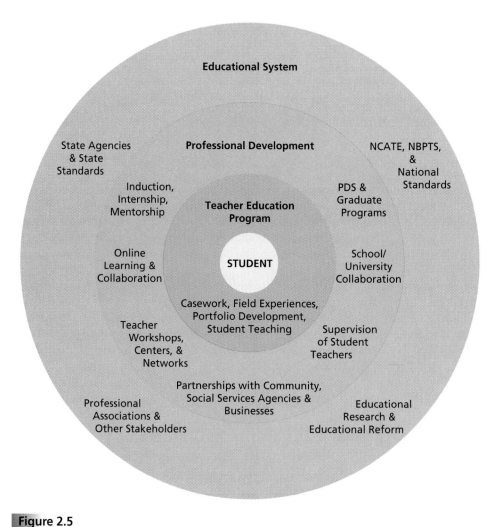

Figure 2.5

Professional development: from teacher education student to practitioner

Teacher Workshops

The quality of **inservice workshops** is uneven, varying with the size of school district budgets and the imagination and knowledge of the administrators and teachers who arrange them. It is significant that the most effective inservice programs tend to be the ones that teachers request—and often design and conduct.

Some workshops focus on topics that all teachers (regardless of subject or level) can benefit from: classroom management, writing-across-the-curriculum, multicultural education, and strategies for teaching students with learning disabilities in the general education classroom, for example. Other workshops have a sharper focus and are intended for teachers of a subject at a certain level—for example, whole-language techniques for middle school students, discovery learning for high school science students, and student-centered approaches to teaching literature in the high school classroom.

Teacher Centers

Teacher centers provide opportunities for teachers "to take the lead in the decision making and implementation of staff development programs based on the needs of teachers. [They] provide the structure for teachers to take charge of their own professional growth" (Teacher Centers of New York State 1999). In contrast to inservice programs, these are more clearly initiated and directed by teachers. Some centers cooperate with a local or neighboring college of education and include members of the faculty on their planning committees.

Many teachers find teacher centers stimulating because they offer opportunities for collegial interaction in a quiet, professionally oriented setting. The busy, hectic pace of life in many schools, teachers often find, provides little time for professional dialogue with peers. Furthermore, in the teacher center, teachers are often more willing to discuss openly areas of weakness in their performance. As one teacher put it:

> At the teacher center I can ask for help. I won't be judged. The teachers who have helped me the most have had the same problems. I respect them, and I'm willing to learn from them. They have credibility with me.

Professional Development Schools

Professional development schools (PDSs) have emerged recently as a way to link school restructuring and the reform of teacher education in America. These school–university partnerships offer teachers the following opportunities:

- Fine learning programs for diverse students
- Practical, thought-provoking preparation for novice teachers
- New understanding and professional responsibilities for experienced educators
- Research projects that add to all educators' knowledge about how to make schools more productive (Holmes Group n.d., 1).

For example, a teacher at a PDS might team with a teacher education professor and teach a university-level course, participate in a collaborative research project, offer a professional development seminar for other teachers, arrange for the teacher educator to demonstrate instructional strategies in his or her classroom, or jointly develop relevant field experiences for prospective teachers.

Supervision and Mentoring of Student Teachers

After several years in the classroom, teachers may be ready to stretch themselves further by supervising student teachers. Some of the less obvious benefits of doing so are that teachers must rethink what they are doing so that they can explain and sometimes justify their behaviors to someone else, learning about themselves in the process. Furthermore, because they become a model for their student teachers, they continually strive to offer the best example. In exchange, they gain an assistant in the classroom—another pair of eyes, an aid with record keeping—and more than occasionally, fresh ideas and a spirit of enthusiasm.

Graduate Study

A more traditional form of professional development is to do graduate study. With the recent reforms, most states now require teachers to take some graduate courses to keep their certifications and knowledge up to date. Some teachers take only courses that are of immediate use to them; others use their graduate study to prepare for new teaching or administrative positions; and still others pursue doctoral work in order to teach prospective teachers or others in their discipline at the college level.

Study on the Internet

If you have access to the **Internet,** you can locate many possibilities for continuing professional development. Teachers use the Internet to exchange ideas and experiences and to acquire additional expertise in teaching or to share their expertise with others. See the Appendix "Professional Development Opportunities on the Internet," on this book's website. In addition, at the website for *Becoming a Teacher,* you will find a periodically updated list of professional development opportunities available for teachers on the Web. If you decide to visit any of these sites, remember that web sites are frequently changed or withdrawn from the Internet. The web addresses given throughout this book were active at the time of printing. Also, because it is estimated that 10,000 web sites are added each day, you should periodically use key words related to education and your favorite search engine to gather the latest information and resources.

SUMMARY

What Essential Knowledge Do You Need to Teach?

- Professional teachers reflect upon their classroom experiences.
- Teachers need three kinds of knowledge: knowledge of self and students, knowledge of subject, and knowledge of educational theory and research.
- Teachers' self-knowledge influences their ability to understand students.
- The ambiguities of teaching can cause teachers to experience anxiety.
- Elementary teachers can experience loneliness because they are isolated from adults; secondary teachers because of departmentalization.

- Teachers must know their students' aptitudes, talents, learning styles, stage of development, and readiness to learn new material.
- Teachers must understand their subjects deeply so they can modify instructional strategies based on students' perception of content.
- Knowledge of educational theory enables professional teachers to know why certain strategies work.
- Educational research provides teachers with rules of thumb for practice.

What Are Six Ways of Viewing the Teacher Knowledge Base?

- There is no universally accepted definition of "good" teaching.
- The teacher knowledge base (essential knowledge and abilities) can place primary emphasis on personal development, research-based competencies, state standards, job analyses, or the views of professional organizations.
- Many states have developed standards for outcome-based or performance-based teacher education. Outcomes are based on what beginning teachers do in real classrooms.
- The job-analysis view of teaching is based on identifying job dimensions—the knowledge, skills, and attitudes teachers need.
- The National Board for Professional Teaching Standards (NBPTS) has developed standards for voluntary national certification.
- Effective teachers are guided by reflection and a problem-solving orientation.

How Do Reforms in Teacher Education Affect You?

- As part of the educational reform movement, the Holmes Group recommends that teachers obtain a bachelor's degree in an academic field and a master's degree in education.
- The Holmes Group recommends establishing professional development schools linked to colleges of education.
- In *Teachers for Our Nation's Schools,* John Goodlad recommends the creation of Centers of Pedagogy.
- The National Board for Professional Teaching Standards (NBPTS) is developing standards in more than 30 areas across six student age levels.
- State-level professional standards boards set criteria for the certification and professional development of education personnel in some states; in others, state standards boards are limited to advising educational policymakers.

What Can You Learn from Observing in Classrooms?

- The opportunity to observe in classrooms helps some students make a final decision about becoming a teacher.
- Many teacher education programs are providing students with more and earlier opportunities to observe in classrooms.

- Distance-learning classrooms, using compressed video, link teacher education programs to schools off campus.
- Observations can focus on a particular aspect of classroom life or be guided by a set of questions related to a specific area, such as how the teacher motivates students.
- Observation instruments range from informal, qualitative descriptions to formal, quantitative checklists.

How Can You Gain Practical Experience for Becoming a Teacher?

- Teacher education students can gain practical experience through focused classroom observations, microteaching, teaching simulations, analyses of video cases, field-based practica and clinical experiences, and classroom aide programs.
- Distance-learning classrooms, using compressed video, link teacher education programs to schools off-campus.
- In microteaching, students practice specific skills by teaching brief lessons that are later analyzed.
- Computer simulations and virtual reality—as well as written, videotaped, and audiotaped cases—are being used for teaching simulations.
- Journal writing and reflective teaching logs increase the benefits of the student teaching experience.
- To prepare to teach students from diverse backgrounds, teacher education students should actively seek field experiences in multicultural settings.
- Induction programs provide assistance to beginning teachers. Internship programs and school-based teacher education programs provide extensive practical experiences.
- Substitute teaching provides additional practical experience after completing a teacher education program.

How Can You Develop Your Teaching Portfolio?

- A portfolio documents professional growth and development over time.
- A portfolio can be organized around specific outcomes or standards.
- Portfolio contents should represent one's best work.
- Professional portfolios can be used in teacher evaluation, self-evaluation, and hiring.

How Can You Benefit from Mentoring Relationships?

- Ask for advice from teachers you admire.
- Mentoring can be a source of professional growth for experienced teachers.
- Mentoring enables the protégé to "learn the ropes."

What Opportunities for Continuing Professional Development Will You Have?

- Self-assessment is necessary to select appropriate professional development experiences.

- Opportunities for professional development include teacher workshops, teacher centers, professional development schools, supervision and mentoring of student teachers, graduate study, and the Internet.

KEY TERMS AND CONCEPTS

distance learning, 54
educational reform movement, 51
field experiences, 53
Holmes Group, 51
Holmes Partnership, 52
induction programs, 60
inservice workshops, 67
Internet, 68
internship programs, 60
Interstate New Teacher Assessment and Support Consortium (INTASC), 50
job analysis, 48
knowledge base, 46
mentor, 64

mentoring, 64
microteaching, 57
National Board for Professional Teaching Standards (NBPTS), 50
observations, 55
outcome-based teacher education, 48
pedagogical content knowledge, 43
performance-based teacher education, 48
personal development view, 47
practicum, 58
problem-solving orientation, 50

professional development school (PDS), 52
professional portfolio, 62
professional standards boards, 53
reflection, 50
reflective teaching log, 59
research-based competencies, 47
school-based teacher education, 61
self-assessment, 66
substitute teaching, 61
teacher centers, 67
teaching simulations, 57

APPLICATIONS AND ACTIVITIES

Teacher's Journal

1. What does self-knowledge mean to you? Why is self-knowledge important in teaching? What steps can you take to achieve greater self-knowledge?

2. As a teacher, you will encounter challenges related to student variability (differences in developmental needs, interests, abilities, and disabilities) and student diversity (differences in gender, race, ethnicity, culture, and socioeconomic status). To begin thinking about how you will acquire and use knowledge about your students, write a brief profile of yourself as a student in elementary school, in middle school or junior high school, and in high school.

3. Reflect on your education as a teacher. What are your primary concerns about the preparation you are receiving? What experiences do you think will be most helpful to you as you move toward becoming a teacher? What qualities would you look for in a mentor?

4. On the basis of your field experiences to date and the information in Chapters 1 and 2, ask yourself these questions and respond in your journal: Do I have the aptitude to become a good teacher? Am I willing to acquire the essential knowledge and skills teachers need? Do I really want to become a teacher?

Teacher's Database

1. Find out more about the 21st Century Teachers Network, a group of more than 100,000 volunteer teacher leaders at the K–12 level who are pioneering the use of technology to enhance teaching and learning. Each of these leaders will then share their knowledge and expertise by mentoring five of their colleagues.

2. Instead of using "outside experts" to deliver professional development workshops to teachers, some states are implementing teacher networks in which teachers address problems of mutual concern. For example, to help teachers implement portfolio assessments of fourth- and eighth-grade student learning in mathematics and eighth-grade writing, Vermont's Department of Education has developed a teacher network. Teacher leaders from the state's educational regions meet periodically with state department personnel to plan three to four teacher network meetings each year. To learn more about the Vermont network, visit the Vermont Department of Education website.

3. Investigate the California State Telemation Program, a statewide network of teachers who mentor one another. The program focuses on integrating online resources into site-level planning, curriculum development, learning strategies, and student-centered activities.

Observations and Interviews

1. Think about areas for focused observations of teaching, such as classroom management, student involvement, questioning techniques, evaluation, or teacher–student rapport. For one or more areas, brainstorm and order in logical sequence a set of questions you could use to guide your next observations. Include a list of questions to ask the teacher whom you will observe.

2. As a collaborative project with classmates, interview students who have completed student teaching at your college or university. What tips do they have for developing a positive relationship with a cooperating teacher? For establishing rapport with students? For developing confidence in presenting lessons?

3. Arrange to interview a school administrator about the knowledge, skills, and aptitude he or she thinks teachers must have. To help you plan for the interview, ask your instructor for handout master M2.2, "Interviewing School Administrators about Teachers' Knowledge and Skills." Which of the knowledge and skills discussed in this chapter does the administrator mention? Does he or she mention knowledge and skills not discussed in this chapter?

4. Observe a teacher in the classroom for the purpose of identifying examples that help to answer the following questions. How does the teacher demonstrate or use knowledge of self and students? Knowledge of subject matter? Knowledge of educational theory and research?

5. Observe a classroom in which there is likely to be some teacher–student interaction (for example, questions and answers, discussion, or oral review and feedback). On the basis of the data you collect, what conclusions can you draw about life in this classroom? To help record your observations, ask your instructor for handout master M2.1, "Recording Classroom Interactions."

Professional Portfolio

1. Create a plan for developing your portfolio. What specific outcomes or standards will you use to organize your portfolio entries? What artifacts will you use to demonstrate your professional growth and development?

2. Evaluate the products of your studies in education so far in your preparation for becoming a teacher. Identify a few examples of your best work to include in your portfolio. Also, evaluate your Teacher's Journal, Teacher's Database, and Observations and Interviews for possible inclusions in your portfolio.

Appendix 2.1

Florida Performance Measurement System Screening/Summative Observation Instrument

FRAME FACTOR INFORMATION (PLEASE PRINT)

Teacher's Name

_____ _____ _____
(Last) (First) (Middle)

SS# __ __ __ - __ __ - __ __ __ __

Institution of Graduation _____ Inst. # _____

Graduated from a College of Education ☐ 1. Yes ☐ 2. No

Number of Complete Years of Teaching Experience _____

District Name _____ Number _____

School Name _____ Number _____

Observer's Name

_____ _____ _____
(Last) (First) (Middle)
☐

SS# __ __ __ - __ __ - __ __ __ __

Position ☐ 1. Principal ☐ 2. Ass't Principal ☐ 3. Teacher ☐ 4. Other

Class _____ Grade Level (Specify one level only–For Adult Ed. mark level 13 For Kindergarten or Preschool mark Level 00.)

Subject Area Observed
- ☐ 1. Language Arts
- ☐ 2. Foreign Language
- ☐ 3. Social Sciences
- ☐ 4. Mathematics
- ☐ 5. Science
- ☐ 6. Physical Education, ROTC
- ☐ 7. Business Education, DCT, CBE
- ☐ 8. Industrial Arts/Education
- ☐ 9. Home Economics
- ☐ 10. Other Vocational Ed.
- ☐ 11. Arts
- ☐ 12. Music
- ☐ 13. Exceptional Stud. Ed.
- ☐ 14. Other (Specify) _____

Type of Classroom/Facility in Which the Observation Occurred
- ☐ 1. Regular Classroom—Self-contained, Open, Pod
- ☐ 2. Laboratory or Shop
- ☐ 3. Field, Court, Gymnasium
- ☐ 4. Media Room or Library

Total Number of Students in Class _____

Observation Information Date ___/___/___

Type of Observation ☐ 1. Prof. Orien. ☐ 2. Dis. Assess ☐ 3. Other (Specify) _____

Screening Obs. ☐ 1. ☐ 2. ☐ 3. ☐ 4.

Summative Obs. ☐ 1. ☐ 2. ☐ 3. ☐ 4.

Time Observation Begins __ __:__ __   Observation Ends __ __:__ __

Test Begins __ __:__ __   Test Ends __ __:__ __

Methods Used in the Observed Lesson
- ☐ 1. Lecture
- ☐ 2. Interactive/Discussion
- ☐ 3. Independent Study/Lab or Shop Work

Teacher's Signature _____

Observer's Signature _____

Number of Students Not Engaged

1 ☐   2 ☐   3 ☐   4 ☐

DOMAIN	EFFECTIVE INDICATORS		TOT. FREQ.	FREQUENCY	FREQUENCY	TOT. FREQ.	INEFFECTIVE INDICATORS
3.0 Instructional Organizatrion and Development	1. Begins instruction promptly						1. Delays
	2. Handles materials in an orderly manner						2. Does not organize materials systematically
	3. Orients students to classwork/maintains academic focus						3. Allows talk/activity unrelated to subject
	4. Conducts beginning/ending review						4.
	5. Questions: academic comprehension/ lesson development	a. single factual (Domain 5.0)					5a. Allows unison response
		b. requires analysis/reasons					5b. Poses multiple questions asked as one
							5c. Poses nonacademic questions/nonacademic procedural questions
	6. Recognizes response/amplifies/gives correct feedback						6. Ignores student or response/expresses sarcasm, disgust, harshness
	7. Gives specific academic praise						7. Uses general, nonspecific praise
	8. Provides practice						8. Extends discourse, changes topic with no practice
	9. Gives directions/assigns/checks comprehension of homework, seatwork assignments/gives feedback						9. Gives inadequate directions on homework/no feedback
	10. Circulates and assists students						10. Remains at desk/circulates inadequately
4.0 Presentation of Subject Matter	11. Treats concepts—definition/attributes/examples/ nonexamples						11. Gives definition or example only
	12. Discusses cause-effect/uses linking words/applies law or principle						12. Discusses either cause or effect only/uses no linking word(s)
	13. States and applies academic rule						13. Does not state or does not apply academic rule
	14. Develops criteria and evidence for value judgment						14. States value judgment with no criteria or evidence
5.0 Communication: Verbal and Nonverbal	15. Emphasises important points						15.
	16. Expresses enthusiasm verbally/challenges students						16.
	17.						17. Uses vague/scrambled discourse
	18.						18. Uses loud, grating, high pitched, monotone, or inaudible talk
	19. Uses body behavior that shows interest—smiles, gestures						19. Frowns, deadpan or lethargic
2.0 Management of Student Conduct	20. Stops misconduct						20. Delays desist/doesn't stop misconduct/desists punitively
	21. Maintains instructional momentum						21. Loses momentum—fragments nonacademic directions, over dwells

Observer's Notes: _____

Appendix 2.2

Office of Teacher Education and Certification, 1826 Capital Plaza Tower, 500 Mero Street, Frankfort, KY 40601, (502) 564–4606, (FAX) (502) 564–6470.

Preamble To The New Teacher Standards The New Teacher Standards describe what first-year teachers should know and be able to do in authentic teaching situations and the academic content, teaching behaviors, and instructional processes that are necessary to promote effective student learning. They imply more than the mere demonstration of teaching competencies. They imply a current and sufficient academic content understanding that promotes consistent quality performance on teaching tasks. Authentic teaching tasks provide opportunities and contexts for performances by beginning teachers. In Kentucky, all teaching and learning tasks address Kentucky's academic expectations. These identify what students need to be successful in the world of the future. Thus, teachers design and implement instruction and assess learning that develops students' abilities to:

1. **Use basic communication and mathematics skills** in finding, organizing, expressing, and responding to information and ideas.
2. **Apply core concepts and principles** from science, arts and humanities, mathematics, practical living studies, social studies, and vocational studies.
3. **Become a self-sufficient individual** who demonstrates high self-esteem, a healthy lifestyle, flexibility, creativity, self-control, and independent learning.
4. **Become a responsible group member** who demonstrates consistent, responsive, and caring behavior; interpersonal skills; respect for the rights and responsibilities of others; world views; and an open mind to other perspectives.
5. **Think and solve problems** including the ability to think critically and creatively, develop ideas and concepts, and make rational decisions.
6. **Connect and integrate experiences and new knowledge** throughout the curriculum, question and interpret ideas from diverse perspectives, and apply concepts to real-life situations.

New Teacher Standards

I. Designs/Plans Instruction
The teacher *designs/plans instruction and learning climates* that develop students' abilities to use communication skills, apply core concepts, become self-sufficient individuals, become responsible team members, think and solve problems, and integrate knowledge.

II. Creates/Maintains Learning Climates
The teacher *creates learning climates* that support the development of students' abilities to use communication skills, apply core concepts, become self-sufficient individuals, become responsible team members, think and solve problems, and integrate knowledge.

III. Implements/Manages Instruction
The teacher *introduces/implements/manages instruction* that develops students' abilities to use communication skills, apply core concepts, become self-sufficient individuals, become responsible team members, think and solve problems, and integrate knowledge.

IV. Assesses/Communicates Learning Results
The teacher *assesses learning and communicates results* to students and others with respect to student abilities to use communication skills, apply core concepts, become self-sufficient individuals, become responsible team members, think and solve problems, and integrate knowledge.

V. Reflects/Evaluates Teaching/Learning
The teacher *reflects on and evaluates specific teaching/learning situations* and/or programs.

VI. Collaborates with Colleagues/Parents/Others
The teacher *collaborates with colleagues, parents, and other agencies* to design, implement, and support learning programs that develop students' abilities to use communication skills, apply core concepts, become self-sufficient individuals, become responsible team members, think and solve problems, and integrate knowledge.

VII. Engages in Professional Development
The teacher *evaluates his/her overall performance* with respect to modeling and teaching Kentucky's Learning Goals and *implements a professional development program* that enhances his/her own performance.

VIII. Demonstrates Content Knowledge
The teacher demonstrates a *current* and *sufficient academic knowledge* of certified content areas to develop student knowledge and performance in those areas.

Source: Kentucky Education Professional Standards Board, *Kentucky's New Teacher Standards.* Copyright © 1993 Kentucky Department of Education. Used with permission of the Kentucky Department of Education, Frankfort, Kentucky, 40601.

Appendix 2.3

Interstate New Teacher Assessment and Support Consortium Standards

1. The teacher understands the central concepts, tools of inquiry, and structures of the discipline(s) he or she teaches and can create learning experiences that make these aspects of subject matter meaningful for students.
2. The teacher understands how children learn and develop, and can provide learning opportunities that support their intellectual, social, and personal development.
3. The teacher understands how students differ in their approaches to learning and creates instructional opportunities that are adapted to diverse learners.
4. The teacher understands and uses a variety of instructional strategies to encourage students' development of critical thinking, problem solving, and performance skills.
5. The teacher uses an understanding of individual and group motivation and behavior to create a learning environment that encourages positive social interaction, active engagement in learning, and self-motivation.
6. The teacher uses knowledge of effective verbal, nonverbal, and media communication techniques to foster active inquiry, collaboration, and supportive interaction in the classroom.
7. The teacher plans instruction based upon knowledge of subject matter, students, the community, and curriculum goals.
8. The teacher understands and uses formal and informal assessment strategies to evaluate and ensure the continuous intellectual, social, and physical development of the learner.
9. The teacher is a reflective practitioner who continually evaluates the effects of his/her choices and actions on others (students, parents, and other professionals in the learning community) and who actively seeks out opportunities to grow professionally.
10. The teacher fosters relationships with school colleagues, parents, and agencies in the larger community to support students' learning and well-being.

Source: A Model Standards for Beginning Teacher Licensing and Development: A Resource for State Dialogue. Washington, DC: Interstate New Teacher Assessment and Support Consortium. A project of the Council of Chief State School Officers, 1993, pp. 1–29.

Appendix 2.4

Sample NBPTS Portfolio Exercise

Early Childhood/Generalist

The National Board for Professional Teaching Standards has created Portfolio Samplers to give candidates (or potential candidates) a clear picture of the kinds of exercises they will be expected to complete. The exercise below is an example of a portfolio exercise for the Early Childhood/Generalist certificate for the 1996–97 assessment year.

- **Introduction to Your Classroom Community**—Teachers are asked to show how they structure their time, establish rules and routines and organize space and materials in ways that promote children's social development, mutual respect and emerging independence. Teachers submit a written commentary and an accompanying videotape that highlights their interaction with children.
- **Reflecting on a Teaching and Learning Sequence**—Teachers submit a written commentary and supporting artifacts which show how they nurture children's growth and learning as they explore an extended theme or topic drawn from at least two content areas —social studies and the arts.
- **Engaging Children in Science Learning**—Teachers are asked to feature a learning experience that engages children in the investigation of a science concept. Central to teachers' written responses is a detailed examination of a learning experience they videotape. They are also asked to describe how this learning experience is embedded within an ongoing series of activities designed to promote children's understanding of science concepts and processes. Teachers submit a videotape and a written commentary.
- **Examining a Child's Literacy Development**—Teachers are asked to present the ways in which they foster literacy development in their classroom. They are also asked to analyze selected work samples from one child and discuss the steps they would take to support the featured child's literacy development. Teachers submit a written commentary and the work samples from the selected child.
- **Documented Accomplishments**—Candidates document their work outside the classroom, with families and in the profession. They submit descriptions and documentation of those activities and accomplishments that illustrate their commitments to families and communities of their students and their contributions to the teaching profession. In addition, candidates compose two brief interpretative summaries of their accomplishments, one for accomplishments with families and the community and the other for accomplishments in the profession.

Source: National Board for Professional Teaching Standards, May 16, 1999. http://www.nbpts.org/nbpts/seeking/sample.html.

part two

Foundations of Teaching

dear mentor

On Keeping Up with a
Rapidly Changing Profession

Dear Mentor:

With all we see in the news media about modernizing and changing education to fit today's political agenda, how can educators be sure they are teaching students the "right" curriculum? How can I, as a teacher, be sure that I can keep up with the rapidly changing times? Is it possible that I can find the answers to these questions by studying the history, philosophy, and governance of education?

Sincerely,
Elizabeth Acevedo

Dear Elizabeth:

The questions you pose concerning curriculum and the rapidly changing times and forces in education today are probably among the most difficult for educators to deal with, but at the same time they are part of what makes education so exciting in this era of technology and the information age. I suggest you start with the curriculum that virtually every school system in the United States has today. This curriculum is based on values and knowledge that are grounded in the history of education and in the education philosophies that have been developed through study and research. These values are also the foundation on which you should build your personal teaching style and philosophy.

I think it is also important to recognize that curricula are not static. They are not rigidly bound to just tradition and accepted values. A good curriculum has to be a vibrant, almost living device that allows us to teach the basic ideas, theories, and learning strategies, as well as to incorporate today's growing body of knowledge which is expanding exponentially because of computers and technology. I think that this makes education particularly exciting. To cite just one example, the amount of research done in the past decade concerning the brain and learning is revolutionizing the way we teach today. As educators we have to keep up with this research and use it in the best way possible to educate our students.

This leads me to your second question: How can a teacher be sure to keep up with the rapidly changing times? I think we should take the medical profession as a good example of how and why we must keep up with our ever-changing field. Just as a good doctor follows the advancements made in medicine by reading professional journals, attending professional conferences, and sharing practices and ideas with colleagues, we as educators have to do the same. We must realize that as professional educators, we have a responsibility to our students to provide them with the best education possible, and we cannot do this unless we are constantly learning, and studying, and improving our profession. We have to make a commitment to learning and incorporate it into our professional development, as well as to instill it into our students' thinking. After all, I think a good teacher would want to be a learner for life and would want to encourage his or her students to be lifelong learners, too.

I hope these thoughts will help you in your quest to become a good teacher. Your questions already indicate that you possess the reflective abilities that all good educators must have. Best of luck to you in the future.

Sincerely,

Joe Bacewicz
Connecticut Teacher of the Year 1999

3

Ideas and Events That Have Shaped Education in the United States

Educational philosophy is a way not only of looking at ideas, but also of learning how to use ideas in better ways.

—Howard A. Ozmon and Samuel M. Craver
Philosophical Foundations of Education,
6th ed., 1999

1. What determines your educational philosophy?

2. What are the branches of philosophy?

3. What are five modern philosophical orientations to teaching?

4. What psychological orientations have influenced teaching philosophies?

5. How can you develop your educational philosophy?

6. What were teaching and schools like in the American colonies (1620–1750)?

7. What were the goals of education during the Revolutionary Period (1750–1820)?

8. How was the struggle won for state-supported common schools (1820–1865)?

9. How did compulsory education change the schools and the teaching profession (1865–1920)?

10. What were the aims of education during the Progressive Era (1920–1945)?

11. How did education change during the modern postwar era (1945–2000)?

Y ou are having an animated conversation in the teacher's lounge with four colleagues, Mary, Juan, Karen, and Hal, about educational reform and the changes sweeping across our nation's schools. The discussion was sparked by a television special everyone watched last night about new approaches to teaching and assessing students' learning.

"I was really glad to see teachers portrayed in a professional light," you say. "The message seemed to be 'Let's get behind teachers and give them the support and resources they need to implement new ideas and technologies. Effective schools are important to our nation's well-being.'"

"I think it's just a case of schools trying to jump on the bandwagon," Hal says. "All this talk about restructuring schools, developing partnerships with the community, and using technology—they're supposed to be the silver bullets that transform education. These ideas just take time away from what we should be doing, and that's teaching kids how to read, write, and compute. If we don't get back to what really matters, our country is going to become a second-rate power in the world . . . that's my educational philosophy."

"But times have changed; the world is a different place," Mary says. "Look at how the Internet has changed things in just a few years. We can't return to the 'good old days.' Students need to learn how to learn; they need to learn how to solve problems that we can't even imagine today."

"Just a minute," Juan interjects. "I don't think the 'good old days' ever were. That's a nostalgia trap. What kids need is to see how education is the key to understanding themselves and others. If we can't get along as human beings on this planet, we're in trouble. Look at the ethnic cleansing in Kosovo, the killing in Rwanda, Angola, Northern Ireland. . . . Sure, we've got the Internet and all this technology, but as a species we haven't evolved at all."

"Of course we can't return to the past," Karen says, "but we can learn a lot from it. That's one of the main purposes of education . . . to see how the great ideas can help us improve things. Like I tell my students, there isn't one problem today that Shakespeare didn't have tremendous insights into 400 years ago—racism, poverty, war."

"Well, all I know is that when I started teaching thirty years ago, we taught the basics," Hal says. "It was as simple as that. We were there to teach, and the kids, believe it or not, were there to learn. Nowadays, we have to solve all of society's problems—eliminate poverty, racism, crime, or whatever."

Hal pauses a moment and then turns his attention to you. "It all changed in the 1980s and 1990s; we got involved in all this reform stuff . . . restructuring schools, empowering teachers, developing partnerships—I don't know where it's all going. What do you think . . . what's your educational philosophy?"

What do you say?

Mary is correct when she says we cannot return to the past, to the "good old days." On the other hand, Karen is also correct when she says we should learn from the past. We cannot understand schools today without a look at what they were yesterday. The current system of public and private education in the United States is an ongoing reflection of its philosophical and historical foundations and of the aspirations and values brought to this country by its founders and generations of settlers. Developing an appreciation for the ideas and events that have shaped education in the United States is an important part of your education as a professional.

Still, you may wonder, what is the value of knowing about the philosophy and history of U.S. education? Will that knowledge help you to be a better teacher? First, knowledge of the ideas and events that have influenced our schools will help you evaluate more effectively current proposals for change. You will be in a better position to evaluate changes if you understand how schools have developed and how current proposals might relate to previous change efforts. Second, awareness of ideas and events that have influenced teaching is a hallmark of professionalism in education.

The first half of this chapter presents several basic philosophical concepts that will help you answer five important questions that teachers must consider as they develop an educational philosophy:

- What should the purposes of education be?
- What is the nature of knowledge?
- What values should students adopt?
- What knowledge is of most worth?
- How should learning be evaluated?

The second half presents brief overviews of six periods of education in the United States. For each period, we discuss the philosophical concepts, social forces, events, and persons that, in our judgment, have had the greatest impact on education in our country.

What Determines Your Educational Philosophy?

In simplest terms, **educational philosophy** consists of what you believe about education—the set of principles that guides your professional action. Every teacher, whether he or she recognizes it, has a philosophy of education—a set of beliefs about how human beings learn and grow and what one should learn in order to live the good life. Teachers differ, of course, in regard to the amount of effort they devote to the development of their personal philosophy or educational platform. Some feel that philosophical reflections have nothing to contribute to the actual act of teaching. (This stance, of course, is itself a philosophy of education.) Other teachers recognize that teaching, because it is concerned with *what ought to be,* is basically a philosophical enterprise.

Your behavior as a teacher is strongly connected to your personal beliefs and your beliefs about teaching and learning, students, knowledge, and what is worth knowing (see Figure 3.1). Regardless of where you stand in regard to these five dimensions of teaching, you should be aware of the need to reflect continually on *what* you believe and *why* you believe it.

Beliefs about Teaching and Learning

One of the most important components of your educational philosophy is how you view teaching and learning. In other words, what is the teacher's primary role? Is the teacher a subject matter expert who can efficiently and effectively impart knowledge to students? Is the teacher a helpful adult who establishes caring relationships with students and nurtures their growth in needed areas? Or is

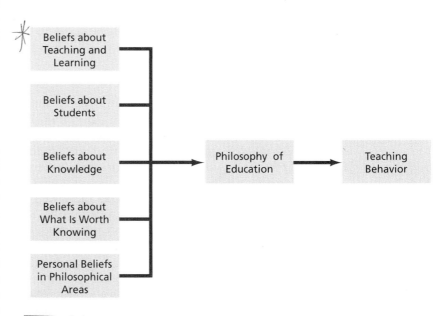

Figure 3.1

The influence of the teacher's educational beliefs on teaching behavior

How can the world wide web enhance your study of and interest in the philosophy and history of education?

The World Wide Web (WWW) has increased dramatically the amount of information that is easily available to anyone with a computer. The WWW, in a manner perhaps more dramatic than the invention of the printing press in the middle of the fifteenth century, has brought limitless information and expertise to people around the globe.

However, you might wonder, is there any connection between the WWW and the philosophy and history of education? Can the WWW enhance your study of and interest in these two areas? Prior to the availability of the WWW, it may have been more difficult for a student to develop an interest in the philosophy and history of education and to see their relevance to becoming a teacher. Only the most diligent students had the time, energy, and interest to do library research in these areas. Moreover, the outcomes of their research were limited to the size of the library collections they were using.

Today, however, the WWW makes available to you in a digitized form almost the entirety of human culture. This means that you can easily access *more* information that is *more relevant* to your interests, experiences, and professional goals. The WWW makes available to you not only vast information on the philosophy and history of education, but also an extensive collection of original primary sources. For example, during June 1999, before this book went to press, the following links were available at the "New This Month" page of The History of Education Site, an international archive of links and source materials about the history of education and the history of childhood maintained by University Nijmegen in the Netherlands. The "History of Education Site" is international in scope; however, half of the forty links for June 1999 addressed education in the United States.

- *Riding the Rails: Teenagers on the Move During the Great Depression*—includes excerpts from letters written by some of the quarter million teenage "hoboes" who roamed the United States in the 1930s.
- *The Games We Used to Play*—the games, especially street play, of city children in the United States during the 1960s.
- *The American Colonist's Library*—primary source texts on early education in the United States.
- *The 1642 Massachusetts Bay School Law*—copy of the Massachusetts Act of 1642.
- *Curriculum of the Boston Latin Grammar School*—course of study from 1712.
- *Classic Writings on School Choice*—historical source

the teacher a skilled technician who can manage the learning of many students at once?

Some teachers emphasize the individual student's experiences and cognitions. Others stress the student's behavior. Learning, according to the first viewpoint, is seen as the changes in thoughts or actions that result from personal experience; that is, learning is largely the result of internal forces within the individual. In contrast, the other view defines learning as the associations between various stimuli and responses. Here, learning results from forces that are external to the individual.

Beliefs about Students

Your beliefs about students will have a great influence on how you teach. Every teacher formulates an image in his or her mind of what students are like—their dispositions, skills, motivation levels, and expectations. What you believe students are like is based

texts from the 1700s and 1800s that presented ideas similar to today's school choice programs.

- *Thoughts upon the Mode of Education Proper in a Republic*—1786 essay by Benjamin Rush on schooling in the United States.
- *Horn Book*—a commercial woodcutter's website on how to obtain an exact copy of a horn book.
- *Comic Books and Juvenile Delinquency*—a 1955 report by the United States Senate Committee on the Judiciary.
- *History of Gifted Education*—annotated bibliography on the history of gifted education in the United States since 1950.
- *The Renaissance Trilogy: A Brief History of Education During Technology Shifts*—discussion on the influence of technology on education during three historical periods: Renaissance I (the printing press), Renaissance II (the WWW), and Renaissance III (the holodeck of the future [first described on the TV show *Star Trek*], which will allow people to create alternative realities in total-immersion, simulated, and safe environments).
- *Nineteenth-Century American Children and What They Read*—excerpts from pre-1860 children's books and magazines.
- *Carrie Berry Diary*—1864–65 diary of a 10-year-old Atlanta girl describing the effects of the Civil War on her school life.
- *The Teacher: Moral Influences Employed in the Instruction and Government of the Young*—1873 handbook for use in teacher education.
- *Explorations in Learning and Instruction*—information on important figures in the history of instructional psychology, theory, and design, including Skinner, Thorndike, Vygotsky, and Piaget.
- *Radical Educators in New York City, 1909–1915*—describes the establishment of a "Modern School" by innovative educators.
- *The History of Women in Education*—abstracts of articles from 1997 symposium.
- *Essay on Education, Applicable to Children in General; the Defective; the Criminal; the Poor; the Adult and Aged*—chapter from 1825 book.

on your unique life experiences, particularly your observations of young people and your knowledge of human growth and development.

Negative views of students may promote teacher–student relationships based on fear and coercion rather than on trust and helpfulness. Extremely positive views may risk not providing students with sufficient structure and direction and not communicating sufficiently high expectations. In the final analysis, the truly professional teacher—the one who has a carefully thought-out educational philosophy—recognizes that, although children differ in their predispositions to learn and grow, they all *can* learn.

Beliefs about Knowledge

How a teacher views knowledge is directly related to how he or she goes about teaching. If teachers view knowledge as the sum total of small bits of subject matter or discrete facts, their students will most likely spend a great deal of time learning that information in a straightforward, rote manner.

Other teachers view knowledge more conceptually, that is, as consisting of the big ideas that enable us to understand and influence our environment. Such teachers would want students to be able to explain how legislative decisions are made in the state capital, how an understanding of the eight parts of speech can empower the writer and vitalize one's writing, and how chemical elements are grouped according to their atomic numbers.

Finally, teachers differ in their beliefs as to whether students' increased understanding of their own experiences is a legitimate form of knowledge. Knowledge of self and one's experiences in the world is not the same as knowledge about a particular subject, yet personal knowledge is essential for a full, satisfying life.

Beliefs about What Is Worth Knowing

As we saw in this chapter's opening scenario, teachers have different ideas about what should be taught. Hal believes it is most important that students learn the basic skills of reading, writing, and computation. These are the skills they will need to be successful in their chosen occupations, and it is the school's responsibility to prepare students for the world of work. Karen believes that the most worthwhile content is to be found in the classics or the Great Books. Through mastering the great ideas from the sciences, mathematics, literature, and history, students will be well prepared to deal with the world of the future. Mary is most concerned with students learning how to reason, communicate effectively, and solve problems. Students who master these cognitive processes will have learned how to learn—and this is the most realistic preparation for an unknown future. Last, Juan is concerned with developing the whole child and teaching students to become self-actualizing. Thus, the curriculum should be meaningful and contribute to the student's efforts to become a mature, well-integrated person.

What Are the Branches of Philosophy?

To provide you with further tools to formulate and clarify your educational philosophy, this section presents brief overviews of six areas of philosophy that are of central concern to teachers: metaphysics, epistemology, axiology, ethics, aesthetics, and logic. Each area focuses on one of the questions that have concerned the world's greatest philosophers for centuries: What is the nature of reality? What is the nature of knowledge and is truth ever attainable? According to what values should one live? What is good and what is evil? What is the nature of beauty and excellence? What processes of reasoning will yield consistently valid results?

Metaphysics

Metaphysics is concerned with explaining, as rationally and as comprehensively as possible, the nature of reality (in contrast to how reality *appears*). What is reality? What is the world made of? These are metaphysical questions. Metaphysics also is concerned with the nature of being and explores questions such as, What does it mean to exist? What is humankind's place in the scheme of things? Metaphysical questions such as these are at the very heart of educational philosophy. As two educational philosophers put it: "Our ultimate preoccupation in educational theory is with the most primary of all philosophic problems: metaphysics, the study of ultimate reality" (Morris and Pai 1994, 28).

Metaphysics has important implications for education because the school curriculum is based on what we know about reality. And what we know about reality is driven by the kinds of questions we ask about the world. In fact, any position regarding what schools should teach has behind it a particular view of reality, a particular set of responses to metaphysical questions.

Epistemology

The next major set of philosophical questions that concerns teachers is called **epistemology.** These questions focus on knowledge: What knowledge is true? How does knowing take place? How do we know that we know? How do we decide between opposing views of knowledge? Is truth constant, or does it change from situation to situation? What knowledge is of most worth?

How you answer the epistemological questions that confront all teachers will have significant implications for your teaching. First, you will need to determine what is true about the content you will teach; then you must decide on the most appropriate means of conveying this content to students. Even a casual consideration of epistemological questions reveals that there are many ways of knowing about the world, at least five of which are of interest to teachers:

1. *Knowing Based on Authority*—for example, knowledge from the sage, the poet, the expert, the ruler, the textbook, or the teacher.
2. *Knowing Based on Divine Revelation*—for example, knowledge in the form of supernatural revelations from the sun god of early peoples, the many gods of the ancient Greeks, or the Judeo-Christian god.
3. *Knowing Based on Empiricism (Experience)*—for example, knowledge acquired through the senses, the informally gathered empirical data that direct most of our daily behavior.
4. *Knowing Based on Reason and Logical Analysis*—for example, knowledge inferred from the process of thinking logically.
5. *Knowing Based on Intuition*—for example, knowledge arrived at without the use of rational thought.

Axiology

The next set of philosophical problems concerns values. Teachers are concerned with values because "school is not a neutral activity. The very idea of schooling expresses a set of values. [We] educate and we are educated for some purpose we consider good. We teach what we think is a valuable set of ideas. How else could we construct education? (Nelson, Carlson, and Palonsky 2000, 304).

Among the axiological questions teachers must answer for themselves are: What values should teachers encourage students to adopt? What values raise humanity to our highest expressions of humaneness? What values does a truly educated person hold?

Axiology highlights the fact that the teacher has an interest not only in the *quantity* of knowledge that students acquire but also in the *quality* of life that becomes possible because of that knowledge. Extensive knowledge may not benefit the individual if he or she is unable to put that knowledge to good use. This point raises additional questions: How do we define quality of life? What curricular experiences contribute most to that quality of life? All teachers must deal with the issues raised by these questions.

Ethics   While axiology addresses the question "What is valuable?", **ethics** focuses on "What is good and evil, right and wrong, just and unjust?"

A knowledge of ethics can help the teacher solve many of the dilemmas that arise in the classroom. Frequently, teachers must take action in situations where they are unable to gather all of the relevant facts and where no single course of action is totally right or wrong. For example, a student whose previous work was above average plagiarizes a term paper: Should the teacher fail the student for the course if the example of swift, decisive punishment will likely prevent other students from plagiarizing? Or should the teacher, following her hunches about what would be in the student's long-term interest, have the student redo the term paper and risk the possibility that other students might get the mistaken notion that plagiarism has no negative consequences? Another ethical dilemma: Is an elementary mathematics teacher justified in trying to increase achievement for the whole class by separating two disruptive girls and placing one in a mathematics group beneath her level of ability?

Aesthetics   The branch of axiology known as **aesthetics** is concerned with values related to beauty and art. Although we expect that teachers of music, art, drama, literature, and writing regularly have students make judgments about the quality of works of art, we can easily overlook the role that aesthetics ought to play in *all* areas of the curriculum.

Aesthetics can also help the teacher increase his or her effectiveness. Teaching, because it may be viewed as a form of artistic expression, can be judged according to artistic standards of beauty and quality. In this regard, the teacher is an artist whose medium of expression is the spontaneous, unrehearsed, and creative encounter between teacher and student.

What might this teacher want her students to learn about aesthetics? How were aesthetic values reflected in the K–12 curricula you experienced?

Logic   Logic is the area of philosophy that deals with the process of reasoning and identifies rules that will enable the thinker to reach valid conclusions. The two kinds of logical thinking processes that teachers most frequently have students master are *deductive* and *inductive* thinking. The deductive approach requires the thinker to move from a general principle or proposition to a specific conclusion that is valid. By contrast, inductive reasoning moves from the specific to the general. Here, the student begins by examining particular examples that eventually lead to the acceptance of a general proposition. Inductive teaching is often referred to as discovery teaching —by which students discover, or create, their own knowledge of a topic.

Perhaps the best-known teacher to use the inductive approach to teaching was the Greek philosopher Socrates (ca. 470–399 B.C.). His method of teaching, known today as the Socratic method, consisted of holding philosophical conversations (dialectics) with his pupils. The legacy of Socrates lives in all teachers who use his questioning strategies to encourage students to think for themselves. Figure 3.2 presents guidelines for using **Socratic questioning** techniques in the classroom.

The Spirit and Principles of Socratic Questioning

- Treat all thoughts as in need of development.
- Respond to all answers with a further question (that calls on the respondent to develop his or her thinking in a fuller and deeper way).
- Treat all assertions as a connecting point to further thoughts.
- Recognize that any thought can only exist fully in a network of connected thoughts. Stimulate students—by your questions—to pursue those connections.
- Seek to understand—where possible—the ultimate foundations for what is said or believed.
- Recognize that all questions presuppose prior questions and all thinking presupposes prior thinking. When raising questions, be open to the questions they presuppose.

Figure 3.2

The spirit and principles of Socratic questioning
Source: Richard Paul and Linda Eider, "The Art of Socratic questioning," *Critical Thinking,* Fall 1995, 16.

What Are Five Modern Philosophical Orientations to Teaching?

Five major philosophical orientations to teaching have been developed in response to the branches of philosophy we have just examined. These orientations, or schools of thought, are perennialism, essentialism, progressivism, existentialism, and social reconstructionism. The following sections present a brief description of each of these orientations, moving from those that are teacher-centered to those that are student-centered (see Figure 3.3).

Socrates
(ca. 470–399 B.C.)

Perennialism

Perennialism, as the term implies, views truth as constant, or perennial. The aim of education, according to perennialist thinking, is to ensure that students acquire knowledge of unchanging principles or great ideas. Like Karen, whom you met briefly in this chapter's opening scenario, perennialists believe that the great ideas continue to have the most potential for solving the problems of any era.

The curriculum, according to perennialists, should stress students' intellectual growth in the arts and sciences. To become "culturally literate," students should encounter in these areas the best, most significant works that humans have created. Thus, a high school English teacher would require students to read Melville's *Moby Dick* or any of Shakespeare's plays rather than a novel on the current best-seller list.

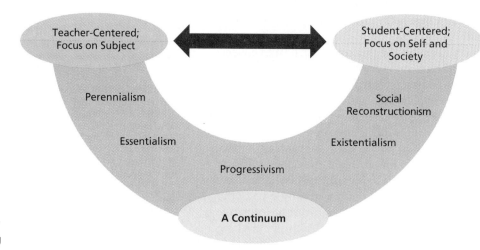

Figure 3.3

Five philosophical orientations to teaching

The figure shows a continuum with the following labels:

Teacher-Centered; Focus on Subject ← → Student-Centered; Focus on Self and Society

Perennialism

Essentialism

Social Reconstructionism

Existentialism

Progressivism

A Continuum

Similarly, science students would learn about the three laws of motion or the three laws of thermodynamics rather than build a model of the space shuttle.

Robert Maynard
Hutchins (1899–1977)

Perennialist Educational Philosophers   Two of the best known advocates of the perennialist philosophy have been Robert Maynard Hutchins (1899–1977) and, more recently, Mortimer Adler. As president of the University of Chicago from 1929 to 1945, Hutchins (1963) developed an undergraduate curriculum based on the study of the Great Books and discussions of these classics in small seminars. Noted educational philosopher Mortimer Adler, along with Hutchins, was instrumental in organizing the Great Books of the Western World curriculum. Through focusing study on over 100 enduring classics, from Plato to Einstein, the Great Books approach aims at the major perennialist goal of teaching students to become independent and critical thinkers. It is a demanding curriculum, and it focuses on the enduring disciplines of knowledge rather than on current events or student interests.

Essentialism

Essentialism, which has some similarities to perennialism, is a conservative philosophy of education originally formulated as a criticism of progressive trends in schools by William C. Bagley (1874–1946), a professor of education at Teachers College, Columbia University. Essentialists, like Hal whom you met in this chapter's opening scenario, believe that human culture has a core of common knowledge that schools are obligated to transmit to students in a systematic, disciplined way. Unlike perennialists, who emphasize a set of external truths, essentialists stress what they believe to be the essential knowledge and skills (often termed "the basics") that productive members of our society need to know.

William C. Bagley
(1874–1946)

According to essentialist philosophy, schooling should be practical and provide children with sound instruction that prepares them to live life; schools should not try to influence or set social policies. Critics of essentialism, however, charge that such a tradition-bound orientation to schooling will indoctrinate students and rule out the possibility of change. Essentialists respond that, without an essentialist approach, students will be indoctrinated in humanistic and/or behavioral curricula that run counter to society's accepted standards and need for order.

Progressivism

Progressivism is based on the belief that education should be child-centered rather than focused on the teacher or the content area. The writing of John Dewey (1859–1952) in the 1920s and 1930s contributed a great deal to the spread of progressive ideas. Briefly, Deweyan progressivism is based on three central assumptions:

1. The content of the curriculum ought to be derived from students' interests rather than from the academic disciplines.
2. Effective teaching takes into account the whole child and his or her interests and needs in relation to cognitive, affective, and psychomotor areas.
3. Learning is essentially active rather than passive.

How might you explain what is happening in this classroom from the perspective of progressivism? From the perspective of perennialism? From the perspective of essentialism?

Progressive Strategies   The progressive philosophy also contends that knowledge that is true in the present may not be true in the future. Hence, the best way to prepare students for an unknown future is to equip them with problem-solving strategies that will enable them to discover meaningful knowledge at various stages of their lives.

Educators with a progressive orientation give students a considerable amount of freedom in determining their school experiences. Contrary to the perceptions of many, though, progressive education does not mean that teachers do not provide structure or that students are free to do whatever they wish. Progressive teachers begin where students are and, through the daily give-and-take of the classroom, lead students to see that the subject to be learned can enhance their lives.

In a progressively oriented classroom, the teacher serves as a guide or resource person whose primary responsibility is to facilitate student learning. The teacher helps students learn what is important to them rather than passing on a set of so-called enduring truths. Students have many opportunities to work cooperatively in groups, often solving problems that the group, not the teacher, has identified as important.

John Dewey
(1859–1952)

Existentialism   Existential philosophy is unique in that it focuses on the experiences of the individual. Other philosophies are concerned with developing systems of thought for identifying and understanding what is common to *all* reality, human existence, and values. **Existentialism,** on the other hand, offers the individual a way of thinking about *my* life, what has meaning for *me*, what is true for *me*. In general, existentialism emphasizes creative choice, the subjectivity of human experiences, and concrete acts of human existence over any rational scheme for human nature or reality.

Jean-Paul Sartre
(1905–1980)

Maxine Green
(b. 1917)

The writings of Jean-Paul Sartre (1905–1980), well-known French philosopher, novelist, and playwright, have been most responsible for the widespread dissemination of existential ideas. According to Sartre (1972), every individual first exists and then he or she must decide what that existence is to mean. The task of assigning meaning to that existence is the individual's alone; no preformulated philosophical belief system can tell one who one is. It is up to each of us to decide who we are.

Life, according to existential thought, has no meaning, and the universe is indifferent to the situation humankind finds itself in. Moreover, "existententialists [believe] that too many people wrongly emphasize the optimistic, the good, and the beautiful—all of which create a false impression of existence" (Ozmon and Craver 1999, 253). With the freedom that we have, however, each of us must commit him- or herself to assign meaning to his or her *own* life. As Maxine Greene, an eminent philosopher of education whose work is based on existentialism, states: "We have to know about our lives, clarify our situations if we are to understand the world from our shared standpoints . . ." (1995, 21). The human enterprise that can be most helpful in promoting this personal quest for meaning is the educative process. Teachers, therefore, must allow students freedom of choice and provide them with experiences that will help them find the meaning of their lives. This approach, contrary to the belief of many, does not mean that students may do whatever they please; logic indicates that freedom has rules, and respect for the freedom of others is essential.

Existentialists judge the curriculum according to whether or not it contributes to the individual's quest for meaning and results in a level of personal awareness that Greene (1995) terms "wide-awakeness." The ideal curriculum is one that provides students with extensive individual freedom and requires them to ask their own questions, conduct their own inquiries, and draw their own conclusions.

Social Reconstructionism

As the name implies, **social reconstructionism** holds that schools should take the lead in changing or reconstructing society. Theodore Brameld (1904–1987), acknowledged as the founder of social reconstructionism, based his philosophy on two fundamental premises about the post–World War II era: (1) We live in a period of great crisis, most evident in the fact that humans now have the capability of destroying civilization overnight, and (2) humankind also has the intellectual, technological, and moral potential to create a world civilization of "abundance, health, and humane capacity" (Brameld 1959, 19). In this time of great need, then, social reconstructionists like Juan, whom we met in this chapter's opening scenario, believe that schools should become the primary agent for planning and directing social change. Schools should not only *transmit* knowledge about the existing social order; they should seek to *reconstruct* it as well.

Social Reconstructionism and Progressivism Social reconstructionism has clear ties to progressive educational philosophy. Both provide opportunities for extensive interactions between teacher and students and among students themselves. Furthermore, both place a premium on bringing the community, if not the entire world, into the classroom. Student experiences often include field trips, community-based projects of various sorts, and opportunities to interact with people beyond the four walls of the classroom.

According to Brameld and social reconstructionists such as George Counts, who wrote *Dare the School Build a New Social Order?* (1932), the educative process should provide students with methods for dealing with the significant crises that confront the world: war, economic depression, international terrorism, hunger, inflation, and ever-accelerating technological advances. The logical outcome of such education would be the eventual realization of a world-wide democracy (Brameld 1956). Unless we actively seek to create this kind of world through the intelligent application of present knowledge, we run the risk that the destructive forces of the world will determine the conditions under which humans will live in the future.

George Counts
(1889–1974)

What Psychological Orientations Have Influenced Teaching Philosophies?

In addition to the five philosophical orientations to teaching described in previous sections of this chapter, several schools of psychological thought have formed the basis for teaching philosophies. These psychological theories are comprehensive world views that serve as the basis for the way many teachers approach teaching practice. Psychological orientations to teaching are concerned primarily with understanding the conditions that are associated with effective learning. In other words, what motivates students to learn? What environments are most conducive to learning? Chief among the psychological orientations that have influenced teaching philosophies are humanistic psychology, behaviorism, and constructivism.

Humanistic Psychology

Humanistic psychology emphasizes personal freedom, choice, awareness, and personal responsibility. As the term implies, it also focuses on the achievements, motivation, feelings, actions, and needs of human beings. The goal of education, according to this orientation, is individual self-actualization.

Humanistic psychology is derived from the philosophy of **humanism,** which developed during the European Renaissance and Protestant Reformation and is based on the belief that individuals control their own destinies through the application of their intelligence and learning. People "make themselves." The term "secular humanism" refers to the closely related belief that the conditions of human existence relate to human nature and human actions rather than to predestination or divine intervention.

In the 1950s and 1960s, humanistic psychology became the basis of educational reforms that sought to enhance students' achievement of their full potential through self-actualization (Maslow 1954, 1962; Rogers 1961). According to this psychological orientation, teachers should not force students to learn; instead, they should create a climate of trust and respect that allows students to decide what and how they learn, to question authority, and to take initiative in "making themselves." Teachers should be what noted psychologist Carl Rogers calls "facilitators," and the classroom should be a place "in which curiosity and the natural desire to learn can be nourished and enhanced" (1982, 31). Through their nonjudgmental understanding of students, humanistic teachers encourage students to learn and grow.

Behaviorism

Behaviorism is based on the principle that desirable human behavior can be the product of design rather than accident. According to behaviorists, it is an illusion to say that humans have a free will. Although we may act as if we are free, our behavior is really *determined* by forces in the environment that shape our behavior. "We are what we are and we do what we do, not because of any mysterious power of human volition, but because outside forces over which we lack any semblance of control have us caught in an inflexible web. Whatever else we may be, we are not the captains of our fate or the masters of our soul" (Power 1982, 168).

B. F. Skinner
(1904–1990)

Founders of Behavioristic Psychology   John B. Watson (1878–1958) was the principal originator of behavioristic psychology and B. F. Skinner (1904–1990) its best-known promoter. Watson first claimed that human behavior consisted of specific stimuli that resulted in certain responses. In part, he based this new conception of learning on the classic experiment conducted by Russian psychologist Ivan Pavlov (1849–1936). Pavlov had noticed that a dog he was working with would salivate when it was about to be given food. By introducing the sound of a bell when food was offered and repeating this several times, Pavlov discovered that the sound of the bell alone (a conditioned stimulus) would make the dog salivate (a conditioned response). Watson came to believe that all learning conformed to this basic stimulus-response model (now termed classical or type S conditioning).

Skinner went beyond Watson's basic stimulus-response model and developed a more comprehensive view of conditioning known as operant (or type R) conditioning. Operant conditioning is based on the idea that satisfying responses are conditioned, unsatisfying ones are not. In other words, "The things we call pleasant have an energizing or strengthening effect on our behaviour" (Skinner 1972, 74). Thus the teacher can create learners who exhibit desired behaviors by following four steps:

1. Identify desired behaviors in concrete (observable and measurable) terms.
2. Establish a procedure for recording specific behaviors and counting their frequencies.
3. For each behavior, identify an appropriate reinforcer.
4. Ensure that students receive the reinforcer as soon as possible after displaying a desired behavior.

Constructivism

In contrast to behaviorism, constructivism focuses on processes of learning rather than on learning behavior. According to **constructivism**, students use cognitive processes to *construct* understanding of the material to be learned—in contrast to the view that they *receive* information transmitted by the teacher. Constructivist approaches support student-centered rather than teacher-centered curriculum and instruction. The student is the key to learning.

Unlike behaviorists who concentrate on directly observable behavior, constructivists focus on the mental processes and strategies that students use to learn. Our understanding of learning has been extended as a result of advances in **cognitive science**—the study of the mental processes students use in thinking and remembering. By drawing from research in linguistics, psychology, anthropology, neurophysiology, and computer science, cognitive scientists are developing new models for how people think and learn.

Teachers who base classroom activities on constructivism know that learning is an active, meaning-making process, that learners are not passive recipients of information. In fact, students are continually involved in making sense out of activities around them. Thus the teacher must *understand students' understanding* and realize that students' learning is influenced by prior knowledge, experience, attitudes, and social interactions.

How Can You Develop Your Educational Philosophy?

As you read the preceding brief descriptions of five educational philosophies and three psychological orientations to teaching, perhaps you felt that no single philosophy fit perfectly with your image of the kind of teacher you want to become. Or, there may have been some element of each approach that seemed compatible with your own emerging philosophy of education. In either case, don't feel that you need to identify a single educational philosophy around which you will build your teaching career. In reality, few teachers follow only one educational philosophy, and, as Figure 3.4 shows, educational philosophy is only one determinant of the professional goals a teacher sets.

Most teachers develop an *eclectic* philosophy of education, which means they develop their own unique blending of two or more philosophies. To help you identify the philosophies most consistent with your beliefs and values about educational goals, curriculum, and teachers' and students' roles in learning, complete the Philosophic Inventory found on this book's website. The self-knowledge you glean from completing the inventory and the philosophical constructs presented in the first half of this chapter provide a useful framework for studying the six periods in the historical development of schools that follow. For example, you will be able to see how philosophical orientations to education waxed and waned during each period—whether it was the peren-

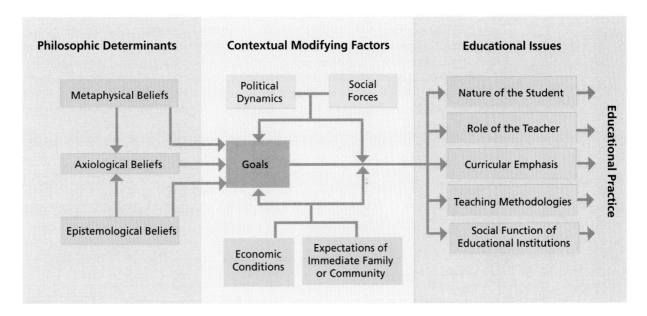

Figure 3.4

The relationship of philosophy to educational practice
Source: George R. Knight, *Issues & Alternatives in Educational Philosophy, 3rd ed.* Berrien Springs, MI: Andrews University Press, p. 34.

These children are active learners in a real or relevant context, and they are constructing their own meanings through direct experience. How might this lesson be seen as an eclectic blend of progressive, existential, and constructivist ideals?

nialism and essentialism that characterized colonial schools, the progressivism of the 1920s and 1930s, the essentialism of the 1950s and 1980s, the humanism and social reconstructionism of the 1960s, or the constructivism of the 1990s.

What Were Teaching and Schools Like in the American Colonies (1620–1750)?

Education in colonial America had its primary roots in English culture. The settlers of our country initially tried to develop a system of schooling that paralleled the British two-track system. If students from the lower classes attended school at all it was at the elementary level for the purpose of studying an essentialist curriculum of reading, writing, and computation and receiving religious instruction. Students from the upper classes had the opportunity to attend Latin grammar schools, where they were given a college-preparatory education that focused on perennialist subjects such as Latin and Greek classics.

Above all, the colonial curriculum stressed religious objectives. Generally, no distinction was made between secular and religious life in the colonies. The religious motives that impelled the Puritans to endure the hardships of settling in a new land were reflected in the schools' curricula. The primary objective of elementary schooling was to learn to read so that one might read the Bible and religious catechisms and thereby receive salvation.

Colonial Schools

In the New England colonies (Massachusetts Bay, New Hampshire, and Connecticut), there was a general consensus that church, state, and schools were interrelated. As a result, town schools were created throughout these colonies to teach children the basics of reading and writing so they could learn the scriptures. The Puritan view of the child included the belief that people are inherently sinful. Even natural childhood play was seen as devil-inspired idleness. The path to redemption lay in learning to curb one's natural instincts and behave like an adult as quickly as possible.

The middle colonies (New York, New Jersey, Pennsylvania, and Delaware) were more diverse, and groups such as the Irish, Scots, Swedes, Danes, Dutch, and Germans established **parochial schools** based on their religious beliefs. Anglicans, Lutherans, Quakers, Jews, Catholics, Presbyterians, and Mennonites in the Middle Colonies tended to establish their own schools. In the largely Protestant southern colonies (Virginia, Maryland, Georgia, and North and South Carolina), wealthy plantation owners believed the primary purpose of education was to promote religion and to prepare their children to attend colleges and universities in Europe. The vast majority of small farmers received no formal schooling and the children of African slaves received only the training they needed to serve their masters.

No one type of schooling was common to all the colonies. The most common types, however, were the dame schools, the reading and writing schools, and the Latin grammar schools. **Dame schools** provided initial instruction for boys and, often, the only schooling for girls. These schools were run by widows or housewives in their homes and supported by modest fees from parents. Classes were usually held in the kitchen, where children learned only the barest essentials of reading, writing, and arithmetic during instruction lasting for a few weeks to one year. Females might also be taught sewing and basic homemaking skills. Students often began by learning the alphabet from a **horn book.** Developed in medieval Europe, the horn book was a copy of the alphabet covered by a thin transparent sheet made from a cow's horn. The alphabet and the horn covering were attached to a paddle-shaped piece of wood.

Reading and writing schools offered boys an education that went beyond what their parents could teach them at home or what they could learn at a dame school. Reading lessons were based on the Bible, various religious catechisms, and the *New England Primer,* first printed in 1690. The **Primer** introduced children to the letters of the alphabet through the use of illustrative woodcuts and rhymed couplets. The first couplet began with the pronouncement that

N NOAH did view / The old world & new

O Young OBADIAS, / DAVID, JOSIAS / All were pious.

P PETER deny'd / His Lord and cry'd.

Q Queen ESTHER sues / And saves the *Jews.*

R Young pious RUTH, / Left all for Truth.

S Young SAM'L dear / The Lord did fear.

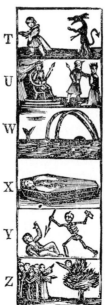

T Young TIMOTHY / Learnt sin to fly.

U VASTHI for Pride, / Was set aside.

W Whales in the Sea, / GOD's Voice obey.

X XERXES did die, / And so must I.

Y While youth do cheer / Death may be near.

Z ZACCHEUS he / Did climb the Tree / Our Lord to see.

What do these two pages from a 1727 edition of *The New England Primer* suggest about the curriculum and aims of education in early schools in the United States?

> In Adam's fall
> We sinned all.

And the final one noted that

> Zaccheus he
> Did climb the Tree
> His Lord to see.

The *Primer* also presented children with large doses of stern religious warnings about the proper conduct of life.

The **Latin grammar school,** comparable to today's secondary school, was patterned after the classical schools of Europe. Boys enrolled in the Latin grammar schools at the age of seven or eight, whereupon they began to prepare to enter Harvard College (established in 1636). Following graduation from Harvard, they would assume leadership roles in the church.

The Origins of Mandated Education

Universal compulsory education had its origins in the **Massachusetts Act of 1642.** Prior to this date, parents could decide whether they wished their children to be educated at home or at a school. Church and civic leaders in the colonies, however, decided that education could no longer remain voluntary. They saw that many children were receiving inadequate training. Moreover, they realized that organized schools would serve to strengthen and preserve Puritan religious beliefs.

The Puritans decided to make education a civil responsibility of the state. The Massachusetts General Court passed a law in 1642 that required each town to determine whether young people could read and write. Parents and apprentices' masters whose children were unable "to read and understand the principles of religion and the capital laws of the country" (Rippa 1997, 36) could be fined and, possibly, lose custody of their children.

Although the Act of 1642 did not mandate the establishment of schools, it did make it clear that the education of children was a direct concern of the local citizenry. In 1648, the Court revised the 1642 law, reminding town leaders that "the good education of children is of singular behoof and benefit to any commonwealth" and that some parents and masters were still "too indulgent and negligent of their duty" (Cohen 1974, 394–95). As the first educational law in this country, the Massachusetts Act of 1642 was a landmark.

The **Massachusetts Act of 1647,** often referred to as the Old Deluder Satan Act (because education was seen as the best protection against the wiles of the devil), mandated the establishment and support of schools. In particular, towns of fifty households or more were to appoint a person to instruct "all such children as shall resort to him to write and read." Teachers were to "be paid either by the parents or masters of such children, or by the inhabitants in general" (Rippa 1997, 36).

Education for African Americans and Native Americans

At the close of the American Revolution, nearly all of the half million African Americans were slaves who could neither read nor write (Button and Provenzo 1989). In most cases, those who were literate had been taught by their masters or through small, church-affiliated programs. Literate Native Americans and Mexican Americans usually had received their training at the hands of missionaries. One of the first schools for African Americans was started by Elias Neau in New York City in 1704. Sponsored by the Church of England, Neau's school taught African and Native Americans how to read as part of the Church's efforts to convert students.

Other schools for African and Native Americans were started by the Quakers, who regarded slavery as a moral evil. Though Quaker schools for African Americans existed as early as 1700, one of the best known was founded in Philadelphia in 1770 by Anthony Benezet, who believed that African Americans were ". . . generously sensible, humane, and sociable, and that their capacity is as good, and as capable of improvement as that of white people" (Button and Provenzo 1989, 45). Schools modeled on the Philadelphia African School opened elsewhere in the Northeast, and "Indian schools" also were founded as philanthropic enterprises.

From the seventeenth to the late-twentieth centuries, schools were segregated by race. The first recorded official ground for school segregation dates back to a decision of the Massachusetts Supreme Court in 1850. When the Roberts family sought to send their daughter Sarah to a white school in Boston, the court ruled that "equal, but separate" schools were being provided and that the Roberts therefore could not claim an injustice (*Roberts v. City of Boston* 1850). From the beginning, however, schools were not equal, and students did not have equal educational opportunity.

What Were the Goals of Education during the Revolutionary Period (1750–1820)?

Education in the United States during the Revolutionary period was characterized by a general waning of European influences on schools. Though religious traditions that had their origins in Europe continued to affect the curriculum, the young country's need to develop agriculture, shipping, and commerce also exerted its influence on the curriculum. By this time, the original settlers who had emigrated from Europe had been replaced by a new generation whose most immediate roots were in the new soil of the United States. This new, exclusively American, identity was also enhanced by the rise of civil town governments, the great increase in books and newspapers that addressed life in the new country, and a turning away from Europe toward the unsettled west. The colonies' break with Europe was most potently demonstrated in the American Revolution of 1776.

Following independence, many leaders were concerned that new disturbances from within could threaten the well-being of the new nation. To preserve the freedoms that had been fought for, a system of education became essential. Through education, people would become intelligent, participating citizens of a constitutional democracy. Among these leaders were Benjamin Franklin, Sarah Pierce, Thomas Jefferson, and Noah Webster.

Benjamin Franklin's Academy

Benjamin Franklin (1706–1790) designed and promoted the Philadelphia Academy, a private secondary school, which opened in 1751. This school, which replaced the old

Benjamin Franklin
(1706–1790)

Latin grammar school, had a curriculum that was broader and more practical and also focused on the English language rather than Latin. The academy was also a more democratically run institution than previous schools had been. Though **academies** were largely privately controlled and privately financed, they were secular and often supported by public funds. Most academies were public in that anyone who could pay tuition could attend, regardless of church affiliation (Rippa 1997, 65).

In his *Proposals Relating to the Education of Youth in Pennsylvania,* written in 1749, Franklin noted that "the good Education of youth has been esteemed by wise men in all ages, as the surest foundation of the happiness both of private families and of commonwealths" (Franklin 1931, 151).

Franklin's proposals for educating youth called for a wide range of subjects that reflected perennialist and essentialist philosophical orientations: English grammar, composition, and literature; classical and modern foreign languages; science; writing and drawing; rhetoric and oratory; geography; various kinds of history; agriculture and gardening; arithmetic and accounting; and mechanics.

Sarah Pierce's Female Academy

English **academies,** often called people's colleges, multiplied across the country, reaching a peak of 6,185 in 1855, with an enrollment of 263,096 (Spring 1997, 22). Usually, these academies served male students only; a notable exception was Sarah Pierce's Litchfield Female Academy in Litchfield, Connecticut. Pierce (1767–1852) began her academy in the dining room of her home with two students; eventually, the academy grew to 140 female students from nearly every state and from Canada (Button and Provenzo 1989, 87).

For the most part, however, girls received little formal education in the seventeenth and eighteenth centuries and were educated for entirely different purposes than were boys. As the following mission statement for Pierce's Academy suggests, an essentialist, rather than perennialist, curriculum was appropriate for girls:

Emma Willard
(1787–1870)

> Our object has been, not to make learned ladies, or skillful metaphysical reasoners, or deep read scholars in physical science: there is a more useful, tho' less exalted and less brilliant station that woman must occupy, there are duties of incalculable importance that she must perform: that station is home; these duties, are the alleviation of the trials of her parents; the soothing of the labours & fatigues of her partner; & the education for time and eternity of the next generation of immortal beings . . . (Button and Provenzo 1989, 88).

Some women enrolled in **female seminaries,** first established in the early nineteenth century to train women for higher education and public service outside of the home. Educational opportunities for women expanded in conjunction with social reform movements that gradually led to greater political equality for women, including the right to vote in the twentieth century. For example, Troy Seminary, founded in 1821 by educator and poet Emma Willard (1787–1870), became one of the first women's colleges in the country.

Thomas Jefferson's Philosophy

Thomas Jefferson (1743–1826), author of the Declaration of Independence, viewed the education of common people as the most effective means of preserving liberty. As historian S. Alexander Rippa put it, "Few statesmen in American history have so vigorously strived for an ideal; perhaps none has so consistently viewed public education as the indispensable cornerstone of freedom" (1997, 55).

For a society to remain free, Jefferson felt, it must support a continuous system of public education. He proposed to the Virginia legislature in 1779 his Bill for the More General Diffusion of Knowledge. This plan called for state-controlled elementary schools that would teach, with no cost to parents, three years of reading, writing, and arithmetic to all white children. In addition, twenty state grammar schools would be created in which selected poor students would be taught free for a maximum period of six years.

Jefferson was unsuccessful in his attempt to convince the Virginia House of Burgesses of the need for a uniform system of public schools as outlined in his bill. Jefferson was, however, able to implement many of his educational ideas through his efforts to found the University of Virginia. He devoted the last years of his life to developing the university, and he lived to see the university open with forty students in March 1824, one month before his eighty-first birthday.

Thomas Jefferson (1743–1826)

Noah Webster's Speller

In the years following the Revolution, several textbooks were printed in the United States. Writers and publishers saw the textbook as an appropriate vehicle for promoting democratic ideals and cultural independence from England. Toward this end, U.S. textbooks were filled with patriotic and moralistic maxims. Among the most widely circulated books of this type were Noah Webster's *Elementary Spelling Book* and *The American Dictionary*.

Webster (1758–1843) first introduced his speller in 1783 under the cumbersome title, *A Grammatical Institute of the English Language*. Later versions were titled the *American Spelling Book* and the *Elementary Spelling Book*. Webster's speller earned the nickname "the old blue-back" because early copies of the book were covered in light blue paper and later editions covered with bright blue paper.

In the introduction to his speller, Webster declared that its purpose was to help teachers instill in students "the first rudiments of the language, some just ideas of religion, morals and domestic economy" (Button and Provenzo 1989, 65). Throughout, the little book emphasized patriotic and moralistic virtues. Short, easy-to-remember maxims taught pupils to be content with their lot in life, to work hard, and to respect the property of others.

Noah Webster (1758–1843)

How Was the Struggle Won for State-Supported Common Schools (1820–1865)?

The first state-supported high school in the United States was the Boston English Classical School, established in 1821. The opening of this school, renamed English High School in 1824, marked the beginning of a long, slow struggle for state-supported **common schools** in this country. Those in favor of free common schools tended to be city residents and nontaxpayers, democratic leaders, philanthropists and humanitarians, members of various school societies, and working people. Those opposed were rural residents and taxpayers, members of old aristocratic and conservative groups,

Should school attendance beyond the elementary level become voluntary?

Should every child in the United States over twelve years old be required to attend high school? Should only those students who choose to be in school be permitted to attend? Should school attendance beyond the elementary level become voluntary?

Compulsory school attendance became a feature of education in the United States during the common schools movement, which was launched to educate the populace so that they could participate in the newly formed democratic government. In 1852 Horace Mann pushed the Massachusetts legislature to pass a law requiring at least twelve weeks of schooling a year for children between ages eight and fourteen. By 1918 all of the other states had passed similar laws.

Over the years, individuals and groups dissatisfied with the schooling system in the United States have argued in favor of voluntary school attendance for a variety of reasons. Some believed that schools forced students to be too conforming and obedient. Others believed that compulsory attendance was simply a means of keeping disruptive adolescents off the streets. Today, many who home school their children believe schools are unsafe, unhealthy, and poor settings for learning. On the other hand, opponents of voluntary school attendance say that the nation will be lost if citizens abdicate responsibility for the education of children over thirteen and release them to society with no further guidance. We would be giving up on them and limiting their futures, they say. Where do you stand on this issue? Should school attendance beyond the elementary level become voluntary?

No, school attendance beyond elementary school should not become voluntary.

Opponents of voluntary school attendance believe that the original reason for requiring students to continue their schooling past the age of twelve remains valid today. Citizens need to be informed and able to think critically if democracy is to prevail. This necessity is especially important today because of the increasing complexity and diversity in society. As extensive immigration to the United States continues, new citizens and their children need to learn about the history, government, and values of their new land. In addition, the growing influence and sophistication of the news media requires an educated citizenry that can resist intellectual manipulation. Thus compulsory school attendance should be continued for the common good of the United States.

In addition, many who oppose the idea of voluntary attendance believe strongly that the core of U.S. society is weak today, lacking such values of the past as honesty, perseverance, integrity, generosity, compassion, and service. Drugs, violence, sexual promiscuity, and the absence of ethics and morals have taken their toll, resulting in a society that is self-indulgent, irresponsible, and impatient for immediate gratification. Too many parents are unwilling to place demands on their children. In such a weakened society, is it wise to make school attendance after the age of twelve voluntary? Will parents choose the easy way out and let their children drop out of school when they are thirteen?

Furthermore, which children would remain in school if attendance were voluntary, the sons and daughters of the wealthy or of the poor? Will the children who leave school when they are thirteen be short-changed in their career options? Will they be able to keep up with the expansion of technology and access to information? Will they acquire the knowledge and thinking skills necessary to make the important, complex decisions in their lives? Will they be able to negotiate as well in our increasingly complex society? Opponents to voluntary school attendance after elementary school think not. They fear that the costs for those who leave and for society as whole would be extensive and irreparable.

Yes, school attendance beyond the elementary level should become voluntary.

"Education is wasted on the young!" say many people who returned to college after being in the work world. They were more motivated to learn, brought more life experiences to their studies, used their time more efficiently, and earned higher grades after being out in the world for a while. Would adolescents discover the same thing if they weren't required to move on to middle or junior high school after elementary school? Instead of forcing thirteen-year-olds to stay in school, shouldn't we encourage them to travel, engage in meaningful service, or experience the work world before continuing their education? Their readiness to learn and their appreciation of the educational opportunities they were given would be greatly enhanced if that were the case, say those who favor voluntary school attendance.

The proponents also ask, "Do all adolescents benefit from having a secondary education?" Some students know exactly what they want to learn, but they are not able to find the instruction they desire in their high schools. Most secondary schools do not offer classes in such areas as paramedics, auto design, marketing, investments, computer graphics, song writing, art design, architecture, guitar playing, fashion design, script writing, film animation, flight training, river boat piloting, auto racing, skiing, broadcasting, scuba diving, parachuting, abnormal psychology, child development, and parenting. A resurgence of the apprenticeships of our colonial past may be the answer for some groups of today's young people.

Proponents of voluntary attendance argue that public schools would be more effective if they didn't have to deal with uncooperative students who wanted to leave but couldn't. These resistant students take teachers' and principals' time from the students who are there to learn. How much more productive schools would be if they were filled only with students motivated to learn! Educators, too, would find their work more rewarding, and teaching would become a more inviting profession. In addition, parent involvement in school would increase, because parents had chosen to have their children continue in school.

The tax money saved from having fewer students in school could enrich school offerings and extend students'

educational experiences. The extra money could even be spent on creative education and training alternatives that would appeal to and benefit those who chose to leave. Making school attendance voluntary after the age of twelve could result in a revitalized education system.

Where do you stand on this issue?

1. With which position do you agree and why?

2. What would you add to the list of subjects desired by students but not currently taught in secondary schools?

3. What do you think of the compromise position of giving people in the United States the option of having ten years of free education that they could take whenever they choose?

4. What other solutions can you suggest for helping students who don't want a traditional secondary education?

Recommended Sources

Mann, H. (1846). The education of free men. *Tenth annual report.*

Mann, H. (1848) The education of free men. *Twelfth annual report.*

McGhan, B. (1997, Winter.) Compulsory school attendance: an idea past its prime? *The Educational Forum.*

Noll, J. W. (ed.). *Taking sides: clashing views on controversial educational issues,* 10th ed. Guilford, CT: McGraw-Hill, 1999.

owners of private schools, members of conservative religious sects, Southerners, and non-English-speaking residents. By far the most eloquent and effective spokesperson for the common school was Horace Mann.

Horace Mann's Contributions

Horace Mann (1796–1859) was a lawyer, Massachusetts senator, and the first secretary of a state board of education. He is best known as the champion of the common

Horace Mann
(1796–1859)

school movement, which has led to the free, public, locally controlled elementary schools we know today. Mann worked tirelessly to convince people that their interests would be well served by a system of universal free schools for all:

> It [a free school system] knows no distinction of rich and poor, of bond and free, or between those, who, in the imperfect light of this world, are seeking, through different avenues, to reach the gate of heaven. Without money and without price, it throws open its doors, and spreads the table of its bounty, for all the children of the State (Mann 1868, 754).

Improving Schools   In 1837, Mann accepted the position of Secretary of the Massachusetts State Board of Education. At the time, conditions in Massachusetts schools were deplorable, and Mann immediately began to use his new post to improve the quality of schools. Through the twelve annual reports he submitted while secretary and through *The Common School Journal,* which he founded and edited, Mann's educational ideas became widely known in this country and abroad.

In his widely publicized *Fifth Report* (published in 1841), Mann told the moneyed conservative classes that support of common public schools would provide them "the cheapest means of self-protection and insurance." Where could they find, Mann asked, "any police so vigilant and effective, for the protection of all the rights of person, property and character, as such a sound and comprehensive education and training, as our system of Common Schools could be made to impart?" (Rippa 1997, 95).

In his *Seventh Report* (published 1843), Mann extolled the virtues of schools he had visited in Prussia that implemented the humanistic approaches of noted Swiss educator Johann Heinrich Pestalozzi (1746–1827). "I heard no child ridiculed, sneered at, or scolded, for making a mistake," Mann wrote (Rippa 1997, 96).

The Normal School   During the late 1830s, Mann put forth a proposal that today we take for granted. Teachers, he felt, needed more than a high school education to teach; they should be trained in professional programs. The French had established the *école normale* for preparing teachers, and Mann and other influential educators of the period, such as Catherine Beecher (1800–1878), whose sister, Harriet Beecher Stowe (1811–1896), wrote *Uncle Tom's Cabin,* believed that a similar program was needed in the United States. Through her campaign to ensure that women had access to an education equal to that of men and her drive to recruit women into the teaching profession, Beecher contributed significantly to the development of publicly funded schools for training teachers (Holmes and Weiss 1995).

The first public **normal school** in the United States opened in Lexington, Massachusetts, on July 3, 1839. The curriculum consisted of general knowledge courses plus courses in pedagogy (or teaching) and practice teaching in a model school affiliated with the normal school. In 1849, Electa Lincoln Walton (1824–1908), an 1843 graduate of the normal school, became acting head administrator and the first woman to administer a state normal school. Walton was energetic and determined to succeed, as her journal reveals:

> Many people think women can't do much. I'd like to show them that they can keep a Normal School and keep it well too . . . I will succeed . . . I will never be pointed at as an example of the incompetency of woman to conduct a large establishment well" (Holmes and Weiss 1995, 42).

When Mann resigned as secretary in 1848, his imprint on education in the United States was broad and deep. As a result of his unflagging belief that education was the "great equalizer of the conditions of men—the balance wheel of the social machinery" (Mann 1957, 87), Massachusetts had a firmly established system of common schools and led the way for other states to establish free public schools.

Reverend W. H. McGuffey's Readers

Reverend William Holmes McGuffey (1800–1873) had perhaps the greatest impact on what children learned in the new school. Far exceeding Noah Webster's speller in sales were the famous **McGuffey readers.** It has been estimated that 122 million copies of the six-volume series were sold after 1836. The six readers ranged in difficulty from the first-grade level to the sixth grade level. Through such stories as "The Wolf," "Meddlesome Matty," and "A Kind Brother," the readers emphasized virtues such as hard work, honesty, truth, charity, and obedience.

Absent from the McGuffey readers were the dour, pessimistic views of childhood so characteristic of earlier primers. Nevertheless, they had a religious, moral, and ethical influence over millions of American readers. Through their reading of the "Dignity of Labor," "The Village Blacksmith," and "The Rich Man's Son," for example, readers learned that contentment outweighs riches in this world. In addition to providing explicit instructions on right living, the McGuffey readers also taught countless children and adults how to read and study.

Justin Morrill's Land-Grant Schools

The common school movement and the continuing settlement of the West stimulated the development of public higher education. In 1862, the **Morrill Land-Grant Act,** sponsored by Congressman Justin S. Morrill (1810–1898) of Vermont, provided federal land for states either to sell or to rent in order to raise funds for the establishment of colleges of agriculture and mechanical arts. Each state was given a land subsidy of 30,000 acres for each representative and senator in its congressional delegation. Eventually, seven and a half million dollars from the sale of over seventeen million acres was given to land-grant colleges and state universities. The Morrill Act of 1862 set a precedent for the federal government to take an active role in shaping higher education in the United States. A second Morrill Act in 1890 provided even more federal funds for land-grant colleges.

How Did Compulsory Education Change Schools and the Teaching Profession (1865–1920)?

From the end of the Civil War to the end of World War I, publicly supported common schools steadily spread westward and southward from New England and the Middle Atlantic states. Beginning with Massachusetts in 1852, compulsory education laws were passed in thirty-two states by 1900 and in all states by 1930.

Because of compulsory attendance laws, an ever-increasing proportion of children attended school. In 1869–70, only 64.7 percent of five- to seventeen-year-olds attended public school. By 1919–20, this proportion had risen to 78.3 percent; and in 1995–96, it was 91.7 percent (National Center for Education Statistics 1999, 50). The growth in enrollment on the high school level was exceptional. Historical data from the National Center for Education Statistics (1999) enable us to determine that between

1880 and 1920, the population in the United States increased 108 percent, and high school enrollment increased 1,900 percent!

As common schools spread, school systems began to take on organizational features associated with today's schools: centralized control; increasing authority for state, county, and city superintendencies; and a division of labor among teachers and administrators at the individual school site. Influenced by the work of Frederick W. Taylor (1856–1915), an engineer and the founder of **scientific management,** school officials undertook reforms based on management principles and techniques from big business. For example, they believed that top-down management techniques should be applied to schools as well as factories.

Higher Education for African Americans

In *Up from Slavery,* Booker T. Washington (1856–1915) recounts how he walked part of the 500 miles from his home in West Virginia to attend the Hampton Normal and Agricultural Institute of Virginia, one of the country's first institutions of higher education for African Americans. Four years after graduating from Hampton, Washington returned to be the school's first African American instructor.

Washington had a steadfast belief that education could improve the lives of African Americans just as it had for white people: "Poverty and ignorance have affected the black man just as they affect the white man. But the day is breaking, and education will bring the complete light" (Rippa 1997, 122). In 1880, Washington helped to found the Tuskegee Institute, an industrial school for African Americans in rural Alabama. According to Washington, the Institute would play a key role in bringing about racial equality:

> The Tuskegee idea is that correct education begins at the bottom, and expands naturally as the necessities of the people expand. As the race grows in knowledge, experience, culture, taste, and wealth, its wants are bound to become more and more diverse; and to satisfy these wants there will be gradually developed within our ranks—as already has been true of the whites—a constantly increasing variety of professional and business men and women (Button and Provenzo 1989, 274).

Not all African Americans shared Washington's philosophy and goals. William E. Burghardt DuBois (1868–1963), the first African American to be awarded a Ph.D. and one of the founders of the National Association for the Advancement of Colored People (NAACP), challenged Booker T. Washington's views on education. In his book *The Souls of Black Folks,* DuBois criticized educational programs that seemed to imply that African Americans should accept inferior status and develop manual skills. DuBois called for the education of the most "talented tenth" of the African American population to equip them for leadership positions in society as a whole.

Margarethe Schurz
(1832–1876)

The Kindergarten

Early childhood education also spread following the Civil War. Patterned after the progressive, humanistic theories of the German educator Friedrich Froebel (1782–1852), the **kindergarten,** or "garden where children grow," stressed the motor development and self-activity of children before they began formal schooling at the elementary level. Through play, games, stories, music, and language activities, a foundation beneficial to the child's later educational and social development would be laid. After founding the first kindergarten in 1837, Froebel developed child-centered curriculum materials that were used in kindergartens in the the United States and throughout the world.

Margarethe Schurz (1832–1876), a student of Froebel, opened the first U.S. kindergarten in her home at Watertown, Wisconsin, in 1855. Her small neighborhood class was conducted in German. In 1860, Elizabeth Palmer Peabody (1804–1891), sister-in-law of Horace Mann and the American writer Nathaniel Hawthorne, opened the first private English-speaking kindergarten in this country in Boston. Initially, kindergartens were privately supported, but in St. Louis in 1873, Susan Blow (1843–1916) established what is commonly recognized as the first successful public kindergarten in the United States. She patterned her kindergarten after one she visited while in Germany. So successful was her kindergarten that by 1879, a total of 131 teachers were working in fifty-three kindergarten classes (Button and Provenzo 1989, 169). The United States Bureau of Education recorded a total of twelve kindergartens in the country in 1873, with seventy-two teachers and 1,252 students. By 1997, enrollments had mushroomed to 2,847,000 in public kindergartens and 575,000 in private kindergartens (National Center for Education Statistics 1999, 61).

The Professionalization of Teaching

During the later 1800s, professional teacher organizations began to have a great influence on the development of schools in America. The National Education Association (NEA), founded in 1857, and the American Federation of Teachers (AFT), founded in 1916, labored diligently to professionalize teaching and to increase teachers' salaries and benefits.

By the early 1900s, the demand for teachers had grown dramatically. An increasing number of women entered the teaching field at this time, beginning a trend often referred to as the "feminization of teaching." Female teachers were given less respect from the community than their male predecessors, though they were still more highly regarded than women who worked in factories or as domestics. In addition, they were expected to be of high moral character. They were subjected to a level of public scrutiny hard to imagine today, as illustrated by the following Professional Reflection.

 **Professional Reflection**   **Reflecting on changes in the image of teachers**

The following is a public school contract that teachers were required to sign in 1927. Analyze the contract and then write a one-paragraph description of the image of teachers and teaching reflected in the contract. How does this image differ from the current image of teachers and teaching?

Teacher Contract

I promise to take vital interest in all phases of Sunday-school work, donating of my time, service, and money without stint for the uplift and benefit of the community.

I promise to abstain from all dancing, immodest dressing, and any other conduct unbecoming a teacher and a lady.

I promise not to go out with any young men except in so far as it may be necessary to stimulate Sunday-school work.

I promise not to fall in love, to become engaged or secretly married.

I promise not to encourage or tolerate the least familiarity on the part of any of my boy pupils.

I promise to sleep at least eight hours a night, to eat carefully, and to take every precaution to keep in the best of health and spirits, in order that I may be better able to render efficient service to my pupils.

I promise to remember that I owe a duty to the townspeople who are paying me my wages, that I owe respect to the school board and the superintendent that hired me, and that I shall consider myself at all times the willing servant of the school board and the townspeople.

Source: Willard Waller, *The Sociology of Teaching,* New York: John Wiley, 1932, p. 43. Copyright 1932 by John Wiley.

Margaret Haley

Women became influential in shaping educational policies during the early 1900s, in part through the women's suffrage movement that led to the right to vote. Women such as Ella Flagg Young (1845–1918), superintendent of Chicago schools from 1909 to 1915, and Catherine Goggin and Margaret Haley, leaders of the Chicago Teachers Federation, played important roles in the governance of Chicago schools (Holmes and Weiss 1995; Button and Provenzo 1989). Another Chicagoan and visionary educational leader, Jane Addams (1860–1935), founded Hull House, a social and educational center for poor immigrants. In *Democracy and Social Ethics* (published in 1902), Addams drew from her training as a social worker and developed a philosophy of socialized education that linked schools with other social service agencies and institutions in the city. At the ceremony to present her the Nobel Peace Prize in 1931, Addams was described as "the foremost woman of her nation" (Rippa 1997, 142).

What Were the Aims of Education during the Progressive Era (1920–1945)?

The philosophy of progressivism had a profound influence on the character of education in the United States from the end of World War I to the end of World War II. During the late nineteenth and early twentieth centuries, supporters of the **progressive movement** were intent on social reform to improve the quality of American life. As pointed out earlier, educational progressives believed that the child's interests and practical needs should determine the focus of schooling. In 1919, the Progressive Education Association was founded and went on to devote the next two decades to implementing progressive theories in the classroom that they believed would lead to the improvement of society.

Teachers in progressive schools functioned as guides rather than taskmasters. They first engaged students through providing activities related to their natural interests, and then they moved students to higher levels of understanding. To teach in this manner was demanding: "Teachers in a progressive school had to be extraordinarily talented and well educated; they needed both a perceptive understanding of children and a wide knowledge of the disciplines in order to recognize when the child was ready to move through an experience to a new understanding, be it in history or science or mathematics or the arts" (Ravitch 1983, 47).

John Dewey's Laboratory School

As pointed out earlier in this chapter, progressive educational theories were synthesized most effectively and eloquently by John Dewey (1859–1952). Born in the year that Darwin's *Origin of Species* was published, Dewey graduated from the University of Vermont when he was twenty. He later earned a doctorate at Johns Hopkins University, where his thinking was strongly influenced by the psychologist William James.

From 1894 to 1904, Dewey served as head of the departments of philosophy, psychology, and pedagogy at the University of Chicago. From 1904 until he retired in 1930, Dewey was a professor of philosophy at Columbia University. Dewey's numerous writings have had a profound impact on U.S. schools. In his best known works, *The School and Society* (1900) and *The Child and the Curriculum* (1902), Dewey states that school and society are connected and that teachers must begin with an understanding of the child's world, the psychological dimension, and then progress to the logical dimension represented by the accumulated knowledge of the human race.

What hallmarks of progressive education are evident in this photograph of one of the first classrooms in the country operated according to Dewey's philosophy? How would a progressive classroom look today?

While at the University of Chicago, Dewey and his wife, Alice, established a Laboratory School for testing progressive principles in the classroom. The school opened in 1896 with two instructors and sixteen students and by 1902 had grown to 140 students with twenty-three teachers and ten university graduate students as assistants. The children, four to fourteen years old, learned traditional subjects by working cooperatively in small groups of eight to ten on projects such as cooking, weaving, carpentry, sewing, and metalwork (Rippa 1997).

Maria Montessori's Method

While Dewey's ideas provided the basis for the development of progressive education in the United States, progressive educators in Europe were similarly developing new approaches that would also impact American education. Chief among these was Maria Montessori (1870–1952), an Italian physician who was influenced by Rousseau and believed that children's mental, physical, and spiritual development could be enhanced by providing them with developmentally appropriate educational activities.

At Montessori's school for poor preschool-age children in Rome, teachers created learning environments based on students' levels of development and readiness to learn new material. According to the **Montessori method,** prescribed sets of materials and physical exercises are used to develop students' knowledge and skills, and students are allowed to use or not use the materials as they see fit. The materials arouse students' interest, and the interest motivates them to learn. Through highly individualized instruction, students develop self-discipline and self-confidence. Montessori's ideas spread throughout the world; by 1915, almost 100 Montessori schools were operating in the

Maria Montessori (1870–1952)

United States (Webb, Metha, and Jordan 1999). Today, Montessorian materials and activities are a standard part of the early childhood and elementary curricula in public schools throughout the nation.

Education of Immigrants and Minorities

The diversity of America's school population increased dramatically during the late nineteenth and early twentieth centuries. Latin Americans, Eastern Europeans, and Southern Europeans followed earlier waves of Western- and Northern-European immigrants such as the Irish and Germans. As with Native American education, the goal of immigrant education was rapid assimilation into an English-speaking Anglo-European society that did not welcome racially or ethnically different newcomers.

Also at stake was the preservation or loss of traditional culture. In some areas, school policies included the punishment of Cuban and Puerto Rican children, for example, for speaking Spanish in school, and children learned to mock their unassimilated parents. In other areas, efforts were made to exclude certain groups, such as Asians, and ethnic enclaves established separate schools for the purpose of preserving, for example, traditional Chinese culture.

By the time Native Americans were granted U.S. citizenship in 1924, confinement on reservations and decades of forced assimilation had devastated Native American cultures and provided few successful educational programs. In 1928, a landmark report titled *The Problem of Indian Administration* recommended that Native American education be restructured. Among the recommendations were the building of day schools in Native American communities and the reform of boarding schools for Native American children. In addition, the report recommended that school curricula be revised to reflect tribal cultures and the needs of local tribal communities. Another fifty years passed before the recommendations began to be implemented.

How Did Education Change during the Modern Postwar Era (1945–2000)?

Throughout the twentieth century, many long-standing trends in U.S. education continued. These trends may be grouped and summarized in terms of three general patterns, shown in Figure 3.5. At the same time, the decades since the end of World War II have seen a series of profound changes in U.S. education. These changes have addressed three as yet unanswered questions: (1) How can full and equal educational opportunity be extended to all groups in our culturally pluralistic society? (2) What knowledge and skills should be taught in our nation's schools?(3) How should knowledge and skills be taught?

The 1950s:
Defense Education and School Desegregation

Teachers and education were put in the spotlight in 1957 when the Soviet Union launched the first satellite, named Sputnik, into space. Stunned U.S. leaders immediately blamed the space lag on inadequacies in the education system. The Soviet Union was first into space, they maintained, because the progressive educational philosophy had

Americanization

- Americanizing of European educational institutions and instructional models
- Americanizing of English language textbooks and curriculum
- Cultural assimilation of immigrants and others through education
- Aims of education based on moral didacticism and pragmatism
- Aims of education relating to child development and child welfare
- Aims of education relating to success in a society based on capitalism
- Aims of education relating to citizenship in a democracy

Democratization

- Steady growth of compulsory, free, secular, publicly funded education
- Preservation of state, local, and parental control of schooling and schools
- Protection of teachers' and students' rights under the U.S. Constitution
- Shifts in educational reform initiatives that reflect a two-party electoral system
- Continual expansion of early childhood education
- Continual expansion of opportunities for higher education and adult education
- Traumatic periodic extensions of educational opportunity to "other" Americans (women; racial, ethnic, and language minorities; people with disabilities)

Professionalization

- Professionalizing of teaching as an occupation
- Professionalizing of teacher organizations and associations
- Growth in scientific and bureaucratic models for the management of schools
- Rising standards for qualifications to teach
- Continual development of institutions and programs for teacher education
- Greater application of theory and research on teaching and learning
- Generally rising status and salaries for teachers as members of a profession

Figure 3.5

Three general patterns of trends in American education

undermined academic rigor. For example, students in the United States were taught less science, mathematics, and foreign language than their European counterparts.

The federal government appropriated millions of dollars over the next decade for educational reforms that reflected the essentialist educational philosophy. Through provisions of the **National Defense Education Act of 1958,** the U.S. Office of Education sponsored research and innovation in science, mathematics, modern foreign languages, and guidance. Out of their work came the new math; new science programs; an integration of anthropology, economics, political science, and sociology into new social studies programs; and renewed interest and innovations in foreign language instruction. Teachers were trained in the use of new methods and materials at summer workshops, schools were given funds for new equipment, and research centers were established. In 1964, Congress extended the act for three years and expanded Title III of the act to include money for improving instruction in reading, English, geography, history, and civics.

The end of World War II also saw the beginning of school **desegregation.** On May 17, 1954, the United States Supreme Court rejected the "separate but equal" doctrine that had been used since 1850 as a justification for excluding African Americans from attending school with whites. In response to a suit filed by the National Association for the Advancement of Colored People (NAACP) on behalf of a Kansas family, Chief Justice Earl Warren declared that to segregate school children "from others of similar age and qualifications solely because of their race generates a feeling of inferiority as to their status in the community that may affect their hearts and minds in a way unlikely ever to be undone" (***Brown v. Board of Education of Topeka*** 1954).

keepers of the dream

Marian Wright Edelman

Founder of Children's Defense Fund

> *"You never, ever forget."*

Marian Wright Edelman knew discrimination even as a child. When she was five she was scolded by a friend for drinking from a water fountain reserved for whites only in a downtown department store in her hometown of Bennettsville, South Carolina. When she went to the movies there, she was not permitted to sit in seats on the first floor—they, too, were reserved for whites only. But the incident that angered her the most was seeing discrimination in the rescue workers at the scene of an accident on the highway near her home. The ambulance picked up the slightly injured white truck driver and left behind the seriously hurt black migrant workers who had been in the car the truck had hit. "I remember watching children like me bleeding," she recalls, "I remember the ambulance driving off. You never, ever forget" (Terry 1993, 4).

When she was fourteen, her father suffered a heart attack and was rushed to a hospital. Riding in the ambulance with him, Edelman listened to his dying wish for her, "Don't let anything get in the way of your education." Ten days after his death the Supreme Court outlawed school segregation in its *Brown v. Board of Education* decision.

Edelman followed her father's advice, graduating first from Spelman College and then from Yale Law School. When she obtained her law degree she returned to Mississippi, where she became the first African American woman to be admitted to the state's bar. After the Voting Rights Act of 1965 was passed, Edelman took up the cause of the poor.

Recognizing the need for a lobbying agency for children, she founded the Children's Defense Fund in Washington D.C. As its president she seeks "to educate the nation about the needs of children and encourage preventive investment in children before they get sick, drop out of school, suffer too-early pregnancy or family breakdown, or get into trouble."

Edelman's message for teachers is to see that all children, especially those who are poor, are taught how to read, write, and compute so that they can have positive and healthy options in their future. She believes strongly that

> all Americans must commit personally and as voters to a national crusade of conscience and action that will ensure that no child is left behind. Only we—individually and collectively—can transform our nation's priorities and assure its future as we face a new century and begin a new millennium.

(Edelman 1992, 20)

The Supreme Court's decision did not bring an immediate end to segregated schools. Though the court one year later ordered that desegregation proceed with "all deliberate speed," opposition to school integration arose in school districts across the country. Some districts, whose leaders modeled restraint and a spirit of cooperation, desegregated peacefully. Other districts became battlegrounds, characterized by boycotts, rallies, and violence.

The 1960s:
The War on Poverty and the Great Society

The 1960s, hallmarked by the Kennedy administration's spirit of action and high hopes, provided a climate that supported change. Classrooms were often places of pedagogical experimentation and creativity reminiscent of the progressive era. The open-education movement, team teaching, individualized instruction, the integrated-day concept, flexible scheduling, and nongraded schools were some of the innovations that teachers were asked to implement. These structural, methodological, and curricular changes implied the belief that teachers were capable professionals.

The image of teachers in the 1960s was enhanced by the publication of several books by educators who were influenced by the progressivist educational philosophy and humanistic psychology. A. S. Neill's *Summerhill* (1960), Sylvia Ashton-Warner's *Teacher* (1963), John Holt's *How Children Fail* (1964), Herbert Kohl's *36 Children* (1967), James Herndon's *The Way It Spozed to Be* (1969), and Jonathan Kozol's *Death at an Early Age* (1967)—a few of the books that appeared at the time—gave readers inside views of teachers at work and teachers' perceptions of how students learn.

The administrations of Presidents Kennedy and Johnson funneled massive amounts of money into a War on Poverty. Education was seen as the key to breaking the transmission of poverty from generation to generation. The War on Poverty developed methods, materials, and programs such as subsidized breakfast and lunch programs, Head Start, Upward Bound, and the Job Corps that would be appropriate to children who had been disadvantaged due to poverty.

The War on Poverty has proved much more difficult to win than imagined, and the results of such programs nearly forty years later have been mixed. The three- to six-year-olds who participated in Head Start did much better when they entered public schools; however, academic gains appeared to dissolve over time. Although the Job Corps enabled scores of youth to avoid a lifetime of unemployment, many graduates returned to the streets where they eventually became statistics in unemployment and crime records. The education of low-income children received a boost in April 1965 when Congress passed the **Elementary and Secondary Education Act.** As part of President Johnson's Great Society program, the act allocated funds on the basis of the number of poor children in school districts. Thus schools in poverty areas that frequently had to cope with such problems as low achievement, poor discipline, truancy, and high teacher turnover rates received much needed assistance in addressing their problems.

In 1968, the Elementary and Secondary Education Act was amended with Title VII, the Bilingual Education Act. This act provided federal aid to low-income children "of limited English-speaking ability." The act did not spell out clearly what bilingual education might mean other than to say that it provided money for local school districts to "develop and carry out new and imaginative elementary and secondary school programs" to meet the needs of non-English-speaking children. Since the passing of Title VII, debate over the ultimate goal of bilingual education has been intense: Should it help students to make the *transition* to regular English-speaking classrooms, or should it help such students *maintain* their non-English language and culture?

The 1970s:
Accountability and Equal Opportunity

The 1970s was a mixed decade for U.S. education, marked by drops in enrollment, test scores, and public confidence, as well as progressive policy changes that promoted a more equal education for all in the United States. Calls for "back to basics" and teacher accountability drives initiated by parents, citizens groups, and politicians who were unhappy with the low academic performance level of many students dominated this troubled decade at the height of the Vietnam conflict. For the first time in polling history, more than half of the U.S. adults polled in 1975 reported that they regarded themselves as better educated than the younger generation (Gallup 1975).

Financial difficulties also confronted the schools. National Center for Education Statistics data reveal that, instead of increasing as it had since 1940, the enrollment of children in prekindergarten through grade 8 in public and private schools declined by nearly five million during the 1970s (National Center for Education Statistics 1999, 12). Schools found themselves with a reduction in state aid, which was determined on the basis of pupil attendance figures. Financial problems were exacerbated by reduced support from local taxpayers, who resisted tax increases for the schools because they were stressed by their own economic problems, or had lost confidence in the schools, or because fewer of them had children in school. Consequently, this further reduced the ability to meet the needs of students.

Many parents responded to the crisis by becoming education activists, seeking or establishing alternative schools, or joining the home education movement led by John Holt, who by then had given up on reforming schools. These parents held a poor image of teachers and schools; they believed that they could provide a better education for their children than public school teachers could. Those who kept their children in the public schools demanded teacher **accountability,** which limited teachers' instructional flexibility and extended their evaluation paperwork. Basal readers and teacher-proof curricular packages descended on teachers, spelling out with their cookbook directions the deeper message that teachers were not to be trusted to teach on their own. Confidence in teachers reached a low point.

In addition, during the late 1960s and early 1970s increasing numbers of young people questioned what the schools were teaching and how they were teaching it. Thousands of them mobilized in protest against an establishment that, in their view, supported an immoral, undeclared war in Vietnam and was unconcerned with the oppression of minorities at home. In their search for reasons why these and other social injustices were allowed to exist, many militant youth groups singled out the schools' curricula. From their perspective, the schools taught subjects irrelevant to finding solutions to pressing problems.

What impact has Title IX had on the education of females? What does equal educational opportunity for female and male students really mean?

Responding in good faith to their critics' accusations, schools greatly expanded their curricular offerings and instituted a wide variety of instructional strategies. In making these changes, however, school personnel gradually realized that they were alienating other groups: taxpayers who accused schools of extravagant spending; religious sects who questioned the values that children were being taught; **back-to-basics** advocates who charged that students were not learning how to read, write, and compute; and citizens who were alarmed at steadily rising school crime, drugs, and violence.

Despite the siege on teachers and schools, however, the reforms of the 1960s and 1970s did result in a number of improvements that have lasted into the present. More young people graduate from high school now than in previous decades, more teachers have advanced training, school buildings are better equipped, and instructional methods and materials are both more relevant to learners and more diverse.

For those people who had been marginalized by the educational system, the federal acts that were passed in the 1970s brought success and encouragement: the Title IX Education Amendment prohibiting sex discrimination (1972), the Indian Education Act (1972), the Education for All Handicapped Children Act (1975), and the Indochina Migration and Refugee Assistance Act (1975).

Title IX of the Education Amendments Act, which took effect in 1975, stated that "no person in the United States shall, on the basis of sex, be excluded from participation in, be denied the benefits of, or be subjected to discrimination under any education program or activity receiving Federal financial assistance."

The **Education for All Handicapped Children Act** (Public Law 94–142), passed by Congress in 1975, extended greater educational opportunities to children with disabilities. This act (often referred to as the **mainstreaming** law) specifies extensive due process procedures to guarantee that children with special needs will receive a free, appropriate education in the least restrictive educational environment. Through the act's provisions, parents are involved in planning educational programs for their children.

The 1980s: A Great Debate

The first half of the 1980s saw a continuation, perhaps even an escalation, of the criticisms aimed at the schools during the two previous decades. With the publication in 1983 of the report by the National Commission on Excellence in Education, *A Nation at Risk: The Imperative for Educational Reform,* a great national debate was begun on how to improve the quality of schools. *A Nation at Risk* and dozens of other national reports on U.S. schools gave evidence to some that the schools were failing miserably to achieve their goals.

Responses included more proposals for curriculum reform. Mortimer Adler's *Paideia Proposal* (1982) called for a perennialist core curriculum based on the Great Books. *High School: A Report on Secondary Education in America* (1983), written by Ernest Boyer for the Carnegie Foundation for the Advancement of Teaching, suggested strengthening the academic core curriculum in high schools, a recommendation that was widely adopted. In 1986, former Secretary of the U.S. Department of Education William Bennett advocated a perennialist high-school curriculum that he described in *James Madison High* (1987). Educators at the middle-school level began to create small learning communities, eliminate tracking, and develop new ways to enhance student self-esteem as a result of the Carnegie Council on Adolescent Development report *Turning Points: Preparing American Youth for the 21st Century* (1989). These and other reform reports that swept the nation during the 1980s made a lasting imprint on education in the United States.

The 1990s and into the Twenty-First Century: Teacher Leadership

The push to reform schools begun in the 1980s has continued into the twenty-first century, and teaching is being transformed in dramatic ways. In response to chal-

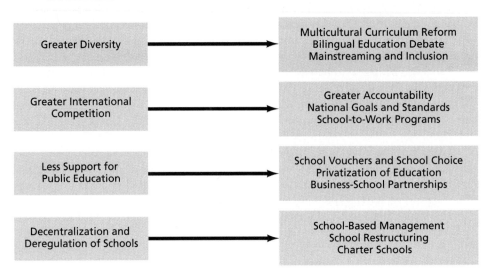

CHALLENGES	RESPONSES
Greater Diversity	Multicultural Curriculum Reform Bilingual Education Debate Mainstreaming and Inclusion
Greater International Competition	Greater Accountability National Goals and Standards School-to-Work Programs
Less Support for Public Education	School Vouchers and School Choice Privatization of Education Business-School Partnerships
Decentralization and Deregulation of Schools	School-Based Management School Restructuring Charter Schools

Figure 3.6

The 1990s: A sampler of trends in education

lenges such as greater diversity, greater international competition, less support for public education, and decentralization and deregulation of schools, innovative approaches to teaching and learning are being developed throughout the United States (see Figure 3.6). Teachers are going beyond the classroom and assuming leadership roles in school restructuring and educational reform—roles that we examine more fully in Chapters 12 and 13. Through collaborative relationships with students, principals, parents, and the private sector, teachers are changing the nature of their profession. As one high school teacher said in the late 1990s: "I see it [change] happening. Not overnight, but I think it's going to. When I first started teaching in the early sixties, I would never have envisioned things changing as much as they have" (Grant and Murray 1999, 212).

SUMMARY

What Determines Your Educational Philosophy?

- An educational philosophy is a set of beliefs about education, a set of principles to guide professional action.
- A teacher's educational philosophy is made up of personal beliefs about teaching and learning, students, knowledge, and what is worth knowing.

What Are the Branches of Philosophy?

- The branches of philosophy and the questions they address are (1) metaphysics (What is the nature of reality?), (2) epistemology (What is the nature of knowledge and is truth attainable?), (3) axiology (What values should one live by?), (4) ethics (What is good and evil, right and wrong?), (5) aesthetics (What is beautiful?), and (6) logic (What reasoning processes yield valid conclusions?).

What Are Five Modern Philosophical Orientations to Teaching?

- *Progressivism*—The aim of education should be based on the needs and interests of students.

- *Perennialism*—Students should acquire knowledge of enduring great ideas.

- *Essentialism*—Schools should teach students, in a disciplined and systematic way, a core of "essential" knowledge and skills.

- *Social reconstructionism*—In response to the significant social problems of the day, schools should take the lead in creating a new social order.

- *Existentialism*—In the face of an indifferent universe, students should acquire an education that will enable them to assign meaning to their lives.

What Psychological Orientations Have Influenced Teaching Philosophies?

- *Humanism*—Children are innately good, and education should focus on individual needs, personal freedom, and self-actualization.

- *Behaviorism*—By careful control of the educational environment and with appropriate reinforcement techniques, teachers can cause students to exhibit desired behaviors.

- *Constructivism*—Teachers should "understand students' understanding" and view learning as an active process in which learners construct meaning.

How Can You Develop Your Educational Philosophy?

- Instead of basing their teaching on only one educational philosophy, most teachers develop an eclectic educational philosophy.

- Professional teachers continually strive for a clearer, more comprehensive answer to basic philosophical questions.

What Were Teaching and Schools Like in the American Colonies (1620–1750)?

- Colonial education was patterned after the British two-track system and its primary objective was to promote religion.

- Puritans believed children were naturally corrupt and sinful and should be disciplined sternly at the dame schools, reading and writing schools, and Latin grammar schools common to the colonies.

- Mandated education in the United States had its origins in two colonial laws: the Massachusetts Acts of 1642 and 1647.

- At the end of the American Revolution, the few African and Native Americans who were literate were taught at church-sponsored schools that were segregated by race.

What Were the Goals of Education during the Revolutionary Period (1750–1820)?

- During the Revolutionary period, characterized by a declining European influence on American education, education in the new democracy was shaped by the ideas of Benjamin Franklin, Thomas Jefferson, and Noah Webster.

- Educational opportunities for women were often limited to preparing them for family life.

How Was the Struggle Won for State-Supported Common Schools (1820–1865)?

- Horace Mann, a strong advocate for state-supported, free common schools, believed that teachers should receive post secondary training in normal schools.

- The six-volume McGuffey reader, with its moral lessons and emphasis on virtue, determined much of what children learned at school.

- The Morrill Land-Grant Act, passed in 1862, provided federal land for colleges and set a precedent for federal involvement in education.

How Did Compulsory Education Change Schools and the Teaching Profession (1865–1920)?

- The spread of common schools and dramatic increases in their enrollments led to the use of scientific management techniques for their operation.

- Booker T. Washington, founder of the Tuskegee Institute, believed education could prepare African Americans to live peaceably with whites, while W. E. B. DuBois believed African Americans should educate themselves for leadership positions and not accept inferior status.

- Kindergartens became common and used child-centered curricula patterned after German educator Friedrich Froebel's ideas.

- The National Education Association (NEA) and the American Federation of Teachers (AFT) were founded to professionalize teaching and increase teachers' salaries and benefits.

What Were the Aims of Education during the Progressive Era (1920–1945)?

- John Dewey's Laboratory School at the University of Chicago, a model of progressive education, offered a curriculum based on children's interests and needs.

- Progressive educator Maria Montessori developed age-appropriate materials and teaching strategies that were implemented in the United States and throughout the world.

- Public criticism of progressive education led to its decline at the start of World War II. School enrollments became increasingly diverse as a result of immigration, and a goal of education was the rapid assimilation of all groups into an English-speaking Anglo-European culture.

How Did Education Change during the Modern Post-War Era (1945–2000)?

- The Soviet Union's launching of Sputnik in 1957 sparked educational reform, particularly in science, mathematics, and foreign language education. Schools were ordered to desegregate with "all deliberate speed" as a result of a 1954 decision by the Supreme Court in *Brown v. Board of Education of Topeka*.

- Innovative curricula and instructional strategies were used in many classrooms of the 1960s. The Elementary and Secondary Education Act of 1965, part of President Johnson's Great Society and War on Poverty programs, provided federal money to improve the education of poor children.

- Alarmed by declining test scores, the public became critical of schools during the 1970s and demanded accountability. An array of federal legislation was passed to provide equal educational opportunity for all students.

- *A Nation at Risk* and other reports during the 1980s addressed weaknesses in U.S. schools and sparked a "Great Debate" on how to improve U.S. education.

- In response to continuing challenges to education, teachers during the 1990s took leadership roles in school restructuring, school governance, curriculum change, and other aspects of educational reform.

KEY TERMS AND CONCEPTS

academies, 100
accountability, 114
aesthetics, 80
axiology, 87
back-to-basics movement, 114
behaviorism, 93
Brown v. Board of Education of Topeka, 111
cognitive science, 94
common schools, 101
constructivism, 94
dame schools, 97
desegregation, 111
Education for All Handicapped Children Act, 115
educational philosophy, 83
Elementary and Secondary Education Act, 113
epistemology, 87
essentialism, 90
ethics, 88
existentialism, 91
female seminaries, 100
horn book, 97
humanism, 93
humanistic psychology, 93
kindergarten, 106
Latin grammar school, 98
logic, 89
mainstreaming, 115
Massachusetts Act of 1642, 98
Massachusetts Act of 1647, 98
McGuffey readers, 105
metaphysics, 86
Montessori method, 109
Morrill Land-Grant Act, 105
National Defense Education Act, 111
normal schools, 104
parochial schools, 97
perennialism, 89
Primer, 97
progressive movement, 108
progressivism, 91
reading and writing schools, 97
scientific management, 106
social reconstructionism, 92
Socratic questioning, 89
Title IX, 115

APPLICATIONS AND ACTIVITIES

Teacher's Journal

1. Imagine that you are a colleague of Hal, who was profiled in this chapter's opening scenario. Write a memo to him in which you react to his philosophical orientation to teaching.

2. Recall one of your favorite teachers in grades K–12. Which of the educational philosophies or psychological orientations to teaching described in this chapter best captures that teacher's approach to teaching? Write a descriptive sketch of that teacher "in action."

3. Based on what you have read in this chapter, identify several broad or long-term trends in the development of U.S. education that continue even today. How are those trends reflected in educational policies and practices through the decades? For example, you might identify the professionalization of teaching as a long-term trend. How is this trend evident at different points in the past and now? How might this trend be manifested in the future?

4. Write a personal history of your experience as a student, focusing on the age or grade level of the students you plan to teach. Conclude with an analysis of how you expect your experience as a student will influence you as a teacher.

5. What does the history of textbooks tell us about education in the United States? What values and priorities do textbooks today seem to reflect in comparison to textbooks of the seventeenth, eighteenth, and nineteenth centuries?

6. Develop a proposal for researching the impact of the past on teaching today and record it in your teacher's journal. For suggestions on choosing a specific topic, locating information, and conducting the research, ask your instructor for Handout M 3.1, "Researching Impacts of the Past on Teaching Today."

Teacher's Database

1. Use your favorite WWW search engine to go to the home page of the American Philosophical Association (APA), Philosophy in Cyberspace, The History of Education Site, or another professional organization devoted to educational philosophy or history and compile a list of online publications, associations, and reference materials that you could use in developing your educational philosophy further.

2. Explore encyclopedias, bibliographies, periodicals, news sources, and online reference works to research in greater detail the contributions of a pioneer in education or a historical development described in Chapter 3.

Observations and Interviews

1. Interview a teacher for the purpose of understanding his or her educational philosophy. Formulate your interview questions in light of the philosophical concepts discussed in this chapter. Discuss your findings with classmates.

2. Administer a philosophical inventory (see the appendix "Using a Philosophic

Inventory" on this book's website) to a group of teachers at a local school. Analyze the results and compare your findings with classmates. To guide you in this school-based activity, ask your instructor for Handout M3.2, "Administering an Educational Philosophy Inventory."

3. Observe the class of a teacher at the level at which you plan to teach. Which of the five philosophies or three psychological orientations to teaching discussed in this chapter most characterizes this teacher? To help you with this activity, ask your instructor for Handout M3.3, "Identifying Educational Philosophies in Action."

4. Visit a school and interview the principal about the school's educational philosophy. Ask him or her to comment on what is expected of teachers in regard to achieving the goals contained in the statement of philosophy.

5. Interview veteran teachers and administrators at a local school and ask them to comment on the changes in education that they have observed and experienced during their careers. In particular, compare their remarks to this chapter's discussion of education during the post-World War II era, using this chapter's descriptions of the era to guide your questions. What events do respondents identify as having had the greatest impact on their teaching? Tape record, videotape, or transcribe respondents' stories to share with classmates.

6. As a collaborative project with classmates, conduct on-site interviews and observations for the purpose of researching the history of a particular school and its culture or way of life. You might also collaborate with teachers and students of history or social studies at the school to help you in your investigation. For more specific guidelines, ask your instructor for Handout M3.4, "Researching the History of a School."

Professional Portfolio

1. Prepare a written (or videotaped) statement in which you describe a key element of your educational philosophy. To organize your thoughts, focus on *one* of the following dimensions of educational philosophy:

   - Beliefs about teaching and learning
   - Beliefs about students
   - Beliefs about knowledge
   - Beliefs about what is worth knowing
   - Personal beliefs about the six branches of philosophy

   Develop your statement of philosophy throughout the course, covering all dimensions. On completion of your teacher-education program, review your portfolio entry and make any appropriate revisions. Being able to articulate your philosophy of education and your teaching philosophy will be an important part of finding your first job as a teacher.

2. Prepare a video- or audiotaped oral history of the school experiences of older members of the community. Focus on a topic or issue of special interest to you and prepare some questions and probes in advance. For instance, you might be interested in an aspect of curriculum or student relations. Analyze the oral histories in relation to the development of education in the United States and videotape or tape record your analysis.

4

Social Realities Confronting Today's Schools

The educational system is part of the common life and cannot escape suffering the consequences that flow from the conditions prevailing outside the school building.

—John Dewey
"Introduction," *The Use of Resources in Education*

focus questions

J eff Banks, a history teacher at Southside High School, enters the faculty lunchroom and sees his friends, Sue Anderson, Nancy Watkins, and Bret Thomas, at their usual table in the corner. Southside is located in a medium-size city in the Southeast. The school, in the center of a low- to middle-income area known as Lawndale, has an enrollment of almost 1,900 students. About 70 percent of these self-identify as Anglo-European Americans, with the remaining 30 percent about evenly divided between African Americans and Mexican Americans. Southside has a reputation for being a "good" school—for the most part, students are respectful of their teachers. Parents, many of whom work in the several small factories found in Lawndale, generally support the school and are involved in school activities in spite of their heavy work schedules. The consensus among teachers is that most Southside parents recognize that education is the key if their children are to "better themselves" and move out of Lawndale.

As soon as Jeff is within earshot of his friends, he knows they are talking about last week's tragic shooting at a high school in Colorado. During a rampage that lasted several hours at the school, two boys killed twelve fellow students, one teacher, and then themselves.

"It's so scary," Sue says, "Who knows, something like that could happen right here at Southside. We have no idea what kids have to deal with today."

"Yeah, we have no idea who might snap," says Bret. "With a lot of these school shootings lately, it seems to be a kid that no one would have expected. Quiet, polite, good student—you just never know."

"In some cases, that's true," Jeff says, placing his lunch tray on the table and then sitting down between Sue and Bret. "But a lot of time there are signs. A lot of these kids are loners and outcasts; they're into violent video games, cults, drugs, guns, you name it."

"What I want to know," says Sue, "is how we can prevent something like that from happening here? Since the Colorado shootings, there have been bomb scares, threats, guns confiscated at dozens of schools around the country."

"Well, I don't think metal detectors, more police in schools, and stiffer penalties for kids who bring guns to school are necessarily the answers," says Bret. "The question is, Why are kids doing this?"

"Right, how can we prevent things like this?" says Jeff.

"If we're going to change things," says Sue, "we've got to figure out ways to identify and help kids who feel so desperate that they turn to violence."

"Well, that's all well and good," says Nancy with a sigh. "But I don't see where all of this is going to lead. Our responsibility as teachers is to educate our kids. We're not psychiatrists or social workers. We can't change society. Besides, we've got youth agencies, centers for families in crisis, and all kinds of social service agencies."

What is the role of schools at the start of the twenty-first century? Should teachers play a role in addressing social problems such as violence in our society? What would you say to a teacher who expresses views such as Nancy's?

The discussion among Jeff and his fellow teachers highlights the expectation of much of the public that schools (and teachers) have a responsibility to address problems that confront modern society. Those who agree with Nancy's point of view tend to believe that schools should teach only content to students. Others, however, believe that teachers have an obligation to address domestic social problems. Underlying both positions are conflicting views on the aims of education.

What Are the Aims of Education Today?

In the United States, people agree that the purpose of schools is to educate. Unlike other institutions in society, schools have been developed exclusively to carry out that very important purpose. That we are not always in agreement about what the aims of education should be, however, is illustrated by the fact that we disagree about what it means to be an educated person. Is a person with a college degree educated? Is the person who has overcome, with dignity and grace, extreme hardships in life educated?

Debate about the **aims of education** is not new. Fourth century B.C. philosopher Aristotle, for example, expressed the dilemma this way: "The existing practice [of education] is perplexing; no one knows on what principle we should proceed—should the useful in life, or should virtue, or should the higher knowledge, be the aim of our training; all three opinions have been entertained" (1941, 1306). Definitive answers to Aristotle's questions have not been achieved; instead, each generation has developed its own response to what the aims of education should be.

Education for National Goals

In 1994, President Clinton signed into law the **Goals 2000: Educate America Act,** a comprehensive funding program to help schools achieve a set of eight national goals (see following), six of which were developed at a 1989 educational summit meeting convened by President Bush for the fifty state governors. The goals place a high priority on increasing student achievement in English, mathematics, science, history, and geography; creating more effective learning environments in the nation's schools; providing for teachers' professional development; and increasing parental involvement.

By the year 2000, the following goals were to be accomplished:

1. *School readiness*—All children in the United States will start school ready to learn.
2. *School completion*—The high school graduation rate will increase to at least 90 percent.
3. *Student achievement and citizenship*—All students will leave grades 4, 8, and 12 having demonstrated competency in challenging subject matter, including English, mathematics, science, foreign languages, civics and government, economics, arts, history, and geography; and every school in the United States will ensure that all students learn to use their minds well, so they may be prepared for responsible citizenship, further learning, and productive employment in our nation's modern economy.
4. *Mathematics and science*—United States students will be first in the world in mathematics and science achievement.
5. *Adult literacy and lifelong learning*—Every adult in the United States will be literate and will possess the knowledge and skills necessary to compete in a global economy and to exercise the rights and responsibilities of citizenship.
6. *Safe, disciplined, and alcohol- and drug-free schools*—Every school in the United States will be free of drugs, violence, and the unauthorized presence of firearms and alcohol and will offer a disciplined environment conducive to learning.
7. *Teacher education and professional development*—The nation's teaching force will

have access to programs for the continued improvement of their professional skills and the opportunity to acquire the knowledge and skills needed to instruct and prepare all U.S. students for the next century.

8. *Parental participation*—Every school will promote partnerships that will increase parental involvement and participation in promoting the social, emotional, and academic growth of children.

In February 1999, the National Education Goals Panel acknowledged that the goals would not be met and passed a resolution to rename the National Education Goals as "America's Education Goals" and to continue striving to meet the goals "beyond the year 2000 without a specific deadline for their achievement." Although some states reached some goals by 2000, none achieved all eight. Schools in North Carolina, South Carolina, California, Colorado, and Texas showed the most signs of improvement during the 1990s. Though the goals were not met, the panel pointed out that America's Education Goals made significant contributions in the following areas: launching and supporting the academic standards movement, legitimizing "benchmarking" and state and international comparisons, increasing the attention paid to early childhood education, and focusing and sustaining educational reform (National Education Goals Panel 1999).

Education for Prosocial Values

Although there is widespread debate about what academic content the schools should teach, the public agrees that schools should teach **prosocial values** such as honesty, patriotism, fairness, and civility. The well-being of any society requires support of such values; they enable people from diverse backgrounds to live together peacefully. One poll of the public, for example, revealed that 90 percent or more of the public believed that the following values should be taught in public schools: respect for others, industry or hard work, persistence or the ability to follow through, fairness in dealing with others, compassion for others, and civility and politeness (Elam, Rose, and Gallup 1994). The strong support for these prosocial values reflects the public's belief that the schools should play a key role in promoting the democratic ideal of equality for all.

Education for Socialization

Schools are places where the young become socialized—where they learn to participate intelligently and constructively in the nation's society. This purpose is contained in the national educational goal that calls for schools to prepare students for "responsible citizenship, further learning, and productive employment in our nation's modern economy." Table 4.1 shows the percentage of the public in 1998 who believed that the practice of good citizenship was a "very important" measure of school effectiveness, even more important than going on to postsecondary education, getting a job, or scoring well on standardized tests.

Additionally, schools, more than any other institution in our society, assimilate persons from different ethnic, racial, religious, and cultural backgrounds and pass on the values and customs of the majority. The Los Angeles Unified School District, for example, recently reported that its students represented nine major language groups and 171 languages. It is through the schools that persons from such diverse

Table 4.1

What are the most important criteria for measuring school effectiveness?

	Very Important %	Somewhat Important %	Not Very Important %	Not at All Important %	Don't Know %
Percentage of students who graduate from high school	82	14	2	1	1
Percentage of high school graduates who practice good citizenship	79	15	3	1	2
Percentage of high school graduates who go on to college or junior college	71	24	3	1	1
Percentage who graduate from college or junior college	69	25	3	1	2
Percentage of graduates who get jobs after completing high school	63	28	5	2	2
Scores that students receive on standardized tests	50	34	9	3	4

Source: L. C. Rose and A. M. Gallup, "The 30th Annual Phi Delta Kappa/Gallup Poll of the Public's Attitudes toward the Public Schools," *Phi Delta Kappan,* September 1998, p. 48.

backgrounds learn English and learn about the importance Americans attach to the Fourth of July or Veterans Day; about the contributions of George Washington, Abraham Lincoln, or Dr. Martin Luther King, Jr.; and about the basic workings of capitalism and democracy.

Education for Achievement

Of the various aims that the schools have, achievement is the most universally agreed on. For most people, the primary purpose of schools is to impart to students the academic knowledge and skills that will prepare them either for additional schooling or for the world of work. Regardless of political ideology, religious beliefs, and cultural values, people want their schools to teach academic content. When asked whether they favor establishing national standards for measuring the academic performance of public schools, 77 percent of respondents in a public poll said they favored such a measure (Rose, Gallup, and Elam 1997).

Education for Personal Growth

Society places great value on the dignity and worth of the individual. Accordingly, one aim of schools is to enable the young to become all that they are capable of becoming. Unlike socialization or achievement, the emphasis on personal growth puts the individual first, society second. According to this view, the desired outcomes of education go beyond achievement to include the development of a positive self-concept and interpersonal skills, or what psychologist Daniel Goleman has termed **"emotional intelligence."** According to Goleman (1997, 1998), schools should emphasize five dimensions of emotional intelligence: self-awareness, handling emotions, motivation, empathy, and social skills. Emotional intelligence is essential for achievement in school, job success, marital happiness, and physical health; it enables students to live independently and to seek out the "good" life according to their own values, needs, and wants. The knowledge and skills students acquire at schools are seen as enabling them to achieve personal growth and self-actualization.

Education for Social Change

Schools also provide students with the knowledge and skills to improve society and the quality of life and to adapt to rapid social change. Naturally, there exists a wide range of opinion about how society might be improved. Some teachers, like Jeff, Sue, and Bret in this chapter's opening scenario, believe that one purpose of schooling is to address social problems such as violence in society; while other teachers, such as their friend, Nancy, believe schools should teach academic content and not try to change society. Less controversial have been efforts to prepare students to serve others through volunteerism and to participate actively in the political life of the nation. During the early 1990s, some high schools began to direct every student to complete a service requirement to help students see that they are not only autonomous individuals but also members of a larger community to which they are accountable. Other schools began to introduce service-learning activities into their curricula. **Service learning** provides students with opportunities to deliver service to their communities while engaging in reflection and study on the meaning of those experiences. Service learning brings young people into contact with the elderly, the sick, the poor, and the homeless, as well as acquaints them with neighborhood and governmental issues.

Education for Equal Educational Opportunity

Ample evidence exists that certain groups in U.S. society are denied equality of opportunity economically, socially, and educationally. For example, if we look at the percentage of children three to four years old who participate in early childhood programs such as Head Start, nursery school, and prekindergarten—experiences that help children from less advantaged backgrounds start elementary school on an equal footing with other children—we find that children from lower-income families are less likely to have such opportunities (see Table 4.2). In addition, there is a positive relationship between parents' educational attainment and their children's enrollment in early childhood programs; also, Latino children are less likely to be enrolled than white or African American children.

Extensive programs at the federal, state, and local levels have been developed to provide equity for all in the United States—regardless of race, ethnicity, language,

Table 4.2

Percentage of three- and four-year-olds enrolled in early childhood programs by selected student characteristics: 1991, 1993, 1995, and 1996

Selected Student Characteristics	3-year-olds				4-year-olds			
	1991	1993	1995	1996	1991	1993	1995	1996
Total	**31.4**	**34.1**	**37.4**	**36.7**	**52.7**	**55.3**	**60.9**	**57.7**
Race/Ethnicity								
White	33.4	33.7	40.2	39.6	52.4	53.7	60.8	58.8
Black	31.6	41.9	41.1	40.5	57.4	62.9	68.2	67.8
Hispanic	19.8	27.2	21.2	22.1	47.5	48.9	49.0	45.3
Household Income								
$10,000 or less	25.4	32.7	26.2	26.0	43.3	52.6	54.3	52.7
10,001–20,000	23.2	21.6	27.0	28.0	45.0	47.2	52.3	45.3
2,001–35,000*	21.3	22.2	27.7	30.8	48.0	47.8	49.7	50.6
35,001–50,000*	33.4	37.9	38.1	42.2	52.3	57.2	59.5	58.2
50,001 or more	52.9	58.7	61.2	55.0	74.8	73.2	80.7	75.8
Parents' Highest Education Level								
Less than high school diploma	17.3	17.1	16.0	22.0**	33.1	42.8	42.4**	47.3**
High school diploma or GED	23.0	23.0	26.3	28.9	40.8	43.2	51.1	47.3
Some college/vocational/technical	31.0	35.9	35.6	34.5	56.3	61.1	63.3	59.8
Bachelor's degree	41.5	41.1	51.7	49.6	67.2	64.1	70.7	62.6
Graduate/professional school	53.0	61.9	60.8**	60.4	72.0	73.3	77.9	78.1

*The middle two income ranges in 1991 were $20,001–30,000 and $30,001–50,000, respectively.
**Interpret with caution; standard errors are large due to small sample sizes.
Note: Included in the total but now shown separately are children from other racial/ethnic groups. Age is as of December 31 of the prior year.

Source: U.S. Department of Education, National Center for Education Statistics, *National Household Education Survey (NHES),* 1991 (Early Childhood Education File), 1993 (School Readiness File), 1995 (Early Childhood Program Participation File), and 1996 (Parent and Family Involvement in Education File). Reported in *The Condition of Education 1998.* Washington, DC: National Center for Education Statistics, 1998.

gender, or religion. The United States has always derived strength from the diversity of its people, and all students should receive a quality education so that they may make their unique contributions to society.

The goal of providing equal educational opportunity for all has long distinguished education in the United States from that found in most other countries. Since the 1850s, schools in the United States have been particularly concerned with providing children from diverse backgrounds the education they need to succeed in our society. As James Banks (1999, 4) suggests, "Education within a pluralistic society should affirm and help students understand their home and community cultures. [To] create and maintain a civic community that works for the common good, education in a democratic society should help students acquire the knowledge, attitudes, and skills needed to participate in civic action to make society more equitable and just."

How Can Schools Be Described?

Given the wide variation in schools and their cultures, many models have been proposed for describing the distinguishing characteristics of schools. Schools can be categorized according to the focus of their curricula; for example, high schools may be college prep, vocational, or general. Another way to view schools is according to their organizational structure; for example, open schools or magnet schools. A **magnet school** allows students from an entire district to attend a school's specialized program. Some magnet schools are organized around specific academic disciplines such as science, mathematics, or the basic skills; others focus on the performing and visual arts, health professions, computers, or international studies and languages.

Metaphors for Schools

Other models view schools metaphorically; that is, what is a school like? Some schools, for example, have been compared to factories; students enter the school as raw material, move through the curriculum in a systematic way, and exit the school as finished products. Terrence Deal and Kent Peterson (1999, 21) have suggested that exemplary schools "become like tribes or clans, with deep ties among people and with values and traditions that give meaning to everyday life." Others have suggested that schools are like banks, gardens, prisons, mental hospitals, homes, churches, families, and teams.

In the school-as-family metaphor, for example, the effective school is a caring community of adults who attend to the academic, emotional, and social needs of the children and youth entrusted to their care.

Schools and Social Class

In spite of a general consensus that schools should promote social change and equal opportunity, some individuals believe that schools "reproduce" the existing society by presenting different curricula and educational experiences to students from different socioeconomic classes. Students at a school in an affluent suburb, for example, may study chemistry in a well-equipped lab and take a field trip to a high-tech industry to see the latest application of chemical research, while students at a school in an impoverished inner-city neighborhood learn chemistry from out-of-date texts, have no lab in which to conduct experiments, and take no field trips because the school district has no funds. Schools, in effect, preserve the stratification within society and maintain the differences between the "haves" and the "have-nots." As Joel Spring puts it: "the affluent members of U.S. society can protect the educational advantages and, consequently, economic advantages, of their children by living in affluent school districts or by using private schools. [T]heir children will attend the elite institutions of higher education, and their privileged educational background will make it easy for them to follow in the footsteps of their parent's financial success" (Spring 1999, 290–91).

A useful way to talk about the relationship between schooling and social class in the United States is suggested by the four categories of schools Jean Anyon (1996) found in her study of several elementary schools in urban and suburban New Jersey. Anyon maintains that schools reproduce the existing society by presenting different curricula and educational experiences to students from different socioeconomic classes.

Anyon studied a small group of schools in one metropolitan area and her criteria are linked almost exclusively to socioeconomic status. Few schools actually fit the categories in all ways.

The first kind of school she calls the *working-class school*. In this school, the primary emphasis is on having students follow directions as they work at rote, mechanical activities such as completing dittoed worksheets. Students are given little opportunity to exercise their initiative or to make choices. Teachers may make negative, disparaging comments about students' abilities and, through subtle and not-so-subtle means, convey low expectations to students. Additionally, teachers at working-class schools may spend much of their time focusing on classroom management, dealing with absenteeism, and keeping extensive records.

The *middle-class school* is the second type identified by Anyon. Here, teachers emphasize to students the importance of getting right answers, usually in the form of words, sentences, numbers, or facts and dates. Students have slightly more opportunity to make decisions, but not much. Most lessons are textbook based. Anyon points out that "while the teachers spend a lot of time explaining and expanding on what the textbooks say, there is little attempt to analyze how or why things happen. . . . On the occasions when creativity or self-expression is requested, it is peripheral to the main activity or it is 'enrichment' or 'for fun'" (Anyon 1996, 191).

The *affluent professional school,* unlike the previous two types of schools, gives students the opportunity to express their individuality and to make a variety of choices. Fewer rules govern the behavior of students in affluent professional schools, and teacher and student are likely to negotiate about the work the student will do.

Anyon provides the following definition of the fourth type of school she identified, the *executive elite school:*

> In the executive elite school, work is developing one's analytical intellectual powers. Children are continually asked to reason through a problem, to produce intellectual products that are both logically sound and of top academic quality (Anyon 1996, 196).

In the affluent professional and executive elite schools, teacher–student relationships are more positive than those in the working-class and middle-class schools. Teachers are polite to their students, seldom give direct orders, and almost never make sarcastic or nasty remarks. However schools are categorized, it seems clear that they reflect the socioeconomic status of the communities they serve.

What Are Schools Like as Social Institutions?

Schools are social institutions. An **institution** is an organization established by society to maintain and improve its way of life. Schools are the institutions our society has established for the purpose of educating the young. For the last 200 years, American schools have developed complex structures, policies, and curricula to accomplish this mission. "The Institutional Structure of Education in the United States" is shown in Figure 4.1 on page 132.

The School as a Reflection of Society

As you might expect, schools mirror the national culture and the surrounding local culture and other special interests. Private, parochial, and religious schools, for example, are often maintained by groups that see the school as a means of perpetuating their preferred way of life. One example of how schools reflect contemporary priorities in life in the United States is the growing number of public schools located in shopping malls. In commenting on his experiences at a school located in the Land-

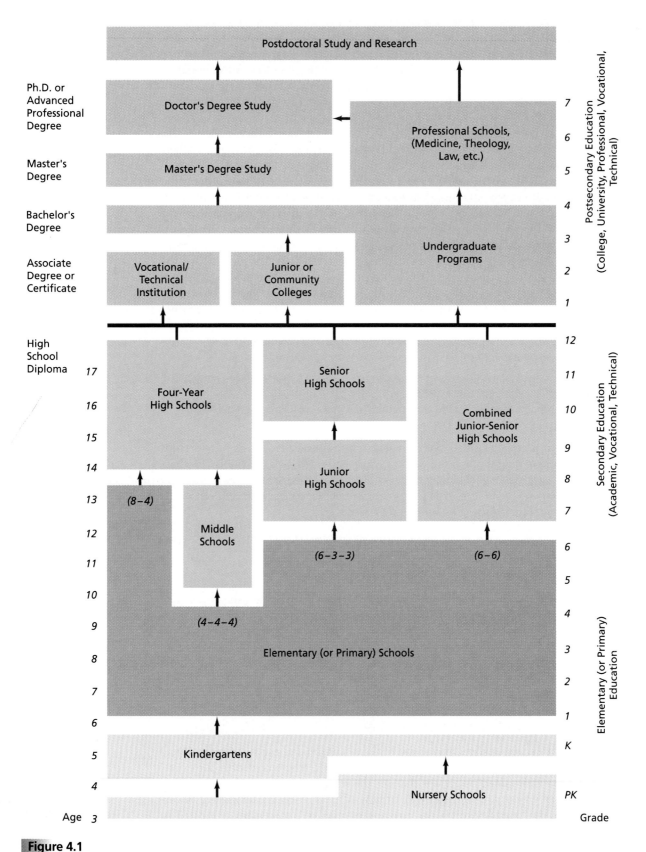

Figure 4.1

The institutional structure of education in the United States

mark Shopping Mall in Northern Virginia, a student is able to say that the goal of count-less students around the country is his reality: "As well as getting an education, I get a job" (Spring 1996, 4). Nevertheless, as Mary Henry (1993, 29) points out, "Schools are . . . not simply puppets of the dominant mainstream society. They have their own unique concerns and their own 'poetry' of people and events. Whether public or private, all schools are not the same."

Rural, Suburban, and Urban Schools Schools also reflect their location. Schools in rural, urban, and suburban settings often have significantly different cultures. Rural schools are often the focal point for community life and reflect values and beliefs that tend to be more conservative than those associated with urban and suburban schools. While the small size of a rural school may contribute to the development of a family-like culture, its small size may also make it difficult to provide students with an array of curricular experiences equal to that found at larger schools in more populated areas. In contrast, large suburban or urban schools may provide students with more varied learning experiences, but these schools may lack the cohesiveness and community focus of rural schools.

Schools and Community Environments The differences among the environments that surround schools can be enormous. Urban schools found in or near decaying centers of large cities often reflect the social problems of the surrounding area, such as drug abuse, crime, and poverty. One of the most serious problems confronting education in the United States is the quality of such schools. Across the country—in Chicago, New York, Los Angeles, St. Louis, Detroit, and Cleveland—middle-class families who can afford to, move away from urban centers or place their children in private schools. As a result, students in urban school districts are increasingly from low-income backgrounds.

In *Savage Inequalities,* Jonathon Kozol documents the startling contrast between the neighborhoods that surround impoverished inner-city schools and those that surround affluent suburban schools. In comparing New Trier High School in affluent Winnetka, Illinois, and Chicago's DuSable High School, an inner-city school at which the first author of this textbook taught for eight years, Kozol points out that New Trier is in a neighborhood of "circular driveways, chirping birds and white-columned homes" (1991, 62). In contrast, DuSable's surroundings are "almost indescribably despairing"; across the street from the school is "a line of uniform and ugly 16-story buildings, the Robert Taylor Homes, which constitute . . . the city's second-poorest neighborhood" (1991, 68, 71).

Though some communities may impact their schools in undesirable

In what ways do schools reflect their communities and the wider American society? What difference might the community make for this school? for the students who attend it? for the teachers who work there?

Do students in urban schools have equal access to up-to-date technologies?

According to a 1999 report on the use of technology in urban schools, large size, poverty, limited resources, outdated equipment, lack of training for teachers, political infighting, and entrenched bureaucracies limit students' access to advanced technologies to enhance their learning. Although the report found that urban districts had some "lighthouse schools" in which technology was fully integrated into the curriculum, many schools had woefully inadequate technology. In the high schools of one city, there was one classroom computer for every 209 students. Some schools in another city had no technology —no computer, no fax machine, no television/VCR; and more than three-quarters of the computers in the city's schools were older models such as Apple IIe's and 286 PCs. Yet another city reported in its inventory of technology in the schools that only half of its more than 42,000 computers were powerful enough to run spreadsheets and database programs or log onto the Internet.

What technologies do you think should be available to *all* students to enhance their learning? What technologies should be available to *all* teachers? What would be the impact on *your* current ability to learn if you had access only to outdated equipment, or none at all? What leadership roles can teachers in urban schools take to increase their students' access to advanced technologies?

Source: Based on *Barriers and Breakthroughs: Technology in Urban Schools,* Education Writers Association, April 1999. Available from the Education Writers Association, 1331 H Street NW #307, Washington, DC 20005, (202) 637-9700; fax (202) 637-9707; ewa@crosslink.net.

---

ways, many teachers at such schools find their work professionally stimulating and growth-enhancing. As one teacher said:

> I taught in two different environments—middle school in an inner city and high school in a more rural area. I think that combination was the experience that made me become a teacher. When I did my student teaching, I enjoyed it so much, and I realized I had a knack for it. When recruiters looked at my résumé, they were impressed that I had two different experiences I could draw from and elaborate on. I know that's how I got my job (Sallie Mae Corporation 1995, 8).

The Culture of the School

Although schools are very much alike, each school is unique. Each has a culture of its own—a network of beliefs, values and traditions, and ways of thinking and behaving that distinguishes it from other schools.

Much like a community, a school has a distinctive culture—a collective way of life. Terms that have been used to describe **school culture** include *climate, ethos, atmosphere,* and *character.* Some schools may be characterized as community-like places where there is a shared sense of purpose and commitment to providing the best education possible for all students. Other schools lack a unified sense of purpose or direction and drift, rudderless, from year to year. Still others are characterized by internal conflict and divisiveness and may even reflect what Deal and Peterson (1999) term a "toxic" school culture; students, teachers, administrators, and parents may feel that the school is not sufficiently meeting their needs. The following excerpt from the mission statement of an award-winning school in the high desert of Northern Arizona illustrates several qualities of a school culture that nurtures students:

> The Ganado Primary School's mission is to provide opportunities for children to make sense of their world, to respect themselves and others, to respect their environment, and to appreciate and understand their cultural and linguistic heritage. [Our] mission is to help everyone [children, teachers, and administrators] negotiate their experiences with the content of the classroom, instructional style, and the social, emotional, physical and professional interactions of school life. We believe that a relaxed atmosphere [characterized by] surprise, challenge, hard work, celebration, humor, satisfaction, and collegiality is the natural order of the day for all (Deal and Peterson 1999, 17).

The Physical Environment   The physical environment of the school both reflects and helps to create the school's overall culture. "Whether school buildings are squeezed between other buildings or located on sprawling campuses, their fenced-in area or other physical separation distinguishes them from the community-at-large" (Ballantine 1997, 210). Some schools are dreary places or, at best, aesthetically bland. The tile floors, concrete block walls, long, straight corridors, and rows of fluorescent lights often found in these schools contribute little to their inhabitants' sense of beauty, concern for others, or personal comfort.

Other schools are much more attractive. They are clean, pleasant, and inviting; and teachers and students take pride in their building. Overall, the physical environment has a positive impact on those who spend time in the school; it encourages learning and a spirit of cohesiveness.

Formal Practices of Schools   The formal practices of schools are well known to anyone who has been educated in U.S. schools. With few exceptions, students attend school from six years of age through sixteen at least, and usually to eighteen, Monday through Friday, September through May, for twelve years. For the most part, students are assigned to grade level on the basis of age rather than ability or interest. Assignment to individual classes or teachers at a given grade level, however, may be made on the basis of ability or interest.

Teachers and students are grouped in several ways in the elementary school and in one dominant pattern in junior and senior high school. At the elementary school level, the **self-contained classroom** is the most traditional and prevalent arrangement. In this type of classroom, one teacher teaches all or nearly all subjects to a group of about twenty-five children, with the teacher and students remaining in the same classroom for the entire day. Often art, music, physical education, and computer skills are taught in other parts of the school, so students may leave the classroom for scheduled periods. Individual students may also attend special classes for remedial or advanced instruction, speech therapy, or instrumental music and band lessons.

In **open-space schools,** students are free to move among various activities and learning centers. Instead of self-contained classrooms, open-space schools have large instructional areas with movable walls and furniture that can be rearranged easily. Grouping for instruction is much more fluid and varied. Students do much of their work independently, with a number of teachers providing individual guidance as needed.

In middle schools and junior and senior high schools, students typically study four or five academic subjects taught by teachers who specialize in them. In this organizational arrangement, called **departmentalization,** students move from classroom to classroom for their lessons. High school teachers often share their classrooms with other teachers and use their rooms only during scheduled class periods.

School Traditions   **School traditions** are those elements of a school's culture that are handed down from year to year. The traditions of a school reflect what students, teachers, administrators, parents, and the surrounding community believe is important and valuable about the school. One school, for example, may have developed a tradition of excellence in academic programs; another school's traditions may emphasize the performing arts; and yet another may focus on athletic programs. Whatever a school's traditions, they are usually a source of pride for members of the school community.

Ideally, traditions are the glue that holds together the diverse elements of a school's culture. They combine to create a sense of community, identity, and trust among people affiliated with a school. Traditions are maintained through stories that are handed down, rituals and ceremonial activities, student productions, and trophies and artifacts that have been collected over the years. For example, Joan Vydra, now principal of Briar Glen Elementary School in Wheaton, Illinois, initiated Care Week as part of the fall tradition at her former school, Hawthorne Elementary. Influenced by the work of Nel Noddings (featured as the "Keeper of the Dream" in Chapter 9), Vydra believed that a tradition of care would nurture student success. On the first day of Care Week, students learned the importance of caring for themselves; on Tuesdays, caring for their families; on Wednesdays, caring for each other; on Thursdays, caring for the school; and on Fridays, caring for those served by local charities (Deal and Peterson 1999).

The Culture of the Classroom

Just as schools develop their unique cultures, each classroom develops its own culture or way of life. The culture of a classroom is determined in large measure by the manner in which teacher and students participate in common activities. In addition, "the environment of the classroom and the inhabitants of that environment—students and teachers—are constantly interacting. Each aspect of the system affects all others" (Woolfolk 1998, 440).

The quality of teacher–student interactions is influenced by the physical characteristics of the setting (classroom, use of space, materials, resources, etc.) and the social dimensions of the group (norms, rules, expectations, cohesiveness, distribution of power and influence). These elements interact to shape **classroom culture.** Teachers who appreciate the importance of these salient elements of classroom culture are more likely to create environments that they and their students find satisfying and growth-promoting. For example, during the second month of student teaching in the second grade, "Miss Martin" reflects on her efforts to create classroom culture characterized by positive teacher–student interactions:

> I started off with a big mistake. I tried to be their friend. I tried joining with them in all the jokes and laughter that cut into instruction time. When this didn't work, I overcompensated by yelling at them when I needed them to quiet down and get to work. I wasn't comfortable with this situation. I did not think it was like me to raise my voice at a child. I knew I needed to consider how they felt. I realized that if I were them, I'd hate me, I really would. In desperation, I turned to my education textbooks for advice.
>
> This was a huge help to me, but a book can only guide you. It can't establish a personality for you or even manage your classroom for you. You have to do that yourself and as lovingly and effectively as possible. But I had so much trouble

finding a middle ground: love them, guide them, talk to them, manage them, but don't control them (Rand and Shelton-Colangelo 1999, 8–9).

Similarly, a beginning teacher at an experimental school describes the classroom culture she wants to create: "What I'm trying to get to in my classroom is that they have power. I'm trying to allow students to have power—to know what their knowledge is and to learn to create their own ideas as opposed to my being the one who is the only holder of ideas in the universe. I want to transfer the authority back to them" (Dollase 1992, 101). The efforts of this teacher to create an empowering classroom culture were supported by the culture of the school itself: "Because her comments reflect the prevailing view of this small, neo-progressive public school, she is able to implement her philosophy in her upper-level middle school classroom. [T]he structure of the school and the organization of the school day, which permits more personalization and more time with each class, are school variables that allow her a chance to succeed in redefining the authority relationships in her class" (Dollase 1992, 101).

What Characteristics Distinguish Successful Schools?

Like Miss Martin referenced above, you may be uncertain at this point in your professional education of your ability to develop a positive classroom climate at a school. However, a great many schools in all settings and with all kinds of students are highly successful, including inner-city and isolated rural schools and schools that serve pupils of all socioeconomic, racial, and ethnic backgrounds. What are the characteristics of these schools? Do they have commonalities that account for their success?

Measures of Success

First, we must define what we mean by a *successful school*. One measure of success, naturally, is that students at these schools achieve at a high level and complete requirements for graduation. Whether reflected in scores on standardized tests or other documentation of academic learning gains, students at these schools are learning. They are achieving literacy in reading, writing, computation, and computer skills. They are learning to solve problems, think creatively and analytically, and, most importantly, they are learning to learn.

Another valid measure of success for a school is that it achieves results that surpass those expected from comparable schools in comparable settings. The achievement of students goes beyond what one would expect. In spite of surrounding social, economic, and political forces that impede the educative process at other schools, these schools are achieving results.

Finally, **successful schools** are those that are improving, rather than getting worse. School improvement is a slow process, and schools that are improving—moving in the right direction rather than declining—are also successful.

Research on School Effectiveness

During the 1980s and early 1990s, much research was conducted to identify the characteristics of successful (or effective) schools. The characteristics of successful schools were described in different ways in several research projects. The following is a synthesis of those findings.

- *Strong leadership*—Successful schools have strong leaders—individuals who value education and see themselves as educational leaders, not just as managers or bureaucrats. They monitor the performance of everyone at the school—teachers, staff, students, and themselves. These leaders have a vision of the school as a more effective learning environment, and they take decisive steps to bring that about.
- *High expectations*—Teachers at successful schools have high expectations of students. These teachers believe that all students, rich or poor, can learn, and they communicate this to students through realistic, yet high, expectations.
- *Emphasis on basic skills*—Teachers at successful schools emphasize student achievement in the basic skills of reading, writing, and mathematical computation.
- *Orderly school environment*—The environments of successful schools are orderly, safe, and conducive to learning. Discipline problems are at a minimum, and teachers are able to devote greater amounts of time to teaching.
- *Frequent, systematic evaluation of student learning*—The learning of students in successful schools is monitored closely. When difficulties are noticed, appropriate remediation is provided quickly.
- *Sense of purpose*—Those who teach and those who learn at successful schools have a strong sense of purpose. From the principal to the students, everyone at the school is guided by a vision of excellence.
- *Collegiality and a sense of community*—Teachers, administrators, and staff at successful schools work well together. They are dedicated to creating an environment that promotes not only student learning but also their own professional growth and development.

Research has also focused on strategies for making schools more effective. Since the early 1990s, school districts across the nation have been participating in **school restructuring** that changes the way students are grouped, uses of classroom time and space, instructional methods, and decision making. A synthesis of research (Newmann and Wehlage 1995) conducted between 1990 and 1995 on restructuring schools identified four characteristics of successful schools:

- *Focus on student learning*—Planning, implementation, and evaluation focus on enhancing the intellectual quality of student learning. All students are expected to achieve academic excellence.
- *Emphasis on authentic pedagogy*—Students are required to think, to develop in-depth understanding, and to apply academic learning to important, realistic problems. Students might, for example, conduct a survey on an issue of local concern, analyze the results, and then present their findings at a town council meeting.
- *Greater school organizational capacity*—The ability of the school to strive for continuous improvement through professional collaboration is enhanced. For example, teachers exchange ideas to improve their teaching; they seek feedback from students, parents, and community members; and they attend conferences and workshops to acquire new materials and strategies.
- *Greater external support*—The school receives critical financial, technical, and political support from outside sources.

In short, the cultures of effective schools encourage teachers to grow and develop in the practice of their profession.

What Social Problems Affect Schools and Place Students at Risk?

A complex and varied array of social issues impact schools. These problems often detract from the ability of schools to educate students according to the seven aims discussed at the beginning of this chapter: national goals, prosocial values, socialization, achievement, personal growth, social change, and equal opportunity. Furthermore, schools are often charged with the difficult (if not impossible) task of providing a front-line defense against such problems.

One of the most vocal advocates of the role of schools in solving social problems was George S. Counts, who said in his 1932 book *Dare the School Build a New Social Order?* that "If schools are to be really effective, they must become centers for the building, and not merely the contemplation, of our civilization" (p. 12). Many people, however, believe that schools should not try to build a new social order. They should be concerned only with the academic and social development of students—not with solving society's problems. Nevertheless, the debate over the role of schools in regard to social problems will continue to be vigorous. For some time, schools have served in the battle against social problems by offering an array of health, education, and social service programs. Schools provide breakfasts, nutritional counseling, diagnostic services related to health and family planning, after-school child care, job placement, and sex and drug education, to name a few. In the following sections we examine several societal problems that directly influence schools, teachers, and students.

Identifying Students at Risk

An increasing number of young people live under conditions characterized by extreme stress, chronic poverty, crime, and lack of adult guidance. As James Garbarino (1999, 19) points out in *Lost Boys: Why Our Sons Turn Violent and How We Can Save Them:* "In almost every community in America, growing numbers of kids live in a socially toxic environment." Frustrated, lonely, and feeling powerless, many youths escape into music with violence-oriented and/or obscene lyrics, violent video games, cults, movies and television programs that celebrate gratuitous violence and sex, and cruising shopping malls or "hanging out" on the street. Others turn also to crime, gang violence, promiscuous sex, or substance abuse. Not surprisingly, these activities place many young people at risk of dropping out of school. In fact, it is estimated that the following percentages of fourteen-year-olds are likely to exhibit one or more at-risk behaviors (substance abuse, sexual behavior, violence, depression, or school failure) and to experience serious negative outcomes as a result: 10 percent at very high risk, 25 percent at high risk, 25 percent at moderate risk, 20 percent at low risk, and 20 percent at no risk (Dryfoos 1998).

Grouped by race/ethnicity or family income, students drop out of school at varying rates. Table 4.3, for example, shows that between 1972 and 1996, the dropout rate for Latinos has been consistently higher than the rates for other groups. Also, while the dropout rate for African American students declined significantly during that period, African American students were still more likely overall to drop out of school than their white peers. Lastly, the data reveal that students from low-income families are more likely to drop out than their counterparts from middle- and high-income families. **Students at risk** of dropping out tend to get low grades, perform below grade level academically, are older than the average student at their grade level because of previous retention, and have behavior problems in school.

Table 4.3

Event dropout rates* for those in grades ten through twelve, ages fifteen to twenty-four, by race/ethnicity and family income: October 1972–96

| October | Total | Race/Ethnicity** | | | Family Income*** | | |
		White	Black	Hispanic	Low	Middle	High
1972	6.1	5.3	9.5	11.2	14.1	6.7	2.5
1974	6.7	5.6	11.6	9.9	—	—	—
1976	5.9	5.6	7.4	7.3	15.4	6.8	
1976	6.7	5.6	10.2	12.3	17.4	7.3	3.0
1960	6.1	5.2	6.2	11.7	15.6	6.4	2.5
1962	5.5	4.7	7.6	9.2	15.2	5.6	1.6
1964	5.1	4.4	5.7	11.1	13.9	5.1	1.6
1966	4.7	3.7	5.4	11.9	10.9	5.1	1.6
1966	4.8	4.2	5.9	10.4	13.7	4.7	1.3
1990	4.0	3.3	5.0	7.9	9.5	4.3	1.1
1991	4.0	3.2	6.0	7.3	10.6	4.0	1.0
1992	4.4	3.7	5.0	6.2	10.9	4.4	1.3
1993	4.5	3.9	5.8	6.7	12.3	4.3	1.3
1994****	5.3	4.2	6.6	10.0	13.0	5.2	2.1
1995****	5.7	4.5	6.4	12.4	13.3	5.7	2.0
1996****	5.0	4.1	6.7	9.0	11.1	5.1	2.1

— Not available.

*The event dropout rate is the percentage of those in grades ten–twelve, ages fifteen–twenty-four, who were enrolled the previous October, but who were not enrolled and had not graduated the following October.

**Included in the total but not shown separately are dropouts from other racial/ethnic groups.

***Low income is the bottom 20 percent of all family incomes; high income is the top 20 percent of all family incomes; and middle income is the 60 percent in between.

****Beginning in 1994, new survey collection techniques and population weighting were used.

Note: Beginning in 1992, the Current Population Survey (CPS) changed the questions used to obtain the educational attainment of respondents to this indicator for further discussion.

Source: U.S. Department of Education, National Center for Education Statistics, *Dropout Rates in the United States: 1996* (based on the October Current Population Surveys). Reported in *Condition of Education 1998,* National Center for Education Statistics.

Many youth take more than the typical four years to complete high school, or they eventually earn a high school equivalency certificate (GED). If these alternative routes to high school completion are considered, however, there are still significant differences among racial/ethnic groups. For example, in 1997, 92.9 percent of whites between the ages of 25 and 29 had completed high school, compared to 86.9 percent of African Americans and 61.8 percent of Latinos (National Center for Education Statistics 1998a).

Many children in the United States live in families that help them grow up healthy, confident, and skilled, but many do not. Instead, their life settings are characterized by problems of alcoholism or other substance abuse, family or gang violence, unemployment, poverty, poor nutrition, teenage parenthood, and a history of school failure. Such children live in communities and families that have many problems and frequently become dysfunctional, unable to provide their children with the support and guidance they need. According to *Kids Count Data Book, 1999,* "13 percent, or 9.2 million, of our children are growing up with a collection of disadvantages that could curtail, if not scuttle, their chances to become productive adult participants in the mainstream of America's future" (Annie E. Casey Foundation 1999, 1).

Children who experience the negative effects of poverty are from families of all ethnic and racial groups. As Marian Wright Edelman (November 9, 1997, B5), founder and president of the Children's Defense Fund, said:

> Since 1973, families headed by someone younger than 30 have suffered a collapse in the value of their incomes, a surge in poverty, and a stunning erosion of employer-provided health benefits for their children. . . . Virtually every category of young families with young children has suffered major losses in median incomes: whites (22 percent), Hispanics (28 percent), and blacks (46 percent). . . . Low-income children are two or three times more likely to suffer from health problems, including infant death, iron deficiency, stunted growth, severe physical or mental disabilities, and fatal accidental injuries . . . the risk of students falling behind in school goes up by 2 percentage points for every year spent in poverty.

The life experiences of students who are at risk of dropping out can be difficult for teachers to imagine; and, as the following comments by a student teacher in an inner-city third-grade classroom illustrate, encountering the realities of poverty for the first time can be upsetting:

> Roughly 85 percent of [students are] living in poverty. The entire school population is eligible for free or reduced lunch. I was horrified. I guess I was a little ignorant of other people's situations.

> [Some] students came in wearing the same clothes for a week. Others would come in without socks on. No pencils, crayons, scissors, or glue. Some without breakfast, lunch, or a snack. My heart bled every day. I found myself becoming upset about their lives. I even found myself thinking about them at night and over the weekend. [I] noticed that they were extremely bright students, but their home life and economic status hindered them from working to their potential. Some of my students couldn't even complete their homework because they had no glue, scissors, or crayons at home (Molino 1999, 55).

Children and Poverty

Although the United States is one of the richest countries in the world, it has by no means achieved an enviable record in regard to poverty among children. According to the U.S. Census Bureau, 21 percent of children under eighteen years of age, or 14.7 million, lived in families below the poverty line in 1998 (see Figure 4.2). In the District

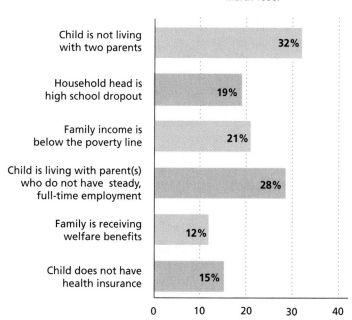

Figure 4.2

Percentage of children with certain risks
Source: U.S. Census Bureau, *Current Population Survey,* March 1998.

Pharoah's Perspective

The following case is excerpted from journalist Alex Kotlowitz's book *There Are No Children Here: The Story of Two Boys Growing up in the Other America*. Pharoah, eleven, and Lafeyette, fourteen, lived with their mother, LaJoe, and their triplet younger sisters in the Henry Horner Homes, a decaying public housing project in one of Chicago's toughest neighborhoods. Pharoah, enthusiastic about school, had participated in a spelling bee in fourth grade but ended up losing a bid for a ribbon because of his stuttering problem. This year, having drilled extensively with his friend and fellow contestant, Clarise, he was determined to win.

On Friday, March 3, the day of the spelling bee, Pharoah looked his best. The night before he had washed his good clothes in the bathtub and then dried them with a fan. This morning, he ironed his evergreen-colored sweater and a pair of new blue jeans on the family's makeshift ironing board, a broken microwave oven. . . .

When Pharoah got to school, Clarise couldn't believe her eyes. She'd never seen Pharoah looking so natty. . . . The judge ran through the rules, though Pharoah and Clarise hardly listened. Pharoah was too busy thinking about not stuttering. When his turn came, he stood poised and ready.

"*Acceptable,*" the judge said. "*Acceptable.*" Pharoah drew a deep breath and took his time.

"*Acceptable,*" Pharoah repeated. "A-C-C-E-P"—He pulled the microphone down toward him so that his voice would be amplified –"T-A-B-L-E. *Acceptable.*" He went to the back of the line. [The contest continued until everyone was eliminated except Clarise and Pharoah. And then Clarise won. . . .] The two children embraced each other, their faces radiant in victory.

"Congratulations," they muttered to each other.

In his joy Pharoah alternately skipped and ran home from school. . . . He couldn't wait to tell his mother of his triumph and show her his award. . . .

Pharoah pushed open the door to the apartment, which his mother left unlocked when school let out. Everyone and everything was eerily quiet. The television was turned down. The triplets were in their room. . . . Lafeyette sat perched by the window . . . his arms around his bent knees. He strained to hear the conversation at the kitchen table between LaJoe, Rochelle, and a neighbor, Clementine, whom everyone called Dutt; it was conducted in hollow whispers.

Pharoah first stood at the entranceway . . . and then went to his mother's side, thrusting the ribbon in her lap. "I-I-I c-c-came in second place." In his excitement and in the spooky stillness, his stutter had returned.

LaJoe returned Pharoah's smile. "Second place; that's still good." [Pharoah shared the details of the final minutes of his loss.]. . . "I-I-I-I knew right away it was wrong. My-my-my, you know, my heart, my heart was beating so fast," he told her, the words streaming out of his mouth.

Pharoah realized that something was terribly wrong. He didn't want to ask. No one seemed to care about his spelling bee triumph. No one wanted to hear what he had to say. Dutt was weeping. Lafeyette, while he had one ear to the conversation, stared vacantly out the window; he didn't even congratulate Pharoah. LaJoe tucked Pharoah's red ribbon into her pocketbook. (She would later display it in the living room alongside three achievement certificates earned by the triplets.) The family had just minutes earlier learned of Craig Davis's death the night before.

LaJoe turned from Pharoah to Dutt, whose daughter had been Craig's girlfriend and who felt partly responsible for Craig's death. Last night, when Craig came over to the house to visit her daughter, she had gotten into a minor spat with the boy, so he had left. If she had let him stay, she told LaJoe, maybe he wouldn't have been shot. LaJoe tried to comfort her. . . .

For much of the rest of the afternoon, the three women remained at the table, sometimes talking, sometimes sitting in silence. . . . In the meantime, Pharoah had shuffled out the door, unnoticed. This was not the time or place to celebrate his spelling victory. He went to play with Porkchop in the second-floor hallway. "I don't like to see nobody sad," he said later.

Questions

1. How does Pharoah reveal that he is still a child even though he needs to deal with adult-size realities?

2. In what ways is Pharoah at risk? How might his school address his needs?

3. What does this episode tell you about the role that school can play in the lives of children affected by poverty and violence?

4. How could teachers promote the involvement of parents like LaJoe in events in their school?

5. How should classroom teachers respond to tragedies such as the shooting death of Craig Davis? How can they help the schoolmates of such victims?

Source: Adapted from *There Are No Children Here: The Story of Two Boys Growing up in the Other America,* by Alex Kotlowitz. Selections taken from pgs. 199–203. Copyright © 1991 by Alex Kotlowitz. Used by permission of Doubleday, a division of Random House, Inc.

of Columbia, 40 percent lived in poverty; 32 percent in Louisiana; and 30 percent in New Mexico and Mississippi (Annie E. Casey Foundation 1999).

Despite the healthy economy during the last half of the 1990s, it was estimated that every night about 600,000 people, 15 percent of whom are children, were homeless (Department of Health and Human Services, 1999). And, not surprisingly, the incidence of child abuse, poor health, underachievement in school, and attendance problems is higher among these children than it is among children with homes.

Family Stress

The stress placed on families in a complex society is extensive and not easily handled. For some families, such stress can be overwhelming. The structure of families who are experiencing the effects of financial problems, substance abuse, or violence, for example, can easily begin to crumble.

The National Clearinghouse on Child Abuse and Neglect (NCCAN) reported that state Child Protective Service (CPS) agencies investigated an estimated two million reports of alleged child maltreatment, involving approximately three million children in 1996. Of these children, CPS determined that almost one million were victims of substantiated or indicated abuse or neglect, an increase of approximately 18 percent since 1990 (National Clearinghouse on Child Abuse and Neglect 1998). Clearly, the burden of having to cope with such abuse in the home environment does not prepare a child to come to school to learn.

Stress within the family can have a significant negative effect on students and their ability to focus on learning while at school. Such stress is often associated with health and emotional problems, failure to achieve, behavioral problems at school, and dropping out of school.

With the high rise in divorce and women's entry into the workforce, family constellations have changed dramatically. No longer is a working father, a mother who stays at home, and two or three children the only kind of family in the United States. The number of single-parent families, stepparent families, blended families, and extended families has increased dramatically during the last decade. Figure 4.2 shows that one in three families with children was headed by a single parent in 1998.

Just as there is diversity in the composition of today's families, so, too, there is diversity in the styles with which children are raised in families. Because of the number of working women and single-parent homes, an alarming number of children are unsupervised during much of the day. It has been estimated that there may be as many as five million such **latchkey children** between the ages of five and fourteen (Child Care Bureau 1997). To meet the needs of latchkey children, many schools offer before- and after-school programs.

In addition, many middle-class couples are waiting longer to have children. Although children of such couples may have more material advantages, they may be "impoverished" in regard to the reduced time they spend with their parents. To maintain their life-style, these parents are often driven to spend more time developing their careers. As a result, the care and guidance their children receive is inadequate, and "Sustained bad care eventually leads to a deep-seated inner sense of insecurity and inadequacy, emotional pain, and a troublesome sense of self" (Comer 1997, 83). To fill the parenting void that characterizes the lives of an increasing number of children from all economic classes, schools and teachers are being called on to play an increased role in the socialization of young people.

Table 4.4

Percentage of students who reported using alcohol or drugs any time during the previous thirty days, by type of drug and grade: School years 1991–97

Type of Drug and Grade	1991	1992	1993	1994	1995	1996	1997
Alcohol							
8th-graders	25.1	26.1	24.3*	25.5*	24.6*	26.2*	24.5*
10th-graders	42.8	39.9	38.2*	39.2*	38.8*	40.4*	40.1*
12th-graders	54.0	51.3	48.6*	50.1*	51.3*	50.8*	52.7*
Marijuana/hashish							
8th-graders	3.2	3.7	5.1	7.8	9.1	11.3	10.2
10th-graders	8.7	8.1	10.9	15.8	17.2	20.4	20.5
12th-graders	13.8	11.9	15.5	19.0	21.2	21.9	23.7
Any illicit drug other than marijuana							
8th-graders	3.8	4.7	5.3	5.6	6.5	6.9	6.0
10th-graders	5.5	5.7	6.5	7.1	8.9	8.9	8.8
12th-graders	7.1	6.3	7.9	8.8	10.0	9.5	10.7
Stimulants							
8th-graders	2.6	3.3	3.6	3.6	4.2	4.6	3.8
10th-graders	3.3	3.6	4.3	4.5	5.3	5.5	5.1
12th-graders	3.2	2.8	3.7	4.0	4.0	4.1	4.8
LSD							
8th-graders	0.6	0.9	1.0	1.1	1.4	1.5	1.5
10th-graders	1.5	1.6	1.6	2.0	3.0	2.4	2.8
12th-graders	1.9	2.0	2.4	2.6	4.0	2.5	3.1
Cocaine							
8th-graders	0.5	0.7	0.7	1.0	1.2	1.3	1.1
10th-graders	0.7	0.7	0.9	1.2	1.7	1.7	2.0
12th-graders	1.4	1.3	1.3	1.5	1.6	2.0	2.3
Tranquilizers							
8th-graders	0.8	0.8	0.9	1.1	1.2	1.5	1.2
10th-graders	1.2	1.5	1.1	1.5	1.7	1.7	2.2
12th-graders	1.4	1.0	1.2	1.4	1.8	2.0	1.8
Cigarettes							
8th-graders	14.3	15.5	16.7	18.6	19.1	21.0	19.4
10th-graders	20.8	21.5	24.7	25.4	27.9	30.4	29.8
12th-graders	28.3	27.8	29.9	31.2	33.5	34.0	36.5
Inhalants							
8th-graders	4.4	4.7	5.4	5.6	6.1	5.8	5.6
10th-graders	2.7	2.7	3.3	3.6	3.5	3.3	3.0
12th-graders	2.4	2.3	2.5	2.7	3.2	2.5	2.5

*In 1993, the questions regarding alcohol consumption changed: therefore, data for alcohol use from 1993 through 1997 may not be comparable to earlier years. For example, in 1993, the original wording produced an estimate of 26 percent for alcohol use of eighth graders. The new wording produced an estimate of 24 percent.

Note: Only drug use not under a doctor's orders is included.

Source: National Center for Education Statistics, *The Condition of Education 1998, Supplemental Table 46-2.* Washington, DC: National Center for Education Statistics, 1998.

Substance Abuse

One of the most pressing social problems confronting today's schools is the abuse of illegal drugs, tobacco, and alcohol. Though drug abuse by students moved from the top-ranked problem facing local schools according to the 1996 Gallup Poll of public's attitudes toward the public schools to the fourth-ranked problem in the 1998 poll, drug use among students actually increased during the 1990s. The National Education Goals Panel reported that the percentage of tenth graders who reported using illicit drugs increased from 24 percent in 1991 to 40 percent in 1997, and the percentage reporting that someone offered to sell or give them an illegal drug at school during the previous year rose from 18 percent in 1992 to 33 percent in 1997 (National Education Goals Panel 1998, 15). Table 4.4 (see p. 145) shows the percentages of eighth, tenth, and twelfth graders who reported using alcohol or drugs between 1991 and 1997.

The use of drugs among young people varies from community to community and from year to year, but overall it is disturbingly high. Mind-altering substances used by young people include the easily acquired glue, white correction fluid, and felt marker, as well as marijuana, amphetamines, and cocaine. The abuse of drugs not only poses the risks of addiction and overdosing, but is also related to problems such as HIV/AIDS, teenage pregnancy, depression, suicide, automobile accidents, criminal activity, and dropping out of school.

For an alarming number of young people, drugs are seen as a way of coping with life's problems.

Violence and Crime

While the nation experienced a decline in serious violent crimes during the 1990s, crime rates among adolescents rose during the same period. Nearly one million adolescents between the ages of twelve and nineteen are victims of violent crimes each year (Hamburg 1997), and since World War II, there has been a sevenfold increase in serious assaults by juveniles in the United States (Garbarino 1999). Each year, almost 5 percent of high school seniors report being injured with a weapon during the previous twelve months, 13 percent threatened with a weapon, and 12 percent injured without a weapon (National Center for Education Statistics 1998a). Figure 4.3 shows the extent of criminal incidents in public schools by seriousness of crimes, instructional level, and location.

In addition, the U.S. Department of Justice estimates that there are more than 30,500 gangs and approximately 816,000 gang members (Moore and Terrett, 1999). An eleven-city survey of eighth graders found that 9 percent were currently gang members, and 17 percent said they had belonged to a gang at some point in their lives (Esbensen and Osgood 1997). Gang membership is perceived by many youth as providing them with several advantages: a sense of belonging and identity, protection from other gangs, opportunities for excitement, or a chance to make money through selling drugs or participating in other illegal activities. Though few students are gang members, a small number of gang-affiliated students can disrupt the learning process, create disorder in a school, and cause others to fear for their physical safety. Strategies for reducing the effect of gang activities on schools include the identification of gang members, implementing dress codes that ban styles of dress identified with gangs, and quickly removing gang graffiti from the school.

The nation's concern about school crime and safety heightened as a result of a string of school shootings between 1996 and 1999. Among the communities that had to

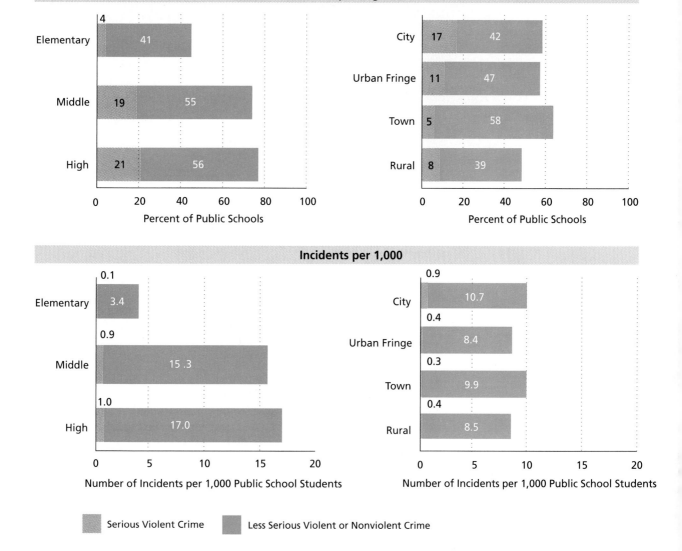

Public Schools Reporting Incidents

Elementary: 4 | 41
Middle: 19 | 55
High: 21 | 56

Percent of Public Schools

City: 17 | 42
Urban Fringe: 11 | 47
Town: 5 | 58
Rural: 8 | 39

Percent of Public Schools

Incidents per 1,000

Elementary: 0.1 | 3.4
Middle: 0.9 | 15.3
High: 1.0 | 17.0

Number of Incidents per 1,000 Public School Students

City: 0.9 | 10.7
Urban Fringe: 0.4 | 8.4
Town: 0.3 | 9.9
Rural: 0.4 | 8.5

Number of Incidents per 1,000 Public School Students

Serious Violent Crime   Less Serious Violent or Nonviolent Crime

Note: Serious violent crimes include murder, rape or other types of sexual battery, suicide, physical attack or fight with a weapon, or robbery. Less serious or nonviolent crimes include physical attack or fight without a weapon, theft/larceny, and vandalism. Schools were asked to report crimes that took place in school buildings, on school buses, on school grounds, and at places holding school-sponsored events.

Figure 4.3

Percentage of public schools reporting one or more criminal incidents to police and number of incidents reported per 1,000 students by seriousness of crimes, instructional level, and urbanicity: 1996–97
Source: Reported in *Indicators of School Crime and Safety, 1998.* Washington, DC: U.S. Departments of Education and Justice, 1998, p. 15.

cope with such tragic incidents were Moses Lake, Washington (1996); Pearl, Mississippi (1997); West Paducah, Kentucky (1997); Jonesboro, Arkansas (1998); Springfield, Oregon (1998); and Littleton, Colorado (1999).

Alarmed by the rise in school violence, President Clinton asked the U.S. Departments of Justice and Education to begin preparing an *Annual Report on School Safe-*

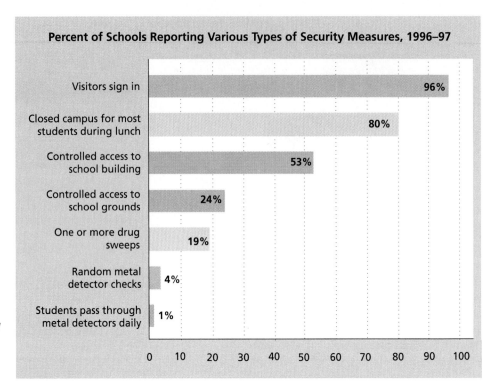

Percent of Schools Reporting Various Types of Security Measures, 1996–97

- Visitors sign in — 96%
- Closed campus for most students during lunch — 80%
- Controlled access to school building — 53%
- Controlled access to school grounds — 24%
- One or more drug sweeps — 19%
- Random metal detector checks — 4%
- Students pass through metal detectors daily — 1%

Figure 4.4

Security measures
Source: Indicators of School Crime and Safety, 1998. Washington, DC: National Center for Education Statistics.

ty, the first of which was released in 1998. In addition, shortly after the killings in Colorado, Clinton convened a White House conference on youth violence that included representatives from the gun manufacturing, television, movie, and video games industries. Since the recurring question after each instance of horrific school violence was why, there was a renewed effort to understand the origins of youth violence. Indeed, the entire nation debated gun control measures; the influence of violence in television, movies, and point-and-shoot video games; and steps that parents, schools, and communities could take to curb school crime and violence. Figure 4.4 shows the percentage of schools reporting various types of security measures.

The increased use of guns by children and youth to solve conflicts is one consequence of the "gun culture" in the United States, in which it is estimated that nearly 40 percent of homes have at least one gun (Garbarino 1999). On the issue of television violence, the American Psychological Association reviewed research studies and concluded that television violence *alone* is responsible for up to 15 percent of all aggressive behavior by children and youth (Garbarino 1999). Lastly, David Grossman, a military psychologist, and his colleague pointed out that violent point-and-shoot video games are similar to those used to "desensitize" soldiers to shoot at human figures (Grossman and Siddle 1999).

As a result of the school shootings listed earlier and the public's concern with school crime and violence, many schools developed crisis management plans to cope with violent incidents on campus. Schools also reviewed their ability to provide students, faculty, and staff with a safe environment for learning; for example, Appendix 4.1 presents a "School Safety Checklist" excerpted from the National Education Association's *School Safety Check Book*. Additionally, to help troubled youth *before* they commit violence, educators familiarized themselves with research-identified risk factors for violence such as the following: economic and social deprivation, family history of substance abuse and/or crime, lack of effective parenting and parental rejection, victimization by physical or sexual abuse, observation of domestic violence, early conduct problems, academic failure, substance abuse, gang affiliation, and possessing of guns (Washington State Department of Health, Non-Infectious Disease and Conditions Epidemiology Section 1994).

Professional Reflection   Identifying the factors behind youth violence

In *Lost Boys: Why Our Sons Turn Violent and How We Can Save Them*, James Garbarino presents ten "facts of life" for violent boys. After reading the list, consider the following questions: What steps can teachers and other adults take to reduce the influence of these factors on individual youth? What kinds of academic and counseling services might be helpful for students prone to violence? How should schools involve the parents and/or guardians of violence-prone youth?

1. Child maltreatment leads to survival strategies that are often antisocial and/or self-destructive.
2. The experience of early trauma leads boys to become hypersensitive to arousal in the face of threat and to respond to such threats by disconnecting emotionally or acting out aggressively.
3. Traumatized kids require a calming and soothing environment to increase the level at which they are functioning.
4. Traumatized youth are likely to evidence an absence of future orientation.
5. Youth exposed to violence at home and in the community are likely to develop juvenile vigilantism, in which they do not trust an adult's capacity and motivation to ensure safety, and as a result believe they must take matters into their own hands.
6. Youth who have participated in the violent drug economy or chronic theft are likely to have distorted materialistic values.
7. Traumatized youth who have experienced abandonment are likely to feel life is meaningless.
8. Issues of shame [and humiliation] are paramount among violent youth . . . [they] share a common sense of inner crisis, a crisis of shame and emptiness. These boys are ashamed of who they are inside, and their efforts to compensate for that shame drive their violence.
9. Youth violence is a boy's attempt to achieve justice as he perceives it.
10. Violent boys often seem to feel they cannot afford empathy.

Source: James Garbarino, *Lost Boys: Why Our Sons Turn Violent and How We Can Save Them.* New York: The Free Press, 1999, pp. 217–30.

Teen Pregnancy

Each year more than one million U.S. teenagers (one in nine women between the ages of fifteen and nineteen) become pregnant, and about 85 percent of these pregnancies are unintended. This figure includes about 18 percent of all African American women

Should metal detectors be installed in schools?

Ten days after the Columbine High School shooting spree in 1999 that took the lives of fourteen students and a teacher and wounded over twenty others, the U.S. Secretary of Education, Richard Riley, sought to make sense of the tragedy. Speaking at Walt Whitman High School in Bethesda, Maryland, he told his audience, "We have always had schoolyard fights, but now there is a new level of fear because of these weapons of deadly violence." Crime statistics at the time indicated an actual decline in the juvenile violence rate, but lethality had increased, mainly due to guns.

"Guns and youth are a particularly deadly combination," observed a report by the Center for the Study and Prevention of Violence at the University of Colorado at Boulder. "Guns give youth the feeling of power, and during adolescence, abstract reasoning about the consequences of gun use and the capacity to read social cues are incomplete." The need to separate the two is obvious. But the way to do that is a challenge. Should metal detectors be installed in schools? Are there less ominous ways to handle the problem? Can schools be kept safe without becoming fortresses?

our society, should we not provide the same for our children and youth?

Metal detectors and similar devices are technological advances that help reduce crime in a variety of settings. In addition to the security they provide in airports, they prevent people from taking library books they haven't checked out and protect stores from shoplifters. Just as we have learned to accept metal detectors in libraries, airports, and stores, so their presence in schools would soon be hardly noticed.

Model programs that have decreased student weapon violations by 70 to 86 percent include weapon scanning with metal detectors along with random searches conducted by police. Other features of such model programs include eliminating building areas that cannot be viewed by surveillance cameras and training school security officers by local police forces. These model programs also call for teachers and students to be trained in how to handle dangerous situations and ways to avoid them. The installation of metal detectors is clearly where protection from school violence must begin.

Metal detectors should be installed in schools.

A shooting in a school is like an earthquake in a city: It shakes the very foundation of what was thought to be solid, secure, and safe. Children and youth need to feel confident that their school is a safe and secure place. The thought of requiring students to spend their days in environments that make them vulnerable to violence is abhorrent. Expecting students to tackle their studies and find learning engaging when they are fearful for their lives is ludicrous. And yet that is exactly what we are doing if we fail to install metal detectors in schools.

After bombings occurred in air travel, metal detectors were installed in airports in order to protect passengers. Few complained, realizing that the personal inconvenience assured them of greater protection and peace of mind. They accepted the need to lose a liberty for the good of all. If adults are granted such protection from the violence in

Metal detectors should not be installed in schools.

Using metal detectors to prevent school violence is like putting an adhesive bandage on an infected wound. Not only will it not remedy the problem, but it could also make it even worse. Students who have not considered bringing a weapon to school might decide to do so simply to challenge the system. Like gang members who write graffiti on dangerous highway overpasses, similar minds will be motivated to find ways to bypass the metal detector. Metal detectors also present a foreboding welcome to a school campus and convey to students the messages "We have problems here" and "We don't trust you."

Instead, the way to prevent school violence is to get to the heart of students' problems. What causes the anger and alienation that eventually explodes in destructive, and sometimes deadly, acts? Teaching students how to solve their problems, handle disappointments, and seek help when it's needed are ways in which some schools have tried

to reduce violence. Conflict management, peace building, using literature to teach empathy, forbidding teasing, and anti-bullying programs are other approaches.

In his speech at Walt Whitman High, Secretary Riley
urged community members, parents, and students themselves to play active roles in reversing the trend toward
greater violence. "I ask all Americans to believe as I do in
this generation of young people. . . . We must send . . . a
powerful message of hope and security. We will do everything we can to protect you, to listen to you, and to reach
out to you so that you feel connected. . . . This is why I ask
parents again and again to slow down your lives." He told
students to speak to adults when they believe something
violent is about to happen. He never mentioned metal
detectors, and rightly so. Finding ways to reduce alienation
and create community in our schools is a better approach
to promoting school safety.

Where do you stand on this issue?

1. With which position do you agree? Why?

2. What are "zero tolerance" policies and should
   they be used?

3. How can teachers help prevent violence in
   schools?

4. How do schools and airports compare in their
   needs for metal detectors?

5. What compromise position can you suggest?

Recommended Sources

Center for the Study and Prevention of Violence, University
of Colorado at Boulder (1991, April 21). Response to the
Columbine school incident.

Department of Education (1999, April 30). Safe schools,
healthy schools: remarks as prepared for delivery by U.S.
Secretary of Education Richard W. Riley

Walters, L. S. (1999, January/February). What makes a good
school violence prevention program? *Harvard Education
Letter.*

ages fifteen to nineteen, 16 percent of Latina women, and 8 percent of Anglo-European
women (Alan Guttmacher Institute 1999). Indeed, most teachers of adolescents today
may expect to have at least some students who are, or have been, pregnant.

Since peaking in 1990, the teenage pregnancy, birth, and abortion rates have
declined 17 percent; about 20 percent of this decrease is the result of decreased sexual
activity and 80 percent the result of more effective contraceptive practices among sexually active teenagers (Alan Guttmacher Institute 1999). Nevertheless, teen pregnancies
remain a serious problem in society. Because the physical development of girls in adolescence may not be complete, complications can occur during pregnancy and in the
birthing process. Also, adolescents are less likely to receive prenatal care in the crucial
first trimester; they tend not to eat well-balanced diets; and are not free of harmful
substances such as alcohol, tobacco, and drugs, which are known to be detrimental to
a baby's development. These young mothers "are at risk for chronic educational,
occupational, and financial difficulties, and their offspring are also at risk for medical,
educational, and behavioral problems" (Durlak 1995, 66). Because most teen mothers
drop out of school, forfeiting their high school diplomas and limiting their access to

decent, higher-paying job opportunities, they and their children stay at the bottom of the economic ladder.

Students with HIV/AIDS

One of the most challenging social problems confronting the schools is providing for the education of children who have HIV/AIDS (human immunodeficiency virus/ acquired immune deficiency syndrome). With AIDS, nearly always fatal, the body is no longer able to defend itself against disease. Many school districts have been involved in litigation over the right of children with HIV/AIDS to attend school, and the condom-distribution programs that a few school systems have initiated to stem the spread of the HIV virus have been challenged in the courts.

According to the Centers for Disease Control and Prevention (CDC), the number of AIDS cases continues to increase at an alarming rate. During 1998, 48,269 persons were reported with AIDS, bringing the total number of persons reported with AIDS since the beginning of the epidemic to 688,200. In 1998, the World Health Organization reported that, worldwide, as many as 42 million people had been infected with HIV since the epidemic began, and that each day 16,000 more become infected and 1,600 babies are born with HIV.

Increasingly, states are beginning to require that schools provide information on HIV/AIDS and how to avoid the disease. The CDC reported in 1998 that about 87 percent of states required a separate health education course between grades six and twelve, and that HIV education was a part of almost all of those required courses. In addition, the CDC found that more than half of schools had a written policy on HIV infection and students and school staff (Centers for Disease Control and Prevention 1998a). To promote the development and implementation of HIV education programs for school-age populations, the CDC funds an HIV education coordinator in each state.

Suicide among Children and Youths

The increase in individual and multiple suicides is alarming. The National Institute for Mental Health (1999) reported that suicide is the third leading cause of death among youth ages fifteen to twenty-four and accounts for more than 4,000 deaths yearly for this group. The Institute also estimated that there are eight to twenty-five attempted suicides for one completion. According to the Centers for Disease Control and Prevention (1998b), about 21 percent of high school students seriously considered committing suicide in 1997; about 16 percent made a specific suicide plan; about 8 percent actually attempted suicide; and about 3 percent required medical attention as a result of their suicide attempt.

Although female students are almost two times more likely than male students to have seriously considered attempting suicide during the preceding twelve months, about six times as many male students as females actually commit suicide. Latino students are about two times more likely than white students to attempt suicide, and students in grade nine are about four times more likely than students in grade twelve to make a suicide attempt that requires medical attention (Centers for Disease Control and Prevention 1998b). Also, lesbian and gay youth are two to three times more likely to attempt suicide than their heterosexual peers, and they account for up to 30 percent of all completed suicides among youth (Besner and Spungin 1995).

What Are Schools Doing to Address Societal Problems?

Responding to the needs of at-risk students will be a crucial challenge for schools, families, and communities during the twenty-first century. Since most children attend school, it is logical that this pre-existing system be used for reaching large numbers of at-risk children (and, through them, their families). During the last decade, many school districts have taken innovative steps to address societal problems that impact students' lives.

Though programs that address social problems are costly, the public believes that schools should be used for the delivery of health and social services to students and their families. According to the 1995 Gallup Poll of the Public's Attitudes toward the Public Schools, for example, 91 percent of respondents said that "serving the emotional and health needs of students" is "very important" or "somewhat important" (Elam and Rose 1995, 44). However, there is some disagreement about the extent to which school facilities should be used for anything but meeting students' educational needs. For example, in a publication titled *Putting Learning First,* the Committee for Economic Development (1994, 1) stated, "Schools are not social service institutions; they should not be asked to solve all our nation's social ills and cultural conflicts." In isolated instances, community groups and school boards have resisted school-based services such as family planning clinics and mental health services. Meanwhile, increases in state funding and foundation support to provide school-based health, mental health, and social services have tended to dissipate most of this resistance (Dryfoos 1998).

Intervention Programs

Under pressure to find solutions to increasing social problems among children and adolescents, educators have developed an array of intervention programs. In general, the aim of these programs is to address the behavioral, social, and academic adjustment of at-risk children and adolescents so they can receive maximum benefit from their school experiences.

In the following sections, we briefly review several comprehensive strategies that have proven effective in addressing academic, social, and behavioral problems among children and adolescents; these approaches to intervention are peer counseling, full-service schools, and school-based interprofessional case management. Chapter 14 presents additional information about recent, innovative steps schools are taking for the *prevention* of the effects of social problems on students. Also see Appendix 4.2 for "Selected Resources for Meeting Needs of Students Placed at Risk"—a list of publications, organizations, and online locations that are good sources of information on the problems children and youth may encounter.

Peer Counseling   To address the social problems that affect students, some schools have initiated student-to-student **peer counseling** programs—usually monitored by a school counselor or other specially trained adult. In peer counseling programs, students can address problems and issues such as low academic achievement, interpersonal problems at home and at school, substance abuse, and career planning. Evidence indicates that both peer counselors and students experience increased self-esteem and greater ability to deal with problems.

When peer counseling is combined with cross-age tutoring, younger students can learn about drugs, alcohol, premarital pregnancy, delinquency, dropping out, HIV/AIDS,

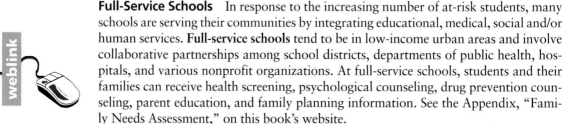

What approach to the education of students at risk does the scene in this photograph represent? What other risk factors affect children and youths? What are some other effective approaches for helping students at risk to succeed in school?

suicide, and other relevant issues. Here the groups are often college-age students meeting with those in high school, or high school students meeting with those in junior high school or middle school. In these preventative programs, older students sometimes perform dramatic episodes that portray students confronting problems and model strategies for handling the situations presented.

Full-Service Schools   In response to the increasing number of at-risk students, many schools are serving their communities by integrating educational, medical, social and/or human services. **Full-service schools** tend to be in low-income urban areas and involve collaborative partnerships among school districts, departments of public health, hospitals, and various nonprofit organizations. At full-service schools, students and their families can receive health screening, psychological counseling, drug prevention counseling, parent education, and family planning information. See the Appendix, "Family Needs Assessment," on this book's website.

One example of a full-service school is award-winning Salome Urena Middle Academy (SUMA), a middle school serving a Dominican community in Washington Heights, New York. Open six days per week, fifteen hours per day, year round, SUMA offers before-school and after-school child care. Through seventy-five partnerships with various community groups and agencies, SUMA offers a comprehensive, integrated array of programs and services to children and their families. Students may enroll in their choice of four academies—business; community service; expressive arts; and mathematics, science, and technology. A Family Institute offers English as a second language, Spanish, aerobics, and entrepreneurial skills. At a Family Resource Center, social workers, paraprofessionals, parents, and other volunteers offer help with immigration, employment, and housing. Next to the Family Resource Center, a clinic provides dental, medical, and mental health services. Each year, the school's more than 1,200 students, their parents, and siblings are served at a cost significantly less than the per-pupil expenditures in most suburban schools. Moreover, according to an evaluation conducted by Fordham University, the school has realized a significant increase in attendance, a major reduction in misbehavior, and a modest increase in test scores (Dryfoos 1994, 1998; Karvarsky 1994).

School-Based Interprofessional Case Management In responding to the needs of at-risk students, it has been suggested that schools "will need to reconceptualize the networks of community organizations and public services that might assist, and they will need to draw on those community resources" (Edwards and Young 1992, 78). One such approach to forming new home/school/community partnerships is known as **school-based interprofessional case management.** The approach uses professionally trained case managers who work directly with teachers, the community, and the family to coordinate and deliver appropriate services to at-risk students and their families. The case management approach is based on a comprehensive service delivery network of teachers, social agencies, and health service agencies.

One of the first case-management programs in the country is operated by the Center for the Study and Teaching of At-Risk Students (C-STARS) and serves 20 school districts in the Pacific Northwest. Center members include Washington State University, the University of Washington, a community-based organization, and Washington State's Department of Social and Health Services. Working with teachers and other school personnel, an interprofessional case management team fulfills seven functions to meet the needs of at-risk students: assessment, development of a service plan, brokering with other agencies, service implementation and coordination, advocacy, monitoring and evaluation, and mentoring. Program evaluation data have shown significant measurable improvements in student's attendance, academic performance, and school behavior.

Compensatory Education

To meet the learning needs of at-risk students, several federally funded **compensatory education programs** for elementary and secondary students have been developed, the largest of which is Title I. Launched in 1965 as part of the Elementary and Secondary Education Act (ESEA) and President Lyndon Johnson's Great Society education program, Title I (called Chapter I between 1981 and 1994) was designed to improve the basic skills (reading, writing, and mathematics) of low-ability students from low-income families. Each year, more than five million students (about 10 percent of enrollments) in nearly all school districts benefit from Title I programs. The Educational Excellence for All Children Act of 1999, President Clinton's plan for reauthorizing the Elementary and Secondary Education Act, including Title I, called for dramatic new steps to improve education for at-risk students. The $8 billion program called for an end to "social promotion" in schools and higher standards for teacher quality and training. Moreover, school districts would be required to show by 2002 that their Title I schools are treated the same as their other schools regarding staff qualifications, curricula, and the condition and safety of school buildings (*Education Week* 1999c).

Students who participate in Title I programs are usually taught through "pull-out" programs, in which they leave the regular classroom to receive additional instruction individually or in small groups. Title I teachers, sometimes assisted by an aide, often have curriculum materials and equipment not available to regular classroom teachers.

Research on the effectiveness of Title I programs has been inconclusive, with some studies reporting achievement gains not found in other studies. Recent research has found positive effects on students' achievement in the early grades, but these gains tend to dissipate during the middle grades. The pattern of short-lived gains is strongest for students attending urban schools that serve a high proportion of families in poverty (Levine and Levine 1996). Some critics of Title I and other compensatory education programs such as Head Start for preschool children, Success for All for preschool and elementary children, and Upward Bound for high school students argue that they are stopgap measures at best. Instead, they maintain, social problems such as poverty, the breakdown of families, drug abuse, and crime that contribute to poor school performance should be reduced.

Alternative Schools and Curricula

To meet the needs of students whom social problems place at risk, many school districts have developed alternative schools and curricula. Usually, an **alternative school** is a small, highly individualized school separate from the regular school; in other cases, the alternative school is organized as a **school-within-a-school**. Alternative school programs usually provide remedial instruction, some vocational training, and individualized counseling. Since they usually have much smaller class sizes, alternative school teachers can monitor students' progress more closely and, when problems do arise, respond more quickly and with greater understanding of student needs.

One exemplary alternative school is the Buffalo Alternative High School serving at-risk seventh to twelfth grade students in the Buffalo, New York, Public School District. To reach students who are not successful at regular schools, the Buffalo program offers individualized instruction, small class sizes, and various enrichment programs delivered in what school staff describe as a "supportive, noncoercive, nontraditional setting." Most students are expected to return to their regular schools after a minimum of four weeks. Students must earn 600 "points" (based on attendance, punctuality, attitude, behavior, and performance) to return to their regular school.

In addition, the Buffalo Alternative High School operates eight satellite schools in nonschool buildings throughout Buffalo. Among these programs are:

- *SAVe (Suspension Avoidance Vehicle)*—a two-week program students complete before returning to their sending school or enrolling in the Alternative High School
- *City-as-School*—students serve as interns in the public and private sectors and earn academic credit
- *SMART (Students Moving Ahead Through Remediation Testing)*—seventh- and eighth-grade students held behind can qualify for promotion to the appropriate grade
- *Bilingual Satellite*—educational services provided to Spanish-speaking students

While they don't work in alternative school settings, many highly effective regular teachers have developed alternative curricula to meet the unique learning needs of students at risk. Many teachers, for example, link students' learning to the business, civic, cultural, and political segments of their communities. The rationale is that connecting at-risk students to the world beyond their schools will enable them to see the relevance of education.

SUMMARY

What Are the Aims of Education Today?

■ Though debate about the aims of education continues, the public believes that schools have a responsibility to address problems confronting American society.

■ One perspective on the aims of education is Goals 2000, a set of national goals in the following areas: school readiness; school completion; student achievement and citizenship; achievement in mathematics and science; adult literacy and lifelong learning; safe, disciplined, and alcohol- and drug-free schools; teacher education and professional development; and parental participation.

■ In 1999, the National Education Goals Panel acknowledged that the National Goals would not be reached by 2000 and passed a resolution to rename them "America's Education Goals," with no specific date for their achievement.

■ Agreement exists regarding six additional broad educational aims—education for prosocial values, socialization, achievement, personal growth, social change, and equal opportunity.

How Can Schools Be Described?

■ Schools can be categorized according to the focus of their curricula and according to their organizational structures.

■ Metaphors for schools have suggested that schools are like families, tribes or clans, banks, gardens, prisons, and so on, with the school-as-family metaphor often describing schools that are successful.

■ Some people believe that schools reproduce the existing social class structure, that they maintain the differences between the "haves" and "have-nots." For example, Anyon's four categories of schools—working-class schools, middle-class schools, affluent professional schools, and executive elite schools—illustrate the relationship between schooling and social class.

What Are Schools Like as Social Institutions?

■ As social institutions that contribute to the maintenance and improvement of society, schools mirror the national American culture and the surrounding local culture.

■ Schools develop their own unique cultures, and the community environment that surrounds a school can impact it positively or negatively.

■ Elements of a school's physical environment such as self-contained classrooms, open-space arrangements, and departmentalization contribute to a school's character and culture. Similarly, each classroom develops its own culture, which is influenced by the physical setting and the social dimensions of the group.

What Characteristics Distinguish Successful Schools?

■ Three aspects of successful schools have been suggested: (1) their students manifest a high level of learning; (2) their results surpass those for comparable schools; and (3) they are improving rather than getting worse.

- Research has identified seven characteristics of effective schools: strong leadership, high expectations, emphasis on basic skills, orderly school environment, frequent and systematic evaluation of student learning, sense of purpose, and collegiality and a sense of community.

- Research indicates that successfully restructured schools emphasize student learning, authentic pedagogy, building organizational capacity, and external support.

What Social Problems Affect Schools and Place Students at Risk?

- Among the many social problems that impact the school's ability to educate students are poverty, family stress, substance abuse, violence and crime, teen pregnancy, HIV/AIDS, and suicide.

- Children at risk, who represent all ethnic and racial groups and all socioeconomic levels, tend to get low grades, underachieve, be older than other students at the same grade level, and have behavior problems at school.

What Are Schools Doing to Address Social Problems?

- Schools have developed intervention and prevention programs to address social problems. Three effective intervention programs are peer counseling, full-service schools, and school-based interprofessional case management.

- Since 1965, an array of federally funded compensatory education programs has provided educational services to improve the basic skills of low-ability students from low-income families.

- Many school districts have developed alternative schools or schools-within-a-school that provide highly individualized instructional and support services for students who have not been successful in regular schools. Also, highly effective teachers modify their techniques and develop alternative curricula to meet the needs of students at risk.

KEY TERMS AND CONCEPTS

aims of education, 125
alternative school, 156
classroom culture, 136
compensatory education
   programs, 155
departmentalization, 135
emotional intelligence, 128
full-service schools, 154
Goals 2000: Educate
   America Act, 125

institution, 131
latchkey children, 144
magnet school, 130
open-space schools, 135
peer counseling, 153
prosocial values, 126
school-based
   interprofessional case
   management, 155
school culture, 134

school restructuring, 138
school traditions, 136
school-within-a-school, 156
self-contained
   classroom, 135
service learning, 128
students at risk, 139
successful schools, 137

APPLICATIONS AND ACTIVITIES

Teacher's Journal

1. Collect and summarize several newspaper and magazine articles that contain references to the public's expectations of education and the schools. To what extent do the articles address the four aims discussed in this chapter? To what extent do they identify social problems that schools are expected to address?

2. Identify and then defend your choice of school reforms that you consider most important for improving the quality of education in the United States. What aims of education do your choices reflect?

3. Reflect on your experiences with the impact of social problems on teaching and learning at the elementary, middle, or high school levels. Select one of the social issues or problems discussed in this chapter and describe its influences on you or your peers.

Teacher's Database

1. Join or start an interactive online discussion on one or more of the following topics discussed in this chapter. You might join a newsgroup already in progress or request discussion partners via an e-mail mailing list or via any one of the message board opportunities that are offered at many of the sites you have already explored. You might also establish a communication link among your classmates or with students in other schools who are taking a similar course.

Goals 2000	HIV/AIDS
teen pregnancies	effective schools
at-risk students	family stress
substance abuse	latchkey children
crime and violence in schools	youth suicide
school restructuring	school-based clinics
children in poverty	alternative schools

Formulate a research question concerning demographic aspects of students and their families, and go online to gather current national and state statistics on topics related to your question. For example, your question might relate to one or more of the above topics.

2. Develop a collaborative project with classmates to investigate and report on issues in drug abuse prevention, at-risk intervention, or violence prevention. Begin by exploring two sites maintained by the U.S. government: Children, Youth and Families Education and Research Network (CYFERNet); and Children, Youth, and Families at Risk (CYFAR). Both sites have extensive resources, databases, and services for at-risk children, youth, and their families.

weblink

Observations and Interviews

1. Visit a school in your community recognized as successful or effective. What evidence do you find of the characteristics of successful schools (or successfully restructured schools) discussed in this chapter? Are there other characteristics you would add to the list based on your observations? To guide your observations and collaborate with classmates, ask your instructor for Handout M4.1, "Observing Characteristics of Effective Schools."

2. Reflect on your experiences relating to social problems at the elementary, middle, or high school levels. Then gather statistics and information about how a local school or local school district is responding to the social problems discussed in this chapter. To help you identify the kind of information to gather, ask your instructor for Handout M4.2, "Analyzing Impacts of Social Problems on Schools."

3. Obtain at least one statement of philosophy, or mission statement, from a school with which you are familiar. Analyze the statement(s), identifying and highlighting portions that refer to the major aims of education discussed in this chapter (national goals, prosocial values, socialization, achievement, personal growth, social change, and equal educational opportunity).

4. Write an essay describing the characteristics of an ideal school in which you would like to teach.

Professional Portfolio

1. Analyze a school as a social institution. How is the school organized in terms of roles and statuses? How does the school's organization and functioning reflect the wider society as well as the community in which it is located? What characteristics of the school and its people relate to the urban, rural, or suburban nature of the school environment? Does the school match one of the four categories of schools identified by Jean Anyon on the basis of social class?

2. Develop a case study of a school's culture. Visit a local school or base your study on a school you have attended. Organize your case in terms of the following categories of information:

   Environment—How would you describe the school facility or physical plant and its material and human resources? How is space organized? What is the climate of the school?

   Formal Practices—What grades are included at the school? How is the school year organized? How is time structured? How are students and teachers grouped for instruction?

   Traditions—What events and activities and products seem important to students, teachers, and administrators? What symbols, slogans, and ceremonies identify membership in the school? How do community members view and relate to the school?

   Draw conclusions from your case study: What aspects of the school culture seem to support learning and academic achievement? On the basis of your case study, draft a position statement on the kind of culture you would like to create or promote in your classroom.

Appendix 4.1

School Safety Checklist

Give your school a thorough crime prevention inspection now. Use this checklist as a
guideline to determine your school's strengths and weaknesses.

	Yes	No
1. Is there a policy for dealing with violence and vandalism in your school? (The reporting policy must be realistic and strictly adhered to.)	_____	_____
2. Is there an incident reporting system?	_____	_____
3. Is the incident reporting system available to all staff?	_____	_____
4. Is there statistical information available as to the scope of the problems at your school and in the community?	_____	_____
5. Have the school, school board and administrators taken steps or anticipated any problems through dialogue?	_____	_____
6. Does security fit into the organization of the school? (Security must be designed to fit the needs of the administration and made part of the site.)	_____	_____
7. Are the teachers and administrators aware of laws that pertain to them? To their rights? To students' rights? Of their responsibility as to enforcement of and respect for rules, regulations, policies, and the law?	_____	_____
8. Is there a working relationship with your local law enforcement agency?	_____	_____
9. Are students and parents aware of expectations and school discipline codes?		
10. Are there any actual or contingency action plans developed to deal with student disruptions and vandalism?	_____	_____
11. Is there a policy as to restitution or prosecution of perpetrators of violence and vandalism?	_____	_____
12. Is there any in-service training available for teachers and staff in the areas of violence and vandalism and other required reporting procedures?	_____	_____
13. Is there a policy for consistent monitoring and evaluation of incident reports?	_____	_____
14. Is the staff trained in standard crime prevention behavior?	_____	_____

Source: Excerpted from *The School Safety Check Book* by the National School Safety Center, 141
Duesenberg Dr., Suite 16, Westlake Village, CA, 91362, http://www.nssc1.org.

Appendix 4.2

Selected Resources for Meeting Needs of Students Placed at Risk

Organizations

American Red Cross
431 18th Street NW
Washington, DC 20006
(703) 206-6750

Center for Research on the Education of Students Placed At Risk
Johns Hopkins University
3003 North Charles Street, Suite 200
Baltimore, MD 21218
(410) 516-8800

Child and Family Policy Center
218 6th Avenue Suite 1021
Des Moines, IA 50309-4006
(515) 280-9027

Children's Defense Fund
25 E Street, NW
Washington, DC 20001
(202) 628-8787

The Family Resource Coalition of America
200 South Michigan Avenue
Chicago, IL 60604
(312) 341-0900

Foundation for Child Development
345 E. 46th Street Suite 700
New York, NY 10017
(212) 697-3150

National Coalition of Hispanic and Human Service Organizations
1501 16th Street
NW Washington, DC 20036
(202) 387-5000

National Community Education Association
3929 Old Lee Highway, Suite 91A
Fairfax, VA 22030
(703) 359-8973

National Institute on the Education of At-Risk Students
U.S. Department of Education

OERI/At-Risk Room
610 555 New Jersey Avenue, NW
Washington, DC 20208-5521

Books on Teaching Students at Risk

101 Ways to Develop Student Self-Esteem and Responsibility. Jack Canfield and Frank Siccone. Boston: Allyn and Bacon, 1994.

Against The Odds: How "At-risk" Children Exceed Expectations. Janie Bempechat. San Francisco: Jossey-Bass, 1998

Assessment and Instruction of Culturally and Linguistically Diverse Students with or At-risk of Learning Problems: From Research to Practice. Virginia Gonzalez, Rita Brusca-Vega, and Thomas Yawkey. Boston: Allyn and Bacon, 1997.

At-risk Students: Tools for Teaching in Problem Settings. Susan L. Peterson. San Francisco: International Scholars Publications, 1998.

Beyond Discipline: From Compliance to Community. Alfie Kohn. Alexandria, VA: Association for Supervision and Curriculum Development, 1996.

Building a Full-Service School: A Step-by-Step Guide. Carol Calfee, Frank Wittwer, and Mimi Meredith. San Francisco: Jossey-Bass, 1998.

Education Reform and Students at Risk. Robert J. Rossi and Samuel C. Stringfield. Washington, DC: U.S. Department of Education, 1997.

Get to School Safely! Washington, DC: National Institute on the Education of At-Risk Students.

Hope at Last for At-Risk Youth. R.D. Barr and W.H. Parrett. Boston: Allyn and Bacon, 1995.

Last Chance High: How Girls and Boys Drop In and Out of Alternative Schools. Kelly Deiredre. New Haven, CT: Yale University Press, 1993.

Mentoring Students at Risk: An Underutilized Alternative Education Strategy for K-12 Teachers. Gary Reglen. Springfield, IL: Charles C. Thomas Publishers, 1998.

The New Circles of Learning: Cooperation in the Classroom and School. David W. Johnson, Roger T.

Johnson, and Edythe J. Holubec. Alexandria, VA: Association for Supervision and Curriculum Development, 1994.

Open Lives, Safe Schools. Donovan R. Walling (Ed.). Bloomington, IN: Phi Delta Kappa Educational Foundation, 1996.

Reducing School Violence through Conflict Resolution. David W. Johnson and Roger T. Johnson. Alexandria, VA: Association for Supervision and Curriculum Development, 1995.

Resiliency in Schools: Making It Happen for Students and Educators. Nan Henderson and Mike M. Milstein. Thousand Oaks, CA: Corwin Press, 1996.

Safe Passage: Making It Through Adolescence in a Risky Society. Joy G. Dryfoos. New York: Oxford University Press, 1998.

A School for Healing: Alternative Strategies for Teaching At-risk Students. Rosa L. Kennedy and Jerome H. Morton. New York: P. Lang, 1999.

The School Safety Handbook: Taking Action for Student and Staff Protection. Kenneth Lane, Michael D. Richardson, and Dennis W. Van Berkum (Eds.). Lancaster, PA: Technomic Publishing Company, 1996.

Students at Risk. H. Lee Manning and Leroy G. Baruth. Boston: Allyn and Bacon, 1995.

Talk It Out: Conflict Resolution in the Elementary Classroom. Barbara Porro. Alexandria, VA: Association for Supervision and Curriculum Development, 1996.

Teaching Mainstreamed, Diverse, and At-risk Students in the General Education Classroom. Sharon Vaughn, Candace S. Bos, and Jeanne S. Schumm. Boston: Allyn and Bacon, 1997.

Teaching Social Competence: A Practical Approach for Improving Social Skills in Students At-risk. Dennis R. Knapczyk and Paul Rodes. Pacific Grove, CA: Brooks/Cole, Pub. Co., 1996.

Toward Resiliency: At-risk Students Who Make It to College. Laura J. Horn, Xianglei Chen, and Clifford Adelman. Washington, DC: U.S. Department of Education.

Treating Adolescent Substance Abuse: Understanding the Fundamental Elements. George R. Ross. Boston: Allyn and Bacon, 1994.

Using Educational Technology with At-risk Students: A Guide for Library Media Specialists and Teachers. Roxanne B. Mendrinos. Westport, CT: Greenwood Press, 1997.

Waiting for a Miracle: Why Schools Can't Solve Our Problems—And How We Can. James P. Comer. New York: Dutton, 1997.

5

Struggles for Control of Schools in the United States

In the late 1990s, we asked teachers to estimate the current status of the teacher empowerment reform effort at their school. . . . Two-thirds of the teachers responded that the reforms had been incorporated either in a robust and major way or in a partial but still significant way.

—Gerald Grant and Christine E. Murray
Teaching in America: The Slow Revolution

1. Who is involved in the struggles for control of schools in the United States?

2. What is the role of the local community in school governance?

3. What powers and influence do states have in governing schools?

4. What assistance do regional education agencies provide?

5. How does the federal government influence education?

6. How are schools financed in the United States?

7. What are some trends in funding for equity and excellence?

focus questions

O n entering the teachers' lounge during your planning period, you can tell immediately that the four teachers in the room are having a heated discussion.

"I don't see how you can say that teachers have much control over the schools," says Kim, a language arts teacher who came to the school three years ago. "It's all so political. The feds, our legislators, the school board—it's the politicians who really control the schools. This April all my kids have to take a test based on the new state standards—we didn't write the standards, it was the politicians. They exploit the schools just so they can get elected."

"If you want to know who *really* controls the schools," Enrique, a mathematics teacher, says, "it's big business. The politicians are actually their pawns. Big business is concerned about international competition—so, they exert tremendous pressure on the politicians who, in turn, lean on the teachers. And then. . ."

"Just a minute," says Frank, raising his hand to silence Enrique. Frank is one of the school's lead teachers and chair of the site-based council. "Maybe that's the way things were in the past, but things *are* changing. I'm not saying that politics or big business doesn't influence the schools, but we have a lot of influence over what we teach and how. Look at our site-based council and all the decisions we've made during the last two years—block scheduling, teaching teams, a common planning time, and integrated curricula."

"Right, teaching really is changing," says Roberta, a science teacher and multimedia coordinator for the school. She motions for you to have a seat at the table. Feeling a bit uncomfortable at the intensity of the discussion, but anxious to fit in with your new colleagues, you take a seat. "When I first started teaching ten years ago," Roberta continues, "I never thought I'd see as many changes as I've seen in the last few years."

"Name one change," says Kim. "Things are still top-down. The politicians, the governor, the school board, the superintendent, the principal—they all tell us what to do."

"Well, like Frank said, look at all the decisions our site-based council has made," Roberta answers. "Plus, just think about the National Board for Professional Teaching Standards—now we've got the option of becoming board certified, just like lawyers have the bar exam and architects have their licensing exam. Also, the majority of the board is made up of teachers, and they helped to develop the standards."

"Good example," Frank says. "Already there's a few thousand board-certified teachers, and there's supposed to be more than 100,000 by 2005. I'm working on my portfolio so I can apply next year."

"It's just a matter of time before board-certified teachers come to have more leverage in controlling the schools," says Roberta. "With more and more districts moving to some sort of school choice, the school that has more board-certified teachers is going to attract more students. So, teachers with board certification will be able to set the conditions under which they work. The market value of board certification is going to rise."

"Exactly," says Frank. "Right now in North Carolina, board-certified teachers get a 12 percent increase in pay."

"Well, I don't quite share your optimism about how teachers are going to have all this influence," says Kim. "Look at every presidential election—the Democrats and Republicans always try to exploit education. So, they talk about all the changes they'd make . . . higher standards, more accountability for teachers, more input for parents, and so on. Plus all politicians—whether they're running for president, governor, or whatever—they use education to build their political careers, and teachers are the ones who have to implement their utopian ideas."

"I agree to some extent," says Roberta. "Politicians will always use education for their own ends. But that's just rhetoric; what's really happening, bit by bit, is that teachers are becoming much more influential."

"Let's just ask this new teacher here," says Frank as he smiles and nods in your direction. "Don't you think teachers have a lot of influence over how schools are run? During the rest of your career, you'll be involved in school governance, won't you?"

Frank, Roberta, Enrique, and Kim look at you, awaiting your response. What do you say?

Who Is Involved in the Struggles for Control of Schools in the United States?

Professional teachers recognize the need to understand the many complex political forces that currently influence schools in the United States (see Figure 5.1). For example, the opening scenario for this chapter illustrates how teachers and various political interest groups seek to influence policies related to school governance. Clearly, teachers have much to gain from becoming politically involved; and, as the title of a guide to political action for teachers suggests, *You Can Make a Difference* (Keresty, O'Leary, and Wortley 1998). (Appendix 5.1 presents "Guidelines for Teachers to Think and Act Politically" and "25 Ways to Become Involved.")

During the twenty-first century, struggles for control of schools in the United States will continue. Among the groups that will continue to have a keen concern for shaping educational policies, at least nine can be identified:

1. *Parents*—Concerned with controlling local schools so that quality educational programs are available to their children
2. *Students*—Concerned with policies related to freedom of expression, dress, behavior, and curricular offerings
3. *Teachers*—Concerned with their role in school reform, improving working conditions, terms of employment, and other professional issues
4. *Administrators*—Concerned with providing leadership so that various interest groups, including teachers, participate in the shared governance of schools and the development of quality educational programs
5. *Taxpayers*—Concerned with maintaining an appropriate formula for determining local, state, and federal financial support of schools

Figure 5.1

Political influences on the schools

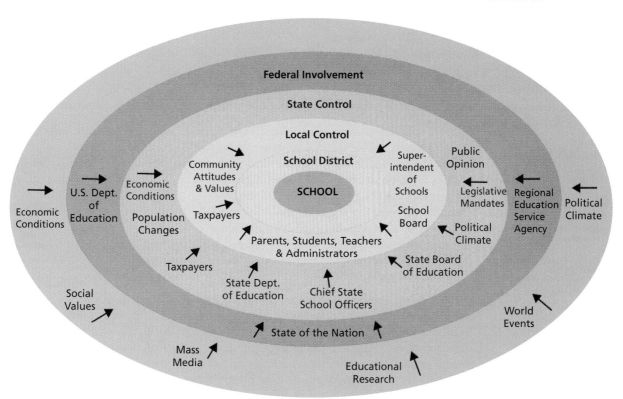

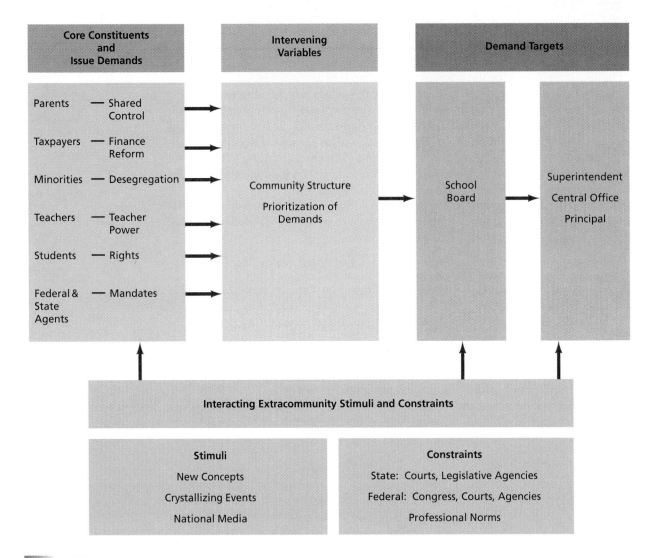

Core Constituents and Issue Demands	Intervening Variables	Demand Targets
Parents — Shared Control		
Taxpayers — Finance Reform	Community Structure	School Board
Minorities — Desegregation	Prioritization of Demands	Superintendent Central Office Principal
Teachers — Teacher Power		
Students — Rights		
Federal & State Agents — Mandates		

Interacting Extracommunity Stimuli and Constraints

Stimuli	Constraints
New Concepts	State: Courts, Legislative Agencies
Crystallizing Events	Federal: Congress, Courts, Agencies
National Media	Professional Norms

Figure 5.2

School politics
Source: Adapted from Frederick M. Wirt and Michael W. Kirst, *The Political Dynamics of American Education.* 2d ed. (Berkeley, CA: McCutcheon, 1997), p. 34. Used with permission.

6. *State and federal authorities*—Concerned with the implementation of court orders, guidelines, and legislative mandates related to the operation of schools
7. *Minorities and women*—Concerned with the availability of equal educational opportunity for all and with legal issues surrounding administrative certification, terms of employment, and evaluation
8. *Educational theorists and researchers*—Concerned with using theoretical and research-based insights as the bases for improving schools at all levels
9. *Businesses and corporations*—Concerned with receiving from the schools graduates who have the knowledge, skills, attitudes, and values to help an organization realize its goals

Out of the complex and often turbulent interactions of these groups, school policies are developed. And, as strange as it may seem, no one of these groups can be said to control today's schools. As Seymour Sarason (1997, 36), author of several books on the complexities of educational change, points out, education in the United States *"is a system in which accountability is so diffused that no one is accountable"* (italics in original). Those who we might imagine control schools—principals, superintendents, and boards of education—are in reality responding to shifting sets of conditions created by those who have an interest in the schools. In addition, schools are influenced by several out-of-school factors—what sociologists have termed *environmental press*. Because schools reflect the society they serve, they are influenced directly and indirectly by factors such as those illustrated in Figure 5.1.

Clearly, it is difficult to untangle the web of political forces that influence schools. Figure 5.2 shows graphically how school authorities are confronted with the difficult task of funneling the input from various sources into unified, coherent school programs. In the next four sections of this chapter, we examine the many political forces that impinge on the schools by looking at how they are influenced at the local, state, federal, and regional levels.

What Is the Role of the Local Community in School Governance?

The Constitution does not address the issue of public education, but the Tenth Amendment is used as the basis for giving states the responsibility for the governance of education, that is, the legal authority to create and manage school systems. In addition, as seen in Figure 5.2, various individuals and groups, though not legally empowered, do exercise local control over schools by trying to influence those legally entitled to operate the schools.

The Tenth Amendment gives to the states all powers not reserved for the federal government and not prohibited to the states. The states have, in turn, created local school districts, giving them responsibility for the daily operation of public schools. As a result of efforts to consolidate districts, the number of local public school districts has declined from 119,001 in 1937–38 to 14,841 in 1996–97 (National Center for Education Statistics 1998a, 97).

Local School District

Local school districts vary greatly in regard to demographics such as number of school-age children; educational, occupational, and income levels of parents; operating budget; number of teachers; economic resources; and number of school buildings. Some serve ultrawealthy communities, others impoverished ghetto neighborhoods or rural areas. Their operations include 487 one-teacher elementary schools in this country (National Center for Education Statistics 1999) as well as scores of modern, multi-building campuses in heavily populated areas. The largest school districts are exceedingly complex operations with multimillion-dollar-a-year operating budgets (see Table 5.1) The largest—the New York City school system—has more than a million pupils (from 190 countries), more than 57,000 teachers (a number that exceeds the number of *students* in Cincinnati; Minneapolis; Portland, Oregon; Sacramento; Seattle; and St. Louis), 1,100 schools, and total annual expenditures of almost $9 billion. The New York system, overseen by a Schools Chancellor, consists of 32 community school districts, each with its own superintendent.

School districts also differ in regard to their organizational structures. Large urban systems, which may contain several districts, tend to have more complex distribution of roles and responsibilities than do smaller districts. Appendix 5.2 presents a typical organizational structure for a school district of about 20,000 pupils, while the Appendix "New York City Board of Education" on this book's web site presents the organizational structure for the New York City Board of Education.

School Board

A **school board,** acting as a state agent, is responsible for the following important activities: approving the teachers, administrators, and other school personnel hired by the superintendent; developing organizational and educational policies; and determining procedures for the evaluation of programs and personnel.

In most communities, school board members are elected in general elections. In some urban areas, however, board members are selected by the mayor. Board members typically serve a minimum of three to five years, and their terms of office are usually staggered. School boards usually range in size from five to fifteen members, with five or seven frequently suggested as the optimum size. Board members in urban areas usually are paid, but in most other areas are not.

A national survey of school board members revealed that women constituted 39.1 percent of school boards and men 54.1 percent (nonresponses and rounding account for the other 6.8 percent). The survey also revealed that minority membership on school boards was 10.9 percent. School board members were somewhat atypical of the general population in other ways: They were older (46.6 percent were between forty-one and fifty years old, with another 24.2 percent between fifty-one and sixty), and they were more affluent—the family income of 45.3 percent of 1998 board members was over $80,000, and over $100,000 for 28 percent (*American School Board Journal* 1998, A15).

Nearly all school board meetings are open to the public; in fact, many communities even provide radio and television coverage. Open meetings allow parents and interested citizens an opportunity to express their concerns and to get more information about problems in the district.

Criticism of school boards has increased recently, with some critics suggesting that school boards should focus more on removing barriers to student learning (Mental Health in Schools Center 1998). Other critics have pointed out that school boards often

- fail to provide far-reaching or politically risky leadership for reform;
- have become another level of administration, often micromanaging districts;
- are so splintered by members' attempts to represent special interests or meet their individual political needs that boards cannot govern effectively;
- are not spending enough time on educating themselves about issues or about education policy making; and
- exhibit serious problems in their capacity to develop positive and productive, lasting relationships with superintendents (Danzberger 1994a, 369).

Some states have taken steps to reform school boards. For example, West Virginia implemented legislation in 1994 to restructure school boards "so that they become well-informed, responsive, policy-making bodies." Board members now serve for four years rather than six, and they must complete training focused on "boardmanship and governing effectiveness" (Danzberger 1994b, 394).

Superintendent of Schools

Though school boards operate very differently, the **superintendent** is invariably the key figure in determining a district's educational policy. The superintendent is the chief administrator of the school district, the person charged with the responsibility of seeing to it that schools operate in accord with federal and state guidelines as well as policies set by the local school board. Though the board of education delegates broad powers to the superintendent, his or her policies require board approval.

How the superintendent and his or her board work together appears to be related

Table 5.1

Selected data for the ten largest public school systems, 1996–1997

School System	Total Enrollment	Number of Teachers*	Pupil/ Teacher Ratio	Number of Schools	Total Expenditures in Thousands	Expenditure per Pupil
New York City	1,063,561	57,338	18.5	1,120	$8,938,067	$7,617
Los Angeles Unified	667,305	28,492	23.4	642	$3,395,358	$5,176
City of Chicago	469,098	23,433	20.0	567	$2,527,901	$6,064
Miami-Dade County	341,117	17,241	19.8	322	$2,209,145	$5,734
Broward County, FL	218,608	10,341	21.1	193	$1,248,289	$5,140
Philadelphia	212,150	11,144	19.0	259	$1,102,589	$5,104
Houston Independent School District	209,375	11,853	17.7	286	$1,050,508	$4,785
Hawaii Public Schools	187,653	10,576	17.7	249	$1,110,820	$5,595
Detroit Public Schools	182,316	8,808	20.7	279	$1,224,334	$6,953
Clark County, NV	179,106	8,875	20.2	211	$787,854	$4,584

*Data exclude teachers reported as working in school district offices rather than in schools.

Source: U.S. Department of Education, National Center for Education Statistics, Common Core of Data survey. (Table prepared February 1999.) Adapted from *Digest of Education Statistics 1998*, Washington, DC: National Center for Education Statistics, U.S. Department of Education, pp. 99–115.

to the size of the school district, with superintendents and school boards in larger districts more likely to be in conflict. School boards in smaller districts, however, are more effective when they do oppose the superintendent. In large districts, the board's own divisiveness makes it less likely that the board will successfully oppose the superintendent (Wirt and Kirst 1997).

Superintendents must have great skill to respond appropriately to the many external political forces that demand their attention, and conflict is inevitable. Effective superintendents demonstrate that they are able to play three roles simultaneously: politician, manager, and teacher. It is a demanding position, and turnover is high; for example, between 1980 and 1995, the New York City school system had ten chancellors (Hurwitz, April 1999).

The Role of Parents

Parents may not be involved legally in the governance of schools, but they do play an important role in education. One characteristic of successful schools is that they have developed close working relationships with parents. Additionally, children whose parents or guardians support and encourage school activities have a definite advantage in school.

Through participation on school advisory and site-based councils, parents are making an important contribution to restructuring and school reform efforts around the country. In addition, groups such as the Parent-Teacher Association (PTA), Parent-Teacher Organization (PTO), or Parent Advisory Council (PAC) give parents the opportunity to communicate with teachers on matters of interest and importance to them.

Marcia McVey
School District Superintendent

"... getting involved in the community ..."

On the shelves in Marcia McVey's office are dozens of statues of elephants. They vary in size and material—wood, ceramic, cloth, and crystal. The collection began when she was named superintendent of the Duarte, California, Independent School District. In her interview with the school board, the body that selects the superintendent, she had used an elephant metaphor to convey her vision for the district's future. She explained that most people in a school district are like people who focus on only one part of the elephant instead of the whole animal. As a consequence, different people have different pictures of the elephant—or the school district. However, she personally enjoys having the big picture and seeing the elephant whole.

In her extended metaphor, the personnel office of the school district is the heart of the elephant, the school board its head, the principals and teachers its legs, and the children the body. "It takes all parts to make the body move ahead," she told the board. Then she suggested that this elephant was ailing and that she saw herself as an elephant doctor.

The board unanimously selected her to be superintendent and, during their first closed session, presented her with a beautiful statue of an elephant. Later they gave her a matching elephant in recognition of one of her early accomplishments as superintendent. She soon discovered that elephants were the gift of choice whenever someone at work wanted to celebrate her birthdays and achievements or simply to thank her. Over the five years of McVey's superintendency her unplanned collection grew to over 100 elephants, a tangible expression of appreciation from the board members, district office administrators, principals, teachers, clerks, parents, and custodians whose lives she touched.

McVey's career path in education is like a tour through a school district's organization chart. She began as a classroom teacher and for ten years taught grades 4 through 11. Then she worked for three years as a school counselor in an intermediate school and as its assistant principal for a year. Over the next ten years she served as principal at two elementary schools. During that time, she took a year's leave of absence to work at the state level on the California State Department of Education Task Force on Conflict Resolution in the Secondary Schools. Then she left elementary school administration to work in the district office as the Director of Curriculum and Instruction

Through these groups, parents can become involved in the life of the school in a variety of ways—from making recommendations regarding school policies to providing much-needed volunteer services, or to initiating school-improvement activities such as fund-raising drives.

Many parents are also influencing the character of education through their involvement with the growing number of private, parochial, for-profit, and charter schools. In addition, many parents are activists in promoting school choice, voucher systems, and the home schooling movement. In their effort to influence schools in the United States, some parents even join well-funded conservative think tanks that launch sophisticated national campaigns to remove from public schools practices and materials that they believe have links to secular humanist or New Age beliefs. According to a book titled *School Wars: Resolving Our Conflicts over Religion and Values*, educational reform initiatives targeted by activist parents have included "outcome-based education, the whole language approach [to teaching reading], thinking skills programs, imagery

K–12. Four years later she began what, in retrospect, seems like a march to the superintendency—three years as assistant superintendent in one district, four years as assistant superintendent in another, two years as deputy superintendent, and then the superintendency that launched her elephant collection! After retiring from the superintendency, having served 36 years in K–12 education, she began teaching future principals and superintendents in the Education Administration Department of a local university. Her graduate students say that she challenges them, pushes them to do their best, and cares about them as people, taking their concerns seriously and helping them locate the right administration position for them. The fifteen students in her first university class continue to communicate with her by e-mail.

When she is asked which of the education positions she has held she liked best, she replies that *each* was the best: "I've always loved what I was doing. As a counselor, I could be a spokesperson for the students; as a principal, I loved working with a team—the parents, teachers, students, everyone. The work as director of curriculum was challenging, and it impacted a whole school district. We decided what the curriculum should be, developed it, and helped see that it was implemented. That was fun. As the superintendent I worked with teams again, empowering principals, getting involved in the community, and communicating regularly with the school board."

Discussing key issues she dealt with as superintendent, McVey noted three areas—money, people, and instruction. Challenges in the first area included, "seeing that positive collective bargaining agreements were negotiated in a timely and fair manner and having to communicate to employees why there wasn't sufficient funding for salary increases. Secondary and integral to this one was building a team, so valued employees didn't leave the district." And of course, balancing the budget was always a challenge.

People-related challenges were "establishing and maintaining credible personnel procedures and practices; keeping the board and all the stakeholders of a school district and the larger community up to date on all of the issues; and being accountable for the progress of the students."

In the area of instruction, McVey had to keep up with the textbook selection process, staff development, and budgets related to new textbook adoptions. A particular challenge in this area was implementing technology and instructional programs. McVey was involved in every aspect, from overseeing the wiring in all the aging buildings for new technology, acquiring hardware, gaining clerical support for the new programs, and implementing staff training and evaluation, to "finding money, establishing consortia and partnerships to make it all work."

Woven throughout McVey's comments is her appreciation of the human dimension of her work. She clearly enjoyed her superintendency—and all the education positions she has held—because of the people. "Helping people be the best that they can be has been the whole purpose of my work."

techniques, self-esteem programs, the teaching of evolution, global education and multiculturalism, and sex education" (Gaddy, Hall, and Marzano 1996, 93).

School Restructuring

At many schools across the country exciting changes are taking place in regard to how schools are controlled locally. To improve the performance of schools, to decentralize the system of governance, and to enhance the professional status of teachers, some districts are **restructuring** their school systems. Restructuring goes by several names: shared governance, administrative decentralization, teacher empowerment, professionalization, bottom-up policymaking, school-based planning, school-based management, and shared decision making. What all these approaches to school governance have in common is allowing those who know students best—teachers, principals, aides, custodians, librarians, secretaries, and parents—greater freedom in deciding how to meet students' needs.

In a synthesis of research on school restructuring at more than 1,500 schools, the Center on Organization and Restructuring of Schools at the University of Wisconsin found that the following structural conditions enhance a school's "professional community" and increase students' learning:

- Shared governance that increases teachers' influence over school policy and practice
- Interdependent work structures, such as teaching teams, which encourage collaboration
- Staff development that enhances technical skills consistent with school missions for high-quality learning
- Deregulation that provides autonomy for schools to pursue a vision of high intellectual standards
- Small school size, which increases opportunities for communication and trust
- Parent involvement in a broad range of school affairs (Newmann and Wehlage 1995, 52).

School-Based Management

One of the most frequently used approaches to restructuring schools is **school-based management (SBM).** Most SBM programs have three components in common:

1. Power and decisions formerly made by the superintendent and school board are delegated to teachers, principals, parents, community members, and students at local schools. At SBM schools, teachers can become directly involved in making decisions about curriculum, textbooks, standards for student behavior, staff development, promotion and retention policies, teacher evaluation, school budgets, and the selection of teachers and administrators.
2. At each school, a decision-making body (known as a board, cabinet, site-based team, or council)—made up of teachers, the principal, and parents—implements the SBM plan.
3. SBM programs operate with the whole-hearted endorsement of the superintendent of schools.

Chicago School Reform   A pioneer in school-based management has been the City of Chicago Public Schools. For years, the Chicago Public School System has been beset by an array of problems: low student achievement, periodic teacher strikes, budget crises, a top-heavy central bureaucracy, and schools in the decaying inner city that seemed beyond most improvement efforts. In response to these problems, the late Mayor Harold Washington appointed a fifty-five-member committee of business, education, and community leaders to develop a school reform proposal. Among the group's recommendations was the creation of a **local school council (LSC)** for each of the city's more than 550 schools, with the majority of council members being parents of schoolchildren.

In December 1988, the Illinois state legislature passed the Chicago School Reform Act, "an undertaking of enormous scope" (Bryk et al 1998, 28) and believed by some to be "the most fundamental restructuring since the early part of the twentieth century" (Moore 1992, 153). Among the provisions of the act were the following:

- School budgets would be controlled by a local school council made up of six parents, two community members, two school employees, and the principal.

- The council had the authority to hire and fire the principal.
- The council, with input from teachers and the principal, had the authority to develop an improvement plan for the local school.
- New teachers would be hired on the basis of merit, not seniority.
- Principals could remove teachers forty-five days after serving them official notice of unsatisfactory performance.
- A Professional Personnel Advisory Committee of teachers would have advisory responsibility for curriculum and instruction.

What are the goals of school restructuring? In school-based management, who participates in the governance and management of schools? How is school-based management different from the school board model of local governance?

The first six years of the Chicago Reform Act produced few concrete improvements. In 1995, frustrated with the district's chronic fiscal problems and inability to increase student achievement, the Illinois legislature gave Mayor Richard M. Daley control over Chicago's schools. Daley created a five-member "reform board of trustees" and appointed a chief executive officer (CEO) who advocated "a balance between local control and central-office control" (Hendrie, May 5, 1999).

By many accounts, the Chicago reform efforts during the last half of the 1990s were a continuing "struggle about how to improve an urban school system" (Hendrie, May 5, 1999). Friction between the mayor's management team and the parent-dominated LSCs intensified with each report that an LSC member had abused his or her authority. As a former chairwoman of a high school council said, "I've seen LSC members who had personal agendas, and I have seen them destroy schools" (Hendrie, May 5, 1999). In response to these allegations, Mayor Daley introduced a bill to allow recourse to principals fired by their LSCs, an action that the director of the Chicago Association of Local School Councils described as "just the first attempt at destroying local school councils" (Hendrie, May 5, 1999).

To date, the overall effectiveness of the Chicago program has been mixed. While the Reform Act called for all Chicago schools to reach national norms within five years, this goal was not reached (Bryk et al. 1994; Walberg and Niemiec 1994; 1996). Eight years after the reform effort was launched, the CEO of Chicago schools even admitted that "not a lot of progress has been made. . . . the bottom line is only 77 of the [557] schools have more than half of the kids at or above national averages" (Hendrie, May 5, 1999). However, "of the schools most in need of change—schools where student achievement had been well below national norms—one third had developed strong democratic support and participation within their school communities [and] were following a systemic approach toward reform. Another third displayed some of these characteristics but were not as far along in implementing change" (Hess 1995, 111). Though it has yet to result in increased student achievement, the Chicago experiment is clearly one of the more dramatic efforts to empower parents and make them full partners in the educative process.

What Powers and Influence Do States Have in Governing Schools?

Above the level of local control, states have a great influence on the governance of schools. Throughout the 1990s, the influence of the state on educational policy increased steadily. In fact, by the end of the 1990s, many states were exerting unprecedented control over public school classrooms, causing one expert in school finance to comment: "I don't think the public realizes the sea change that's occurred in who's responsible for schools. While we talk about local control, what we have is anything but local control" (*Education Week* 1999b). For example, forty-eight states had statewide academic standards in 1999 (Iowa and Nebraska were the exceptions), and thirty-nine had mandated tests aligned to those standards; also, nineteen states required high school exit exams, while eight others were considering exit exams. Moreover, twenty-three states had passed legislation allowing them to take over academically failing school districts (eleven states had done so by 1999), and ten states allowed takeovers of individual schools that were failing (*Education Week* 1999b).

In response to criticisms of U.S. education, many of which pointed to the nation's frequent low ranking in international comparisons of achievement, many states launched extensive initiatives to improve education, such as the following:

- Increased academic standards
- Greater accountability for teachers
- Testing students in teacher education programs prior to graduation
- Frequent assessments of students' mastery of basic skills
- Professional development as a criterion for continued employment of teachers
- Recertification of experienced teachers

As mentioned previously, the Tenth Amendment to the Constitution allows the states to organize and to administer education within their boundaries. To meet the responsibility of maintaining and supporting schools, the states have assumed several powers:

- The power to levy taxes for the support of schools and to determine state aid to local school districts
- The power to set the curriculum and, in some states, to identify approved textbooks
- The power to determine minimum standards for teacher certification
- The power to establish standards for accrediting schools
- The power to pass legislation necessary for the proper maintenance and support of schools

To carry out the tasks implied by these powers, the states have adopted a number of different organizational structures. Most states, however, have adopted a hierarchical structure similar to that presented in the Appendix, "Organizational Structure of a Typical State School System," on this book's web site.

The Roles of State Government in Education

Various people and agencies within each state government play a role in operating the educational system within that state. Though state governments differ in many respects, the state legislature, the state courts, and the governor have a direct, critical impact on education in their state.

The Legislature   In nearly every state, the legislature is responsible for establishing and maintaining public schools and for determining basic educational policies within the state. To accomplish these ends, the legislature has the power to enact laws related to education. Among the policies that the state legislature may determine are the following:

- How the state boards of education will be selected and what their responsibilities will be
- How the chief state school officer will be selected and what his or her duties will be
- How the state department of education will function
- How the state will be divided into local and regional districts
- How higher education will be organized and financed
- How local school boards will be selected and what their powers will be

In addition, the legislature may determine how taxes will be used to support schools, what will or will not be taught, the length of the school day and school year, how many years of compulsory education will be required, and whether or not the state will have community colleges and/or vocational/technical schools. Legislatures may also make policies that apply to such matters as pupil attendance, admission, promotion, teacher certification, teacher tenure and retirement, and collective bargaining.

The Courts From time to time, state courts are called on to uphold the power of the legislature to develop laws that apply to schools. The state courts must determine, however, that this power does not conflict with the state or federal constitution. It is important to remember, too, that the role of state courts is not to develop laws but to rule on the reasonableness of laws that apply to specific educational situations.

Perhaps no state court had a greater impact on education during the first half of the 1990s than the Kentucky Supreme Court. In 1989, the Court ruled that the state's entire school system was "inadequate." Naming the state superintendent and the state education agency as part of the problem and pointing out that Kentucky schools were ineffective and inequitable, the Court labeled the school system "unconstitutional." The Court called on the governor and the legislature to develop an entirely new system of education for the state. A twenty-two-member task force, appointed by the governor and the legislature, then developed the 906-page **Kentucky Education Reform Act (KERA)** passed in 1990. KERA required each school to form a school-based management council by 1996 with authority to set policy in eight areas: curriculum, staff time, student assignment, schedule, school space, instructional issues, discipline, and extracurricular activities. Three teachers, two parents (elected by their peers), and the principal comprised each council.

Almost ten years after its adoption, KERA had dramatically equalized funding across the state, and some school districts made substantial gains in funding for students. Though variations among district spending on education still existed, these were no longer based on "the traditional determinants of educational financing . . . local income and property wealth. Now districts with low incomes or little property value per student are just as likely to have high educational spending as are wealthy districts" (Hoyt 1999, 36). In addition, teacher salaries and student/teacher ratios improved compared to national averages. However, student achievement, as measured by test score gains or graduation rates, had not improved (Hoyt 1999).

The Governor Though the powers of governors vary greatly from state to state, a governor can, if he or she chooses, have a far-reaching impact on education within the state. The governor may appoint and/or remove educators at the state level, and in some states the governor may even appoint the chief state school officer. Furthermore, in every state except North Carolina, the governor may use his or her veto power to influence the legislature to pass certain laws related to education. Governors are also extremely influential because they make educational budget recommendations to legislatures, and, in many states, they may elect to use any accumulated balances in the state treasury for education. Governors can also have a significant impact on matters related to curriculum and instruction within the state and, indeed, across the nation. For example, in the mid-1990s, Roy Romer, governor of Colorado, was instrumental in organizing ACHIEVE, an effort by U.S. governors and corporate leaders to raise academic standards and develop accountability systems for schools. In addition, the **National Governors' Association (NGA)** is active in teacher education and school reforms.

State Board of Education

The **state board of education,** acting under the authority of the state legislature, is the highest educational agency in a state. Every state, with the exception of Wisconsin, has a state board of education. In most states there are two separate boards, one responsible for elementary through secondary education, the other for higher education.

The method of determining board members varies from state to state. In some states, the governor appoints members of the state board; in other states, members are selected through general elections. Two states have *ex officio* members who, by virtue of the positions they hold, automatically serve on the board. Most states have either seven- or nine-member boards.

People disagree on which is better: electing or appointing board members. Some believe that election to the state board may cause members to be more concerned with politics than with education. Others argue that elected board members are more aware of the wishes of the public whom the schools are supposed to serve. People in favor of appointing members to the state board suggest that appointment increases the likelihood that individuals will be chosen on the basis of merit rather than politics.

The regulatory and advisory functions generally held by state boards are as follows:

- Ensuring that local school districts adhere to legislation concerning educational policies, rules, and regulations
- Setting standards for issuing and revoking teaching and administrative certificates
- Establishing standards for accrediting schools
- Managing state monies appropriated for education
- Developing and implementing a system for collecting educational data needed for reporting and program evaluation
- Advising the governor and/or the state legislature on educational issues
- Identifying both short- and long-range educational needs in the state and developing plans to meet those needs
- Hearing all disputes arising from the implementation of its educational policies

State Department of Education

The educational program of each state is implemented by the state's department of education, under the leadership of the chief state school officer. State departments of education have a broad set of responsibilities, and they affect literally every school, school district, and teacher education program in a state. In general, the state board of education is concerned with policymaking, the **state department of education** with the day-to-day implementation of those policies. Perhaps the greatest boost for the development of state departments of education came with the federal government's Elementary and Secondary Education Act of 1965 (see Chapter 3). This act and its subsequent amendments required that local applications for federal funds to be used for innovative programs and for the education of disadvantaged, disabled, bilingual, and migrant students first receive approval from state departments of education.

Today, the responsibilities of state departments of education include (1) certifying teachers, (2) distributing state and federal funds to school districts, (3) reporting to the public the condition of education within the state, (4) ensuring that school districts adhere to state and federal guidelines, (5) accrediting schools, (6) monitoring student transportation and safety, and (7) sponsoring research and evaluation projects to improve education within the state.

Perhaps the most significant index of the steady increase in state control since the 1980s is the fact that the states now supply the majority of funding for schools. During the twenty-first century, the power and influence of state departments of education will continue to be extensive.

Chief State School Officer

The **chief state school officer** (known as the commissioner of education or superintendent of public instruction in many states) is the chief administrator of the state department of education and the head of the state board of education. In twenty-five states, the state board of education appoints the chief state school officer; in fifteen, the office is filled through a general election; and in the remaining ten, the governor appoints an individual to that position (personal communciation, Council of Chief State School Officers June 7, 1999).

Though the specific responsibilities of the chief state school officer vary from state to state, most individuals in this position hold several responsibilities in common:

1. Serving as chief administrator of the state department of education and state board of education
2. Selecting state department of education personnel
3. Recommending educational policies and budgets to the state board
4. Interpreting state school laws and state board of education policies
5. Ensuring compliance with state school laws and policies
6. Mediating controversies involving the operation of schools within the state
7. Arranging for studies, committees, and task forces to address educational problems and recommend solutions
8. Reporting on the status of education to the governor, legislature, state board, and public

What Assistance Do Regional Education Agencies Provide?

When one thinks of how schools are governed and the sources of political pressure applied to them, one typically thinks of influences originating at three levels: local, state, and federal. There is, however, an additional source of control—the regional, or intermediate, unit. The intermediate unit of educational administration, or the **Regional Educational Service Agency (RESA),** is the least understood branch of the state public school system. Through the intermediate unit, local school districts can receive supportive services that, economically and logistically, they could not provide for themselves.

Presently, about half of the states have some form of intermediate or regional unit. The average unit is made up of twenty to thirty local school districts and covers a fifty-square-mile area. The intermediate or regional unit has many different names: educational service district (in Washington), county education office (in California), education service center (in Texas), intermediate school district (in Michigan), multicounty educational service unit (in Nebraska), and board of cooperative educational services (in New York).

The primary role of the intermediate unit is to provide assistance directly to districts in the areas of staff development, curriculum development, instructional media, and program evaluation. Intermediate or regional units also help school districts with their school improvement efforts by providing help in targeted areas such as bilingual education, vocational education, educational technology, and the education of gifted and talented students and students with disabilities. Although intermediate units do monitor local school districts to see that they follow state educational guidelines, local districts, in fact, exert great influence over RESAs by identifying district-level needs that can be met by the intermediate unit.

How Does the Federal Government Influence Education?

Since the birth of the United States, the federal government has played a major role in shaping the character of schools. This branch of government has always recognized that the strength and well-being of the country are directly related to the quality of its schools. The importance of a quality education, for example, has been highlighted by many U.S. Supreme Court rulings supporting the free speech rights of teachers and students under the First Amendment and the right of all citizens to equal educational opportunity under the Fourteenth Amendment. During the twenty-first century it is clear that the nation will face unprecedented levels of both global competition and the need for greater international cooperation. A rapidly changing, increasingly complex society will require a better-educated workforce to compete and cooperate successfully.

The federal government has taken aggressive initiatives to influence education at several points in U.S. history, such as the allocation of federal money to improve science, mathematics, and foreign language education after Russia launched the world's first satellite. During World War II, the federal government funded several new educational programs. One of these, the Lanham Act (1941), provided funding for (1) the training of workers in war plants by U.S. Office of Education personnel, (2) the construction of schools in areas where military personnel and workers on federal projects resided, and (3) the provision of child care for the children of working parents.

Another influential and extensive federal program in support of education was the Servicemen's Readjustment Act, popularly known as the **G.I. Bill of Rights.** Signed into law by President Franklin D. Roosevelt in 1944, the G.I. Bill has provided millions of veterans with payments for tuition and room and board at colleges and universities and at technical schools. Similar legislation was later passed to grant educational benefits to veterans of the Korean and Vietnam conflicts. Not only did the G.I. Bill stim-

highlights

How should federal revenues be distributed to the states for the purchase of educational technology?

It has been suggested that "school technology has become the educational initiative *du jour* for lawmakers across the nation and of every political stripe. They might argue vehemently about school choice and national standards, but they're in almost total agreement when it comes to the need for computers and other kinds of technology in the classroom" (White 1997). In spite of this widespread support for technology in the schools, the percentage of high-tech schools differs significantly from state to state (see the accompanying table).

Percentage of High-Tech Schools*

Alabama	6%	Montana	20%
Alaska	32%	Nebraska	36%
Arizona	13%	Nevada	15%
Arkansas	10%	New Hampshire	14%
California	10%	New Jersey	14%
Colorado	29%	New Mexico	18%
Connecticut	14%	New York	15%
Delaware	17%	North Carolina	24%
Florida	29%	North Dakota	31%
Georgia	23%	Ohio	13%
Hawaii	26%	Oklahoma	10%
Idaho	27%	Oregon	24%
Illinois	26%	Pennsylvania	12%
Indiana	23%	Rhode Island	10%
Iowa	25%	South Carolina	14%
Kansas	25%	South Dakota	18%
Kentucky	18%	Tennessee	27%
Louisiana	7%	Texas	15%
Maine	25%	Utah	20%
Maryland	19%	Vermont	22%
Massachusetts	14%	Virginia	23%
Michigan	16%	Washington	20%
Minnesota	36%	West Virginia	12%
Mississippi	7%	Wisconsin	19%
Missouri	16%	Wyoming	31%

*Schools with a computer network system, Internet access, and better-than-average availability of computers and CD-ROMs. Based on mail and phone survey responses from 55,000 schools.

Source: Market Data Retrieval for the Milken Exchange on Education Technology, 1997. Taken from *Education Week on the Web* (http://www.edweek.org/sreports/tc/policy/po-t.htm). Used by permission of the publisher.

One approach to reducing these inequities would be to earmark federal funds for educational technology. In fact, a survey revealed that 61 percent of voters would be willing to pay $100 more in federal taxes if the additional money were used *only* to equip public schools with computers and up-to-date technology (see the accompanying figure). What would be an equitable way to distribute federal money to the states for the purchase of educational technology? In developing your solution, keep in mind two points: (1) "many states have little information on how much technology is in their schools, much less whether it is being used effectively," and "states are taking widely differing approaches to increasing [educational technology]. Many [are] emphasizing multimedia computers; others are putting their money into Internet access or distance learning" (White 1997).

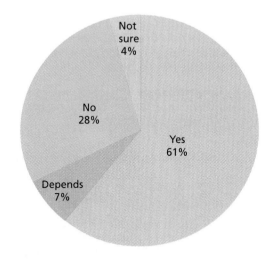

Financial support

Would you be willing to pay $100 more in federal taxes if the additional money were used *only* to equip public schools with computers and up-to-date technology?
Note: 1,012 voters polled by telephone.
Source: Peter D. Hart Research Associates Inc. for the Milken Exchange on Education Technology, 1997. Taken from *Education Week on the Web* (http://www.ed.week.org/sreports/tc/policy/po-c2.htm. Used by permission of the publisher.)

ulate the growth of colleges and universities in the United States, but it also opened higher education to an older and nontraditional student population.

The executive, legislative, and judicial branches of the federal government influence education in four ways:

1. *Exert moral suasion*—develop a vision and promote educational goals for the nation; for example, William Bennett, Secretary of Education during the Reagan administration, referred to the "Bully Pulpit" he used to promote policies and programs
2. *Provide categorical aid*—assist school systems with funding if they adopt federally endorsed programs, methods, or curricula
3. *Regulate*—withhold federal funds if a school system fails to follow legal statutes related to equal educational opportunity
4. *Fund educational research*—identify and then fund research projects related to federal goals for education

The Impact of Presidential Policies

Presidential platforms on education often have a profound effect on education. Ronald Reagan's two terms of office (1980–1988) and George Bush's term (1988–1992), for example, saw a significant shift in the federal government's role in education. In general, these two administrations sought to scale back what some viewed as excessive federal involvement in education. During Bill Clinton's two terms of office (1992-2000), the federal government assumed a more active role in ensuring equal educational opportunity. As President Clinton (1999) said of the "Educational Excellence for All Children Act of 1999," his proposal to reauthorize the Elementary and Secondary Education Act (ESEA):

[T]his legislation strengthens accountability for results. It says that states and school districts that choose to accept federal aid must take responsibility for turning around failing schools, or shutting them down. It says they must give parents report cards not just on their children, but on the children's schools. It says school districts must have strong discipline codes that are fair, consistent, and focused on prevention. It says they must make sure that teachers actually know the subjects they are teaching. It says they must stop the practice of social promotion, not by holding students back, but by making sure they have the support to meet the higher standards.

"To meet our responsibility to create twenty-first century schools for all our children, we have to do a far, far better job of spending the $15 billion in federal aid we send to our schools every year." (White House press briefing, May 19, 1999.)

U.S. Department of Education

In addition to supporting educational research, disseminating the results of research, and administering federal grants, the U.S. Department of Education advises the president on setting a platform for his educational agenda. For example, Secretary of Education Richard Riley and President Clinton promoted the following educational initiatives for fiscal year 1999:

1. All students will read independently and well by the end of third grade.
2. All students will master challenging mathematics, including the foundations of algebra and geometry, by the end of eighth grade.
3. By eighteen years of age, all students will be prepared for and able to afford college.
4. All states and schools will have challenging and clear standards of achievement and accountability for all children, and effective strategies for teaching those standards.
5. There will be a talented, dedicated, and well-prepared teacher in every classroom.
6. Every classroom will be connected to the Internet by 2000 and all students will be technologically literate.
7. Every school will be strong, safe, drug-free, and disciplined.

 **Professional Reflection** | **Examining the tension between federal and state roles in education**

At times, the roles of the federal and state governments in education are in conflict. As the trend continues toward increased state control over educational policies, teachers and students may be increasingly affected by partisan politics. For example, in 1996, legislators in one state were unable to override the governor's veto of the state's participation in the Goals 2000 program. The governor, claiming that Goals 2000 would give the federal government too much control over education in the state, said, "Our children's future is more important than a few pennies per child in federal funding accompanied by dictates. Now is no time to turn control of our reforms over to federal bureaucrats and politicians. . ." (*Education Week* 1996b, 14).

In your teacher's journal, identify some issues of state versus federal control that might affect you as a prospective teacher and later as a professional educator. For each issue you identify, do you support greater states' rights or greater federal involvement? Explain your reasons.

How Are Schools Financed in the United States?

To provide free public education to all school-age children in the United States is a costly undertaking. Schools must provide services and facilities to students from a wide range of ethnic, racial, social, cultural, linguistic and individual backgrounds. Expenditures for these services and facilities have been rising rapidly and are expected to continue rising through 2008 (see Figure 5.3). Total expenditures for public elementary and secondary schools in 1997–98 were $351 billion, and the total **expen-**

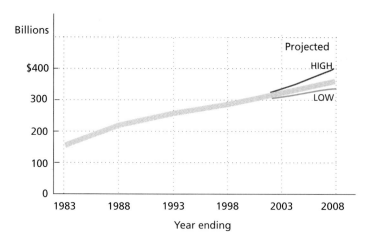

Figure 5.3

Current expenditures of public schools (in constant 1995–96 dollars), with alternative projections: 1982–83 to 2007–08
Source: Projections of Education Statistics to 2008, Figure 51. Washington DC: National Center for Education Statisitics, 1998

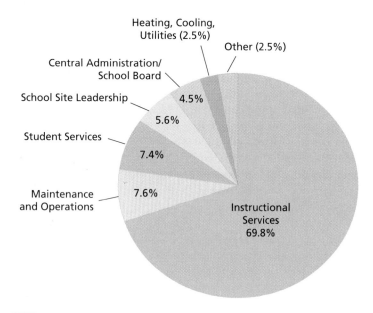

Figure 5.4

Average allocation of the 1996–97 school district operating budget
Source: Educational Research Service (ERS) National Survey of School District Budgets, 1996–97. In Nancy Protheroe, *School Administration under Attack: What Are the Facts?* Copyright © by Educational Research Service, p. 32. Used with permission.

diture per pupil was $7,502 (in constant 1997-98 dollars) (National Center for Education Statistics 1999, 35). Figure 5.4 shows how the budget for a typical school district is allocated.

Financing an enterprise as vast and ambitious as the United States system of free public schools has not been easy. It has proved difficult both to devise a system that equitably distributes the tax burden for supporting schools and to provide equal educational services and facilities for all students. And, "rather than one national education system [in the United States], there are fifty state systems that raise revenues from local, state, and federal sources. Dollars are distributed quite unequally across the states, districts, and schools. And only a small fraction of the education dollar supports regular classroom instruction—significant proportions are spent in schools, but outside of the classroom" (Odden and Busch 1998, 4). Moreover, there has been a tendency for the financial support of schools to be outpaced by factors that continually increase the cost of operating schools, such as inflation, rising enrollments, and the need to update aging facilities. According to the 1999 Gallup Poll of the public's attitudes toward the public schools, lack of financial support/funding/money was seen as the number three problem (after lack of discipline/more control and fighting/violence/gangs) confronting local schools. Moreover, "finances/funding" topped the list of what the public views as the "main obstacle" to improving schools in their communities.

A combination of revenues from local, state, and federal sources is used to finance public elementary and secondary schools in the United States. As Table 5.2 shows, schools received almost half of their 1995–96 funding from the state, 45.9 percent from local and other sources, and 6.6 percent from the federal government. Since 1980, schools have received almost equal funding from local and state sources; prior to that date, however, schools received most of their revenues from local sources, and early in the twentieth century, nearly all school revenues were generated from local property taxes. The 1998 Gallup Poll revealed that the public is undecided about the best way to finance schools: 21 percent

Table 5.2

**Revenues for public elementary and secondary schools, by source of funds:
1919–20 to 1995–96**

School Year	Percentage Distribution		
	Federal	State	Local (including intermediate)*
1919–20	0.3	16.5	83.2
1929–30	0.4	16.9	82.7
1939–40	1.8	30.3	68.0
1949–50	2.9	39.8	57.3
1959–60	4.4	39.1	56.5
1969–70	8.0	39.9	52.1
1979–80	9.8	46.8	43.4
1989–90	6.1	47.1	46.8
1992–93	7.0	45.8	47.2
1993–94	7.1	45.2	47.8
1994–95**	6.8	46.8	46.4
1995–96	6.6	47.5	45.9

*Includes a relatively small amount from nongovernmental private sources (gifts and tuition and transportation fees from patrons). These sources accounted for 2.6 percent of total revenues in 1995–96.

**Revised from previously published figures.

Note: Beginning in 1980–81, revenues for state education agencies are excluded. Beginning in 1988–89, data reflect new survey collection procedures and may not be entirely comparable with figures for earlier years. Because of rounding, details may not add to totals.

Source: U.S. Department of Education, National Center for Education Statistics, *Statistics of State School Systems: Revenues and Expenditures to Public Elementary and Secondary Education;* and Common Core of Data surveys. (Table prepared June 1998.) Excerpted from National Center for Education Statistics, *Digest of Education Statistics 1998,* Washington, DC: U.S. Department of Education, 1999, p. 169.

believed local property taxes should provide funding; 33 percent, state taxes; and 37 percent, federal taxes.

Revenues for education are influenced by many factors, including the apportionment of taxes among the local, state, and federal levels; the size of the tax base at each level; and competing demands for allocating funds at each level. In addition, funding for education is influenced by the following factors:

- The rate of inflation
- The health of the national economy
- The size of the national budget deficit
- Taxpayer revolts to limit the use of property taxes to raise money, such as Proposition 13 in California and Oregon's property tax limitation
- Changes in the size and distribution of the population
- School-financed lawsuits to equalize funding and ensure educational opportunity. (As of 1999, the systems of school finance in eighteen states had been overturned by court rulings, and more than twenty lawsuits seeking reform of state financing of K–12 education were pending [*Education Week* 1999b]).

Local Funding

At the local level, most funding for schools comes from **property taxes** that are determined by the value of property in the school district. Property taxes are assessed against real estate and, in some districts, also against personal property such as cars, household furniture and appliances, and stocks and bonds. Increasing taxes to meet the rising costs of operating local schools or to fund needed improvements is often a heated issue in many communities.

Although property taxes provide a steady source of revenue for local school districts, there are inequities in the ways in which taxes are determined. By locating in areas where taxes are lowest, for example, businesses and industries often avoid paying higher taxes while continuing to draw on local resources and services. In addition, the fair market value of property is often difficult to assess, and groups within a community sometimes pressure assessors to keep taxes on their property as low as possible. Most states specify by law the minimum property tax rate for local school districts to set. In many districts, an increase in the tax rate must have the approval of voters. Some states place no cap, or upper limit, on tax rates, and other states set a maximum limit.

State Funding

Most state revenues for education come from sales taxes and income taxes. Sales taxes are added to the cost of items such as general goods, gasoline, amusements, alcohol, and insurance. Income taxes are placed on individuals (in many states) and on business and industry.

As mentioned previously, states contribute nearly 50 percent of the resources needed to operate the public schools. The money that a state gives to its cities and towns is known as **state aid.** Table 5.3 compares selected states on the percent of education funds received from federal, state, local and intermediate, and private sources in relation to total expenditures for 1995–96. The table also shows how total expenditures may vary widely from state to state as well as the per-pupil amount retained for the administration of state education agencies.

How does federal funding influence schools at the local level? How does federal funding help to reduce inequities among schools?

Federal Funding

The role of the federal government in providing resources for education has been limited. As Table 5.2 shows, the federal share of funding for public elementary and secondary schools peaked in 1979–80 at 9.8 percent and had declined to 6.6 percent by 1995–96. Prior to 1980 the federal government had in effect bypassed the states and provided funding for local programs that were administered through various federal agencies, such as the Office of Economic Opportunity (Head Start, migrant education, and Follow Through) and the Department of Labor (Job Corps

Table 5.3

Revenues for public elementary and secondary schools by source and per-pupil funds retained for administration of state education agencies for selected states and the District of Columbia

		Percent of Total Revenues 1995–1996				
State	Revenues	Federal	State	Local & Intermediate	Private*	Total state administration funds per student, 1995–1996
Alaska	$1,183,127,000	11.1	66.1	20.2	2.5	$314
California	$30,858,564,000	8.9	55.8	34.2	1.2	$28
Connecticut	$4,786.247,000	3.7	38.0	55.5	2.8	$286
District of Columbia	$675,409,000	8.1	—	91.5	0.5	—
Louisiana	$3,934,998,000	12.1	50.3	34.9	2.6	$45
Nebraska	$1,876,494,000	5.6	31.6	56.9	5.9	$73
New York	$25,849,431,000	5.8	39.7	53.5	0.9	$68
Oregon	$3,366,831,000	6.5	54.1	35.8	3.6	$120
Texas	$21,689,792,000	7.2	42.9	47.2	2.6	$17
Washington	$6,327,993,000	5.8	68.0	23.1	3.1	$22

*Includes revenues from gifts, and tuition and fees from patrons.
Note: Excludes revenues for state education agencies. Because of rounding, details may not add to totals.

Source: U.S. Department of Education, National Center for Education Statistics, Common Core of Data survey; and U.S. General Accounting Office, *Education Finance, Extent of Federal Funding in State Education Agencies.* Excerpted from National Center for Education Statistics, *Digest of Education Statistics 1998,* Washington, DC: U.S. Department of Education, 1999, pp. 170, 172.

and the Comprehensive Employment Training Act [CETA]). Since the Reagan administration (1980–88), federal aid has increasingly been given directly to the states in the form of **block grants,** which a state or local education agency may spend as it wishes with few limitations. The 1981 **Education Consolidation and Improvement Act (ECIA)** gave the states a broad range of choices in spending federal money. The ECIA significantly reduced federal aid to education, however, thus making state aid to education even more critical.

Though a small proportion of the funds for schools comes from the federal level, the federal government has enacted supplemental programs to help meet the educational needs of special student populations. Such programs are often referred to collectively as **entitlements.** The most significant is the Elementary and Secondary Education Act of 1965. Title I of the act allocates a billion dollars annually to school districts with large numbers of students from low-income families. Among the other funded entitlement programs are the Vocational Education Act (1963), the Manpower Development and Training Act (1963), the Economic Opportunity Act (1964), the Bilingual Education Act (1968), the Indian Education Act (1972), and the Education for All Handicapped Children Act (1975).

The federal government also provides funding for preschool programs such as Project Head Start. Originally started under the Economic Opportunity Act of 1964 to provide preschool experiences to poor children, Head Start was later made available to children whose parents were above the poverty level. Under the Clinton administration, funding for Head Start more than doubled, increasing from $2.2 billion in fiscal year 1992 to $4.66 billion in 1999. Reauthorized by Congress in 1998, Head Start served an estimated 830,000 children and their families that year. The Head Start Act Amendments of 1994 also established the Early Head Start program, designed to serve pregnant women and children under three from low-income families. In fiscal year 1998, Early Head Start funding totaled $279 million, and 39,000 children were served by the program (U.S. Department of Health and Human Services October 27, 1998).

What Are Some Trends in Funding for Equity and Excellence?

The fact that schools have had to rely heavily on property taxes for support has resulted in fiscal inequities for schools. Districts with higher property wealth are able to generate more money per pupil than districts with lower property values. The degree of inequity between the wealthiest and the poorest districts, therefore, can be quite large. In some states, for example, the ability of one district to generate local property tax revenues may be several times greater than another district's. Moreover, unequal educational funding in the United States makes it one of the most inequitable countries in the world (Odden and Busch 1998).

In *Savage Inequalities: Children in America's Schools,* noted educator Jonathan Kozol (1991) presents a compelling analysis of the inequities in school funding. He found that the amount of money spent on each school age child ranged from $1,500 to $15,000, depending on where the child lived. Disputing those who claim that parental values, not high spending on education, determines how much children learn, Kozol points out that high spending on education in affluent districts does coincide with high achievement.

Tax Reform and Redistricting

To correct funding inequities, several court suits were initiated during the 1970s. In the 1971 *Serrano v. Priest* case in California, it was successfully argued that the relationship between spending and property wealth violated the state's obligation to provide equal protection and education. The California Supreme Court ruled in a six-to-one decision that the quality of a child's education should not be dependent on the "wealth of his parents and neighbors." The court also recognized that communities with a poor tax base could not be expected to generate the revenues of more affluent districts. Nevertheless, the Court did not forbid the use of property taxes to fund education.

Then, in 1973, the U.S. Supreme Court decided in *San Antonio Independent School District v. Rodriguez* that fiscal inequities stemming from unequal tax bases did not violate the Constitution. That court's decision reversed a lower court's ruling claiming that school financing on the basis of local property taxes was unconstitutional.

Regardless of the mixed outcomes of court challenges, many state legislatures have enacted school finance equity reforms during the last fifteen years. A few states (California, Hawaii, New Mexico, Washington, and West Virginia, for example) have led the way by developing programs to ensure statewide financial equality. These states have **full-funding programs** in which the state sets the same per-pupil expenditure level for all schools and districts.

Other states have adopted new funding formulas to try to broaden their revenue base. Level funding augmented by sales taxes, cigarette taxes, state lottery revenues, property taxes on second homes, and school-choice plans are among the solutions tried. One of the most dramatic changes in educational funding occurred in Michigan in 1993 with the passage of Proposal A, a plan that greatly reduced school funding from local property taxes and increased funding from the state's sales tax.

Since each state has been free to determine the number of districts within its boundaries—the number varied from 1,043 in Texas to 1 in Hawaii in 1996–97 (National Center for Education Statistics 1999, 98)—a common approach to achieving equal funding is **redistricting,** redrawing school district boundaries to reduce the range of variation in the ability of school districts to finance education. Redistricting not only equalizes funding; it can also reduce the cost of maintaining and operating schools if smaller districts are combined. The per-pupil cost of instruction, supplies, and equipment is usually lower in large districts. In addition, greater resources often allow larger districts to offer a broader curriculum and higher salaries to attract more qualified teachers.

Vertical Equity

Other states have developed various mechanisms for providing **vertical equity,** that is, for allocating funds according to legitimate educational needs. Thus, additional support is given to programs that serve students from low-income backgrounds; those with limited English proficiency, or special gifts and talents; and those who need special education or vocational programs.

Additional state-appropriated funds to cover the costs of educating students with special needs are known as **categorical aid.** Funding adjustments are also made to compensate for differences in costs within a state—higher expenses due to rural isolation or the higher cost of living in urban areas, for example. Some states even conduct periodic regional cost-of-living analyses, which are then used to determine adjustments in per-pupil funding.

School Choice

One of the most bitter struggles for control of schools in the United States during the last half of the 1990s centered around **school choice,** the practice of allowing parents to choose the schools their children attend. According to the 1999 Phi Delta Kappa/Gallup Poll of the public's attitudes toward the public schools, 51 percent were in favor of allowing parents to send their school-age children to any public, private, or church-related school they choose, with the government paying all or part of the tuition (Rose and Gallup 1999, 53).

Debate continues about whether school choice programs will, in fact, promote equity and excellence. Advocates of school choice believe that giving parents more options will force public schools to adjust to free-market pressures—low-performing schools would have to improve or shut down. Moreover, they contend that parents whose children must now attend inferior, and sometimes dangerous, inner-city schools would be able to send their children elsewhere. In addition, some supporters see choice as a way to reduce the influence of top-heavy school bureaucracies and teachers' unions—as Florida's governor stated in defense of his school choice proposal: "We must dismantle the bureaucracy and make our schools parent–oriented and performance-driven" (National Governor's Association 1998).

School Vouchers:
Pro or Con?

Magnet schools, charter schools, and voucher plans are school choice initiatives designed to improve education, especially in urban areas. In its simplest form, school choice permits parents to enroll their children in schools outside their neighborhoods or districts. The rationale is that if parents have a choice in the matter, they will more strongly support the schools they select for their children, and that teachers and principals will make greater efforts to be effective and inviting in order to gain student enrollments.

Magnet schools were introduced in the 1970s as a means of facilitating school integration in the nation's inner cities. Students of all races were drawn to their specialized curricula, thematic foci, unique teaching/learning approaches, positive climates, enthusiastic teachers, and images of excellence. Their success was evident. "Virtually all magnets have long waiting lists," Morton Inger reported in a 1991 issue of *ERIC Digest*.

Charter schools were developed in the 1990s to improve school effectiveness by granting freedom from many state and local restrictions. Charter schools were required only to be nonsectarian and democratic. Given a three- to five-year time limit to show results, designers of charter schools were energized by the opportunity to develop alternative schools that fit their beliefs. From 1991, when the first charter-school legislation was adopted in Minnesota, to 1998 "the U.S. charter-school movement . . . produced 800 schools in 29 states and the District of Columbia, enrolling 100,000 students," according to a report by Margaret Hadderman (1998).

Voucher plans are the most controversial of the school choice initiatives. They involve giving parents cash certificates, vouchers, or tax credits from public funds to pay to send their children to schools of their choice—private or public. Milton Friedman, a conservative economist who first suggested the plan in 1955, believed that schools would improve significantly if they were operated by private enterprise instead of the government. The challenge to the public school system in the United States and the constitutional legalities of voucher plans have stirred heated debates ever since. In 1999, five state supreme courts and one appeals court reviewed the legality of using vouchers to send students to religious schools. Their deci-

sions were mixed, and the debate continues. Where do you stand on this issue? Are you in favor of or against school vouchers?

The Pro Voucher Position

Use of school vouchers would strengthen the education system in the United States. The principles of the free market system would make schools more accountable and attractive to their clients—students and parents. Schools that provide an inadequate education would lose students and eventually close. Thus ineffective schools would disappear and effective ones would be positively reinforced both fiscally and psychologically.

Under a voucher system, teachers and administrators would be more sensitive to students' needs and more anxious to obtain parents' support. School sites would become safer, more attractive, and student-centered. The curricula and teaching methods would resemble those that made magnet schools such a success. Religious schools would thrive as more parents used vouchers to select them. And parent–teacher partnerships would strengthen school cultures.

Academic standards would be raised for all students. Block grants, used already to equalize educational opportunities for children in poor districts, would provide financial incentives that travel with students to their schools of choice. Their stature in the schools would be enhanced, and teachers would take extra measures to see that they learned. Kevin Walters reported in 1999, "Choice plans in Cambridge, Massachusetts, have increased overall student achievement while closing the educational gap between white and black students. East Harlem, New York, has seen a five-fold increase in the rate of students reading at or above grade level since initiating a school choice plan" (Nathan 1990).

Teachers' unions argue against the voucher system by expressing concern for students, but their resistance seems self-serving. The unions would lose money and influence when the number of public school educators drops as more parents use vouchers to buy private education, the unions claim. However, the teaching profession itself would grow in stature under a voucher system, with inadequate teachers who are resistant to change leaving the profession and effective ones remaining.

The Anti-Voucher Position

Vouchers would destroy the public education system in the United States and disrupt the social fabric of the nation. With parents free to choose from an array of options, schools would become segregated on the basis of race, ethnicity, social class, religion, language, and special interests. The safeguards of separation of church and state would be lost. And without a common curriculum and shared schooling experiences, groups in a diverse society would become further alienated from one another. The original purpose of public schools, to educate the citizenry, would not be fulfilled, and a common understanding of the principles of democracy would be endangered.

Public schools themselves would suffer, especially in urban centers. Besides losing out financially from declining enrollment, schools would lose their best students and academic standards would decline. Students with special learning, emotional, or physical needs could have difficulty being admitted to private schools, and the extra expenses of the services they need would tax the public schools' diminishing funds.

Better educated and wealthier parents would have the time to visit schools and make knowledgeable decisions for their children. Poorer parents could remain uninformed or be misled by unethical promoters of inadequate schools. Their poor school choices would short-change their children and, in turn, perpetuate the separation between economic classes in U.S. society.

The teaching profession itself would also suffer. Teachers who remained in public schools would be stressed by increased responsibilities and reduced support, consequences of reduced public funding. Those who moved to private schools would be stressed by the insecurity of having no union to represent them. The instability and unpredictability that a voucher system would bring could keep people from entering the teaching profession and might drive good teachers away.

Finally, the serious problems in schools today are too great and too intertwined with society's problems to be resolved by simply giving parents more options. As John Lewis (1995) has written, "'School choice' is a strategy that does not deal with the problems facing our schools, but in fact runs from them." Citizens need to work together and not splinter into groups to best serve their children and country.

Where do you stand on this issue?

1. Are you for or against school voucher plans? Why?

2. Which arguments for each position do you think are most persuasive?

3. What other drawbacks or strengths would a voucher system bring?

4. If you were a parent with a voucher to spend for your child's education, what qualities would you seek in the school of your choice?

5. If you were a teacher in a voucher system, which type of school would you prefer to work in and why?

Recommended Sources

Cookson, P. W., Jr., and Shroff, S. M. (1997). Recent experience with urban school choice plans. *ERIC/CUE Digest, No. 127.*

Hadderman, M. (1998). Charter schools. *ERIC Digest, No. 118.*

Morton, I. (1999). Improving urban education with magnet schools. *ERIC/CUE Digest, No. 76.*

Lewis, J. F. (1995, September). Saying no to vouchers: What is the price of democracy? *NASSP Bulletin.*

Walters, K. (1995, September). Saying yes to vouchers: Perception, choice, and the educational response. *NASSP Bulletin.*

Noll, J. W. (1999). *Taking sides: Clashing views on controversial educational issues,* 10th ed. Guilford, CT: McGraw-Hill.

Nathan, J. (1990). Progress, problems, and prospects of state education plans. In W. Boyd and H. Walberg (Eds.). *Choice in education: Potential and problems.* Berkeley, CA: McCutchan.

On the other hand, opponents believe that school choice would have disastrous consequences for public schools and lead to students being sorted by race, income, and religion. School choice, they argue, would subsidize the wealthy by siphoning money away from the public schools and further widen the gap between rich and poor districts. Moreover, opponents point out that research does not indicate that school choice would improve education (Smith and Meier 1995), nor would it promote educational equity:

> Since poor parents lack the supplemental resources that rich people have for help-ing their children, it is foolish to argue that [school choice] would help to equalize educational opportunities. (For example, rich parents can afford the extra costs for transportation, clothing, and educational supplies when they send their children to a distant, private school; poor parents cannot) (Berliner and Biddle 1995, 175).

Other critics contend that school choice could lead to the creation of segregated schools and schools that would be more committed to competing for education dollars and the most able, manageable students. Still others point out that, while school choice is offered as a solution to the U.S. education crisis (Chubb and Moe 1990), our nation's school system is not failing, it is *perceived* as failing. As David Berliner and Bruce Biddle (1995, 4) point out in *The Manufactured Crisis: Myths, Fraud, and the Attack on America's Public Schools*, "When one actually *looks* at the evidence [for a failing school system], one discovers that most of the claims of the Manufactured Crisis are, indeed, myths, half-truths, and sometimes outright lies."

Voucher Systems

One approach to providing educational equity that has generated considerable con-troversy is the **voucher system** of distributing educational funds. Although various plans have been proposed, one of the most common would give states the freedom to dis-tribute money directly to parents in the form of vouchers. Parents would then use the vouchers to enroll their children in schools of their choice. The most controversial vouch-er proposals would allow parents to choose from among public as well as private (sec-ular, parochial, for-profit, and charter) schools; others would limit parents' choice to public schools.

Half of the respondents to the 1999 Phi Delta Kappa/Gallup Poll were asked if they favored vouchers that would pay *full tuition* at private or church-related schools —47 percent favored such a voucher system, 48 percent opposed it, and 5 percent said they "don't know." The other half of respondents were asked if they favored vouch-ers that would pay *partial tuition*—52 percent were in favor, 45 percent were opposed, and 3 percent said they didn't know (Rose and Gallup 1999, 53–54).

In the late 1990s, debates about vouchers regularly made the national news. New Mexico's provoucher governor clashed with the state's legislature over private school vouchers (*Education Week* 1999a). After months of contentious debate, Florida became the first state to offer state-paid tuition to children in failing public schools to attend a public, private, or religious school of choice (*The Miami Herald,* 1999). And, for months, the media covered New York City Schools Chancellor Rudolph Crew's oppo-sition to Mayor Rudolph W. Giuliani's plan to "give poorer parents the same oppor-tunity to make choices about their children's education that the richest and most affluent parents in new York City have" (*Education Week* 1999e).

It is clear that the debate over school choice will continue for the foreseeable future. Gradually, support for school choice appears to be increasing—as of 1999, twenty states allowed some form of "interdistrict" transfer, which would allow students to attend public schools outside of their home district, and an equal number of states were con-sidering choice plans. In fact, Grant and Murray (1999, 235) suggest that "It is conceivable that by 2020 as many as a quarter of all students could be enrolled in some 'school of choice,' whether private or public."

Corporate-Education Partnerships

To develop additional sources of funding for equity and excellence, many local school districts have established partnerships with the private sector. Businesses may contribute funds or materials needed by a school, sponsor sports teams, award scholarships, provide cash grants for pilot projects and teacher development, and even construct school buildings. One example of a corporate-education partnership is Thomas Jefferson High School for Science and Technology, a college preparatory magnet school in Alexandria, Virginia. Twenty-five local and multinational businesses, including AT&T, Mobil, Boeing, Honeywell, and Exxon, raised almost a million dollars for the school. State-of-the-art facilities include a $600,000 telecommunications lab with a television studio, radio station, weather station, and a satellite earth station. The school has a biotech laboratory for genetic engineering experiments in cloning and cell fission as well as labs for research on energy and computers.

Corporate contributions to education total more than $2 billion annually, with about 9 percent going to elementary and secondary education and the rest to colleges, including grants to improve teacher preparation. A survey of Fortune 500 and Service 500 companies found that 78 percent contributed money to education, 64 percent contributed materials or equipment, 26 percent offered teachers summer employment, and 12 percent provided executives-on-loan to schools (Hopkins and Wendel 1997, 15).

If schools in the United States are to succeed in meeting the challenges of the twenty-first century, they will need to be funded at a level that provides quality educational experiences to students from a diverse array of backgrounds. Though innovative approaches to school funding have been developed, much remains to be done before both excellence and equity characterize all schools in the United States.

SUMMARY

Who Is Involved in the Struggles for Control of Schools in the United States?

- Parents, students, teachers, administrators, taxpayers, state and federal authorities, minorities and women, educational theorists and researchers, and businesses and corporations are among the groups that exert political influence on education.

- Schools reflect the society they serve and thus are influenced by out-of-school factors such as the mass media, demographic shifts, international events, and social issues.

What Is the Role of the Local Community in School Governance?

- Local school districts, which vary greatly in size, locale, organizational structure, demographics, and wealth, are responsible for the management and operation of schools.

- Local schools boards, whose members are usually elected, set educational policies for a district; however, many people believe that boards should be reformed to be more well informed and responsive.

- The superintendent, the chief administrator of a local district, has a complex array of responsibilities and must work cooperatively with the school board and others in an environment that is often politically turbulent.

- Through groups like the PTA or PTO, some parents are involved in local school activities and reform efforts; others are involved with private schools; and some actively promote alternative approaches to education such as school choice, voucher systems, and home schooling.

- As part of the restructuring movement, schools are changing their policies for governance, curricula, and community collaboration; the Chicago School Reform Act is one example of restructuring based on school-based management that empowers teachers, principals, parents, community members, and students at local schools.

What Powers and Influence Do States Have in Governing Schools?

- The state legislature, state courts, and the governor significantly influence education by setting policies related to the management and operation of schools within a state; many states have even passed legislation allowing them to take over academically failing school districts or individual schools.

- The state board of education, the highest educational agency in a state, regulates education and advises the governor and others on important educational policies.

- The state department of education implements policies related to teacher certification, allocation of state and federal funds, enforcement of state and federal guidelines, school accreditation, and research and evaluation projects to improve education.

- The chief state school officer oversees education within a state and, in collaboration with the governor, legislature, state board of education, and the public, provides leadership to improve education.

What Assistance Do Regional Education Agencies Provide?

- The Regional Educational Service Agency (RESA), an intermediate unit of educational administration in about half of the states, provides assistance to two or more school districts for staff development, curriculum development, instructional media, and program evaluation.

How Does the Federal Government Influence Education?

- The federal government influences education at the state level through funding general and categorical programs, establishing and enforcing standards and regulations, conducting and disseminating educational research, providing technical assistance to improve education, and encouraging equity and excellence for the nation's schools.

- The national legislature, federal and Supreme courts, and the president significantly influence education by exerting moral suasion for the improvement of schools, providing categorical aid for federal programs, ensuring that school systems follow legal statutes, and funding educational research.

- The U.S. Department of Education supports and disseminates educational research through ERIC, administers federal grants in education, and assists the president in developing and promoting a national agenda for education.

- At times, the roles of the federal and state governments in education are in conflict.

How Are Schools Financed in the United States?

- Schools are supported with revenues from the local, state, and federal levels, with most funding now coming from the state level.

- Local funding is provided through property taxes, which in many instances results in inequitable funding for schools located in areas with an insufficient tax base.

- One challenge to financing schools has been the development of an equitable means of taxation for the support of education.

What Are Some Trends in Funding for Equity and Excellence?

- Many state legislatures have enacted tax reforms including full-funding programs which set the same per-pupil expenditures for all schools and districts. Some states have achieved greater equity through redistricting—redrawing district boundaries to reduce funding inequities.

- Some states achieve vertical equity by providing additional funding, or categorical aid, to educate students with special needs. Also, many local districts and schools receive additional funding through partnerships with the private sector.

- School choice and voucher programs are two controversial approaches to providing parents the freedom to select the schools their children attend.

KEY TERMS AND CONCEPTS

block grants, 187
categorical aid, 189
chief state school
    officer, 179
Education Consolidation
    and Improvement Act
    (ECIA), 187
entitlements, 187
expenditure per pupil, 183
full-funding programs, 188
G.I. Bill of Rights, 180
Kentucky Education
    Reform Act (KERA), 177

local school council
    (LSC), 174
local school districts, 169
National Governors'
    Association (NGA), 178
property taxes, 186
redistricting, 189
Regional Educational
    Service Agency
    (RESA), 180
restructuring, 173
school-based management
    (SBM), 174

school board, 170
school choice, 189
state aid, 186
state board of
    education, 178
state department of
    education, 179
superintendent, 170
vertical equity, 189
voucher system, 192

APPLICATIONS AND ACTIVITIES

Teacher's Journal

1. In *Conflict of Interests: The Politics of American Education*, 3rd ed., Joel Spring (1998, 50) points out that

   > Differing political groups struggle to have their ideas emphasized in schools. Politicians attempt to win votes by claiming that their educational policies will improve schools and society. Ethnic politicians demand language and cultural policies in schools that will maintain the cohesiveness of their particular constituencies. And a long-standing conflict exists between business interests and workers over the content of education. Many workers want schools to be avenues of economic mobility for their children, while many businesspeople want the schools to focus on job training to meet corporate needs.

   Describe some examples of how politicians, workers, and business people are currently using schools to promote their interests within your state. Which actions do you support? Which do you oppose?

2. From the many political forces that influence schools (see Figure 5.1, page 167), select one factor and describe how it is currently influencing education at the national level. How is this factor influencing schools at the local level in your area?

3. Imagine that you are given vouchers to send your child to any school in your state. What factors would you consider in making your choice? Compare your list with the following list, most important coming first, from a recent survey of parents: quality of teaching staff, maintenance of school discipline, courses offered, size of classes, and test scores of students. What are the similarities and differences between the lists? What do the differences reveal about your view of education and schools?

4. Think of businesses and agencies in your community that might be good partners for a school. Select one of them and develop a proposal outlining the nature, activities, and benefits (to both) of the partnership you envision.

Teacher's Database

1. Use the Internet and the World Wide Web to gather information about the structure of education and school funding in your state. How many districts are in your state? Which is the largest? What are enrollment figures, trends, and projections for your state? What are the figures for household income and poverty rate? What proportion of school funding in your state is from the local, state, and federal levels? What are the total expenditures and per-pupil expenditures?

   Begin your data search at the U.S. Department of Education's National Center for Education Statistics (NCES) where you will find NCES data from the *Digest of Education Statistics,* the *Condition of Education, Youth Indicators, Projections of Education Statistics,* the *Directory of Department of Education Publications,* the *Directory of Current OERI-Funded Projects,* and the *Directory of Computer Data Files.*

2. Find information on sources of funding for education, education budgets, and issues of education finance. Begin at the U.S. Department of Education and then go to the Budget home page of the Department.

Observations and Interviews

1. Visit a private (secular, parochial, for-profit, or charter) school. Find out how teachers and other staff members are hired and how the school is organized and governed. How does the management and operation of this school differ from public schools?

2. Interview a school superintendent and ask him or her to comment on how federal, state, and local forces affect education in the district. To what extent do influences at these three levels help (and/or hinder) the district in accomplishing its goals?

3. Interview a teacher and ask how legislation at the federal and state levels affects the teacher's work. Would the teacher like to see the federal government more or less involved in education? Report your findings to the rest of the class.

4. Attend a meeting of a local school board and observe the communication and decision-making process at that meeting. To help you make this observation, ask your instructor for Handout M5.1, "Observing Community-Based Decision Making on Education."

5. To understand how school-based decision making works, observe a meeting of a site-based council (SBC) or local school council (LSC). For guidance in making this observation, ask your instructor for Handout M5.2, "Observing School-Based Decision Making."

Professional Portfolio

Prepare a profile of a school district. The district may be in your home town, your college or university community, or a community in which you would like to teach. Information on the district may be obtained from your university library, public library, school district offices, state board of education, or professional teacher associations.

Keeping in mind that school district statistics are more readily available in some cases than in others, your profile might include the following types of information:

- Organizational chart showing (if possible) personnel currently assigned to each position
- Tables showing numbers of school buildings, students, teachers, administrators, support personnel, and so forth
- Graduation/dropout rate
- Scores on standardized achievement tests
- Total annual budget
- Expenditures per pupil
- Entitlement programs
- Demographic characteristics of population living in the area served by the district —age, race/ethnicity, socioeconomic status, unemployment rate, and so forth
- Volunteer groups serving schools in the district
- Pupil-teacher ratio
- Percent of ethnic minority students, students with disabilities, and so forth
- Percent of students going on to college

Appendix 5.1

Guidelines for Teachers to Think and Act Politically

- Learn from those who have come before you.
- Find your main focus and organize around that.
- Provide leadership and direction.
- Build a coalition.
- Know who is making the decisions and who/what will influence them.
- Speak simply and forcefully.
- Be a lion.
- Look organized and be organized.
- Do it because it's the right thing to do.

Twenty-Five Ways to Become Involved

1. Attend organizational meetings.
2. Encourage others to become involved.
3. Organize a phone tree of supporters.
4. Keep each other informed on what is happening in individual schools and areas.
5. Get parents to agree to speak at school board meetings.
6. Provide transportation for parents and children to school board meetings.
7. Arrange for translators for limited-English-speaking parents at school board meetings.
8. Help parents and students prepare what they will say at school board meetings.
9. Attend school board meetings.
10. Write letters to parents.
11. Write letters to the superintendent.
12. Write letters to school board members.
13. Write letters to newspaper editors.
14. Write and send a survey to parents of present and former students.
15. Collect returned surveys to present to school board.
16. Call the school board members.
17. Call TV and radio stations.
18. Encourage parents to call school board members and the superintendent.
19. Encourage teachers in your school to call school board members and the superintendent.
20. Organize other teachers in your school to attend and to speak at school board meetings.
21. Be a liaison with specific school board members.
22. Work with your union.
23. Be creative.
24. Attend and speak at staff and committee meetings at the school and district level.
25. Provide refreshments.

Source: Adapted by permission of Barbara Keresty, Susan O'Leary, and Dale Wortley, *You Can Make a Difference: A Teacher's Guide to Political Action.* Portsmouth, NH: Heinemann, 1998, pp. 29–49; 58–59. Used by permission of the publisher Heinemann, a division of Reed Elsevier Inc.

Appendix 5.2

Typical Organizational Structure for a Medium-Size School District (20,000 Pupils)

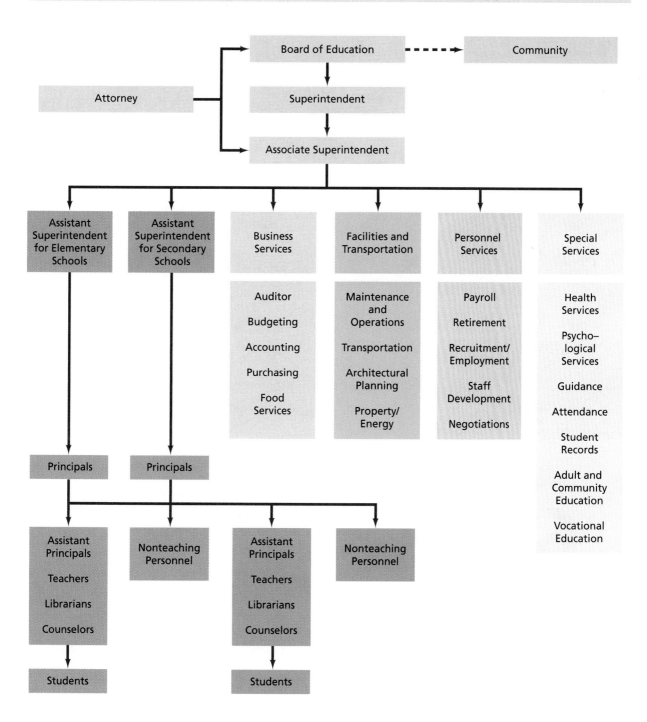

6

Ethical and Legal Issues in Education in the United States

Teachers [must] balance public obligations with their personal beliefs and purposes in teaching.
—David T. Hansen
The Call to Teach

focus questions

1. Why do you need a professional code of ethics?

2. What are your legal rights as a teacher?

3. Do student teachers have the same rights?

4. What are your legal responsibilities as a teacher?

5. What are the legal rights of students and parents?

6. What are some issues in the legal rights of school districts?

The day has ended and you are grading papers while waiting to meet with Cassandra, one of your fifth-grade students, and her mother. Cassandra's mother called you at home yesterday to arrange the meeting. When you asked her about the purpose of the meeting, she was vague and offered only that Cassandra had recently had "some trouble" with one of her classmates, Robert.

A quick glance at the clock tells you they should arrive at any moment. To prepare for the meeting, you stop grading papers and reflect on what you know about the situation between Cassandra and Robert.

Because he was held back in the third grade, Robert is almost two years older than his classmates. Though physically more mature than the other boys in your class, Robert's social skills are less developed. Although he acts silly and immature from time to time, Robert has not been a behavior problem . . . at least not until a week ago, when Cassandra told you what happened on the playground.

Last Monday at the end of the day, Cassandra told you that Robert had "talked mean" to her during recess on the playground. When you questioned Cassandra to find out exactly what Robert said, her answers were hard to follow. At first, it seemed that, whatever words were exchanged, they were not unlike the taunts boys and girls hurl back and forth daily on playgrounds across the country. As you continued to press for details, however, Cassandra began to talk, again vaguely, about how Robert had "talked dirty" to her. Further questioning of Cassandra still failed to give you a clear picture of what happened on the playground.

Based on what you learned from talking with Cassandra, you decided to give Robert a stern reminder about appropriate ways of talking to other people. The following morning you did just that.

Robert listened respectfully and seemed genuinely contrite. He promised to leave Cassandra alone while they were on the playground. The conversation ended with you telling Robert that his behavior on the playground and in the classroom would be monitored closely.

During the following week, it appeared that the friction between Robert and Cassandra had ended. As far as you could tell, the matter was over.

When Cassandra and her mother entered the room, you knew immediately that both were upset. Cassandra looked like she was on the verge of tears, and her mother looked angry.

"Tell your teacher what you told me," Cassandra's mother began, as she and her daughter seated themselves at two student desks in front of your desk.

"Well," Cassandra began slowly, almost whispering, "Robert bothered me on the playground yesterday." Cassandra started breathing more deeply as she struggled to continue. "He came over to me and. . . ." Cassandra stared at the top of her desk while searching for additional words to express what she wanted to say.

"What she means to tell you," said Cassandra's mother, "is that Robert rubbed up against her and said he wanted to have sex with her. She was sexually harassed."

On hearing what Robert is alleged to have done, you are shocked. What should you do? How does a teacher tell the difference between sexual harassment and the teasing and name calling that are an inescapable part of growing up? Should you try to determine the truth of the allegations before involving the principal? What are your responsibilities to Cassandra and her mother? What are your responsibilities to Robert? How should your school handle the matter?

The preceding scenario, based partially on actual events that culminated with the filing of a lawsuit against a school board *(Davis v. Monroe County Board of Education* 1999) and a U.S. Supreme Court ruling in 1999, highlights the role that legal issues can play in the lives of teachers and students. In this instance, a fifth-grade Georgia girl said she endured a five-month "barrage of sexual harassment and abuse" from a classmate. The boy allegedly touched the girl's breasts, rubbed against her suggestively, and repeatedly said he wanted to have sex with her. The lawsuit claimed that the girl's mother reported each incident to school officials but the boy was never disciplined; as a result, the girl's grades fell and she became mentally and emotionally upset. The sharply divided Supreme Court (five majority and four dissenting) ruled that school districts can be sued under Title IX in cases involving student-on-student sexual harassment, if the district acts with "deliberate indifference" to the harassment. (Title IX prohibits discrimination on the basis of sex in programs that receive federal money.)

In this chapter we examine significant ethical and legal issues that affect the rights and responsibilities of teachers, administrators, students, and parents. Teachers must act in accordance with a wide range of federal and state legislation and court decisions. As a teacher, you may need to deal with such legal issues as the teacher's responsibility for accidents, discriminatory employment practices, freedom of speech, desegregation, student rights, and circumstances related to job termination or dismissal. Without knowledge of the legal dimensions of such issues, you will be ill-equipped to protect your rights and the rights of your students.

What ethical dilemmas might this experiment pose for a teacher? How might you respond? On what moral or ethical grounds would you base your response? What legal concerns might be involved?

Why Do You Need a Professional Code of Ethics?

The actions of professional teachers are determined not only by what is legally required of them, but also by what they know they *ought* to do. They do what is legally right, and they *do the right thing.* A specific set of values guides them. A deep and lasting commitment to professional practice characterizes their work. They have adopted a high standard of professional ethics and they model behaviors that are in accord with that code of ethics.

At present, the teaching profession does not have a uniform **code of ethics** similar to the Hippocratic oath, which all doctors are legally required to take when they begin practice. However, the largest professional organization for teachers, the National Education Association (NEA) has a code of ethics for its members (see Appendix 6.1) that includes the following statement: "The educator accepts the responsibility to adhere to the highest ethical standards."

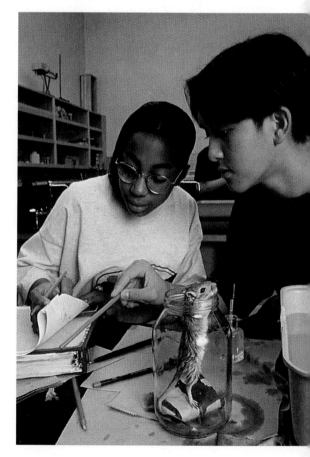

Ethical Teaching Attitudes and Practices

Teaching is an ethical enterprise—that is, a teacher has an obligation to act ethically, to follow what he or she knows

Lisa's Ethical Challenge

The following case is from Laurie Olsen's book *Made in America: Immigrant Students in Our Public Schools.* In a two-year ethnographic study of life in an urban high school, Olsen explored "what it is like to go to school and to teach in school during a time of increasingly complex cultural relations, and amidst the pressures of a large urban, fiscally strapped public school system" (p. 9). What she found questions the ethics of current school structures and practices and warns of their consequent impact on the future of the United States. Lisa Stern, a new teacher in the school, confronts one ethical challenge in the selection that follows.

At Madison High, it is the responsibility of ninth-grade English teachers to determine what academic level students should be placed in for tenth-grade English and social studies. Their tenth-grade level is most often the level at which they continue throughout high school. Students placed in "skills" classes (remedial classes) stay there. Students placed in "honors" classes end up with the courses needed for admission to four-year universities. Students in the "regular" track have some opportunity for sliding downward into "skills" classes or climbing "upward" into college-preparatory classes. Most, however, appear to stay in the regular track. There is no formal policy or criteria determining how these decisions should be made.

When Lisa Stern first began teaching social studies at Madison High, as a brand-new teacher, she was assigned to teach three tenth-grade "skills" classes. It was the tradition that first-year teachers would be assigned these courses, reputed to be the toughest in the school. A faculty member consoled her: "I'm sorry you're stuck with the garbage kids. You'll be able to teach other students after a few years."

Fresh out of graduate school, Stern had read research about the ways in which the division of students into academic tracks is detrimental to students in the bottom levels, and the fact that such tracking often relegates students of color and poor students to an inferior education. She decided to conduct some research of her own with the students at Madison High. Stern surveyed six classes: two skills classes, two "regular" classes, and two honors classes. The survey asked, "What level do you think this class is? (high, medium, or low)?" "How far did your mother go in school?" "How far did your father go in school?" and "Has your family ever been consulted about the level of history class you are taking?"

The results were stark. Students knew clearly what level they were placed in. All of the skills class students' parents did not finish high school or graduated from high school but did not go to college. Almost all of the students in the honors classes had at least one parent who completed college. Most of the honor's-class students' parents seemed to be aware they were taking honors classes. Only one skills-class student thought his parents were aware that he was in a "lower"–level history class. To Stern, this was clear evidence that the school was just perpetuating a class system: the children of people who have had access to higher education also get prepared for higher education, and the children of people who have not had higher education don't get prepared for higher education.

Determined to do something about the tracking of students in social studies, Stern put together the survey results and some of the research on tracking. She recounts bringing it first to her department with a proposal to detrack the tenth-grade social studies classes. She received a lukewarm reaction, and the suggestion that she take it to the next level—the districtwide Social Studies Curriculum Council. An associate superintendent told her, "there is no evidence that would support detracking social studies." He brought in a parent of an honors student to speak on behalf of gifted and talented students and their need for honors classes. The Curriculum Council told her, "we don't know enough to make a decision." A vote was taken, and nineteen people abstained.

The next day at school, Stern was met in the hall by the principal. He told her that what she was doing was misguided: "You're going to hurt our kids who want to get into college. We need honors classes here. You're just hurting our kids. I'm going to fight you on this all the way."

Stern was so upset that she dropped the subject. No one ever mentioned it to her again—not the principal, not the department faculty who had passed her along to the Curriculum Council, not the members of the Curriculum Council who abstained on her proposal. Yet, the memory of that experience continued to affect Stern deeply throughout her years of teaching at the school.

Questions:

1. Who had a say in the placement of students in tracks and who made the policies regarding tracking at Madison High? How could these procedures be improved?

2. What arguments for their positions did Lisa and her principal offer? With whom do you agree?

3. How do the behaviors of Lisa's department colleagues, the associate superintendent, the Curriculum Council members who abstained, and the principal compare with the principles of the NEA Code of Ethics (Appendix 6.1)?

4. Did Lisa approach making a policy change in the best way? If not, what should she have done instead?

Source: Laurie Olsen, *Made in America: Immigrant Students in Our Public Schools.* New York: The New Press, 1997. Selection section, pp. 192–93. Copyright © 1997 *Made in America,* by Laurie Olsen. Reprinted by permission of The New Press.

to be the most appropriate professional action to take. The best interests of students, not the teacher, provide the rule of thumb for determining what is ethical and what is not. Behaving ethically is more than a matter of following the rules or not breaking the law—it means acting in a way that promotes the learning and growth of students and helps them realize their potential.

Unethical acts break the trust and respect on which good student-teacher relationships are based. An example of unethical conduct would be to talk publicly about Cassandra's allegations against Robert (described in this chapter's opening scenario). Other examples would be using grades as a form of punishment, expressing rage in the classroom, or intentionally tricking students on tests. You could no doubt think of other examples from your own experience as a student.

Ethical Dilemmas in Classroom and School

Teachers routinely encounter **ethical dilemmas** in the classroom and in the school. They often have to take action in situations in which all the facts are not known or for which no single course of action can be called right or wrong. At these times it can be quite difficult to decide what an ethical response might be. Dealing satisfactorily with ethical dilemmas in teaching often requires the ability to see beyond short-range consequences to consider long-range consequences.

Consider, for example, the following three questions based on actual case studies. On the basis of the information given, how would you respond to each situation?

1. Should the sponsor of the high school literary magazine refuse to print a well-written story by a budding writer if the piece appears to satirize a teacher and a student?
2. Is a reading teacher justified in trying to increase achievement for an entire class by separating two disruptive students and placing one in a reading group beneath his reading level?
3. Should a chemistry teacher punish a student (on the basis of circumstantial, inconclusive evidence) for a laboratory explosion if the example of decisive, swift punishment will likely prevent the recurrence of a similar event and thereby ensure the safety of all students?

What Are Your Legal Rights as a Teacher?

It is frequently observed that with each freedom comes a corresponding responsibility to others and to the community in which we live. As long as there is more than one individual inhabiting this planet, there is a need for laws to clarify individual rights and responsibilities. This necessary balance between rights and responsibilities is perhaps more critical to teaching than to any other profession. As education law experts Martha McCarthy, Nelda Cambron-McCabe, and Stephen Thomas (1998, 309) point out: "Although public educators do not shed their constitutional rights as a condition of public employment, under certain circumstances restrictions on these freedoms are justified by overriding governmental interests."

While schools do have limited "power over" teachers, teachers' rights to **due process** cannot be violated. Teachers, like all citizens, are protected from being treated arbitrarily by those in authority. A principal who disagrees with a teacher's methods cannot suddenly fire that teacher. A school board cannot ask a teacher to resign merely by claiming that the teacher's political activities outside of school are "disruptive" of the educational process. A teacher cannot be dismissed for "poor" performance without ample documentation that the performance was, in fact, poor and without sufficient time to meet clearly stated performance evaluation criteria.

Certification

Karla Brown is a junior high school English teacher and lives in a state with a law specifying that a teacher must show proof of five years of successful teaching experience for a teaching certificate to be renewed. Last year was Karla's fifth year of teaching, and her principal gave her an unsatisfactory performance rating. Karla's principal told her that her teaching certificate cannot be renewed. Is the principal correct?

Karla's principal is mistaken about the grounds for nonrenewal of a teaching certificate. According to the state's law, *unsuccessful* performance, or a failure to complete the school year, is grounds for nonrenewal of a certificate—not performance that is judged to be *unsatisfactory*. Because state laws vary and unsuccessful performance is defined differently in different states, however, Karla's principal might have been correct if she taught in another state.

No teacher who meets all of a state's requirements for initial certification can arbitrarily be denied a certificate. And once obtained, a certificate may not be revoked without due process of law. For a certificate to be revoked, the reason must be job-related and demonstrably impair the teacher's ability to perform satisfactorily. In this regard, the case of a California teacher whose certificate was revoked because someone admitted to having a homosexual relationship with the teacher is often cited. The court determined that the teacher's homosexual conduct was not an impairment to the teacher's performance and ordered the certificate restored (*Morrison v. State Board of Education* 1969). When courts have upheld the refusal to hire and the right to terminate homosexual teachers, these decisions have been influenced by factors such as sexual involvement with students or public acts of indecency (McCarthy, Cambron-McCabe, and Thomas 1998). Several states (California, Connecticut, Hawaii, Massachusetts, Minnesota, New Jersey, and Wisconsin) and the District of Columbia have laws that prohibit discrimination on the basis of sexual orientation in regard to employment, housing, and education. In states that have such antidiscrimination laws, "it will be difficult, if not impossible . . . to uphold the denial of employment or the discharge of homosexuals with respect to teaching positions in the public schools" (LaMorte 1999, 213).

Teachers' Rights to Nondiscrimination

Harold Jones has met all the qualifications for teaching but is denied certification because he has a prison record. Several years ago he was convicted of a felony. Harold claims he is being discriminated against because of his past. Is he right?

States may impose certain limitations on initial certification as long as those limitations are not discriminatory in regard to race, religion, ethnic origin, sex, or age. Nearly all the states, for example, require that applicants for a teaching certificate pass a test that covers basic skills, professional knowledge, or academic subject areas. Qualifications for initial certification may also legally include certain personal qualities. The case of Harold Jones at the beginning of this section, for example, is based on an Oregon case involving a man who had successfully completed a teacher training program but was denied a certificate because he had once been found guilty of a felony and served a term in prison. The Oregon State Board of Education raised some legitimate questions regarding the moral character of the applicant. The court held that a criminal conviction is proof of bad moral character, and his character flaw is irremediable regardless of the passage of time and subsequent legal behavior. As a result, he was unable to obtain the teaching certificate he needed to be hired as a teacher (*Application of Bay v. State Board of Education* 1963).

The right to **nondiscrimination** in regard to employment is protected by Title VII of the Civil Rights Act of 1964, which states:

> It shall be an unlawful employment practice for an employer (1) to fail or refuse to hire or to discharge any individual, or otherwise to discriminate against any individual with respect to his compensation, terms, conditions, or privileges of employment, because of such individual's race, color, religion, sex, or national origin; or (2) to limit, segregate, or classify his employees or applicants for employment in any way which would deprive or tend to deprive any individual of employment opportunities or otherwise adversely affect his status as an employee, because of such individual's race, color, religion, sex, or national origin.

Teaching Contracts

A **teaching contract** represents an agreement between the teacher and a board of education. For a contract to be valid, it must contain these five basic elements:

1. *Offer and acceptance*—The school board has made a formal offer and the employee has accepted the contract terms.
2. *Competent parties*—The school board is not exceeding the authority granted to it by the state and the teacher meets the criteria for employment.
3. *Consideration*—Remuneration is promised to the teacher.
4. *Legal subject matter*—The contract terms are neither illegal nor against public policy.
5. *Proper form*—The contract adheres to state contract laws.

Before you sign a teaching contract, it is important that you read it carefully and be certain that it is signed by the appropriate member(s) of the board of education or board of trustees. Ask for clarification of any sections you don't understand. It is preferable that any additional nonteaching duties be spelled out in writing rather than left to an oral agreement. Because all board of education policies and regulations will be part of your contract, you should also read any available teacher handbook or school policy handbook.

The importance of carefully reading a contract and asking for clarification is illustrated in the following case:

> Victor Sanchez had just begun his first year as an English teacher at a high school in a city of about 300,000. Victor became quite upset when he learned that he had been assigned by his principal to sponsor the poetry club. The club was to meet once a week after school. Victor refused to sponsor the club, saying that the contract he had signed referred only to his teaching duties during regular school hours. Could Victor be compelled to sponsor the club?

Certain assignments, though not specified in a contract, may be required of teachers in addition to their regular teaching load, as long as there is a reasonable relationship between the teacher's classroom duties and the additional assignment. Furthermore, such assignments can include supervision of school events on weekends as well. Though Victor's contract did not make specific reference to club sponsorship, such a duty would be a reasonable addition to his regular teaching assignment.

When school authorities have assigned teachers to additional duties not reasonably related to their teaching, the courts have tended to rule in favor of teachers who file suit. For example, a school's directive to a tenured teacher of American history to assume the additional role of basketball coach was not upheld by a court of appeals (*Unified School Dist. No. 241 v. Swanson* 1986).

Due Process in Tenure and Dismissal

Tenure is a policy that provides the individual teacher with job security by (1) preventing his or her dismissal on insufficient grounds and (2) providing him or her with due process in the event of dismissal. Tenure is granted to teachers by the local school district after a period of satisfactory teaching, usually two to five years. In most cases, tenure may not be transferred from one school district to another.

The following case highlights the importance of tenure to a teacher's professional career:

> A teacher was dismissed from his teaching position by the school board after it learned that the teacher was a homosexual. The teacher filed suit in court, claiming that his firing was arbitrary and violated the provisions of tenure that he had been granted. The school board, on the other hand, maintained that his conduct was inappropriate for a teacher. Was the school board justified in dismissing the teacher?

The events in this case were actually heard by a court, which ruled that the teacher was unfairly dismissed (*Burton v. Cascade School Dist. Union High School No. 5* 1975). The court said that the board violated the teacher's rights as a tenured employee by failing to show "good and just cause" for dismissal. The teacher was awarded the balance due under his contract and an additional one-half year's salary. In a similar case, however, a court upheld the dismissal of a teacher whose sexual orientation was the target of parents' complaints and students' comments. The court ruled that the teacher could no longer effectively carry out his teaching duties (*Gaylord v. Tacoma School District No. 10* 1977).

The practice of providing teachers with tenure is not without controversy. Some critics point out that tenure policies make it too difficult to dismiss incompetent teachers and that performance standards are high in many other fields that do not provide employees with job security. Generally, however, the courts have held the position that tenure is a property right "from which students ultimately benefit" (Essex 1999, 179).

Just about every state today has a tenure law that specifies that a teacher may be dismissed with good cause; what counts as a good cause varies from state to state. The courts have ruled on a variety of reasons for **dismissal:** (1) insubordination, (2) incompetence or inefficiency, (3) neglect of duty, (4) conduct unbecoming a teacher, (5) subversive activities, (6) retrenchment or decreased need for services, (7) physical and/or mental health, (8) age, (9) causing or encouraging disruption, (10) engaging in illegal activities, (11) using offensive language, (12) personal appearance, (13) sex-related activities, (14) political activities, and (15) use of drugs or intoxicants.

For a tenured teacher to be dismissed, a systematic series of steps must be followed so that the teacher receives due process and his or her constitutionally guaranteed rights are not violated. Due process involves a careful, step-by-step examination of the charges brought against a teacher. Most states have outlined procedures that adhere to the following nine steps:

1. The teacher must be notified of the list of charges.
2. Adequate time must be provided for the teacher to prepare a rebuttal to the charges.
3. The teacher must be given the names of witnesses and access to evidence.
4. The hearing must be conducted before an impartial tribunal.
5. The teacher has the right to representation by legal counsel.
6. The teacher (or legal counsel) can introduce evidence and cross-examine adverse witnesses.
7. The school board's decision must be based on the evidence and findings of the hearing.
8. A transcript or record must be maintained of the hearing.
9. The teacher has the right to appeal an adverse decision.

These steps notwithstanding, it should be noted that "the definition [of due process] in each instance depends largely on a combination of the specific facts in a situation, the law governing the situation, the particular time in history in which judgment is being rendered, and the predilections of the individual judge(s) rendering the decision" (LaMorte 1999, 6), as the following case illustrates:

> Near the start of his fifth year of teaching at an elementary school in a small city, and two years after earning tenure, Mr. Mitchell went through a sudden and painful divorce. A few months later a woman whom he had met around the time of his divorce moved into the house he was renting.
>
> For the remainder of the school year he and the woman lived together. During this time, he received no indication that his lifestyle was professionally unacceptable, and his teaching performance remained satisfactory.
>
> At the end of the year, however, Mr. Mitchell was notified that he was being dismissed because of immoral conduct; that is, he was living with a woman he was not married to. The school board called for a hearing and Mr. Mitchell presented his side of the case. The board, nevertheless, decided to follow through with its decision to dismiss him. Was the school board justified in dismissing Mr. Mitchell?

Though at one time teachers could readily be dismissed for living, unmarried, with a member of the opposite sex, a lifestyle such as Mr. Mitchell's is not that unusual today. Because the board had not shown that Mr. Mitchell's alleged immoral conduct had a negative effect on his teaching, his dismissal would probably not hold up in court, unless the community as a whole was upset by his behavior. Moreover, Mr. Mitchell could charge that his right to privacy as guaranteed by the Ninth Amendment to the Constitution had been violated. Overall, it appears that the decision to dismiss Mr. Mitchell was arbitrary and based on the collective bias of the board. Nevertheless, teachers should be aware that courts frequently hold that teachers are role models, and the local community determines "acceptable" behavior both in school and out of school.

Teachers also have the right to organize and to join teacher organizations without fear of dismissal. In addition, most states have passed collective bargaining laws that require school boards to negotiate contracts with teacher organizations. Usually, the teacher organization with the most members in a district is given the right to represent teachers in the collective bargaining process.

An important part of most collective bargaining agreements is the right of a teacher to file a grievance, a formal complaint against his or her employer. A teacher may not be dismissed for filing a grievance, and he or she is entitled to have the grievance heard by a neutral third party. Often, the teachers' union or professional association that negotiated the collective bargaining agreement will provide a teacher who has filed a grievance with free legal counsel.

One right that teachers are not granted by collective bargaining agreements is the right to strike. Like other public employees, teachers do not have the legal right to strike in most states. Although teachers have a limited right to strike in a few states, "extensive restrictions have been placed on its use" (McCarthy, Cambron-McCabe, and Thomas 1998, 433). Teachers who do strike run the risk of dismissal (*Hortonville Joint School District No. 1 v. Hortonville Education Association* 1976), though when teacher strikes occur a school board cannot possibly replace all the striking teachers.

Academic Freedom

A teacher of at-risk students at an alternative high school used a classroom management/motivational technique called "Learnball." The teacher divided the class into teams, allowed students to elect team leaders and determine class rules and grading exercises, and developed a system of rewards that included listening to the radio and shooting baskets with a foam ball in the classroom. The school board ordered the teacher not to use the Learnball approach. Did the teacher have the right to continue using this teaching method?

This case is based on actual events involving a teacher in Pittsburgh. The teacher brought suit against the board to prevent it from imposing a policy that banned Learnball in the classroom. The teacher cited the principle of **academic freedom** and claimed that teachers have a right to use teaching methods and materials to which school officials might object. A U.S. District Court, however, upheld the school board policy against Learnball (*Murray v. Pittsburgh Board of Public Education* 1996).

Although the courts have held that teachers have the right to academic freedom, it is not absolute and must be balanced against the interests of society. In fact, education law expert Michael LaMorte (1999, 189–90) suggests that the concept of academic freedom "is no longer as strong a defense as it once was"; for this defense to prevail "it must be shown that the teacher did not defy legitimate state and local curriculum directives; followed accepted professional norms for that grade level and subject matter; discussed matters which were of public concern; and acted professionally and in good faith when there was no precedent or policy."

Famous Cases   A landmark case involving academic freedom focused on John Scopes, a biology teacher who challenged a Tennessee law in 1925 that made it illegal to teach in a public school "any theory which denies the story of the Divine Creation of man as taught in the Bible, and to teach instead that man is descended from a lower order of animals." Scopes maintained that Darwin's theory about human origins had scientific merit and that the state's requirement that he teach the biblical account of creation violated his academic freedom.

Scopes's trial, which came to be known as the Monkey Trial, attracted national attention. Prosecuting Scopes was the "silver-tongued" William Jennings Bryan, a famous lawyer, politician, and presidential candidate. The defending attorney was Clarence Darrow.

Scopes believed strongly in academic freedom and his students' right to know about scientific theories. He expressed his views in his memoirs, *Center of the Storm*:

Especially repulsive are laws restricting the constitutional freedom of teachers. The mere presence of such a law is a club held over the heads of the timid. Legislation that tampers with academic freedom is not protecting society, as its authors piously proclaim. By limiting freedom they are helping to make robot factories out of schools; ultimately, this produces nonthinking robots rather than the individualistic citizens we desperately need—now more than ever before (1966, 277).

The Monkey Trial ended after eleven days of heated, eloquent testimony. Scopes was found guilty of violating the Butler Act and was fined $100. The decision was later reversed by the Tennessee Supreme Court on a technicality.

Since the Scopes trail, controversy has continued to surround the teaching of evolution. In many states during the 1980s, for example, religious fundamentalists won rulings that required science teachers to give equal time to both creationism and evolutionism in the classroom. The Supreme Court, however, in *Edwards v. Aguillard* (1987) ruled that such "balanced treatment" laws were unconstitutional. In the words of the Court: "Because the primary purpose of the [Louisiana] Creationism Act is to advance a particular religious belief, the Act endorses religion in violation of the First Amendment." In 1996, controversy over evolution again emerged in Tennessee when lawmakers defeated, by a 20 to 13 vote, legislation that would allow districts to dismiss teachers for "insubordination" if they taught evolution as fact.

Another case suggesting that a teacher's right to academic freedom is narrow and limited is *Krizek v. Cicero-Stickney Township High School District No. 201* (1989). In this instance, a District Court ruled against a teacher whose contract was not renewed because she showed her students an R-rated film *(About Last Night)* as an example of a modern-day parallel to Thornton Wilder's play *Our Town*. Although the teacher told her students that they would be excused from viewing the film if they or their parents objected, she did not communicate directly with their parents. The teacher's attempt to consider the objections of students and parents notwithstanding, the Court concluded that

> . . . the length of the film indicates that its showing was more than an inadvertent mistake or a mere slip of the tongue, but rather was a planned event, and thus indicated that the teacher's approach to teaching was problematic. . . .

Though concerned more with the right of a school to establish a curriculum than with the academic freedom of teachers per se, other cases have focused on the teacher's use of instructional materials. In *Mozert v. Hawkins County Board of Education* (1987, 1988), for example, a group of Tennessee parents objected to "secular humanist" reading materials used by their children's teachers. In *Smith v. Board of School Commissioners of Mobile County* (1987), 624 parents and teachers initiated a court suit alleging that forty-four history, social studies, and home economics texts used in the Mobile County, Alabama, public schools encouraged immorality, undermined parental authority, and were imbued with the "humanist" faith. In both cases, the courts supported the right of schools to establish a curriculum even in the face of parental disapproval. In *Smith v. Board of School Commissioners of Mobile County* (1987) the Eleventh Circuit Court stated that "[i]ndeed, given the diversity of religious views in this country, if the standard were merely inconsistency with the beliefs of a particular religion there would be very little that could be taught in the public schools. . . ."

States' Rights   The preceding cases notwithstanding, the courts have not set down specific guidelines to reconcile the teacher's freedom with the state's right to require teachers to follow certain curricular guidelines. The same federal court, for example, heard a similar case regarding a high school teacher who wrote a vulgar word for sexual intercourse on the blackboard during a discussion of socially taboo words. The court actually sidestepped the issue of academic freedom and ruled instead that the regulations authorizing teacher discipline were unconstitutionally vague and, therefore, the teacher could not be dismissed. The court did, however, observe that a public school teacher's right to traditional academic freedom is "qualified," at best, and the "teacher's right must yield to compelling public interests of greater constitutional significance."

In reviewing its decision, the court also said, "Nothing herein suggests that school authorities are not free after they have learned that the teacher is using a teaching method of which they disapprove, and which is not appropriate to the proper teaching of the subject, to suspend him [or her] until he [or she] agrees to cease using the method" (*Mailloux v. Kiley* 1971).

Although some teachers have been successful in citing academic freedom as the basis for teaching controversial subjects, others have been unsuccessful. Teachers have been dismissed for ignoring directives regarding the teaching of controversial topics related to sex, polygamy, race, and religion. Though the courts have not been able to clarify just where academic freedom begins and ends, they have made it clear that the state does have a legitimate interest in what is taught to impressionable children.

 **Professional Reflection**   **Evaluating statements about academic freedom**

Edward B. Jenkinson (1995, 70–73) suggests that the following statements about the "schoolbook protest movement" and its attempts to restrict teachers' academic freedom are myths and/or misunderstandings:

- Protesters are primarily concerned with "filth."
- Parents have the right to request that books be removed.
- Schoolbook protesters play by the rules.
- Public schools preach "alien religions."
- Public schools may not mention the Bible or religions.

Do you agree with Jenkinson? What examples can you provide to support his observations? How should a teacher respond to a perceived attempt to restrict his or her academic freedom? Are censorship attempts always a threat to academic freedom?

Do Student Teachers Have the Same Rights?

Do student teachers have the same legal status as certified teachers? Read the following case:

> Meg Grant had really looked forward to the eight weeks she would spend as a student teacher in Mrs. Walker's high school English classes. Meg knew that Mrs. Walker was one of the best supervising teachers she might have been paired with, and she was anxious to do her best.
>
> In Mrs. Walker's senior class, Meg planned to teach *Brave New World*. Mrs. Walker pointed out to Meg that this book was controversial and some parents might object. She asked Meg to think about selecting an additional title that students could read if their parents objected to *Brave New World*. Meg, however, felt that Mrs. Walker was bowing to pressure from conservative parents, so she decided to go ahead and teach the book.
>
> Two weeks later Meg was called down to the principal's office where she was confronted by an angry father who said, "You have no right to be teaching my daughter this Communist trash; you're just a student teacher." What should Meg do? Does she have the same rights as a fully certified teacher?

Legal Advice for Student Teachers

1. Read the teacher's handbook, if one is available, and discuss its contents with the cooperating teacher. Be sure you understand its requirements and prohibitions.

2. Thoroughly discuss school safety rules and regulations. Be certain you know what to do in case of emergency, before assuming complete control of the classroom.

3. Be aware of the potential hazards associated with any activity and act accordingly to protect children from those dangers.

4. Be certain you know what controls the district has placed on the curriculum you will be teaching. Are there specific texts and/or methodologies that district policy requires or prohibits?

5. Be certain that student records are used to enhance and inform your teaching. Make certain that strict confidentiality is respected.

6. Document any problems you have with students, or as a teacher, in case you are called upon to relate details at a later time.

Figure 6.1

Legal advice for student teachers
Source: Julie Mead and Julie Underwood, "A Legal Primer for Student Teachers." In Gloria Slick (Ed.), *Emerging Trends in Teacher Preparation: The Future of Field Experiences.* Thousand Oaks, CA: Corwin Press, Inc., 1995, pp. 49–50.

In some states, a student teacher such as Meg might have the same rights and responsibilities as a fully certified teacher; in others, her legal status might be that of an unlicensed visitor. The most prudent action for Meg to take would be to apologize to the father and assure him that if any controversial books are assigned in the future, alternative titles would be provided. In addition, Meg should learn how important it is for a student teacher to take the advice of his or her supervising teacher.

The exact status of student teachers has been the subject of controversy in many states. In fact, one study found that the authority of student teachers to teach was established by law in only forty states, and no state had a statutory provision regulating the dismissal of a student teacher, the assignment of a student teacher, or the denial of the right to student teach (Morris and Curtis 1983). Nevertheless, student teachers should be aware that a potential for liability exists with them just as it does with certified teachers.

One area of debate regarding student teachers is whether they can act as substitutes for their cooperating teachers or even other teachers in a school building. Unfortunately, many school districts have no policy regarding this practice. Depending on statutes in a particular state, however, a student teacher may substitute under the following conditions:

- A substitute teacher is not immediately available.
- The student teacher has been in that student teaching assignment for a minimum number of school days.
- The supervising teacher, the principal of the school, and the university supervisor agree that the student teacher is capable of successfully handling the teaching responsibilities.
- A certificated classroom teacher in an adjacent room or a member of the same teaching team as the student teacher is aware of the absence and agrees to assist the student teacher if needed.
- The principal of the school or the principal's representative is readily available in the building.
- The student teacher is not paid for any substitute service (Shoop and Dunklee 1992, 98).

Given the ambiguous status of student teachers, it is important that you begin your student teaching assignment with a knowledge of the legal aspects of teaching and a clear idea of your rights and responsibilities. To accomplish this, read the "NEA Bill of Rights for Student Teachers" in Appendix 6.2 and follow the recommendations in Figure 6.1 made by school law experts Julie Mead and Julie Underwood.

What Are Your Legal Responsibilities as a Teacher?

Teachers are, of course, responsible for meeting the terms of their teaching contracts. As noted previously, teachers are responsible for duties not covered in the contract if they are reasonably related to teaching. Among these duties may be club sponsorship; lunchroom, study hall, or playground duty; academic counseling of students; and record keeping.

Teachers are also legally responsible for the safety and well-being of students assigned to them. Although it is not expected that a teacher be able to control completely the behavior of young, energetic students, a teacher can be held liable for any injury to a student if it is shown that the teacher's negligence contributed to the injury.

Avoiding Tort Liability

An eighth-grade science teacher in Louisiana left her class for a few moments to go to the school office to pick up some forms. While she was gone, her students continued to do some laboratory work that involved the use of alcohol-burning devices. Unfortunately, one girl was injured when she tried to relight a defective burner. Could the teacher be held liable for the girl's injuries?

The events described above actually occurred in 1974 *(Station v. Travelers Insurance Co.)*. The court that heard the case determined that the teacher failed to provide adequate supervision while the students were exposed to dangerous conditions. Considerable care is required, the court observed, when students handle inherently dangerous objects, and the need for this care is magnified when students are exposed to dangers they don't appreciate.

At times, teachers may have concerns about their liability for damages as a result of their actions. The branch of law concerned with compensating an individual who suffers losses resulting from another's negligence is known as tort law. "A tort is a civil wrong in which one suffers loss as a result of the improper conduct of another" (LaMorte 1999, 384). The harm inflicted on the injured party may be the result of "intentional wrongdoing, recklessness, or simple carelessness" (Imber and van Geel 1993, 575). According to **tort liability** law, an individual who is negligent and at fault in the exercise of his or her legal duty may be required to pay monetary damages to an injured party. Generally, the standard of behavior applied by the courts is that the injury "must be avoidable by the exercise of reasonable care" (McCarthy, Cambron-McCabe, and Thomas 1998, 436). However, teachers are held to a higher standard than ordinary citizens, and certain teachers (e.g., physical education and chemistry teachers) are held to an even higher standard because of

Should this teacher/coach have any concerns about tort liability? How might this teacher reduce the risk of liability?

Table 6.1

Selected court decisions in which school personnel were found negligent for failure to meet a "standard of care"

1. A woodworking instructor allowed a student to operate a table saw without the use of a safeguard, which resulted in serious damage to his proximal interphalangeal joint. *Barbin v. State,* 506 So. 2d 88 (1st Cir. 1987).

2. A student dislocated his shoulder during an intramural football game, when the school provided no protective equipment and improper supervision of the game. *Locilento v. John A. Coleman Catholic High School,* 523 N.Y.S. 2d 198 (A.D. 3d Dept. 1987).

3. An eleven-year-old student suffered serious head injuries from a blow in the head during a kick game and was without medical attention for more than an hour. The one-hour delay caused a hematoma to grow from the size of a walnut to that of an orange. *Barth v. Board of Education,* 490 N.E. 2d 77 (Ill.app. 186 Dist. 1986).

4. An eight-year-old girl was seriously burned when her costume caught fire from a lighted candle on her teacher's desk. *Smith v. Archbishop of St. Louis,* 632, S.W. 2d 516 (Mo. app. 1982).

5. A twelve-year-old boy was killed when he fell through a skylight at school while retrieving a ball. *Stahl v. Cocalico School District,* 534 A. 2d 1141 (Pa. Cmwlth. 1987).

6. A boy was seriously injured while playing on school grounds when he fell into a hole filled with glass, trash, and other debris, due to the absence of school officials to warn him of the dangerous condition. *Dean v. Board of Education,* 523 A. 2d 1059 (Md. App. 1987).

7. A female student was in route to class when she pushed her hand through a glass panel in a smoke-colored door, causing severe and permanent damage. *Bielaska v. Town of Waterford,* 491 A. 2d 1071 (Conn. 1985).

8. A high school student was seriously injured when he was tackled and thrown to the ground during a touch football game in gym class, based on inadequate supervision when the players began to use excessive force. *Hyman v. Green,* 403 N.W. 2d 597 (Mich. App. 1987).

Source: From Nathan L. Essex, *School Law and the Public Schools: A Practical Guide for Educational Leaders.* Boston: Allyn and Bacon, 1999, pp. 110, 126. Copyright © 1999 by Allyn & Bacon. Reprinted by permission.

the increased risk of injury involved in the classes they teach. Table 6.1 presents several examples of cases in which students were injured and educators were found to have breached their duty of care.

Negligence In contrast to the decision reached by the Louisiana court mentioned earlier, the courts have made it clear that there are many accidents that teachers cannot reasonably foresee that do result in student injuries. For example, a teacher on playground duty was found to be not negligent when a student threw a rock that struck another student in the eye. After the teacher walked past a group of boys, one boy threw a small rock that hit a larger rock on the ground and then bounced up to hit the other boy in the eye. The court ruled that "[w]here the time between an act of a student and injury to a fellow student is so short that the teacher had no opportunity to prevent injury, it cannot be said that negligence of the teacher is a proximate cause of the injury" (*Fagen v. Summers* 1972). In another case, the court ruled that a New York teacher could not have anticipated that the paper bag she asked a student to pick up contained a broken bottle upon which the student cut herself (*West v. Board of Education of City of New York* 1959). In two almost identical cases, the courts ruled that a teacher of a class with a good behavior record could not reasonably be expected to anticipate that a student would be injured by a pencil thrown by a classmate while the teacher was momentarily out of the room attending to her usual duties (*Ohman v. Board of Education* 1950; *Simonetti v. School District of Philadelphia* 1983).

When a court considers a case involving tort liability, evidence is examined to determine whether the responsible party (the school district, the administrator, or the teacher) acted negligently. For a school official to be considered liable, the following must be shown to be present:

1. A legal duty to conform to a standard of conduct for the protection of others
2. A failure to exercise an appropriate standard of care
3. A causal connection, often referred to as "proximate cause," between the conduct and the resultant injury
4. Actual loss or damage as a result of the injury (LaMorte 1999, 400–01)

As a teacher, you should be especially alert when conditions exist that might lead to accidental injury of one or more students. You will have a duty in regard to your pupils, and you could be held liable for injuries that students incur as a result of your **negligence.** This does not mean, however, that your liability extends to any and all injuries your students might suffer; only if you fail to provide the same degree of care for pupils that a reasonable and prudent person would have shown in similar circumstances can you be held liable. Our review of court cases involving the tort liability of teachers suggests that most cases involve at least one of the following:

■ Inadequate supervision
■ Inadequate instruction
■ Lack of or improper medical treatment of pupils
■ Improper disclosure of defamatory information concerning pupils—for example, release of school records that contain negative statements about a student

Teachers' concern about their potential monetary liability for failing to act reasonably and prudently in preventing injury to their students has been lessened by the availability of liability insurance. Many professional organizations for teachers offer liability coverage as part of their membership benefits, and teachers may also purchase individual liability insurance policies. In addition, some states that provide school districts with full or partial immunity from tort liability are considering extending the same protection to school employees. Georgia, for example, has extended immunity to teachers and principals (LaMorte 1999).

Educational Malpractice   Since the mid-1970s several plaintiffs have charged in their **educational malpractice** suits that schools should be responsible for a pupil whose failure to achieve is significant. In the first of such cases, the parents of Peter W. Doe charged that the San Francisco Unified School District was negligent because it allowed him to graduate from high school with a fifth-grade reading level and this handicap would not enable him to function in adult society. In particular, they charged that the "defendant school district, its agents and employees, negligently and carelessly failed to provide plaintiff with adequate instruction, guidance, counseling and/or supervision in basic academic skills such as reading and writing, although said school district had the authority, responsibility, and ability [to do so]." They sought $500,000 for the negligent work of the teachers who taught Peter.

Table 6.2

Physical and behavioral indicators of child abuse and neglect

Type of Child Abuse/Neglect	Physical Indicators	Behavioral Indicators
Physical Abuse	Unexplained bruises and welts:	Wary of adult contacts
	■ on face, lips, mouth	Apprehensive when other children cry
	■ on torso, back, buttocks, thighs	Behavioral extremes:
	■ in various stages of healing	■ aggressiveness
	■ clustered, forming regular patterns	■ withdrawal
	■ reflecting shape of article used to inflict (electric cord, belt buckle)	■ overly compliant
	■ on several different surface areas	Afraid to go home
	■ regularly appear after absence, weekend, or vacation	Reports injury by parents
	■ human bite marks	Exhibits anxiety about normal activities, e.g., napping
	■ bald spots	Complains of soreness and moves awkwardly
	Unexplained burns:	Destructive to self and others
	■ cigar, cigarette burns, especially on soles, palms, back, or buttocks	Early to school or stays late as if afraid to go home
	■ immersion burns (sock-like, glove-like, doughnut-shaped on buttocks or genitalia)	Accident prone
	■ patterned like electric burner, iron, etc.	Wears clothing that covers body when not appropriate
	■ rope burns on arms, legs, neck, or torso	Chronic runaway (especially adolescents)
	Unexplained fractures:	Cannot tolerate physical contact or touch
	■ to skull, nose, facial structure	
	■ in various stages of healing	
	■ multiple or spiral fractures	
	Unexplained lacerations or abrasions:	
	■ to mouth, lips, gums, eyes	
	■ to external genitalia	
	Consistent hunger, poor hygiene, inappropriate dress	
Physical Neglect	Consistent lack of supervision, especially in dangerous activities or long periods	Begging, stealing food
	Unattended physical problems or medical needs	Constant fatigue, listlessness, or falling asleep
	Abandonment	States there is no caretaker at home
	Lice	Frequent school absence or tardiness
	Distended stomach, emaciated	Destructive, pugnacious
		School dropout (adolescents)
		Early emancipation from family (adolescents)

In evaluating the claim of Peter W. Doe and his parents, the court pointed out that the alleged injury was not within the realm of tort law and that many factors beyond a school's responsibility or control can account for lack of achievement. The court did not hold the school responsible for Peter's lack of achievement and made it clear that to do so would be to set a precedent with potentially drastic consequences: "To hold

Table 6.2 continued

Type of Child Abuse/Neglect	Physical Indicators	Behavioral Indicators
Sexual Abuse	Difficulty in walking or sitting ■ torn, stained, or bloody underclothing Pain or itching in genital area Bruises or bleeding in external genitalia, vaginal, or anal areas Venereal disease Frequent urinary or yeast infections Frequent unexplained sore throats	Unwilling to participate in certain physical activities Sudden drop in school performance Withdrawal, fantasy, or unusually infantile behavior Crying with no provocation Bizarre, sophisticated, or unusual sexual behavior or knowledge Anorexia (especially adolescents) Sexually provocative Poor peer relationships Reports sexual assault by caretaker Fear of or seductiveness toward males Suicide attempts (especially adolescents) Chronic runaway Early pregnancies
Emotional Maltreatment	Speech disorders Lags in physical development Failure to thrive (especially in infants) Asthma, severe allergies, or ulcers Substance abuse	Habit disorders (sucking, biting, rocking, etc.) Conduct disorders (antisocial, destructive, etc.) Neurotic traits (sleep disorders, inhibition of play) Behavioral extremes: ■ compliant, passive ■ aggressive, demanding Overly adaptive behavior: ■ inappropriately adult ■ inappropriately infantile Developmental lags (mental, emotional) Delinquent behavior (especially adolescents)

Source: Adapted from Cynthia Crosson Tower, *The Role of Educators in the Prevention and Treatment of Child Abuse and Neglect,* The User Manual Series, 1992. Washington, DC: U.S. Department of Health and Human Services; and Derry Koralek, *Caregivers of Young Children: Preventing and Responding to Child Maltreatment,* The User Manual Series, 1992. Washington, DC: U.S. Department of Health and Human Services.

[schools] to an actionable duty of care, in the discharge of their academic functions, would expose them to the tort claims—real or imagined—of disaffected students and parents in countless numbers. . . . The ultimate consequences, in terms of public time and money, would burden them—and society—beyond calculation" (*Peter Doe v. San Francisco Unified School District* 1976).

Reporting Child Abuse

Teachers, who are now *required* by law to report any suspected child abuse, are in positions to monitor and work against the physical, emotional, and sexual abuse and the neglect and exploitation of children. Teachers' professional journals and information from local, state, and federal child welfare agencies encourage teachers to be more observant of children's appearance and behavior in order to detect symptoms of child abuse. Such sources often provide lists of physical and behavioral indicators of potential child abuse, similar to that shown in Table 6.2 on page 218–219. Many communities, through their police departments or other public and private agencies, provide programs adapted for children to educate them about their rights in child-abuse situations and to show them how to obtain help.

Schools usually have a specific process for dealing with suspected abuse cases, involving the school principal and nurse as well as the reporting teacher. Because a child's physical welfare may be further endangered when abuse is reported, caution and sensitivity are required. Teachers are in a unique position to help students who are victims of child abuse, both because they have daily contact with them and because children learn to trust them.

Observing Copyright Laws

The continuing rapid development of technology has resulted in a new set of responsibilities for teachers in regard to observing **copyright laws** pertaining to the use of photocopies, videotapes, and computer software programs. In 1976 Congress revised the Copyright Act by adding the doctrine of **fair use**. Although the fair use doctrine cannot be precisely defined, it is generally interpreted as it was in *Marcus v. Rowley* (1983)—that is, one may "use the copyrighted material in a reasonable manner without [the copyright holder's] consent" as long as that use does not reduce the demand for the work or the author's income.

With the vast amount of material (in text, audio, video, and graphic formats) now distributed in digital form over the Internet, teachers must consider copyright laws and restrictions that apply to the use of this material. Unfortunately, the Copyright Act does not provide guidelines for the use of intellectual property found on the Internet. In any case, teachers should understand that ". . . when [their] computer displays a home page on the Internet, [the] computer is presenting a copy of the page that 'exists' on a remote computer. . . . [They] are viewing a published copy of an original document" (Schwartz and Beichner 1999, 199), and the doctrine of fair use applies to the use of such materials.

Photocopies   To clarify the fair use doctrine as it pertained to teachers photocopying instructional materials from books and magazines, Congress endorsed a set of guidelines developed by educators, authors, and publishers. These guidelines allow teachers to make single copies of copyrighted material for teaching or research but are more restrictive regarding the use of multiple copies. The use of multiple copies of a work must meet the tests of brevity, spontaneity, and cumulative effect.

- *Brevity* means that short works can be copied. Poems or excerpts cannot be longer than 250 words, and copies of longer works cannot exceed 1,000 words or 10 percent of the work (whichever is less). Only one chart or drawing can be reproduced from a book or an article.
- The criterion of *spontaneity* means that the teacher doing the copying would not have time to request permission from the copyright holder.

highlights

What ethical and legal issues will you face regarding the use of computer software?

With the explosion of computer-based technology in schools, teachers face a new ethical and legal issue—adhering to copyright laws as they relate to computer software. Making an illegal copy of software on a computer hard drive—in effect, stealing another person's "intellectual property"—is quite easy. In fact, "It is very common for otherwise ethical and moral people to ask for and/or offer illegal copies of software to one another" (Schwartz and Beichner 1999, 193). It is therefore important that, as a teacher, you be an exemplar of ethical behavior regarding copyrighted computer software. Just as you would not allow students to plagiarize written material or submit work that was not their own, you should follow the same standard of behavior regarding the use of computer software.

Currently, the Copyright Act is being revised to reflect how the doctrine of fair use should be applied to digital data. "Revisions to the Copyright Act will require a balancing of authors' interests in compensation for intellectual work and educators' continuing concern for 'fair use'" (McCarthy, Cambron-McCabe, and Thomas 1998, 265–66). Two questions currently not answered by copyright law as it pertains to the educational use of computer software are the legality of (1) installing a single program on several computers in a laboratory and (2) modifying the program for use in a computer network.

Imagine that during your first year of teaching a colleague suggests using a software program in one (or both) of the preceding ways. Analyze your colleague's suggestion in light of the following excerpt from the Copyright Act, which presents four factors that are considered to determine whether use of copyrighted material constitutes fair use or an infringement:

(1) the purpose and character of the use, including whether such use is of a commercial nature or is for non-profit educational purposes; (2) the nature of the copyrighted work; (3) the amount and substantiality of the portion used in relation to the copyrighted work as a whole; and (4) the effect of the use on the potential market for or value of the copyrighted work.

How do you respond to your colleague's suggestion? What is the rationale for your response?

▪ The criterion of *cumulative effect* limits the use of copies to one course and limits the material copied from the same author, book, or magazine during the semester. Also, no more than nine instances of multiple copying per class are allowed during a semester.

Videotapes   Guidelines for the use of videotapes made by teachers of television broadcasts were issued by Congress in 1981 (see the Appendix, "Guidelines for Off-Air Recordings", on this book's website). Videotaped material may be used in the classroom only once by the teacher within the first ten days of taping. Additional use is limited to reinforcing instruction or evaluation of student learning, and the tape must be erased within forty-five days.

Computer Software   Computer software publishers have become concerned about the abuse of their copyrighted material. Limited school budgets and the high cost of

Table 6.3

Common types of commercial software licenses

License Type	What Is Permitted	Suitability for Schools
Single-User License	Permits installation on one and only one computer.	Not usually economical for schools.
Multiple-User License (sometimes called a "Lab Pack")	Permits installation on up to a specified number of computers (typically 5, 10, 50, etc.).	Economical and commonly found in K–12 schools.
Network License	Permits installation on a network. License will specify the maximum number of simultaneous users.	Economical and commonly found in larger K–12 schools if they are networked.
Site License	Permits installation on any and all computers owned by the institution.	Not typically used in K–1 2 schools. More common for college campuses.

Source: From James E. Schwartz and Robert J. Beichner, *Essentials of Educational Technology.* Boston: Allyn and Bacon, 1999, p. 195. Copyright © 1999 by Allyn and Bacon.

computer software have led to the unauthorized reproduction of software. To address the problem, the Copyright Act was amended in 1980 to apply the fair use doctrine to software. Accordingly, a teacher may now make one backup copy of a program. If a teacher were to make multiple copies of software, the fair use doctrine would be violated because the software is readily accessible for purchase and making multiple copies would substantially reduce the market for the software. Software publishers have several different options for licensing their software to schools (see Table 6.3), and teachers should be aware of the type of license that has been purchased with each software program they use.

The increased practice of networking computer programs—that is, storing a copy of a computer program on a network file server and serving the program to a computer on the network—is also of concern to software publishers. As yet, the practice has not yet been tested in the courts. As more public schools develop computer networks, however, the issue of networked software will most likely be debated in the courts.

Electronic Mail and the Internet   With the huge increase in the transmission of documents via electronic mail (e-mail) and the Internet, copyright laws have been extended to cyberspace. Material "published" online may include a statement by the author(s) that the material is copyright protected and may not be duplicated without permission. In other cases, the material may include a statement such as the following: "Permission is granted to distribute this material freely through electronic or by other means, provided it remains completely intact and unaltered, the source is acknowledged, and no fee is charged for it." If the material is published without restrictions on the Internet, one may assume that the author waives copyright privileges; however, proper credit and a citation should accompany the material if it is reproduced.

Publishing on the Internet   Thousands of teachers and their students around the globe are publishing material at their home pages on the Internet. Teacher- and student-produced materials can be copyright protected by including a statement that the materials may not be duplicated without permission. In addition, teachers should be careful not to include information that would enable someone to identify children in a class. Children's last names should never be published, nor should photos of children be published with any identifying information.

What Are the Legal Rights of Students and Parents?

As a prospective teacher, you have an obligation to become familiar with the rights of students. Since the 1960s students have increasingly confronted teachers and school districts with what they perceived to be illegal restrictions on their behavior. In this section we discuss briefly some of the major court decisions that have clarified students' rights related to freedom of expression, suspension and expulsion, search and seizure, privacy, and nondiscrimination.

Freedom of Expression

The case of *Tinker v. Des Moines Independent Community School District* (1969) is perhaps the most frequently cited case concerning students' **freedom of expression.** The Supreme Court ruled in *Tinker* that three students, ages thirteen, fifteen, and sixteen, had been denied their First Amendment freedom of expression when they were suspended from school for wearing black arm bands in protest of the Vietnam War. The court ruled that neither teachers nor students "shed their rights to freedom of speech or expression at the schoolhouse gate." In addition, the court found no evidence that the exercise of such a right interfered with the school's operation.

Censorship   One area of student expression that has generated frequent controversy is that of student publications. Prior to 1988, the courts generally made it clear that student literature enjoyed constitutional protection, and it could only be regulated if it posed a substantial threat of school disruption, if it was libelous, or if it was judged vulgar or obscene *after publication.* However, school officials could use "prior **censorship**" and require students to submit literature before publication if such controls were necessary to maintain order in the school.

Within these guidelines, students frequently successfully defended their right to freedom of expression. For example, the right of high school students to place in the school newspaper an advertisement against the war in Vietnam was upheld (*Zucker v. Panitz* 1969). Students were also upheld in their right to distribute information on birth control and on laws regarding marijuana (*Shanley v. Northeast Independent School District* 1972). And other cases upheld the right of students to publish literature that was critical of teachers, administrators, and other school personnel (*Scoville v. Board of Education of Joliet Township High School District 204* 1971; *Sullivan v. Houston Independent School District* 1969).

In January of 1988, however, the Supreme Court, in a five-to-three ruling in *Hazelwood School District v. Kuhlmeier,* departed from the earlier *Tinker* decision and gave public school officials considerable authority to censor school-sponsored student publications. The case involved a Missouri high school principal's censorship of articles in the school newspaper, the *Spectrum,* on teenage pregnancy and the impact of divorce on students. The principal believed the articles were inappropriate because they might identify pregnant students and because references to sexual activity and birth control were inappropriate for younger students. Several students on the newspaper staff distributed copies of the articles on their own and later sued the school district, claiming that their First Amendment rights had been violated.

Writing for the majority in *Hazelwood School District v. Kuhlmeier* Justice Byron White (who had voted with the majority in *Tinker*) said school officials could bar "speech that is ungrammatical, poorly written, inadequately researched, biased or prejudiced, vulgar or profane, or unsuitable for immature audiences." White also pointed out that *Tinker* focused on a student's right of "personal expression," and the Missouri case dealt with school-sponsored publications that were part of the curriculum and bore the "imprimatur of the school." According to White, "Educators do not offend the First Amendment by exercising editorial control over the style and content of student speech in school-sponsored expressive activities so long as their actions are reasonably related to legitimate pedagogical concerns."

A case involving an attempt to regulate an "underground" student newspaper entitled *Bad Astra,* however, had a different outcome. Five high school students in Renton, Washington, produced a four-page newspaper at their expense, off school property, and without the knowledge of school authorities. *Bad Astra* contained articles that criticized school policies, a mock poll evaluating teachers, and several poetry selections. The students distributed 350 copies of the paper at a senior class barbecue held on school grounds.

After the paper was distributed, the principal placed letters of reprimand in the five students' files, and the district established a new policy whereby student-written, non-school-sponsored materials with an intended distribution of more than ten were subject to predistribution review. The students filed suit in federal district court, claiming a violation of their First Amendment rights. The court, however, ruled that the new policy was "substantially constitutional." Maintaining that the policy was unconstitutional, the students filed an appeal in 1988 in the Ninth Circuit Court and won. The court ruled that *Bad Astra* was not "within the purview of the school's exercise of reasonable editorial control" (*Burch v. Barker* 1987, 1988).

Dress Codes   Few issues related to the rights of students have generated as many court cases as have dress codes and hairstyles. The demand on the courts to hear such cases prompted Supreme Court Justice Hugo L. Black to observe that he did not believe "the federal Constitution imposed on the United States Courts the burden of supervising the length of hair that public school students should wear" (*Karr v. Schmidt* 1972). In line with Justice Black's observation, the Supreme Court has repeatedly refused to review the decisions reached by the lower courts.

In general, the courts have suggested that schools may have dress codes as long as such codes are clear, reasonable, and students are notified. However, when the legality of such codes has been challenged, the rulings have largely indicated that schools may not control what students wear unless it is immodest or is disruptive of the educational process.

Students in private schools, however, do not have First Amendment protections provided by *Tinker v. Des Moines Independent Community School District* because private schools are not state affiliated. As a result, students at private schools can be required to wear uniforms, and "[d]isagreements over 'student rights' . . . are generally resolved by applying contract law to the agreement governing the student's attendance" (LaMorte 1999, 98).

At one time, educators' concerns about student appearance may have been limited to hairstyles and immodest dress; however, today's educators, as Michael LaMorte

(1996, 93) points out, may be concerned about "T-shirts depicting violence, drugs (e.g., marijuana leaves), racial epithets, or characters such as Bart Simpson; ripped, baggy, or saggy pants or jeans; sneakers with lights; colored bandannas, baseball or other hats; words shaved into scalps, brightly colored hair, distinctive haircuts or hairstyles, or ponytails for males; exposed underwear; Malcolm X symbols; Walkmen, cellular phones, or beepers; backpacks; tatoos, unusual-colored lipstick, pierced noses, or earrings; and decorative dental caps."

Since gangs, hate groups, and violence in and around public schools have become more prevalent during the last decade, rulings that favor schools are becoming more common when the courts "balance the First Amendment rights of students to express themselves against the legitimate right of school authorities to maintain a safe and disruption-free environment" (LaMorte 1999, 147). This balance is clearly illustrated in *Jeglin v. San Jacinto Unified School District* (1993). In this instance, a school's dress code prohibiting the wearing of clothing with writing, pictures, or insignia of professional or college athletic teams was challenged on the grounds that it violated students' freedom of expression. The court acknowledged that the code violated the rights of elementary and middle school students, but not those of high school students. Gangs, known to be present at the high school, had intimidated students and faculty in connection with the sports-oriented clothing. The court ruled that the curtailment of students' rights did not "demand a certainty that disruption will occur, but only the existence of facts which might reasonably lead school officials to forecast substantial disruption."

After the Colorado high school shootings in 1999, which left fouteen students and a teacher dead—including the two gunmen who were members of a clique called the "Trench Coat Mafia"—many school districts made their rules for student dress more restrictive. Ten days after the shootings, a federal judge who upheld a school's decision to suspend a student for wearing a T-shirt that said "Vegan" (a vegetarian who doesn't eat animal products), said "gang attire has become particularly troubling since two students wore trench coats in the Colorado shooting." And, in Jonesboro, Arkansas, where four students and a teacher were shot and killed the previous year, a group of boys and girls identifying themselves as the "Blazer Mafia" were suspended for ten days (Portner, May 12, 1999).

To reduce disruption and violence in schools, some school districts and policy makers have considered requiring students to wear uniforms. During his last term in office, President Clinton frequently expressed his support for school uniforms; for example, during a conversation with high school students in Alexandria, Virginia, two days after the Colorado shootings, he had this to say about the effects of the nation's first mandatory school uniform policy in Long Beach, California: "it [the uniform policy] distinguished [students] from the gangs, which created a safety problem . . . it made all the kids safe. And it lowered dropouts, it increased attendance, it reduced discipline problems" (1999). The U.S. Department of Education, which has developed guidelines for schools that wish to implement a uniform policy, reported in 1998 that 4 percent of public elementary schools and 4 percent of middle schools required students to wear uniforms.

Due Process in Suspension and Expulsion

In February and March of 1971, a total of nine students received ten-day suspensions from the Columbus, Ohio, public school system during a period of citywide unrest. One student, in the presence of his principal, physically attacked a police officer who

Should schools require students to wear uniforms?

"**W**hen students trade in their unofficial uniforms of baggy pants, message T-shirts, backward baseball caps, and name-brand sneakers for a school-sanctioned outfit of white dress shirts, ties, and dark pants or skirts, do they behave better and take school more seriously?" *American Teacher* writer Daniel Gursky (1996) asks the question and responds affirmatively. Observing that few teachers object, he quips: "Given rampant disorder among students, why criticize something that appears to make a difference?" Others disagree and regard the apparent rush to adopt school uniform policies as a simplistic response to a complex problem and a fad lacking in foundation.

In 1994 the school system in Long Beach, California, adopted a uniform policy for all of its K–8 students. In 1995, California passed a state law that permitted the state's schools to require students to wear uniforms. Soon after, according to the U.S. Department of Education's *Manual on Uniforms,* (1996) Florida, Georgia, Indiana, Louisiana, Maryland, New York, Tennessee, Utah and Virginia enacted similar laws, and major school systems in cities like Baltimore, Cincinnati, Detroit, Los Angeles, Memphis, Miami, Milwaukee, Nashville, Phoenix, Seattle, and St. Louis joined in with voluntary or mandatory uniform policies. *Education Week* reported on May 12, 1999, that "20 percent of the nation's school districts use uniforms, most of them voluntarily."

Implemented into these programs are "opt out" provisions, which allow students—with their parents' permission —to sidestep the uniform requirement. In addition, most programs include assistance for families unable to purchase the required uniforms.

Are these states going in the right direction by encouraging school uniforms? Should schools require students to wear uniforms?

Schools should require students to wear uniforms.

Schools should require students to wear uniforms in order to "deter violence, promote discipline, and foster a better learning community." President Clinton used these words in a memorandum to his Secretary of Education in February 1996: "Too often, we learn that students resort to violence and theft simply to obtain designer clothes or fancy sneakers. Too often, we learn that clothing items worn at school, bearing special colors or insignias, are used to identify gang membership or instill fear among students and teachers alike. If school uniforms can help deter school violence, promote discipline, and foster a better learning environment, then we should offer our strong support to the schools and parents that try them" (Noll 1999, 306).

The concern for safety that stemmed from the school shootings in Moses Lake, Washington; Pearl, Mississippi; Jonesboro, Arkansas; and Springfield, Oregon, was heightened to alarm status after the April 20, 1999, shootings in Littleton, Colorado, by two students in the "Trench Coat Mafia" at Columbine High School. In their vigilance following that event, school authorities around the country cracked down on any hints of similar violence.

With a mandatory school uniform program, inciting attire would be forbidden. Safety would be enhanced in two ways: (1) gangs and other dissident groups would not be able to display their "colors" at school, and (2) outsiders not wearing uniforms would stand out on campus. With a glance, teachers, school officials, and campus security could spot strangers (and potential violence). According to Jessica Portner's *Education Week* report of May 12, 1999, "In the four years since the Long Beach district adopted a uniform of black pants, white shirts, and red jackets, the number of assaults has dropped 85 percent, district figures show." With the absence of expensive sportswear to fight over and the increase in parent participation in designing and implementing the uniform program, more ordinary school discipline problems would also be reduced.

School learning would be enhanced in subtle ways. Just as clergy and university faculty in academic regalia move with a dignity absent when they wear casual clothes to wash cars or play sports, so too will students stand taller and conduct themselves more seriously when they dress up for school. Also, in uniforms students look equal and thus are likely to receive more equitable attention and instruction. That, combined with a learning environment that feels safer, should raise students' academic achievements.

Schools should not require students to wear uniforms.

Schools should not require students to wear uniforms. To do so tramples students' rights of free expression and subjects them to a conformity that is unhealthy, interrupting the development of adolescents' identity and independence. Uniforms can also be personally demoralizing. With them authorities send the message that the student cannot be trusted and needs to be controlled, much as prisoners do.

Mandatory uniform programs can also be degrading for students in families that cannot afford to purchase uniforms. Even though in most programs financial support is available to those in need, the stigma of receiving the assistance can be embarrassing, even humiliating.

Researchers question schools' claims that their uniform programs increase achievement, attendance, good discipline, and students' sense of safety. One contradiction to these claims is reported in *Education Week*: "Researchers David Brunsma and Kerry Rockquemore analyzed data on nearly 5,000 10th graders who took part in a federal study that began in 1988. They found that sophomores in schools requiring uniforms were not less likely than their more casually dressed peers to fight, smoke, drink alcohol, take drugs, or otherwise get in trouble at school. And they were no more likely to attend school regularly or score higher on standardized tests. In fact, the data showed that achievement scores were slightly lower for students made to wear uniforms" (Viadero 1999, p. 23).

Noll reports Dennis L. Evans' argument that "the successful programs that have been cited are mostly in elementary schools where the problems that the uniforms will allegedly solve do not exist; among adolescent gangs school uniforms will be cosmetic at best and will not change gang mentality" (Noll 1999, 307).

The lack of careful research and evaluation of the effectiveness of existing school uniform programs, the infringement on free expression, the curtailment of students' development of identity and independence, and the criticism that such programs are superficial, cause opponents to say no to requiring students to wear uniforms.

Where do you stand on this issue?

1. What is your experience with school uniforms?
2. Which position do you agree with and why?
3. Which arguments are most persuasive to you?
4. Propose a compromise position on this issue.
5. What other approaches could you develop to deter violence, promote discipline, and create a productive learning environment in schools?

Recommended Sources

Guskey, D. (1996, March). 'Uniform' improvement? *Education Digest.*

Noll, J. W. (1999). *Clashing views on controversial educational issues,* 10th ed. Guilford, CT: McGraw-Hill.

Paliokas, K. L. and Rist, R. C. Do they reduce violence—or just make us feel better? *Education Week 61*(7), 46–9.

Portner, J. (1999, May 12). Schools ratchet up the rules on student clothing, threats. *Education Week.*

U.S. Department of Education. (1996, February) *Manual on school uniforms.*

Viadero, D. (1999, January) *Education Week 10*(4), 23.

was trying to remove a disruptive student from a high school auditorium. Four others were suspended for similar conduct. Another student was suspended for his involvement in a lunchroom disturbance that resulted in damage to school property. All nine students were suspended in accordance with Ohio law. Some of the students and their parents were offered the opportunity to attend conferences prior to the start of the suspensions, but none of the nine was given a hearing. Asserting that their constitutional rights had been denied, all nine students brought suit against the school system.

In a sharply divided five-to-four decision, the Supreme Court ruled that the students had a legal right to an education, and that this "property right" could be removed only through the application of procedural due process. The court maintained that suspension is a "serious event" in the life of a suspended child and may not be imposed by the school in an arbitrary manner (*Goss v. Lopez* 1975).

As a result of cases such as *Goss v. Lopez,* every state has outlined procedures for school officials to follow in the suspension and expulsion of students. In cases of short-term suspension (defined by the courts as exclusion from school for ten days or less), the due process steps are somewhat flexible and determined by the nature of the infraction and the length of the suspension. As Figure 6.2 shows, however, long-term suspension (more than ten days) and expulsion require a more extensive due process procedure. The disciplinary transfer of a disruptive student to an alternative school, designed to meet his or her needs, is not considered an expulsion (LaMorte 1999).

In response to an increase of unruly students who disrupt the learning of others, a few districts and states have granted teachers the authority to suspend students for up to ten days. Teachers in Cincinnati and Dade County, Florida, for example, have negotiated contracts that give them authority to remove disruptive students from their classrooms; however, district administrators decide how the students will be disciplined. In 1995, Indiana became the first state to grant teachers the power to suspend students, and the following year New York's governor proposed legislation to allow teachers to remove students from their classrooms for up to ten days for "committing an act of violence against a student, teacher, or school district employee; possessing or threatening to use a gun, knife, or other dangerous weapon; damaging or destroying school district property; damaging the personal property of teachers or other employees; or defying an order from a teacher or administrator to stop disruptive behavior" (Lindsay 1996, 24).

Figure 6.2

Due process in suspension and expulsion
Source: Adapted from Martha M. McCarthy, Nelda H. Cambron-McCabe, and Stephen B. Thomas, *Public School Law: Teachers' and Students' Rights.* Boston: Allyn and Bacon, 1998, pp. 301, 205.

At minimum, students should be provided with:

Suspension for 10 days or fewer

■ Oral or written notification of the nature of the violation and the intended punishment.

■ An opportunity to refute the charges before an objective decisionmaker (such a discussion may immediately follow the alleged rule infraction).

■ An explanation of the evidence on which the disciplinarian is relying.

Long-term suspension and expulsion

■ Written notice of the charges, the intention to expel, and the place, time, and circumstances of the hearing, with sufficient time for a defense to be prepared.

■ A full and fair hearing before an impartial adjudicator.

■ The right to legal counsel or some other adult representation.

■ The right to be fully apprised of the proof or evidence.

■ The opportunity to present witnesses or evidence.

■ The opportunity to cross-examine opposing witnesses.

■ Some type of written record demonstrating that the decision was based on the evidence presented at the hearing.

Reasonable Search and Seizure

As a teacher you have reason to believe that a student has drugs, and possibly a dangerous weapon, in his locker. Do you have the right to search the student's locker and seize any illegal or dangerous items? According to the Fourth Amendment, citizens are protected from **search and seizure** conducted without a search warrant. With the escalation of drug use in schools and school-related violence, however, cases involving the legality of search and seizure in schools have increased. These cases suggest guidelines that you can follow if confronted with a situation such as that described here.

The case of *New Jersey v. T.L.O.* (1985) involved a fourteen-year-old student (T.L.O.) whom a teacher found smoking a cigarette in a rest room. The teacher took the student to the principal's office, whereupon the principal asked to see the contents of her purse. On opening the purse, the principal found a pack of cigarettes and what appeared to be drug paraphernalia and a list titled "People who owe me money." T.L.O. was arrested and later found guilty of delinquency charges.

After being sentenced to one year's probation, T.L.O. appealed, claiming that the evidence found in her purse was obtained in violation of the Fourth Amendment and that her confession to selling marijuana was tainted by an illegal search. The United States Supreme Court found that the search had been reasonable. The Court also developed a two-pronged test of "reasonableness" for searches: (1) A school official must have a reasonable suspicion that a student has violated a law or school policy and (2) the search must be conducted using methods that are reasonable in scope.

Another case focused on the use of trained dogs to conduct searches of 2,780 junior and senior high school students in Highland, Indiana. During a two-and-a-half- to three-hour period, six teams with trained German shepherds sniffed the students. The dogs alerted their handlers a total of 50 times. Seventeen of the searches initiated by the dogs turned up beer, drug paraphernalia, or marijuana. Another eleven students singled out by the dogs, including thirteen-year-old Diane Doe, were strip searched in the nurse's office. It turned out that Diane had played with her dog, who was in heat, that morning and that the police dog had responded to the smell of the other dog on Diane's clothing.

Diane's parents later filed suit, charging that their daughter was searched illegally. The court ruled that the use of dogs did not constitute an unreasonable search, nor did holding students in their homerooms constitute a mass detention in violation of the Fourth Amendment. The court did, however, hold that the strip searches of the students were unreasonable. The court pointed out that the school personnel did not have any evidence to suggest that Diane possessed contraband because, prior to the strip search, she had emptied her pockets as requested. Diane was awarded $7,500 in damages (*Doe v. Renfrow* 1980, 1981).

Court cases involving search and seizure in school settings have maintained that school lockers are the property of the schools, not students, and may be searched by school authorities if reasonable cause exists. In addition, students may be sniffed by police dogs if school authorities have a reasonable suspicion that illegal or dangerous items may be found. Lastly, courts have tended not to allow strip searches; however, as *Cornfield v. Consolidated High School District No. 230* (1993) illustrates, strip searches may be constitutional depending upon the circumstances giving rise to the search, the age of the student, and the severity of the suspected infraction. In *Cornfield*, the court allowed a strip search of a 16-year-old student suspected of "crotching" drugs. The court's decision was influenced by "allegations of several recent prior incidents such as dealing in drugs, testing positive for marijuana, possession of drugs, having 'crotched' drugs during a police raid at his mother's house, failing a urine analysis for cocaine, unsuccessful completion of a drug rehabilitation program, and a report by a bus driver that there was a smell of marijuana where the student sat on the bus" (LaMorte 1999, 144–45).

In general, the courts have tried to balance the school's need to obtain information and the student's right to privacy. To protect themselves from legal challenges related to searches, educators should follow guidelines that have been suggested by school law experts:

What are students' rights with regard to their persons, lockers, personal property, and records in school and on school grounds? How are school districts' rights of search and seizure decided? In what ways have students' rights to privacy been upheld?

- Inform students and parents at the start of the school year of the procedures for conducting locker and personal searches.
- Base any search on "reasonable suspicion."
- Conduct any search with another staff member present.
- Avoid strip searches or mass searches of groups of students.
- Require that police obtain a search warrant before conducting a search in the school.

Some schools use drug testing as a requirement for either attendance or interscholastic participation, including sports competition, or as a means of discipline. A 1988 court case upheld a urinalysis drug test for randomly selected student athletes because those who tested positively were suspended only from participating in sports for a period of time and no disciplinary or academic penalties were imposed (*Schaill v. Tippecanoe School Corporation* 1988). Similarly, the U.S. Supreme Court reversed a lower court's ruling and stated that a school district's desire to reduce drug use justified the degree of intrusion required by random tests of student athletes' urine (*Acton v. Vernonia School District* 1995). A few school districts have attempted to implement mandatory drug testing of teachers. So far the courts have upheld the decision rendered in *Patchogue-Medford Congress of Teachers v. Board of Education of Patchogue-Medford Union Free School District* (1987) that drug testing of teachers violates the Fourth Amendment's prohibition of unreasonable searches.

Privacy

Prior to 1974 students and parents were not allowed to examine school records. On November 19, 1974, Congress passed the Family Educational Rights and Privacy Act (FERPA), which gave parents of students under eighteen and students eighteen and older the right to examine their school records. Every public or private educational institution must adhere to the law, known as the **Buckley Amendment,** or lose federal money.

Under the Buckley Amendment, schools must do the following:

1. Inform parents or eligible students of their rights.
2. Facilitate access to records by parents or eligible students by providing information on the types of educational records that exist and the procedures for gaining access to them.
3. Permit parents or eligible students to review educational records, request changes, request a hearing if the changes are disallowed, and add their own statement by way of explanation, if necessary.
4. Ensure that the institution does not give out personally identifiable information without the prior written, informed consent of a parent or an eligible student.
5. Allow parents and eligible students to see the school's record of disclosures (Fischer and Sorenson 1996, 89).

The Buckley Amendment actually sets forth the minimum requirements that schools must adhere to, and many states and school districts have gone beyond these minimum guidelines in granting students access to their records. Most high schools, for example, now grant students under eighteen access to their educational records, and all students in Virginia, elementary through secondary, are guaranteed access to their records.

A number of exceptions are allowed by the Buckley Amendment. The teacher's gradebook, psychiatric or treatment records, notes or records written by the teacher for his or her exclusive use or to be shared with a substitute teacher, or the private notes of school law enforcement units, for example, are not normally subject to examination (Fischer and Sorenson 1996).

Students' Rights to Nondiscrimination

Schools are legally bound to avoid discriminating against students on the basis of race, sex, religion, disability, marital status, or infection with a noncommunicable disease such as HIV/AIDS. One trend that has confronted schools with the need to develop more thoughtful and fair policies has been the epidemic in teenage pregnancies.

In regard to students who are married, pregnant, or parents, the courts have been quite clear: Students in these categories may not be treated differently. A 1966 case in Texas involving a sixteen-year-old mother established that schools may provide separate classes or alternative schools on a *voluntary* basis for married and/or pregnant students. However, the district may not *require* such students to attend separate schools, nor may they be made to attend adult or evening schools (*Alvin Independent School District v. Cooper* 1966).

The courts have made an about-face in their positions on whether students who are married, pregnant, or parents can participate in extracurricular activities. Prior to 1972 participation in these activities was considered a privilege rather than a right, and restrictions on those who could participate were upheld. In 1972, however, cases in Tennessee, Ohio, Montana, and Texas established the right of married students (and, in one case, a divorced student) to participate (*Holt v. Sheldon* 1972; *Davis v. Meek* 1972; *Moran v. School District No. 7* 1972; and *Romans v. Crenshaw* 1972). Since then, restrictions applicable to extracurricular activities have been universally struck down.

Since the mid-1980s, many school districts have become embroiled in controversy over the issue of how to provide for the schooling of young people with HIV/AIDS and whether school employees with HIV/AIDS should be allowed to continue working. As one observer put it:

> Public schools now face the difficulty of balancing two equal and opposing rights: the right of a student with AIDS to an education and the right of students who are not infected with HIV to be protected against infection. The latter right is fueled by fear that one can be infected with HIV through casual contact, even though no medical evidence has found or remotely suggested that HIV can be transmitted through casual contact. The practical result of attempts to balance those rights has been to open a floodgate to discrimination against students infected with this insidious virus (Alali 1995, 3).

In rulings on HIV/AIDS-related cases, the courts have sided with the overwhelming medical evidence that students with AIDS pose no "significant risk" of spreading the disease. "To date, courts have revealed a high degree of sensitivity to students with HIV or AIDS and to their being included in the public school mainstream" (LaMorte 1999, 338). In 1987, for example, a judge prevented a Florida school district from requiring that three hemophiliac brothers who were exposed to HIV/AIDS through transfusions be restricted to homebound instruction (*Ray v. School District of DeSoto County* 1987).

To stem the spread of HIV/AIDS, school systems in many large cities—New York, Los Angeles, San Francisco, and Seattle, to name a few—have initiated programs to distribute condoms to high school students. According to a 1994 poll by Public Agenda, 55 percent of Americans believe it is appropriate to allow schools to distribute condoms to students, while 43 percent oppose it (Public Agenda 1994, 28).

New York's condom-distribution program, which initially did not require parental consent, was challenged in 1993 (*Alfonso v. Fernandez*). The court ruled that the program was a "health issue" and that the district could not dispense condoms without prior parental approval. The court maintained that the program violated parents' due process rights under the Fourteenth Amendment to raise their children as they see fit; however, the program did not violate parents' or students' freedom of religion. Three years later, however, the U.S. Supreme Court declined to review a Massachusetts high court ruling that upheld a school board's decision to place condom machines in high school restrooms and allow junior- and senior-level students to request condoms from the school nurse (*Curtis v. School Committee of Falmouth* 1996).

What Are Some Issues in the Legal Rights of School Districts?

Clearly, the law touches just about every aspect of education in the United States today. Daily, the media remind us that ours is an age of litigation; no longer are school districts as protected as they once were from legal problems. Corporal punishment, sexual harassment, religious expression, and home schooling are among the issues in the legal rights of school districts.

Corporal Punishment

The practice of **corporal punishment** has had a long and controversial history in education in the United States. Currently, policies regarding the use of corporal punishment vary widely from state to state, and even from district to district.

Critics believe that corporal punishment "is neither a necessary nor an effective response to misbehavior in school" (Slavin 2000, 391), and some believe the practice is "archaic, cruel, and inhuman and an unjustifiable act on the part of the state" (LaMorte 1999, 129). In spite of such arguments against its effectiveness, corporal punishment continues to be widespread. Nevertheless, almost half of the states and many school districts currently ban corporal punishment, and many others restrict its use (LaMorte 1999).

The most influential Supreme Court case involving corporal punishment is *Ingraham v. Wright,* decided in 1977. In Dade County, Florida, in October 1970, junior high school students James Ingraham and Roosevelt Andrews were paddled with a wooden paddle. Both students received injuries as a result of the paddlings, with Ingraham's being the most severe. Ingraham, who was being punished for being slow to respond to a teacher's directions, refused to assume the "paddling position" and had to be held over a desk by two assistant principals while the principal administered twenty "licks." As a result, Ingraham "suffered a hematoma requiring medical attention and keeping him out of school for several days."

The court had two significant questions to rule on in *Ingraham:* Does the Eighth Amendment's prohibition of cruel and unusual punishment apply to corporal punishment in the schools? And, if it does not, should the due process clause of the Fourteenth Amendment provide any protection to students before punishment is administered? In regard to the first question, the Court, in a sharply divided five-to-four decision, ruled that the Eighth Amendment was not applicable to students being disciplined in school, only to persons convicted of crimes. On the question of due process, the Court said, "We conclude that the Due Process clause does not require notice and a hearing prior to the imposition of corporal punishment in the public schools, as that practice is authorized and limited by the common law." The Court also commented on the severity of the paddlings in *Ingraham* and said that, in such cases, school personnel "may be held liable in damages to the child and, if malice is shown, they may be subject to criminal penalties."

Though the Supreme Court has upheld the constitutionality of corporal punishment, many districts around the country have instituted policies banning its use. Where corporal punishment is used, school personnel are careful to see that it meets criteria that have emerged from other court cases involving corporal punishment:

1. It is consistent with the existing statutes.
2. It is a corrective remedy for undesirable behavior.
3. It is neither cruel nor excessive.
4. There is no permanent or lasting injury.
5. Malice is not present.
6. The punishment is suitable for the age and sex of the child.
7. An appropriate instrument is used (O'Reilly and Green 1983, 144–45).

Sexual Harassment

Though few victims report it, sexual harassment affects about four out of every five teenagers in schools across the nation, according to a survey of eighth- through eleventh-graders sponsored by the American Association of University Women (1993). Students' responses were based on the following definition: "Sexual harassment is unwanted and unwelcome sexual behavior which interferes with your life" (American Association of University Women 1993, 6). Although most teens report that they are harassed by their schoolmates, one-fourth of the girls and one-tenth of the boys said they had been harassed by school employees. Figure 6.3 shows the percentage of students reporting various types of **sexual harassment.** In addition, the survey indicated that only 7 percent of the victims told the school about the sexual harassment, and more than half didn't even know whether their school had a policy on sexual harassment.

Data from the AAUW study were further analyzed by four University of Michigan researchers who came to the surprising conclusion that "the large majority of adolescents who experience harassment have also harassed someone else during their school life. Over half of all students, equivalent by gender, have experienced harassment both as victim and perpetrator" (Lee, Chen, and Smerdon 1996, 399–400). They also concluded that "we cannot say which came first, harassing others or being harassed" and that their findings "run counter to any explanation of sexual harassment based solely on differential social or power status" (399). To address the alarming problem of sexual harassment in schools, the University of Michigan team recommended the following:

- The discussion of sexuality, both wanted and unwanted, should be included in the formal and informal curriculum.
- Helping students understand, recognize, and address their own ambivalence about sexual harassment (indeed, about sexuality generally) should be a meaningful component of every secondary school's curriculum.
- Adults in schools should serve as models for respectful cross-status relations (Lee, Chen, and Smerdon 1996, 410).

As our discussion of this chapter's opening scenario pointed out, a landmark Supreme Court Case (*Davis v. Monroe County Board of Education* 1999) ruled by a narrow 5 to 4 margin that educators can be held liable if they fail to take steps to end peer sexual harassment. In their majority opinion, five justices disagreed with the claim by the other four justices that "nothing short of expulsion of every student accused of misconduct involving sexual overtones would protect school systems from liability or damages." Instead, their ruling was intended "only for harassment that is so severe, pervasive, and objectively offensive that it effectively bars the victim's access to an educational opportunity or benefit."

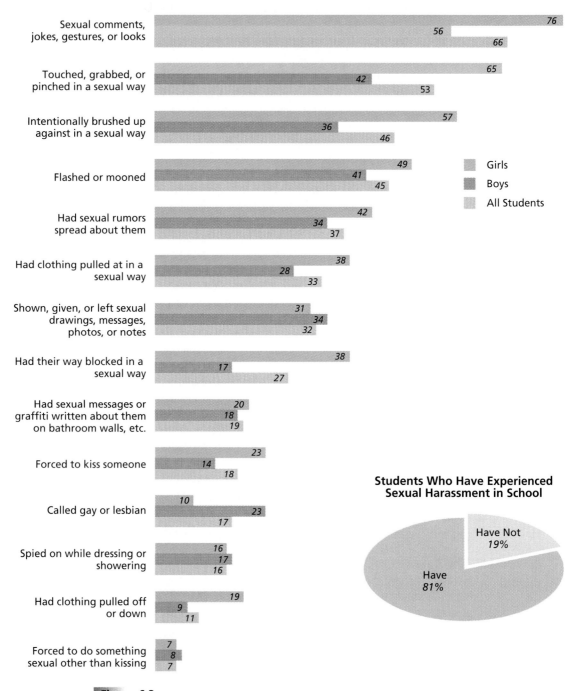

Teen Sexual Harassment
Types of Sexual Harassment Experienced in School
(percent of eighth through eleventh graders polled)

Sexual comments, jokes, gestures, or looks — 76 / 56 / 66

Touched, grabbed, or pinched in a sexual way — 65 / 42 / 53

Intentionally brushed up against in a sexual way — 57 / 36 / 46

Flashed or mooned — 49 / 41 / 45

Had sexual rumors spread about them — 42 / 34 / 37

Had clothing pulled at in a sexual way — 38 / 28 / 33

Shown, given, or left sexual drawings, messages, photos, or notes — 31 / 34 / 32

Had their way blocked in a sexual way — 38 / 17 / 27

Had sexual messages or graffiti written about them on bathroom walls, etc. — 20 / 18 / 19

Forced to kiss someone — 23 / 14 / 18

Called gay or lesbian — 10 / 23 / 17

Spied on while dressing or showering — 16 / 17 / 16

Had clothing pulled off or down — 19 / 9 / 11

Forced to do something sexual other than kissing — 7 / 8 / 7

Girls / Boys / All Students

Students Who Have Experienced Sexual Harassment in School

Have Not 19%

Have 81%

Figure 6.3

Teen sexual harassment
Source: American Association of University Women, *Hostile Hallways: The AAUW Survey on Sexual Harassment in America's School,* New York: Louis Harris and Associates, Inc.,1993, pp. 7, 9.

The dissenting justices, however, expressed concern about the "avalanche of liability now set in motion" and the "potentially crushing financial liability" for schools.

A female plaintiff who pleads only that a boy called her offensive names, that she told a teacher, that the teacher's response was unreasonable, and that her school performance suffered as a result, appears to state a successful claim.... After today, Johnny will find that the routine problems of adolescence are to be resolved by invoking a federal right to demand assignment to a desk two rows away.

To highlight their concern about the effects of the ruling, the dissenting Justices also noted that shortly after a U.S. Department of Education warning that schools could be liable for peer sexual harassment, a North Carolina school suspended a six-year-old boy who kissed a female classmate on the cheek.

In addition to harassment by the opposite sex, same-sex harassment, usually against gay and lesbian students, is a problem at some schools. Since the mid-1990s, several school districts have faced lawsuits filed by gay and lesbian students who claimed that school officials failed to protect them from verbal and physical antigay harassment. For example, in 1999 six gay and lesbian teenagers in Morgan Hill, California, filed a complaint in a U.S. District Court charging that school officials failed to protect them from years of antigay harassment. One of the complainants alleged that teachers regularly witnessed the harassment but did nothing to stop it: "Most [teachers] just don't want the hassle; others will acknowledge that they are homophobic, that they just don't like gays and lesbians." Moreover, the student found that administrators also refused to get involved: "Taking these things [i.e., complaints about antigay harassment] to the administrators and having them, my protectors, say 'Go back to class and stop talking about it' affected me more than anything. I learned that teachers won't do anything for you if they don't get any backup from the administration" (Ruenzel 1999). A 1996 verdict awarding almost $1 million to a gay student by a U.S. District Court was the first time a federal jury found school officials responsible for antigay harassment committed by students (Jacobson, November 22, 1996). Currently, at least five states and several school districts have education policies that prohibit discrimination based on sexual orientation.

Increased reports of sexual harassment of students by educators and a Supreme Court ruling in 1992 *(Franklin v. Gwinnett County Public Schools)* that students could sue and collect damages for harassment under Title IX of the Education Act of 1972 are causing some teachers to be apprehensive about working closely with students, and a small number of teachers even report that they fear being falsely accused by angry, disgruntled students. As a school superintendent put it, "There's no question but that the attitudes of personnel in schools are changing because of the many cases [of sexual harassment] that have come up across the country. I think all of us are being extremely cautious in how we handle students and in what we say and do with students and employees" (*Spokesman Review* 1993, 1A). To address the problem, many school districts have suggested guidelines that teachers can follow to show concern for students, offer them encouragement, and congratulate them for their successes.

Religious Expression

Conflicts over the proper role of religion in schools are among the most heated in the continuing debate about the character and purposes of education in the United States. Numerous school districts have found themselves embroiled in legal issues related to school prayer, Bible reading, textbooks, creationism, singing of Christmas carols, distribution of religious literature, New Age beliefs, secular humanism, religious holidays, use of school buildings for religious meetings, and the role of religion in moral education, to name a few. On the one hand, conservative religious groups wish to restore prayer and Christian religious practices to the public schools; on the other, secular liberals see religion as irrelevant to school curricula and maintain that public schools should not promote religion. In addition, somewhere between these two positions are those who believe that, while schools should not be involved in the *teaching of* religion, they should *teach about* religion.

During the last fifty years, scores of court cases have addressed school activities related to the First Amendment principle of separation of church and state. As Michael Imber and Tyll van Geel put it: "By far the most common constitutional objection raised against a school program in the latter half of the twentieth century is that it fails to respect the wall of separation between church and state" (1993, 88). In one of these landmark cases (*Engel v. Vitale* 1962), the United States Supreme Court ruled that recitation of a prayer said in the presence of a teacher at the beginning of each school day was unconstitutional and violated the First Amendment which states: "Congress shall make no law respecting an establishment of religion, or prohibiting the free exercise thereof." Justice Hugo Black, who delivered the opinion of the Court, stated ". . . it is no part of the business of government to compose official prayers for any group of the American people to recite as a part of a religious program carried on by government."

The following year, the U.S. Supreme Court ruled that Bible reading and reciting the Lord's Prayer in school were unconstitutional (*School District of Abington Township v. Schempp* 1963). In response to the district's claim that unless these religious activities were permitted a "religion of secularism" would be established, the Court stated that "We agree of course that the State may not establish a 'religion of secularism' in the sense of affirmatively opposing or showing hostility to religion, thus 'preferring those who believe in no religion over those who do believe.' We do not agree, however, that this decision in any sense has that effect."

To determine whether a state has violated the separation of church and state principle, the courts refer to the decision rendered in *Lemon v. Kurtzman* (1971). In this instance, the U.S. Supreme Court struck down an attempt by the Rhode Island legislature to provide a 15 percent salary supplement to teachers of secular subjects in nonpublic schools and Pennsylvania legislation to provide financial supplements to nonpublic schools through reimbursement for teachers' salaries, texts, and instructional materials in certain secular subjects. According to the three-part test enunciated in *Lemon v. Kurtzman*, governmental practices "must (1) reflect a clearly secular purpose; (2) have a primary effect that neither advances nor inhibits religion; and (3) avoid excessive entanglement with religion" (LaMorte 1999, 39). Though criticized vigorously by several Supreme Court justices since 1971, the so-called **Lemon test** has not been overruled.

During the mid-1990s, the courts heard several cases addressing the question of whether parents' right to direct their children's upbringing meant they could demand curricula and learning activities that were compatible with their religious beliefs. Without exception, the courts have rejected "parent-rights" cases against the schools; those rights, according to a U.S. Court of Appeals ruling in support of a schoolwide assembly on HIV/AIDS, "do not encompass a broad-based right to restrict the flow of information in the public schools" (*Brown v. Hot, Sexy and Safer Productions, Inc.* 1996). In a similar case, parents objected to a Massachusetts school district's policy of distributing condoms to junior and senior high school students who requested them. The state's Supreme Judicial Court rejected the parental rights argument and their argument that the program infringed on their First Amendment right to free exercise of religion: "Parents have no right to tailor public school programs to meet their individual religious or moral preferences" (*Curtis v. School Committee of Falmouth* 1996).

Home Schooling

One spinoff of the public's heightened awareness of the problems that schools face has been the decision by some parents to educate their children in the home. While most home-schoolers view home schooling as an opportunity to provide their children with a curriculum based on religious values, "a new breed of home-schooler is emerging, motivated not by religious doctrine but by more practical concerns ranging from school violence to poor academic quality to overzealous peer pressure" (Schnaiberg 1996, 24). Estimates of the number of school-age children being taught at home vary; however, the National Home Education Research Institute (NHERI) estimated that about 1.5 million students were home schooled in 1999.

Table 6.4

Educator's rights and responsibilities

Legislation or Court Ruling	How It Affects Educators
Application of Bay v. State Board of Education, 1963	A past criminal conviction is grounds for being denied a teaching certificate.
Title VII of the Civil Rights Act of 1964	Educators are guaranteed nondiscrimination in hiring situations.
Morrison v. State Board of Education, 1969	An educator's conduct in his/her personal life is not an impairment to professional performance or grounds for revoking a teaching certificate.
Mailloux v. Kiley, 1971	School authorities are free to suspend teachers who use teaching methods of which they disapprove.
Station v. Travelers Insurance Co., 1974	Teachers must provide adequate supervision while students are exposed to dangerous conditions.
Burton v. Cascade School Dist. Union High School, 1975	A tenured teacher cannot be dismissed unless the employer shows "good and just cause."
Hortonville Joint School District No 1. v. Hortonville Education Association, 1976	Teachers working under collective bargaining agreements may be dismissed for striking.
*Peter Doe v. San Francisco Unified School Disttrict,*1976	A school cannot be held responsible for a student's lack of achievement.
Copyright Act of 1980	The fair use doctrine applies to software as well as print materials.
Marcus v. Rowley, 1983	Teachers can make "fair use" of copyrighted material.
Unified School Dist. No. 241 v. Swanson, 1986	Schools cannot assign duties to teachers that are not reasonably related to their teaching.
Edwards v. Aguillard, 1987	"Balanced treatment" laws that mandate curricula that advance particular religious beliefs are unconstitutional.
Mozer v. Hawkins County Board of Education, 1987, 1988 and *Smith v. Board of School Commissioners of Mobile County,* 1987	A school may establish a curriculum despite parental disapproval.
Krizek v. Cicero-Stickney Township High School District No. 20 1989	Teachers must notify students' parents before using materials that might be found objectionable in the classroom.
Murray v. Pittsburgh Board of Public Education, 1996	Teachers may not have the right to use teaching methods and materials to which school officials object.
Davis v. Monroe County Board of Education, 1999	School districts can be sued in cases involving student-on-student sexual harassment, if the district acts with "deliberate indifference."

Home schooling is legal in all the states and the District of Columbia; however, how it is regulated, and whether resources are allocated, vary greatly. In 1999, NHERI reported that forty-one states had no minimum academic requirements for parents who decided to home-school their children. More than 60 percent of the states have home-schooling statutes or regulations, and half of the states require that home-schooled students participate in standardized testing (LaMorte 1999). In most states, home-schoolers must demonstrate that their instruction is "equivalent" to that offered in the public schools, a standard set in *New Jersey v. Massa* (1967).

Legal support for home schools has been mixed. In 1994, home-schoolers in Maine defeated legislative attempts to require that home schools be visited monthly by public school officials. In 1993 and 1994, legislation to require home-school teachers to be state certified were defeated in South Dakota and Kansas, and similar laws were overturned in Iowa and North Dakota. However, a federal district court upheld a West Virginia statute making children ineligible for home schooling if their standardized test scores fell below the 40th percentile (*Null v. Board of Education* 1993). In Iowa, mandatory home-schooling reports to the state were upheld in *State v. Rivera* (1993); home-schoolers in that state must submit course outlines, weekly lesson plans, and provide the amount of time spent on areas of the curriculum. And, a Maryland law requiring the state's monitoring of home schooling was upheld despite a parent's claim that the state's curriculum promoted atheism, paganism, and evolution (*Battles v. Anne Arundel County Board of Education* 1996).

Table 6.4 (page 237) lists chronologically and summarizes the key legislation and court decisions affecting educators that are discussed in this chapter.

As the preceding cases related to home schooling show, school law is not static—instead, it is continually evolving and changing. In addition, laws pertaining to education vary from state to state. Therefore, it is important for the beginning teacher to become familiar with current publications on school law in his or her state.

SUMMARY

Why Do You Need a Professional Code of Ethics?

- A professional code of ethics guides teachers' actions and enables them to build relationships with students based on trust and respect.

- A code of ethics helps teachers see beyond the short-range consequences of their actions to long-range consequences, and it helps them respond appropriately to ethical dilemmas in the classroom.

What Are Your Legal Rights as a Teacher?

- The right to due process protects teachers from arbitrary treatment by school districts and education officials regarding certification, nondiscrimination, contracts, tenure, dismissal, and academic freedom.

- Several court rulings have illustrated how the constitutional rights of teachers must be balanced against a school's need to promote its educational goals.

Do Student Teachers Have the Same Rights?

■ Many states have not clarified the legal status of student teachers to teach. However, student teachers should be aware that a potential for liability exists for them just as it does with certified teachers, and they should clarify their rights and responsibilities prior to beginning student teaching.

■ Depending on state statutes, a student teacher may substitute under certain conditions for a cooperating teacher.

What Are Your Legal Responsibilities as a Teacher?

■ Teachers are responsible for meeting the terms of their teaching contracts, including providing for their students' safety and well-being.

■ Three legal responsibilities that concern teachers are: avoiding tort liability (specifically, negligence and educational malpractice), recognizing the physical and behavioral indicators of child abuse and then reporting suspected instances of such abuse, and observing copyright laws as they apply to photocopies, videotapes, computer software, and materials published on the Internet.

What Are the Legal Rights of Students and Parents?

■ Students' rights related to freedom of expression, suspension and expulsion, search and seizure, privacy, and nondiscrimination are based on several landmark legal decisions.

■ Generally, students' freedom of expression can be limited if it is disruptive of the educational process or incongruent with the school's mission.

■ Students can be neither suspended nor expelled without due process.

■ Courts have developed a two-pronged test for search and seizure actions involving students: (1) School officials must have "reasonable" suspicion that a student has violated a law or school policy, and (2) the search must be done using methods that are reasonable and appropriate, given the nature of the infraction.

■ Under the Buckley Amendment, students have the right to examine their school records, and schools may not give out information on students without their prior written consent.

■ Schools may not discriminate against students on the basis of race, sex, religion, disability, marital status, or infection with a noncommunicable disease such as HIV/AIDS.

What Are Some Issues in the Legal Rights of School Districts?

■ In spite of its proven ineffectiveness, corporal punishment has been upheld by the Supreme Court; however, almost half of the states and many school districts ban it, and many others restrict its use.

■ About four out of five teenagers are affected by sexual harassment. According to a landmark Supreme Court decision in 1999, school officials can be held responsible if they fail to act on reports of sexual harassment of students by their peers.

Schools can also be held responsible for the sexual harassment of students by professional staff, according to a 1992 Supreme Court decision.

■ Courts have ruled that school officials can be held responsible if they fail to take steps to protect gay and lesbian students from antigay harassment.

■ The First Amendment principle of separation of church and state has been applied to numerous court cases involving religious expression in the public schools. Court rulings banning school prayer, Bible reading, and other religious activities are often based on the three-part test developed in Lemon v. Kurtzman (1971). The courts have ruled consistently against parents who demand curricula and learning activities that are compatible with their religious beliefs.

■ Home schooling is legal in all states, though most require home-schoolers to demonstrate that their instruction is "equivalent" to that in public schools.

KEY TERMS AND CONCEPTS

academic freedom, 211
Buckley Amendment, 230
censorship, 223
code of ethics, 203
collective bargaining, 210
copyright laws, 220
corporal punishment, 232
dismissal, 209

due process, 206
educational
    malpractice, 217
ethical dilemmas, 206
fair use, 220
freedom of expression, 223
grievance, 210
Lemon test, 236

negligence, 217
nondiscrimination, 208
search and seizure, 228
sexual harassment, 223
teaching contract, 208
tenure, 209
tort liability, 215

APPLICATIONS AND ACTIVITIES

Teacher's Journal

1. Read the NEA Code of Ethics for Teachers in Appendix 6.1. Record in your journal examples of situations you observed or experienced in which you feel a teacher may have violated NEA principles. Include one example involving Principle I, a teacher's commitment to students, and one example involving Principle II, a teacher's commitment to the profession. Conclude your analysis of these cases with a personal statement about your goals for ethical conduct as a teacher.

2. What limits do you believe should be placed on *what* teachers teach? on *how* they teach? Which of the legal cases on academic freedom discussed in this chapter support your views?

3. A California school district suspended a fourteen-year-old student for writing two essays with violent content for an English assignment. In one essay titled "Goin' Postal" a boy goes to school with a gun and shoots the principal seven times (Walsh 1999d). How should teachers respond to student work—essays, creative writing, videos, and so forth—that has violent content?

4. What is your position regarding corporal punishment? Are there circumstances under which its use is justified?

5. Review the section on the legal rights of students (pp. 223–232). Can you recall a time when you believe your rights as a student (or the rights of a classmate) were denied? Describe those events. What court cases and parts of the U.S. Constitution would apply to the events you describe?

Teacher's Database

1. Conduct an Internet search on one or more of the topics listed below or on another topic from Chapter 6. Narrow your search to issues and information relating to school law and the legal rights and responsibilities of school districts and schools, teachers and administrators, and students and parents. Include a search of news sources, such as *Education Week* on the Web, for summaries of recent court rulings pertaining to education and school law. The texts of many policies, laws, and U.S. Supreme Court decisions are also available online. You may wish to select a particular court case from Chapter 6 to investigate.

   Topics on legal issues to search from Chapter 6:

academic freedom	expulsion	school uniforms
censorship	free speech	search and seizure
collective bargaining	gay and lesbian rights	sexual harassment
copyright law	home schooling	suspension
corporal punishment	nondiscrimination	teacher dismissal
creation science	privacy	teacher tenure
dress codes	professional ethics	
due process	school prayer	

2. Using an index system or a keyword search engine, locate and visit the websites of three or more of the following educational journals and publications. At each site, download or record information related to one or more of the education law issues discussed in Chapter 6.

American Educator	*Instructor*
American School Board Journal	*Kappa Delta Phi Record*
Childhood Education	*Phi Delta Kappan*
Educational Leadership	*PTA Today*
Elementary School Journal	*Teacher Magazine*
High School Journal	*Young Children*

Observations and Interviews

1. Interview several students at a middle school or high school to get their views regarding the legal rights of students, discussed in this chapter. You may wish to develop a questionnaire that explores students' opinions in depth on a particular issue, such as freedom of expression or religion in the schools. Or you might get students' reactions to one of the legal cases summarized in this chapter. Present the results of your interview or survey to your classmates.

2. During an observation of a teacher's day, identify an ethical dilemma that the

teacher confronts. Describe the dilemma and the teacher's response in a journal entry. To help you with this activity, ask your instructor for Handouts M6.1, "Identifying Ethical Dilemmas in Teaching," and M6.2, "Analyzing Teachers' Responses to Ethical Dilemmas."

3. Interview a school superintendent or principal to find out about any instances of actual or threatened litigation that occurred in the district during the last year or so. Ask him or her to identify procedures the district has in place to ensure due process for teachers and students. Report your findings.

Professional Portfolio

Survey a group of students, teachers, and/or parents regarding a legal issue in education. Among the legal issues and questions you might address are the following:

■ Should tenure for teachers be abolished? Does tenure improve the quality of education students receive?

■ Under what circumstances should restrictions be placed on what teachers teach and how they teach?

■ Should parents be allowed to provide home schooling for their children?

■ Are parents justified in filing educational malpractice suits if their children fail to achieve in school?

■ Under what circumstances should restrictions be placed on students' freedom of expression?

■ Should schools have the right to implement dress codes? guidelines for students' hairstyles? school uniforms?

■ Should corporal punishment be banned? If not, under what circumstances should it be used?

■ How should schools combat the problem of sexual harassment?

■ To combat drug abuse, should schools implement mandatory drug testing of students? of teachers?

■ Should students have access to their educational records? should their parents or guardians?

■ As part of an HIV/AIDS prevention program, should condoms be distributed to high school students? Should parental approval be required for participation?

The report summarizing the results of your survey should include demographic information such as the following for your sample of respondents: gender, age, whether they have children in school, level of education, and so on. When you analyze the results, look for differences related to these variables.

Appendix 6.1

Preamble

The educator, believing in the worth and dignity of each human being, recognizes the supreme importance of the pursuit of truth, devotion to excellence, and the nurture of democratic principles. Essential to these goals is the protection of freedom to learn and to teach and the guarantee of equal educational opportunity for all. The educator accepts the responsibility to adhere to the highest ethical standards.

The educator recognizes the magnitude of the responsibility inherent in the teaching process. The desire for the respect and confidence of one's colleagues, of students, of parents, and of the members of the community provides the incentive to attain and maintain the highest possible degree of ethical conduct. The Code of Ethics of the Education Profession indicates the aspiration of all educators and provides standards by which to judge conduct.

The remedies specified by the NEA and/or its affiliates for the violation of any provision of this code shall be exclusive and no such provision shall be enforceable in any form other than one specifically designated by the NEA or its affiliates.

Principle I

Commitment to the Student   The educator strives to help each student realize his or her potential as a worthy and effective member of society. The educator therefore works to stimulate the spirit of inquiry, the acquisition of knowledge and understanding, and the thoughtful formulation of worthy goals.

In fulfillment of the obligation to the student, the educator:

1. Shall not unreasonably restrain the student from independent action in the pursuit of learning
2. Shall not unreasonably deny the student access to varying points of view
3. Shall not deliberately suppress or distort subject matter relevant to the student's progress
4. Shall make reasonable effort to protect the student from conditions harmful to learning or to health and safety
5. Shall not intentionally expose the student to embarrassment or disparagement
6. Shall not on the basis of race, color, creed, sex, national origin, marital status, political or religious beliefs, family, social or cultural background, or sexual orientation unfairly:
   (a) Exclude any student from participation in any program
   (b) Deny benefits to any student
   (c) Grant any advantage to any student
7. Shall not use professional relationships with students for private advantage
8. Shall not disclose information about students obtained in the course of professional service, unless disclosure serves a compelling professional purpose or is required by law

Principle II

Commitment to the Profession   The education profession is vested by the public with a trust and responsibility requiring the highest ideals of professional service.

In the belief that the quality of the services of the education profession directly influences the nation and its citizens, the educator shall exert every effort to raise professional standards, to promote a climate that encourages the exercise of professional judgment, to achieve conditions that attract persons worthy of the trust to careers in education, and to assist in preventing the practice of the profession by unqualified persons.

In fulfillment of the obligation to the profession, the educator:

1. Shall not in an application for a professional position deliberately make a false statement or fail to disclose a material fact related to competency and qualifications
2. Shall not misrepresent his/her professional qualifications
3. Shall not assist any entry into the profession of a person known to be unqualified in respect to character, education, or other relevant attribute
4. Shall not knowingly make a false statement concerning the qualifications of a candidate for a professional position
5. Shall not assist a noneducator in the unauthorized practice of teaching
6. Shall not disclose information about colleagues obtained in the course of professional service unless disclosure serves a compelling professional purpose or is required by law
7. Shall not knowingly make false or malicious statements about a colleague
8. Shall not accept any gratuity, gift, or favor that might impair or appear to influence professional decisions or actions

Source: Code of Ethics of the Education Profession, adopted by the NEA Representative Assembly, 1975. The National Education Association, Washington DC. Used with permission.

Appendix 6.2

NEA Bill of Rights for Student Teachers

As a citizen, a student, and a future member of the teaching profession, the individual student teacher has the right:

1. To freedom from unfair discrimination in admission to student teaching and in all aspects of the field experience. Student teachers shall not be denied or removed from an assignment because of race, color, creed, sex, age, national origin, marital status, political or religious beliefs, social or cultural background, or sexual orientation. Nor shall their application be denied because of physical handicap unless it is clear that such handicap will prevent or seriously inhibit their carrying out the duties of the assignment.

2. To be informed in advance of the standards of eligibility for student teaching and of the criteria and procedures for evaluation of his or her classroom performance.

3. To be consulted in advance and have effective voice in decisions regarding assignment, with respect to subject, grade level, school, and cooperating teacher.

4. To be assigned to a cooperating teacher who volunteers to work with the student-teaching program, who is fully qualified to do so, and is appropriately remunerated for the work and given sufficient time to carry out its responsibilities.

5. To be reimbursed by the college or university for any financial hardship caused by the student-teaching assignment; for example, for the costs of traveling excessive distances to the cooperating school district, or for the expenses incurred when the student teacher is assigned to a location so remote from his or her college/university that it is necessary to establish residence there, in addition to the college or university residence.

6. To be informed, prior to the student-teaching period, of all relevant policies and practices of the cooperating school district, including those regarding personnel, curriculum, student requirements, and student-teaching program.

7. To confidentiality of records. Except with the express permission of the student teacher, the college or university shall transmit to the cooperating school district only those student records that are clearly necessary to protect the health and welfare of the student teacher, the cooperating teacher, the students, and others in the cooperating school. All persons having access to the records of student teachers shall respect the confidentiality of those records, as required by law.

8. To be admitted to student teaching and to remain in the student-teaching assignment in the absence of a showing of just cause for termination or transfer through fair and impartial proceedings.

9. To a student-teaching environment that encourages creativity and initiative. The student teacher should have the opportunity, under the perceptive supervision of the cooperating teacher, to develop his or her own techniques of teaching.

10. To a student-teaching environment that encourages the free exploration of ideas and issues as appropriate to the maturity of the students and the topics being studied.

11. To carry out the student-teaching assignment in an atmosphere conducive to learning and to have authority under supervision of the cooperating teacher, to use reasonable means to preserve the learning environment and protect the health and safety of students, the student teacher, and others.

12. To participate, with the cooperating teacher and college/university supervisor, in planning the student-teaching schedule to include in addition to work with the assigned cooperating teacher, observation of other classes, attendance at professional meetings, and involvement, as appropriate, in extracurricular activities that will enrich and broaden the range of the field experience.

13. To be assigned to duties that are relevant to the student teacher's learning experience. Student teachers shall not be required to act as substitute teacher or teacher aide, nor to handle any non-teaching duties that are not part of the cooperating teacher's duties.

14. To request transfer in the event of prolonged illness of, or serious personality conflict with the cooperating teacher and to have that request given favorable consideration without damage to any party's personal or professional status.

15. To a cessation of student-teaching responsibilities in the event and for the duration of a teacher strike at the cooperating school or school district to which the student teacher is assigned. If the strike is a prolonged one, the college or university has the responsibility to reassign the student teacher to another school district.

16. To the same liability protections as are provided by the school district for regularly employed certified teachers.

17. To influence the development and continuing evaluation and improvement of the student teacher program, including the formulation and systematic review of standards of student teacher eligibility, and criteria and procedures of student teacher evaluation. Such influence shall be maintained through representation of student teachers and recent graduates of the student-teacher program on committees established to accomplish these purposes.

18. To frequent planning and evaluative discussions with the cooperating teacher.

19. To systematic, effective supervision by the college/ university supervisor. Such supervision shall include (1) regularly scheduled classroom observations of sufficient frequency and length to permit thorough insight into the strengths and weaknesses of the student teacher's performance; (2) conferences with college/university supervisor immediately following observation, or as soon thereafter as possible, to discuss results of observation; and (3) regularly scheduled three-way evaluation conferences among student teacher, college supervisor, and cooperating teacher, to ensure that the student teacher is fully apprised of his or her progress and is given substantive assistance in assessing and remedying the weaknesses and reinforcing the strengths of his or her performance.

20. To see, sign, and affix written responses to evaluations of his or her classroom performance.

21. To an equitable and orderly means of resolving grievances relating to the student-teaching assignment. The college/university grievance procedure shall incorporate due process guarantees, including the right to be informed in writing of the reasons for any adverse action regarding his or her assignment, and to appeal any such action, with the right to have both student and teacher representation on committees formulated to hear and adjudicate student teacher grievances.

22. To be free to join, or not to join, on or off campus organizations, and to enjoy privacy and freedom of lifestyle and conscience in out-of-school activities, unless it is clearly evident that those activities have a harmful effect on the student teacher's classroom performance.

Source: National Education Association, 1201 16th Street NW, Washington, DC, 1977.

The Art
of Teaching

dear mentor

On Becoming a Master Teacher

Dear Mentor,

I have been a student at California State University—
Los Angeles for two years. I would like to find out how
to become a master teacher. What is the profile of a
master teacher?

Sincerely,

Darryl Hampton

D ear Darryl,

Congratulations on being a second-year university student with the goal of becoming a teacher. Teaching is a valuable profession and one that will require your heart, talent, and energy.

Regarding how to become a master teacher, I think you've taken an important first step by asking the question. Look for master teachers and observe them. Keep in mind what good teaching looks like. Seek a mentor and make time for the relationship.

As you begin your career, it is important that you know and use the academic standards for your subject area—whether is it elementary education, middle school math, or high school English. Your lesson plans should show how you will teach students the learning strategies they will need to meet those standards. Join the academic professional organization in your subject area. The members can become an expert support group.

Also, take time to observe and learn about your school's culture. Seek to understand the school's community. From there, decide how you can be a positive contributor to both your school and community.

Believe in your ability to teach. When a challenge faces you, use your problem-solving skills. For example, in your class there could be a student who is reading below grade level. Use a variety of instructional methods to engage the student, and continue to explore other approaches to teaching reading skills. Read articles, attend professional development classes, or consult with your school district's or university's reading specialists. For, you see, as a teacher, your learning is ever-growing.

But most important of all, believe in your students' desire to learn. That has become my driving force. My students motivate and inspire me to become a better teacher for them. As the professional in the classroom, a teacher must provide a safe and caring environment that encourages learning and effort. It is not enough to instill high dreams. We must equip our students with academic skills so that they have the tools to reach those dreams.

Incorporate your talents and interests into your teaching. That's one way to show your students a connection between what they learn in school and the real world.

In closing, I want to share with you some advice for new teaches that my second and third graders gave: "I would suggest patience and thoughtfulness, and make them laugh a little." "If a student needs help don't tell them the answer; just help them with the problem." So Darryl, you see, students really want a teacher's help.

Above all, remember to celebrate successes, because encouragement is never wasted.

Sincerely,

Janice James
1999 Kentucky Teacher of the Year

7

Teaching Diverse Learners

Prejudice is a burden which confuses the past, threatens the future, and renders the present inaccessible.
—Maya Angelou

focus questions

1. How is diversity embedded in the culture of the United States?

2. What does equal educational opportunity mean?

3. What is meant by bilingual education?

4. What is multicultural education?

5. How is gender a dimension of multicultural education?

Today I strolled into Sojourner Truth High School with a bit of concern. I had been student teaching for the spring semester at the same high school I had attended myself as a teenager and was really enjoying the experience, looking forward to it every day. Since February, I have been responsible for teaching five freshman world history classes to a group of inner-city students. The classes are made up of mostly African Americans like myself as well as a small percentage of Caribbean, Hispanic, Asian, and Polish American students. I care for these students and am committed to making a difference in their lives.

Ms. Callaway, my cooperating teacher, puts a lot of faith and trust in my approach to teaching. She told me that the students sorely need African American males in positions of authority who can relate to their problems. She stressed that the students look up to me and enjoy my innovative lessons.

I know that I have in fact reached some of the students, and I am proud of my teaching successes. The students seem to be really learning by relating history to their everyday lives. I have spent many long hours trying to make history come alive for them. I want the students to see history as *theirs,* and I believe that I am meeting with much success, at least on the academic front.

But my zeal and eagerness are nevertheless starting to wear down. My growing lack of enthusiasm, I have realized, is due to the daily blatant disregard and disrespect that students have for themselves and others.

I find it difficult to teach a lesson without constantly reminding my class, "Watch your mouth!" "Take your hat off, please," and "Please be respectful of other folks' differences." All day long, in and out of class, I directly and indirectly hear conversations heavily laced with profanity, disrespect, and insults. I know that this kind of talk will not help my students advance themselves in the outside world. I know that for them to succeed, I need to help them gain self-esteem and to project a better image to others.

At first, I thought that maybe if I set a good example each and every day by using proper speech, not wearing my hat in the building, and respecting my peers and all of the students, I could help. After all, I had graduated from this same school and could serve as a role model of someone who had gone to college and gained a profession. But without fail, there was little improvement.

My failure to reach my students has caused me many sleepless nights. I worry that knowledge and love for history is not enough. So much is stacked against my students that they need every edge they can get. I remember Ms. Jefferson, a teacher at this very school, now retired, who inspired me to make profound changes in my own life. I want to do for my students what Ms. Jefferson did for me, but I feel that I am reaching a dead end.

One day, out of frustration, I simply asked the students, "Why do you think that it is so necessary to use profanity in the classroom?"

I listened to their answers: "It's a habit!" "It's the way I express myself!" "I can't help it!" "I don't know; it's the way I talk!"

So I went on to ask, "Why do guys wear their hats in the building?" They pretty much all agreed that it was done "to be cool" and as a "habit."

"But how," I responded, "are you guys going to go to college if you are trying so hard to be cool all the time and can't control your mouths or your dress?"

They said they liked the way they talked and dressed and didn't need college.

Then I asked, "Well, why do you think that it's a must to insult or hurt someone's feelings?"

Everyone agreed that it was done because "it's fun."

"But what happens when someone's feelings are really hurt or the insults get out of hand?" I persisted.

"Well, I guess I got to kick his #@@###**!" was the only response.

Deep down inside, I know there must be some hope for these kids, but I do not know where to begin or what else to do. I feel helpless. (Curtis Parker quoted in Rand and Shelton-Colangelo, 1999, 87–88).

The above reflections by Curtis Parker on his student teaching experience highlight how important it is for teachers to be able to communicate with students from diverse cultural backgrounds. Although Curtis is momentarily discouraged by his inability to get his students to stop using profanity and to improve their behavior, he may actually be influencing his students more than he realizes. It is possible, for example, that some of Curtis's students really do understand the important lesson in life he is trying to teach them; however, their strong need not to risk disapproval of their peers prevents them from changing their behavior at this time. At the very least, Curtis's students know that he cares genuinely about their education, that he wants to learn about their lives, and, though he disapproves of some of their behavior, he does not disapprove of them. Finally, as Curtis notes, his students are "relating history to their everyday lives" and he is "meeting with much success"—two solid indicators that he is building positive relationships with his students and will continue to become an increasingly influential role model in their lives.

This chapter looks at cultural diversity in the United States and the challenges of equalizing educational opportunity for all students. Professional teachers, such as Curtis is well on his way toward becoming, see cultural diversity as an asset to be preserved and valued, not a liability. The United States has always derived strength from the **diversity** of its people, and *all* students should receive a high-quality education so that they may make their unique contributions to society.

How Is Diversity Embedded in the Culture of the United States?

The percentage of ethnic minorities in the United States has been growing steadily since the end of World War II. According to the U.S. Census Bureau, there were more than 25 million foreign-born people living in the United States in 1999, and there was a net increase of one international migrant every 30 seconds. Twenty percent of U.S. senators are grandchildren of immigrants, a claim that can be made by no other nation in the world about its leading legislative body (Wirt and Kirst 1997). In addition, the Census Bureau estimates that

- By 2010, blacks and Hispanics will equal the number of whites.
- By 2025, half of U.S. youth will be white and half "minority."
- By 2050, no one group will be a majority among adults.

As a result, the number of students from diverse cultural backgrounds is increasing in most schools in the United States (see Figure 7.1). The District of Columbia now has minority group enrollments of 96.0 percent; Hawaii, 76.5 percent; New Mexico, 56.9 percent; and Mississippi, 56.1 percent (National Center for Education Statistics 1999). Most students in urban school districts are members of groups traditionally thought of as minorities. Among the urban school districts where non-Hispanic white students currently number less than 20 percent are Atlanta, Baltimore, Chicago, Detroit, Houston, Los Angeles, Miami, New Orleans, Oakland, Richmond, and San Antonio (National Center for Education Statistics 1999).

Clearly, the increasing diversity of U.S. society has extensive implications for schools. There is, for example, an increased demand for bilingual programs and teachers. All but a few school districts face a critical shortage of minority teachers. And, there is a need to develop curricula and strategies that address the needs and backgrounds

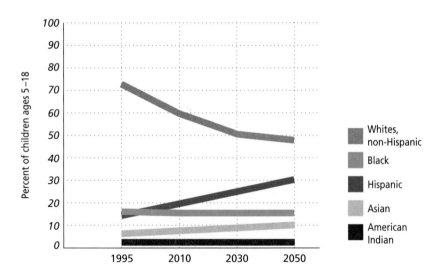

Figure 7.1

Changing school population

Note: Hispanic Americans can be of any race; figures for Anglo-European Americans are non-Hispanics; Asian Americans include Pacific Islanders; Native Americans include Eskimos and Aleuts. Percents do not add to 100 because the Hispanic population includes members of several races, including blacks and whites.

Source: Census Bureau Projections.

of all students—regardless of their social class, gender, sexual orientation, or ethnic, racial, or cultural identity.

The Meaning of Culture

As we pointed out in Chapter 4's discussion of the aims of education, one mission of schools is to maintain the culture of the United States. But what is the U.S. culture? Is there a single culture to which everyone in the country belongs? Before we can answer that question we must define the term *culture*. Simply put, **culture** is *the way of life* common to a group of people. It consists of the values, attitudes, and beliefs that influence their traditions and behavior. It is also a way of interacting with and looking at the world. Though at one time it was believed that the United States was a "melting pot" in which ethnic cultures would melt into one, ethnic and cultural differences have remained very much a part of life in the U.S. A "salad-bowl" analogy captures more accurately the **cultural pluralism** of U.S. society. That is, the distinguishing characteristics of cultures are to be preserved rather than blended into a single culture.

Dimensions of Culture　Within our nation's boundaries, we find cultural groups that differ according to other distinguishing factors, such as religion, politics, economics, and geographic region. The regional culture of New England, for example, is quite different from that of the Southeast. Similarly, Californians are culturally different from Iowans.

However, everyone in the United States does share some common dimensions of culture. James Banks, an authority on multicultural education, has termed this shared culture the "national macroculture" (Banks 1999). In addition to being members of the national macroculture, people in the United States are members of ethnic groups. An ethnic group is made up of individuals within a larger culture who share a self-defined racial or cultural identity and a set of beliefs, attitudes, and values. Members of an ethnic group distinguish themselves from others in the society by physical and social attributes. In addition, you should be aware that the composition of ethnic groups can change over time, and that there is often as much variability within groups as between them.

Cultural Identity　In addition to membership in the national macroculture, each individual participates in an array of subcultures, each with its customs and beliefs. Collectively, these subcultures determine an individual's **cultural identity,** an overall sense of who one is. Other possible elements that might shape a person's cultural identity include age, racial identity, exceptionalities, language, gender, sexual orientation, income level, and beliefs and values. These elements have different significances for different people. For example, the cultural identity of some people is most strongly determined by their occupations; for others by their ethnicity; and for others by their religious beliefs.

Remember that your future students will have their own complex cultural identities, which are no less valid for being different. For some of them, these identities may make them feel "disconnected" from the attitudes, expectations, and values conveyed by the school. For example,

Students in today's classrooms have diverse cultural identities. As a teacher, what steps will you take to integrate *all* students into the classroom?

> Students who come from homes where languages other than English are the medium of communication, who share customs and beliefs unique to their cultural community and/or home countries, or who face the range of challenges posed by economic insecurity will not often find much of their family, community, or national existence reflected in the school setting. Often these students feel that school is itself foreign, alienating, and unrelated to their beliefs and concerns (Rice and Walsh 1996, 9).

As a teacher, you will be challenged to understand the subtle differences in cultural identities among your students and to create a learning environment that enables all students to feel comfortable in school and "connected to" their school experiences.

Language and Culture   Culture is embedded in language, a fact that has resulted in conflict among different groups in our society. Some groups, although they support the preservation of ethnic cultures, believe that members of non-English-speaking groups must learn English if they are to function in U.S. society. There is also conflict between those who wish to preserve linguistic diversity and those who wish to establish English as a national language.

Much of the debate has focused on **bilingual education,** that is, using two languages as the medium of instruction. Bilingual education is designed to help students maintain their ethnic identity and become proficient in both English and the language of the home, to encourage assimilation into the mainstream culture and integrate the home language and culture with a new one. Some people are staunchly opposed to any form of bilingual education, and others support it as a short-term way to teach English to students.

Language diversity is an important dimension of U.S. cultural diversity regardless. Many students come from homes where English is not spoken. The National Clearinghouse for Bilingual Education reported that there were nearly 3.5 million **limited English proficient (LEP)** students—those with limited ability to understand, read, or speak English and who have a first language other than English—in public and nonpublic schools in 1998, or about 7.4 percent of the total enrollment (Macías et al 1998). Currently, one in seven U.S. residents speaks a language other than English at

Table 7.1

Fifty languages with greatest number of speakers in the U.S. after English; and percent of five- to seventeen-year-olds year olds who speak a non-English language at home, by state

Language	Number of Speakers	Language	Number of Speakers
1. Spanish	17,339,172	26. Gujarathi	102,418
2. French	1,702,176	27. Ukranian	95,568
3. German	1,547,099	28. Czech	92,485
4. Italian	1,308,648	29. Pennsylvania Dutch	83,525
5. Chinese	1,249,213	30. Miao (Hmong)	81,877
6. Tagalog	843,251	31. Norwegian	180,723
7. Polish	723,483	32. Slovak	80,388
8. Korean	626,478	33. Swedish	77,511
9. Vietnamese	507,069	34. Serbocroation	70,964
10. Portugese	429,860	35. Kru	65,848
11. Japanese	427,657	36. Rumanian	65,265
12. Greek	388,260	37. Lithuanian	55,781
13. Arabic	355,150	38. Finnish	54,350
14. Hindi (Urdu)	331,484	39. Panjabi	50,005
15. Russian	241,798	40. Formosan	46,044
16. Yiddish	213,064	41. Croatian	45,206
17. Thai (Laotian)	206,266	42. Turkish	41,876
18. Persian	201,865	43. Ilocano	41,131
19. French Creole	187,658	44. Bengali	38,101
20. Armenian	149,694	45. Danish	35,639
21. Navajo	148,530	46. Syriac	35,146
22. Hungarian	147,902	47. Samoan	34,914
23. Hebrew	144,292	48. Malayalam	33,949
24. Dutch	142,684	49. Cajun	33,670
25. Mon-Khmer (Cambodian)	127,441	50. Amharic	31,505

home, most frequently Spanish; and in eleven states, 15 or more percent of five- to seventeen-year-olds speak a non-English language at home (see Table 7.1).

Students differ among themselves not only regarding the first language spoken in the home, but also in the *language patterns* they acquire from the culture within which they are raised. Researchers have found that children from working-class backgrounds tend to develop "restricted" language patterns with their use of English, while children from middle-class backgrounds tend to develop more "elaborated" language patterns (Bernstein 1996; Heath 1983). In many cases, children encounter a mismatch between the language patterns used in the home and those they are expected to use in school, and this mismatch can be "a serious stumbling block for working-class and nonwhite pupils" (MacLeod 1995, 18).

Students' language patterns became a topic of national debate in late 1996 when

Table 7.1 continued

State	Percent of 5–17-Year-Olds Who Speak Non-English Language at Home	State	Percent of 5–17-Year-Olds Who Speak Non-English Language at Home
Alabama	3.0	Montana	3.9
Alaska	9.5	Nebraska	3.6
Arizona	22.8	Nevada	11.8
Arkansas	3.0	New Hampshire	4.4
California	35.0	New Jersey	19.4
Colorado	8.4	New Mexico	29.5
Connecticut	14.9	New York	23.3
Delaware	6.5	North Carolina	4.7
D.C.	11.8	North Dakota	2.7
Florida	17.8	Ohio	5.0
Georgia	4.5	Oklahoma	4.6
Hawaii	14.9	Oregon	7.0
Idaho	5.8	Pennsylvania	6.8
Illinois	14.4	Rhode Island	16.3
Indiana	4.9	South Carolina	3.5
Iowa	3.9	South Dakota	4.1
Kansas	5.3	Tennessee	3.2
Kentucky	2.8	Texas	28.2
Louisiana	5.5	Utah	5.5
Maine	4.4	Vermont	3.1
Maryland	8.4	Virginia	7.0
Massachusetts	15.3	Washington	8.8
Michigan	5.4	West Virginia	2.7
Minnesota	5.1	Wisconsin	5.5
Mississippi	3.0	Wyoming	3.9
Missouri	3.6		

Source: U.S. Bureau of the Census, United States Department of Commerce, 1998.

the Oakland, California, school district passed a resolution on "ebonics" (a blend of the words *ebony* and *phonics)*, also known as "black English." The resolution, which recognized ebonics as the "primary language" of many of the district's 28,000 African American students, called for them to be taught in their primary language and suggested that some students might be eligible for state and federal bilingual education or ESL money. Critics of the resolution, including U.S. Secretary of Education Richard W. Riley, pointed out that "black English" is a nonstandard form of English or a dialect of English and not a foreign language. Other critics were concerned that students and teachers would be taught ebonics. In the midst of intense national debate, the district revised the resolution so that it no longer called for students to be taught in their "primary language"; instead, the district would implement new programs to move students from the language patterns they bring to school toward proficiency in standard English. Other dialects of English and their use in the classroom have been debated from time to time—for example, "Chicano English," "Cajun English," or Hawaiian Creole English (more popularly known as "pidgin English").

The Concept of Multiculturalism   **Multiculturalism** is a set of beliefs based on the importance of seeing the world from different cultural frames of reference and on recognizing and valuing the rich array of cultures within a nation and within the global community. For teachers, multiculturalism affirms the need to create schools where differences related to race, ethnicity, gender, disability, and social class are acknowledged and all students are viewed as valuable members and as human resources for enriching the teaching–learning process. Furthermore, a central purpose of teaching, according to the multiculturalist view, is to prepare students to live in a culturally pluralistic world—a world that "contrasts sharply with cultural assimilation, or 'melting pot' images, where ethnic minorities are expected to give up their traditions and blend in or be absorbed by the mainstream society or predominant culture" (Bennett 1999, 11).

For teachers, multiculturalism also means actively seeking out experiences within other cultures that lead to increased understanding of and appreciation for those ways of life. To provide such cross-cultural experiences for their students, several teacher education programs have developed "cultural immersion" experiences that enable prospective teachers to live in their students' neighborhoods and communities while student teaching. The University of Alaska-Fairbanks Teachers for Alaska Program, for example, enables students to live in remote Alaskan Native villages during their year-long student teaching experience. In the Urban Education Program of the Associated Colleges of the Midwest, prospective teachers live in a former convent in a multiracial, economically diverse neighborhood in Chicago. There the students teach and participate in structured activities that take them into the city's other ethnic neighborhoods. Students at Indiana University can choose among three unique student teaching experiences: the Native American Reservation Project, the Overseas Project, and the Bilingual/Bicultural Project. Through student teaching on a reservation, in another country, or on the Rio Grande border, students have a life-altering cultural immersion experience. As a student who participated in the Native American Reservation Project and now teaches high school in Indianapolis put it: "Before we went to the reservation, people [came] back to IU who said that it would change your life. We thought, 'Oh yeah, sure.' But it really does. A day doesn't go by when I don't think of those students, of that place" (Indiana University 1999).

Ethnicity and Race

Your understanding of the distinction between ethnicity and race will enable you to provide students with educational experiences that reflect ethnic and racial diversity in meaningful ways. **Ethnicity** refers to "a shared feeling of common identity, a sense of peoplehood, and a shared sense of interdependence of fate. These feelings derive, in part, from a common ancestral origin, a common set of values, and a common set of experiences" (Banks 1999, 71).

On the other hand, **race** is a subjective concept that is used to distinguish among human beings on the basis of biological traits and characteristics. Numerous racial categories have been proposed, but because of the diversity among humans and the mixing of genes that has taken place over time, no single set of racial categories is universally accepted. Since many genetic factors are invisible to the naked eye (DNA, for example), noted anthropologist Ashley Montagu has suggested that there could be as few as three "races" (Negroid, Caucasoid, and Mongoloid) or as many as 300, depending on the kind and number of genetic features chosen for measurement. In his classic book, *Man's Most Dangerous Myth: The Fallacy of Race*, Montagu pointed out that

> It is impossible to make the sort of racial classification which some anthropologists and others have attempted. The fact is that all human beings are so . . . mixed with regard to origin that between different groups of individuals . . . "overlapping" of physical traits is the rule (1974, 7).

To reflect the realities of racial identities in the United States, the questionnaire for Census 2000 was changed so that people with a "mixed race" background could select "one or more races" for their racial identity. In addition, the "Spanish/Hispanic/Latino" category allowed respondents to choose among the following: Mexican, Mexican American, and Chicano; Puerto Rican; Cuban; and "other" Spanish/Hispanic/Latino. Similarly, respondents who self-identified as "Asian or Pacific Islander" had the following choices: Asian Indian, Chinese, Filipino, Japanese, Korean, Vietnamese, "other" Asian, Native Hawaiian, Guamanian or Chamorro, Samoan, and "other" Pacific Islander.

There are many ethnic groups in U. S. society, and everyone belongs to at least one. However, as James Banks points out:

> an individual American is ethnic to the extent that he or she functions within ethnic subsocieties and shares their values, behavioral styles, and cultures. An individual, however, may have a low level of ethnicity or psychological identification with his or her ethnic group or groups (1997, 9).

It is also clear that racial and ethnic identities in the United States are becoming more complex. We now know that "racial and ethnic identities derive their meanings from social and historical circumstances, that they can vary over time, and that they can sometimes even be slipped on and off like a change of clothing" (Coughlin 1993, A7). For example, a third-generation descendent of a Japanese immigrant may choose to refer to him- or herself as a Japanese American, an American, or an Asian American. Furthermore, it is evident that "specific racial categories acquire and lose meaning over time" (Coughlin 1993, A7), and the use of ethnic and racial labels and expressions of group membership is largely self-selected and arbitrary.

The Concept of Minorities

To understand the important concept of **minorities,** it may help to remember that even though the term *minority* technically refers to any *group* numbering less than half of the total population, in certain parts of the country "minorities" are actually the majority. However, more important than the numbers themselves is an appreciation of how many groups of people have continuously struggled to obtain full educational, economic, political, and social opportunities in society. Along with minority racial and ethnic groups, others who have traditionally lacked power in U.S. public life are immigrants, the poor, children and the elderly, non-English speakers, members of minority religions, and women. Groups that have been most frequently discriminated against in terms of the quality of education they have received include African Americans, Spanish-speaking Americans, Native Americans, Asian Americans, exceptional learners, people with disabilities, and females. There is mounting evidence that many students from these groups continue to receive a substandard education that does not meet their needs or help empower them to participate fully and equally in life in the United States.

Minority Groups and Academic Achievement   Minority-group students are disproportionately represented among students who have failed to master minimum competencies in reading, writing, and mathematics. It has been estimated that ethnic

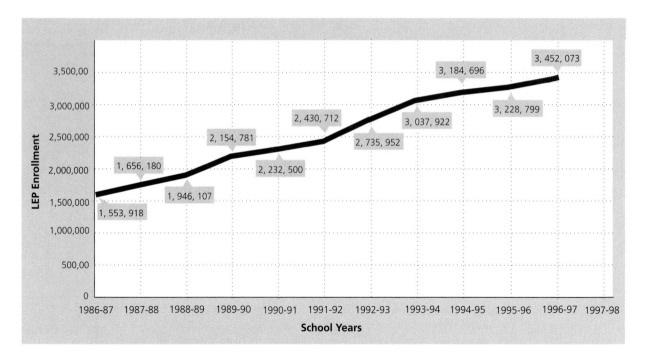

Figure 7.2

LEP enrollment growth from 1986–87 to 1996–97

Sources: B. Donly, et al. *Summary of Bilingual Education State Educational Agency Program Survey of States' LEP Persons and Available Educational Services 1993–94.* Prepared under contract for the U.S. Department of Education by Development Associates, Inc. in Arlington, VA, 1995; R. F. Macias, et al. *Summary Report of the Survey of the States' Limited English Proficient Students and Available Educational Programs and Services, 1996–97.* Washington, DC: National Clearinghouse for Bilingual Education, 1998.

minority students are two to four times more likely than others to drop out of high school. In addition, "in many schools across the nation, racial and language minority students are overrepresented in special education and experience disproportionately high rates of suspension and expulsion" (Bennett 1999, 15). Nevertheless, there has been a trend of "modest growth in achievement among students from minority groups and from 'less advantaged' backgrounds" (Berliner and Biddle 1995, 27).

When we consider the lower achievement levels of minority students, it is important to note the much higher incidence of poverty among minority families and the research showing that socioeconomic status—not race, language, or culture—contributes most strongly to students' achievement in school (Coleman et al. 1966; National Center for Education Statistics 1980; Jencks et al. 1972; Jencks and Phillips 1998). Understandably, it is difficult for poor children to learn well if they endure the stress of living in crime-ridden neighborhoods, dwelling in dilapidated homes, or going to school hungry.

Language Minorities   According to the 1990 census, one in seven U.S. residents aged five years or older spoke a language other than English at home. Various bilingual education programs have been developed to meet the special needs of **language-minority students,** those whose language of the home is a language other than English, and students with limited English proficiency (LEP). Figure 7.2 shows LEP enrollment growth from 1986–87 to 1996–97. Though most bilingual education programs serve

Spanish-speaking students, there are bilingual education programs for the more than ninety other language groups in the United States.

Stereotyping and Racism

Although teachers should expand their knowledge of and appreciation for the diverse cultural backgrounds of their students, they should also guard against forming stereotypes or overgeneralizations about those cultures. **Stereotyping** is the process of attributing behavioral characteristics to all members of a group. In some cases, stereotypes are formed on the basis of limited experiences with and information about the group being stereotyped, and the validity of these stereotypes is not questioned.

Within any cultural group that shares a broad cultural heritage, however, considerable diversity exists. For example, two Puerto Rican children who live in the same community and attend the same school may appear alike to their teachers when, in reality, they are very different. One may come from a home where Spanish is spoken and Puerto Rican holidays are observed; the other child may know only a few words of Spanish and observe only the holidays of the majority culture.

In addition to being alert for stereotypes they and others may hold, teachers should learn to recognize **individual racism,** the prejudicial belief that one's ethnic or racial group is superior to others, and **institutional racism,** "established laws, customs, and practices which systematically reflect and produce racial inequalities in American society . . . whether or not the individuals maintaining those practices have racist intentions" (Jones 1981, 118).

In light of the arbitrariness of the concept of race, James A. Banks points out, "In most societies, *the social significance of race is much more important than the presumed physical differences among groups*" (1997, 74, italics in original). Unfortunately, many people attach great importance to the concept of race. If you believe "that human groups can be validly grouped on the basis of their biological traits and that these identifiable groups inherit certain mental, personality, and cultural characteristics that determine their behavior" (Banks 1997, 78) then you hold racist beliefs. When people use such beliefs as a rationale for oppressing other groups, they are practicing racism. Appendix 7.1 presents a checklist for a small-group activity that can help you become more aware of individual and institutional racism.

As a teacher, you will not be able to eliminate stereotypic thinking or racism in society. However, you have an obligation to all your students to see that your curriculum and instruction are free of any forms of stereotyping or racism. The following Professional Reflection will help you examine, and possibly reassess, your cultural attitudes and values and determine whether you have stereotypes about other cultural groups.

 **Professional Reflection** — Reflecting on your cultural identity

In a Teacher's Journal entry, describe your cultural identity. Who are you? What beliefs, customs, and attitudes are part of your culture? Which of these are most important to your cultural identity?

Next, think of the ethnic and cultural groups in the United States with which you are unfamiliar. When you become a teacher, some of your students may be from these groups. What are some stereotypes about these groups that you tend to believe? How might these stereotypes influence your teaching and teaching effectiveness? How will you test or change your beliefs as part of the process of becoming a teacher?

What Does Equal Educational Opportunity Mean?

To provide equal educational opportunity to all students means that teachers and schools promote the full development of students as individuals, without regard for race, ethnicity, gender, sexual orientation, socioeconomic status, abilities, or disabilities. More specifically, educators fulfill this important mission by continually evaluating the appropriateness of the curricular and instructional experiences they provide to each student.

In the following sections, we review the progress that has been made to provide students from diverse groups with equal educational opportunity, and we focus on strategies for teaching in diverse classrooms. The strategies we present for each group draw from research that suggests that particular learning styles *may be* associated with specific ethnic groups in U.S. society (Shade 1982; Hale-Benson 1986; Bennett 1999). These strategies should not lead you to assume, however, that *all* students from a certain group learn in a particular way. As Christine I. Bennett, an expert on multicultural education, points out:

> The notion that certain learning styles are associated with different ethnic groups is both promising and dangerous. Promise lies in the realization that low academic achievement among some ethnic minorities may sometimes be attributed to conflicts between styles of teaching and learning, not low intelligence. This leads to the possibility that teachers will alter their own instructional styles to be more responsive to the learning needs of students. Danger lies in the possibility that new ethnic stereotypes will develop while old ones are reinforced, as in "Blacks learn aurally," "Asians excel in math," "Mexican American males can't learn from female peer tutors," and "Navajos won't ask a question or participate in a discussion" (Bennett 1999, 63).

We omit Anglo-European Americans from our review, not because students from this very diverse group always have had equal educational opportunities, but because this group represents the historically dominant culture. To a great extent, it has determined the curricular and instructional practices found in schools.

Like the groups we discuss, however, "Anglo-European American" is not a single, monolithic culture. Americans whose ethnic heritage is English, Polish, German, Italian, Irish, Czechoslovakian, Russian, or Swedish, for example, often differ greatly in religious and political traditions, beliefs, and values. Their individual ethnic identity may or may not be strengthened by recent immigrants from their country of origin. European ethnics have, nevertheless, assimilated into the mainstream U.S. society more completely than others.

Education and African Americans

Of the more than 273 million persons living in the United States, approximately 13 percent are African Americans. According to U.S. Census Bureau projections, the African American population in the United States is expected to increase from 36 million (13 percent of the total population) in 2001 to 45 million (14 percent of the total) in 2020, and then to 55 million (15 percent of the total) in 2040. The incidence of social problems such as unemployment, crime, drug abuse, poverty, inadequate housing, and school dropouts is proportionally greater for African Americans than for whites. The struggle of African Americans to improve their quality of life after the end of slavery has been hampered for generations by persistent racism, discrimination, poverty, crime, unemployment, and underemployment.

The civil rights movement of the 1960s and 1970s made it clear that African Americans had been denied full access to many aspects of U.S. life, including the right to a good education. A 1976 report by the United States Commission on Civil Rights, for example, revealed that a Southern school district in the 1930s spent nearly eighteen times as much for the education of white pupils as it did for the education of African Americans.

What is the legacy of school desegregation today? What are some outcomes of education research and curriculum reform related to the African-American experience?

The Desegregation Era   Perhaps the most blatant form of discrimination against African Americans has been school segregation and unequal educational opportunity. As you learned in Chapter 3, the attempt was made to justify segregation by the idea of separate-but-equal schools. It was not until the National Association for the Advancement of Colored People (NAACP) brought suit on behalf of a Kansas family (*Brown v. Board of Education of Topeka, Kansas*) in 1954 that the concept of separate-but-equal schools was decidedly struck down.

The parents of Linda Brown felt that the education their fourth-grader was receiving in the segregated Topeka schools was inferior. When their request that she be transferred to a white school was turned down, they filed suit. In a landmark decision, the U.S. Supreme Court ruled that segregated schools are "inherently unequal" and violate the equal protection clause of the Fourteenth Amendment. U.S. citizens, the justices asserted, have a right to receive an equal opportunity for education.

As a result of opportunities created during the civil rights movement, a substantial number of African Americans are now members of the middle class. Affirmative action programs have enabled many African Americans to attain high-ranking positions in the business, medical, legal, and educational professions. Such gains lead James Banks to point out that

> [A]ny accurate and sophisticated description of the status of African Americans on the threshold of the twenty-first century must describe not only the large percentage of Blacks who are members of the so-called underclass, but also the smaller and significant percentage of African Americans who have entered the middle and upper classes and who function in the mainstream society. Many of the children of the new middle class are not only unacquainted with poverty, but also have been socialized in mainstream middle- and upper-class communities. They have little first-hand experience with traditional African American culture (Banks and Banks 1997, 228–29).

Resegregation of Schools in the United States   As the United States continues to become more ethnically and racially diverse, there is evidence that schools have been "resegregating" during the last ten years, according to *Resegregation in American*

Schools, a Harvard University report released in June 1999 (Orfield and Yun 1999). The report included the following findings:

- Latinos attend the most severely segregated schools (see Figure 7.3).
- Since the late 1980s, schools in the South have been resegregating.
- As African Americans and Latinos move to the suburbs, they are attending segregated schools, especially in urban areas.
- States with a high proportion of African American students made progress toward desegregation in the 1970s; however, all showed increases in school segregation between 1980 and 1996.
- Segregated schools, with the exception of those for white students, tend to have a high concentration of poverty, which has a negative influence on student achievement.

One reason for the trend back to resegregation has been Supreme Court rulings that removed judicial supervision of school districts' efforts to desegregate—for example, *Board of Education of Oklahoma City Public Schools v. Dowell*, 1991 and *Freeman v. Pitts*, 1992. In addition, the Supreme Court ruled in *Missouri v. Jenkins*, 1995, that Kansas City schools did not have to maintain desegregation through a magnet school approach until actual benefits for African American students were shown. Such rulings by the Supreme Court prompted the filing of many lawsuits to end desegregation in several large school districts.

The Learning Needs of African American Students   Research on factors related to students' success in school suggests that schools are monoethnic and do not take into account the diverse needs of ethnic minority-group students (Bennett 1999). In the case of African American students, the failure of the school curriculum to address their learning needs may contribute to high dropout rates and below-average achievement. For example, research indicates that teaching strategies that emphasize cooperation—not competition—often result in higher achievement among African American (and Mexican American) students (Aronson and Gonzalez 1988). In addition, it has been suggested that because many African Americans have grown up in an oral tradition, they may learn better through oral/aural activities—for example, reading aloud

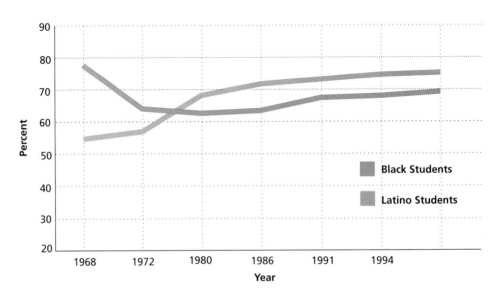

Figure 7.3

Percent of African American and Latino students in 50–100% minority schools, 1968–96
Source: Gary Orfield and John T. Yun, *Resegregation in American Schools.* Cambridge, MA: The Civil Rights Project, Harvard University, June 1999. Used by permission of the publisher.

and listening to audiotapes (Bennett 1999). However, one should not assume that all African Americans learn better aurally.

Afrocentric Schools   To address the educational inequities that African American and other minority-group students may experience as a result of segregation, many communities have tried to create more ethnically and racially diverse classrooms through the controversial practice of busing students to attend schools in other neighborhoods. Also, some African Americans have recently begun to call for **Afrocentric schools**—that is, schools that focus on African American history and cultures for African American pupils. Proponents believe that the educational needs of African American students can be met more effectively in schools that offer Afrocentric curricula.

Private Afrocentric schools, or "black academies," have sprung up across the country in recent years, many supported by the growing number of African Americans who practice Islam, a religion based on the teachings of the prophet Mohammed. Curricula in these schools emphasize the people and cultures of Africa and the history and achievements of African Americans. Teaching methods are often designed for culture-based learning styles, such as choral response, learning through movement, and sociality.

Education and Latino and Hispanic Americans

Hispanic Americans, the fastest growing minority group in the United States, account for about 10 percent of the population, and it has been estimated that an additional five million illegal aliens who speak Spanish may be in the country. By 2010, the Hispanic population is expected to be 14 percent, surpassing African Americans as the nation's largest minority group. The U.S. Census Bureau estimates that the Hispanic American population in the United States will increase from 32 million (12 percent of the total population) in 2001 to 52 million (16 percent of the total) in 2020, and then to 80 million (22 percent of the total) in 2040.

Included in the category of Hispanic Americans are people who call themselves Latinos and Chicanos and who report their ancestry as Mexican, Puerto Rican, Cuban, Central American, or South American. Five states have populations that are more than 10 percent Hispanic: California, Texas, New Mexico, Arizona, and Colorado. Many states have passed English-only laws and made efforts to restrict Hispanic immigrants' access to education. Prior to 1983, six states had English-language laws; however, efforts by political action groups such as U.S. English, founded by the late Senator S.I. Hayakawa of California in 1983, were instrumental in getting English-only laws passed in 25 states by 1999, including California and Colorado. Arizona's 1988 Official English amendment was overturned by the Arizona State Supreme Court in 1998. In addition, California voters approved Proposition 187 in 1994, which prevents public schools from educating the children of illegal aliens.

Socioeconomic Factors   Although some Spanish-speaking immigrants come to the United States hoping to escape a life of poverty in their home country, many others come because they have relatives in the United States or they wish to take advantage of business opportunities in this country. For those Spanish-speaking immigrants who lack job skills and have little education, however, adjusting to the complexities and demands of life in the United States may be difficult.

Socioeconomic factors affect the education of some Hispanics, such as the children of migrant farm workers. Among the estimated one million or so migrant farm workers in this country, more than 70 percent are Spanish-speaking. The dropout rate among all migrant workers is 90 percent, and 50 percent leave school before finishing the ninth grade (Bennett 1999). Migrant children are handicapped by the language barrier, deprivation resulting from poverty, and irregular school attendance. Some states have educational intervention programs in place for reaching this group.

The Learning Needs of Spanish-Speaking Students   What can easily happen to Spanish-speaking learners if they are taught by teachers who are not sensitive to their learning needs is illustrated in Christine I. Bennett's portrait of Jesús, a student with limited English proficiency (LEP):

> Jesús Martinez was a bright, fine-looking six-year old when he migrated with his family from Puerto Rico to New York City. At a time when he was ready to learn to read and write his mother tongue, Jesús was instead suddenly thrust into an English-only classroom where the only tool he possessed for oral communication (the Spanish language) was completely useless to him. Jesús and his teacher could not communicate with each other because each spoke a different language and neither spoke the language of the other. Jesús felt stupid, or retarded; his teacher perceived him to be culturally disadvantaged and beyond her help. However, she and the school officials agreed to allow him to "sit there" because the law required that he be in school (Bennett 1999, 7).

Bennett also captures well the dilemma that many Spanish-speaking LEP students find themselves in: "Students with limited English proficiency are often caught up in conflicts between personal language needs—for example, the need to consolidate cognitive skills in the native language—and a sociopolitical climate that views standard English as most desirable and prestigious" (Bennett 1999, 387). The degree to which students from Spanish-speaking backgrounds are motivated to learn English varies from group to group. Mexican American students who live in the southwest may retain the Spanish language to maintain ties with family and friends in Mexico. Recently arrived Cubans, on the other hand, may have a stronger motivation to learn the language of their new country. In regard to what they wish to learn, children take their cues from the adults around them. If their parents or guardians and friends and relatives have learned English and are bilingual, then they will be similarly motivated. Many Hispanic Americans who value assimilation over their traditional culture favor English-only education.

However, the limited English proficiencies of many children raised in native Spanish-speaking families contribute significantly to the difficulties they have in school. To address the needs of these students, federally funded bilingual-bicultural programs encourage teachers to view bicultural knowledge as a bridge to the school's curriculum. Bilingual education is examined in detail later in this chapter.

Education and Asian Americans and Pacific Islanders

Asian Americans and Pacific Islanders represent about 3 percent of the total population of the United States. The U.S. Census Bureau estimates that the Asian and Pacific Islander population in the United States will increase from 11.6 million (4 percent of the total population) in 2001 to 19.6 million (6 percent of the total) in 2020, and then to 29 million (8 percent of the total) in 2040. This group, comprising at least 34 ethnic groups that speak more than 300 languages and dialects (Asian Americans/Pacific Islanders in Philanthropy 1997), is tremendously diverse and includes people from South

Asia, primarily Bangladesh, India, and Pakistan; Southeast Asia, including Indochina (Laos, Thailand, Indonesia, Malaysia, and Vietnam) and the Philippines; East Asia, including China, Hong Kong, Japan, Korea, and Taiwan; and the Pacific Islands, including Hawaii, Guam, and Samoa. About 55 percent of the total Asian American and Pacific Islander population lives in the western United States, compared to 22 percent of the total population (U.S. Census Bureau 1999).

Historical, Cultural, and Socioeconomic Factors The three largest Asian American groups are Chinese (23.8 percent of Asian Americans), Filipinos (20.4 percent), and Japanese (12.3 percent) (U.S. Census Bureau 1998). Although these groups differ significantly, each "came to the United States seeking the American dream, satisfied important labor needs, and became victims of an anti-Asian movement designed to prevent their further immigration to the United States. [They] also experienced tremendous economic, educational, and social mobility and success in U.S. society" (Banks 1997, 438).

The California gold rush of 1849 brought the first immigrants from Asia, Chinese men who worked in mines, on railroads, and on farms, and who planned to return to their families and homeland. Early Chinese immigrants encountered widespread discrimination in their new country, with anti-Chinese riots occurring in San Francisco, Los Angeles, and Denver between 1869 and 1880. In 1882, Congress passed the Immigration Act, which ended Chinese immigration until 1902. The Chinese were oriented toward maintaining traditional language and religion and established tight-knit urban communities, or "Chinatowns." Recently, many upwardly mobile, professional Chinese Americans have been assimilated into suburban communities, while newly arrived, working-class immigrants from China and Hong Kong are settling in redeveloped Chinatowns.

Japanese immigrants began to arrive in Hawaii and the U.S. mainland in the late 1800s; most worked in agriculture, fisheries, the railroads, or industry and assimilated rapidly despite racial discrimination. The San Francisco Board of Education, for example, began to segregate all Japanese students in 1906, and the Immigration Act of 1924 ended Japanese immigration until 1952. During World War II, the United States was at war with Japan. In response to war hysteria over the "yellow peril," the United States government interned 110,000 Japanese Americans, most of them American-born, in ten detention camps from 1942 to 1946. Since World War II, Japan has developed into one of the world's leading economic and technological powers—an accomplishment that has contributed, no doubt, to a recent decline in Japanese immigration to the United States.

Filipinos began to immigrate to Hawaii and the mainland as field laborers during the 1920s. They, too, encountered racism; in 1934 Congress passed the Tydings-McDuffie Act, which limited Filipino immigration to the United States to 50 persons annually. The following year, President Franklin Roosevelt signed the Repatriation Act, which provided free transportation to Filipinos willing to return to the Philippines. While most early Filipino immigrants had little education and low income, recent immigrants have tended to be professional, technical workers who hope to obtain employment in the United States more suitable for their education and training than they could in the Philippines (Banks 1997).

Teacher's Concerns about Asian American Students Asian Americans are frequently stereotyped as hard-working, conscientious, and respectful of authority, what Sue and Sue (1999) term a "model minority." In fact, 42.2 percent of Asian Americans 25 years and over have a bachelor's degree or more, compared to 23.9 percent of the total population (U.S. Census Bureau 1999). The unreliability of such stereotypes notwithstanding, Asian American parents do tend to require their children to respect authority and value education. However, "for many Asian American students, this image is a destructive myth," according to a report titled *An Invisible Crisis: The Educational Needs of Asian Pacific American Youth.* "As their schools fail them, these children become increasingly likely to graduate with rudimentary language skills, to drop out of school, to join gangs, or to find themselves in the low-paying occupations and on the margins of American life" (Asian Americans/Pacific Islanders in Philanthropy 1997). Families often pressure children to be successful academically through sacrifice and hard work. At the same time, there has been an increase in the number of Asian American youth who are in conflict with their parents' way of life. Leaders in Asian American communities have expressed concern about increases in dropout rates, school violence, and declining achievement. Some Indochinese Americans, for example, face deep cultural conflict in schools. Values and practices that are accepted in U.S. culture, such as dating and glorification of the individual, are sources of conflict between many Indochinese students and their parents.

Teachers need to be sensitive to cultural conflicts that may contribute to problems in school adjustment and achievement for Asian American students and realize that

> Stereotypes about Asian "whiz kids" and jealousy over the relatively high percentages of Asian Americans in the nation's colleges and universities may blind some non-Asian parents, fellow students, and teachers to the deep cultural conflict many Southeast Asian Americans face in our schools (Bennett 1999, 150).

To help Asian American students adjust to the U.S. culture, Qiu Liang offers teachers the following advice based on his school experiences as a Chinese immigrant:

> They [teachers] should be more patient [with an immigrant child] because it is very difficult for a person to be in a new country and learn a new language. Have patience.

> If the teacher feels there is no hope in an immigrant child, then the child will think, "Well, if the teacher who's helping me thinks that I can't go anywhere, then I might as well give up myself" (Igoa 1995, 99–100).

Similarly, Dung Yoong offers these recommendations based on her educational experiences as a Vietnamese immigrant:

> Try to get them to talk to you. Not just everyday conversation, but what they feel inside. Try to get them to get that out, because it's hard for kids. They don't trust —I had a hard time trusting and I was really insecure because of that.

> [P]utting an immigrant child who doesn't speak English into a classroom, a regular classroom with American students, is not very good. It scares [them] because it is so different. [Teachers] should start [them] slowly and have special classes where the child could adapt and learn a little bit about American society and customs (Igoa 1995, 103).

Education and Native Americans and Alaskan Natives

Native Americans and Alaskan Natives peopled the Western hemisphere more than 12,000 years ago. Today, they represent less than 1 percent of the total U.S. population, or about 2 million people (U.S. Census Bureau 1999). This group consists of 517 federally recognized and 365 state-recognized tribes, each with its own language, religious beliefs, and way of life. The four largest groups are the Cherokee Nation of Oklahoma, over 308,000 members; the Navajo Nation, 219,000; the Chippewa Nation, 104,000; and the Sioux Nation of the Dakotas, 103,000 (U.S. Census Bureau 1993). Approximately 760,000 Native Americans live on 275 reservations located primarily in the West. More than half of the Native American and Alaskan Native population lives in six states: Alaska, Arizona, California, New Mexico, Oklahoma, and Washington (Manning and Baruth 1996). Though most Native Americans live in cities, many are establishing connections with reservation Indians as a means of strengthening their cultural identities.

Native Americans are an example of the increasing ambiguity of racial and ethnic identities in the United States. For example, controversy exists over who is Native American. "Some full-blooded native people do not regard a person with one-quarter native heritage to qualify, while others accept $\frac{1}{128}$" (Bennett 1999, 132). While most Native Americans consider a person with one-quarter or more tribal heritage to be a member, the U.S. Census Bureau considers anyone who claims native identity to be a member. An expert on Native Americans and Alaskan Natives, Arlene Hirschfelder, points out that fifty-two legal definitions of Native Americans have been identified (Hirschfelder 1986). Native Americans were declared U.S. citizens in 1924, and native nations have been recognized as independent, self-governing territories since the 1930s (Bennett 1999).

Historical, Cultural, and Socioeconomic Factors Perhaps more than any other minority group, Native Americans have endured systematic long-term attempts to eradicate their languages and cultures. Disease, genocide, confinement on reservations, and decades of forced assimilation have devastated Native American cultures. In 1492, native people used 2 billion acres of land; currently, they own about 94 million acres of land, or about 5 percent of U.S. territory (Bennett 1999). Today, the rates of unemployment, poverty, and lack of educational attainment among Native Americans are among the nation's highest. Since the 1970s, however, there has been a resurgence of interest in preserving or restoring traditional languages, skills, and land claims.

There are hundreds of Native American languages, which anthropologists have attempted to categorize into six major language families (Banks 1999). Older tribal members fluent in the original tribal language and younger members often speak a form of so-called "reservation English." The challenge of educating Native Americans from diverse language backgrounds is further complicated by the difference in size of various Native American populations. These range from the more than 300,000 Cherokee to the 200 or so Supai of Arizona. As a result of the extreme diversity among Native Americans, it has even been suggested that "There is no such thing as an 'Indian' heritage, culture, or value system. [N]avajo, Cherokee, Sioux, and Aleut children are as different from each other in geographic and cultural backgrounds as they are from children growing up in New York City or Los Angeles" (Gipp 1979, 19).

Education for Native American children living on reservations is currently administered by the federal government's Bureau of Indian Affairs (BIA). The **Indian Education Act of 1972** and its **1974 amendments** supplement the BIA's educational programs and provide direct educational assistance to tribes. The act seeks to improve Native American education by providing funds to school districts to meet the special needs of Native American youth, to Indian tribes and state and local education agencies to improve education for youth and adults, to colleges and universities for the purpose of training teachers for Indian schools, and to Native American students to attend college.

Research on Native American Ways of Knowing Considerable debate has occurred over the best approaches for educating Native Americans. For example, Banks points

out that "since the 1920s, educational policy for Native Americans has vacillated between strong assimilationism to self-determination and cultural pluralism" (Banks 1999, 22). In any case, the culture-based learning styles of many Native Americans and Alaskan Natives differ from that of other students. The traditional upbringing of Native American children generally encourages them to develop a view of the world that is holistic, intimate, and shared. "They approach tasks visually, seem to prefer to learn by careful observation which precedes performance, and seem to learn in their natural settings experientially" (Swisher and Deyhle 1987, 350). Bennett suggests the following guideline to ensure that the school experiences of Native American students are in harmony with their cultural backgrounds: "An effective learning environment for Native Americans is one that does not single out the individual but provides frequent opportunities for the teacher to interact privately with individual children and with small groups, as well as opportunities for quiet, persistent exploration" (Bennett 1999, 206).

Increasingly, Native Americans are designing multicultural programs to preserve their traditional cultures and ways of knowing. Although these programs are sometimes characterized as emphasizing separatism over assimilation, for many Native Americans they are a matter of survival. The Heart of the Earth Survival School in Minneapolis, for example, was created to preserve the languages and cultures of the northern Plains Indians. Native American teachers at the school provide bilingual instruction in Ojibwe and Dakota. Students are encouraged to wear traditional dress and practice traditional arts, such as drumming and dancing.

Cultural preservation is also the primary concern at Alaskan Native schools in remote parts of western Alaska and Cherokee schools in the Marietta Independent School District of Stillwell, Oklahoma. In Alaska, elders come into the classroom to teach children how to skin a seal, an education that few Alaskan Native children receive today at home. In Oklahoma, schools try to keep alive the diverse languages of peoples forced to relocate to reservations there from the Southwestern United States in the last century. Students of mixed Cherokee, Creek, and Seminole descent become fluent and literate in the Cherokee language.

What factors contribute to below-average achievement levels of Native American children? How do forces toward assimilation and cultural preservation coexist in the Native American experience?

What Is Meant by Bilingual Education?

Bilingual education programs are designed to meet the learning needs of students whose first language is not English by providing instruction in two languages. Regardless of the instructional approach used, one outcome for all bilingual programs is for students to become proficient in English. Additionally, students are encouraged to become **bicultural,** that is, able to function effectively in two or more linguistic and cultural groups.

In 1968, Congress passed the Bilingual Education Act, which required that language-minority students be taught in both their native language and English. In

Four Types of Bilingual Education Programs

Immersion programs: Students learn English and other subjects in classrooms where only English is spoken. Aides who speak the first language of students are sometimes available, or students may also listen to equivalent audiotaped lessons in their first language.

Transition programs: Students receive reading lessons in their first language and lessons in English as a Second Language (ESL). Once they sufficiently master English, students are placed in classrooms where English is spoken and their first language is discontinued.

Pull-out programs: On a regular basis, students are separated from English-speaking students so that they may receive lessons in English or reading lessons in their first language. These are sometimes called sheltered English programs.

Maintenance programs: To maintain the student's native language and culture, instruction in English and instruction in the native language are provided from kindergarten through twelfth grade. Students become literate.

Figure 7.4

Four types of bilingual education programs

response to the Act, school districts implemented an array of bilingual programs that varied greatly in quality and effectiveness. As a result, many parents filed lawsuits, claiming that bilingual programs were not meeting their children's needs. In 1974, the Supreme Court heard a class action suit *(Lau v. Nichols)* filed by 1,800 Chinese students in San Francisco who charged that they were failing to learn because they could not understand English. The students were enrolled in all-English classes and received no special assistance in learning English. In a unanimous ruling, the Court asserted that federally funded schools must "rectify the language deficiency" of students who "are certain to find their classroom experiences wholly incomprehensible." That same year, Congress adopted the Equal Educational Opportunity Act (EEOA), which stated in part that a school district must "take appropriate action to overcome language barriers that impede equal participation by its students in its instructional programs."

Bilingual programs, most of which serve Latino and Hispanic American students, are tremendously varied and reflect "extreme differences in student composition, program organization, teaching methodologies and approaches, and teacher backgrounds and skills" (Griego-Jones 1996, 115). Generally, however, four types of bilingual education programs are currently available to provide special assistance to the 3.5 million language-minority students in the United States (see Figure 7.4). Only about 315,000 students actually participate in some kind of bilingual program.

Research and Debate on Bilingual Programs

Research on the effectiveness of bilingual programs is mixed (Rothstein 1998). Some who have examined the research conclude that bilingual programs have little effect on achievement (Rossell 1990; Baker 1991). Others have found that well-designed bilingual programs do increase students' achievement and are superior to monolingual programs (Willig 1987; Schmidt 1991; Cziko 1992; Nieto 1992; Trueba, Cheng, and Kenji 1993).

Considerable debate surrounds bilingual programs in the United States. Those in favor of bilingual education make the following points:

Is multicultural education unifying or divisive?

Multicultural education is an outgrowth of the Civil Rights Movement that began in the 1960s. African Americans and other groups in U.S. society had been denied equal access to voting rights, housing, work opportunities, public transportation, education, health care, and various other services. Multicultural education emerged as a reform effort designed to equalize school experiences, curricula, and educational decision-making powers for all groups. It became formalized in teacher education programs with the 1977 adoption by the National Council for Accreditation of Teacher Education of a standard for multicultural education that read: "The institution gives evidence of planning for multicultural education in its teacher education curricula including both the general and professional studies components" (*Standards for the Accreditation of Teacher Education* 1977, 4).

Since then, educators have paid increasing attention to defining and implementing multicultural education. James Banks, an influential advocate and a scholar/author, broadened the initial concept to include not only (1) the integration of multicultural content into a school's curricula but also "(2) the knowledge construction process, (3) prejudice reduction, (4) an equity pedagogy, and (5) an empowering school culture and social structure" (Banks 1993, 112). Similarly, Carl Grant (1978), another strong voice in the multicultural field, emphasized the need to regard multicultural education as not simply an add-on program but as a transformation of the whole system of and approach to education. Proponents say multicultural education is unifying because it recognizes and celebrates all citizens of the United States and equalizes power for all in the U.S. democracy.

Opponents believe multicultural education is divisive, replacing a common Western perspective and traditional values with an array of outlooks and beliefs. Christine Sleeter reports that those who are most critical believe that multicultural education is "the politically charged work of an extremist lunatic fringe of radicals who represent neither the public at large nor the majority of African Americans and Latinos" (1999, 266). Others think that it shifts the education balance too far toward diversity by overemphasizing race and ethnicity.

Where do you stand? Does multiculturalism promote unity or does it cause divisiveness?

Multicultural education is unifying.

The United States has been multicultural, from its earliest days. Many colonists came to this continent seeking refuge from religious persecution in their former homelands. They differed from one another in their historical backgrounds, languages, and beliefs; yet, over time those in the thirteen colonies worked and fought together to become one nation united under the principles of the Declaration of Independence.

Two groups, the indigenous Native American tribes and the African slaves brought to the Americas, were left out of that unifying equality. Over the years other groups from Mexico, South America, Asia, Europe, and countries around the world came to the United States to gain equality and freedom, only to discover that they, too, were left out and marginalized in a racially and ethnically divided country. According to these people and their supporters, the country needed to recognize each group's worth and extend its privileges to all people. Education in diversity was one way to do this. As Banks (1997) wrote, "Multicultural education seeks to extend to all people the ideals that were meant only for an elite few at the nation's birth."

Without multicultural education, schools perpetuate inequality in U.S. society. Academic tracking, curricula devoid of diverse perspectives, culturally biased tests, and prejudicial treatment of racial and ethnic groups cause diverse groups to become invisible or second class in the school culture and society. With multicultural education, greater unity of all groups can occur.

Finally, because familiarity enhances understanding and suppression breeds mistrust, having students learn about cultural groups different from their own can yield positive results. They become more accepting of others when they know their beliefs, lifestyles, manners, history, and values and realize the commonalties we all share. As Banks observed, "The major goal of multicultural education is to restructure schools so that all students will acquire the knowledge, attitudes, and skills needed to function in an ethnically and racially diverse nation and world."

Multicultural education is divisive.

Criticism of multicultural education has increased in recent years. In a search through the literature, Sleeter located "two critiques published in journals in the 1970s, six in the 1980s and fifty-one between 1990 and 1992 alone" (1999, 266). In addition to the charge that the multicultural movement is led by a small group of radicals who do not represent the views of their own races and ethnicities, critics claim that multiculturalism threatens the preservation of Western ideals.

Even some who favor multicultural education believe that others are overemphasizing diversity. Diane Ravitch (1990), an advocate for what she terms "pluralism" with the goal of attaining "a richer common culture," argues that multiculturalism is being replaced with a "particularism" that rejects the belief that a "common culture is possible or desirable." Others note that focusing on diversity makes learning unfocused and superficial.

Unity comes about from having a unified curriculum. Mortimer J. Adler (1994) proposed that one course of study for all was the better answer and that studying a focused curriculum was more effective. Noting the impossibility of studying all cultures in depth, Adler wrote in 1984, "What we face is several lifetimes of work to master diverse histories, each remote from that of New England or Texas, between which we ourselves see enough differences to require special effort in the teaching of a unified American history."

James William Noll (1999) raises a deeper issue behind the question of whether multicultural education is unifying or divisive: "Is the nation strengthened and its minority populations empowered by the process of assimilation into a culture with primarily Western European origins? Or is the United States—which is an immigrant nation—constantly redefined by the cultural influences that come to its shores?"

Where do you stand on this issue?

1. What do you believe is the place of multicultural education for the United States today?

2. In your opinion, why is criticism of multicultural education increasing?

3. Which position do you hold: (a) Assimilation of all ethnic groups should be the nation's goal, or (b) the nation should be "redefined by the cultural influences that come to its shores"? Why do you maintain this position?

4. What would be the consequences of fully implementing either position proposed in question 3?

5. Propose a compromise position.

Recommended Sources

Adler, M. J. (1984). *The paideia program: An educational syllabus.* New York: Macmillan.

Banks, J. A. (1993, September). Multicultural education: Development, dimensions, and challenges. *Phi Delta Kappan.*

Grant, C. A. (1978). Education that is multicultural: Isn't that what we mean? *Journal of Teacher Education, 29*(5), 45–48.

Noll, J. W. (1999). *Taking sides: Clashing views on controversial issues,* 10th ed. Guilford, CT: Dushkin/McGraw-Hill.

Ravitch, D. (1990). Multiculturalism: e pluribus plures. *American Scholar, 59*(3), 337–355.

Sleeter, C. E. (1999). Curriculum controversies in multicultural education. In M. J. Early and K. J. Rehage (Eds.). *Issues in curriculum: A selection of chapters from past NSSE yearbooks.* (pp. 257–80). Chicago: University of Chicago Press.

Standards for the Accreditation of Teacher Education (1977). Washington, DC: National Council for the Accreditation of Teacher Education.

- Students are better able to learn English if they are taught to read and write in their native language.
- Bilingual programs allow students to learn content in their native language rather than delaying that learning until they master English.
- Further developing competencies in students' native languages provides important cognitive foundations for learning English and academic content.

- Second-language learning is a positive value and should be as valid for a Spanish-speaker learning English as for an English-speaker learning Spanish.
- Bilingual programs support students' cultural identity, social context, and self-esteem.

On the other hand, those opposed to bilingual programs make the following points:

- Public schools should not be expected to provide instruction in all the first languages spoken by their students, nor can schools afford to pay a teacher who might teach only a few students.
- The cost of bilingual education is high. Bilingual programs divert staff and resources away from English-speaking students.
- If students spend more time exposed to English, they will learn English more quickly.
- Bilingual programs emphasize differences among and barriers between groups; they encourage separateness rather than assimilation and unity.
- Bilingual education is a threat to English as the nation's first language.

Advice for Monolingual Teachers

Although the future of bilingual education in the United States is uncertain, teachers must continue to meet the needs of language-minority students. These needs are best met by teachers who speak their native language as well as English. However, this is often not possible, and monolingual teachers will find increasing numbers of LEP students in their classrooms. See the Appendixes, "Creating Classroom Environments that Support Second-Language Learners," and "Strategies for Enhancing the Learning and Literacy of Second-Language Learners" on this book's web site. Developed by bilingual/ESL education expert Gisela Ernst and her colleagues, these strategies can be used whether or not a teacher is bilingual.

What Is Multicultural Education?

Multicultural education is committed to the goal of providing all students—regardless of socioeconomic status, gender, sexual orientation or ethnic, racial, or cultural backgrounds—with equal opportunities to learn in school. Multicultural education is also based on the fact that students do not learn in a vacuum—their culture predisposes them to learn in certain ways. And finally, multicultural education recognizes that current school practices have provided, and continue to provide, some students with greater opportunities for learning than students who belong to other groups. The suggestions in the Appendixes referenced above are examples of multicultural education in practice.

As multiculturalism has become more pervasive in U.S. schools, controversy over the need for multicultural education and its purposes has emerged (see Where Do You Stand? feature, pp. 270–271). Carl Grant has identified as "myths" the following six arguments against multicultural education: "(1) It is both divisive and so conceptually weak that it does little to eliminate structural inequalities; (2) it is unnecessary because the United States is a melting pot; (3) multiculturalism—and by extension multicultural education—and political correctness are the same thing; (4) multicultural education rejects the notion of a common culture; (5) multicultural education is a 'minority thing'; and (6) multicultural education will impede learning the basic skills" (Grant 1994, 5). Though multicultural education is being challenged by those who promote these beliefs, we believe that public dialogue and debate about how schools can more effectively address diversity is healthy—an indicator that our society is making real progress toward creating a culture that incorporates the values of diverse groups.

Dimensions of Multicultural Education

According to James A. Banks, "Multicultural education is a complex and multidimensional concept" (Banks 1999, 13). More specifically, Banks suggests that multicultural education may be conceptualized as consisting of five dimensions: (1) content integration, (2) knowledge construction, (3) prejudice reduction, (4) an equity pedagogy, and (5) an empowering school culture (see Figure 7.5). As you progress through your teacher-

Figure 7.5

Banks' dimensions of multicultural education
Source: From James A. Banks, and Cherry A. McGee Banks. *Multicultural Education: Issues and Perspectives,* 3d ed. Copyright © 1997 by Allyn & Bacon. Reprinted by permission, p. 24.

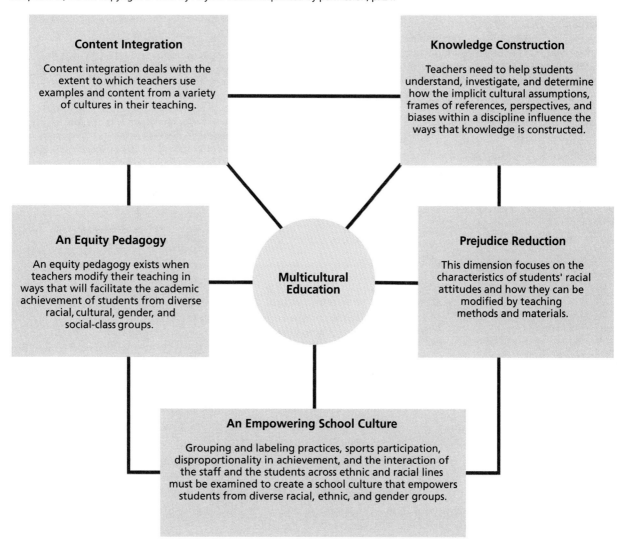

Content Integration

Content integration deals with the extent to which teachers use examples and content from a variety of cultures in their teaching.

Knowledge Construction

Teachers need to help students understand, investigate, and determine how the implicit cultural assumptions, frames of references, perspectives, and biases within a discipline influence the ways that knowledge is constructed.

An Equity Pedagogy

An equity pedagogy exists when teachers modify their teaching in ways that will facilitate the academic achievement of students from diverse racial, cultural, gender, and social-class groups.

Multicultural Education

Prejudice Reduction

This dimension focuses on the characteristics of students' racial attitudes and how they can be modified by teaching methods and materials.

An Empowering School Culture

Grouping and labeling practices, sports participation, disproportionality in achievement, and the interaction of the staff and the students across ethnic and racial lines must be examined to create a school culture that empowers students from diverse racial, ethnic, and gender groups.

Peter White: Opportunity Creator
1999 National Teacher of the Year Finalist

"I have journeyed with my students . . ."

Peter White, the 1999 New York State Teacher of the Year, believes in preparing students for a broader and more compassionate life by learning first-hand about the realities and challenges people face in the world outside the classroom. His preferred mode of teaching his high school social studies students is action learning. "Together we have traveled to New York City and Boston countless times, uncovering their history, architecture, economics, cultural and ethnic diversity, law, beauty, parks, museums, and mass transit, maps, and personal safety," he says. From such experiences his students not only learn their school subjects memorably, but they also strengthen their self-reliance, discover new career options, and learn about diversity.

Through service learning endeavors, White's students also develop an appreciation for the spirit and courage of people in other cultures. White explains: "I have journeyed with my students to the poorest regions of our hemisphere. We have seen the real world and how people eke out a living on less than $100 a year. We have lived with and worked side by side with the shoeless, roofless, hungry, patient, brave, caring, uplifting people of Nicaragua. We visit to help and to learn. All are significantly moved by these experiences."

In trips to the village of Chacraseca, Nicaragua, White guides students, other teachers, and volunteers in supporting schools, planting gardens, and helping in bakeries. In a letter nominating White for 1999 National Teacher of the Year, one of the adult volunteers on several of these trips describes the history of the Northport High School group called "Students for 60,000" that White founded and leads:

> "The organization, which began in 1987, had at first the modest goal of supplying winter coats to some of the estimated 60,000 homeless people in New York City. Since then, under [Peter White's] committed guidance, the club has branched out to a wide variety of services and educational projects. These involve nutrition networks on Long Island, a migrant workers' group, schools in Brooklyn, and homeless shelters in Manhattan."

In 1992, White took his first group for a week-long trip to Chacraseca. Over the following years his groups "fund-

education program and eventually begin to prepare curriculum materials and instructional strategies for your multicultural classroom, remember that integrating content from a variety of cultural groups is just one dimension of multicultural education. Multicultural education is not "something that is done at a certain time slot in the school day where children eat with chopsticks or listen to Peruvian music . . . [it is] something that is infused throughout the school culture and practiced daily" (Henry 1996, 108).

Multicultural education promotes students' positive self-identity and pride in their heritage, acceptance of people from diverse backgrounds, and critical self-assessment. In addition, multicultural education can prompt students, perhaps with guidance from their teachers, to take action against prejudice and discrimination within their school. Indeed, as Joel Spring says, "multicultural education should create a spirit of tolerance and activism in students. An understanding of other cultures and of differing cultural frames of reference will . . . spark students to actively work for social justice" (Spring 1998, 163). For example, students might reduce the marginalization of minority-group students in their school by inviting them to participate in extracurricular and after-school activities.

ed and/or constructed three schools, a health clinic, ten wells/pumps, a rural electrification project, 11 playgrounds, 11 school comedores (dining rooms), and purchased land for agricultural development to meet nutritional needs of hungry school children. . . . Now more than 800 children are eating a substantial meal every school day."

White also is the lead teacher in his school's model law program, which began in 1985. After teaching the course a few times he realized that he needed more expertise, so he attended law school and passed the bar exam in two states. His students learn criminal law, trial practice, torts, contracts, property law, family law, education law, and legal research and writing.

A strong believer in the richness in diversity, White is against tracking students because it "creates a sense of superiority in some and inferiority in others." He explains the benefits of having mixed ability groups together:

"Recently, in my American Law class, where sophisticated legal topics are covered, I had 26 students. Six were special education students, with learning and emotional problems. The majority were from the middle to upper-middle academic ranks. Several were honor students, one the editor of the school's newspaper, and another the valedictorian from a class of 400 students. The intermixture of these diverse personalities and learning types was terrific. There were times when some could not grasp a concept and the others helped them understand. At other times, the so-called underachievers took to their feet and were successful in trial competitions, giving the others a 'how-to' lesson. Each learned from the other."

White's respect for students and appreciation of their abilities to grapple with life's challenging realities shape his response to the problem of violence on school campuses. He says,

"We have some troubled and disaffected students and parents who need help. I believe that the solution lies more with identification, intervention, and treatment than with heightened security and a police-type presence. In schools where administrators speak to each other in military jargon on walkie-talkies, students often feel mistrusted and alienated, and learning suffers. Young people need to be trusted in order to become trustworthy, they need to be respected in order to be respectful, and they need to be given real decisions to make in order to be able to make sound decisions later on in life."

Being an "opportunity creator," White believes, is his greatest accomplishment as a teacher. "I try to create opportunities for students to grow, learn, and use the real world to improve academic skills and develop as people." His students are the benefactors, and so are many in the world beyond his classroom.

Multicultural Curricula

As a teacher you will teach students who historically have not received full educational opportunity—students from the many racial and ethnic minority groups in the United States, students from low-income families or communities, students with exceptional abilities or disabilities, students who are gay or lesbian, and students who are male or female. You will face the challenge of reaching out to all students and teaching them that they are persons of worth who can learn.

In your diverse classroom your aim is not to develop a different curriculum for each group of students—that would be impossible and would place undue emphasis on differences among students. Rather, your curriculum should help increase students' awareness and appreciation of the rich diversity in U.S. culture. A **multicultural curriculum** addresses the needs and backgrounds of all students regardless of their cultural identity. As Banks suggests, the multicultural curriculum "enable[s] students to derive valid generalizations and theories about the characteristics of ethnic groups and to learn how they are alike and different, in both their past and present experiences. . . . [It] focus[es] on a range of groups that *differ* in their racial characteristics, cultural experiences, languages, histories, values, and current problems" (Banks 1997, 15). Teachers who provide multicultural education recognize the importance of asking questions such as those posed by Valerie Ooka Pang: "Why is a child's home language important to keep? What strengths does culture give children? What impact does culture have on learning? What does racism, sexism, or classism look like in schools?" (Pang 1994, 292).

In developing a multicultural curriculum, you should be sensitive to how your instructional materials and strategies can be made more inclusive so that they reflect cultural perspectives, or "voices," that previously have been silent or marginalized in discussions about what should be taught in schools and how it should be taught. "Nondominant groups representing diversity in the school whose voices traditionally have not been heard include those defined by race, language, gender, sexual orientation, alternative family structures, social class, disability, bilingualism, and those with alien or refugee status" (Henry 1996, 108). Effective teachers attend to these previously unheard voices not as an act of tokenism but with a genuine desire to make the curriculum more inclusive and to "create space for alternative voices, not just on the periphery but in the center" (Singer 1994, 286).

Multicultural Instructional Materials and Strategies

To create classrooms that are truly multicultural, teachers must select instructional materials that are sensitive, accurately portray the contributions of ethnic groups, and reflect diverse points of view. (See the Appendix, "Selected Resources for Multicultural Education" on this book's web site.) Teachers must also recognize that "[s]ome of the books and other materials on ethnic groups published each year are insensitive, inaccurate, and written from mainstream and insensitive perspectives and points of view" (Banks 1997, 124). Some guidelines for selecting multicultural instructional materials follow:

- Books and other materials should accurately portray the perspectives, attitudes, and feelings of ethnic groups.
- Fictional works should have strong ethnic characters.
- Books should describe settings and experiences with which all students can identify and yet should accurately reflect ethnic cultures and lifestyles.
- The protagonists in books with ethnic themes should have ethnic characteristics but should face conflicts and problems universal to all cultures and groups.
- The illustrations in books should be accurate, ethnically sensitive, and technically well done.
- Ethnic materials should not contain racist concepts, clichés, phrases, or words.
- Factual materials should be historically accurate.
- Multiethnic resources and basal textbooks should discuss major events and documents related to ethnic history (Banks 1997, 125–26).

Yvonne Wilson, a first-grade teacher in Talmoon, Minnesota, and an Ojibwe Indian, points out that a teacher's willingness to learn about other cultures is very important to students and their parents:

People in the community know if you are trying to understand their culture. Students also see it. Becoming involved—going to a powwow or participating in other cultural events—shows people that here is a teacher who is trying to learn about our culture.

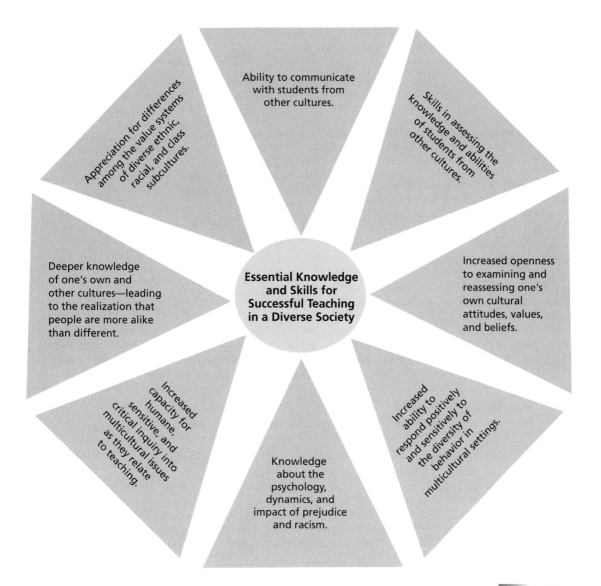

Ability to communicate with students from other cultures.

Skills in assessing the knowledge and abilities of students from other cultures.

Appreciation for differences among the value systems of diverse ethnic, racial, and class subcultures.

Essential Knowledge and Skills for Successful Teaching in a Diverse Society

Deeper knowledge of one's own and other cultures—leading to the realization that people are more alike than different.

Increased openness to examining and reassessing one's own cultural attitudes, values, and beliefs.

Increased capacity for humane, sensitive, and critical inquiry into multicultural issues as they relate to teaching.

Increased ability to respond positively and sensitively to the diversity of behavior in multicultural settings.

Knowledge about the psychology, dynamics, and impact of prejudice and racism.

Figure 7.6

Essential knowledge and skills for successful teaching in a diverse society
Source: Adapted from Forrest W. Parkay and Henry T. Fillmer, "Improving Teachers' Attitudes toward Minority-Group Students: An Experiential Approach to Multicultural Inservice," *New Horizons Journal of Education* (November 1984), pp. 178–79

Participating wholeheartedly in cross-cultural experiences will help you to grow in the eight areas outlined in Figure 7.6 as essential for successful teaching in a diverse society.

How Is Gender a Dimension of Multicultural Education?

Though it may be evident that gender affects students' learning in many ways, it may not be evident that gender is an important dimension of multicultural education. However, as Tozer, Violas, and Senese point out:

Traditional definitions of culture have centered around the formal expression of a people's common existence—language, art, music, and so forth. If culture is more broadly defined to include such things as ways of knowing, ways of relating to oth-

highlights

Does gender equity exist in the use of educational technology?

Considerable evidence indicates that boys tend to have more experience with and positive attitudes toward computer technology than girls (Bitter and Pierson 1999; Comber et al 1997; Hammett 1997; Valenza 1997; Whitley 1997). In addition, boys participate in more elective technology courses and activities than girls. A partial explanation for this difference may stem from the fact that "Software generally tends to emphasize male-dominated activities. Games often include violence and competition as motivation. These software characteristics tend to attract males" (Bitter and Pierson 1999, 240). Also, some computer software and online advertisements promote gender stereotypes (Knupfer 1998). In addition, Cornelia Brunner and Dorothy Bennett (1997) suggest that the attitude of girls toward technology might reflect a tendency in schools to celebrate the speed and power of the machine (the "masculine view") rather than the social function of technology (the "feminine view").

In any case, as the use of technologies continues to become more widespread in society and schools, teachers must make a special effort to ensure that girls have equal access to technology and that their technology-related experiences are positive and growth-enhancing. What steps will you take to ensure that your use of technology reflects gender equity? How will you encourage your students, regardless of gender, to acquire additional knowledge and skills with computers?

ers, ways of negotiating rights and privileges, and modes of conduct, thought, and expression, then the term "culture" applies not only to ethnic groups but to people grouped on the basis of gender. [G]ender entails cultural as well as physiological dimensions (Tozer, Violas, and Senese 1993, 310).

Gender Differences

Cultural differences between males and females are partially shaped by society's traditional expectations of them. Through **sex role stereotyping** families, the media, the schools, and other powerful social forces condition boys and girls to act in certain ways regardless of abilities or interests. As we mentioned in Chapter 4, one of the aims of schools is to socialize students to participate in society. One dimension of the **sex role socialization** process conveys to students certain expectations about the way boys and girls are "supposed" to act. Girls are supposed to play with dolls, boys with trucks. Girls are supposed to be passive, boys active. Girls are supposed to express their feelings and emotions when in pain, boys to repress their feelings and deny pain.

Students may be socialized into particular gender-specific roles as a result of the curriculum materials they use at school. By portraying males in more dominant, assertive ways and portraying females in ways that suggest that they are passive and helpless, textbooks can subtly reinforce expectations about the way girls and boys "should" behave. Within the last few decades, though, publishers of curriculum materials have become more vigilant about avoiding these stereotypes.

Gender and Education

As noted in Chapter 3, it was not until Title IX of the Education Amendments Act was passed in 1972 that women were guaranteed equality of educational opportunity in educational programs receiving federal assistance. Title IX has had the greatest impact on athletic programs in schools; for example, in 1973, 800,000 girls played high school sports; and in 1997, 2.5 million girls participated (*Health* 1999). The law requires that both sexes have equal opportunities to participate in and benefit from the availability of coaches, sports equipment, resources, and facilities. For contact sports such as football, wrestling, and boxing, sports that were not open to women, separate teams are allowed.

The right of females to equal educational opportunity was further enhanced with the passage of the **Women's Educational Equity Act (WEEA)** of 1974. This act provides the following opportunities:

- Expanded math, science, and technology programs for females
- Programs to reduce sex-role stereotyping in curriculum materials
- Programs to increase the number of female educational administrators
- Special programs to extend educational and career opportunities to minority, disabled, and rural women
- Programs to help school personnel increase educational opportunities and career aspirations for females
- Encouragement for more females to participate in athletics

What impact has civil rights legislation had on the education of females? Why and in what ways does gender bias persist in many U.S. classrooms and schools?

Despite reforms stemming from WEEA, several reports in the early 1990s criticized schools for subtly discriminating against girls in tests, textbooks, and teaching methods. Research on teacher interactions in the classroom seemed to point to widespread unintentional gender bias against girls. Two of these studies, *Shortchanging Girls, Shortchanging America* (1991) and *How Schools Shortchange Girls* (1992), both commissioned by the American Association of University Women (AAUW), claimed that girls were not encouraged in math and science and that teachers favored boys' intellectual growth over that of girls.

In the mid-1990s, however, some gender equity studies had more mixed findings. In their analysis of data on achievement and engagement of 9,000 eighth-grade boys and girls, University of Michigan researchers Valerie Lee, Xianglei Chen, and Becky A. Smerdon concluded that "the pattern of gender differences is inconsistent. In some cases, females are favored; in others males are favored" (Lee, Chen, and Smerdon 1996). Similarly, University of Chicago researchers Larry Hedges and Amy Nowell found in their study of thirty-two years of mental tests given to

boys and girls that, while boys do better than girls in science and mathematics, they were "at a rather profound disadvantage" in writing and scored below girls in reading comprehension (Hedges 1996, 3).

Additional research and closer analyses of earlier reports on gender bias in education were beginning to suggest that boys, not girls, were most "shortchanged" by the schools (Sommers, 1996). Numerous articles as well as a 1999 PBS series that began with a program titled "The War on Boys" challenged the conclusions of the earlier AAUW report, *How Schools Shortchange Girls*. Other commentary discounted gender bias in the schools as a fabrication of radical feminism; among the first to put forth this view was Christina Hoff Sommers' (1994) controversial book, *Who Stole Feminism? How Women Have Betrayed Women*; and, more recently, Judith Kleinfeld's (1998) *The Myth That Schools Shortchange Girls: Social Science in the Service of Deception* and Cathy Young's (1999) *Ceasefire!*

To examine gender issues in the public schools, *The Metropolitan Life Survey of the American Teacher, 1997* surveyed 1,306 students in grades 7–12 and interviewed 1,035 teachers in grades 6–12. The analysis of data indicated that:

(1) contrary to the commonly held view that boys are at an advantage over girls in school, girls appear to have an advantage over boys in terms of their future plans, teachers' expectations [see Figure 7.7], everyday experiences at school and interactions in the classroom; (2) minority girls [African Americans and Hispanics only] hold the most optimistic views of the future and are the group most likely to focus on education goals; (3) minority boys are the most likely to feel discouraged about the future and the least interested in getting a good education; and (4) teachers nationwide view girls as higher achievers and more likely to succeed than boys. [These] findings appear to contradict those from other studies which conclude that girls have lower expectations than boys, feel less confident, perceive competitiveness as a barrier to learning and believe that society discourages them from pursuing their goals (Louis Harris and Associates 1997, 3).

To shed light on gender differences in academic achievement, Warren Willingham and Nancy Cole (1997) conducted a seminal study of the scores of 15 million students in the fourth, eighth, and twelfth grades on hundreds of standardized exams used by schools and college placement exams such as the SAT. Contrary to long-standing assumptions that there are pronounced differences between the performance of males and females on standardized tests, their study found that "There is not a dominant picture of one gender excelling over the other and, in fact, the average performance difference across all subjects is essentially zero." Boys and girls, Willingham and Cole found, were fairly evenly matched in verbal and abstract reasoning, math computation, and the social sciences. The superiority of boys in

Figure 7.7

Teachers' opinions on who aims higher: boys or girls
Source: The Metropolitan Life Survey of the American Teacher 1997: Examining Gender Issues in Public Schools. New York: Louis Harris and Associates, Inc., 1997, p. 52.

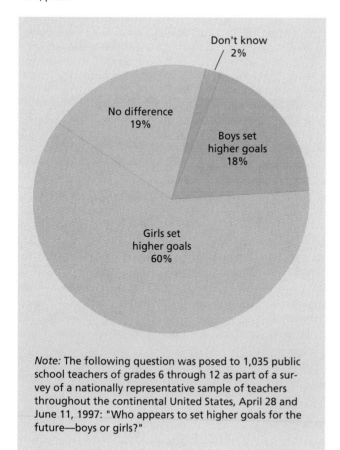

Note: The following question was posed to 1,035 public school teachers of grades 6 through 12 as part of a survey of a nationally representative sample of teachers throughout the continental United States, April 28 and June 11, 1997: "Who appears to set higher goals for the future—boys or girls?"

math and science was found to be surprisingly slight and "significantly smaller than 30 years ago." Boys were found to have a clear advantage in mechanical and electronic ability and knowledge of economics and history, while girls had a clear advantage in language skills, especially writing, and a "moderate edge" in short-term memory and perceptual speed. Furthermore, the authors concluded that gender differences in test scores are not the result of bias in the exams; instead, the differences are genuine and would be reflected also in more carefully designed tests.

Gender-Fair Classrooms and Curricula

Although research and debate about the bias boys and girls encounter in school will no doubt continue, it is clear that teachers must encourage girls and boys to develop to the full extent of their capabilities and provide them an education that is free from **gender bias**—subtle favoritism or discrimination on the basis of gender.

Following is a list of basic guidelines for creating a **gender-fair classroom.** Adherence to these guidelines will help teachers "address the inequities institutionalized in the organizational structure of schools, the curriculum selected to be taught, the learning strategies employed, and their ongoing instructional and informal interactions with students" (Stanford 1992, 88).

- Become aware of differences in interactions with girls and boys.
- Promote boys' achievement in reading and writing and girls' achievement in mathematics and science.
- Reduce young children's self-imposed sexism.
- Teach about sexism and sex role stereotyping.
- Foster an atmosphere of collaboration between girls and boys.

See the Appendix "Selected Resources for Achieving Gender Equity" on this book's web site.

Sexual Orientation   In addition to gender bias, some students experience discrimination on the basis of their sexual orientation. To help all students realize their full potential, teachers should acknowledge the special needs of gay, lesbian, and bisexual students for "there is an invisible gay and lesbian minority in every school, and the needs of these students [a]re often unknown and unmet" (Besner and Spungin 1995, xi). One study of 120 gay and lesbian students ages fourteen to twenty-one found that only one-fourth said they were able to discuss their sexual orientation with school counselors, and less than one in five said they could identify someone who had been supportive of them (Tellijohann and Price 1993). Moreover, a similar study of lesbian and gay youth reported that 80 percent of participants believed their teachers had negative attitudes about homosexuality (Sears 1991).

Based on estimates that as much as 10 percent of society may be homosexual, a high school with an enrollment of 1,500 might have as many as 150 gay, lesbian, and bisexual students (Besner and Spungin 1995; Stover 1992). The National Education Association, the American Federation of Teachers, and several professional organizations have passed resolutions urging members and school districts to acknowledge the special needs of these students.

The nation's first dropout prevention program targeting gay, lesbian, and bisexual students was implemented in the Los Angeles school system. Known as Project 10, the program focuses on education, suicide prevention, dropout prevention, creating a safe environment for homosexual students, and HIV/AIDS education (Uribe and Harbeck 1991). In 1993, Massachusetts became the first state to adopt an educational policy prohibiting discrimination against gay and lesbian students and teachers. At one Massachusetts high school, gay and straight students created the Gay-Straight Alliance (GSA), a school-sanctioned student organization that gives students a safe place to discuss sexual orientation issues (Bennett 1997).

Homosexual students can experience school-related problems and safety risks. The hostility gay, lesbian, and bisexual youth can encounter may cause them to feel confused, isolated, and self-destructive (Alexander 1998; Jordan, Vaughan, and Woodworth 1997; Edwards 1997; Anderson, 1997). Teachers and other school personnel can provide much-needed support. Informed, sensitive, and caring teachers can play an important role in helping all students develop to their full potential. Such teachers realize the importance of recognizing diverse perspectives, and they create inclusive classroom environments that encourage students to respect differences among themselves and others and to see the contributions that persons from all groups have made to society.

SUMMARY

How Is Diversity Embedded in the Culture of the United States?

■ The percentage of ethnic minorities in the United States has been growing steadily since World War II. By 2025, half of U.S. youth will be white and half "minority;" and by 2050, no one group will be a majority among adults in the United States. Currently, the majority of students in several states and many urban districts are from groups traditionally thought of as minority.

■ Culture is defined as the way of life common to a group of people, including beliefs, attitudes, habits, values, and practices.

■ Dimensions of cultural identity include beliefs, attitudes, and values; racial identity; exceptionalities; language; gender; ethnicity; income level; and occupation.

■ Ethnicity refers to a commonly shared racial or cultural identity and a set of beliefs, values, and attitudes. The concept of *race* is used to distinguish among people on the basis of biological traits and characteristics. A minority group is a group of people who share certain characteristics and are fewer in number than the majority of a population.

■ The lower achievement levels of certain minority-group students compared to those of their Anglo-European American and Asian American counterparts reflect the strong connection between socioeconomic status (SES) and achievement, since the incidence of poverty is highest among minority families.

■ Stereotyping is the process of attributing certain behavioral characteristics to all members of a group, often on the basis of limited experiences with and information about the group being stereotyped. Individual racism is the prejudicial belief that one's own ethnic or racial group is superior to others, and institutional racism refers to laws, customs, and practices that lead to racial inequalities.

What Does Equal Educational Opportunity Mean?

- Equal educational opportunity means that teachers promote the full development of students without regard for race, ethnicity, gender, sexual orientation, socioeconomic status, abilities, or disabilities.

- Past evidence indicates that four minority groups in the United States have been denied equality of educational opportunity through various forms of racism, discrimination, and neglect: African Americans, Latino and Hispanic Americans, Asian Americans and Pacific Islanders, and Native Americans and Alaskan Natives. Teachers can meet the needs of students from these groups by becoming familiar with their cultural and linguistic backgrounds and learning styles.

- In spite of increasing diversity in the United States, there has been a trend during the last ten years for schools to "resegregate," perhaps as a result of Supreme Court rulings that removed judicial supervision of school district efforts to desegregate.

What Is Meant by Bilingual Education?

- Bilingual education programs provide instruction in a student's first language and English. The goal of bilingual programs is for students to learn English and become bicultural, able to function effectively in two or more linguistic/cultural groups. Four approaches to bilingual education are immersion, maintenance, pullout, and transition programs.

- Some research has found that bilingual programs have a positive effect on achievement, while others have found little effect. In light of inconclusive outcomes and mixed support, there has been a continuing debate over bilingual education in the United States.

What Is Multicultural Education?

- Five dimensions of multicultural education have been suggested: content integration, knowledge construction, prejudice reduction, an equity pedagogy, and an empowering school culture.

- A multicultural curriculum addresses the needs and backgrounds of all students—regardless of their cultural identity—and expands students' appreciation for diversity. Effective multicultural materials and instructional strategies include the contributions of ethnic groups and reflect diverse points of view or "voices" that previously may have been silenced or marginalized in society.

How Is Gender a Dimension of Multicultural Education?

- Gender includes ways of knowing and "modes of conduct, thought, and expression"; these are dimensions of culture.

- The behavior of boys and girls in our society is influenced by *sexism, sex role socialization,* and *sex role stereotyping.*

- Both boys and girls experience inequities in the classroom; teachers, however, can provide both sexes with an education free of *gender bias* by creating gender-fair classrooms and curricula.

■ Teachers should acknowledge the special needs of students who are gay, lesbian, or bisexual, and provide them with safe, supportive learning environments.

KEY TERMS AND CONCEPTS

Afrocentric schools, 263
bicultural, 268
bilingual education, 253
cultural identity, 252
cultural pluralism, 252
culture, 252
diversity, 251
ethnic group, 252
ethnicity, 256
gender bias, 281
gender-fair
    classroom, 281

Indian Education Act of
    1972 and 1974
    Amendments, 267
individual racism, 259
institutional racism, 259
language-minority
    students, 258
limited English proficiency
    (LEP), 253
minorities, 257
multicultural
    curriculum, 275

multicultural
    education, 272
multiculturalism, 256
National Assessment of
    Educational Progress
    (NAEP), 284
race, 256
sex role socialization, 278
sex role stereotyping, 278
stereotyping, 259
Women's Educational
    Equity Act (WEEA), 279

APPLICATIONS AND ACTIVITIES

Teacher's Journal

1. Reflecting on your experiences in schools and the five dimensions of multicultural education (see Figure 7.5 on page 273), describe the steps your teachers took to create an empowering school culture and social climate.

2. During your school years, did you ever experience discrimination as a member of a "different" group? Write about one outstanding incident that you feel affected your performance as a student.

3. As a teacher, what activities and materials might you use in a specific learning context to reduce the prejudices of students toward groups different from theirs?

4. Describe an example of sex-role stereotyping or gender bias that you experienced or observed in a school setting and how you felt about it.

Teacher's Database

1. Conduct an online keyword search for sources of information on one or more of the following diversity topics from Chapter 7. Share your findings with classmates before narrowing your search:

gender equity   English as a Second Language (ESL)
cultural diversity   bilingual education
multicultural education   English for Students of Other Languages (ESOL)

2. Using one of the diversity topics listed above, go online to gather current national

and state statistics related to that topic. For example, you may gather relevant data at one or more of the following sites:

National Center for Education Statistics   U.S. Bureau of the Census

National Center for Education Information   National Data Resource Center

National Assessment of Educational Progress

Observations and Interviews

1. If possible, visit a school that has an enrollment of students whose cultural or socioeconomic backgrounds differ from your own. What feelings and questions about these students emerge as a result of your observations? How might your feelings affect your teaching and teaching effectiveness? How might you go about finding answers to your questions?

2. Interview a teacher at the school identified in the above activity.. What special satisfactions does he or she experience from teaching at the school? What significant problems relating to diversity does he or she encounter, and how are they dealt with?

Professional Portfolio

Prepare an annotated directory of local resources for teaching students about diversity, implementing multicultural curricula, and promoting harmony or equity among diverse groups. For each entry, include an annotation—that is, a brief description of the resource materials and their availability.

Resources for your personalized directory should be available through local sources such as your university library, public library, community agencies, and so on. Among the types of resources you might include are the following:

- Films, videos, audiocasettes, books, and journal articles

- Simulation games designed to improve participants' attitudes toward diversity

- Motivational guest speakers from the community

- Ethnic museums and cultural centers

- Community groups and agencies dedicated to promoting understanding among diverse groups

- Training and workshops in the area of diversity

Appendix 7.1

Can you recognize racism?

Instructions

First work alone. Put a check before each statement you think is an example of racism. Then work with your small group and try to agree on the examples of racism. (Your group will receive a packet of statement cards to make the task easier.) Choose one member of your group to share your decisions with everyone.

1. Which of the following quotations or descriptive statements are examples of racism?
   Indicate these with a check (✓).

   _____ "A black family moved into our neighborhood this week."

   _____ The principal interviewed two equally outstanding candidates, one black and the other Latino. She selected the black teacher because her school had several Latino teachers but no black teachers.

   _____ In 1882 immigration laws excluded the Chinese, and the Japanese were excluded in 1908.

   _____ During the 1960s civil rights movement, Mrs. Viola Liuzzo, a white civil rights worker from Michigan, was shot by white southern segregationists.

   _____ Between 1892 and 1921 nearly 2,400 African Americans were lynched by vigilante mobs who were never brought to justice.

   _____ "The best basketball players on our team this year are black."

   _____ The band director discouraged black students from playing the flute or piccolo because he believed it was too difficult for them to excel on these instruments.

   _____ When Mrs. Wallace, an African American woman from Detroit, visited a predominantly white university in northern Michigan to see her son play basketball, she was seriously injured in a car accident. She refused a blood transfusion because she was afraid of being contaminated by white blood.

   _____ When Stacey Russell, an African American undergraduate, went through rush, the girls of an all-white sorority decided not to pledge her because several members threatened to move out if they did.

   _____ The geography textbook described the peoples of Nigeria as primitive and underdeveloped.

   _____ The children who attended an elementary school in southwest Texas spoke only Spanish at home. When they came to school all the books and intelligence tests were in English. Nearly all of the children were placed in remedial classes or in classes for the mentally retarded.

   _____ Mr. Jones said, "It is true that Indians who still live on reservations live in extreme poverty. But this is because they refuse to give up their traditions and a culture which is obsolete in the modern world."

   _____ The U.S. Constitution allowed each slave to be counted as three-fifths of a person.

   _____ The reporter wrote that "Toni Morrison is a brilliant writer who accurately portrays much of the black experience in America."

   _____ When John brought home a new friend, his father was shocked and angry. Peter, the new friend, was of Japanese origin and John's father had been seriously wounded by the Japanese in World War II. John's father refused to allow Peter to visit again.

_____   In 1896 the Supreme Court ruled that separate facilities for the races were legal as long as they were *equal*. This resulted in separate schools, churches, restaurants, restrooms,
_____   swimming pools, theaters, doctors' offices, neighborhoods, Bibles used in court, and so forth.

_____   When Mary Adams wanted to find a place in the school cafeteria, the only vacant chair was at a table seating five black girls. Mary, who is white, was afraid to join them.

In California today, approximately 10 percent of the population is black, while 41 percent of those in prison are black. Blacks generally have more financial difficulty than whites in hiring a lawyer and plea bargaining.

2. Select one member to write your group's decisions below on the decision sheet and another person to share the results with the rest. Be prepared to explain your reasons if necessary.

a. The following statements are examples of either individual or institutional racism: (Write numbers and a word or two for description, and arrange them according to those that refer to racist individuals or to racist policies and institutions.)

Individual Racism	Institutional Racism

b. The group's definition of racism is:

_____

c. The main difference between individual and institutional racism is:

_____

d. Examples of individual and institutional racism in our community are:
Individual racism:

_____

_____

_____

Institutional racism:

_____

_____

_____

Source: From Christine I. Bennett, *Comprehensive Multicultural Education: Theory and Practice,* 4th ed. Boston: Allyn and Bacon, 1999, pp. 312-314. Copyright © 1999 by Allyn and Bacon. Reprinted by permission.

8

Addressing Learners' Individual Needs

I was . . . fortunate that I chose theoretical physics, because it is all in the mind. So my disability has not been a serious handicap.

—Stephen W. Hawking
A Brief History of Time: From the Big Bang to Black Holes

focus
questions

1. How do students' needs change as they develop?

2. How do students vary in intelligence?

3. How do students vary in ability and disability?

4. What are special education, mainstreaming, and inclusion?

5. How can you teach all learners in your inclusive classroom?

It's late Friday afternoon, the end of the fourth week of school, and you've just finished arranging your classroom for the cooperative learning groups you're starting on Monday. Leaning back in the chair at your desk, you survey the room and imagine how things will go on Monday. Your mental image is positive, with one possible exception—eleven-year-old Rick. Since the first day of school, he's been very disruptive. His teacher last year described him as "loud, aggressive, and obnoxious."

Since school began, Rick has been belligerent and noncompliant. For the most part, he does what he wants, when he wants. As far as you know, he has no close friends; he teases the other kids constantly and occasionally gets into fights.

Rick's parents divorced when he was in the second grade. His father was given custody of Rick and his younger sister. Two years later, Rick's father married a woman with three children of her own. You've heard that Rick's two new half-brothers, thirteen and fifteen years old, are "out of control," and the family has been receiving counseling services from the local mental health clinic.

Rick's school records indicate that other teachers have had trouble with him in the past. Academically, he's below his classmates in all subjects except physical education and art. Comments from two of his previous teachers suggest Rick has a flair for artwork. Last year, Rick was diagnosed with mild learning and behavior disorders.

Mr. Chavez, the school psychologist, and Ms. Tamashiro, the school's inclusion facilitator, have been working with you on developing an individualized education program (IEP) for Rick. In fact, before school on Monday, you're meeting with Ms. Tamashiro to discuss how to involve Rick in the cooperative learning groups. You're anxious to get her suggestions, and you're confident that with her help and Mr. Chavez's, you can meet Rick's learning needs.

As the preceding scenario about Rick suggests, teachers must understand and appreciate students' unique learning and developmental needs. They must be willing to learn about students' abilities and disabilities and to explore the special issues and concerns of students at three broad developmental levels—childhood, early adolescence, and late adolescence. The need to learn about the intellectual and psychological growth of students at the age level you plan to teach is obvious. In addition, understanding how their interests, questions, and problems will change throughout their school years will better equip you to serve them in the present. In this chapter, we look at how students' needs change as they develop and how their needs reflect various intelligences, abilities, and disabilities.

How Do Students' Needs Change as They Develop?

Development refers to the predictable changes that all human beings undergo as they progress through the life span—from conception to death. Although developmental changes "appear in orderly ways and remain for a reasonably long period of time" (Woolfolk 1998, 24), it is important to remember that students develop at different rates. Within a given classroom, for example, some students will be larger and physically more mature than others; some will be socially more sophisticated; and some will be able to think at a higher level of abstraction.

As humans progress through different **stages of development,** they mature and learn to perform the tasks that are a necessary part of daily living. There are several different types of human development. For example, as children develop physically, their bodies undergo numerous changes. As they develop cognitively, their mental capabilities expand so that they can use language and other symbol systems to solve problems. As they develop socially, they learn to interact more effectively with other people—as individuals and in groups. And, as they develop morally, their actions come to reflect a greater appreciation of principles such as equity, justice, fairness, and altruism.

Because no two students progress through the stages of cognitive, social, and moral development in quite the same way, teachers need perspectives on these three types of development that are flexible, dynamic, and, above all, useful. By becoming familiar with models of cognitive, social, and moral development, teachers at all levels, from preschool through college, can better serve their students. Three such models are Piaget's theory of **cognitive development,** Erikson's stages of **psychosocial development,** and Kohlberg's stages of **moral reasoning.**

Piaget's Model of Cognitive Development

Jean Piaget (1896–1980), the noted Swiss biologist and epistemologist, made extensive observational studies of children. He concluded that children reason differently from adults and even have different perceptions of the world. Piaget surmised that children learn through actively interacting with their environments, much as scientists do, and proposed that a child's thinking progresses through a sequence of four cognitive stages (see Figure 8.1). According to Piaget's theory of cognitive development, the rate of progress through the four stages varies from individual to individual.

During the school years, students move through the **preoperational stage,** the **concrete operations stage,** and the **formal operations stage;** yet, because of individual interaction with the total environment, each student's perceptions and learning will be unique. According to Piaget,

> The principal goal of education is to create [learners] who are capable of doing new things, not simply repeating what other generations have done—[learners] who are creative, inventive, and discoverers. [We] need pupils who are active, who learn early to find out by themselves, partly by their own spontaneous activity and partly through material we set up for them; who learn early to tell what is verifiable and what is simply the first idea to come to them (quoted in Ripple and Rockcastle 1964, 5).

Figure 8.2 presents guidelines for teaching children at the preoperational stage, the concrete operations stage, and the formal operations stage.

Jean Piaget
(1896–1980)

Erikson's Model of Psychosocial Development

Erik Erikson's model of psychosocial development delineates eight stages, from infancy to old age (see Table 8.1, p. 294). For each stage a **psychosocial crisis** is central in the individual's emotional and social growth. Erikson expresses these crises in polar terms; for instance, in the first stage, that of infancy, the psychosocial crisis is trust versus mistrust. Erikson explains that the major psychosocial task for the infant is to develop a sense of trust in the world but not to give up totally a sense of distrust. In the tension between the poles of trust and mistrust, a greater pull toward the more positive pole is considered healthy and is accompanied by a virtue. In this case, if trust prevails, the virtue is hope. Shortly before his death in 1994 at the age of 91, Erikson postulated a ninth stage in the human life cycle, *gerotranscendence*, during which some people mentally transcend the reality of their deteriorating bodies and faculties. In the final chapter of an extended version of Erikson's *The Life Cycle Completed*, first published in 1982, his wife and lifelong colleague, Joan M. Erikson (1901–1997), described the challenge of the ninth stage:

Erik Erikson
(1902–1994)

> Despair, which haunts the eighth stage, is a close companion in the ninth, because it is almost impossible to know what emergencies and losses of physical ability

1. **Sensorimotor Intelligence (birth to 2 years):**
Behavior is primarily sensory and motor. The child does not yet "think" conceptually; however, "cognitive" development can be observed.

2. **Preoperational Thought (2–7 years):**
Development of language and rapid conceptual development are evident. Children begin to use symbols to think of objects and people outside of their immediate environment. Fantasy and imaginative play are natural modes of thinking.

3. **Concrete Operations (7–11 years):**
Children develop ability to use logical thought to solve concrete problems. Basic concepts of objects, number, time, space, and causality are explored and mastered. Through use of concrete objects to manipulate, children are able to draw conclusions.

4. **Formal Operations (11–15 years):**
Cognitive abilities reach their highest level of development. Children can make predictions, think about hypothetical situations, think about thinking, and appreciate the structure of language as well as use it to communicate. Sarcasm, puns, argumentation, and slang are aspects of adolescents' speech that reflect their ability to think abstractly about language.

Figure 8.1

Piaget's stages of cognitive growth

are imminent. As independence and control are challenged, self-esteem and confidence weaken. Hope and trust, which once provided firm support, are no longer the sturdy props of former days. To face down despair with faith and appropriate humility is perhaps the wisest course (Erikson, 1997 105–6).

When we examine the issues and concerns of students in childhood and early and late adolescence later in this chapter, we will return to Erikson's model of psychosocial development. For further information on this significant and useful theory of development, we recommend that you read Erikson's first book, *Childhood and Society* (1963).

Guidelines for Teaching School-Age Children at Piaget's Three Stages of Cognitive Growth

Teaching the Child at the Preoperational Stage

1. Use concrete props and visual aids whenever possible.
2. Make instruction relatively short, using actions as well as words.
3. Don't expect the students to be consistent in their ability to see the world from someone else's point of view.
4. Be sensitive to the possibility that students may have different meanings for the same word or different words for the same meaning. Students may also expect everyone to understand words they have invented.
5. Give children a great deal of hands-on practice with the skills that serve as building blocks for more complex skills such as reading comprehension.
6. Provide a wide range of experiences in order to build a foundation for concept learning and language.

Teaching the Child at the Concrete-Operational Stage

1. Continue to use concrete props and visual aids, especially when dealing with sophisticated material.
2. Continue to give students a chance to manipulate and test objects.
3. Make sure presentation and readings are brief and well organized.
4. Use familiar examples to explain more complex ideas.
5. Give opportunities to classify and group objects and ideas on increasingly complex levels.
6. Present problems that require logical, analytical thinking.

Teaching the Child at the Formal Operations Stage

1. Continue to use concrete-operational teaching strategies and materials.
2. Give students the opportunity to explore many hypothetical questions.
3. Give students opportunities to solve problems and reason scientifically.
4. Whenever possible, teach broad concepts, not just facts, using materials and ideas relevant to the students' lives.

Figure 8.2

Guidelines for teaching school-age children at Piaget's three stages of cognitive growth
Source: Excerpted from Anita E. Woolfolk, *Educational Psychology,* 7th ed. Boston: Allyn and Bacon, 1998, pp. 33, 36, 39. Copyright © 1998 by Allyn and Bacon. Reprinted by permission.

Kohlberg's Model of Moral Development

According to Lawrence Kohlberg (1927–1987), the reasoning process people use to decide what is right and wrong evolves through three levels of development. Within each level, Kohlberg has identified two stages. Table 8.2 shows that at Level I, the preconventional level, the individual decides what is right on the basis of personal needs and rules developed by others. At Level II, the conventional level, moral decisions reflect a desire for the approval of others and a willingness to conform to the expectations of family, community, and country. At Level III, the postconventional level, the individual has developed values and principles that are based on rational, personal choices that can be separated from conventional values.

Kohlberg suggests that "over 50 percent of late adolescents and adults are capable of full formal reasoning [i.e., they can use their intelligence to reason abstractly, form hypotheses, and test these hypotheses against reality], but only 10 percent of these adults display principled (Stages 5 and 6) moral reasoning" (2000, 138–39). In addition, Kohlberg found that maturity of moral judgment is not highly related to IQ or verbal intelligence.

Some individuals have criticized Kohlberg's model as being too systematic and

Lawrence Kohlberg
(1927–1987)

Table 8.1

Erikson's eight stages of psychosocial development

Stage	Psychosocial Crisis	Approximate Age	Important Event	Description
1. Infancy	Basic trust versus basic mistrust	Birth to 12–18 months	Feeding	The infant must form a first loving, trusting relationship with the caregiver or develop a sense of mistrust.
2. Early Childhood	Autonomy versus shame/doubt	18 months to 3 years	Toilet training	The child's energies are directed toward the development of physical skills, including walking, grasping, controlling the sphincter.
3. Play Age	Initiative versus guilt	3 to 6 years	Independence	The child learns control but may develop shame and doubt if not handled well.
4. School Age	Industry versus inferiority	6 to 12 years	School	The child continues to become more assertive and to take more initiative but may be too forceful, which can lead to guilt feelings.
5. Adolescence	Identity versus role confusion	Adolescence	Peer relationships	The child must deal with demands to learn new skills or risk a sense of inferiority, failure, and incompetence.
6. Young Adult	Intimacy versus isolation	Young adulthood	Love relationships	The teenager must achieve identity in occupation, gender roles, politics, and religion.
7. Adulthood	Generativity versus stagnation	Middle adulthood	Parenting/ Mentoring	The young adult must develop intimate relationships or suffer feelings of isolation. Each adult must find some way to satisfy and support the next generation.
8. Mature Love	Ego integrity versus despair	Late adulthood	Reflection on and acceptance of one's life	The culmination is a sense of acceptance of oneself as one is and a sense of fulfillment.

Source: Adapted from Lester A. Lefton, *Psychology,* 7th ed. Boston: Allyn and Bacon, 1999. Copyright © 1999 by Allyn and Bacon. Reprinted by permission

---

sequential, limited because it focuses on moral reasoning rather than actual behavior, or biased because it tends to look at moral development from a male perspective (Bracey 1993). Carol Gilligan, for example, suggests that male moral reasoning tends to address the rights of the individual while female moral reasoning addresses the individual's responsibility to other people. In her book, *In a Different Voice: Psychological Theory and Women's Development* (1993), Gilligan refers to women's principal moral voice as the "ethics of care," which emphasizes care of others over the more male-oriented "ethics of justice." Thus, when confronted with a moral dilemma, females tend to suggest solutions based more on altruism and self-sacrifice than on rights and rules (Gilligan 1993).

The question remains, can moral reasoning be taught? Can teachers help students develop so that they live according to principles of equity, justice, caring, and empathy? Kohlberg suggests the following three conditions that can help children internalize moral principles:

Table 8.2

Kohlberg's theory of moral reasoning

1. Preconventional Level of Moral Reasoning

Child is responsive to cultural rules and labels of good and bad, right or wrong, but interprets these in terms of consequences of action (punishment, reward, exchanges of favors).

Stage 1: Punishment-and-obedience orientation
Physical consequences of action determine its goodness or badness. Avoidance of punishment and deference to power are valued.

Stage 2: The instrumental-relativist orientation
Right action consists of that which satisfies one's own needs and occasionally the needs of others. Reciprocity is a matter of "You scratch my back and I'll scratch yours."

II. Conventional Level of Moral Reasoning

Maintaining the expectations of the individual's family, group, or nation is perceived as valuable, regardless of consequences.

Stage 3: The interpersonal concordance or "good boy–nice girl" orientation
Good behavior is that which pleases or helps others and is approved by them.

Stage 4: The "law and order" orientation
Orientation toward fixed rules and the maintenance of the social order. Right behavior consists of doing one's duty and showing respect for authority.

III. Postconventional, Autonomous, or Principled Level of Moral Reasoning

Effort to define moral principles that have validity and application apart from the authority of groups.

Stage 5: The social-contract, legalistic orientation
Right action defined in terms of rights and standards that have been agreed on by the whole society. This is the "official" morality of the American government and Constitution.

Stage 6: The universal-ethical-principle orientation
Right is defined by conscience in accord with self-chosen *ethical principles* appealing to logic and universality.

Source: Adapted from Lawrence Kohlberg, *"The Cognitive-Developmental Approach to Moral Education,"* in *Curriculum Planning: A Contemporary Approach,* 7th ed., Forrest W. Parkay and Glen Hass (eds.). Boston: Allyn and Bacon, 2000, p. 137. The original version appeared in *Journal of Philosophy, 70*(18), 1973, pp.631–32.

1. Exposure to the next higher stage of reasoning
2. Exposure to situations posing problems and contradictions for the child's current moral structure, leading to dissatisfaction with his [her] current level
3. An atmosphere of interchange and dialogue combining the first two conditions, in which conflicting moral views are compared in an open manner (Kohlberg 2000, 144).

One approach to teaching values and moral reasoning is known as **character education,** a movement that stresses the development of students' "good character." According to *A Nation of Spectators,* a 1998 report by the National Commission on Civic Renewal, the need for character education to make a "comeback" in our society is clear:

Is character education an effective way to improve society?

Character education and the teaching of moral values have been part of the educational system in the United States from the nation's earliest days. The main reason colonial schools were created was to see that children learned to read the Bible so they could lead good lives and find salvation. "When struggles eventually arose over whose Bible to use and which doctrines to teach, William McGuffey stepped onto the stage in 1836 to offer his *McGuffey Readers,* ultimately to sell more than 100 million copies" (Lickona 1993, p.6). These books mixed heroic tales, homilies, and poetry with popular Bible stories to teach children the importance of being honest, industrious, courageous, kind, obedient, and courteous.

Over the years, the ties to religion in U.S. education weakened and were replaced first with an emphasis on acquiring knowledge for an informed citizenship, then on knowledge for occupational purposes, and then, in the 1960s, on knowledge for individual growth and self-fulfillment. Today, with increases in racism, hate crimes, gang activity, and random violence and an erosion of ethical behavior and common decency, many people call for a return to teaching values and morals in schools. In 1999, all fifty states had some form of character education in their public schools, and in Georgia and Alabama such programs were mandatory. In the same year the federal government gave $5.2 million to support school character education programs, and that figure was expected to double in the year 2000 according to a *Time* magazine report (Ferguson et al. 1999).

Proponents regard character education as a necessary and effective way to improve society. Opponents disagree, believing that character education is too authoritarian in its implementation, narrow in its perspective, and intrusive into family matters. Where do you stand on this issue? Do you think character education will improve society?

Carnegie Foundation for the Advancement of Teaching wrote, "Education unguided by an ethical compass is potentially more dangerous than ignorance itself." In his book *The Basic School,* Boyer (1995) stressed that schools should not concern themselves only with teaching and instruction but also with giving students an appreciation for the dignity of human life and empowering them to make a difference in society.

Today's proponents observe that educators do teach values in school whether they do so intentionally or not. The way teachers do things in school—often referred to as the hidden curriculum—can teach students that people are not equal, working independently is better than helping others (the latter is "cheating"), external rewards should be sought, competition is good, obedience should be paid to authorities, one should take care of "Number 1," and winning is everything. The proponents argue that since educators are teaching values anyway—even some values we wish they weren't teaching—they should do so consciously and deliberately with a formal program.

They also point out that today's students come from a different family and social environment than their predecessors did. The increased number of single-parent families and families with both parents working outside the home and the decrease in extended families living together combine to empty homes of adults to guide students in their moral development. Schools must pick up the slack and give students the moral direction and tools they need to negotiate today's increasingly complex and morally challenging society. These proponents suggest that schools plan their programs with the assistance of parents, determining together the goals to pursue and the values to emphasize. They argue that to fail to offer character education in schools and instead leave it to parents already stressed by finances and overwork is to place at risk a safe and healthy future for the nation's children and youth.

Character education is an effective way to improve society.

Proponents of character education believe that morals and ethics are inherent and necessary aspects of education. Theodore Roosevelt once said, "To educate a person in mind and not in morals is to educate a menace to society." Similarly, Ernest Boyer, the late president of the

Character education is not an effective way to improve society.

In his book *Answering the "Virtuecrats": A Moral Conversation on Character Education,* Robert Nash writes, "In the extreme, much character education is unnecessarily apocalyptic and narrow in its cultural criticism, inherently authoritarian in its convictions, excessively nostalgic and premodern in its understanding of virtue, too closely aligned with a reactionary (or a radical) politics, anti-intellectual in its curricular initiatives, hyperbolic in its moral claims, dangerously antidemocratic, and overly simplistic in its contention that training and imitation alone are sufficient for instilling moral character" (1997, 10). He critiques the works of authors in three schools of moral education—conservative, liberal, and libertarian—and proposes his own approach, the cultivation of a "democratic character," a pragmatic means of coping with conflicting perspectives and the potential of "unruly disagreements" in a pluralistic society.

The loudest cry of opponents is that moral development is a family matter and not the school's. They complain that schools already infringe on families more than they should and that teachers should not take time away from academics to teach moral values. Many parents worry that their children will be taught values that contradict their religious beliefs. Others ask the question, "Whose values will be taught?"

Alfie Kohn, in an article entitled "How Not to Teach Values," asks a related question: "Which values will be taught?" (1997). He believes that most character education programs are based on a conservative perspective and require obedience to authority. He describes the typical method of instruction in character education programs as "tantamount to indoctrination. The point is to drill students in specific behaviors rather than to engage them in deep, critical reflection about certain ways of being." He asks his readers to speculate on "the concrete differences between a school dedicated to turning out students who are empathic and skeptical and a school dedicated to turning out students who are loyal, patriotic, obedient, and so on." Kohn proposes that the better way to teach values is to lead students to ask themselves "what kind of person one ought to be, which traditions are worth keeping, and how to proceed when two basic values seem to be in conflict." Such discussions, character education opponents argue, should take place in the family and places of worship, not in schools.

Where do you stand on this issue?

1. Which position best reflects your own?
2. Which values, if any, would you like to see emphasized in schools today?
3. List several values that have a religious basis and several that apply to all people.
4. What methods could be used to teach character education through critical thinking?
5. Distinguish between indoctrination, instruction, and learning in a character education program.

Recommended Sources

Boyer, E. (1995). *The basic school: A community for learning.* New York: The Carnegie Foundation for Excellence in Teaching.

Ferguson, A., Barovick, H., Hylton, A., Monroe, S., and Morse, J. (1999, May 24). Character goes back to school, *Time, 153,* Issue 20, pp. 68–69.

Kohn, A. (1997 February). How not to teach values: A critical look at character education, *Phi Delta Kappan.*

Lickona, T. (1993). The return of character education, *Educational Leadership, 51*(3), 6–11.

Nash, R. J. (1997). *Answering the virtuecrats: A moral conversation on character education.* New York: Teachers College Press.

Related Resources

Building Character with Literacy. (Available from Young People's Press. 1731 Kettner Bldv., San Diego, CA 92101. 1-800-231-9774.)

The Moral Intelligence of Children. Robert Coles. (Available from Random House.)

Giraffe Project. (Available from P.O. Box 759, Langley, WA 98260. 360-221-7989. e-mail: medlock@giraffe.org.)

Eleven Principles of Effective Character Education. Thomas Lickona and Catherine Lewis. Video commissioned by the Character Education Partnership. (Available from National Professional Resources, 25 South Regent Street; Port Chester, NY 10573. 1-800-453-7461.)

Building Character in Schools. Kevin Ryan and Karen E. Bohlin. (Available from Jossey-Bass, San Francisco.)

Related Web Pages

Use your favorite search engine or check the Allyn and Bacon website to find the websites of the following resources:

- The Basic School Network at the National Association of Elementary School Principals
- Center for Advancement of Character and Ethics at Boston University
- Center for Research on Ethics and Values at Azusa Pacific University
- Character Education Partnership
- International Center for Character Education at the University of San Diego

On the eve of the twenty-first century, America is prosperous, secure, and free. [But] when we assess our country's civic and moral condition, we are deeply troubled. Neighborhood and community ties have frayed. Many of our streets and public spaces have become unsafe. Our character-forming institutions are enfeebled. Much of our popular culture is vulgar, violent, and mindless. Much of our public square is coarse and uncivil. Political participation is at depressed levels last seen in the 1920s. Public trust in our leaders and institutions has plunged (National Commission on Civic Renewal 1998).

There is no single way for teachers to develop students' character; however, in comments made shortly after the shooting deaths of fourteen students and a teacher at Columbine High School in Colorado, well-known sociologist and organizer of several White House conferences on character education Amitai Etzioni said, "What schools should help youngsters develop—if schools are going to help lower the likelihood of more Columbines—are two crucial behavior characteristics: the capacity to channel impulses into prosocial outlets, and empathy with others" (Etzioni 1999). In addition, Figure 8.3 illustrates twelve strategies Thomas Lickona suggests teachers can use to create moral classroom communities.

Some teachers, such as those at Dry Creek Elementary School in Clovis, California, Alexander Dumas School (K–8) in Chicago, and Allen Elementary School in inner-city Dayton, Ohio, emphasize specific moral values in their curricula. At Franklin Elementary School, a charter school near Boston, teachers and students focus on a virtue a month as well as a virtue a week. The parents who founded the school organized the curriculum around the four cardinal virtues of the ancient Greeks: fortitude, justice, temperance, and prudence (Lickona 1998).

Maslow's Model of a Hierarchy of Needs

Students' developmental levels also vary according to how well their biological and psychological needs have been satisfied. Psychologist Abraham Maslow (1908–1970) formulated a model of a **hierarchy of needs** (see Figure 8.4) that suggests that people are motivated by basic needs for survival and safety first. When these basic needs have been met sufficiently, people naturally seek to satisfy higher needs, the highest of which is self-actualization—the desire to use one's talents, abilities, and potentialities to the fullest. Students whose needs for safety have been fairly well satisfied will discover strong needs for friendship, affection, and love, for example. If efforts to satisfy the various needs are thwarted, the result can be maladjustment and interruption or delay in the individual's full and healthy development.

The hierarchy of needs model has particular relevance for teachers because students differ markedly in terms of where they are on Maslow's hierarchy of needs. Many families lack the resources to provide adequately for children's basic needs. Children from families that are concerned with day-to-day survival may not receive the support that could help them succeed in school. They come to school tired and hungry and may have trouble paying attention in class. Others may be well fed and clothed but feel unsafe, alien, or unloved; they may seek to protect themselves by withdrawing emotionally from activities around them.

Developmental Stresses and Tasks of Childhood

During Erikson's school-age stage, children strive for a sense of industry and struggle against feelings of inferiority. If successful, they gain the virtue of competence, believ-

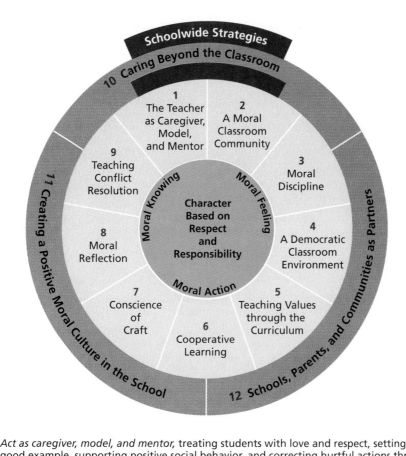

1. *Act as caregiver, model, and mentor,* treating students with love and respect, setting a good example, supporting positive social behavior, and correcting hurtful actions through one-on-one guidance and whole-class discussion.

2. *Create a moral community,* helping students know one another as persons, respect and care about one another, and feel valued membership in, and responsibility to, the group.

3. *Practice moral discipline,* using the creation and enforcement of rules as opportunities to foster moral reasoning, voluntary compliance with rules, and a respect for others.

4. *Create a democratic classroom environment,* involving students in decision making and the responsibility for making the classroom a good place to be and learn.

5. *Teach values through the curriculum,* using the ethically rich content of academic subjects (such as literature, history, and science) as vehicles for teaching values and examining moral questions.

6. *Use cooperative learning* to develop students' appreciation of others, perspective taking, and the ability to work with others toward common goals.

7. *Develop the "conscience of craft"* by fostering students' appreciation of learning, capacity for hard work, commitment to excellence, and sense of work as affecting the lives of others.

8. *Encourage moral reflection* through reading, research, essay writing, journal keeping, discussion, and debate.

9. *Teach conflict resolution,* so that students acquire the essential moral skills of solving conflicts fairly and without force.

10. *Foster caring beyond the classroom,* using positive role models to inspire altruistic behavior and providing opportunities at every grade level to perform school and community service.

11. *Create a positive moral culture in the school,* developing a schoolwide ethos that supports and amplifies the values taught in classrooms.

12. *Recruit parents and the community as partners in character education,* letting parents know that the school considers them their child's first and most important moral teacher.

Figure 8.3

A comprehensive approach to values and character education
Source: Thomas Lickona, *Educating for Character: How Our Schools Can Teach.* New York: Bantam Books, 1991, p. 69. Copyright © 1991 by Thomas Likona. Used by permission of Bantam Books, a division of Random House, Inc.

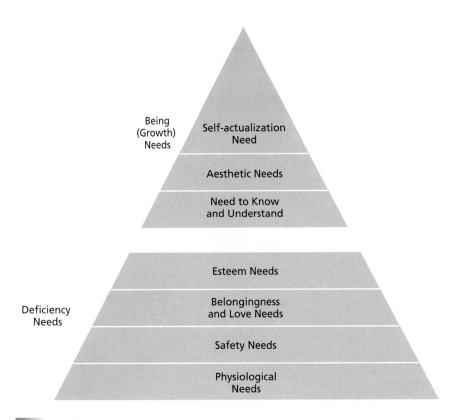

Figure 8.4

Maslow's hierarchy of needs. Note: The four lower-level needs are called deficiency needs because the motivation to satisfy them decreases when they are met. On the other hand, when being (growth) needs are met, motivation to fulfill them increases.

Source: Based on Abraham H. Maslow, *Toward a Psychology of Being,* 3rd ed. New York: John Wiley & Sons, 1999; and *Motivation and Personality,* 3rd ed. Addison-Wesley Publishing Company, 1987.

ing in their abilities to do things. If children find evidence that they are inferior to others, if they experience failure when they try new tasks, and if they struggle without ever gaining a sense of mastery, then they feel incompetent.

Children gain the sense of industry needed at this age by playing seriously, mastering new skills, producing products, and being workers. When they first go to school they are oriented toward accomplishing new things (some kindergartners expect to learn to read on their first day of school and are disappointed when they don't). For young schoolchildren, the idea of work is attractive; it means that they are doing something grown-up.

Is childhood a time of carefree play or a period of stress? Certainly the answer depends on the life circumstances and personality of the individual child. In a study of stressful events in the lives of more than 1,700 children in the second through the ninth grades in six countries, Karou Yamamoto and his associates found that the most stressful events "threaten[ed] one's sense of security and occasion[ed] personal denigration and embarrassment" (Yamamoto et al. 1996, 139). Other studies have shown that serious stress is experienced by latchkey children, for example, who are left on their own or in each others' care for part or all of the day.

Developmental Stresses and Tasks of Adolescence

Many psychologists believe that adolescence contains two distinct stages: an early period covering the ages of ten to twelve through the ages of fourteen to sixteen, and a late period from approximately fifteen to sixteen through nineteen. Although a continuity exists in each individual's life, the psychosocial issues of adolescence—coping with change and seeking identity—vary in form and importance as individuals progress through the transition from childhood to adulthood.

In Erik Erikson's model of the eight stages of humans, identity versus role diffusion is the psychosocial crisis for the adolescent years. Although the quest for identity is a key psychosocial issue for both early and late adolescence, many believe that Erikson's identity-versus-role diffusion stage fits best for early adolescence. During this time, young adolescents, using their new thinking abilities, begin integrating a clearer sense of personal identity. Erikson's role diffusion refers to the variety of roles that adolescents have available to them.

According to Erikson's theory, when adolescents identify themselves with a peer group, with a school, or with a cause, their sense of fidelity—the "virtue" of this stage—is clear and strong. At this stage adolescents are loyal and committed, sometimes to people or ideas that may dismay or alarm their parents, sometimes to high ideals and dreams.

In late adolescence, the quest for identity shifts from relying on others to self-reliance. Young people continue to work on strengthening their sense of identity in late adolescence, but as they do so they draw less on the reactions of their peers and more on their own regard for what matters. Although late adolescents possess an array of interests, talents, and goals in life, they share a desire to achieve independence. More like adults than children, late adolescents are anxious to use newly acquired strengths, skills, and knowledge to achieve their own purposes, whether through marriage, parenthood, full-time employment, education beyond high school, a career, or military service.

What needs must this child satisfy for healthy development? What childhood stresses does she face? What developmental tasks must she accomplish in her psychosocial development? What needs, stresses, and developmental tasks will affect this child as an adolescent? Why is information about development important to teachers?

The vulnerability of today's adolescents is portrayed graphically in *Great Transitions: Preparing Adolescents for a New Century,* a report by the Carnegie Council on Adolescent Development: "Altogether, nearly half of American adolescents are at high or moderate risk of seriously damaging their life chances. The damage may be near-term and vivid, or it may be delayed, like a time bomb set in youth" (Carnegie Council on Adolescent Development 1995). The list of alarming concerns in adolescence includes academic failure and retention, accidents, anorexia, assaultive behavior, criminal activity, cultism, depression, discipline problems, dropouts, drug abuse, homicides, incest, prostitution, runaways, school absenteeism, suicide, teenage pregnancy, vandalism, and the contraction of sexually transmitted diseases.

What can teachers do to help children and adolescents develop to their full potential? To help prevent the problems that place them at risk, an energetic, creative, and multifaceted approach is necessary. Figure 8.5 presents several strategies for helping students develop competence, positive self-concepts, and high esteem and for intervening to prevent or address problems that place them at risk.

How Do Students Vary in Intelligence?

In addition to developmental differences, students differ in terms of their intellectual capacity. Unfortunately, test scores, and sometimes intelligence quotient (IQ) scores, are treated as accurate measurements of students' intellectual ability because of their convenience and long-time use. What is intelligence and how has it been redefined to account for the many ways in which it is expressed? Though many definitions of intel-

1. **Provide opportunities and encouragement for students to develop competence.**

   - Provide a learning environment in which students can risk making mistakes.
   - Assign work that students can perform successfully and still be challenged.
   - Have realistic but high expectations for students.
   - Express belief in students' ability to succeed.
   - Encourage industry by letting students work on goals or projects of their choosing.
   - Provide opportunities for students to take special responsibility.
   - Assign older students to work with younger ones.
   - Reward industry and competence.

2. **Promote the development of positive self-concept and high self-esteem.**

   - Give praise more than criticism.
   - Take students and their work seriously.
   - Respect students' dignity.
   - Plan individual and group activities that boost morale.
   - Provide opportunities for students to interact and work cooperatively.
   - Teach and model acceptance of human diversity and individuality.
   - Develop systems for the recognition and reward of individual and group achievement.
   - Support students' efforts to achieve and appropriately express independence.

3. **Intervene to prevent or address problems that place students at risk.**

   - Provide a safe and structured learning environment where students feel secure.
   - Practice effective leadership and classroom management.
   - Provide opportunities to discuss preferences, values, morals, goals, and consequences.
   - Teach and model critical thinking, decision making, and problem solving.
   - Teach and model prosocial attitudes and behaviors and conflict resolution strategies.
   - Provide information on subjects of special concern to students and parents.
   - Cultivate family involvement.
   - Collaborate, consult, network, and refer on behalf of students.

Figure 8.5

What teachers can do to help children and adolescents develop.

ligence have been proposed, the term has yet to be completely defined. One view is that **intelligence** is the ability to learn. As David Wechsler, the developer of the most widely used intelligence scales for children and adults, said: "Intelligence, operationally defined, is the aggregate or global capacity to act purposefully, to think rationally, and to deal effectively with the environment" (Wechsler 1958, 7). Other definitions of intelligence that have been proposed are the following:

- Goal-directed adaptive behavior
- Ability to solve novel problems
- Ability to acquire and think with new conceptual systems
- Problem-solving ability
- Planning and other metacognitive skills
- Memory access speed
- What people think intelligence is
- What IQ tests measure
- The ability to learn from bad teaching (Woolfolk 1998, 109)

Intelligence Testing

The intelligence tests that we now use can be traced to the 1905 Metrical Scale of Intelligence designed by French psychologists Alfred Binet and Theodore Simon, who were part of a Paris-based commission that wanted a way to identify children who would need special help with their learning. Binet revised the scale in 1908, which was adapted for American children in 1916 by Lewis Terman, a psychologist at Stanford University. Terman's test was, in turn, further adapted, especially by the U.S. Army, which transformed it into a paper-and-pencil test that could be administered to large groups. The use of such intelligence tests has continued throughout the years. Approximately 67 percent of the population have an IQ between 85 and 115—the range of normal intelligence.

Individual intelligence tests are presently valued by psychologists and those in the field of special education because they can be helpful in diagnosing a student's strengths and weaknesses. However, group intelligence tests given for the purpose of classifying students into like-score groups have received an increasing amount of criticism.

The most significant and dramatic criticism of group IQ tests has been that test items and tasks are culturally biased, drawn mostly from white middle-class experience. Thus the tests are more assessments of how informed students are about features in a specific class or culture than of how intelligent they are in general. This complaint became a formal, legal challenge when, on the basis of their IQ test scores, a group of African American children were put into special classes for mentally retarded children. Their parents brought the complaint to the courts in 1971 and persisted with it all the way to the federal appellate court, where a decision was eventually made in their favor in 1984. In that well-known case, *Larry P. v. Riles* (1984), the court decided that IQ tests were discriminatory and culturally biased. However, in another case, *PASE v. Hannon* (1980), an Illinois district court ruled that when IQ tests were used in conjunction with other forms of assessment, such as teacher observation, they were not discriminatory for placement purposes. Although the criticism continues, a number of psychometricians are seeking other solutions by attempting to design culture-free intelligence tests.

Multiple Intelligences

Many theorists believe that intelligence is a basic ability that enables one to perform mental operations in the following areas: logical reasoning, spatial reasoning, number ability, and verbal meaning. However, "the weight of the evidence at the present time is that intelligence is multidimensional, and that the full range of these dimensions is not completely captured by any single general ability" (Sternberg 1996, 11). Howard Gardner, for example, believes that human beings possess at least eight separate forms of intelligence; "each intelligence reflects the potential to solve problems or to fashion products that are valued in one or more cultural settings. [Each] features its own distinctive form of mental representation" (Gardner 1999, 71–72). Drawing on the theories of others and research findings on savants, prodigies, and other exceptional individuals, Gardner originally suggested in *Frames of Mind* (1983) that human beings possessed seven human intelligences: logical-mathematical, linguistic, musical, spatial, bodily-kinesthetic, interpersonal, and intrapersonal. In the mid-1990s, he identified an eighth intelligence, that of the naturalist; and in his most recent book, *The Disciplined Mind*, he suggests that "it is possible that human beings also exhibit a ninth, existential intelligence—the proclivity to pose (and ponder) questions about life, death, and ultimate realities" (Gardner 1999, 72). According to Gardner, every person possesses the eight intelligences (see Figure 8.6), yet each person has his or her particular blend of the intelligences.

Gardner's theory of **multiple intelligences** is valuable for teachers. As Robert Slavin suggests, "Teachers must avoid thinking about children as smart or not smart

Linguistic intelligence allows individuals to communicate and make sense of the world through language. Poets exemplify this intelligence in its mature form. Students who enjoy playing with rhymes, who pun, who always have a story to tell, who quickly acquire other languages—including sign language— all exhibit linguistic intelligence.

Musical intelligence allows people to create, communicate, and understand meanings made out of sound. While composers and instrumentalists clearly exhibit this intelligence, so do the students who seem particularly attracted by the birds singing outside the classroom window or who constantly tap out intricate rhythms on the desk with their pencils.

Logical-mathematical intelligence enables individuals to use and appreciate abstract relations. Scientists, mathematicians, and philosophers all rely on this intelligence. So do the students who "live" baseball statistics or who carefully analyze the components of problems—either personal or school-related—before systematically testing solutions.

Spatial intelligence makes it possible for people to perceive visual or spatial information, to transform this information, and to recreate visual images from memory. Well-developed spatial capacities are needed for the work of architects, sculptors, and engineers. The students who turn first to the graphs, charts, and pictures in their textbooks, who like to "web" their ideas before writing a paper, and who fill the blank space around their notes with intricate patterns are also using their spatial intelligence.

Bodily-kinesthetic intelligence allows individuals to use all or part of the body to create products or solve problems. Athletes, surgeons, dancers, choreographers, and craftspeople all use bodily-kinesthetic intelligence. The capacity is also evident in students who relish gym class and school dances, who prefer to carry out class projects by making models rather than writing reports, and who toss crumpled paper with frequency and accuracy into wastebaskets across the room.

Interpersonal intelligence enables individuals to recognize and make distinctions about others' feelings and intentions. Teachers, parents, politicians, psychologists, and salespeople rely on interpersonal intelligence. Students exhibit this intelligence when they thrive on small-group work, when they notice and react to the moods of their friends and classmates, and when they tactfully convince the teacher of their need for extra time to complete the homework assignment.

Intrapersonal intelligence helps individuals to distinguish among their own feelings, to build accurate mental models of themselves, and to draw on these models to make decisions about their lives. Although it is difficult to assess who has this capacity and to what degree, evidence can be sought in students' uses of their other intelligences—how well they seem to be capitalizing on their strengths, how cognizant they are of their weaknesses, and how thoughful they are about the decisions and choices they make.

Naturalist intelligence allows people to distinguish among, classify, and use features of the environment. Farmers, gardeners, botanists, geologists, florists, and archaeologists all exhibit this intelligence, as do students who can name and describe the features of every make of car around them.

Figure 8.6

The eight intelligences
Source: Project SUMIT (Schools Using Multiple Intelligence Theory), "Theory of Multiple Intelligences."

because there are many ways to be smart (Slavin 2000, 130). Some students are talented in terms of their interpersonal relations and exhibit natural leadership abilities. Others seem to have a high degree of what Peter Salovey and David Sluyter (1997) term *emotional intelligence*—awareness of and ability to manage their feelings. Differences in musical, athletic, and mechanical abilities can be recognized by even the minimally informed observer. Because these intelligences are not tested or highlighted, they may go unnoticed and possibly wasted.

However, keep in mind Gardner's "reflections" twelve years after the publication of *Frames of Mind* (Gardner 1995, 206):

> MI [multiple intelligence] theory is in no way an educational prescription. [E]ducators are in the best position to determine the uses to which MI theory should be put. . . .

Learning Styles

Students vary greatly in regard to **learning styles,** the approaches to learning that work best for them. These differences have also been called *learning style preferences* or *cognitive styles* (Woolfolk 1998). The National Task Force on Learning Style and Brain Behavior suggests that there is a "consistent pattern of behavior and performance by which an individual approaches educational experiences. It is the composite of characteristic cognitive, affective, and physiological behaviors that serve as relatively stable indicators of how a learner perceives, interacts with, and responds to the learning environment."

Students' learning styles are determined by a combination of hereditary and environmental influences. Some more quickly learn things they hear; others learn faster when they see material in writing. Some need a lot of structure; others learn best when they can be independent and follow their desires. Some learn best in formal settings; others learn best in informal, relaxed environments. Some need almost total silence to concentrate; others learn well in noisy, active environments. Some are intuitive learners; some prefer to learn by following logical, sequential steps.

There is no one "correct" view of learning styles to guide teachers in their daily decision making. Culture-based differences in learning styles are subtle, variable, and difficult to describe; and learning styles change as the individual matures. Moreover, critics maintain that there is little evidence to support the validity of dozens of conceptual models for learning styles and accompanying assessment instruments. Nevertheless, you should be aware of the concept of learning styles and realize that any given classroom activity may be more effective for some students than for others. Knowledge of your own and your students' learning styles will help you to individualize instruction and motivate your students.

 **Professional Reflection** **Identifying your learning style preferences**

Describe your preferred learning environment. Where, when, and how do you learn best? Does certain lighting, food, or music seem to enhance your learning? Think about how you acquire new information—do you prefer being analytical and abstract or commonsensical and concrete? Do you prefer thinking about things or doing things? Do you prefer to learn alone, in a small group, or in a large group? When given an assignment, do you prefer a lot of structure and details, or do you prefer more unstructured or open-ended assignments?

How Do Students Vary in Ability and Disability?

Students also differ according to their special needs and talents. Some enter the world with exceptional abilities or disabilities; others encounter life experiences that change their capabilities significantly, and still others struggle with conditions that medical scientists have yet to understand. Where possible, all children and youth with exceptionalities are given a public education in the United States.

Exceptional Learners

Children "who require special education and related services if they are to realize their full human potential" (Hallahan and Kauffman 2000, 7) are referred to as **exceptional learners.** They are taught by special education teachers and by regular teachers into whose classrooms they have been integrated or *included*. Among the many exceptional children that teachers may encounter in the classroom are students who have physical, mental, or emotional disabilities and students who are gifted or talented.

Special-needs students are often referred to synonymously as *handicapped* or *disabled*. However, it is important for teachers to understand the following distinction between a disability and a handicap:

> A disability . . . results from a loss of physical functioning (e.g., loss of sight, hearing, or mobility) or from difficulty in learning and social adjustment that significantly interferes with normal growth and development. A handicap is a limitation imposed on the individual by environmental demands and is related to the individual's ability to adapt or adjust to those demands (Hardman, Drew, and Egan 1999, 3).

For example, Stephen W. Hawking, the gifted physicist who provides the epigraph for this chapter, has amyotrophic lateral sclerosis (also known as Lou Gehrig's disease), which requires him to use a wheelchair for mobility and a speech synthesizer to communicate. If Hawking had to enter a building accessible only by stairs, or if a computer virus infected his speech synthesizer program, his disability would then become a handicap.

In addition, teachers should know that current language use emphasizes the concept of "people first." In other words, a disabling condition should not be used as an adjective to describe a person. Thus, one should say "a child with a visual impairment," not a "blind child" or even a "visually impaired child."

Teachers should also realize that the definitions for disabilities are generalized, open to change, and significantly influenced by the current cultural perception of normality. For example, the American Association on Mental Retardation (AAMR) has changed its definition of mental retardation seven times since 1950 to reflect shifting views of people with cognitive disabilities.

Cautions about labeling should also apply to gifted and talented students. Unfortunately, people commonly have a negative view of gifted and talented youngsters. Like many ethnic groups, gifted students are "different" and thus have been the target of many myths and stereotypes. However, a landmark study of 1,528 gifted males and females begun by Lewis Terman (Terman, Baldwin, and Bronson 1925; Terman and Oden 1947, 1959) in 1926 and to continue until 2010 has "exploded the myth that high-IQ individuals [are] brainy but physically and socially inept. In fact, Terman found that children with outstanding IQs were larger, stronger, and better coordinated than other children and became better adjusted and more emotionally stable adults" (Slavin 2000, 428).

Students with Disabilities

Table 8.3 shows that the percentage of all students participating in federally supported education programs for **students with disabilities** increased from 8.33 percent in 1976–77 to 12.98 percent in 1996–97. More than 5.9 million students participated in these programs in 1997 (National Center for Education Statistics 1999).

Various tests and other forms of assessment are used to identify persons in the categories of disability listed in Table 8.3. The following brief definitional characteristics of these categories are based on the Individuals with Disabilities Education Act (IDEA) and definitions used by professional organizations dedicated to meeting the needs of persons in each category.

1. *Specific learning disabilities (LD)*—Learning is significantly hindered by difficulty in listening, speaking, reading, writing, reasoning, or computing

Table 8.3

Percent of children 0 to 21 years old in federal programs for students with disabilities, 1976–77 to 1996–97*

Type of Disability	1976–77	1980–81	1984–85	1988–89	1992–93	1996–97
Specific learning disabilities	1.80	3.58	4.67	4.94	5.50	5.81
Speech or language impairments	2.94	2.86	2.87	2.41	2.33	2.29
Mental retardation	2.16	2.03	1.77	1.40	1.21	1.27
Serious emotional disturbance	0.64	0.85	0.95	0.94	0.94	0.98
Hearing impairments	0.20	0.19	0.18	0.14	0.14	0.15
Orthopedic impairments	0.20	0.14	0.14	0.12	0.12	0.14
Other health impairments	0.32	0.24	0.17	0.11	0.15	0.35
Visual impairments	0.09	0.08	0.07	0.06	0.05	0.06
Multiple disabilities	—	0.17	0.17	0.21	0.24	0.21
Deaf-blindness	—	0.01	****	****	****	****
Autism and other	—	—	—	—	0.04	0.10
Preschool disabled**	***	***	***	0.98	1.38	1.62
All disabilities	8.33	10.13	11.00	11.26	12.08	12.98

*Includes students served under Chapter I and Individuals with Disabilities Education Act (IDEA), formerly the Education of the Handicapped Act.
**Includes preschool children 3–5 years and 0–5 years served under Chapter I and IDEA, respectively.
***Prior to 1987–88, these students were included in the counts by handicapping condition. Beginning in 1987–88, states were no longer required to report preschool handicapped students (0–5 years) by handicapping condition.
****Less than .005 percent.
—Data not available.

NOTE—Counts are based on reports from the 50 states and District of Columbia only (i.e., figures from U.S. territories are not included). Increases since 1987–88 are due in part to new legislation enacted in 1986, which mandates public school special education services for all children with disabilities ages 3 through 5. Some data have been revised from previously published figures. Because of rounding, details may not add to totals.

Source: U.S. Department of Education, Office of Special Education and Rehabilitative Services, *Annual Report to Congress on the Implementation of The Individuals with Disabilities Education Act,* various years, and unpublished tabulations; and National Center for Education Statistics, Common Core of Data survey. This table was prepared May 1998. Taken from National Center for Education Statistics, *Digest of Education Statistics, 1998.* Washington, DC: National Center for Education Statistics, 1999, p. 66.

2. *Speech or language impairments*—Significant difficulty in communicating with others as a result of speech or language disorders
3. *Mental retardation*—Significant limitations in cognitive ability
4. *Serious emotional disturbance (SED)*—Social and/or emotional maladjustment that significantly reduces the ability to learn
5. *Hearing impairments*—Permanent or fluctuating mild to profound hearing loss in one or both ears
6. *Orthopedic impairments*—Physically disabling conditions that affect locomotion or motor functions
7. *Other health impairments*—Limited strength, vitality, or alertness caused by chronic or acute health problems
8. *Visual impairments*—Vision loss that significantly inhibits learning
9. *Multiple disabilities*—Two or more interrelated disabilities
10. *Deaf-blindness*—Vision and hearing disability that severely limits communication
11. *Autism and other*—Significantly impaired communication, learning, and reciprocal social interactions

As Figure 8.7 shows, students with learning disabilities account for about 51 percent of all students ages six through twenty-one with disabilities. Since the term **learning disability (LD)** was first introduced in the early 1960s, there has been no universally accepted definition. The National Joint Committee on Learning Disabilities states that

> Learning disabilities is a general term that refers to a heterogeneous group of disorders manifested by significant difficulties in the acquisition and use of listening, speaking, reading, writing, reasoning, or mathematical skills. These disorders are intrinsic to the individual, presumed to be due to central nervous system dysfunction, and may occur across the life span. Problems in self-regulatory behaviors, social perception, and social interaction may exist with learning disabilities but

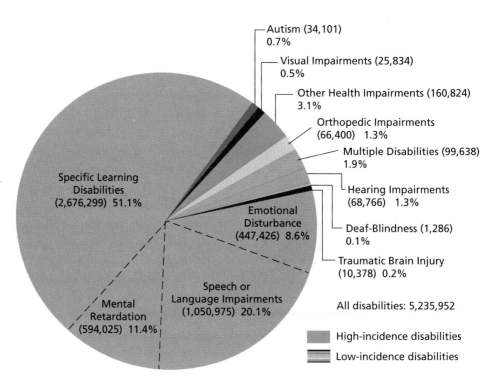

Figure 8.7

Number of children ages 6–21 served under IDEA (Individuals with Disabilities Education Act) by disability
Source: Based on data presented in the *Twentieth Annual Report to Congress on the Implementation of the Individuals with Disabilities Act: To Assure the Free Appropriate Public Education of All Children with Disabilities.* U.S. Department of Education, 1998.

do not, by themselves, constitute a learning disability (National Joint Committee on Learning Disabilities 1997).

Imagine that you are concerned about two of your new students—Mary and Bill. Mary has an adequate vocabulary and doesn't hesitate to express herself, but her achievement in reading and mathematics doesn't add up to what you believe she can do. Often, when you give the class instructions, Mary seems to get confused about what to do. In working with her one-on-one, you've noticed that she often reverses letters and numbers the way much younger children do—she sees a *b* for a *d* or a 6 for a 9. Mary may have a learning disability, causing problems in taking in, organizing, remembering, and expressing information. Like Mary, students with learning disabilities often show a significant difference between their estimated intelligence and their actual achievement in the classroom.

Bill presents you with a different set of challenges. He is obviously bright, but he frequently seems to be "out of sync" with classroom activities. He gets frustrated when he has to wait for his turn. He sometimes blurts out answers before you've even asked a question. He can't seem to stop wiggling his toes and tapping his pencil, and he often comes to school without his backpack and homework. Bill may have **attention deficit hyperactivity disorder (ADHD)**, one of the most commonly diagnosed disabilities among children. Students with ADHD have difficulty remaining still so they can concentrate. Students with an **attention deficit disorder (ADD)** have difficulty focusing their attention long enough to learn well. Children with ADD/ADHD do not qualify for special education unless they also have another disability in a federally defined category.

Treatment for students with ADD/ADHD includes behavior modification and medication. Since the early 1980s, Ritalin has become the most commonly prescribed drug for ADD/ADHD, and more than one million American children are currently estimated to take Ritalin to increase their impulse control and attention span.

By being alert for students who exhibit several of the following characteristics, teachers can help in the early identification of students with learning disabilities so they can receive the instructional adaptations or special education services they need.

- Significant discrepancy between potential and academic achievement
- Distractibility or inability to pay attention for as long as peers do
- Hyperactive behavior, exhibited through excessive movement
- Inattentiveness during lectures or class discussions
- Impulsiveness
- Poor motor coordination and spatial relation skills
- Inability to solve problems
- Poor motivation and little active involvement in learning tasks
- Overreliance on teacher and peers for class assignments
- Evidence of poor language and/or cognitive development
- Immature social skills
- Disorganized approach to learning
- Substantial delays in academic achievement (Smith 1998, 139)

Students Who Are Gifted and Talented

You are concerned about the poor performance of Paul, a student in your eighth-period high school class. Paul is undeniably bright. When he was ten, he had an IQ of 145 on the Stanford-Binet. Last year, when he was sixteen, he scored 142. Paul's father is a physi-

cian, and his mother is a professor. Both parents clearly value learning and are willing to give Paul any needed encouragement and help.

Throughout elementary school, Paul had an outstanding record. His teachers reported that he was brilliant and very meticulous in completing his assignments. He entered high school amid expectations by his parents and teachers that he would continue his outstanding performance. Throughout his first two years of high school, Paul never seemed to live up to his promise. Now, halfway through his junior year, Paul is failing English and geometry. Paul seems to be well adjusted to the social side of school. He has a lot of friends and says he likes school. Paul explains his steadily declining grades by saying that he doesn't like to study.

Paul may be gifted. **Gifted and talented students,** those who have demonstrated a high level of attainment in intellectual ability, academic achievement, creativity, or visual and performing arts, are evenly distributed across all ethnic and cultural groups and socioeconomic

Gifted and talented students benefit from accelerated and enriched learning experiences. What are some forms of acceleration and enrichment that you will offer your students?

classes. Although you might think it is easy to meet the needs of gifted and talented students, you will find that this is not always the case. "Students with special gifts or talents often challenge the system of school, and they can be verbally caustic. Their superior abilities and unusual or advanced interests demand teachers who are highly intelligent, creative, and motivated" (Hallahan and Kauffman 2000, 497). The ability of such students to challenge the system is reflected in a recent U.S. Department of Education study that found that gifted and talented elementary schoolchildren have mastered 35 percent to 50 percent of the grade curriculum in five basic subject areas *before* starting the school year.

There are many forms that giftedness may take; Joseph S. Renzulli (1998), Director of the National Research Center on the Gifted and Talented at the University of Connecticut, for example, suggests two kinds of giftedness: "schoolhouse giftedness [which] might also be called test-taking or lesson-learning giftedness" and "creative-productive giftedness." The trend during the last few decades has been to broaden our view of what characterizes giftedness.

Drawing from the work of Renzulli and his colleagues, Woolfolk (1998) defines *giftedness* "as a combination of three basic characteristics: above-average general ability, a high level of creativity, and a high level of task commitment or motivation to achieve in certain areas. Truly gifted children are not the students who simply learn quickly with little effort. The work of gifted students is original, extremely advanced for their age, and potentially of lasting importance" (Woolfolk 1998, 126).

Variations in criteria used to identify gifted and talented students are especially evident in the reported incidence of giftedness from state to state; for example, North Dakota identifies only 1.0 percent of its students as gifted and talented, while Wisconsin identifies 15.0 percent (National Center for Education Statistics 1999, 67). Depending on the criteria used, estimates of the number of gifted and talented students range from 3 to 5 percent of the total population.

Strategies for teaching students who are gifted and talented begin with effective teachers. Educational psychologist Anita Woolfolk suggests that "Teaching methods for gifted students should encourage abstract thinking (formal-operational thought), creativity, and independence, not just the learning of greater quantities of facts. In working with gifted and talented students, a teacher must be imaginative, flexible, and unthreatened by the capabilities of these students. The teacher must ask, What does this child need most? What is she or he ready to learn? Who can help me to challenge them?" (Woolfolk 1998, 129).

Research indicates that effective teachers of the gifted and talented have many of the same characteristics as their students (Davis and Rimm 1998; Piirto 1999). In fact, Feldhusen (1997) suggests that teachers of gifted students should be gifted themselves and should possess the following characteristics:

- Be highly intelligent
- Have cultural and intellectual interests
- Strive for excellence and high achievement
- Be enthusiastic about talent
- Relate well to talented people
- Have broad general knowledge

Several innovative approaches exist for meeting the educational needs of gifted students.

Acceleration—Accelerated programs for intellectually precocious students have proven successful. For example, an analysis of 314 studies of the academic, psychological, and social effects of acceleration practices at the elementary and secondary levels found "generally positive academic effects for most forms of acceleration" and no negative effects on socialization or psychological adjustment (Rogers 1991). In addition, the analysis identified the following acceleration options as the most beneficial at different grade levels:

- *Elementary school*—early entrance, grade-skipping, nongraded classes, and curriculum compacting (modifying the curriculum to present it at a faster pace).
- *Junior high school*—grade-skipping, grade telescoping (shortening the amount of time to complete a grade level), concurrent enrollment in a high school or college, subject acceleration, and curriculum compacting.
- *Senior high school*—concurrent enrollment, subject acceleration, advanced placement (AP) classes, mentorships, credit by examination, and early admission to college.

One example of acceleration is a suburban Chicago alternative school where high-potential at-risk students work at their own pace in high-tech classrooms. They engage in "integrative accelerative learning," which offers advanced curricula and encourages individual creativity, positive reinforcement, and relaxation. At the National Research Center on Gifted and Talented Education, teachers in experimental classrooms practice thematic "curriculum compacting," which encourages brighter students to forge ahead in the regular curriculum while all students work to their strengths and less able students still get the time and attention they need. Also, many colleges and universities now participate in accelerated programs whereby gifted youth who have outgrown the high school curriculum may enroll in college courses.

Self-directed or independent study—For some time, self-directed or independent study has been recognized as an appropriate way for teachers to maintain the interest of gifted students in their classes. Gifted students usually have the academic backgrounds and motivation to do well without constant supervision and the threat or reward of grades.

Individual education programs—Since the passage of PL 94-142 and the mandating of Individual Education Programs (IEPs) for special education students, IEPs have been promoted as an appropriate means for educating gifted students. Most IEPs for gifted students involve various enrichment experiences, self-directed study, and special, concentrated instruction given to individuals or small groups in pull-out programs. For example, at Columbia Teachers College in New York, economically disadvantaged students identified as gifted participate in Project Synergy, which pairs students with mentors who nurture their talents and guide them through advanced academic content.

Alternative or magnet schools—Several large-city school systems have developed magnet schools organized around specific disciplines, such as science, mathematics, fine arts, basic skills, and so on. The excellent programs at these schools are designed to attract superior students from all parts of the district. Many of these schools offer outstanding programs for gifted and talented youth. Gary Davis and Sylvia Rimm, experts in education for the gifted and talented, say that such schools "are indeed relevant, and they do meet students' needs" (Davis and Rimm 1998, 137).

What Are Special Education, Mainstreaming, and Inclusion?

Prior to the twentieth century, children with disabilities were usually segregated from regular classrooms and taught by teachers in state-run and private schools. Today, an array of programs and services in general and special education classrooms is aimed at developing the potential of exceptional students. Three critical concepts to promote the growth, talents, and productivity of exceptional students are special education, mainstreaming, and inclusion.

Special education refers to "specially designed instruction that meets the unusual needs of an exceptional student" (Hallahan and Kauffman 2000, 12). Teachers who are trained in special education become familiar with special materials, techniques, and equipment and facilities for students with disabilities. For example, children with visual impairment may require reading materials in large print or Braille; students with hearing impairment may require hearing aids and/or instruction in sign language; those with physical disabilities may need special equipment; those with emotional disturbances may need smaller and more highly structured classes; and children with special gifts or talents may require access to working professionals. "Related services—special transportation, psychological assessment, physical and occupational therapy, medical treatment, and counseling—may be necessary if special education is to be effective" (Hallahan and Kauffman 1997, 14).

Special Education Laws

Until 1975, the needs of students with disabilities were primarily met through self-contained special education classes within regular schools. That year, however, Congress passed the **Education for all Handicapped Children Act (Public Law 94-142).** This act guaranteed to all children with disabilities a free and appropriate public education. The law, which applied to every teacher and every school in the country, outlined extensive procedures to ensure that exceptional students between the ages of three and eighteen were granted due process in regard to identification, placement, and educational services received. As a result of PL 94-142, the participation of students with disabilities in all classrooms and school programs became routine.

In 1990, PL 94-142 was replaced by the **Individuals with Disabilities Education Act (IDEA).** IDEA included the major provisions of PL 94-142 and extended the availability of a free, appropriate education to youth with disabilities between the ages of three and twenty-one years of age. IDEA, which is one of the most important and far-

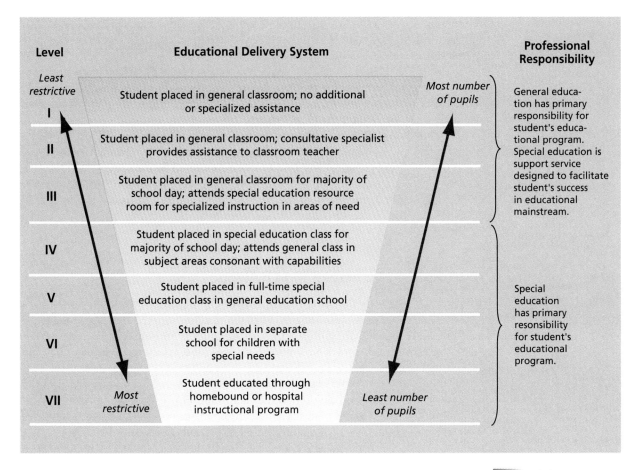

Level	Educational Delivery System	Professional Responsibility

Least restrictive

I — Student placed in general classroom; no additional or specialized assistance — *Most number of pupils*

II — Student placed in general classroom; consultative specialist provides assistance to classroom teacher

III — Student placed in general classroom for majority of school day; attends special education resource room for specialized instruction in areas of need

General education has primary responsibility for student's educational program. Special education is support service designed to facilitate student's success in educational mainstream.

IV — Student placed in special education class for majority of school day; attends general class in subject areas consonant with capabilities

V — Student placed in full-time special education class in general education school

VI — Student placed in separate school for children with special needs

VII — *Most restrictive* — Student educated through homebound or hospital instructional program — *Least number of pupils*

Special education has primary resonsibility for student's educational program.

Figure 8.8

Educational service options for students with disabilities
Source: Michael L. Hardman, Clifford J. Drew, and M. Winston Egan, *Human Exceptionality: Society, School, and Family,* 6th ed. Boston: Allyn and Bacon, 1999, p. 28. Copyright © 1999 by Allyn and Bacon. Reprinted by permission.

reaching pieces of educational legislation ever passed in this country, has several provisions with which all teachers should be familiar. In 1997, the **Amendments to the Individuals with Disabilities Education Act (IDEA 97)** were passed. IDEA 97, which went beyond IDEA's focus on public school *access* for students with disabilities to emphasize educational *outcomes,* modified eligibility requirements, IEP guidelines, public and private placements, student discipline guidelines, and procedural safeguards.

Least restrictive environment—IDEA requires that all children with disabilities be educated in the **least restrictive environment.** In other words, a student must be mainstreamed into a general education classroom whenever such integration is feasible and appropriate and the child would receive educational benefit from such placement. Figure 8.8 shows the educational service options for students with disabilities, from the least restrictive to the most restrictive. About 95 percent of students with disabilities receive their education in general education classes, with the remaining 5 percent in a residential facility, day school, or hospital/homebound program (U.S. Department of Education 1998).

Individualized education plan—Every child with a disability is to have a written **individualized education plan (IEP)** that meets the child's needs and specifies educational goals, methods for achieving those goals, and the number and quality of special educational services to be provided. The IEP must be reviewed annually by five parties: (1) a parent or guardian, (2) the child, (3) a teacher, (4) a professional who has recently evaluated the child, and (5) others, usually the principal or a special-education resource person from the school district.

Related services— IDEA 97 ensures that students with disabilities receive any related services, including "transportation, and such developmental, corrective, and other supportive services as may be required to assist a child with a disability to benefit from special education" (Amendments to IDEA 97).

Confidentiality of records—IDEA also ensures that records on a child are kept confidential. Parental permission is required before any official may look at a child's records. Moreover, parents can amend a child's records if they feel information in it is misleading, inaccurate, or violates the child's rights.

Due process—IDEA gives parents the right to disagree with an IEP or an evaluation of their child's abilities. If a disagreement arises, it is settled through an impartial due process hearing presided over by an officer appointed by the state. At the hearing, parents may be represented by a lawyer, give evidence, and cross-examine, and are entitled to receive a transcript of the hearing and a written decision on the case. If either the parents or the school district disagree with the outcome, the case may then be taken to the civil courts.

Meeting the Mainstreaming Challenge

To help teachers satisfy the provisions of IDEA, school districts across the nation have developed inservice programs designed to acquaint classroom teachers with the unique needs of students with disabilities. In addition, colleges and universities with preservice programs for educators have added courses on teaching students with special educational needs.

The guidelines for IDEA suggest that schools must make a significant effort to include, or mainstream, *all* children in the classroom. However, it is not clear how far schools must go to meet this **mainstreaming** requirement. For example, should children with severe disabilities be included in general education classrooms if they are unable to do the academic work? Recent court cases have ruled that students with severe disabilities must be included if there is a potential benefit for the child, if the class would stimulate the child's language development, or if other students could act as appropriate role models for the child. In one case, the court ordered a school district to place a child with an IQ of 44 in a regular second-grade classroom and rejected as exaggerated the district's claim that the placement would be prohibitively expensive (*Board of Education, Sacramento City Unified School District v. Holland*, 1992). In another case, the court rejected a school district's argument that inclusion of a child with a severe disability would be so disruptive as to significantly impair the learning of the other children (*Oberti v. Board of Education of the Borough of Clementon School District*, 1992).

To meet the mainstreaming challenge, teachers must have knowledge of various disabilities and the teaching methods and materials appropriate for each. Since teachers with negative attitudes toward students with special needs can convey these feelings to all students in a class and thereby reduce the effectiveness of mainstreaming (Lewis and Doorlag 1999), general education teachers must have positive attitudes toward students receiving special education. An accepting, supportive climate can significantly enhance the self-confidence of students with disabilities.

In addition, Hallahan and Kauffman suggest that all teachers should be prepared to participate in the education of exceptional learners. Teachers should be willing to do the following:

1. Make maximum effort to accommodate individual students' needs
2. Evaluate academic abilities and disabilities
3. Refer [students] for evaluation [as appropriate]
4. Participate in eligibility conferences [for special education]

5. Participate in writing individualized education programs
6. Communicate with parents or guardians
7. Participate in due process hearings and negotiations
8. Collaborate with other professionals in identifying and making maximum use of exceptional students' abilities (Hallahan and Kauffman 2000, 20–22)

The Debate Over Inclusion

While mainstreaming refers to the application of the least restrictive environment clause of PL 94-142, **inclusion** goes beyond mainstreaming to integrate all students with disabilities into general education classes and school life with the active support of special educators and other specialists and service providers, as well as **assistive technology** and adaptive software. Advocates of inclusion believe that "if students cannot meet traditional academic expectations, then those expectations should be changed. They reject the mainstreaming assumption that settings dictate the type and intensity of services and propose instead the concept of inclusion" (Friend and Bursuck 1999, 4).

Full inclusion goes even further and calls for "the integration of students with disabilities in the general education classrooms at all times regardless of the nature or severity of the disability" (Friend and Bursuck 1999, 4). According to the full-inclusion approach, if a child needs support services, these are brought *to the child*; the child does not have to participate in a pull-out program to receive support services. Advocates of full inclusion maintain that pull-out programs stigmatize participating students because they are separated from their general-education classmates, and pull-out programs discourage collaboration between general and special education teachers. Those who oppose full inclusion maintain that classroom teachers, who may be burdened with large class sizes and be assigned to schools with inadequate support services, often lack the training and instructional materials to meet the needs of all exceptional students.

In addition, some parents of children with disabilities believe that full inclusion could mean the elimination of special education as we know it along with the range of services currently guaranteed by federal special education laws. Full inclusion, they reason, would make them depend upon individual states, not the federal government, to meet their children's needs. Moreover, some parents believe that special education classes provide their children with important benefits. For example, in 1994, parents of exceptional children attending Vaughn Occupational High School in Chicago protested a decision by the Chicago Board of Education to include the children in neighborhood schools. The Chicago Board was responding to the Illinois State Board of Education's threat to withhold state and federal funds from the school if students were not included in regular classrooms. In response, the parents picketed a Chicago Board of Education meeting with signs reading "The board's inclusion is exclusion." One parent expressed concern that inclusion would deny her son essential vocational training: "I know [my son] won't go to college so I don't expect that, just for him to learn everyday living and work skills" (Spring 1998, 140).

The general public also has reservations about full inclusion. According to the 1998 Phi Delta Kappa/Gallup Poll of the Public's Attitudes toward the Public Schools, 65 percent believed exceptional students should be educated in special classes of their own; 26 percent believed they should be put in the same classes with regular students; and 9 percent said they "don't know" (Rose and Gallup 1998, 53). Nevertheless, the trend toward full inclusion continues.

How do classroom teachers feel about inclusion? Lin Chang, an eighth-grade teacher, addresses the concerns general education teachers may have about the availability of resources to help them be successful in inclusive classrooms.

> At first I was worried that it would all be my responsibility. But after meeting with the special education teacher, I realized that we would work together and I would have additional resources if I needed them (Vaughn, Bos, and Schumm 1997, 18).

In addition, the following comments by Octavio Gonzalez, a ninth-grade English teacher who has three students with disabilities in two of his five sections of English, express the satisfaction that teachers can experience in inclusive classrooms:

> At first I was nervous about having students with disabilities in my class. One of the students has a learning disability, one student has serious motor problems and is in a wheelchair, and the third student has vision problems. Now I have to say the adaptations I make to meet their special learning needs actually help all of the students in my class. I think that I am a better teacher because I think about accommodations now (Vaughn, Bos, and Schumm 1997, 18).

Equal Opportunity for Exceptional Learners

Like many groups in our society, exceptional learners have often not received the kind of education that most effectively meets their needs. Approximately 10 percent of the population aged three to twenty-one is classified as exceptional; that is, "they require special education because they are markedly different from most children in one or more of the following ways: They may have mental retardation, learning disabilities, emotional or behavioral disorders, physical disabilities, disorders of communication, autism, traumatic brain injury, impaired hearing, impaired sight, or special gifts or talents" (Hallahan and Kauffman 2000, 7).

Just as there are no easy answers for how teachers should meet the needs of students from diverse cultural backgrounds, there is no single strategy for teachers to follow to ensure that all exceptional students receive an appropriate education. The key, however, lies in not losing sight of the fact that *the most important characteristics of exceptional children are their abilities* (Hallahan and Kauffman 2000, 6).

To build on students' strengths, classroom teachers must work cooperatively and collaboratively with special education teachers, and students in special education programs must not become isolated from their peers. In addition, teachers must understand how some people can be perceived as "different" and presumed to be "handicapped" because of their appearance or physical condition. Evidence suggests, for example, that people who are short, obese, or unattractive are often victims of discrimination, as are people with conditions such as AIDS, cancer, multiple sclerosis, or epilepsy. Significantly, many individuals with clinically diagnosable and classifiable impairments or disabilities do not perceive themselves as *handicapped*. The term itself means permanently unable to be treated equally.

Officially labeling students has become a necessity with the passage of the laws that provide education and related services for exceptional students. The classification labels help determine which students qualify for the special services, educational programs, and individualized instruction provided by the laws, and they bring to educators' attention many exceptional children and youth whose educational needs could be overlooked, neglected, or inadequately served otherwise. Detrimental aspects include the fact that classification systems are imperfect and have arbitrary cutoff points that sometimes lead to injustices. Also, labels tend to evoke negative expectations, which can cause teachers to avoid and underteach these students, and their peers to isolate or reject them, thereby stigmatizing individuals, sometimes permanently. The most serious detriment, however, is that students so labeled are taught to feel inadequate, inferior, and limited in terms of their options for growth.

How Can You Teach All Learners in Your Inclusive Classroom?

Teachers have a responsibility to address all students' developmental, individual, and exceptional learning needs. Although addressing the range of student differences in the inclusive classroom is challenging, it can also be very rewarding. Consider the comments of three first-year teachers who reflect on their successes with diverse learners:

> I taught a boy with ADD. His first-grade teacher segregated him from other students, but I had him stay with his peer group. Soon, I heard from other teachers that he was not being a troublemaker anymore. By year's end, he had published his own booklet for a writing project.

> I had a troubled student who dropped out of school mid-year after I had spent a considerable amount of time working with him. He went to court over a trespassing charge, so I went to court with him. His mother wrote me a letter saying I had been such a positive influence on him and she was very grateful. It was the relationships I was able to establish with these kids that meant so much to me. The opportunity to take kids with disciplinary problems and make them your kids—to get them to trust you and do what they need to do—is the most rewarding part of teaching.

> One little girl in my kindergarten class had neurological problems, but all the children joined together in helping her. By the end of the year, she was kicking and screaming, not because she had to come to school, but because she had to leave! (Sallie Mae Corporation 1994, 5, 11).

Though it is beyond the scope of this book to present in-depth instructional strategies to address students' diverse learning needs, Appendix 8.2 presents "Examples of Instructional Strategies for Teaching All Learners." See the appendix "Selected Resources for Including Exceptional Learners" on this book's website. In addition, attention to three key areas will enable you to create a truly inclusive classroom: collaborative consultation, partnerships with parents, and assistive technology for special learners.

Collaborative Consultation with Other Professionals

One approach to meeting the needs of all students is known as **collaborative consultation,** an approach in which a classroom teacher meets with one or more other professionals (a special educator, school psychologist, or resource teacher, for example) to focus on the learning needs of one or more students. The following first-year teacher describes how collaborative consultation enabled her to meet the needs of a special student.

> I taught a Down's syndrome child who was very frustrated. I convened a meeting that included district experts, his parent, and a resource teacher, suggesting a change

Help! Tell Me about This Kid!

DonnaLee Brown, M.A., is an elementary school counselor with twenty-three years of experience in Texas schools. She compiled this case on the basis of her work with several children in recent years.

Mary Stone, a second grade teacher, had "inherited" Linda on the third day of school. She had heard rumors about the child's difficulties the previous year. She also knew about the special education assessment that was under way and the private ADHD diagnosis she had received. Mary stuck her head in my office with a frantic, "What can you tell me about this kid Linda?"

"Linda? Linda who?"

Mary said plaintively, "All I need is another messed up kid! I've already got Beth, Mario, and Jonathan. And I heard Linda can't even read or write! How can I be expected to include her in group work? And I can't work one-on-one with her all the time!"

Several days later, Mary's calls to me came on a regular basis. "Please come as soon as you can and get Linda! She is wet and smells of urine, and the kids are saying things." And, "Please come. Linda won't do what I tell her to do. She is unteachable!" And, "Linda refuses to talk to me. I ask her a question and she's totally silent. Help!"

When Linda's test results came in, they indicated that her IQ score was above average. They also showed that she had a lot of difficulty with sound/symbol associations but no difficulty reproducing written symbols and doing sequencing of all kinds. She appeared to be disturbed in the area of emotional attachment, and she exhibited oppositional behavior. The last we knew!

I also had regular contact with Linda since she came daily to my office for her dry clothes. While there she would show me magic tricks with Pokémon cards and visit. She

in educational strategy. All agreed to pilot the plan, and things have worked more smoothly ever since. It was a very rewarding experience (Sallie Mae Corporation 1995, 11).

Collaborative consultation is based on mutuality and reciprocity (Hallahan and Kauffman 1994), and participants assume equal responsibility for meeting students' needs. Friend and Bursuck (1999) make the following suggestions for working with a consultant:

1. **Do your homework.** Working with a consultant should be an intervention you seek only after you have attempted to identify and resolve the problem by analyzing the situation yourself, talking about it with parents, presenting it at a grade-level meeting, and so on.

2. **Demonstrate your concern with documentation.** At your initial meeting with a consultant, bring samples of student work, notes recounting specific incidents

described her class as boring, her teacher as stupid, and the work as never-ending. She complained that she had no chance of earning recess, so she decided not to do anything, not even to talk. When Ms. Stone asked her something, she would not answer. Her teacher would then get red in the face and lean really close to her—and that made all the kids laugh. She added, "The kids really like me!"

Working with the class and incorporating several suggestions from me, Mary gradually fit Linda into group work with a peer partner and an agreement from the group about their expectations of Linda: She was to contribute ideas when inspired and was not to be expected to write for the group unless she volunteered. Mary and Linda also agreed that Linda could use head-nodding to signal "yes" or "no" whenever Mary questioned her or gave her directives in class. Linda agreed to accept a "reminder signal" from her peer partner for two bathroom trips a day (before recess and before math).

While all was not perfect, the number of Linda's trips to my office for clean clothes diminished, and Mary's calls for help stopped completely. When Mary did drop by my office, it was more often to share a laugh, celebrate a success, or discuss a new behavior management strategy. I knew Linda was in good hands when Mary began telling *me* about "this kid."

Questions

1. Why do you think Linda prefers to use head-nodding rather than verbal answers?

2. How did Mary involve others in integrating Linda into the class?

3. What accommodations did Mary need to make to work effectively with Linda?

4. How can counselor intervention assist teachers and students like Mary and Linda?

5. What does Linda gain or lose by being included in Mary Stone's class?

in the classroom, records of correspondence with parents, and other concrete information.

3. **Participate actively.** If you clearly describe the problem, contribute specific information about your expectations for how the situation should change, offer your ideas on how best to intervene to resolve the problem, implement the selected strategy carefully, and provide your perception of the effectiveness of the strategy, you will find consultation very helpful.

4. **Carry out the consultant's suggestions carefully and systematically.**

5. **Contact the consultant if problems occur** (Friend and Bursuck 1996, 96).

To enhance the educational experiences of their students with disabilities, general education teachers are often assisted by special educators and other support professionals. The following professionals are among those who consult and/or collaborate with general education teachers:

Consulting teacher—A special educator who provides technical assistance such as arranging the physical setting, helping to plan for instruction, or developing approaches for assessing students' learning

Resource-room teacher—A special educator who provides instruction in a resource room for students with disabilities

School psychologist—Consults with the general education teacher and arranges for the administration of appropriate psychological, educational, and behavioral assessment instruments; may observe a student's behavior in the classroom

Speech and language specialist—Assesses students' communication abilities and works with general education teachers to develop educational programs for students with speech and/or language disorders

Physical therapist—Provides physical therapy for students with physical disabilities

Occupational therapist—Instructs students with disabilities to prepare them for everyday living and work-related activities

Working with Parents

In addition to working with education professionals to meet the learning needs of all students, effective teachers develop good working relationships with parents. Parents of exceptional children can be a source of valuable information about the characteristics, abilities, and needs of their children; they can be helpful in securing necessary services for their children; and they can assist you by reviewing skills at home and praising their children for their learning. The power of partnerships with parents is evident, for instance, in three examples from the U.S. Department of Education's *Schools with IDEAs That Work* (1999b), state-by-state descriptions of schools that work closely with parents to implement IDEA.

- *O'Loughlin Elementary School*—At this award-winning school in Hays, Kansas, parents pay for after school programs such as Young Astronauts and O'Loughlin Singers; and students lead the four parent-teacher conferences per year.
- *Sudduth Elementary School*—Since this rural school of approximately 1,000 students in Starkville, Mississippi, has limited fiscal and human resources, parent volunteers come and go throughout the day; during the first eight weeks of school one year, parents had 1,129 contacts with the school.
- *Mirror Lake Middle School*—At this school in Chugiak, Alaska, parents volunteer in the office, classroom, and other areas of the school; and frequently they help teach lessons and serve as guest speakers in classrooms.

Assistive Technology for Special Learners

The ability of teachers to create inclusive classrooms has increased dramatically as a result of many technological advances that now make it easier for exceptional students to learn and communicate. For example, computer-based word processing and math tutorials can greatly assist students with learning disabilities in acquiring literacy and computational skills. Students with hearing impairments can communicate with other students by using telecommunications equipment, and students with physical disabilities can operate computers through voice commands or with a single switch or key. Among the recent developments in assistive technology are the following:

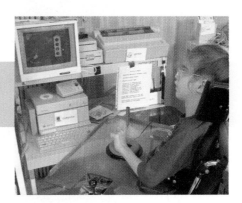

How can word prediction software enhance the writing abilities of students with disabilities?

"What should I write?" "What words will best express what I want to say?" Although most people find these questions at least somewhat difficult to answer, students with disabilities may confront unique challenges when they write. Students with learning disabilities may not be able to retain ideas in their memory long enough to express them in writing; others may have difficulty with spelling; and students with motor disabilities may be challenged when forming letters with pen or pencil or making repetitive keystrokes on a word processor.

Students with disabilities that affect their ability to write can be assisted by word prediction software that reduces the number of keystrokes needed to type words. When writing with word prediction software, a student types the first letter of a word, and then a numbered list of words beginning with that letter appears on the computer screen. If the desired word is on the list, the student enters the number and the word is typed automatically. For example, assume a student wants to write the word *tonight* to complete the sentence "I will watch TV *tonight.*" First, she enters a "t" and the list of common "t" words shown in screen # 1 appears. Since the word *tonight* is not on this list, she types an "o" and screen #2 appears. Since *tonight* is on this list, she types a number "3" and the word is entered automatically. Thus, the seven keystrokes needed to write *tonight* has been reduced to three.

The following list describes additional features of various word prediction software programs.

- *Synthesized speech output*
- *Prediction methods*—Some programs predict on the basis of spelling only, while others consider the words that have come before in the sentence; for example only nouns are listed after the word *a* or *an.*
- *List updating*—After "learning" a student's vocabulary, the word prediction program tailors the word prediction lists to the student's usage. Some programs update automatically, while others allow the user to decide when to update.
- *Prediction window customizing*
- *Keyboard sensitivity adjustment*—Keyboard sensitivity can be adjusted to prevent repetition if keys are not quickly released.

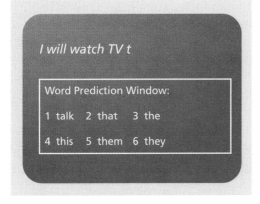

Screen #1

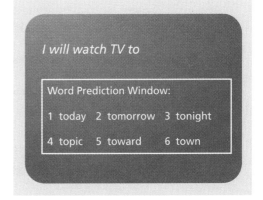

Screen #2

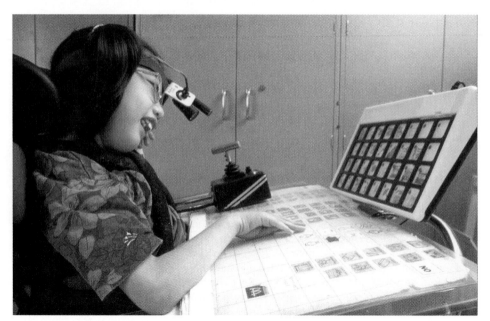

The IEP for this student with multiple disabilities provides for assistive technology, which enables her to create and respond to language.

1. talking word processor
2. speech synthesizer
3. touch-sensitive computer screens
4. computer screen image enlarger
5. teletypewriter (TTY) (connects to telephone and types a spoken message to another TTY)
6. customized computer keyboards
7. ultrasonic head controls for computers
8. voice-recognition computers
9. television closed captioning
10. Kurzweil reading machine (scans print and reads it aloud)

In addition, assistive technology includes devices to enhance the mobility and everyday activities of people with disabilities (wheelchairs, lifts, adaptive driving controls, scooters, laser canes, feeders).

Many technology-related special education resources and curriculum materials are available on the Internet. One of these sites, The National Center to Improve Practice in Special Education through Technology, Media, and Materials, also maintains discussion forums for teachers of students with disabilities. Clearly, the dazzling revolution in microelectronics will continue to yield new devices to enhance the learning of all students.

SUMMARY

How Do Students' Needs Change as They Develop?

■ People move through different stages of cognitive, psychosocial, and moral development throughout their life spans.

- Piaget maintains that children, who reason differently from adults, pass through four stages of cognitive development as they mature. Effective teachers are aware of the characteristics of school-age children's thinking during three of these stages: the preoperational stage, the concrete operations stage, and the formal operations stage.

- According to Erikson's model of psychosocial development, people pass through eight stages of emotional and social development throughout their lives. Each stage is characterized by a "crisis" with a positive and negative pole. Healthy development depends upon a satisfactory, positive resolution of each crisis.

- Kohlberg believes that moral development, the reasoning people use to decide between right and wrong, evolves through three levels. Evidence suggests that males may base their moral reasoning on rights and rules, and females on altruism and self-sacrifice. Many teachers and schools emphasize character education to "teach" moral reasoning and values.

- Maslow suggests that human growth and development depends on how well the individual's biological and psychological needs have been met. According to his hierarchy of needs model, people must satisfy their survival and safety needs before addressing "higher" needs such as self-actualization.

- Teachers must be aware of the developmental stresses and tasks students encounter during childhood and early and late adolescence.

How Do Students Vary in Intelligence?

- There are conflicting definitions of *intelligence;* they range from "what IQ tests measure" to "goal-directed adaptive behavior." Some theorists believe intelligence is a single, basic ability, though recent research suggests that there are many forms of intelligence.

- According to Howard Gardner's theory of multiple intelligences, there are at least eight human intelligences.

- Students differ in their learning styles—the patterns of behavior they prefer to use while learning. Although there is conflict about the concept of learning styles, effective teachers are aware of differences among students regarding their preferences for learning activities.

How Do Students Vary in Ability and Disability?

- Some students are "exceptional" because they have abilities or disabilities that distinguish them from other students. Students with physical, cognitive, or emotional disabilities and students who are gifted and talented have unique learning needs.

- There is a lack of agreement regarding the definition of *learning disability (LD).* Teachers can identify students with learning disabilities by noting difficulties they have acquiring and processing new information. Learning disabilities are the most common disability among students, with attention deficit hyperactivity disorder (ADHD) and attention deficit disorder (ADD) the most common learning disabilities.

- There are many forms of giftedness. Among the approaches used to meet the learning needs of gifted students are acceleration, self-directed or independent study, individual education programs, special or magnet schools, and weekend and summer programs.

What Are Special Education, Mainstreaming, and Inclusion?

■ Special education includes a variety of educational services to meet the needs of exceptional students. Key provisions of the Individuals with Disabilities Education Act (IDEA) include least restrictive environment, individualized education program (IEP), confidentiality of records, and due process.

■ *Mainstreaming* is the process of integrating students with disabilities into regular classrooms.

■ *Inclusion* integrates all students with disabilities into regular classrooms, with the support of special education services as necessary. *Full inclusion* is the integration of students with disabilities in general education classrooms at all times regardless of the severity of the disability.

How Can You Teach All Learners in Your Inclusive Classroom?

■ Though challenging, teachers have a responsibility to create inclusive classrooms that address the developmental, individual, and exceptional learning needs of all students.

■ Through collaborative consultation, an arrangement whereby the regular classroom teacher collaborates with other education professionals, teachers can meet the needs of exceptional students. Collaborative consultation is based on mutuality and reciprocity, and all participants assume responsibility for meeting students' needs.

■ By developing effective relationships with parents of exceptional students, teachers acquire valuable information and support.

■ An array of assistive technologies and resources is available to help exceptional students learn and communicate in inclusive classrooms.

KEY TERMS AND CONCEPTS

Amendments to the Individuals with Disabilities Education Act (IDEA 97), 313
assistive technology, 315
attention deficit disorder (ADD), 309
attention deficit hyperactivity disorder (ADHD), 309
character education, 295

cognitive development, 291
collaborative consultation, 317
concrete operations stage, 291
Education for all Handicapped Children Act (Public Law 94-142), 312
exceptional learners, 306
formal operations

stage, 291
full inclusion, 315
gifted and talented, 310
hierarchy of needs, 298
inclusion, 315
individualized education plan (IEP), 313
Individuals with Disabilities Education Act (IDEA), 312
intelligence, 320

APPLICATIONS AND ACTIVITIES

Teacher's Journal

1. Through a series of vignettes, relate Erikson's stages of psychosocial development to your own experiences as a child and as an adolescent. How did sources of stress, psychosocial crises, and your resolutions of them affect your learning in school?

2. Do you know your IQ or recall participating in an IQ test? How do you regard yourself in terms of intelligence and how did you come by your beliefs about your intelligence? Do you think these beliefs influenced your motivation, choices, and achievement as a student? Do you think they influenced your school or class placements? Do you think they influenced the way your teachers and peers responded to you? What criteria would you use now to evaluate the fairness of IQ testing and the appropriateness of use of IQ scores?

3. Recount an experience you had as an exceptional student or one that involved a person with disabilities. What did you learn from this experience or from your reflection on it that could help you as a teacher?

Teacher's Database

1. Investigate sources of information on students with disabilities or exceptional learners in the ERIC Clearinghouse on Disabilities and Gifted Education. The databases in this clearinghouse are maintained by the Council for Exceptional Children (CEC) in Reston, Virginia.

   Then visit the National Information Center for Children and Youth with Disabilities (NICHCY) on the SpecialNet. This government clearinghouse answers questions about disability issues, refers you to disability organizations, provides fact sheets, and identifies relevant educational resources in your state.

2. "Observe" children online by locating chat rooms by and for children and youth. As an adult you may not be allowed to participate, but in many cases you will be invited to visit (called "lurking" in Internet jargon). What educational interests, needs, and concerns do students share with one another? How might visiting students' sites online be viewed as an extension of your field experiences as an education major or a student teacher? What teacher observation techniques and protocols could you use in this situation? What are some ethical concerns about this practice? How might any new knowledge of students gained in this way help to make you a more effective teacher?

Observations and Interviews

1. Observe in a classroom that has exceptional students. What steps does the teacher take to meet the needs of these students? Interview the teacher to determine what he or she sees as the challenges and rewards of teaching exceptional students.

2. Observe and interview a student in the age group you wish to teach to conduct a brief case study that focuses on common developmental tasks for that age group and the areas of individual differences highlighted in this chapter. Then prepare a written portrait of the student. To help you with this activity, ask your instructor for Handouts M8.1, "Who Are the Students in the Classroom?" and M8.2, "Conversations with Students in the School."

3. Visit a school at the level you plan to teach. Interview the counselor, asking questions about the problems that bring students to the counselor most often. If possible, shadow the school counselor for a day.

4. Attend an extracurricular event such as a high school basketball game or Little League soccer game. Observe the students on the field as well as any students watching the players. Notice the differences among the students in terms of their physical appearance, clothing and hairstyles, athletic abilities, social skills, and evidence of personal interests and confidence. Share your observations in class.

Professional Portfolio

For the grade level and content area you are preparing to teach, identify learning activities that address each of the eight multiple intelligences identified by Gardner. For example, you might plan activities such as the following. For one activity in each category, list the preparations you would need to make and/or the materials you would need to gather, and add this information to your portfolio.

Logical-Mathematical
■ Design an experiment on . . .
■ Describe the rules for a new board game called . . .

Linguistic
■ Write a short story about . . .
■ Write a biographical sketch of . . .

Musical
■ Write song lyrics for . . .
■ Locate music that sounds like . . .

Spatial
■ Draw, paint, or sculpt a . . .
■ Create an advertisement for . . .

Bodily-Kinesthetic
■ Role play a person who is . . .
■ Do a dance that shows . . .

Intrapersonal
■ Assess your ability to . . .

■ Describe how you feel about . . .

Interpersonal
■ Show one or more of your classmates how to . . .
■ In a small group, construct a . . .

Naturalist
■ Identify the trees found in . . .
■ Classify the rocks found in . . .

Appendix 8.1

A sample individualized education plan

Student's Primary Classification: Serious Emotional Disturbance

Secondary Classification: None

Student Name   _Diane_

Date of Birth   _5-3-87_

Primary Language:

HOME   _English_   Student   _English_

Date of IEP Meeting   _April, 27, 2000_

Entry Date to Program   _April, 27, 2000_

Projected Duration of Services   _One school year_

Services Required   _Specify amount of time in educational and/or related services per day or week_

General Education Class   _4—5 hours p/day_

Resource Room   _1—2 hours p/day_

Special Ed Consultation in General Ed Classroom
Co-teaching and consultation with general education teacher in the areas of academic and adaptive skills as indicated in annual goals and short-term objectives.

Self-Contained   _none_

Related Services   _Group counseling sessions twice weekly with guidance counselor. Counseling to focus on adaptive skill development as described in annual goals and short-term objectives_

RE. Program   _45 min. daily in general ed PE class with support from adapted PE teacher as necessary_

Assessment

Intellectual   _WISC-R_

Educational   _Key Math Woodcock Reading_

Behavioral/Adaptive   _Burks_

Speech/Language

Other

Vision   _Within normal limits_

Hearing   _Within normal limits_

Classroom Observation Done

Dates   _1/15–2/25/00_

Personnel Conducting Observation   _School Psychologist, Special Education Teacher, General Education Teacher_

Present Level of Performance Strengths:
1) _Polite to teachers and peers_
2) _Helpful and cooperative in the classroom_
3) _Good grooming skills_
4) _Good in sports activities_

Access to General Education Curriculum
Diane will participate in all content areas within the general education curriculum. Special education supports and services will be provided in the areas of math and reading.

Effect of Disability on Access to General Education Curriculum
Emotional disabilities make it difficult for Diane to achieve at expected grade level performance in general education curriculum in the areas of reading and math. It is expected that this will further impact her access to the general education curriculum in other content areas (such as history, biology, English) as she enters junior high school.

Participation in Statewide or District Assessments
Diane will participate in all state and district wide assessments of achievement. No adaptations or modifications required for participation.

Justification for Removal from General Education Classroom:
Diane's objectives require that she be placed in a general education classroom with support from a special education teacher for the majority of the school day. Based on adaptive behavior assessment and observations, Diane will receive instruction in a resource room for approximately one to two hours per day in the areas of social skill development.

Reports to Parents on Progress toward Annual Goals:
Parents will be informed of Diane's progress through weekly reports of progress on short-term goals, monthly phone calls from general ed teachers, special education teachers, and school psychologist, and regularly scheduled report cards at the end of each term.

Appendix 8.1 *(continued)*

Areas Needing Specialized Instruction and Support

1. Adaptive Skills
   - Limited interaction skills with peers and adults
   - Excessive facial tics and grimaces
   - Difficulty staying on task in content subjects, especially reading and math.
   - Difficulty expressing feelings, needs, and interests
2. Academic Skills
   - Significantly below grade level in math—3.9
   - Significantly below grade level in reading—4.3

Annual Review: _____ Date: _____

Comments/Recommendations

_____

_____

_____

_____

_____

Team Signatures   IEP Review Date _____

LEA Rep. _____

Parent _____

Sp Ed Teacher _____

Gen Ed Teacher _____

School Psych _____

Student (as appropriate) _____

Related Services Personnel (as appropriate) _____

Objective Criteria and Evaluation Procedures _____

IEP—Annual Goals and Short-Term Objectives	Persons Responsible	Objective Criteria and Evaluation Procedures
#1 ANNUAL GOAL: Diane will improve her interaction skills with peers and adults.	General education teacher and special ed teacher (resource room)	Classroom observations and documented data on target behavior
S.T. OBJ. Diane will initiate conversation with peers during an unstructured setting twice daily.	School psychologist consultation	
S.T. OBJ. When in need of assistance, Diane will raise her hand and verbalize her needs to teachers or peers without prompting 80% of the time.		
#2 ANNUAL GOAL: Diane will increase her ability to control hand and facial movements.	General education teacher and special ed teacher (resource room)	Classroom observations and documented data on target behavior
S.T. OBJ. During academic work, Diane will keep her hands in an appropriate place and use writing materials correctly 80% of the time.	School psychologist consultation	
S.T. OBJ. Diane will maintain a relaxed facial expression with teacher prompt 80% of the time. Teacher prompt will be faded over time.		
#3 ANNUAL GOAL: Diane will improve her ability to remain on task during academic work.	General education teacher and special ed teacher (resource room)	Classroom observations and documented data on target behavior
S.T. OBJ. Diane will work independently on an assigned task with teacher prompt 80% of the time.	School psychologist consultation	
S.T. OBJ. Diane will complete academic work as assigned 90% of the time.		

Appendix 8.1 *(continued)*

IEP—Annual Goals and Short-Term Objectives	Persons Responsible	Objective Criteria and Evaluation Procedures
#4 ANNUAL GOAL: Diane will improve her ability to express her feelings. **S.T. OBJ.** When asked how she feels, Diane will give an adequate verbal description of her feelings or moods with teacher prompting at least 80% of the time. **S.T. OBJ.** Given a conflict or problem situation, Diane will state her feelings to teachers and peers 80% of the time.	General education teacher and special ed teacher (resource room) School psychologist consultation	Classroom observations and documented data on target behavior
#5 ANNUAL GOAL: Diane will improve math skills one grade level. **S.T. OBJ.** Diane will improve rate and accuracy in oral 1- and 2-digit division facts to 50 problems per minute without errors. **S.T. OBJ.** Diane will improve her ability to solve word problems involving t—x—v.	Collaboration of general education teacher and special education teacher through co-teaching and consultation	Precision teaching Addison Wesley Math Program Scope and Sequence Districtwide Assessment of Academic Achievement
#6 ANNUAL GOAL: Diane will improve reading skills one grade level. **S.T. OBJ.** Diane will answer progressively more difficult comprehension questions in designated reading skills program. **S.T. OBJ.** Diane will increase her rate and accuracy of vocabulary words to 80 wpm without errors.	Collaboration of general education teacher and special education teacher through co-teaching and consultation	Precision teaching Barnell & Loft Scope and Sequence District wide Assessment of Academic Achievement

Source: Michael L. Hardman, Clifford J. Drew, and M. Winston Egan, *Human Exceptionality: Society, School, and Family,* 6th ed. Boston; Allyn and Bacon, 1999, pp. 123–25. Copyright © 1999 by Allyn and Bacon. Used with permission.

Appendix 8.2

Examples of instructional strategies for teaching all learners

1. Present material on tape for students who cannot read successfully. School volunteers, older students, or parents can be asked to make recordings of assigned material.

2. Allow students to tape record answers if writing is difficult or their handwriting is illegible.

3. Provide lots of visual reminders (pictures, maps, charts, graphs) for students who have trouble listening or attending.

4. Present handouts that are clear, legible, and uncrowded. Blurred copies [can be] very hard for [students with disabilities] to read.

5. Break directions and assignments into small steps. Completion of each step is an accomplishment—reward it.

6. Give tests orally if the child has trouble with reading, spelling, or writing. Testing that demonstrates what the student knows rather than language skills gives you a clearer picture of the student's abilities. The student demonstrates abilities, not disabilities.

7. Emphasize quality rather than quantity of writing.

8. Be consistent with directions, rules, discipline, and organization.

9. Arrange the class schedule so that the exceptional student does not miss important activities when he or she goes to the resource room.

10. Dispense encouragement freely but fairly. If students make errors, help them find the correct answers, and then reward them.

11. Discover the exceptional student's strengths and special interests. Capitalize on them in the regular classroom.

12. Carefully establish routines so that the student does not become further handicapped by the confusion of unclear expectations.

13. Arrange desks, tables, and chairs so every person can be easily seen and every word easily heard. Remember, students with hearing impairments need to see your face as you speak.

14. If possible, schedule difficult subjects when there are no outside noises, such as a class at recess.

15. Provide carrels or screens—an "office"—for students who are easily distracted.

16. When checking students' work, check correct answers rather than incorrect answers. The student is still informed of mistakes, but sees his or her successes emphasized.

17. Allow the exceptional student to tape lectures or arrange for a classmate who writes neatly to use carbon paper. Either the carbon copy or a copy of the teacher's notes can be given to the exceptional student.

18. Correct deficient lighting, glare from windows, and light-blocking partitions. Small light problems can be distractions for some exceptional students.

19. Fit the furniture to the child. Discomfort leads to distraction and restlessness.

20. Generally, become sensitive to the obstacles which prevent the exceptional student from exercising his or her abilities.

Source: Pamela Maniet-Bellerman, *Mainstreaming Children with Disabilities: A Guide to Accompany "L.D." Does NOT Mean Learning Dumb!* Pittsburgh: Upward Bound Press; as presented in R. R. McCown and Peter Roop, *Educational Psychology and Classroom Practice: A Partnership*, Boston: Allyn and Bacon, 1992, pp. 424–425.

9

Creating a Community of Learners

Teacher-oriented, passive-student approaches to instruction are outdated . . . we cannot effectively conduct our classes as if students were sponges who sit passively and absorb attentively.

—A middle school mathematics teacher, quoted in Burden and Byrd (1999, 103)

focus questions

1. What determines the culture of the classroom?

2. How can you create a positive learning environment?

3. What are the keys to successful classroom management?

4. What teaching methods do effective teachers use?

5. What are some characteristics of effective teaching?

September 26

I set up a classroom library. We don't use the reading textbook. What for? Grown-ups don't read textbooks unless they're forced. I told them we could read real books so long as they don't steal any. I make a big show of counting the books at the end of the day. The kids sigh audibly when they're all there. They look beautiful, like a bookstore, facing out in a big wooden display my uncle made for me. Plus, it covers the bullet-riddled window that never was repaired.

We don't call the subjects the old-fashioned names in Room 211. Math is "Puzzling," science is "Mad Scientist Time," social studies is "T.T.W.E." which stands for "Time Travel and World Exploring," language arts is "Art of Language," and reading is "Free Reading Time." I did this because I figured kids at this age come to me with preconceived notions of what they are good at. This way, a kid who thinks she's no good in math might turn out to be good at Puzzling, and so on.

In the morning, three things happen religiously. I say good morning, real chipper, to every single child and make sure they say good morning back. Then I collect "troubles" in a "Trouble Basket," a big green basket into which the children pantomime unburdening their home worries so they can concentrate on school. Sometimes a kid has no troubles. Sometimes a kid piles it in, and I in turn pantomime bearing the burden. This way, too, I can see what disposition the child is in when he or she enters. Finally, before they can come in, they must give me a word, which I print on a piece of tagboard and they keep in an envelope. It can be any word, but preferably one that they heard and don't really know or one that is personally meaningful. A lot of times the kids ask for *Mississippi,* just to make me spell it. We go over the words when we do our private reading conferences. I learned this from reading *Teacher* by Sylvia Ashton-Warner, who taught underprivileged Maori children in New Zealand. She says language should be an organic experience. I love her approach.

It takes a long time to get in the door this way, but by the time we are in, I know every kid has had and given a kind greeting, has had an opportunity to learn something, and has tried to leave his or her worries on the doorstep. Some kids from other classrooms sneak into our line to use the Trouble Basket or to get a word card.

Then the national anthem blares over the intercom. The kids sing with more gusto now that we shout "Play ball!" at the end. We do Puzzling until 10:30, then we alternate Mad Sciencing with T.T.W.E., lunch, reading aloud, Free Reading and journaling, and Art of Language.

At the end of the day, as the kids exit, they fill in the blanks as I call out, "See you in the _____ [morning!]." "Watch out for the _____ [cars!]." Don't say _____ [shut up!]." I love _____ [you!]." This is a game I played with my father at bedtime growing up. It gives the day a nice closure (Codell 1999, 29–31).

T he opening scenario for this chapter, taken from *Educating Esmé: Diary of a Teacher's First Year,* by Esmé Raji Codell, a fifth-grade teacher in Chicago, illustrates how one teacher organized her classroom to create a positive learning environment. Sensitivity to the elements that combine to give a day in the classroom a "nice closure" is the hallmark of a professional, reflective teacher. For teacher education students such as you, making the transition between the study of teaching and actual teaching can be a challenge. The more you understand how "the classroom learning environment develops gradually, in response to the teacher's communication of expectations, modeling of behavior, and approach to classroom management" (Good and Brophy 1997, 129), the better prepared you will be to make the transition smoothly.

What Determines the Culture of the Classroom?

As you learned in Chapter 7, one definition of *culture* is the way of life common to a group of people. In much the same way, each classroom develops its own culture. The culture of a classroom is determined by the manner in which teachers and students participate in common activities.

The activities that teachers and students engage in are influenced by several factors. As a teacher, you will make countless decisions that will shape the physical and social milieus of your classroom. From seating arrangement, to classroom rules and procedures, to the content and relevance of the curriculum, you will have a strong influence on the culture that emerges in your classroom. You will have many methodological choices to make—when to shift from one activity to another, when to use discussion rather than lecture, or whether to make one requirement rather than another.

Classroom Climate

Part of the environment of the classroom is **classroom climate**—the atmosphere or quality of life in a classroom. The climate of your classroom will be determined by how you interact with your students and "by the manner and degree to which you exercise authority, show warmth and support, encourage competitiveness or cooperation, and allow for independent judgment and choice" (Borich 1996, 470).

In addition to promoting learning, the classroom climate should make students feel safe and respected. In light of the finding in *The Metropolitan Life Survey of the American Teacher 1996, Students Voice Their Opinions on: Their Education, Teachers and Schools* that 42 percent of students would give their teachers a grade of "C" or worse on "treating students with respect," it is important that your classroom fosters respect for others and be a place where students feel supported while learning.

Classroom climates are complex and multidimensional; their character is determined by a wide array of variables, many of which are beyond the teacher's control. Nevertheless, our observations of high-performing teachers have confirmed that they take specific steps to create classroom climates with the following eight characteristics:

- A productive, task-oriented focus
- Group cohesiveness
- Open, warm relationships between teacher and students
- Cooperative, respectful interactions among students
- Low levels of tension, anxiety, and conflict
- Humor
- High expectations
- Frequent opportunities for student input regarding classroom activities

These dimensions of classroom climates are within teachers' spheres of influence and are promoted, consciously or unconsciously, by their styles of communicating and treating students. As the following reflections by a student teacher indicate, creating a classroom climate characterized by these eight dimensions is not easy; teachers must make moment-to-moment judgments about what actions will enhance students' motivation to learn.

> The next day, as I was going over the instructions for a science experiment I noticed Sheila and Devon leaning over and whispering. I immediately stopped my presentation and said, "Sheila and Devon, you need to turn around in your seats and stop whispering while I am talking." Both girls rolled their eyes and slowly turned

their bodies around in their seats. Neither of them made eye contact with me as I continued the lesson. Although the class was now quiet, I felt uncomfortable myself. As the students gathered the science materials they needed to carry out the experiment in their cooperative learning groups, I noticed that Theresa was passing a note to Sheila. Trying to hide my anger and frustration, I said, "Theresa, you need to get rid of that note now. You can come up and put it in the wastebasket. It is time to be working on science, not note passing." Although singling out the girls worked in the short term, to tell the truth I did not feel comfortable dealing with the situation as I did.

I didn't want to feel as if I was spending half the time handling misbehavior, but that's just what I was doing. I had learned in school to reach for student strengths, so I am trying to practice the strategy of giving the students a better attitude about themselves through praise. I explained to them that by correcting their behavior I was just trying to create a climate in which they could learn. I am trying to be a supportive teacher who still corrects misbehavior—always with the goal of redirecting students toward meaningful classroom work.

That same afternoon, I began to gather the students together for literature circles. I had four groups reading different novels. Today I was planning to have the students discuss their reactions to the first chapter and make predictions about the rest of the book. For the first five minutes or so, the groups were very productive, and I felt a surge of hope that all would go well. Just then, I noticed Devon lean back in her chair to pass a note to Theresa, who was in a different group. I wanted to shout across the room at them, but I kept my calm and tried to figure out what I should do now (Rand and Shelton-Colangelo 1999, 10–11).

How would you describe this classroom climate using the eight dimensions listed earlier? What changes in the student teacher's behavior could transform the overall climate?

Although teachers influence the classroom climate by the way they regard and treat students, they also shape it by their instructional decisions. David Johnson and Roger Johnson, two researchers in the area of classroom communication and dynamics, delineate three types of interactions promoted by instructional decisions: cooperative or positive interdependence, competitive or negative interdependence, and individualistic or no interdependence (Johnson and Johnson 1999). To illustrate the three types, Johnson and Johnson suggest that a group project to measure classroom furniture would promote cooperative interdependence; a race to be the first student to measure the furniture would call for competitive interdependence; and having a student measure the furniture independently would be an example of no interdependence. Johnson and Johnson believe that teachers should use strategies that foster all three forms of interactions, depending on their instructional goals, but that, ideally, the emphasis should be on furthering cooperative interdependence.

What words would you use to describe the apparent climate of this classroom? In what ways does this classroom appear to be an effective learning environment? What would you look for to determine if this is a caring classroom?

Classroom Dynamics

Interactions between teachers and students are the very core of teaching. The quality of these interactions reveals to students how the teacher feels about them. Teachers who empathize with students, genuinely respect them, and expect them to learn are more likely to develop a classroom climate free of management problems. In classrooms with positive group dynamics, teachers and students work toward a common goal—learning. In classrooms with negative interactions, the energy of teachers and students may be channeled into conflict rather than into learning.

There is no precise formula to guarantee success in the classroom; however, educational psychologist Anita Woolfolk (1998, 427) suggests four "necessary conditions" to increase student learning through positive interactions:

1. The classroom must be relatively organized and free from constant interruptions and disruptions.
2. The teacher must be a patient, supportive person who never embarrasses students for mistakes.
3. The work must be challenging but reasonable.
4. The learning tasks must be authentic.

Teacher Communication   Successful teachers possess effective communication skills. They express themselves verbally and nonverbally (and in writing) in a manner that is clear, concise, and interesting. They "are able to communicate clearly and directly to their students without wandering, speaking above students' levels of comprehension, or using speech patterns that impair the clarity of what is being presented" (Borich 1996, 11). In addition, they are good listeners. Their students feel that not only are they heard, they are understood.

Effective teachers relish the live, thinking-on-your-feet dimensions of classroom communication. Their communication skills enable them to respond appropriately to events that could sabotage the plans of less effective teachers: a student's clowning, announcements on the public address system, interruptions by other teachers or parents, students' private arguments or romances, or simply the mood of the class at that particular time.

Student Interaction   In addition to engaging in positive, success-oriented interactions with their students, effective teachers foster positive, cooperative interactions among students. As a result, students feel supported by their peers and free to devote their attention to learning. Richard Schmuck and Patricia Schmuck (1997) describe the climate of such classrooms as "mature" and "self-renewing." Their research on classroom group processes has led them to identify the four sequential stages of group development portrayed in Figure 9.1.

During Stage 1 of a class's group development, students are on their best behavior. Teachers who are aware of this "honeymoon period" use it to their advantage; they dis-

Figure 9.1

Characteristics of groups at four stages of development

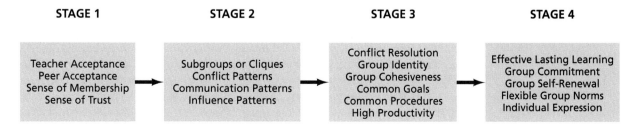

STAGE 1	STAGE 2	STAGE 3	STAGE 4
Teacher Acceptance Peer Acceptance Sense of Membership Sense of Trust	Subgroups or Cliques Conflict Patterns Communication Patterns Influence Patterns	Conflict Resolution Group Identity Group Cohesiveness Common Goals Common Procedures High Productivity	Effective Lasting Learning Group Commitment Group Self-Renewal Flexible Group Norms Individual Expression

cuss and teach classroom rules and procedures, outline their goals, and deliberately set the classroom tone and standards they want. During Stage 2, teachers seeking to promote group development are advised to encourage student participation and communication and to discourage the formation of cliques.

Groups that have met the requirements of the preceding stages move into Stage 3, which lasts for the majority of the expected life of the group (i.e., the semester or the school year). This stage is characterized by the group's willingness to set clear goals, share tasks, and agree on deadlines. At Stage 4, the final stage, group members fully accept responsibility for the group's quality of life, and they continuously strive to improve it.

In addition, teachers who effectively orchestrate group processes in their classrooms recognize that, for good or ill, students as well as teachers exert leadership in classrooms. Wise teachers quickly identify student leaders and develop ways to focus their leadership abilities on the attainment of goals that benefit the entire class. Teachers should also encourage their students to develop leadership skills.

How Can You Create a Positive Learning Environment?

A positive classroom climate and positive classroom dynamics are prerequisites for a good learning environment. Creating and then maintaining a positive learning environment is a multidimensional challenge. While no single set of strategies will ensure success in all situations, educational researchers have identified teacher behaviors that tend to be associated with high levels of student learning. Effective teachers also know how to use these behaviors and *for what purposes* they are best suited. The following sections address three important dimensions of positive learning environments: the caring classroom, the physical classroom environment, and classroom organization, including procedures for grouping students for instruction and managing time.

The Caring Classroom

At this point in your preparation to become a teacher, you may feel uncertain of your ability to create a positive classroom climate and to orchestrate the complex dynamics of the classroom so that you and your students become a cohesive, productive, and mutually supportive group. In your quest to achieve these aims, it will help to remember that an authentic spirit of caring is at the heart of an effective learning environment. "[C]aring interactions between teachers, students, and parents often make the difference between positive school experiences and frustration or alienation" (Chaskin and Rauner 1995, 667–68).

How do teachers establish a **caring classroom?** First, teachers demonstrate caring through their efforts to help all students learn to their fullest potential. "Teachers display genuine caring for students when they find out about students' abilities and motivations. They continue this pervasive caring by providing all their students with the appropriate amount of support, structure, and expectations they need in order to be self-directed, responsible learners" (Zehm and Kottler 1993, 54). In addition, teachers realize that how they speak and listen to students determines the extent to which students believe their teachers care about them. In a synthesis of research on classroom environments that enhance students' learning, Herbert Walberg and Rebecca Greenberg (1997, 46) found that "students learn more when their classes are satisfying, challenging, and friendly and they have a voice in decision making. [When] classes are unfriendly, cliquish, and fragmented, they leave students feeling rejected and therefore impede learning." Table 9.1, based on Walberg and Greenberg's work, presents fifteen dimensions of classroom life and how each influences students' learning at the junior and senior high levels.

While students learn best in caring classrooms, Nel Noddings has suggested that students also must learn to care for others. Toward this end, she recommends reorganizing the school curriculum around "themes of care" and points out that "educators must recognize that caring for students is fundamental in teaching and that developing people with a strong capacity for care is a major objective of responsible education" (Noddings 1995, 678).

The Classroom as a Physical Environment

When you become a teacher, the physical environment you work in will probably be similar to that of schools you attended. However, we encourage you, with the help of

Table 9.1

15 Dimensions of Classroom Environment

Dimension	Percent Positive Influence on Learning	Description
Satisfaction	100% (17)	Students enjoy classroom work and find it satisfying.
Challenge	87 (16)	Students find the work difficult and challenging.
Cohesiveness	86 (17)	Students know one another well and are helpful and friendly toward one another.
Physical Environment	85 (15)	Adequate books, equipment, space, and lighting are available.
Democracy	85 (14)	Students share equally in making decisions that affect the entire class.
Goal Direction	73 (15)	Learning goals are clear.
Competition	67 (9)	Competition among students is minimized.
Formality	65 (17)	Class is informal, with few formal rules to guide behavior.
Speed	54 (14)	Students have sufficient time to finish their work.
Diversity	31 (14)	Students' interests differ and are provided for.
Apathy	14 (15)	Students don't care about what the class does.
Favoritism	10 (13)	All students do not enjoy the same privileges; the teacher has favorites.
Cliquishness	8 (13)	Certain students work only with close friends and refuse to interact with others.
Disorganization	6 (17)	Activities are disorganized and confusing, rather than well organized and efficient.
Friction	0 (17)	Tension and quarreling among students characterize the classroom.

Note: Percent indicates the percentage of research studies that reported a positive influence on learning for that dimension; number in parenthesis indicates number of research studies that investigated that dimension.

Source: Adapted from Herbert J. Walberg and Rebecca C. Greenberg, "Using the Learning Environment Inventory," *Educational Leadership,* May 1997, p. 47.

your students, to make your surroundings as safe, pleasant, and convenient as possible. Fresh air; plants; clean, painted walls; displays of students' work; a comfortable reading or resource area; and a few prints or posters can enhance the quality of teacher–student relationships. Seating arrangements and the placement of other classroom furniture also do much to shape the classroom environment. Although seating by rows may be very appropriate for whole-group instruction or examinations, other arrangements may be more beneficial for other activities. For example, you can enhance small-group activities by moving desks into small clusters in different parts of the room. Figure 9.2 shows the arrangement of a classroom at an exemplary elementary school. The room is designed to encourage students to learn through discovery at learning centers located around the room.

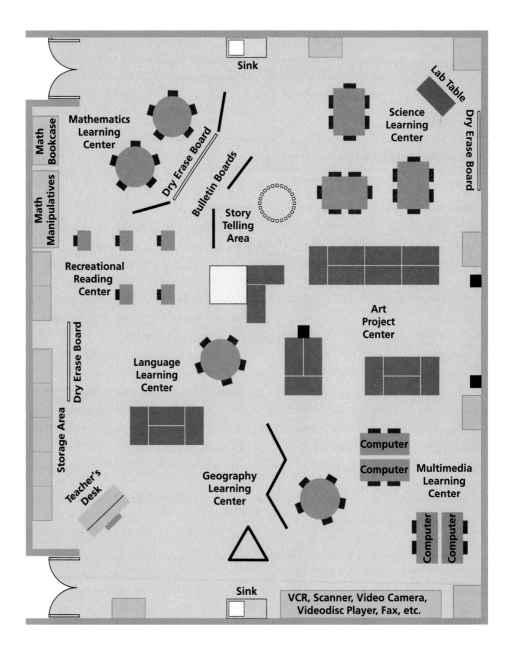

Figure 9.2

Learning centers in an elementary classroom

However you design your classroom, take care to ensure that seating arrangements do not reduce the opportunity of some students to learn. For example, students in some classrooms receive more attention if they are seated in the "action zone," the middle front-row seats and seats on the middle aisle. Teachers often stand near this area and unknowingly give students seated there more opportunities to speak.

Classroom Organization

A factor in positive learning environments is **classroom organization**—the way teachers and students are grouped for instruction, the way learning tasks are structured, and other resources used. The following sections focus on these aspects of classroom organization.

Grouping Students by Ability Two common approaches for grouping students on the basis of shared characteristics are between-class ability grouping, often called tracking, and within-class ability grouping. Students who attend schools where **between-class ability** grouping is practiced are assigned to classes on the basis of ability or achievement (usually determined by scores on standardized tests). Another form of between-class ability grouping, especially at the high school level, is based on students' goals after graduation. Many high schools, for example, have a college preparatory track, a vocational track, and a business education track.

Research suggests that, for the most part, between-class ability grouping does not contribute to greater achievement (Good and Brophy 2000). Supporters nevertheless claim that teachers are better able to meet the needs of students in homogeneous groupings. Among the alternatives to between-class ability grouping are heterogeneous (or mixed-ability) grouping, regrouping by subject area, the Joplin Plan (regrouping students for reading instruction by ability across grade levels), and cooperative learning.

Within-class ability grouping often is used for instruction in reading and mathematics within a class, where a teacher instructs students in homogeneous, small groups. Within-class grouping is used widely in elementary classrooms. Perhaps you can recall learning to read in a small group with a name such as the Eagles, the Redbirds, or the Mustangs. Like tracking, within-class ability grouping can heighten preexisting differences in achievement between groups of students, especially if teachers give high-achieving groups more attention. Also, once students are grouped, they tend not to be regrouped, even when differences in achievement are reduced.

At best, evidence to support student groupings is mixed. Whether students are grouped on the basis of ability, curricular interests, or disabling condition, there is a danger that some group labels can evoke negative expectations, causing teachers to "underteach" certain students, and their peers to isolate or reject them. The most serious consequence, of course, is that students so labeled are taught to feel inadequate, inferior, and limited in their options for growth.

Grouping Students for Cooperative Learning Cooperative learning is an approach to teaching in which students work in small groups, or teams, sharing the work and helping one another complete assignments. Student-Team-Learning, for example, is a cooperative approach teachers use to increase the basic skills achievement of at-risk students. In cooperative learning arrangements, students are motivated to learn in small groups through rewards that are made available to the group as a whole and to individual members of the group. Cooperative learning includes the following key elements:

Nel Noddings
Leader in the Challenge to Care

"Keep reflecting on everything you do. . . ."

Nel Noddings, author of over 100 articles and chapters, a philosophy textbook, and a number of books, including the popular and influential works, *Caring* (1984) and *The Challenge to Care in Schools* (1992), is also the mother of ten children, half of whom are adopted. When Noddings suggests that teachers view education as "parents who are engaged in the task of raising a huge heterogeneous family" (1992, 177), she brings her heart and personal experience to the metaphor.

Noddings, a Stanford University professor, leads a movement to emphasize care in schools. She taught mathematics at the secondary level in New Jersey for many years and then earned a doctorate in philosophy at Stanford University. There she remained, teaching courses in philosophy and education, serving as dean, and writing articles on theories of knowledge.

It was through an effort to combine the twin treasures in her life, her family and her superb analytical training, that Noddings developed the concept of caring. When she introduced the idea, the feedback she received was enthusiastic; the timing of her work was well matched with a growing sense of alarm in the United States over the increase of violence and the erosion of character and moral behavior. Schools unwittingly or unwillingly have contributed to the problem. As Noddings observes, "Secondary schools—where violence, apathy, and alienation are most evident—do little to develop the capacity to care. Today, even elementary teachers complain that the pressure to produce high test scores inhibits the work they regard as central to their mission: the development of caring and competent people" (1995, 679).

Noddings contends that educational efforts should promote more than adequate academic achievement. "We will not achieve even that meager success unless our children believe that they themselves are cared for and learn to care for others" (1995, 675–76). Noddings' perception of caring is not that of soft sentimentality, but rather the quality of care that involves deep commitment. "When we care, we want to do our very best for the objects of our care" (1995, 676). She suggests organizing the curriculum around themes of care: caring for self, for intimate others, for strangers and global others, for the natural world and its nonhuman creatures, for the human-made world, and for ideas (1992). She encourages teachers to collaborate in developing curricula according to these broad themes or to emphasize these common themes in their separate curricula. She also recommends that teachers introduce themes of care in response to events that occur in the school or neighborhood. When faced with a tragedy, schools too often rely on outside experts, "when what children really need is the continuing compassion and presence of adults who represent constancy and care in their lives" (1995, 678).

Noddings' advice to teachers is "to keep reflecting on everything you do to see whether, in fact, what you do does promote the growth of loving, lovable, competent, and caring people. When you examine everything you do—how you grade, the rules you make—from this perspective, you will change the way you operate." She agrees with John Dewey's warning: "What the best and wisest parent wants for his own child, that must the community want for all its children. Any other ideal for our schools is narrow and unlovely; acted upon, it destroys our democracy" (Dewey 1902, 3).

- Small groups (four to six students) work together on learning activities.
- Assignments require that students help one another while working on a group project.
- In competitive arrangements, groups may compete against one another.
- Group members contribute to group goals according to their talents, interests, and abilities.

In addition, cooperative learning is an instructional method that can strengthen students' interpersonal skills. When students from different racial, ethnic, and cultural backgrounds and mainstreamed special-needs students all contribute to a common group goal, friendships increase and group members tend to view one another as more equal in status and worth. The contribution that cooperative learning can make to the culture of the classroom is supported by research that indicates that, under cooperative learning arrangements, "African American, Mexican American, and White students develop more positive racial attitudes and choose more friends from outside racial groups" (Banks 1999, 47). In addition, cooperative learning has "a positive effect on the academic achievement of students of color" (Banks 1999, 48).

Cooperative learning also enables students to learn a variety of roles and responsibilities, as the following comments by a fifth-grade science teacher indicate:

> I have the class divided into groups of five students and each group works as a team. The job duties are as follows: principal investigator (PI), materials manager (MM), reader, recorder, and reporter. The PI is the leader of the group and helps mediate when problems occur. The PI is the only student who can come to me with questions during the actual procedure. This rule enables me to monitor the groups and also teaches the group to work independently.
>
> Students change job duties within their group [for] each activity and every six weeks students change groups. This plan gives each student the experience of working with different classmates as well as learning the responsibility of group participation through performing the different job duties.

Delivering Instruction The delivery of instruction is a key element in creating positive learning environments. What the teacher does and what students do have powerful influences on learning and on the quality of classroom life. A common activity format in elementary schools consists of students doing seatwork on their own or listening to their teachers and participating in whole-class recitations. In addition, students participate in reading groups, games, and discussions; take tests; check work; view films; give reports; help clean up the classroom; and go on field trips.

A teacher must answer the question "What activity will enable me to accomplish my instructional goals?" Teachers also must realize that learning activities should meet *students'* goals; that is, the activities must be meaningful and authentic for students. **Authentic learning tasks** enable students to see the connections between classroom learning and the world beyond the classroom—both now and in the future. To understand how authentic learning tasks can motivate students to learn, reflect upon your own school expe-

Figure 9.3

Level of authentic student performance for students who experience low, average, and high authentic pedagogy in restructuring elementary, middle, and high schools.
Source: Fred M. Newmann and Gary G. Wehlage, *Successful School Restructuring: A Report to the Public and Educators by the Center on Organization and Restructuring of Schools.* University of Wisonsin-Madison: Center on Organization and Restructuring of Schools, 1995, pp. 21, 55.

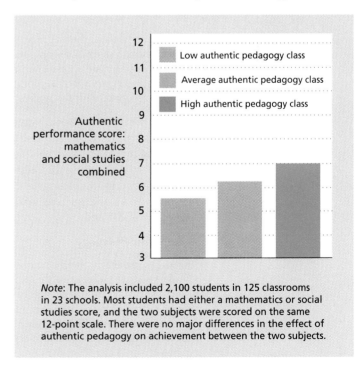

Note: The analysis included 2,100 students in 125 classrooms in 23 schools. Most students had either a mathematics or social studies score, and the two subjects were scored on the same 12-point scale. There were no major differences in the effect of authentic pedagogy on achievement between the two subjects.

riences. Do you recall memorizing facts only because they would appear on a test? Did you ever wonder why a teacher asked you to complete a learning task? Did you ever feel that a teacher asked you to do "busywork"? What kinds of learning tasks motivated you the most?

Herbert A. Thelen (1981, 86) contends that authenticity is "the first criterion all educational activity must meet." According to Thelen, an activity is authentic for a person if he or she "feels emotionally 'involved' and mentally stimulated . . . is aware of choices and enjoys the challenge of making decisions," and feels he or she "has something to bring to the activity and that its outcome will be important" (Thelen 1981, 86). A comprehensive nationwide study of successfully restructured schools reported that "authentic pedagogy" helps students to (1) "construct knowledge" through the use of higher-order thinking, (2) acquire "deep knowledge" (relatively complex understandings of subject matter), (3) engage in "substantive conversations" with teachers and peers, and (4) make connections between substantive knowledge and the world beyond the classroom (Newmann and Wehlage 1995; Newmann et al. 1996). In addition, as Figure 9.3 (see p. 343) shows, high authentic pedagogy classes boost achievement for students at all grade levels. The following Professional Reflection illustrates the differences between high and low authentic pedagogy.

 **How do low and high authentic pedagogy differ?**

Read the following descriptions of low and high authentic pedagogy classes in social studies. What differences do you notice between the two classes? What do you think Mrs. Allen's students thought about the learning tasks they were asked to complete? Ms. Rodriguez's students? When you were a fifth- or sixth-grade student, which teacher would you have preferred? Why?

Low Authentic Pedagogy

The task for a class of fifth graders required them to copy a set of questions about famous explorers from a worksheet and to add the correct short-answer responses in the appropriate spots. The class spent thirty minutes on this exercise, which was part of a larger unit on exploration and which the teacher, Mrs. Allen, described as very consistent with the typical assessment.

During the four times that [researchers] observed Allen's hour-long classes, students read aloud from the textbook, a routine occasionally punctuated with Allen's asking them factual recall questions. During one class, students copied a chart from the board organizing the facts from the reading into categories. After finding more facts to fill up the chart, the students then completed a worksheet crossword puzzle built from the vocabulary words of the lesson (Marks, Newmann, and Gamoran 1996, 59–60).

High Authentic Pedagogy

As an assessment of their learning, Ms. Rodriguez had her class of fifth and sixth graders research and write a paper on ecology, an assignment that occupied forty hours of class time during the twelve-week grading period. Each student produced several drafts of the paper and met individually with the teacher several times to discuss the drafts. Before they began the project, students received eleven pages of written directions on how to research, organize, and write the paper, including a step-by-step checklist for completing the assignment, a sample outline, and sample bibliography entries. The paper counted for 75 percent of the student's grade for the twelve-week period (Marks, Newmann, and Gamoran, 1996, 60).

Structuring the Use of Time How teachers use time affects student learning. **Allocated time** is the time teachers allocate for instruction in various areas of the curriculum. Teachers vary widely in their instructional use of time. Educational researchers Tom Good and Jere Brophy report, for example, that "some students [may receive] as much as four times more instructional time in a given subject than other students in the same grade" (Good and Brophy 1997, 29–30).

Researchers have shown that **time on task**—the amount of time students are actively engaged in learning activities—is directly related to learning. As anyone who has ever daydreamed while appearing to pay attention can confirm, time on task is difficult to measure. In response to this difficulty, researchers have introduced the concept of **academic learning time**—the amount of time a student spends working on academic tasks with a high level of success (80 percent or higher) Not surprisingly, learning time, like allocated time, varies greatly from classroom to classroom. For example, Figure 9.4 shows how the more than 1,000 hours most states mandate for instruction at the elementary level actually result in about 300 hours during which students are truly engaged in meaningful, appropriate tasks.

An additional concept that is proving useful in understanding teachers' use of time in the classroom is known as **opportunity to learn** (OTL). OTL is based on the premise that teachers should use time to provide all students with challenging content

Figure 9.4

How much time is there, anyway?
Source: From Carol Simon Weinstein and Andrew J. Migano, Jr. *Elementary Classroom Management: Lessons from Research and Practice,* 2nd ed., p. 142. Copyright © 1997 by McGraw-Hill Companies. Adapted with permission of The McGraw-Hill Companies.

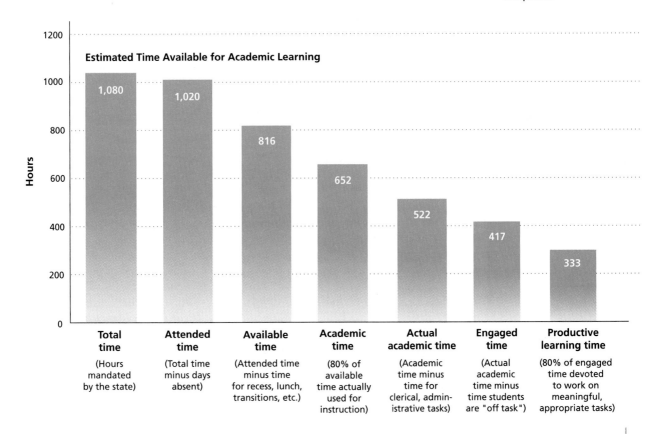

How Can You Create a Positive Learning Environment? **345**

through appropriate instruction. Many states are developing OTL standards for how teachers should use time in the classroom.

To increase the time available for active learning, many high schools have implemented block scheduling arrangements. **Block scheduling** uses longer blocks of time each class period, with fewer periods each day. Longer blocks of time allow more in-depth coverage of subject matter and lead to deeper understanding and higher-level applications. Block scheduling also gives teachers more time to present complex concepts and students more time to practice applying those concepts to authentic problems.

What Are the Keys to Successful Classroom Management?

For most new teachers, classroom management is a primary concern. How can you prevent discipline problems from arising and keep students productively engaged in learning activities? While effective **classroom management** cannot be reduced to a cookbook recipe, there are definite steps you can take to create an effective learning environment in your classroom. First, it is important to understand that classroom management refers to how teachers structure their learning environments to prevent, or minimize, behavior problems; *discipline* refers to the methods teachers use *after* students misbehave. *Classroom management* is prevention-oriented, while *discipline* is control-oriented. Second, it is important to recognize that "the key to good management is use of techniques that elicit student cooperation and involvement in activities and thus *prevent* problems from emerging in the first place" (Good and Brophy 1997, 129). In addition, sound classroom management techniques are based on the guidelines for creating an effective learning environment presented previously in this chapter—in other words, (1) creating a caring classroom, (2) organizing the physical classroom environment, (3) grouping students for instruction, (4) providing authentic learning tasks, and (5) structuring the use of time to maximize students' learning. Positive leadership and preventive planning thus are central to effective classroom management.

The Democratic Classroom

Research findings suggest that teachers who allow students to participate in making decisions about the physical classroom environment, classroom rules and procedures, modifications to the curriculum, and options for learning activities also have fewer discipline problems. Students in **democratic classrooms** have both more power and more responsibility than students in conventional classrooms. On the premise that if students are to live in a democracy, they must learn to manage freedom responsibly, teachers model democracy by giving their students some choices and some control over classroom activities. William Glasser, well-known psychiatrist and author of *Quality School* (1998a), *The Quality School Teacher* (1998b), *Choice Theory* (1998c), and (with Karen Dotson) *Choice Theory in the Classroom* (1998), recommends that teachers develop "quality" classrooms based on democratic principles. According to Glasser, many teachers struggle with classroom management because their actions are guided by stimulus-response theory; that is, they try to coerce students through rewards or punishment, or what many teachers term "logical consequences." Instead, Glasser maintains that teachers should establish "quality' environments in the classroom by following *choice theory*—that is, recognizing that human beings make choices that enable them to create "quality worlds" that satisfy four needs: the need to belong, the need for power, the need for freedom, and the need for fun. From a **choice theory** perspective, misbehavior in the classroom arises when students' learning experiences do not enable them to create quality worlds for themselves. Therefore, teachers "must give up bossing and turn to 'leading'" (Glasser 1997, 600). We follow leaders, Glasser says, because we believe they are concerned about our welfare. To persuade students to do quality schoolwork, teachers must establish warm, noncoercive relationships with students; teach students meaningful skills rather than ask them to memorize information; enable them to experience satisfaction and excitement by working in small teams; and move from teacher evaluation to student self-evaluation.

Preventive Planning

In what other ways can teachers prevent discipline problems from occurring? The key to prevention is excellent planning and an understanding of life in classrooms. In addition, teachers who have mastered the essential teaching skills have fewer discipline problems because students recognize that such teachers are prepared, well organized, and have a sense of purpose. They are confident of their ability to teach all students, and their task-oriented manner tends to discourage misbehavior.

In a seminal study of how teachers prevent discipline problems, Jacob Kounin looked at two sets of teachers: those who managed their classrooms smoothly and productively with few disruptions and those who seemed to be plagued with discipline problems and chaotic working conditions. He found that the teachers who managed their classrooms successfully had certain teaching behaviors in common: (1) they displayed the proverbial eyes-in-the-back-of-the-head, a quality of alertness Kounin referred to as *withitness*, (2) they used individual students and incidences as models to communicate to the rest of the class their expectations for student conduct—Kounin's *ripple effect*, (3) they supervised several situations at once effectively, and (4) they were adept at handling transitions smoothly (Kounin 1970). In addition to the principles of effective classroom management that emerge from Kounin's study, two key elements of preventive planning are establishing rules and procedures and organizing and planning for instruction.

Establishing Rules and Procedures   Educational researchers have found that effective classroom managers have carefully planned rules and procedures, which they teach early in the year using clear explanations, examples, and practice (Evertson et al. 1997; Good and Brophy 1997). Your classroom rules should be clear, concise, reasonable, and few in number. For example, five general rules for elementary-age students might include: (1) be polite and helpful; (2) respect other people's property; (3) listen quietly while others are speaking; (4) do not hit, shove, or hurt others; and (5) obey all school rules. Rules for the secondary level might stipulate the following: (1) bring all needed materials to class; (2) be in your seat and ready to work when the bell rings; (3) respect and be polite to everyone; (4) respect other people's property; (5) listen and stay seated while someone else is speaking; and (6) obey all school rules (Evertson et al. 1997).

It is important to enforce classroom rules consistently and fairly. "Consistency is a key reason why some rules are effective while others are not. Rules that are not enforced or that are not applied evenly and consistently over time result in a loss of prestige and respect for the person who has created the rules and has the responsibility for carrying them out" (Borich 1996, 364).

Procedures—the routines your students will follow as they participate in learning activities—also are essential for smooth classroom functioning and minimizing opportunities for misbehavior. How will homework be collected? How will supplies be distributed? How will housekeeping chores be completed? How will attendance be taken? How do students obtain permission to leave the classroom? Part of developing classroom rules and procedures is to decide what to do when students do not follow them. Students must be made aware of the consequences for failing to follow rules or procedures. For example, consequences for rule infractions can range from an expression of teacher disapproval to penalties such as loss of privileges, detention after school, disciplinary conference with a parent or guardian, or temporary separation from the group.

Organizing and Planning for Instruction The ability to organize instructional time, materials, and activities so that classes run smoothly are skills that will enable you to keep your students engaged in learning, thereby reducing the need for discipline. Time spent planning authentic learning activities that are appropriate to students' needs, interests, and abilities will enable you to enjoy the professional satisfaction that comes from having a well-managed classroom.

In the following, a remedial algebra teacher in an urban school tells how organization and planning helped her effectively teach a class of twenty-seven students, grades 9 through 12, who enrolled in the class "for a myriad of reasons, [including] absenteeism, learning disabilities, failure in college prep classes, unwillingness to do required work in college prep classes, personal problems, nonconformity, and a need for credits":

> I am consistently rewarded by the creative thinking and quickness of these students when they are asked to do something other than listen to my thinking, take notes, and copy examples from the board. I have learned that planning meaningful activities, choosing engaging tasks, organizing small groups and pair problem-solving experiences, valuing thinking, and carefully assessing understanding promote an improved classroom atmosphere where learning is the objective for everyone (Schifter 1996, 75–76).

Effective Responses to Student Behavior

When student misbehavior does occur, effective teachers draw from a repertoire of problem-solving strategies. These strategies are based on their experience and common sense, their knowledge of students and the teaching-learning process, and their knowledge of human psychology. There are many structured approaches to classroom management; some are based on psychological theories of human motivation and behavior, while others reflect various philosophical views regarding the purposes of education. None of these approaches, however, is appropriate for all situations or for all teachers or for all students, and the usefulness of a given method depends, in part, on the teacher's individual personality and leadership style and ability to analyze the complex dynamics of classroom life. In addition, what works should not be the only criterion for evaluating structured or "packaged" approaches to discipline; what they teach students about their self-worth, acting responsibly, and solving problems is also important (Curwin and Mendler 1988, 1989).

Severity of Misbehavior Your response to student misbehavior will depend, in part, on whether an infraction is mild, moderate, or severe and whether it is occurring for the first time or is part of a pattern of chronic misbehaviors. For example, a student who throws a wad of paper at another student might receive a warning for the first infraction, while another student who repeatedly throws objects at other students might receive an after-school detention. Definitions of the severity of misbehavior vary from

Table 9.2

Mild, moderate, and severe misbehaviors and some alternative responses

Misbehaviors	Alternative Responses
Mild misbehaviors	**Mild responses**
Minor defacing of school property or property of others	Warning
Acting out (horseplaying or scuffling)	Feedback to student
Talking back	Time out
Talking without raising hand	Change of seat assignment
Getting out of seat	Withdrawal of privileges
Disrupting others	After-school detention
Sleeping in class	Telephone/note to parents
Tardiness	
Throwing objects	
Exhibiting inappropriate familiarity (kissing, hugging)	
Gambling	
Eating in class	
Moderate misbehaviors	**Moderate responses**
Unauthorized leaving of class	Detention
Abusive conduct toward others	Behavior contract
Noncompliant	Withdrawal of privileges
Smoking or using tobacco in class	Telephone/note to parents
Cutting class	Parent conference
Cheating, plagiarizing, or lying	In-school suspension
Using profanity, vulgar language, or obscene gestures	Restitution of damages
Fighting	Alternative school service (e.g., clean up, tutoring)
Severe misbehaviors	**Severe responses**
Defacing or damaging school property or property of others	Detention
Theft, possession, or sale of another's property	Telephone/note to parents
Truancy	Parent conference
Being under the influence of alcohol or narcotics	In-school suspension
Selling, giving, or delivering to another person alcohol, narcotics, or weapons	Removal from school or alternative school placement
Teacher assault or verbal abuse	
Incorrigible conduct, noncompliance	

Source: Gary Bovich, *Effective Teaching Methods,* 3rd ed. Englewood Cliffs, NJ: Merrill, 1996, p. 527. © 1996. Reprinted by permission of Prentice-Hall, Inc., Upper Saddle River, NJ.

school to school and from state to state. Table 9.2 presents one classification of examples of mild, moderate, and severe misbehaviors and several alternative responses.

Constructive Assertiveness The effectiveness of your responses to students' misbehavior will depend, in part, on your ability to use "constructive assertiveness" (Evertson et al. 1997). Constructive assertiveness "lies on a continuum of social response between aggressive, overbearing pushiness and timid, ineffectual, or submissive responses that allow some students to trample on the teacher's and other students' rights. Assertiveness skills allow you to communicate to students that you are serious about teaching and about maintaining a classroom in which everyone's rights are respected" (Evertson et al, 1997 139). Communication based on constructive assertiveness is neither hostile, sarcastic, defensive, nor vindictive; it is clear, firm, and concise.

Evertson and colleagues (1997) suggest that constructive assertiveness has three basic elements:

- A clear statement of the problem or concern
- Body language that is unambiguous (e.g., eye contact with student, erect posture, facial expressions that match the content and tone of corrective statements)
- Firm, unwavering insistence on appropriate behavior

Lee Cantor developed an approach to discipline based on teacher assertiveness. The approach calls on teachers to establish firm, clear guidelines for student behavior and to follow through with consequences for misbehavior. Cantor (1989, 58) comments on how he arrived at the ideas behind assertive discipline: "I found that, above all, the master teachers were assertive; that is, they *taught* students how to behave. They established clear rules for the classroom, they communicated those rules to the students, and they taught students how to follow them." **Assertive discipline** requires teachers to do the following:

1. Make clear that they will not tolerate anyone preventing them from teaching, stopping learning, or doing anything else that is not in the best interest of the class, the individual, or the teacher.
2. Instruct students clearly and in specific terms about what behaviors are desired and what behaviors are not tolerated.
3. Plan positive and negative consequences for predetermined acceptable or unacceptable behaviors.
4. Plan positive reinforcement for compliance. Reinforcement includes verbal acknowledgment, notes, free time for talking, and, of course, tokens that can be exchanged for appropriate rewards.
5. Plan a sequence of steps to punish noncompliance. These range from writing a youngster's name on the board to sending the student to the principal's office (MacNaughton and Johns 1991, 53).

Teacher Problem Solving   When a teacher's efforts to get a student to stop misbehaving are unsuccessful, a problem-solving conference with the student is warranted. A problem-solving conference may give the teacher additional understanding of the situation, thus paving the way for a solution. A conference also helps teacher and student understand the other's perceptions better and begin to build a more positive relationship.

The goal of a problem-solving conference is for the student to accept responsibility for his or her behavior and make a commitment to change it. While there is no "right way" to conduct a problem-solving conference, Glasser's choice theory lends itself to a conferencing procedure that is flexible and appropriate for most situations. Students will usually make good choices (i.e., behave in an acceptable manner) if they experience success and know that teachers care about them. The following steps are designed to help misbehaving students see that the choices they make may not lead to the results they want.

1. Have the misbehaving student evaluate and take responsibility for his or her behavior. Often, a good first step is for the teacher to ask "What are you doing?" and then "Is it helping you?"

2. Have the student make a plan for a more acceptable way of behaving. If necessary, the student and the teacher brainstorm solutions. Agreement is reached on how the student will behave in the future and the consequences for failure to follow through.
3. Require the student to make a commitment to follow the plan.
4. Don't accept excuses for failure to follow the plan.
5. Don't use punishment or react to a misbehaving student in a punitive manner. Instead, point out to the student that there are logical consequences for failure to follow the plan.
6. Don't give up on the student. If necessary, remind the student of his or her commitment to desirable behavior. Periodically ask "How are things going?"

Developing Your Own Approach to Classroom Management   No approach to classroom management is effective with all students at all times. How you respond to misbehavior in your classroom will depend on your personality, value system, and beliefs about children and will range along a continuum from the "minimum power" of giving students nonverbal cues to the "maximum power" of physical intervention.

Classroom management expert Charles Wolfgang points out that teachers usually present one of three "faces" (or attitudes) to students who misbehave:

1. The *relationship-listening* "face" involves the use of minimum power. This reflects a view that the student has the capabilities to change his or her own behavior, and that if the student is misbehaving, it is because of inner emotional turmoil, flooded behavior, or feelings of inner inadequacy.
2. The *confronting-contracting* "face" is one of "I am the adult. I know misbehavior when I see it and will confront the student to stop this behavior. I will grant the student the power to decide how he or she will change, and encourage and contract with the student to live up a mutual agreement for behavioral change."
3. The *rules and consequences* "face" is one that communicates an attitude of "This is the rule and behavior that I want and I will set out assertively to get this action" (Wolfgang 1999, 5–6).

See the Appendix "Beliefs about Discipline Inventory" on this book's website, so you can determine which "face of discipline" best fits your personality.

In your journey toward becoming a professional teacher, you will develop a repertoire of strategies for classroom management; then, when you encounter a discipline problem in the classroom, you can analyze the situation and respond with an effective strategy. The ability to do so will give you confidence, like the following beginning teacher:

> I went into the classroom with some confidence and left with lots of confidence. I felt good about what was going on. I established a comfortable rapport with the kids and was more relaxed. Each week I grew more confident. When you first go in you are not sure how you'll do. When you know you are doing OK, your confidence improves.

What Teaching Methods Do Effective Teachers Use?

As we pointed out in our discussion of educational philosophy in Chapter 3, beliefs about teaching and learning, students, knowledge, and what is worth knowing influence the instructional methods a teacher uses. In addition, instruction is influenced by variables such as the teacher's style, learners' characteristics, the culture of the school and surrounding community, and the resources available. All of these components contribute to the "model" of teaching the teacher uses in the classroom. A model of teaching provides the teacher with rules of thumb to follow to create a particular kind of learning environment, or, as Bruce Joyce, Marsha Weil, and Emily Calhoun point out in *Models of Teaching* (2000, 13), a model of teaching is "a description of a learning environment." Table 9.3 presents brief descriptions of four widely used models of teaching.

Effective teachers use a repertoire of teaching models and assessment strategies, depending upon their situations and the goals and objectives they wish to attain. Your teaching strategies in the classroom will most likely be eclectic, that is, a combination

Table 9.3

Four instructional models

	Goals and Rationale	Methods
Cooperative Learning	Students can be motivated to learn by working cooperatively in small groups if rewards are made available to the group as a whole and to individual members of the group.	■ Small groups (four to six students) work together on learning activities. ■ Assignments require that students help one another while working on a group project. ■ In competitive arrangements, groups may compete against one another. ■ Group members contribute to group goals according to their talents, interests, and abilities.
Theory into Practice	Teachers make decisions in three primary areas: content to be taught, how students will learn, and the behaviors the teacher will use in the classroom. The effectiveness of teaching is related to the quality of decisions the teacher makes in these areas.	The teacher follows seven steps in the classroom: 1. Orients students to material to be learned 2. Tells students what they will learn and why it is important 3. Presents new material that consists of knowledge, skills or processes students are to learn 4. Models what students are expected to do 5. Checks for student understanding 6. Gives students opportunity for practice under the teacher's guidance 7. Makes assignments that give students opportunity to practice what they have learned on their own
Behavior Modification	Teachers can shape student learning by using various forms of enforcement. Human behavior is learned, and behaviors that are positively reinforced (rewarded) tend to increase and those that are not reinforced tend to decrease.	■ Teacher begins by presenting stimulus in the form of new material. ■ The behavior of students is observed by the teacher. ■ Appropriate behaviors are reinforced by the teacher as quickly as possible.
Nondirective Teaching	Learning can be facilitated if teachers focus on personal development of students and create opportunities for students to increase their self-understanding and self-concepts. The key to effective teaching is the teacher's ability to understand students and to involve them in a teaching–learning partnership.	■ Teacher acts as a facilitator of learning. ■ Teacher creates learning environments that support personal growth and development. ■ Teacher acts in the role of a counselor who helps students to understand themselves, clarify their goals, and accept responsibility for their behavior.

of several models and assessment techniques. Also, as you gain classroom experience and acquire new skills and understanding, your personal model of teaching will evolve, enabling you to respond appropriately to a wider range of teaching situations.

Methods Based on Learning New Behaviors

Many teachers use instructional methods that have emerged from our greater understanding of how people acquire or change their behaviors. **Direct instruction,** for example, is a systematic instructional method that focuses on the transmission of knowledge and skills from the teacher (and the curriculum) to the student. Direct instruction is organized on the basis of observable learning behaviors and the actual products of learning. Generally, direct instruction is most appropriate for step-by-step knowledge acquisition and basic skill development but not appropriate for teaching less structured, higher-order skills such as writing, the analysis of social issues, and problem solving.

Extensive research was conducted in the 1970s and 1980s on the effectiveness of direct instruction (Gagné, 1974, 1977; Good and Grouws, 1979; Rosenshine,1988; Rosenshine and Stevens, 1986). The following eight steps are a synthesis of research on direct instruction and may be used with students ranging in age from elementary to senior high school.

1. Orient students to the lesson by telling them what they will learn.
2. Review previously learned skills and concepts related to the new material.
3. Present new material, using examples and demonstrations.
4. Assess students' understanding by asking questions; correct misunderstandings.
5. Allow students to practice new skills or apply new information.
6. Provide feedback and corrections as students practice.
7. Include newly learned material in homework.
8. Review material periodically.

A direct instruction method called **mastery learning** is based on two assumptions about learning: (1) virtually all students can learn material if given enough time and taught appropriately and (2) students learn best when they participate in a structured, systematic program of learning that enables them to progress in small, sequenced steps (Carroll 1963; Bloom 1981):

1. Set objectives and standards for mastery.
2. Teach content directly to students.
3. Provide corrective feedback to students on their learning.
4. Provide additional time and help in correcting errors.
5. Follow a cycle of teaching, testing, reteaching, and retesting.

In mastery learning, students take diagnostic tests and then are guided to do corrective exercises or activities to improve their learning. These may take the form of programmed instruction, workbooks, computer drill and practice, or educational games. After the corrective lessons, students are given another test and are more likely to achieve mastery.

Methods Based on Child Development

As you learned in Chapter 8, children move through stages of cognitive, psychosocial, and moral development. Effective instruction includes methods that are developmentally appropriate, meet students' diverse learning needs, and recognize the importance of learning that occurs in social contexts. For example, one way that students reach higher levels of development is to observe and then imitate their parents, teachers, and peers, who act as models. As Woolfolk (1998, 229) points out:

> Modeling has long been used, of course, to teach dance, sports, and crafts, as well as skills in subjects such as home economics, chemistry, and shop. Modeling can also be applied deliberately in the classroom to teach mental skills and to broaden horizons—to teach new ways of thinking. Teachers serve as models for a vast range of behaviors, from pronouncing vocabulary words, to reacting to the seizure of an epileptic student, to being enthusiastic about learning.

Effective teachers also use **modeling** by "thinking out loud" and following three basic steps of "mental modeling" (Duffy and Roehler 1989):

1. Showing students the reasoning involved
2. Making students conscious of the reasoning involved
3. Focusing students on applying the reasoning

In this way, teachers can help students become aware of their learning processes and enhance their ability to learn.

Since the mid-1980s, several educational researchers have examined how learners *construct* understanding of new material. "Constructivist views of learning, therefore, focus on how learners make sense of new information—how they construct meaning based on what they already know" (Parkay and Hass 2000, 168). Teachers with this constructivist view of learning focus on students' thinking about the material being learned and, through carefully orchestrated cues, prompts, and questions, help students arrive at a deeper understanding of the material. The common elements of **constructivist teaching** include the following:

- The teacher elicits students' prior knowledge of the material and uses this as the starting point for instruction.
- The teacher not only presents material to students, but he or she also responds to students' efforts to learn the material. While teaching, the teacher must *learn about students' learning.*
- Students not only absorb information, but they also actively use that information to construct meaning.
- The teacher creates a social milieu within the classroom, a community of learners, that allows students to reflect and talk with one another as they construct meaning and solve problems.

Constructivist teachers provide students with support, or "scaffolding," as they learn new material. By observing the child and listening carefully to what he or she says, the teacher provides **scaffolding** in the form of clues, encouragement, suggestions, or other assistance to guide students' learning efforts. The teacher varies the amount of support given on the basis of the student's understanding—if the student understands little, the teacher gives more support; conversely, the teacher gives progressively less support as the student's understanding becomes more evident. Overall, the teacher provides just enough scaffolding to enable the student to "discover" the material on his or her own.

The concept of scaffolding is based on the work of L. S. Vygotsky, a well-known Soviet psychologist. Vygotsky (1978, 1980) coined the term *zone of proximal development* to refer to the point at which students need assistance in order to continue learning. The effective teacher is sensitive to the student's zone of development and ensures

Table 9.4

Using information processing ideas in the classroom

■ Make sure you have the students' attention. For example, begin a lesson by asking a question that stimulates interest in the topic.

■ Help students separate essential from nonessential details and focus on the most important information as it relates to instructional objectives.

■ Help students make connections between new information and what they already know.

■ Provide for repetition and review of information and the practice of skills.

■ Present material in a clear, organized, concrete way. For example, give students a brief outline to follow and summarize lessons.

■ Focus on meaning, not memorization.

Source: Adapted from Anita E. Woolfolk, *Educational Psychology,* 7th ed. Boston: Allyn and Bacon, 1998, p. 265–66.)

that instruction neither exceeds the student's current level of understanding nor underestimates the student's ability.

Methods Based on the Thinking Process

Some instructional methods are derived from the mental processes involved in learning, thinking, remembering, problem solving, and creativity. **Information processing,** for example, is a branch of cognitive science concerned with how people use their long- and short-term memory to access information and solve problems. The computer is often used as an analogy for information-processing views of learning:

> Like the computer, the human mind takes in information, performs operations on it to change its form and content, stores the information, retrieves it when needed, and generates responses to it. Thus, processing involves gathering and representing information, or *encoding;* holding information, or *storage;* and getting at the information when needed, or *retrieval.* The whole system is guided by *control processes* that determine how and when information will flow through the system (Woolfolk 1998, 249-50).

Although several systematic approaches to instruction are based on information processing—teaching students how to memorize, think inductively or deductively, acquire concepts, or use the scientific method, for example—they all focus on how people acquire and use information. Table 9.4 presents general teaching guidelines based on ideas from information processing.

In **inquiry learning** and **discovery learning** students are given opportunities to inquire into subjects so that they "discover" knowledge for themselves. When teachers ask students to go beyond information in a text to make inferences, draw conclusions, or form generalizations; and when teachers do not answer students' questions, preferring instead to have students develop their own answers, they are using methods based on inquiry and discovery learning. These methods are best suited for teaching concepts, relationships, and theoretical abstractions, and for having students formulate and test hypotheses. The following example shows how inquiry and discovery learning in a first-grade classroom fostered a high level of student involvement and thinking.

The children are gathered around a table on which a candle and jar have been placed. The teacher, Jackie Wiseman, lights the candle and, after it has burned brightly for a minute or two, covers it carefully with the jar. The candle grows dim, flickers, and goes out. Then she produces another candle and a larger jar, and the exercise is repeated. The candle goes out, but more slowly. Jackie produces two more candles and jars of different sizes, and the children light the candles, place the jars over them, and the flames slowly go out. "Now we're going to develop some ideas about what has just happened," she says. "I want you to ask me questions about those candles and jars and what you just observed" (Joyce, Weil, and Calhoun 2000, 3).

Methods Based on Peer-Mediated Instruction

Student peer groups can be a deterrent to academic performance (Steinberg et al. 1996), but they can also motivate students to excel. Because school learning occurs in a social setting, **peer-mediated instruction** provides teachers with options for increasing students' learning. Cooperative learning, described earlier in this chapter, is an example of peer-mediated instruction. Another example is **group investigation,** in which the teacher's role is to create an environment that allows students to determine what they will study and how. Students are presented with a situation to which they "react and discover basic conflicts among their attitudes, ideas, and modes of perception. On the basis of this information, they identify the problem to be investigated, analyze the roles required to solve it, organize themselves to take these roles, act, report, and evaluate these results" (Thelen 1960, 82).

The teacher's role in group investigation is multifaceted; he or she is an organizer, guide, resource person, counselor, and evaluator. The method is very effective in increasing student achievement (Sharan and Sharan 1989/90, 17–21), positive attitudes toward learning, and the cohesiveness of the classroom group. The model also allows students to inquire into problems that interest them and enables each student to make a meaningful, authentic contribution to the group's effort based on his or her experiences, interests, knowledge, and skills.

Other common forms of peer-mediated instruction include peer tutoring and cross-age tutoring. In **peer-tutoring** arrangements, students are tutored by other pupils in the same class or the same grade. **Cross-age tutoring** involves, for example, sixth-grade students tutoring second-grade students in reading. Research clearly shows that with proper orientation and training, cross-age tutoring can greatly benefit both "teacher" and learner (Henriques 1997; Schneider and Barone 1997; Utay and Utay 1997; Zukowski 1997). Pilot programs pairing students at risk of dropping out of school with younger children and with special-needs students have proved especially successful.

What Are Some Characteristics of Effective Teaching?

The *outcomes* of effective teaching are relatively easy to enumerate: (1) students acquire an understanding of the subject at hand; (2) they can apply what they have learned to new situations; and (3) they have a desire to continue learning. However, if we wish to identify the *characteristics* of effective teaching, we find ourselves confronted with a more difficult task.

What do effective teachers do when they are teaching? How do they communicate with students? How do they manage classroom activities? What models of teach-

Domain 1: Planning and Preparation	Domain 3: Instruction
■ Demonstrating knowledge of content and pedagogy	■ Communicating clearly and accurately
■ Demonstrating knowledge of students	■ Using questioning and discussion techniques
■ Selecting instructional goals	■ Engaging students in learning
■ Demonstrating knowledge of resources	■ Providing feedback to students
■ Designing coherent instruction	■ Demonstrating flexibility and responsiveness
■ Assessing student learning	

Domain 2: The Classroom Environment	Domain 4: Professional Responsibilities
■ Creating an environment of respect and rapport	■ Reflecting on teaching
■ Establishing a culture for learning	■ Maintaining accurate records
■ Managing classroom procedures	■ Communicating with families
■ Managing student behavior	■ Contributing to the school and district
■ Organizing physical space	■ Growing and developing professionally
	■ Showing professionalism

Figure 9.5

The Praxis framework for teaching
Source: Charlotte Danielson, *Enhancing Professional Practice: A Framework for Teaching.* Alexandria, VA: Association for Supervision and Curriculum Development, 1996.

ing do they use? As the previous discussions of classroom cultures, learning environments, classroom management, and teaching methods suggest, answers to questions such as these are not easy to formulate. However, one broad helpful view of the characteristics that underlie all effective teaching is the "Framework for Teaching," developed as part of the Praxis Series: Professional Assessments for Beginning Teachers. According to the Praxis framework, teachers must be proficient in four domains: planning and preparation, structuring classroom environment, instruction, and professional responsibilities. Teachers must be effective within these domains while taking into account individual, developmental, and cultural differences among students and differences among subjects. Figure 9.5 shows the tasks teachers should be able to perform within the four domains.

Establishing Goals

One characteristic of successful teachers is that they focus on the outcomes—the results or consequences of their teaching. Regardless of the instructional method used, with clear goals to provide guidance, teachers can make good decisions about classroom activities to select or develop.

Goals are general statements of purpose that guide schools and teachers as they develop instructional programs. **Instructional goals** can be derived from the curriculum or content being taught; or, as you saw in Chapter 3, they can be derived from various educational philosophies. Goals range from very broad statements of purpose that apply to a large number of students to those that apply to students in a particular

From this photo, what can you tell about this teacher's proficiency in planning and preparation, structuring classroom environment, instruction, and professional responsibilities?

classroom. In addition, teachers evaluate their teaching by how well students master certain objectives. **Learning objectives** are specific, measurable outcomes of learning that students are to demonstrate. For example, "Students will identify the structural elements of cells and explain their functions" might be a specific objective toward a larger goal of "understanding biological concepts and principles."

Successful teachers also realize that the quality of their teaching depends on what students can *do*, not only on what they *know*. To evaluate their effectiveness in this area, teachers assess students' mastery of performance tasks in which they apply their learning to a new problem. Figure 9.6 illustrates two different approaches to lesson planning that take into account targeted goals, objectives, and performance tasks.

Linking Assessment with Instruction

In assessing students' learning, teachers make judgments about the performance of students and about their own performance as teachers. Successful teachers use **assessment** to evaluate the effectiveness of their teaching because they recognize that how well students learn depends on how well they teach.

To assess students' learning, teachers use measurement and evaluation techniques. **Measurement** is the gathering of quantitative data related to the knowledge and skills students have acquired. Measurement yields scores, rankings, or ratings that teachers can use to compare students. **Evaluation** involves making judgments about or assigning a value to those measurements. **Formative evaluation** occurs when the teacher measures students' learning for instruction. **Summative evaluation** is used by teachers to determine grades at the end of a unit, semester, or year and to decide whether students are ready to proceed to the next phase of their education.

Authentic assessments (sometimes called *alternative assessments*) require students to use higher-level thinking skills to perform, create, or solve real-life problems—not just choose one of several designated responses as on a multiple-choice test. The authentic assessments a teacher might use include evaluating the quality of individual and small-group projects, videotaped demonstrations of skills, or participation in community-based activities. In science, for example, students might design and conduct an experiment; in mathematics, they might explain in writing how they solved a problem. Authentic assessments require students to solve problems or to work on tasks that approximate as much as possible those they will encounter beyond the classroom. **Portfolio assessment** is based on a collection of student work that "tell[s] a story of a learner's growth in proficiency, long-term achievement, and significant accomplishments in a given academic area" (Tombari and Borich 1999, 164). For students, an important part of portfolio assessment is clarifying the criteria used to select work to be included in the portfolio. **Performance assessment** is used to determine what students can do as well as what they know. In some cases, the teacher observes and then evaluates an actual performance or application of a skill; in others, the teacher evaluates a product created by the student.

Examples of Effective Teachers

This chapter concludes with comments by several effective teachers in which they describe strategies that help them create communities of learners. As you read the teachers' comments, identify how each has put into practice many of the concepts discussed in this chapter. In addition, reflect on the degree to which that teacher's approach would "fit" your personality and value system.

Laurie Robben, Fourth Grade Teacher, Greenwich, Connecticut[1]   I am extremely proud of the positive rapport that I have with my students. One way that I instill mutual respect is through classroom meetings. Every Friday, I set aside at least fifteen minutes for a class meeting. We all sit together on the floor, including myself, to show that no one's ideas are more important than another's.

Classroom meetings provide a time for students to share their feelings openly about their school experience, and issues can be positive or negative. An important rule is that if someone wants to say something negative about a particular student, the class is not allowed to talk about that conversation outside the confines of our meeting. This is to prevent a student from being badgered.

One example is Alex, a nine-year old who desperately wants peer attention but resorts to behaving like a clown. In a recent meeting, students told him they were not comfortable with his clowning and wished that he would stop. I asked the class to share times when they enjoyed being with Alex, and they encouraged him to practice those behaviors more frequently. At the end of the meeting, Alex asked his peers, "Could you help me be better and tell me when I'm bugging you?" We talked about how to tell Alex. The class concluded that a person is more likely to respond if you ask nicely ("Alex, this is an example of something that bugs me. Please stop."). Improvement has been apparent since that meeting.

Since we regularly have class meetings, the students will give me updates on past issues, such as "Lunch is better now. Adam doesn't show us the food in his mouth anymore!"

Class meetings show the class that I care about them outside of the traditional academic areas. It also encourages them to listen to one another. And it allows me to use peer influence to encourage behavioral changes. We all win!

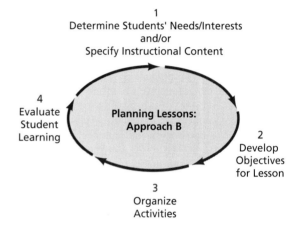

Figure 9.6

Two approaches to planning lessons

---

[1]From Paul Burden and David Byrd, *Methods for Effective Teaching,* 2nd ed. Copyright © 1999 by Allyn and Bacon, p. 120. Reprinted by permission.

Should the use of standardized testing be increased?

Assessment of student learning is essential: students, teachers, school administrators, parents, and the public need to know how schools and students are doing. Not knowing is like shooting arrows at a target out of your line of vision and never being told how close you are to the bull's-eye. Simply to be told "Shoot another one, shoot another one" will not help you get closer to the target. Madeline Hunter, UCLA teacher educator and author of *Enhancing Teaching* (1994), used that illustration to emphasize the importance of feedback. Although most educators agree with Hunter in general principle, they disagree as to which type of assessment is best and how extensive it should be.

Some people favor increasing use of standardized testing and even raising it to the national level. They think that educators in the United States, like the archer who can't see the target, are ignorant of how students compare to others in different schools, cities, states, and nations. Believing that schools would benefit from international comparisons, President Clinton proposed in his 1997 State of the Union address that national tests be given as benchmarks in fourth-grade reading and eighth-grade math. "Seven states and sixteen school districts, which serve approximately 20 percent of the nation's fourth- and eighth-graders and include the nation's three largest districts" signed up to take the tests, according to a 1998 *Phi Delta Kappan* report (Rose and Gallup 1998).

Opponents of increasing the use of standardized testing note that alternative forms of assessment—teacher-constructed tests, student portfolios, evaluations of student performances, and teacher judgments—are better ways to determine how well students are learning. They fear that mandating more standardized testing will discriminate against schools with greater populations of language-minority students and students from lower socioeconomic groups. They also warn that curricula will be narrowed by teaching to the test and express concern that the consequences of poor test results can negatively affect the lives of students and teachers.

Where do you stand on this issue? Should the use of standardized testing be increased?

Yes, the use of standardized testing should be increased.

Educators must be held accountable for student learning. Parents entrust their children to schools to educate them well. The community invests in school buildings, teachers' salaries, and curricular resources, and thus people have a right to know how well the schools are doing. For schools to expect to proceed without any accountability is unreasonable and irresponsible.

Educators themselves also need to know how they are doing. As in Madeline Hunter's archery illustration, if educators do not know whether they are on target, they are unable to improve their performance. Teachers should be continually evaluating their strategies and education programs in terms of the programs' effectiveness in promoting students' learning. If teachers do not do this, students, who are the center of the education enterprise, are the losers. The portion of their lives that students spend in school can be a waste rather than a life-changing boon. For teachers not to take care in assessing their own effectiveness is to risk short-changing children and youth.

The public clearly supports a national testing program. In the 1998 annual Phi Delta Kappa/Gallup Poll (Rose and Gallup 1998), 71 percent of those surveyed favored voluntary national tests. Results from such international comparisons can motivate school districts to engage in effective self-studies and reform. That was the case for Minnesota when its eighth-grade students scored higher than the international average in science but lower in math in the Third International Mathematics and Science Study, a project involving twenty-six countries. Minnesota educators examined the differences in how the two subjects were taught, gained several key insights, and implemented changes accordingly. Rural, urban, and suburban schools across the country can all benefit from such a process.

No, the use of standardized testing should not be increased.

The arguments against using more standardized testing are summarized succinctly and dramatically by George Madaus, Boston College Professor of Education and Director of the Center for the Study of Testing:

The tests can become the ferocious master of the educational process, not the compliant servant they should be. Measurement-driven instruction invariably leads to cramming; narrows the curriculum; concentrates attention on those skills most amenable to testing (and today this means skills amenable to the multiple-choice format); constrains creativity and spontaneity of teachers and students; and, finally, demeans the professional judgment of teachers. (Madaus 1999)

Other opponents are especially concerned about the misuse of the resulting scores. W. James Popham, author of *Testing! Testing! What Every Parent Should Know about School Tests* (1999), points out that "even the standardized test items that actually measure knowledge and skills that might be taught in school will often fail to coincide with the content stressed in a specific school." When that is the case, the school rates poorly in comparison to other schools even though it may have been doing a superior job teaching the content it deems important.

Some districts evaluate teachers in terms of how well their students score on standardized tests, ignoring the fact that the tests are more reflective of "what children bring to school, not what they learn there," Popham argues. He urges teachers to "become thoroughly familiar with the innards of any standardized test being used in their setting. These tests are not sacrosanct instruments." Teachers should investigate a test's history, development, current use, norming population, fit with the school's curriculum and goals, and the number of questions in each skill area. Such knowledge is essential for interpreting the results to children, parents, principals, district administrators—and the news media. The last group can unfairly damage a school's reputation, a realistic fear that drives some administrators to overstress test scores, promoting teaching to the test and narrowing curriculum in the process.

Most important is the impact the scores of questionable standardized tests can have on the education and lives of children and young people. An overreliance on standardized test scores can lead to inappropriate assignments to remediation programs, unjustified retentions of students, increases in dropout rates, and reduced career opportunities for students. Adriana Steinberg, in a 1999 *Harvard Education Letter,* provides one illustration of the human dimension of the problem:

Standardized test scores do not differentiate between a newly mainstreamed bilingual student who rewrites each paper four or five times and meets twice a week after school with a math tutor, but who does not yet know enough academic English to decipher arcane test items, and a student whose disengagement from school and low estimation of his own academic abilities cause him to give up midway through the first section of the test and leave much of the rest blank.

Teachers know better than developers of tests how *their* students are doing, why they are doing well or poor-

ly, and how to assist them individually. Their opinions matter much more than scores on standardized tests taken in an artificial setting on one or two days of the entire school year. Their judgments deserve the public's trust. Standardized testing should not be increased, because teachers need all the time they can get to do their most important work—teaching.

Where do you stand on this issue?

1. What is your position on increasing standardized testing? Why do you hold this position?

2. Which form of assessment has been most helpful to you as a student? How can you tell?

3. Propose a compromise position regarding standardized testing.

4. How would you interpret children's standardized test scores to their parents?

5. Find two examples of standardized tests and evaluate the aspects of tests that Popham cites.

Recommended Sources

Hunter, M. (1994). *Enhancing teaching.* New York: Macmillan.

Madaus, G. F. (1999). *The influence of testing on the curriculum.* In Margaret J. Early and Kenneth J. Rehage (Eds.). *Issues in curriculum: A selection of chapters from past NSSE yearbooks: Ninety-eighth yearbook of the national society for the study of education, Part II.* Chicago: University of Chicago Press.

Popham, W. J. (1999, May 12). Commentary: assessment apathy. *Education Week.*

Rose, L. C. and Gallup, A. M. (1998, September). The 30th annual Phi Delta Kappa/Gallup poll of the public's attitudes toward the public schools. *Phi Delta Kappan.*

Smith, M. S., Stevenson, D. L., and Li, C. P. (1998). Voluntary national tests: Helping schools improve instruction and learning in reading and mathematics. *Phi Delta Kappan, 80*(3), 213–19.

Steinberg, A. (1999, March/April). The human cost of overreliance on tests. *Harvard Education Letter.*

technology

highlights

How do effective teachers use technology to enhance their instruction?

Effective teachers recognize that educational technologies should be used to enhance students' inquiry, reflection, and problem solving rather than merely "grafted" onto existing practices. They also recognize that "schools need not be technology rich to be 'information age.' Rather, the phrase 'information age' signals that the schools focus on developing students' critical habits of mind with regard to ideas and evidence—the ability to use their minds well" (Brunner and Tally 1999, 32).

The following excerpt describes how teachers at the Bank Street School for Children in New York City used the Internet site for *The Wild Ones* (a source of information about endangered species) to promote children's higher-order thinking. The Bank Street teachers used technology for research, recording and sharing data, and as medium for publishing students' work. After reading the excerpt, identify several ways in which you will use technology as a tool to promote inquiry, reflection, and problem solving among your students.

Sixth-grade students [have] recently been studying environmental science in coordination with *The Wild Ones.* In their first project they charted environmental conditions in New York City over six weeks. When they posted their recordings on the Web (in standardized graphs representing temperature, precipitation, pH, humidity, and daylight), students were able to compare, for instance, their own environment's conditions with those posted by students in Bra, Italy. The surprisingly colder temperatures and lesser rainfall in Italy enabled students to speculate about the reasons for the disparity: season, latitude, elevation, ocean-borne weather patterns.

In their second activity, the Bank Street students began a long-term exploration of animal adaptations. Part of their work included trips to the Central Park Zoo to observe animals in the zoo's carefully created and nat-uralistic (if not natural) habitats. *The Wild Ones* Web page shows, through photos and text, the progress of their work. (Students took photographs of the animals themselves; the teacher photographed the process of student work.) First, students are seen at the zoo observing tamarins, monkeys, river otters, and penguins, drawing them, and making notes about their behaviors and their habitats. Next, students are seen back in the classroom, comparing and discussing their observations in small groups, trying to come to consensus about the ways their animal is adapted to its environment, and keeping track of questions or difficulties that emerge. Then students are seen at the computer, typing e-mail questions to *The Wild Ones* scientists who are experts on the animal they are studying.

Finally, students expressed what they had learned in the form of creative articles about their animals. Students used their imaginations in writing about and drawing their animal but were also asked to integrate what they had learned about the way their animal was adapted—through behavior or through bodily form—to its environment. The assignment (and perhaps the promise of Web publication) proved very motivating for students. Taking advantage of the class discussion of upcoming national elections, the teacher encouraged some students to write about "animal politics," prompting them to decide "which candidate will your animal vote for?" (Brunner and Tally 1999, 191–92).

Terri Jenkins, Eighth-Grade Middle School Language-Arts Teacher, Hephzibah, Georgia[2]   Four years ago, I was teaching in an inner city school with 99 percent minority enrollment. From the beginning, I was convinced that all these children could learn. My goal each day was to provide material and present in such a way that

[2]From Paul Burden and David Byrd, *Methods for Effective Teaching,* 2nd ed. Copyright © 1999 by Allyn and Bacon. Reprinted by permission.

ensured every student would experience some degree of success. I will never forget one particular series of lessons.

We began reading "The Graduation" by Maya Angelou, which recounts her own graduation and valedictory address. We then learned the Negro spiritual, "We Shall Overcome." The story and song were inspirational, but they weren't enough. I wanted to make the entire experience personal. I told the class that one day someone sitting in that very classroom would be responsible for giving a valedictory address at his or her own graduation, and that their next assignment was to prepare a speech and present it in class. The speeches were wonderful as I introduced each and every one of them as the valedictorian of that year. As they spoke, I could hear a new determination in their voices; I could see a new pride in their posture.

Three weeks ago, there was a soft tap on my classroom door and a welcomed face appeared. Immediately I recognized Carol, one of those students who had given her valedictory address in my eighth grade classroom almost five years ago. After a big smile and a warm hug, she quietly spoke. "I just had to come by and personally invite you to my graduation on June 5. I'll be giving the valedictory address, and I want you to be there." With that, an irrepressible smile burst across her face. After much earned congratulations, she looked at the tears in my eyes and said, "I did it just for you." Carol had become a believer in her dreams, a believer in herself.

Self-esteem and belief in oneself are essential. I firmly believe that self-esteem must be built through real achievement. I still strive to provide lessons designed to maximize student success and ensure achievement, and I continually verbalize my own convictions that they all can be winners. I make every effort to personalize success in the classroom. I realize that I cannot assure success for every student in my classroom, but I now know that I truly can make a difference.

James P. Anderson, Barbara Floisand, David Martinez, and Dalmar P. Robinson, Alternative High School Teachers, Salt Lake City, Utah[3]   We believe that schools should be democratic institutions. We are a service organization and live in the neighborhood as fellow citizens. Our priorities are as follows: students first, teachers second, classified staff third, and administrators fourth. Above all, every student must be treated fairly and with dignity. We tell students: "You can't pick your parents or where or when you are born. It is perfectly natural to want to belong, to be acknowledged, to succeed, regardless of your circumstances."

Most high school students who find themselves at [our school] have not been successful in the regular school setting. Their self-esteem may be low. They may feel alienated from their peers. Some may believe that society has set them up for failure. [Our] task is to provide a supportive environment that motivates and allows students to recognize windows of opportunity and to reach their educational and career goals.

SUMMARY

What Determines the Culture of the Classroom?

■ From seating arrangements, to classroom rules and procedures, to the content and relevance of the curriculum, teachers make many decisions that influence the culture of the classroom.

---

[3]Anderson, J. P.; Floisand, B.; Martinez, D.; and Robinson, D. P. (1997). Horizonte—where students come first. *Educational Leadership, 54*(7), p. 51.

- Classroom climate refers to the atmosphere or quality of life in a classroom. The climates established by high-performing teachers are characterized by a productive, task-oriented focus; group cohesiveness; open, warm relationships between teacher and students; cooperative, respectful interactions among students; low levels of tension, anxiety, and conflict; humor; high expectations; and frequent opportunities for student input regarding classroom activities.

How Can You Create a Positive Learning Environment?

- An important element of a positive learning environment is a caring classroom climate. Teachers show care for students by providing support, structure, and appropriate expectations.

- The physical environment of a classroom—seating arrangements and the placement of other classroom furniture, for example—can make a positive contribution to students' learning.

- Classroom organization, how students are grouped for instruction and how time is used, is an important element of the effective learning environment. Among the patterns for organizing classrooms are grouping students by ability, grouping students for cooperative learning, using activity formats based on authentic learning tasks, and using time to maximize students' learning.

What Are the Keys to Successful Classroom Management?

- The key to successful classroom management is preventing problems before they occur. Teachers who prevent problems foster effective, harmonious interpersonal interactions; understand how their leadership style influences students; and facilitate the development of the classroom group so that it becomes more cohesive and supportive.

- Teachers who establish a democratic classroom climate that allows students to participate in making decisions about the classroom environment, rules and procedures, curriculum materials, and learning activities have fewer discipline problems.

- When management problems occur, effective teachers use a repertoire of problem-solving skills based on experience, common sense, and understanding of the teaching–learning process. Regardless of the management strategy used, effective teachers base their response to problems on three elements of "constructive assertiveness": a clear statement of the problem or concern; unambiguous body language; and a firm, unwavering insistence on appropriate behavior.

What Teaching Methods Do Effective Teachers Use?

- Although it is difficult to identify all the skills teachers need, research indicates that effective teachers use a repertoire of models of teaching based on students' learning behaviors, child development, the thinking process, and peer mediation.

- Direct instruction and mastery learning are based on the view that learning is the acquisition of new behaviors.

- Modeling, constructivism, and scaffolding are based primarily on an understanding of how students construct meaning as they learn new material.

- Information processing, inquiry learning, and discovery learning are based on our understanding of the cognitive processes involved in learning.

- Peer-mediated instruction, which views learning as taking place in social situations, includes cooperative learning, group investigation, and peer- and cross-age tutoring.

What Are Some Characteristics of Effective Teaching?

- Effective teaching focuses on outcomes—the results or consequences of teaching. Outcomes include clear goals, objectives, and performance tasks that students are to master.

- Successful teachers modify their instruction based on assessments of students' understanding.

- Measurement refers to gathering data related to students' knowledge and skills, while evaluation involves making judgments about or assigning value to those judgments. In addition to traditional tests, teachers can use authentic assessments, portfolio assessments, and performance assessments to measure and evaluate students' learning.

KEY TERMS AND CONCEPTS

academic learning time, 345
allocated time, 345
assertive discipline, 350
assessment, 358
authentic assessments, 343
authentic learning tasks, 341
between-class ability grouping, 341
block scheduling, 346
caring classroom, 338
choice theory, 347
classroom climate, 335
classroom management, 346

classroom organization, 341
constructivist teaching, 354
cooperative learning, 341
cross-age tutoring, 356
democratic classrooms, 346
direct instruction, 353
discovery learning, 355
evaluation, 358
formative evaluation, 358
group investigation, 356
information processing, 355
inquiry learning, 355
instructional goals, 357
learning objectives, 358

mastery learning, 353
measurement, 358
modeling, 354
opportunity to learn (OTL), 345
peer-mediated instruction, 356
peer-tutoring, 356
performance assessment, 358
portfolio assessment, 358
scaffolding, 354
summative evaluation, 358
time on task, 345
within-class ability grouping, 341

APPLICATIONS AND ACTIVITIES

Teacher's Journal

1. Recall the teachers and classmates you had during your school career. Select one class and analyze its group processes in terms of the stages of group development

discussed in this chapter. At what stage of development was the group near the end of the school year? What conditions facilitated or impeded the development of this group?

2. Describe the "ideal" physical classroom environment for you. How would the seating arrangement facilitate the attainment of your instructional goals and objectives? How would you involve students in arranging the classroom?

3. Describe your leadership style as it relates to classroom management. In which aspects of leadership and classroom management do you feel most and least confident? What might you do, or what skills might you acquire, to strengthen your effectiveness in areas you feel you lack confidence? Develop your ideas into a statement of professional goals.

Teacher's Database

1. Visit the home pages of three or more of the following research publications on the Web. These journals focus on educational research, learning theories, student and teacher attitudes and behaviors, and the effectiveness of teaching methods. Some journals especially emphasize the implications of educational psychology theory and research for educational policy and applications to teaching practice. Note the kinds of studies and research topics each selected journal reports. How might articles in these journals help you as an education major? as a classroom teacher? as a teaching professional?

American Educational Research Journal   *Cognition and Instruction*
Contemporary Educational Psychology   *Educational Psychologist*
Educational Psychology Review   *Educational Researcher*
Journal of Educational Psychology   *Review of Research in Education*
Journal of Teaching and Teacher Education   *Social Psychology of Education*
Review of Educational Research

2. What resources are available on the Internet for developments in educational assessment? Begin in the ERIC Clearinghouse on Assessment and Evaluation. This clearinghouse contains the Test Locator service, searchable testing databases, tips on how to best evaluate a test, and information on fair testing practices.

   Then visit CRESST (The National Center for Research on Evaluation, Standards, and Student Testing), which houses a database of alternative approaches to assessment, including portfolio and performance assessments.

Observations and Interviews

1. Observe several teachers at the level for which you are preparing to teach and try to identify the teaching methods they are using as part of their instructional repertoires.

2. Interview a classroom teacher about the assessment of students' learning. How do the assessment methods used by this teacher relate to his or her goals and objectives? To what extent does the teacher use authentic assessments?

Professional Portfolio

Prepare a poster depicting a classroom arrangement appropriate for the subject area and grade level for which you are preparing to teach. The poster should indicate the seating arrangement and location of other classroom furniture. In addition, make a list of classroom rules that will be posted in the room. You may wish to organize the rules according to the following categories.

- Rules related to academic work
- Rules related to classroom conduct
- Rules that must be communicated on your first teaching day
- Rules that can be communicated later

Last, prepare a flow chart depicting routine activities for a typical day. This chart could include procedures for the following:

- Handling attendance, tardy slips, and excuses
- Distributing materials
- Turning in homework
- Doing seatwork or various in-class assignments
- Forming small groups for cooperative learning activities
- Returning materials and supplies at the end of class

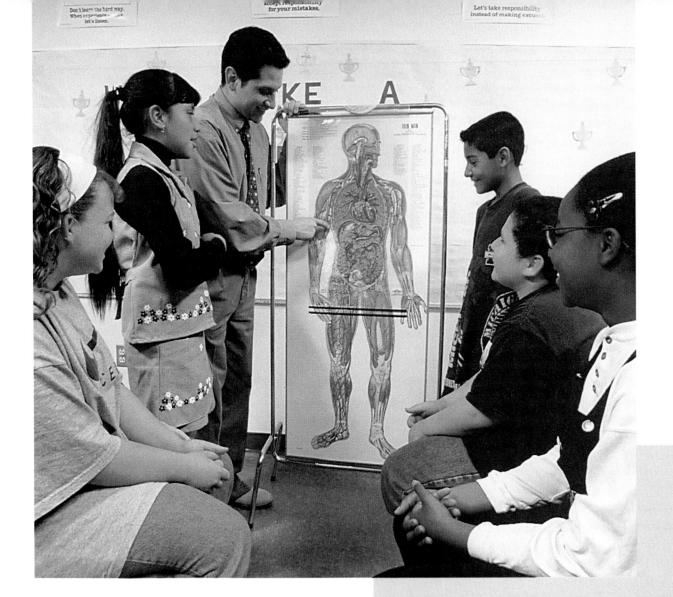

10

Developing and Implementing the Curriculum

An educator is entrusted with the most serious work that confronts humankind: the development of curricula that enable new generations to contribute to the growth of human beings and society.

—William H. Schubert
Curriculum: Perspective, Paradigm, and Possibility

1. What is taught in schools?

2. How is the school curriculum developed?

3. What reform efforts have affected the curriculum?

4. What are some current subject-area trends?

A s a beginning teacher, you are attending your school's open house held one evening during the early fall. From 7:30 to 9:00, teachers stay in their classrooms and visit with parents as they drop by. Several parents have already visited your classroom and heard you explain your curriculum. Judging by their comments and questions, you think they appear to be pleased with what their children are learning.

Shortly before 9:00, the parents of one of your students enter the room. After greeting them, you start to outline the goals and objectives of your curriculum. They listen attentively; the father even jots down a few notes on the cover of the open house program he was given at the orientation session in the auditorium.

"My curriculum is organized around an integrated, thematic approach," you say. "Each theme addresses a key concept—how animals have influenced the lives of human beings on earth, for example. As kids explore each theme, they learn relevant skills from areas such as language, reading, mathematics, science, art, and music."

To illustrate the thematic approach, you direct the parents' attention to a nearby bulletin board display titled "How Do Animals Influence Our Lives?" The bulletin board features children's drawings that are clustered into categories such as "Companionship," "Transportation," "Food," "Work," and "Recreation."

After a brief pause, you continue. "Overall, one of the main goals of my curriculum is for students to go beyond the basics. I want them to know how to use the material they learn, how to solve problems. The curriculum should be a unified whole, rather than separate, disconnected parts."

At this point, your student's mother says, "I'm not sure I agree. The purpose of the curriculum should be to learn the basics. We want our child to do well on the state's test of basic skills. If the curriculum is organized around themes, how can we be sure the kids master the basics?"

"Right," her husband says. "If kids don't do well on the test, they're less likely to continue their education. To focus on anything other than the basics is to emphasize needless frills. That may sound harsh, but that's the way I feel."

How do you justify your curriculum to these parents?

Think back to your experiences as a student at the elementary, middle, junior, and secondary schools you attended. What things did you learn? Certainly, the curriculum you experienced included reading, computation, penmanship, spelling, geography, and history. In addition to these topics, though, did you learn something about cooperation, competition, stress, football, video games, computers, popularity, and the opposite sex? Or, perhaps, did you learn to love chemistry and to hate English grammar?

What Is Taught in Schools?

The countless things you learned in school make up the curriculum that you experienced. Curriculum theorists and researchers have suggested several different definitions for **curriculum,** with no one definition universally accepted. Here are some definitions in current use.

1. A course of study, derived from the Latin *currere,* meaning "to run a course"
2. Course content, the information or knowledge that students are to learn
3. Planned learning experiences
4. Intended learning outcomes, the *results* of instruction as distinguished from the *means* (activities, materials, etc.) of instruction
5. All the experiences that students have while at school

No one of these five is in any sense the "right" definition. The way we define curriculum depends on our purposes and the situation we find ourselves in. If, for example, we were advising a high school student on the courses he or she needed to take in order to prepare for college, our operational definition of curriculum would most likely be "a course of study." However, if we were interviewing sixth-grade students for their views on the K–6 elementary school they had just graduated from, we would probably want to view curriculum as "all the experiences that students have while at school." Let us posit an additional definition of curriculum: *Curriculum refers to the experiences, both planned and unplanned, that enhance (and sometimes impede) the education and growth of students.*

Kinds of Curriculum

Elliot Eisner, a noted educational researcher, has said that "schools teach much more —and much less—than they intend to teach. Although much of what is taught is explicit and public, a great deal is not" (1994, 87). For this reason, we need to look at the four curricula that all students experience. The more we understand these curricula and how they influence students, the better we will be able to develop educational programs that do, in fact, educate.

Explicit Curriculum   The explicit, or overt, curriculum refers to what a school intends to teach students. This curriculum is made up of several components: (1) the goals, aims, and learning objectives the school has for all students, (2) the actual courses that make up each student's course of study, and (3) the specific knowledge, skills, and attitudes that teachers want students to acquire. If we asked a principal to describe the educational program at his or her school, our inquiry would be in reference to the explicit curriculum. Similarly, if we asked a teacher to describe what he or she wished to accomplish with a particular class, we would be given a description of the explicit curriculum.

In short, the **explicit curriculum** represents the publicly announced expectations the school has for its students. These expectations range from learning how to read, write, and compute to learning to appreciate music, art, and cultures other than one's own. In most instances, the explicit curriculum takes the form of written plans or guides for the education of students. Examples of such written documents are course descriptions, curriculum guides that set forth the goals and learning objectives for a school or district, texts and other commercially prepared learning materials, and teachers' lesson plans. Through the instructional program of a school, then, these curricular materials are brought to life.

Hidden Curriculum   The hidden, or implicit, curriculum refers to the behaviors, attitudes, and knowledge the culture of the school unintentionally teaches students (Parkay and Hass 2000). In addition, the **hidden curriculum** addresses "aspects of schooling that are recognized only occasionally and remain largely unexamined, particularly the schools' pedagogical, organizational, and social environments, and their interrelations" (Cornbleth 1990, 48). For example, one study of an "effective" inner-city elementary school revealed that students had "learned" that grades depended as much or more on their attitudes and behavior as on their academic ability. When asked "How do you earn grades for your report card?" the responses of fifth- and sixth-grade students included the following (Felsenthal 1982, 10):

> If you want to earn good grades you got to hand in your work on time. You got to sit up straight and don't talk to no one.

You have to be quiet, be a nice student and know how to write and read and stuff.

As a result of the hidden curriculum of schools, students learn more than their teachers imagine. Although teachers cannot directly control what students learn through the hidden curriculum, they can increase the likelihood that what it teaches will be positive. By allowing students to help determine the content of the explicit curriculum, by inviting them to help establish classroom rules, and by providing them with challenges appropriate for their stage of development, teachers can ensure that the outcomes of the hidden curriculum are more positive than negative.

Null Curriculum   Discussing a curriculum that cannot be observed directly is like talking about dark matter or black holes, unseen phenomena in the universe whose existence must be inferred because their incredible denseness and gravitational fields do not allow light to escape. In much the same way, we can consider the curriculum that we *do not* find in the schools; it may be as important as what we *do* find. Elliot Eisner has labeled the intellectual processes and content that schools do not teach "the **null curriculum**—the options students are not afforded, the perspectives they may never know about, much less be able to use, the concepts and skills that are not a part of their intellectual repertoire" (1994, 106–7).

For example, the kind of thinking that schools foster among students is largely based on manipulations of words and numbers. Thinking that is imaginative, subjective, and poetic is stressed only incidentally. Also, students are seldom taught anthropology, sociology, psychology, law, economics, filmmaking, or architecture.

Eisner points out that "certain subject matters have been traditionally taught in schools not because of a careful analysis of the range of other alternatives that could be offered but rather because they have traditionally been taught. We teach what we teach largely out of habit, and in the process neglect areas of study that could prove to be exceedingly useful to students" (1994, 103).

 **Professional Reflection**   **Identifying kinds of curriculum**

Reflect on your experiences with the curriculum as an elementary, middle, or high school student. Then, focusing on one part of the explicit curriculum that you experienced—a particular subject or a particular class—identify possible aspects of the hidden curriculum and possible areas of null curriculum. What conclusions might you draw about beliefs and values concerning the curriculum held by educators? local communities? the wider society? How did those beliefs and values affect you and your education?

Extracurricular/Cocurricular Programs   The curriculum includes school-sponsored activities—music, drama, special interest clubs, sports, student government, and honor societies, to name a few—that students may pursue in addition to their studies in academic subject areas. When such activities are perceived as additions to the academic curriculum, they are termed *extracurricular*. When these activities are seen as having important educational goals—and not merely as extras added to the academic curriculum—they are termed *cocurricular*. To reflect the fact that these two labels are commonly used for the same activities, we use the term *extracurricular/cocurricular* activities.

Though **extracurricular/cocurricular programs** are most extensive on the secondary level, many schools at the elementary, middle, and junior high levels also provide their students with a broad assortment of extracurricular/cocurricular activities. For those students who choose to participate, such activities provide an opportunity to use social and academic skills in many different contexts.

Research shows that the larger a school is, the less likely it is that a student will take part in extracurricular/cocurricular activities. At the same time, those who do participate tend to have higher self-concepts than those who do not (Coladarci and Cobb 1996). The actual effects that extracurricular/cocurricular activities have on students' development, however, are not entirely clear. Although it is known that students who participate in extracurricular/cocurricular activities tend to receive higher grades than nonparticipants and are more frequently identified as gifted (Jordan and Nettles 1999; Modi, Konstantopoulos, and Hedges 1998; Gerber 1996), it is not known whether participation influences achievement, or whether achievement influences participation. However, research has shown that participation has a positive influence on the decision to remain in school (Mahoney and Cairns 1997), educational aspirations (Modi, Konstantopoulos, and Hedges 1998), and the occupation one aspires to and eventually attains (Holland and Andre 1987; Brown, Kohrs, and Lanzamo 1991). Furthermore, students themselves tend to identify extracurricular/cocurricular activities as a high point in their school careers.

Table 10.1

Percentage of public school seniors participating in selected extracurricular activities by socioeconomic status (SES) of student and affluence of school, 1992

Selected Activity	All Students*	Low SES Students		High SES Students	
		Less Affluent Schools	More Affluent Schools	Less Affluent Schools	More Affluent Schools
Any extracurricular activity	79.9	74.7	73.0	86.8	87.6
Sports (individual and team)	42.4	34.3	33.2	48.6	53.1
Performing arts	27.5	25.0	20.7	32.0	29.2
Academic clubs	26.2	20.2	20.5	36.2	32.3
Vocational/professional clubs	20.8	29.2	25.6	16.0	11.8
Honor societies	18.1	10.3	10.0	30.8	29.9
Publications	17.0	17.6	9.5	22.4	20.0
Student government	15.5	12.6	9.9	17.5	20.9
Service clubs	15.2	10.0	9.4	25.0	21.1
Hobby clubs	8.5	8.2	6.9	9.4	9.6

*Includes students in middle two quartiles.

Source: Educational Policy Issues: Statistical Perspectives: Extracurricular Participation and Student Involvement. Washington, DC: National Center for Education Statistics, 1995.

It is also clear that students who might benefit the most from participating in extracurricular/cocurricular activities—those below the norm in academic achievement and students at risk—tend not to participate. In addition, students from low socioeconomic backgrounds participate less often. Table 10.1 (see page 373), for example, indicates that low-socioeconomic-status tenth-grade students had a lower rate of participation in eight out of nine areas of extracurricular/cocurricular activities.

Curriculum Content

The nation's schools teach what the larger society believes young people should learn. For example, Table 10.2, based on a survey by Public Agenda, shows several curriculum content areas that the public believes are "absolutely essential." Like the parents featured in this chapter's opening scenario, the public believes that the "basics" of reading, writing, and mathematics plus the development of good work habits should be the heart of the curriculum. Additional support for these curriculum goals comes from employers and college professors who deal with students after they graduate from high school. For example, when asked whether public school graduates have the skills needed to succeed "in the work world" or "in college," only 32 percent of employers surveyed and 39 percent of professors believe students have the skills (Public Agenda 1999). The following comments by two parents who participated in an earlier Public Agenda survey typify the concern many people have about the position of the basic skills in the school curriculum:

> Education is becoming more about social issues as opposed to reading, writing, and arithmetic. Some of it's fine, but I think schools need to stay with the basics. . . . You can't get by in the business world on social issues if you can't add and subtract.

> They all talk all the time about this "whole child educational process". . . . It's not your business to make a "whole child." Your business is to teach these students

Table 10.2

What content is essential for the curriculum?

	Absolutely Essential	Important, But Not Essential	Not That Important	Don't Know
Basic reading, writing, and math skills	92%	8%	<0.5%	1%
Good work habits such as being responsible, on time, and disciplined	83%	15%	1%	1%
The value of hard work	78%	20%	1%	1%
Values such as honesty and tolerance of others	74%	23%	2%	1%
Computer skills and media technology	80%	18%	1%	1%

Note: Does not total 100% due to rounding. Methodology: telephone survey of 800 adults.

Source: Adapted from Public Agenda, *Education: A Nation Divided?* New York: Public Agenda, 1999.

how to read, how to write, and give them the basic skills to balance their checkbook. It's not to make new Emersons out of them (Johnson and Immerwahr 1994, 13)

Although much of the public is concerned about a perceived lack of emphasis on the basics in the curriculum, evidence suggests that it may be incorrect to assume that schools need to "get *back* to the basics." As John Goodlad noted of the data reported in *A Place Called School,* a landmark study of 129 elementary, 362 junior high, and 525 senior high classrooms around the country, schools teach the basic skills with remarkable uniformity:

> Our data, whatever the source, reveal not only the curricular dominance of English/language arts and mathematics but also the consistent and repetitive attention to basic facts and skills. Developing "the ability to read, write, and handle basic arithmetical operations" pervades instruction from the first through the ninth grades and the lower tracks of courses beyond (Goodlad 1983a, 14–15).

How Is the School Curriculum Developed?

Although there is no easy-to-follow set of procedures for developing curriculum, Ralph Tyler has provided four fundamental questions that must be answered in developing any curriculum or plan of instruction. These four questions, known as the **Tyler rationale,** are as follows (Tyler 1949, 1):

1. What educational purposes should the school seek to attain?
2. What educational experiences can be provided that are likely to attain these purposes?
3. How can these educational experiences be effectively organized?
4. How can we determine whether these purposes are being attained?

Tyler's classic work has been used by a great number of school systems to bring some degree of order and focus to the curriculum development process.

The Focus of Curriculum Planning

In discussing curriculum development, it is helpful to clarify the focus of curriculum planning. Figure 10.1 illustrates two dimensions of this planning process: the target and the time orientation. The target of curriculum planning may be at the macro- or the micro-level. At the macro-level, decisions about the content of the curriculum apply to large groups of students. The national goals for education and state-level curriculum guidelines are examples of macro-level curricular decisions. At the micro-level, curriculum decisions are made that apply to groups of students in a particular school or classroom. To some extent, all teachers are micro-level curriculum developers—that is, they make numerous decisions about the curricular experiences they provide students in their classrooms.

Another dimension of curriculum planning is the time orientation—does the planning focus on the present or the future? In addition to the national goals and state-level curriculum guidelines, the semester-long or monthly plans or unit plans that teachers make are examples of future-oriented curriculum planning. Present-oriented curriculum planning usually occurs at the classroom level and is influenced by the unique needs of specific groups of students. The daily or weekly curriculum decisions and lesson plans that teachers make are examples of present-oriented curriculum planning.

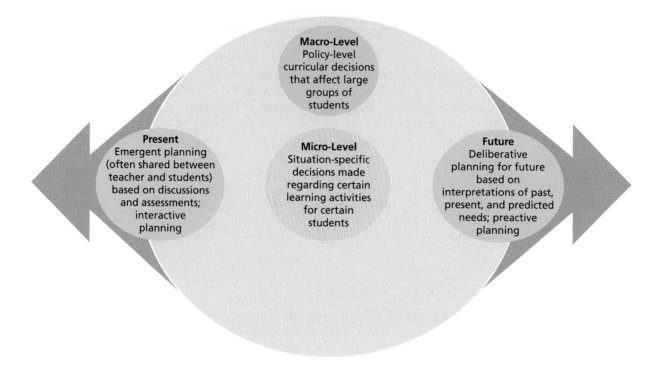

Figure 10.1

Two dimensions of
curriculum planning

Student-Centered versus
Subject-Centered Curricula

A key concern in curriculum development is whether greater emphasis should be given
to the requirements of the subject area or to the needs of the students. It is helpful to
imagine where a school curriculum might be placed on the following continuum.

Student-Centered   Subject-Centered
Curriculum   Curriculum

Although no course is entirely subject- or student-centered, curricula vary considerably in the degree to which they emphasize one or the other. The **subject-centered curriculum** places primary emphasis on the logical order of the discipline students are to
study. The teacher of such a curriculum is a subject-matter expert and is primarily
concerned with helping students understand the facts, laws, and principles of the discipline. Subject-centered curricula are more typical of high school education.

Some teachers develop curricula that reflect greater concern for students and their
needs. Though teachers of the **student-centered curriculum** also teach content, they
emphasize the growth and development of students. This emphasis is generally more
typical of elementary school curricula.

The Integrated Curriculum

The opening scenario for this chapter is based on the integrated approach to developing the school curriculum. Used most frequently with elementary-age students, the **integrated curriculum** draws from several different subject areas and focuses on a theme
or concept rather than on a single subject. Early childhood education expert Suzanne

Krogh (2000, 340) suggests that an integrated approach based on thematic "webs" is a more "natural" way for children to learn:

> [Children] do not naturally learn through isolating specific subjects. These have been determined by adult definition. Children's natural learning is more likely to take place across a theme of interest: building a fort, exploring a sandbox, interacting with the first snow of winter. Teachers can create a good deal of their curriculum by building webs made up of these themes of interest. Done with knowledge and care, a web can be created that incorporates most, or even all, of the required and desired curriculum.

According to a national survey of elementary teachers' views on the integrated curriculum, 89 percent believed that integration was the "most effective" way to present the curriculum. As one teacher who was surveyed said, "I'm not interested in presenting isolated facts which children seem to memorize and forget. I want to help students put each lesson in perspective" (Boyer 1995, 83). In *The Basic School: A Community for Learning*, the late Ernest Boyer suggested that the elementary school curriculum should be integrated according to eight themes or "core commonalities": The Life Cycle, The Use of Symbols, Membership in Groups, A Sense of Time and Space, Response to the Aesthetic, Connections to Nature, Producing and Consuming, and Living with Purpose (Boyer 1995).

Who Plans the Curriculum?

Slightly more than 34 percent of public school teachers in the country believe they have "a good deal of influence" over establishing the curriculum (National Center for Education Statistics 1998a). However, Figure 10.2, based on Boyer's survey of elementary teachers, shows that most teachers believe "groups of teachers working together" should control the curriculum.

Various agencies and people outside the school are involved in curriculum planning. Textbook publishers, for example, influence what is taught because many teachers use textbooks as curriculum guides. The federal government contributes to curriculum planning by setting national education goals, and state departments of education develop both broad aims for school curricula and specific minimum competencies for students to master.

Within a given school, the curriculum-planning team and the classroom teacher plan the curriculum that students actually experience. As a teacher you will draw from a reservoir of curriculum plans prepared by others, thus playing a vital role in the curriculum-planning process. Whenever you make decisions about what material to include in your teaching, how to sequence content, and how much time to spend teaching certain material, you are planning the curriculum.

Figure 10.2

Who do you think best controls the content of the school curriculum?

Source: The Carnegie Foundation for the Advancement of Teaching and the George H. Gallup International Institute, The International Schooling Project, 1994 [United States]. In Ernest L. Boyer, *The Basic School: A Community for Learning.* Princeton, NJ: The Carnegie Foundation for the Advancement of Teaching, 1995, p. 36.

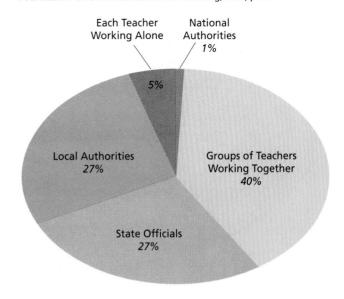

Each Teacher Working Alone — 5%
National Authorities — 1%
Local Authorities — 27%
State Officials — 27%
Groups of Teachers Working Together — 40%

What Influences Curricular Decisions?

From the earliest colonial schools to schools of the twenty-first century, curricula have been broadly influenced by a variety of religious, political, and utilitarian agendas. Figure 10.3 illustrates the influence of community pressures, court decisions, students' life situations, testing results, national reports, teachers' professional organizations, research results, and other factors. The inner circle of the figure represents factors that have a more direct influence on curriculum development (such as students' needs and school district policies). The outer circle represents factors that are more removed from the school setting or have less obvious effects on the curriculum. Individual schools respond to all these influences differently, which further affects their curricula. Let us examine some of these influences in greater detail.

Social Issues and Changing Values   Values that affect curriculum planning include prevailing educational theories and teachers' educational philosophies. In addition, curriculum planners respond to social issues and changing values in the wider society. As a result, current social concerns find their way into textbooks, teaching aids, and lesson plans. Often curriculum changes are made in the hope that changing what students learn will help solve social problems or achieve local, statewide, or national goals.

Because the United States is so culturally diverse, proposed curriculum changes also reflect divergent interests and values. This divergence then leads to controversies over curriculum content and conflicting calls for reform. Recall, for example, the discussion in Chapter 6 of legal issues surrounding the demands of some groups that Christian teachings and observances be included in the public school curricula or that materials regarded as objectionable on religious grounds be censored or banned; or the discussion in Chapter 7 of the trend for states to pass English-only laws and the controversy that erupted in California around the teaching of "ebonics" or "black English." Additional curriculum controversies have arisen over calls for the elimination of all activities or symbols that have their origins in organized religion, including even

Figure 10.3

Influences on the school curriculum

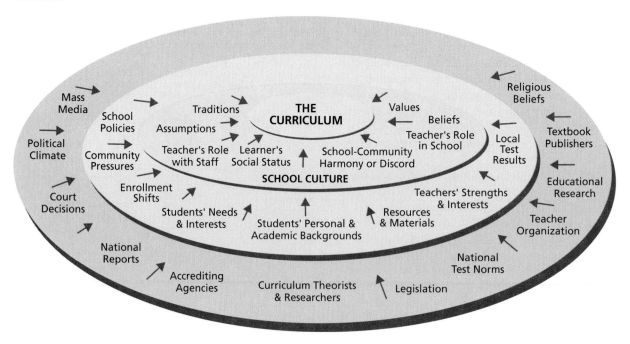

secularized or commercialized ones such as Halloween and the Easter bunny. Curriculum changes to promote greater social integration or equity among racial or ethnic groups may draw complaints of irrelevancy or reverse discrimination. Traditionalists may object to curriculum changes that reflect feminist views.

As you can imagine, consensus on many curriculum reform issues is never achieved. However, because of their public accountability, schools must consider how to respond to those issues. One survey revealed that during a one-year period, half the school districts in Florida received complaints about curriculum content. Included were complaints claiming that the schools were undermining family values, overemphasizing globalism, underemphasizing patriotism, permitting profanity and obscenity, and teaching taboo subjects such as satanism and sex (Sheuerer and Parkay 1992, 112–18). In the end, the creative and evaluative tasks of choosing and developing curriculum materials are a source of both empowerment and frustration for teachers. Budget constraints, social and legal issues, and state and local curriculum mandates often determine curriculum choices.

Textbook Publishing   Textbooks greatly influence the curriculum. According to one study, "with nearly 95 percent of classroom instruction in grades K–8 and 90 percent of homework time derived from printed materials, textbooks predominate the school day" (Venezky 1992, 444). In addition, textbook publishers influence school curricula by providing teaching objectives, learning activities, tests, audiovisual aids, and other supplements to assist their customers.

Like curriculum planners, textbook authors and publishers are influenced by trends in education and by social issues. In response to criticism, for example, publishers now tend to avoid bias in terms of gender, religion, class, race, and culture. However, because the goal of business is profit, publishers are most responsive to market trends and customer preferences. They are often reluctant to risk losing sales by including subjects that are controversial or that may be offensive to their bigger customers. They may also modify textbooks to appeal to decision makers in populous states that make statewide adoptions of textbooks, such as California and Texas. About half the states have statewide adoption policies that school districts must follow in selecting textbooks. In addition, California and Texas are among several states that systematically review state-approved textbooks for accuracy. Texts with too many errors are dropped from state-approved lists, and publishers are levied fines for failing to correct errors (Manzo 1999).

Educators have criticized textbooks for inoffensiveness to the point of blandness, for artificially lowered reading levels (called "dumbing down"), and for pedagogically questionable gimmicks to hold students' attention. "The quality problem [with textbooks also] encompasses [f]actors such as poor writing, poor content 'coverage,' and failure to engage students in the skills needed to create the knowledge contained in a particular area of study" (Sowell 1996, 158). Although the publishing industry continually responds to such criticisms, you would be wise to follow systematic guidelines in evaluating and selecting textbooks and other curriculum materials.

What Reform Efforts Have Affected the Curriculum?

The content of the curricula in America's schools has changed frequently since the colonial period. These modifications came about as the goals of the schools were debat-

Ms. Hyman's ESL Writing Lesson

The following case is a selection from Sara Lawrence Lightfoot's award-winning book, *The Good High School: Portraits of Character and Culture.* Lightfoot, a qualitative researcher and Harvard professor, studied six distinctive high schools in depth to discover the qualities of a "good high school"—two urban, two suburban, and two elite. The ESL (English as a Second Language) writing class that she observed and describes below took place in one of the study's urban schools. The students were in a transitional program, preparing to join classes of native and transitioned English-only speakers.

The brainchild of Ellen Hyman, a dedicated and able teacher, Writing Skills is designed to make students more comfortable with the expressive and descriptive dimensions of English. Using creative pedagogical strategies and curricular ideas, the course builds on the premise that language facility provides reinforcement for self-knowledge and self-confidence. Each class begins with five minutes of journal writing. Both teacher and students join in this activity and students are asked to write about "topics that are relevant" to their lives, such as "Describe your next-door neighbor." Or "We don't have enough holidays. Invent one and tell why and when we celebrate it." Or "Pretend you cut class yesterday. Write an outrageous excuse to your teacher." In responding to these questions, students are encouraged to be spontaneous, truthful, and personal. The journals are not corrected for grammar or spelling, and if the student judges the content to be too personal for the teacher to read, she may fold the page for privacy.

Ms. Hyman, a quietly attractive woman, has a soft, soothing voice and a generous smile. Although there are thirty-two students in the class (twenty-eight Hispanics, three Asians, and one Russian), the intimacy and comfortable exchanges make the group feel much smaller. Students are attentive, but relaxed. They often speak out spontaneously without raising their hands and the dialogue is laced with laughter, but never does the organization, momentum, or focus of the class break down. The lesson centers on increasing the sensory word vocabulary of the students. It follows a series of lessons on learning how to describe "physical details" and precedes a segment on learning "emotional details." The sequence is designed to augment the expressive range of students; offer them more ways of discerning and describing events, people, and feelings.

As part of the lesson on sensory details, Ms. Hyman takes out a small bag of potato chips and says, "After today no more food, I promise." With slight melodrama, she holds the bag up and demonstrates. "I have here an ordinary brand of potato chips." The students laugh enthusiastically, as they appreciate the reference to television commercials. "Let's see if we can describe potato chips using sensory details. . . . Juan, how would you describe by *sight* this potato chip?" "It is brown, round, yellow, with a brown burn spot on it," responds Juan. "Maria touch it, feel it . . . what can you tell me about the feel?" Maria reaches for the chip and describes it as "a little hard, rough . . . I can feel the grains of salt." From the back of the room Roberto calls out, "Hey, over here, I'll try the taste." The class erupts in laughter as the teacher responds to Roberto's offer. The class quiets immediately when Ms. Hyman says, "Listen, boys and girls," and in the silence breaks a single potato chip. "Crunch," says one volunteer; "snap," says another as they try to match the correct word to the sound.

Up at the blackboard, the teacher writes three words on the board and demonstrates their meaning by crushing a potato chip in her hand, letting the pieces fall to the floor, and by shaking the bag. Together they identify "crunchy" (to crush noisily), "crumble" (to break into little pieces), and "rustle" (one thing rubbing softly against the other). Then they figure out which sense (sight, sound, touch, or taste) allows one to make those distinctions. Once they have written the words and meanings in their notebooks, the teacher asks them to repeat the words out loud. Their choral effort is vigorous. As they speak the words with a Spanish lilt, their voices begin to capture the sights and sounds of the potato chip demonstration. The lesson concludes with dramatic exchanges between Ms. Hyman and her rapt students as they collectively develop meanings for "mouth-watering" (something looks so delicious it makes you hungry), "thundering" (what word do you recognize in thundering—take it from there), "screeching" (two cars approach one another—they put on their brakes and swerve away quickly), and "thirst-quenching" (picture yourself on a very hot day—you'd do anything for a cold drink).

The class closes with a brief review of what they have covered and an exclamation and big smile from Juan: "The more you see, the more you feel, the more you write!" The homework assignment is greeted with good-natured groans. With the sound of the bell, students immediately return to Spanish; the tempo is accelerated, expressive gestures reappear, and they feel at home. A dark skinned, shiny-haired girl approaches me and is surprised when I do not understand her Spanish. A friend nearby translates: "Ms. Hyman is great. She gives us a gift."

Questions

1. What were the purposes of the lesson?

2. How did the lesson fit into the larger curriculum plan?

3. How did Ms. Hyman maintain her students' interest in the curriculum?

4. In your own observation and written account of a classroom lesson, practice using portraiture, the style of reporting that Lightfoot uses in this selection.

5. In some states, ESL classes are no longer permitted. What do you think are the consequences of such a legislative decision?

Source: Sara Lawrence Lightfoot, *The Good High School: Portraits of Character and Culture.* New York: Basic Books, 1985. Selections taken from pp. 79–81.

ed, additional needs of society became evident, and the characteristics of student populations shifted. The following list is a sampling of goals the schools have set for themselves at different times in our history:

- Prepare students to carry out religious and family responsibilities
- Provide employers with a source of literate workers
- Desegregate society
- Reduce crime, poverty, and injustice
- Help our country maintain its competitive edge in the world economy
- Provide the scientists needed to keep our country strong
- Educate students for intelligent participation in a democracy

Forrest W. Parkay and Glen Hass (2000, 51) suggest that three interrelated "social forces" influence the school curriculum: "[An] appropriately developed school program —from preschool through the graduate level—must enhance [the student's] ability to accomplish developmental tasks in three areas: *vocation, citizenship, and self-*

Figure 10.4

A chronology of major emphasis in the school curriculum

Religious Emphasis	1620	1620—Emphasis on basic skills needed to learn religious catechisms and read prayers. Curriculum also includes surveying, navigation, and bookkeeping. Education primarily for the elite.
	1640	1636—Latin grammar (college-prep) schools established and, like Harvard and Yale Colleges, emhasize Latin, Greek, theology, and philosophy for those preparing to enter law or religion.
	1660	1647—Massachusetts Law of 1647 mandates a reading and writing teacher for towns of 50 or more families; a Latin teacher for towns of 100 or more. Females taught basics to enable them to carry out religious and family responsibilities.
	1680	
	1700	1700—Public schools teach reading, writing, and basic mathematics (counting, adding, and subtracting) to prepare students for jobs and apprenticeships.
	1720	
	1740	
Political Emphasis on Citizenship	1760	Early 1750s—Academies teach secondary students a practical curriculum (drawing, surveying, navigation, merchant's accounting, etc.) to become tradespeople and workers.
	1780	
	1800	
Vocational Emphasis	1820	1821—First public high school teaches basic skills and history, geography, health, and physical training.
	1840	
	1860	1860—First English-speaking kindergarten emphasizes growth, activity, play, songs, and physical training.
	1880	1874—Free public schooling now includes high schools that place emphasis on vocational education and reading, writing, and mathematics.

fulfillment." The timeline presented in Figure 10.4 shows how school curricula have shifted in their degree of emphasis on these three demands since 1620.

Church, Nation, and School

From 1620 to 1760, the primary aim of the curriculum was to train students in religious beliefs and practices. It was only later that a distinction was made between civil and religious life. Basic skills were taught for the purpose of learning religious catechisms and reading prayers. In addition to taking courses with religious content, students also studied such practical subjects as surveying, navigation, bookkeeping, architecture, and agriculture.

From 1770 to 1860 the development of citizenship provided the curriculum's major focus. The United States had just won its independence from England, and many policymakers believed that literacy was essential to the preservation of freedom. Accord-

Figure 10.4 *(continued)*

Education for Masses	1900	1893—Committee of Ten asserts that high schools are for college-bound and curriculum should emphasize mental disciplines in humanities, language, and science.
		1918—Commission on Reorganization of Secondary Education focuses on individual differences. Curriculum to stress Seven Cardinal Principles.
	1920	
		1930s—Progressive education movement stresses curriculum based on student's needs and interests. Home economics, health, family living, citizenship, and wood shop added
	1940	1940s to the curriculum.
		1957— Russia's Sputnik sparks emphasis on science, mathematics, and languages.
	1960	1960s—Calls for relevancy result in expanded course offererings and electives.
		Mid 1970s—Back-to-basics movement emphasizes reading, writing, mathematics, and oral communication.
	1980	
		1983—*Nation at Risk* report calls for "five new basics" — English, mathematics, science, social studies, and computer science.
		1985—Rigorous core curricula advocated at all levels in an effort to increase standards and to ensure quality.
The Excellence Movement		1989—The Carnegie Council on Adolescent Development report, *Turning Points*, recommends the creation of learning communities and a core academic program for middle-level students.
	1990	1990—President Bush unveils national educational goals in six areas: readiness for school; high school completion; student achievement and citizenship; science and mathmatics; adult literacy and lifelong learning; and safe, disciplined, and drug-free schools.
		1992—President Clinton proposes a program of national service for America's youth.
		1994—Goals 2000:Educate America Act—teachers' professional development and parental involvement added to six National Education Goals.
		Mid 1990s—National standards committees meet in the subject areas. Renewed emphasis on developing curricula for schooling in an increasingly diverse society.
		1996—The President's Educational Technology Initiative: access to technology for all students, Internet access for schools, quality educational software, and teacher training in technology.
	2000	1999—Acknowledging that eight National Education Goals would not be reached by 2000, the Goals Panel renames the goals "America's Educational Goals," with no deadline for achievement.

ingly, students were taught history, geography, health, and physical training, as well as the basic skills of reading, writing, and computation. In 1821, the nation's first public high school was opened in Boston, and two years later the first private normal school for teachers opened in Concord, Vermont. The first English-speaking kindergarten, taught by Elizabeth Peabody, opened in Boston in 1860.

By the beginning of the Civil War, the basic skills of reading, writing, and mathematics were well established in the curriculum. Various types of schools had been incorporated into state systems, and in 1852 the first compulsory school attendance law was passed in Massachusetts. Parents in every section of the country wanted more and better opportunities for their children. Through a curriculum that stressed individual virtue, literacy, hard work, and moral development, reformers wished to improve social conditions and to provide more opportunities for the poor.

The development of citizenship continues to influence school life and school curricula. All students, for example, are required to study U.S. history and the U.S. Constitution at some time during their school career. Presidents' birthdays and national holidays are built into the school year calendar. Issues concerning civil liberties and the expression of patriotism often become educational issues, as in controversies during the last decades over treatment of the American flag and the recitation of the Pledge of Allegiance in schools.

Children and School

Vocational goals for the curriculum were most prominent from 1860 to 1920. The turn of the century brought with it many changes that profoundly influenced the curriculum. The dawning of the machine age altered the nature of industry, transportation, and communication. The growth of cities and the influx of millions of immigrants resulted in new functions for all social institutions, and home life was forever changed. As a result, curricula came to be based on vocationally oriented social and individual need rather than on subject-matter divisions. Subjects were judged by the criterion of social utility rather than by their ability to develop the intellect.

During this period, several national committees met for the purpose of deciding what should be taught in elementary and secondary schools. Initially, these committees espoused goals formed by educators at the college and private secondary school levels—that is, uniform curricula with standardized methods of instruction. Gradually, though, these appointed groups began to recommend curricula that were more flexible and based on the needs of children. This shift is seen clearly in the recommendations made by three of the more influential committees during this period: the Committee of Ten, the Committee of Fifteen, and the Commission on Reorganization of Secondary Education.

The Committee of Ten During 1892–93, the directors of the National Education Association appropriated $2,500 for a **Committee of Ten** to hold nine conferences that focused on the following subjects in the high school curriculum: (1) Latin; (2) Greek; (3) English; (4) other modern languages; (5) mathematics; (6) physics, astronomy, and chemistry; (7) natural history (biology, botany, and zoology); (8) history, civil government, and political science; and (9) geography (physical geography, geology, and meteorology). The group's members decided that the primary function of high schools was to take intellectually elite students and prepare them for life. Their recommendations stressed mental discipline in the humanities, languages, and science.

The Committee of Fifteen The report of the Committee of Ten sparked such discussion that in 1893 the National Education Association appointed the **Committee of Fifteen** to examine the elementary curriculum. In keeping with the view that high schools were college preparatory institutions, the committee's report, published in 1895, called for the introduction of Latin, the modern languages, and algebra into the elementary curriculum. In addition, the curriculum was to be organized around five basic subjects: grammar, literature, arithmetic, geography, and history.

The Reorganization of Secondary Education In 1913 the National Education Association appointed the Commission on the **Reorganization of Secondary Education.** The commission's report, *Cardinal Principles of Secondary Education,* was released in 1918 and called for a high school curriculum designed to accommodate individual differences in scholastic ability. Seven educational goals were to provide the focus for schooling at all levels: health, command of fundamental processes (reading, writing, and computation), worthy home membership, vocation, citizenship, worthy use of leisure time, and ethical character.

Standards and the Schools

From 1920 to the present, schools have become increasingly accountable for providing all students with curricular experiences based on high standards. The following comments made by Roy Romer, former governor of Colorado and a vocal national advocate for higher standards, for example, reflects the nation's concern about current standards in schools (2000, 314–15):

> Setting standards, raising expectations, and assessing student progress in a meaningful way gives students the tools they need to thrive in the twenty-first century and the tools parents and teachers need to help them. [Content] standards are a compilation of specific statements of what students should know or be able to do. They do not represent the totality of what students should learn at school. They are not curriculum. When standards are well conceptualized and written, they can focus the education system on common, explicit goals; ensure that rigorous academic content is taught by all teachers in all classrooms and raise expectations for all students.

To meet these demands for higher standards, schools have undertaken numerous curricular reforms over the years and used more sophisticated methods for measuring the educational outcomes of these reforms.

The Push for Mass Education Since 1920, schools have been expected to provide educational opportunities for all Americans. During this period, curricula have been developed to meet the needs and differences of many diverse student groups: disabled, bilingual, gifted, delinquent, and learning-disabled students, for example. Moreover, these curricula have been used not only in public schools but also in schools that provide alternatives to public education: religious and nonsectarian private schools; night schools; boarding schools; schools without walls; continuation schools; magnet schools; and schools for students who are African American, Native American, or members of other ethnic and racial groups. According to the National Center for Education Statistics, more than 360,000 teachers taught at almost 28,000 private and/or alternative schools in 1998. And, near the end of 1999, researchers at the University of California at Berkeley and Stanford University reported that nearly one-fourth of all children, about

8 million students nationwide, attended alternatives to the nearest public school. So remarkable was the growth in alternative schools during the 1990s, that one of the researchers asserted that "Anyone who claims there is a public school monopoly out there is about 20 years behind" (Fuller et al. 1999).

The Progressive Curriculum   The concern in this country for educating all our youth has drawn much of its initial energy from the progressive education movement. During the 1920s, the Progressive Education Association reacted against the earlier emphasis on the mental disciplines and called for elementary schools to develop curricula based on the needs and interests of all students. Throughout the 1930s, progressive ideas were promoted on the secondary level as well.

Though there was no single set of beliefs that united all Progressives, there was general agreement that students should be involved in activities that parallel those found in society. Furthermore, those activities should engage students' natural interests and contribute to their self-fulfillment. With these guidelines in mind, the progressive education movement expanded the curriculum to include such topics as home economics, health, family living, citizenship, and wood shop. The spirit of the progressive education movement is expressed well in a statement made in 1926 by the Director of the School of Organic Education in Fairhope, Alabama (Johnson 1926, 350–51):

> We believe that education is life, growth; that the ends are immediate; that the end and the process are one. We believe that all children should have the fullest opportunity for self-expression, for joy, for delight, for intellectual stimulus through subject matter, but we do not believe that children should be made self-conscious or externalized by making subject matter an end. Our constant thought is not what do the children learn or do, but what are the "learning" and the "doing" doing to them. . . .
>
> We believe that society owes all children guidance, control, instruction, association, and inspiration—right conditions of growth—throughout the growing years until physical growth is completed. No child may know failure—all must succeed. Not "what do you know" but "what do you need," should be asked, and the nature of childhood indicates the answer.

The Eight-Year Study   One of the most ambitious projects of the progressive education movement was the **Eight-Year Study,** which ran from 1932 to 1940. During this period, thirty public and private high schools were given the opportunity to restructure their educational programs according to progressive tenets and without regard for college and university entrance requirements. Over 300 colleges and universities then agreed to accept the graduates of these schools. The aim of the study, according to its director, was "to develop students who regard education as an enduring quest for meanings rather than credit accumulation" (Aiken 1942, 23). The curricula developed by these schools emphasized problem solving, creativity, self-directed study, and more extensive counseling and guidance for students.

Ralph Tyler evaluated the Eight-Year Study by matching nearly 1,500 graduates of the experimental schools who went on to college with an equal number of college freshmen who graduated from other high schools. He found that students in the experimental group received higher grades in every subject area except foreign languages and had slightly higher overall grade point averages. Even more significant, perhaps, was the finding that the experimental group had higher performance in such areas as problem solving, inventiveness, curiosity, and motivation to achieve. Unfortunately, the Eight-Year Study failed to have any lasting impact on American education—possibly because World War II overshadowed the study's results.

The Push for Excellence   Concern with excellence in our schools ran high during the decade that spanned the late 1950s to the late 1960s. The Soviet Union's launching of the satellite Sputnik in 1957 marked the beginning of a great concern in this country over the content of the schools' curricula. Admiral Hyman G. Rickover was a leading proponent of an academically rigorous curriculum and urged the public to see that our strength as a nation was virtually linked to the quality of our educational system. He wrote in his 1959 book *Education and Freedom* (188):

> The past months have been a period of rude awakening for us. Our eyes and ears have been assaulted by the most distressing sort of news about Russia's giant strides in technology, based on the extraordinary success she has had in transforming her educational system. All but in ruins twenty-five years ago, it is today an efficient machine for producing highly competent scientists and engineers—many more than we can hope to train through our own educational system which we have so long regarded with pride and affection.

> We are slowly thinking our way through a thicket of bitter disappointment and humiliating truth to the realization that America's predominant educational philosophy is as hopelessly outdated today as the horse and buggy. Nothing short of a complete reorganization of American education, preceded by a revolutionary reversal of educational aims, can equip us for winning the educational race with the Russians.

Fueled by arguments like Rickover's, many curriculum reform movements were begun in the 1950s and 1960s. The federal government became involved and poured great sums of money into developing curricula in mathematics, the sciences, modern languages, and, to a lesser extent, English and history. Once again, the focus of the curriculum was on the mental disciplines and the social and psychological needs of children were secondary. Testing and ability grouping procedures were expanded in an effort to identify and to motivate academically able students.

The Inquiry-Based Curriculum   The prevailing view of what should be taught in the schools during this period was influenced significantly by Jerome Bruner's short book, *The Process of Education*. A report on a conference of scientists, scholars, and educators at Woods Hole, Massachusetts, in 1959, Bruner's book synthesized current ideas about intelligence and about how to motivate students to learn. Bruner believed that students should learn the "methods of inquiry" common to the academic disciplines. For example, in an **inquiry-based curriculum,** instead of learning isolated facts about chemistry, students would learn the principles of inquiry common to the discipline of chemistry. In short, students would learn to think like chemists; they would be able to use principles from chemistry to solve problems independently.

Bruner's ideas were used as a rationale for making the curriculum more rigorous at all levels. As he pointed out in an often-quoted statement in *The Process of Education,* "Any subject can be taught effectively in some intellectually honest form to any child at any stage of development" (1960, 33). Bruner advocated a spiral curriculum wherein children would encounter the disciplines at ever-increasing levels of complexity as they progressed through school. Thus elementary students could be taught physics in a manner that would pave the way for their learning more complex principles of physics in high school.

The Relevancy-Based Curriculum   The push for a rigorous academic core curriculum was offset in the mid-1960s by a call for a **relevancy-based curriculum.** Many educators, student groups, and political activists charged that school curricula were unresponsive to social issues and significant changes in our culture. At some schools,

Is raising national educational standards an effective way to improve education?

National concern over the poor educational performance of students in the United States prompted President George Bush to call an education summit in 1989, gathering together the country's fifty state governors to address the problem. The reform agenda that emerged from that meeting, America 2000, consisted of six educational goals that were to be accomplished by the year 2000. These included the goal that U.S. students would be first in the world in mathematics and science achievement, and U.S. students in grades 4, 8, and 12 would have demonstrated "competency in challenging subject matter, including English, mathematics, science, history, and geography." As part of the plan to meet the goals—America 2000: An Education Strategy— two items reflected national standards: a voluntary system of national testing and "New World Standards" in five core subjects.

President-elect Bill Clinton, who attended that education summit, revised the plan when he became president. In 1994, he signed into law the Goals 2000: Educate America Act, which made state participation voluntary. The goals for student achievement were similar to those of the earlier plan with the addition of four more areas for demonstrated competency—foreign languages, the arts, economics, civics and government.

By the late 1990s it was clear that U. S. students would fail to meet the achievement goals set in the original plan and its revision. That was particularly evident in the discouraging results of the Third International Mathematics and Science Study (TIMSS), a rigorous five-year research study of students' performances in over fifty countries. The U.S. twelfth-grade students' performances were "among the lowest of participating countries in general knowledge of mathematics and science and more specific knowledge of physics and advanced math," according to a July 1999 *Bioscience* report (Moreno 1999).

Chester E. Finn, Jr., the former Assistant U.S. Secretary of Education, evaluated the national goals plan and was quoted in a 1999 *Education Week* article (Hoffa 1999) as concluding, "It didn't accomplish what we'd hoped it would accomplish. Instead of doing more of it, let's do something different."

What do you think? Is raising national educational standards the way to improve education? Or not?

Yes, raising educational standards for the nation is an effective way to improve education.

"We are moving in this country from a local to a national view of education and we need better arrangements to guide the way. . . . The challenge is to develop a national agenda for school renewal while retaining leadership at the state and local levels," Ernest Boyer, the late president of the Carnegie Foundation for the Advancement of Teaching, said in 1990. His observation still applies today. Educators need to continue to seek a national perspective, even if efforts have not thus far achieved success.

As a free society in which people can work hard or be lazy, the United States needs goals and high standards to motivate and stretch its people. Without them people can become complacent and satisfied with mediocrity. The country needs to compare its students with those of other countries in order to maximize what schools do. Just as a runner will run faster when paced by another, the U.S. education system will raise its standards when it compares them to those of other countries.

As a diverse society, rich in a variety of ethnicities, religions, nationalities, and language groups, the United States also needs common standards for unity. With increasing immigration to the country which brings diverse groups of people to its urban, rural, and suburban neighborhoods, schools need to provide common knowledge about democracy and the heritage of the country, and shared curricula in the other areas of study. People should share things in common if the United States is to remain "united." And the national curriculum needs to be guided by high educational standards.

As a mobile society, the United States needs common educational standards so that children from one area will not fall behind when they move to another. Children from a farming community in Minnesota should be able to move to the heart of New Orleans without finding themselves behind or ahead of their peers in school. Children from a school in Seattle should be able to move to school in Cinncinatti and recognize the curricula that are studied there. And the educational standards for the common curricula should be high.

With a national curriculum and national standards, the true benefactors will be the nation's children and youth. For a great many, the quality of their education and the options for their lives after school would increase significantly. As an advocate of raising standards and assessing them in order to improve schools, Diane Ravitch observed, "A failing mark on the state test will be only a temporary embarrassment, but a poor education will stigmatize young people for life" (1997).

No, raising educational standards in the nation is not an effective way to improve education.

Schools' inability to achieve the national standards of Goals 2000 is evidence enough that another approach is needed. People have overlooked the lack of uniformity in schools around the country and the needs of the children who come to them. As the book *Savage Inequalities* (Kozol 1992) vividly shows, equal education in the country is an illusion. To compare the performance of a student in the poorest Chicago housing project with that of a student in that city's wealthy suburbs is to see the "savage inequalities" that are repeated throughout the country's education system.

Supporters of the Opportunity to Learn Standards address these inequalities. They believe that any effort to raise educational standards should be accompanied by evaluations of the opportunities to learn that students receive. In a 1995 report, Wendy Schwartz lists twenty-three such opportunities, including:

■ All students should have access to high level courses that will allow them to meet performance and content standards and provide them with good career opportunities

■ Teachers should spend adequate time covering the content in class

■ Pre- and in-service teacher training should lead to mastery of course content and techniques to teach it meaningfully, with particular attention to the material in the content standards

■ Pre- and in-service teacher training should include strategies for reaching diverse student populations and students with different learning styles.

To raise educational standards without equalizing opportunities to learn is to perpetuate the problems and extend the need for school reform.

Critics also complain that those behind the drive to raise education standards nationally minimize the place of diversity in the United States. With University of Washington professor Cherry A. McGee Banks, (1997) they raise the questions: "Whose standards?" "Who benefits from the standards?" and "Whom will the standards harm?" Her concern is that the "standards can increase race and class stratification in U.S. society."

Others argue that raising standards is actually pointless. They note that many of the countries that outperformed the United States on the TIMSS did not have a national standards program. Gerald Bracey concludes that in the United States "states that are scoring high don't need standards and those that are scoring low have too many other, more pressing problems to make use of standards" (1999).

Where do you stand on this issue?

1. What are the key points in each argument?

2. With which argument do you agree most? What other points could you make to defend your position?

3. Propose a means of raising education standards that would not perpetuate class differences.

4. Search the internet for an update on the status of national standards and assessments. Begin by checking the U.S. Department of Education's website.

Recommended Sources

Bracey, G. W. (1999, March). Getting along without national standards. *Phi Delta Kappan, 80*(7), 548–50.

Banks, C. A. M. (1997, Spring). The challenges of national standards in a multicultural society. *Educational Horizons,* 126–32.

Hoff, D. (1999, January 13). With 2000 looming, chances of meeting national goals iffy. *Education Week.*

Moreno, N. P. (1999, July). K–12 science education reform—a primer for scientists. *Bioscience, 49*(7), 569–77.

Noll, J. W. (1999). *Taking sides: clashing views on controversial issues,* 10th ed. Guilford, CT: Dushkin/McGraw-Hill.

Ravitch, D. (1997, December 15). The fight for standards. *Forbes, 160*(13), 106.

Schwartz, W. (1995, December). *Opportunity to learn standards: Their impact on urban education.* ERIC/CUE Digest No. 110.

largely high schools, students actually demonstrated against educational programs they felt were not relevant to their needs and concerns. In response to this pressure, educators began to add more courses to the curriculum, increase the number of elective and remedial courses offered, and experiment with new ways of teaching. This concern with relevancy continued until the back-to-basics movement began in the mid-1970s.

The Core Curriculum   In the early 1980s, the public was reminded anew that the country's well-being depended on its system of education, and once again the schools were found lacking in excellence. Several national reports claimed that curriculum standards had eroded. The 1983 report by the National Commission on Excellence in Education asserted, for example, that secondary school curricula had become "homogenized, diluted, and diffused." And even Admiral Rickover, in his characteristically terse, hard-hitting manner, pointed out in 1983 that school curricula had become less rigorous (Rickover 1983):

> Student performance is lower than in 1957 at the time of Sputnik, when many so-called reforms were initiated. Some curricula involve expensive gimmicks, trivial courses and quick fixes of dubious value. Teachers are often poorly trained and misused on nonacademic tasks. Many students have settled for easy, so-called relevant and entertaining courses. They and their parents are deceived by grade inflation. And the lack of national standards of performance blinds everyone to how poor our education system is.

The push for excellence in the high school curriculum received a boost at the end of 1987 when U.S. Secretary of Education William J. Bennett proposed an academically rigorous **core curriculum** for all high school students. In a U.S. Department of Education booklet entitled *James Madison High School: A Curriculum for American Students,* Bennett described what such a curriculum might look like for an imaginary high school. His course of study called for four years of English consisting of four year-long literature courses; three years each of science, mathematics, and social studies; two years of foreign language; two years of physical education; and one semester each of art and music history. Twenty-five percent of his program would be available for students to use for electives.

Performance-Based Education   One approach to reforming the curriculum to ensure that all students learn and perform at higher levels is known as **performance-based** or **outcome-based education.** The performance-based approach focuses on assessing students' mastery of a set of rigorous learning goals or outcomes. Opponents to performance-based education have expressed concern about the content of the outcomes, who determines them, and how they will be assessed. By 2000, Kentucky, Oregon, Connecticut, and Washington were among the states that had mandated outcomes, while other states had developed outcomes as guidelines for the curriculum. Washington, for example, developed Essential Academic Learning Requirements that all students must meet. The requirements are organized around four over-arching goals:

Students will be able to

1. Read with comprehension, write with skill, and communicate effectively and responsibly in a variety of ways and settings
2. Know and apply the core concepts and principles of mathematics; social, physical and life sciences; civics, history, and geography; arts; and health and fitness
3. Think analytically, logically, and creatively, and integrate experiences and knowledge to form reasoned judgments and solve problems

4. Understand the importance of work and how performance, effort and decisions directly affect future career and educational opportunities

Assessments to measure students' mastery of the Essential Academic Learning Requirements occur at the fourth-, seventh-, and tenth-grade levels. Initially, the assessments were available for voluntary use by schools; by 2008, however, all of the assessments will be required.

What Are Some Current Subject-Area Trends?

The final section of this chapter examines briefly some of the current trends and issues regarding what is taught in elementary, middle, junior high, and high schools. See Appendix 10.1 for selected subject-area references for curriculum planning and see the Appendix "Free Curriculum Materials" on this book's website for information on obtaining free curriculum materials.

Reading and Writing

The importance of attaining a minimum level of literacy in our society cannot be underestimated; the language arts are the tools through which students learn in nearly all other areas of the curriculum. Most students who are deficient in reading and writing skills are at a significant disadvantage when it comes to seeking employment or additional education.

The teaching of reading at all levels should focus on acquiring basic comprehension skills and learning to appreciate literature in its various forms: novels, essays, poetry, short stories, and so on. Reading teachers, however, are currently far from united as to how these aims should be realized. Does instruction in phonics enhance reading comprehension? Is a whole-language approach to the teaching of reading superior to teaching isolated decoding and comprehension skills? Should children be taught the alphabet before learning to read? Although media coverage frequently dichotomizes the teaching of reading between the phonics approach and the whole-language approach, Cheeks, Flippo, and Lindsey (1997, 130) contend that "this polarization is more political than representative of the real issues. Those who advocate for whole language do not believe that phonics is not important. Instead they argue about how it should be presented to students."

The following comments by a first-grade teacher reflect the position that many teachers have taken regarding the "reading wars": "I don't think there is one best method of teaching reading or one best program. What I have done over my twenty-seven years is pick what I think works and incorporate it" (Smolkin 1999, 1A). The eclectic approach to teaching reading is also advocated by the International Reading Association, which stated that "there is no single method or single combination of methods that can successfully teach all children to read. Therefore, teachers must be familiar with a wide range of methods for teaching reading and a strong knowledge of the children in their care so they can create the appropriate balance of methods needed for each child" (International Reading Association 1999). As part of a trend to "deescalate" the reading wars, then, many schools that emphasized a whole-language approach during the 1990s, began to shift to a "balanced" approach at the start of the new decade (see Figure 10.5).

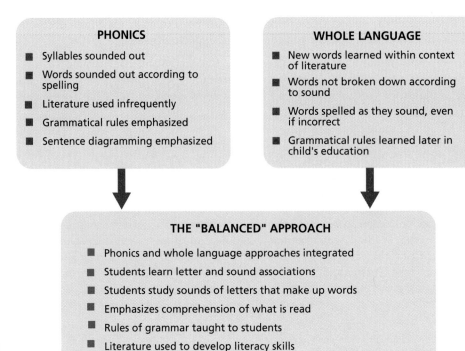

Figure 10.5

A "balanced" approach to teaching reading and writing

Advocates of the **whole-language approach** believe that reading is part of general language development, not an isolated skill students learn apart from listening, speaking, and writing. Teachers in whole-language classrooms seldom use textbooks; instead, young students write stories and learn to read from their writing, and older students read literature that is closely related to their everyday experiences.

Literature-based reading instruction is important. The 1998 National Assessment of Educational Progress (NAEP) in reading, given to fourth- and eighth-, and twelfth-grade students. provided insight into the methods the fourth- and eight-grade teachers used to teach reading. Among the fourth-grade teachers, 57 percent used books (novels, poetry, and nonfiction) every day, while 25 percent used books once or twice a week; among the eighth-grade teachers, 53 percent used books every day, while 27 percent used them once or twice a week (National Assessment of Educational Progress 1999). Results from the 1998 NAEP showed that about 62 percent of fourth-grade students, 74 percent of eighth-grade students, and 77 percent of twelfth-grade students were at or above the "basic" level in reading.

During the last two decades, several new approaches have been incorporated into the language arts curriculum. Many English teachers have reduced the amount of time spent on grammar, electing instead to teach grammar as needed within the context of a writing program. English teachers also have generally broadened their view of literature to include more contemporary forms of writing and the literary contributions of minority or ethnic writers. Teaching in the English classroom now frequently includes such techniques as creative writing, drama, journal writing, guided fantasy exercises, and group discussions. In addition, many teachers are using computers to explore new ways to teach students reading and writing. For example, the 1998 NAEP revealed that about 42 percent of fourth-grade teachers and 20 percent of eighth grade teachers used computer software for reading instruction, and about 60 percent of both fourth-grade and eighth-grade teachers had students use computers to write compositions.

After three years of collaborative development, the International Reading Association and the National Council of Teachers of English released voluntary national standards for English-language arts in 1996. Debate over these standards continues to stimulate discussion and debate about the goals of language arts instruction.

Based on their review of literacy research, Cheeks, Flippo, and Lindsey (1997, 83–84) recommend that teachers do the following to develop children's language abilities.

1. Allow many opportunities for social imaginative play and other verbal peer interaction, which enhance language and cognitive development.
2. Develop learning activities that integrate listening, speaking, reading, and writing (oral and written language).
3. Use art, music, and drama activities to further develop language opportunities.
4. Read many books and stories to children every day.
5. Choose books and stories that you believe will be of high interest to children and will further stimulate their interest in reading books.
6. Give children opportunities to respond to the books and stories you read.
7. Reread favorite stories as often as children request them.
8. Give children opportunities to retell and/or act out stories in their own words after listening to you read them.
9. Give children many opportunities to make their own books. Children can dictate stories as the teacher writes the stories down in the children's own words. Children also can write their own books using scribble writing, pictures, and invented spellings to tell their stories in their own words.
10. Give children many opportunities to share with others the stories they write.
11. Accept "less than perfect" readings, retellings, writing, and other literacy attempts for all children.
12. Provide classroom activities and an environment that enhances the idea that literacy is part of communication and that meaning is essential for communication to take place.

Mathematics

Since it began working on the *Standards 2000* project, a set of preK–12 standards to be released in spring 2000, the National Council of Teachers of Mathematics (NCTM) has made it clear that basic mathematical skills for the new century should consist of more than computation skills. *Standards 2000* emphasizes five mathematical content standards (number and operation; patterns, functions, and algebra; geometry and spatial sense; measurement; and data analysis, statistics, and probability) that students should study with increasing breadth and depth as they move through the grades. In addition, *Standards 2000* emphasizes five mathematical processes through which students should acquire and use their mathematical knowledge: problem solving, reasoning and proof, communication, connections, and representation (National Council of Teachers of Mathematics 1998).

During the 1990s, mathematics programs, from the elementary through secondary levels, still tended to focus on the mechanical acquisition of skills. Some people believed that efforts to increase the mathematics and science competencies of students were not succeeding because textbooks were measuring low-level skills such as memorization—not the higher-order reasoning and problem-solving skills students need. For example, *A Splintered Vision: An Investigation of U.S. Science and Mathematics Education* (1996), a report by the U.S. Department of Education and the International Insti-

Table 10.3

The "good news" and "bad news" about middle-level mathematics textbooks

Good news:	Bad news:
■ There are a few excellent middle grades mathematics textbook series.	■ There are no popular commercial textbooks among the best rated.
■ The best series contains both in-depth mathematics content and excellent instructional support.	■ Most of the textbooks are inconsistent and often weak in their coverage of conceptual benchmarks in mathematics.
■ Most of the textbooks do a satisfactory job on number and geometry skills.	■ Most of the textbooks are weak in their instructional support for students and teachers.
■ A majority of textbooks do a reasonable job in the key instructional areas of engaging students and helping them develop and use mathematical ideas.	■ Many textbooks provide little development in sophistication of mathematical ideas from grades 6 to 8, corroborating similar findings of the Third International Mathematics and Science Study.
	■ A majority of textbooks are particularly unsatisfactory in providing a purpose for learning mathematics, taking account of student ideas, and promoting student thinking.

Note: Thirteen textbooks were evaluated on how likely they are to help students achieve six key learning goals contained in the American Association for the Advancement of Science's *Benchmarks for Science Literacy.*

Source: American Association for the Advancement of Science, Project 2061, *2061 Today: Science Literacy for a Changing Future,* Spring 1999, 9(1), p. 3.

tute of Education, asserted that publishers included shallow analyses of many different topics to appeal to as many school districts as possible. Compared to the mathematics curricula of other nations, the report asserted, the U.S. curriculum in mathematics is "a mile wide and an inch deep." More recently, the American Association for the Advancement of Science conducted a rigorous analysis of thirteen middle school mathematics textbooks and found nine to be "unsatisfactory"; moreover, the four "satisfactory" texts were not widely used (American Association for the Advancement of Science 1999). Table 10.3 presents the "good news" and "bad news" about middle-level mathematics texts.

What is needed is **problem-centered learning,** in which students work in small groups on problems that have many or open-ended solutions. Rather than memorizing facts, working on sets of problems in textbooks, and competing against their classmates, students discover concepts, solve problems similar to those they will encounter in life, and learn to cooperate in small groups. For example, one mathematics-reform group developed a curriculum unit on testing blood for diseases that asks students to use quadratic and cubic equations to decide when to pool samples of blood rather than test each sample individually (Viadero 1996, 33). The use of manipulative materials such as Cuisinnaire rods, balance beams, counting sticks, and measuring scales also has positive effects on students' achievement in mathematics. For instance, Washington State University researcher David Slavit (1998, 280) found that "combining hands-on, visually based activities with mathematical discussions [can increase] students' structural understanding of the geometric concepts of similarity and congruence. Observing students perform these activities confirmed . . . the educational importance of 'doing' mathematics."

Science and Technology

Perhaps more than any other area of the curriculum, the teaching of science in the United States has come under increasingly critical scrutiny. On the elementary level, the science curriculum consists of assorted science-related topics: animals, plants, seasons, light, sound, heat, weather, magnets, the stars and planets, basic electricity, nutrition, oceanography, and so on. These topics are often restudied in greater depth at the middle or junior high level in courses variously titled Earth Science, General Science, Physical Science, or Life Science. At the high school level, students typically may select from only a limited number of basic science courses: Biology, Chemistry, Physical Science, Anatomy and Physiology, and Physics. Many high schools do, however, distinguish between science courses that are applied (for the noncollege-bound) and those that are academic.

Several leading science educators and national committees have recommended changes in the science curriculum. Nearly all stress the need for students to learn more science and to acquire scientific knowledge, skills, and processes through an inquiry, discovery, or problem-centered method. The teacher's primary role is to guide students in their search for knowledge rather than to act solely as a source of information and/or right answers.

To assess students' achievement in science, for example, the 1996 National Assessment of Educational Progress (NAEP) in Science included a "Knowing and Doing Science" dimension that focused on the following goals:

- Students should acquire a rich collection of scientific information that will enable them to move from simply being able to provide reasonable interpretations of observations to providing explanations and predictions.

In what ways might these students be meeting curriculum goals of the National Assessment of Educational Progress in Science?

How can educational software change the roles of teachers and students?

Educational software enables students to experience events or study phenomena that they could not witness firsthand. By integrating educational software into various learning tasks and across subject areas, teachers can provide students with learning experiences that would have been impossible a few years ago. Most important, careful and purposeful use of educational software changes the roles of teachers and students and enhances students' higher order and problem-solving skills.

As you read the following two classroom vignettes, consider how the use of educational software changes the roles of teachers and students. Then, individually or with the rest of your class, reflect on the questions that follow the vignettes.

Vignette #1

When five of her students consistently had trouble understanding early geometry concepts, and all began to have poor attitudes about their own abilities, Ms. Johnson turned to problem-solving software as another tool to provide a useful context for their learning. Over the course of two weeks, she introduced the group to the problem-solving activities in *Snootz Math Trek*.

[Her] students concentrated on only one of the five thinking activities in *Snootz*, the one that dealt with the shape puzzles in Al's Garage. The Snootz characters engaged students, and the exposure to the quality problem-solving activities made light bulbs start going on in their heads.

Speaking with them individually over the next several weeks proved to Ms. Johnson that not only were the students demonstrating proficiency with problem-solving strategies, but they were feeling confident about what they knew. One student even offered to show one of the top math students how to use the software (Bitter and Pierson 1999, 94).

Vignette #2

One of the most difficult areas of the eighth-grade language arts curriculum to teach effectively, according to Mrs. Hancock, is poetry. Students just are not interested. [She] was, therefore, most interested when she found the program *In My Own Voice: Multicultural Poets on Identity*.

Mrs. Hancock feels that all good writers have a writing environment that is comfortable to them and inspires them to write, and she was amazed that this software simulates such a rich environment. In the *Writer Space*, students can access all of the program resources. They can visit a gallery of artistic images and hear the poems that were inspired by the art. Students can study one poet's style by reading a collection of his or her poems

- Appropriate to their age and grade level, students will be assessed on their ability to acquire new information, plan appropriate investigations, use a variety of scientific tools, and communicate the results of their investigations.
- By grade 12, students should be able to discuss larger science- and technology-linked problems not directly related to their immediate experience. Examples include waste disposal, energy uses, air quality, water pollution, noise abatement, and the trade-offs between the benefits and adverse consequences of various technologies (National Assessment of Educational Progress 1996).

Similarly, the American Association for the Advancement of Science issued a set of "benchmarks" based on Project 2061 (2061 refers to the year Halley's comet returns). The Association recommended (1) integrating science and mathematics with other disciplines, (2) preparing students to become inquirers and critical thinkers rather than sources of right answers, and (3) focusing on the contributions science can make to current social issues—population growth, environmental pollution, waste dispos-

and hear in the poet's own words how each poem was created. They can examine the actual text of each poem to see examples of the unique capitalization, punctuation, and physical layout that is acceptable in poetry. Budding poets can even choose from a selection of background music to further frame the writing mood.

Over the next several weeks, students worked individually or in pairs to write and rewrite their own original poems using the writing tool *In My Own Voice*. When they all had a poem they were proud of, Mrs. Hancock planned for one more extension to the project.

The students used another tool program called *Blocks in Motion* to design an electronic illustration to accompany their poems. They used the various backgrounds and motions to create a scene they envisioned when they thought about their poem. Once each student had finished experimenting

and each had designed a finished visual representation of their poem, a recording was made of each student poet reading his or her poem. The audio recordings would play in an electronic slide show of the student creations.

The class held a gallery day when Ms. Johnson invited other classes to visit the poets. Not only had students learned about poetry, but they had personally experienced what it feels like to be a poet (Bitter and Pierson 1999, 100).

1. In addition to the content and processes students learn through the use of educational software, what "lessons" might they learn through the "hidden curriculum" created by educational software?

2. In regard to the subject area and grade level for which you are preparing to teach, what are the advantages and disadvantages of teaching concepts with and without educational software?

3. Based on your experiences, is educational software educationally sound? Does some software rely too heavily on "bells and whistles" to entertain students?

4. To what extent is quality educational software currently available for the subject area and grade level for which you are preparing to teach?

---

al, energy, and birth control. The Association's *Atlas of Science Literacy: Mapping K–12 Learning Goals* illustrates the connections among the benchmarks through the use of "strand maps" in nine areas: seasons, gravity, water cycle, changes in matter, energy, methods in science, proportional reasoning, mental health, and feedback and control (Association for the Advancement of Science 2000). Figure 10.6 presents a strand map for gravity.

Social Studies

Goals for the social studies lack the precision that we find in other subject areas. Consider, for example, Charles Beard's comment in 1938 that the social studies aim at the "creation of rich and many-sided personalities, equipped with practical knowledge and inspired by ideals so that they can make their way and fulfill their mission

Strand Map Legend

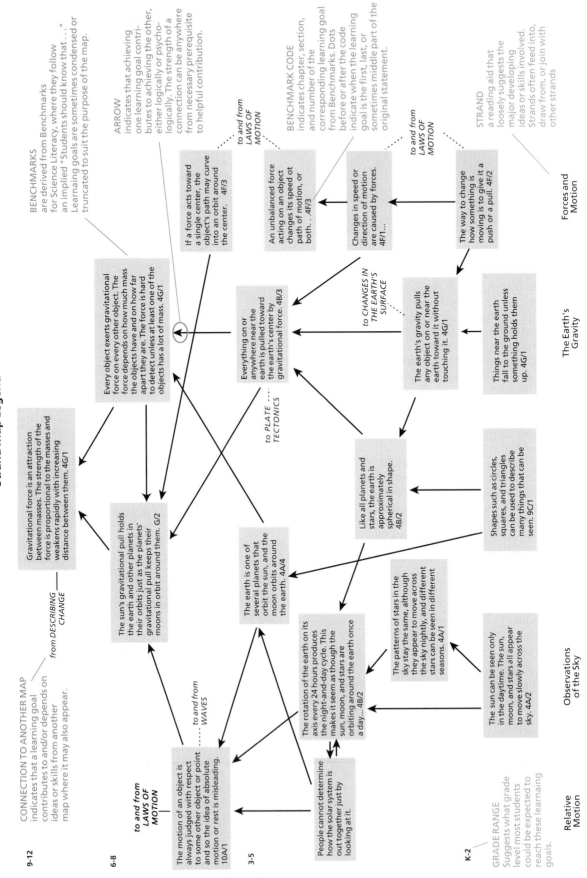

BENCHMARKS
are derived from Benchmarks for Science Literacy, where they follow an implied "Students should know that…" Learning goals are sometimes condensed or truncated to suit the purpose of the map.

ARROW
indicates that achieving one learning goal contributes to achieving the other, either logically or psychologically. The strength of a connection can be anywhere from necessary prerequisite to helpful contribution.

BENCHMARK CODE
indicates chapter, section, and number of the corresponding learning goal from Benchmarks. Dots before or after the code indicate when the learning goal is the first, last, or sometimes middle part of the original statement.

STRAND
a reading aid that loosely suggests the major developing ideas or skills involved. Strands often feed into, draw from, or join with other strands

CONNECTION TO ANOTHER MAP
indicates that a learning goal contributes to and/or depends on ideas or skills from another map where it may also appear.

GRADE RANGE
Suggests what grade level most students could be expected to reach these learning goals.

9-12

6-8

3-5

K-2

from DESCRIBING CHANGE

to and from LAWS OF MOTION

to and from LAWS OF MOTION

to and from LAWS OF MOTION

to CHANGES IN THE EARTH'S SURFACE

to PLATE TECTONICS

to and from WAVES

Forces and Motion

The Earth's Gravity

Observations of the Sky

Relative Motion

If a force acts toward a single center, the object's path may curve into an orbit around the center. 4F/3

An unbalanced force acting on an object changes its speed ot path of motion, or both… 4F/3

Changes in speed or direction of motion are caused by forces. 4F/1…

The way to change how something is moving is to give it a push or a pull. 4F/2

Every object exerts gravitational force on every other object. The force depends on how much mass the objects have and on how far apart they are. The force is hard to detect unless at least one of the objects has a lot of mass. 4G/1

Gravitational force is an attraction between masses. The strength of the force is proportional to the masses and weakens rapidly with increasing distance between them. 4G/1

Everything on or anywhere near the earth is pulled toward the earth's center by gravitational force. 4B/3

The earth's gravity pulls any object on or near the earth toward it without touching it. 4G/1

Things near the earth fall to the ground unless something holds them up. 4G/1

The sun's gravitational pull holds the earth and other planets in their orbits just as the planets' gravitational pull keeps their moons in orbit around them. G/2

Like all planets and stars, the earth is approximately spherical in shape. 4B/2

Shapes such as circles, squares, and triangles can be used to describe many things that can be seen. 9C/1

The earth is one of several planets that orbit the sun, and the moon orbits around the earth. 4A/4

The rotation of the earth on its axis every 24 hours produces the night-and-day cycle. This makes it seem as though the sun, moon, and stars are orbiting around the earth once a day… 4B/2

The patterns of stars in the sky stay the same, although they appear to move across the sky nightly, and different stars can be seen in different seasons. 4A/1

The sun can be seen only in the daytime. The sun, moon, and stars all appear to move slowly across the sky. 4A/2

The motion of an object is always judged with respect to some other object or point and so the idea of absolute motion or rest is misleading. 10A/1

People cannot determine how the solar system is put together just by looking at it.

in a changing society which is part of a world complex" (1938, 179). Or the current position of the National Council for the Social Studies (NCSS) that the aim of the social studies is to "teach students the content knowledge, intellectual skills, and civic values necessary for fulfilling the duties of citizenship in a participatory democracy."

Or finally, the following ten "strands" from the NCSS's (1994) *Expectations of Excellence: Curriculum Standards for Social Studies:*

1. Culture and cultural diversity
2. Human beings' views of themselves over time
3. People, places, and environments
4. Individual development and identity
5. Interactions among individuals, groups, and institutions
6. How structures of power, authority, and governance are changed
7. The production, distribution, and consumption of goods and services
8. Relationships among science, technology, and society
9. Global interdependence
10. Citizenship in a democratic society

The content of traditional social studies courses has remained comparatively unchanged during the last decade. Trends include fewer offerings in ancient history and civics and more offerings in psychology, economics, world cultures, and marriage and the family. Experimental courses or units in subjects such as African American studies, Latino and Hispanic culture, and women's history have been criticized variously as gratuitous, distorting, misrepresentative, ethnocentric, or defamatory. As you read in Chapter 7, the development of a truly multicultural curriculum is a subject of debate. In spite of such debate, however, a Public Agenda survey study of native-born and foreign-born parents' beliefs on whether a set of "American values" should be taught in the schools concluded that

> [There is] a clear-eyed patriotism among parents of all backgrounds; a deep belief that the United States is a unique nation, while acknowledging its faults. Parents want the schools to face those faults, but not to dwell on them—the parents we surveyed want history taught with fairness to all groups, but recoil from strategies that they feared might encourage divisiveness (Public Agenda 1998).

The National Center for History in the Schools at UCLA became embroiled in controversy in 1994 when it issued a set of voluntary U.S. and world history standards. The Council for Basic Education and other groups believed that the standards' authors were overly concerned about including the stories of minorities and women and the discrimination they experienced, with the result that they omitted significant historical figures and positive features of the United States and the West. Others complained that the new standards were "politically correct" to the extent that they contained an anti-Western bias. With input from two independent, bipartisan national review panels appointed by the Council for Basic Education; 33 national education organizations; and more than 1,000 educators, the National Center for History rewrote the standards

Figure 10.6

Atlas of Science Literacy: Strand Map for Gravity
Source: Adapted from *Atlas of Science Literacy: Mapping K–12 Learning Goals,* American Association for the Advancement of Science, Project 2061. New York: Oxford University Press, 2000. Used with permission.

and released the revised edition in 1996 with endorsements from several groups that had criticized the previous standards.

Foreign Languages

As we become increasingly aware of our interconnectedness with other nations, the small number of students who study foreign languages at the elementary through secondary levels is alarming. Support for foreign languages increased briefly immediately following Russia's launching of Sputnik in 1957, but foreign language enrollments declined dramatically during the 1960s and 1970s.

Currently, about 40 percent of high school students enroll in a foreign language course (National Center for Education Statistics 1999), though the majority enroll in one of only three languages: Spanish, French, or German. Only a few schools in the country offer a course in the world's first and third most commonly spoken languages —Mandarin and Hindi. To enhance foreign language instruction in the United States in an era of expanding global interdependence, several states have developed guidelines for foreign language study, and government and private groups are working cooperatively with foreign language organizations to promote the need for foreign language study.

In *Standards for Foreign Language Learning: Preparing for the 21st Century,* the American Council on the Teaching of Foreign Languages (1996) asserted that:

> Language and communication are at the heart of the human experience. The United States must educate students who are linguistically and culturally equipped to communicate successfully in a pluralistic American society and abroad. This imperative envisions a future in which ALL students will develop and maintain proficiency in English and at least one other language, modern or classical. Children who come to school from non-English backgrounds should also have opportunities to develop further proficiencies in their first language.

To reach this goal, the Council recommended that foreign language instruction focus on the following "five C's of foreign language education":

> *Communication:* Communicate in languages other than English
> *Cultures:* Gain knowledge and understanding of other cultures
> *Connections:* Connect with other disciplines and acquire information
> *Comparisons:* Develop insight into the nature of language and culture
> *Communities:* Participate in multilingual communities at home and around the world (American Council on the Teaching of Foreign Languages 1996)

Rarely are students introduced to foreign language study at the optimal time for learning a second language—as early as second grade. The first year of a foreign language, usually Spanish or French, is sometimes offered at the middle school or junior high school level. Students typically study the first part of Spanish I, for example, in the sixth or seventh grade and complete the course next year. As high school freshmen, then, they are ready for Spanish II.

Some schools have broadened their foreign language offerings to include such languages as Russian, Japanese, and Chinese. At a few schools, foreign language study has even become a central part of the curriculum. La Salle Language Academy in Chicago, for example, provides its K–8 students daily instruction in French, Spanish, Italian, or German. In addition, parents are encouraged to take special morning or evening language classes, and seventh- and eighth-grade students may participate in a foreign-exchange program.

The Arts

More than any other area of the curriculum, the arts have held an insecure position. When schools have faced budgetary cutbacks or pressure to raise scores on basic skills tests, a cost-conscious public has often considered the elimination of music and art. Near the end of the 1990s, however, the position of the arts in the curriculum seemed more secure. For example, in 1998 the White House held a special event, "Recognizing the Power of the Arts in Education," and the national *Arts Report Card* was published, asserting that "As a means of encountering the world around us, the arts offer a unique combination of intellectual, emotional, imaginative, and physical experiences. The arts as a means of expression are especially important in the context of current educational reform." In addition, "hard" evidence on the importance of the arts began to appear in the media, academic journals, and various national reports. *Arts Education: Basic to Learning,* a report by the Northwest Regional Educational Laboratory, pointed out that:

■ In 1995 College Board testing, students who studied the arts for at least four years score 59 points higher on the verbal portion of the SAT, and 44 points higher on math, than students with no experience or coursework in the arts.

■ According to a 1997 report from the Department of Education, "Children naturally sing, dance, draw, and role-play in an effort to understand the world around them and communicate their thoughts about it. A growing body of evidence demonstrates that when their caretakers engage them in these activities early in life on a regular basis, they are helping to wire the children's brains for successful learning."

■ In studies at [the] University of California at Irvine, IQ scores go up among college students who listen to classical recordings immediately before testing—a phenomenon nicknamed the "Mozart Effect."

■ Arts education programs are related to safer and more orderly school environments.

■ Schools with strong arts programs report better attendance, increased graduation rates, improved multicultural understanding, greater community support, invigorated faculty, and the development of higher-order thinking skills, creativity, and problem-solving ability among students.

■ The arts serve students with special needs, including those who are in danger of falling through the cracks of the educational system and allow success "for people who have been defined as failures" (Northwest Regional Educational Laboratory, 1999, 5).

Typically, elementary art and music are limited to one period a week, and this instruction is given either by regular teachers or by special teachers who travel from school to school. In addition, most elementary students have occasional opportunities to use crayons, watercolors, clay, and other art materials as they learn in other subject areas. And, from time to time, many children even have the opportunity to experience dance, puppetry, role-playing, pantomime, and crafts.

At the middle and junior high level, instruction in art and music becomes more structured, as well as more voluntary. Students may choose from band, chorus, arts, and crafts. At the high school level, art and music are usually offered as electives. Depending on the school's resources, however, students frequently have a wide assortment of classes to choose from: jazz band, glee club, band, orchestra, drama, chorus, photography, sculpture, ceramics, and filmmaking, to name a few. In addition, middle school and high school students may receive instruction in practical arts, such as sewing, cooking, woodworking and metalworking, automotive shop, print shop, and courses teaching agricultural knowledge and skills. A noteworthy trend is for students of both sexes to take courses in all the practical arts rather than follow traditional sex-role stereotypes; that is, you increasingly find boys and girls both in the kitchen and in the garage.

Art education in U.S. schools began to receive considerable attention when the Getty Education Center for the Arts, funded by the J. Paul Getty Trust, began to call for a "discipline-based" approach to art education. **Discipline-based art programs** emphasize art-making, art criticism, art history, and aesthetics. The Getty Institute has also spearheaded five major efforts to influence the quality of art education in the schools:

- Public advocacy for the value of art in education
- Professional development programs for school administrators and teachers
- Development of the theoretical bases of discipline-based art education
- Development of model programs to demonstrate discipline-based art education in the classroom
- Development of discipline-based curricula

In 1996, the Getty Institute and the College Board launched "The Role of the Arts in Unifying the High School Curriculum," a five-year research and development project to study how the arts can unify the school curriculum across all subject areas. Five high schools, including arts magnet and comprehensive high schools from rural and urban areas in Massachusetts, New Mexico, Texas, Maryland, and Washington, were selected to develop and test model curricula to integrate the arts with subjects such as history, literature, language, and science. Project teams at these schools will share their work with other schools over online school networks.

Physical Education

The ultimate aim of physical education is to promote physical activities that develop a desire in the individual to maintain physical fitness throughout life. More specifically, the National Association for Sport and Physical Education has stated that a physically educated student:

1. Demonstrates competency in many movement forms and proficiency in a few movement forms
2. Applies movement concepts and principles to the learning and development of motor skills
3. Exhibits a physically active lifestyle
4. Achieves and maintains a health-enhancing level of physical fitness
5. Demonstrates responsible personal and social behavior in physical activity settings
6. Demonstrates understanding and respect for differences among people in physical activity settings
7. Understands that physical activity provides opportunities for enjoyment, challenge, self-expression, and social interaction (National Association for Sport and Physical Education 1999)

In addition to their participation in activities, students in physical education programs may receive instruction in health and nutrition, sex education, and driver education.

At one time, physical education programs consisted largely of highly competitive team sports. Many children, less aggressive and competitive than their peers, did not do well in such programs and experienced a lowered sense of self-esteem. Gradually, instructors began to offer activities designed to meet the needs and abilities of all students, not just the athletically talented. In addition to traditional team sports such as football, baseball, and basketball, and individual sports such as swimming and wrestling, many students in grades K–12 may now participate in a broad array of physical activities, including aerobics, archery, badminton, dodgeball, folk and square dancing, gymnastics, handball, hockey, table tennis, golf, racquetball, shuffleboard, skating, volleyball, soccer, and yoga.

In addition to becoming more sensitive to the needs and abilities of individual students, physical education programs were required by law to provide more opportunities for female students. In 1972, Congress enacted Title IX of the Education Amendments Act, which said, "No person in the United States shall, on the basis of sex, be excluded from participation in, be denied benefits of, or be subjected to discrimination under any education or activity receiving federal financial assistance." Following Title IX, girls became much more involved in school athletic programs. The National Federation of State High School Associations, for example, found that 1.85 million young women participated in high school athletics in 1980–81 compared to only 240,000 in 1970–71. In 1999, the National Center for Education Statistics reported that more than 30 percent of female high school seniors participated in school-sponsored athletic activities.

Vocational-Technical Education

In addition to their academic (or college preparatory) curricula, many comprehensive high schools offer programs in vocational-technical education, and some high schools offer only a vocational-technical program. **Vocational-technical education** programs vary from those that actually prepare students to take jobs in business and industry after graduation to those that merely introduce students to career possibilities.

Prior to the 1990s, programs to prepare students for particular jobs or provide them with the basic skills and career awareness to enter the world of work were referred to, generally, as *vocational education*. Since vocational students in comprehensive high schools often have lower achievement levels than students in nonvocational programs, vocational education in the United States has had an "image problem." For example, "Vocational Education's Image for the 21st Century," a position paper by the ERIC Clearinghouse on Adult, Career, and Vocational Education, asserted that "Leaders of the new school reform movement do not give it [vocational education] high priority. They assume that it is separate from general education, has little educational value, and should be replaced by a predominantly academic curriculum. At best, vocational courses are expected to provide students who are not college bound with minimal training for low-status jobs at entry level" (Catri 1999, 1).

In response to such perceptions, many states and school districts changed the name of their vocational education systems and redesigned their curricula during the 1990s. Also, the major professional association for vocational educators, the American Vocational Association, changed its name to the Association for Career and Technical Education in 1999. The most common reason for these changes was public image, "negative baggage" associated with the word *vocational* (Ries 1997).

In the mid 1990s, many high schools formed partnerships with the private sector and began to develop tech-prep and school-to-work programs to address current and future needs in industry. **Tech-prep programs** enable students to prepare for the world of work by spending time at local businesses and industries during their last two years in high school. Thus students acquire their vocational training in actual on-the-job settings rather than in a high school, and they learn to transfer the knowledge and skills learned at school to the job setting. Under a provision of the Carl D. Perkins Vocational and Technical Education Act which became law in 1999, some high schools have worked with community colleges and businesses to develop tech-prep programs that high school juniors and seniors complete at a community college.

School-to-work programs prepare students to enter two-year postsecondary schools or various types of postsecondary training programs. For example, the first author of this text and a colleague helped teachers at Rogers High School in Spokane, Washington, redesign the curriculum according to five "career pathways": Business and Marketing, Communications and Arts, Science and Nature, Health and Human Services, and Industry and Technology. As part of this new "real-world" curriculum, all students would select a career pathway and take courses that prepare them to pursue the pathway at the "entry," "skilled/technical," or "professional" levels after graduation. Within the Business and Marketing pathway, for example, a student at the entry level would take courses to prepare to become a cashier or salesperson; a student at the professional level would take courses appropriate for an eventual career as an accountant or business executive. In addition, students could select from pathway-appropriate opportunities for internships, summer work, and job shadowing.

As the United States continues to be concerned about its productivity compared with other nations, and as employers continue to expect schools to graduate students who have mastered the basic skills and learned how to learn, it seems likely that vocational-technical education will continue to be an important part of the school curriculum. Through school–business partnerships such as the one at Rogers High, a new definition of vocational-technical education will be forged—one based on new, rigorous standards cooperatively developed by educators and employers from various industrial sectors.

SUMMARY

What Is Taught in Schools?

■ There are many different definitions for the term *curriculum*. A general definition is that *curriculum* refers to the experiences, both planned and unplanned, that either enhance or impede the education and growth of students.

■ There are four curricula that all students experience. In addition to learning what teachers intend to teach (the explicit curriculum), students learn from the hidden curriculum, the null curriculum, and extracurricular/cocurricular programs.

■ From school policies to national politics, many factors influence what is taught (and not taught) in the schools.

How Is the School Curriculum Developed?

■ Curricula are based on the needs and interests of students and also reflect a variety of professional, commercial, local, state, national, and international pressures.

■ Teachers must be prepared to assume important roles in the curriculum development process, especially in developing student-centered and integrated curricula.

What Reform Efforts Have Affected the Curriculum?

■ Historical forces affecting the aims of education have influenced curriculum reform. Religion and the need to educate for citizenship in a democracy have played important roles in the development of American school curricula. In any historical period, curriculum content reflects society's beliefs and values about education.

■ Recent systematic efforts to establish curriculum reforms have focused on curriculum standards, core curricula, and education for equity and excellence.

What Are Some Current Subject-Area Trends?

■ Alternative curricula for literacy, multicultural curricula, character education, art as curriculum, problem-centered learning, thinking skills, computer literacy, and career education are examples of curriculum trends today.

■ Curriculum trends also involve, for example, redefining foreign language study and sex/health education, developing school-to-work programs, providing for active and authentic learning, determining what students will need to know and be able to do in the twenty-first century, and establishing national standards in the content areas.

KEY TERMS AND CONCEPTS

APPLICATIONS AND ACTIVITIES

Teacher's Journal

1. List in order of importance the five factors that you believe have the greatest impact on the curriculum. Then list the five factors that you believe *ideally* should have the greatest influence. What differences do you notice between your actual and ideal lists? What might be done to reduce the differences between the two lists?

2. Reflect on the 12,000 or so hours that you have spent as a student in K–12 classrooms. What did the nonexplicit curricula in the classes teach you about yourself?

3. What religious and political emphases affected your learning as a student in elementary school or high school? Which experiences do you view as having been positive? Which do you view as having been negative for you?

4. In your opinion, how should teachers and schools respond to censorship issues in the curricula and complaints about the content of instructional materials?

5. What is your opinion of the current emphasis on preparing students for the world of work as the chief aim of education? What influences have created this emphasis? What curriculum goals might be sacrificed through a focus on turning out good employees?

Teacher's Database

1. Visit the online ERIC Clearinghouse for a curricular area you plan to teach, and record information for your portfolio on the resources available to you as a teacher in that content area.

2. Survey the Internet to begin locating and bookmarking websites, schools, networks, and teacher discussion groups that you could use to help develop a subject-area curriculum for your students. To begin, you might wish to visit some of the online resources for developing and implementing the curriculum presented in the Appendix "Online Resources for Developing and Implementing the Curriculum" on this book's website.

3. Find the professional curriculum standards for your subject area(s) online and compare them to the curriculum standards for that subject area in a state where you plan to teach. For example, you might download the National Council for Teachers of Mathematics (NCTM) standards and then compare them with the mathematics curriculum in the state where you plan to teach.

Observations and Interviews

1. Spend a half-day at school at the level you plan to teach and record your impressions regarding the types of curricula. If possible, chat briefly with administrators, teachers, and students about your impressions. Include observations of students outside the classroom during the school day.

2. As a collaborative project, conduct an informal survey on what people think are the four most important subjects to be taught at the elementary, middle, junior, and senior high levels. Compare your data with the information in this chapter.

3. With classmates, as an experiment, practice the process of curriculum development described in this chapter. Assign some members of the group to observe and report on their observations in relation to concepts presented in in this chapter.

Professional Portfolio

Compare and contrast two or more textbooks or curriculum guides that are currently used by teachers to teach a unit in a subject area and at a grade level you are preparing to teach. Assess the strengths and weaknesses of the unit in each textbook or curriculum guide. Would you use the materials in your classroom? How would you improve them? What other curriculum materials would you incorporate? How would you integrate educational technology? How would you adapt the curriculum for the unit for individual students according to their needs and characteristics?

Appendix 10.1

Selected Subject-Area References for Curriculum Planning

The following are among the many recently published resources available for curriculum planning in the various subject areas. Many of these materials are available in online and CD-ROM versions as well as print.

Reading and Writing

Publications

Becoming a Reader: A Developmental Approach to Reading Instruction, 2nd ed. Michael P. O'Donnell and Margo Wood. Boston: Allyn and Bacon, 1999.

Best Books for Beginning Readers. Thomas G. Gunning. Boston: Allyn and Bacon, 1998.

Children's Inquiry: Using Language to Make Sense of the World. Judith Wells Lindfors. *Teaching for a Tolerant World, Grades K-6*. Judith P. Robertson (Ed.). New York: Teachers College Press, 1999.

Children's Writing: Perspectives from Research. Karin L. Dahl and Nancy Farnan. Newark, DE: International Reading Association, 1998.

Essentials of Children's Literature, 3rd ed. Carol Lynch-Brown and Carl M. Tomlinson. Boston: Allyn and Bacon, 1999.

Essentials of Elementary Language Arts, 2nd ed. Margo Wood. Boston: Allyn and Bacon, 1999.

Ideas Plus: Book Fifteen. Champaign, IL: National Council of Teachers of English, 1997.

Learning in Living Color: Using Literature to Incorporate Multicultural Education into the Primary Curriculum. Alora Valdez. Boston: Allyn and Bacon, 1999.

Literacy Instruction in Half- and Whole-Day Kindergartens: Research to Practice. Lesley Mandel Morrow, Dorothy S. Strickland, and Deborah Gee Woo. Newark, DE: International Reading Association, 1998.

NAEP 1998 Reading Report Card for the Nation and States. Washington, DC: National Assessment of Educational Progress, 1999.

Practical Applications of the Language Experience: Looking Back, Looking Forward. Olga G. Nelson and Wayne M. Linek. Boston: Allyn and Bacon, 1999.

Popular Culture in the Classroom: Teaching and Researching Critical Media Literacy. Donna E. Alvermann, Jennifer S. Moon, and Margaret C. Hagood. Newark, DE: International Reading Association, 1999.

Resilient Children: Stories of Poverty, Drug Exposure, and Literacy Development. Diane Barone. Newark, DE: International Reading Association, 1999.

Scaffolding Emergent Literacy: A Child-centered Approach for Preschool through Grade 5. Anne K. Soderman, Kara M. Gregory, and Louise T. O'Neill. Boston: Allyn and Bacon, 1999.

Teaching Children to Read and Write: Becoming an Influential Teacher, 2nd ed. Boston: Allyn and Bacon, 1999.

Teaching Language Arts: A Student- and Response-Centered Classroom, 3rd ed. Connie Cox. Boston: Allyn and Bacon, 1999.

Teaching Reading in the 21st Century, web ed. Michael F. Graves, Connie Juel, and Bonnie B. Graves. Boston: Allyn and Bacon, 1999.

Teaching Writing in Middle and Secondary Schools: Theory, Research and Practice. Margot Iris Soven. Boston: Allyn and Bacon, 1999.

Writing Framework and Specifications for the 1998 National Assessment of Educational Progress. Washington, DC: National Assessment of Educational Progress, 1999.

Journals

English Education

English Journal

Language Arts

The Reading Teacher

Mathematics

Publications

Activities for Junior High School and Middle School Mathematics, vol. 2. Kenneth E. Easterday, F. Morgan Simpson, and Tommy Smith. Reston, VA: National Council of Teachers of Mathematics, 1998.

Essentials of Elementary Mathematics, 2nd ed. C. Alan Riedesel and James E. Schwartz. Boston: Allyn and Bacon, 1999.

Future Basics: Developing Numerical Power. Randall Charles and Joanne Lobato. Reston, VA: National Council of Supervisors of Mathematics, 1998.

Mathematics in the Middle. Larry Leutzinger (ed.). Reston, VA: National Council of Teachers of Mathematics, and Columbus, OH: National Middle School Association, 1998.

Middle Grades Mathematics Textbooks: A Benchmark-based Evaluation (book and CD-ROM). American Association for the Advancement of Science. New York: Oxford University Press, 1999.

School Policies and Practices Affecting Instruction in Mathematics. Evelyn F. Hawkins, Frances B. Stancavage, and John A. Dossey. Washington, DC: National Assessment of Educational Progress (NAEP), 1998.

Spreadsheet Activities in Middle School Mathematics, 2nd ed., *revised for Macintosh and ClarisWorks.* John C. Russell. Reston, VA: National Council of Teachers of Mathematics, 1998.

Teacher-made Aids for Elementary School Mathematics: Readings from The Arithmetic Teacher *and* Teaching Children Mathematics, *Vol. 3.* Carole J. Reesink (ed.). Reston, VA: National Council of Teachers of Mathematics, 1998.

Teaching Mathematics: A Sourcebook of Aids, Activities, and Strategies, 3rd ed. Max A. Sobel and Evan M. Maletsky. Boston: Allyn and Bacon, 1999.

The Wonderful World of Mathematics: A Critically Annotated List of Children's Books in Mathematics, 2nd ed. Diane Thiessen, Margaret Matthais, and Jacquelin Smith. Reston, VA: National Council of Teachers of Mathematics, 1998.

Journals

Arithmetic Teacher
The Journal of Computers in Mathematics and Science Teaching
Mathematics Teacher
School Science and Mathematics

Science and Technology

Publications

Atlas of Science Literacy: Mapping K–12 Learning Goals. American Association for the Advancement of Science. New York: Oxford University Press, 2000.

Benchmarks for Science Literacy: A Tool for Curriculum Reform. American Association for the Advancement of Science. New York: Oxford University Press, 1993.

Blueprints for Reform: Science, Mathematics, and Technology Education. American Association for the Advancement of Science. New York: Oxford University Press, 1998.

Designs for Science Literacy. American Association for the Advancement of Science. New York: Oxford Uni-

versity Press, 1999.

Discovering Elementary Science: Method, Content, and Problem-solving Activities, 2nd ed. Boston: Allyn and Bacon, 1999.

Essentials of Elementary Science. Daniel C. Dobey, Robert J. Beichner, Sharon L. Raimondi. Boston: Allyn and Bacon, 1999.

Resources for Science Literacy: Professional Development, Helping Teachers Understand and Use Science Literacy Goals. (CD-ROM and companion paperback). American Association for the Advancement of Science. New York: Oxford University Press, 1997.

Science for All Children: Lessons for Constructing Understanding. Ralph Martin, Colleen Sexton, and Jack Gerlovich. Boston: Allyn and Bacon, 1999.

Journals

American Biology Teacher
Physics Teacher
School Science and Mathematics
Science and Children
Science Education
Science Teacher
Studies in Science Education

Social Studies

Publications

Because We Can Change the World: A Practical Guide to Building Cooperative, Inclusive, Classroom Communities. Mara Sapon-Shevin. Boston: Allyn and Bacon, 1999.

Essentials of Elementary Social Studies. Thomas N. Turner. Boston: Allyn and Bacon, 1999.

Classroom-Ready Activities for Teaching History and Geography in Grades 7–12. Thomas P. Ruff and Jennifer T. Nelson. Boston: Allyn and Bacon, 1998.

Global Perspectives for Educators. Carlos F. Diaz, Byron G. Massialas, and John A. Xanthopoulos. Boston: Allyn and Bacon, 1999.

Middle Grades Social Studies: Teaching and Learning for Active and Responsible Citizenship, 2nd ed. Michael G. Allen and Robert L. Stevens. Boston: Allyn and Bacon, 1998.

Teaching for a Tolerant World, Grades K–6. Judith P. Robertson (ed.). Champaign, IL: National Council of Teachers of English, 1999.

Teaching for a Tolerant World, Grades 9–12. Carol

Danks and Leatrice B. Rabinsky (eds.). Champaign, IL: National Council of Teachers of English, 1999.

Journals
History Teacher
Social Education
The Social Studies
Social Studies and the Young Learner
Social Studies Journal

Foreign Languages

Publications
Content-Based Instruction in Foreign Language Education: Models and Methods. Stephen B. Stryker and Betty Lou Leaver. Washington, DC: Georgetown University Press, 1997.
Language and Cognitive Development in Second Language Learning: Educational Implications for Children and Adults. Virginia Gonzalez. Boston: Allyn and Bacon, 1999.
Technology-Enhanced Language Learning. Michael D. Bush and Robert M. Terry (eds.). Lincolnwood, IL: National Textbook Co., 1997.
Understanding Learning Styles in the Second Language Classroom. Joy M. Reide (ed.). Upper Saddle River, NJ: Prentice Hall Regents, 1998.

Journals
Modern Language Journal
Modern Language Quarterly
Modern Languages

The Arts

Publications
The Arts in Children's Lives: Aesthetic Education in Early Childhood. Mary Renck Lalongo and Laurie Nicholson Stamp. Boston: Allyn and Bacon, 1997.
Learning in and Through Arts: A Guide to Discipline-based Art Education. Stephen Mark Dobbs. Los Angeles: Getty Education Institute for the Arts, 1998.
The Quiet Evolution: Changing the Face of Arts Education. Brent Wilson. Los Angeles: Getty Education Institute for the Arts, 1996.

Journals
Art Education
Music Educator's Journal
School Arts

Physical Education

Publications
Concepts of Physical Education: What Every Student Needs to Know. Reston, VA: National Association for Sport and Physical Education, 1998.
Dynamic Physical Education for Elementary School Children, 12th ed. Robert P. Pangrazi. Boston: Allyn and Bacon, 1998.
Eastern District Association's Guidelines for Physical Education Programs: Standards, Objectives, and Assessments for Grades K-12. Steveda F. Chepko and Ree K. Arnold. Boston: Allyn and Bacon, 1999.
Moving into the Future: National Physical Education Standards: A Guide to Content and Assessment. Reston, VA: National Association for Sport and Physical Education, 1995.
Physical Activity for Children: A Statement of Guidelines. Reston, VA: National Association for Sport and Physical Education, 1998.
Physical Education Methods for Classroom Teachers. Human Kinetics with Bonnie Pettifor. Champaign, IL: Human Kinetics, 1999.

Journals
Journal for Physical Education, Recreation and Dance
Journal of Health Education
Research Quarterly for Exercise and Sport Strategies

Vocational Education

Publications
Career and Technical Educator's Survival Guide. Alexandria, VA: Association for Career and Technical Education, 1999.
Curriculum Development in Vocational and Technical Education: Planning, Content, and Implementation, 5th ed. Curtis R. Finch and John R. Crunkilton. Boston: Allyn and Bacon, 1999.
High Skill, High-Wage Jobs. Kristen J. Amundson.

Appendix 10.1 *(continued)*

Alexandria, VA: Association for Career and Technical Education, 1998.

Making the Case—for School-to-Careers and Vocational Education. Alexandria, VA: Association for Career and Technical Education, 1997.

Taking the Worry out of Work-based Learning: The Law, Labor & School-to-Careers. Alice Potosky. Alexandria, VA: Association for Career and Technical Education, 1998.

Teaching Your Occupation to Others: A Guide to Surviving the First Year. Paul A. Bott. Boston: Allyn and Bacon, 1998.

The Dog Did It! And Other Classroom Stories from Vocational Educators. Alexandria, VA: Association for Career and Technical Education, 1998.

Journals
American Vocational Journal
The Career Development Quarterly
Career Education
Journal for Vocational Special Needs Education
Techniques: Connecting Education and Careers

11

Teaching with Technology

Media and technologies [may] greatly expand the range of teaching, learning, and communication modalities available to teachers and students, but at bottom their only value is in helping us to do other things well—engage students deeply in a topic, help them take more responsibility for their learning, help them learn to communicate clearly about their work and their ideas.

—Cornelia Brunner and William Tally
The New Media Literacy Handbook, 1999

1. How are educational technologies influencing schools?

2. What technologies are available for teaching?

3. How do teachers use computers and the Internet?

4. What are the effects of technology on learning?

5. Should technology be at the forefront of efforts to improve schools in the United States?

6. What barriers limit the integration of technology into schools?

At James Madison High School in New York City, tenth-grade students, mostly African American and Latino, file into a networked computer lab and find seats at large new monitors and keyboards. Outside, in the hallways, in the stairwells, and in the foyers, the school resembles a minimum-security-prison facility, with metal detectors at the doors, a police substation located off the foyer, and security guards who move through the halls breaking up small groups of students who are avoiding classes by lounging on stairs and in rest rooms. James Madison is a large school in a middle-income neighborhood, but nearly all the students are poor and working-class. Drugs and violence are a recurrent problem. The computer lab, however, is a relative haven: it is quiet here, and as students enter their names into the computer, they find that the software program greets them warmly by name, remembers exactly where they were when they left off the day before with their work, and gently guides them through well-designed exercises in biology, algebra, and American history, praising successful answers and offering patient prompting and another chance—without a hint of judgment—when they miss an answer. The teacher, who monitors the students' individual workstations from a central machine of his own, moves around the room, helping students with technical problems, finding files, and printing. The students work well and mostly silently until the bell rings fifty minutes after they entered the room. Then they file out to return to their regular classrooms where, despite some dedicated teachers, the crowded, noisy, and sometimes intimidating teaching conditions will ensure that they remain relatively anonymous, and will have little contact with challenging material. In the chaotic context of James Madison, technology is the vehicle of a more individualized, effective—and possibly humane—instruction than students might otherwise get.

At the Richmond Academy, a private school across town from James Madison, ninth-graders file into their social studies classroom and, before class begins, log on to one of six workstations at tables against the walls. They argue noisily about what they are finding as they unearth an archaeological site in ancient Greece. The students have been working on the computer-based archaeology simulation for about three weeks, and teams of students are each responsible for excavating one of four separate quadrants of the site. It is a welcome break for the ninth-graders, who in their other classes spend much of their time taking lecture notes and learning to parse sophisticated texts as part of their college-prep curriculum. Here they are "digging up" pottery shards, fragments of weapons, pieces of masonry, and bits of ancient texts, and trying to identify and interpret each artifact in order to fit it into their emerging picture of the site as a whole. In their research the students visit local museums, consult reference works on Greek history, art, and architecture, and ask other teachers in the school to help translate texts. Cleverly, the students' teachers have filled the site with ambiguous evidence, so that some teams find a preponderance of data suggesting the site was a temple, while others find artifacts mostly suggesting it was a battlefield. In weekly meetings the teams present their latest findings to the rest of the class, and a hot debate ensues as the amateur archaeologists struggle to reconcile the fragmentary and ambiguous data. On this day the classroom is active and noisy, yet controlled, as students take turns at the computer, graph their findings on large wall-charts, call across the room to ask if anyone has a spearhead to compare with one just found, and argue about whose final interpretation of the site will best explain the bulk of the evidence (Brunner and Tally 1999, 23–25).

Source: From *The New Media Literacy Handbook: An Educator's Guide to Bringing New Media into the Classroom,* by Cornelia Brunner and William Tally. Copyright 1999 by Cornelia Brunner and William Tally. Used by permission of Doubleday, a division of Random House, Inc.

In the two contrasting settings above, students are using up-to-date computers in very different ways. The teacher at James Madison High uses computers to present information to students systematically and efficiently; in effect, the computers are an *instructional delivery system*. The instructors at Richmond Academy use computers to stimulate students' higher order thinking, creativity, and problem solving as they evaluate complex, often ambiguous material; here, computers are a *catalyst for group investigation and inquiry*. Although these two examples are strikingly different, they are similar in that teachers at both schools are using the computer as a "tool" to achieve their educational goals and to create particular kinds of learning environments. The computer-based curriculum at James Madison enables the teacher to provide students with a structured, sequential way to acquire information, and the computers provide students with immediate feedback in a nonthreatening manner. Computers serve an entirely different purpose at Richmond—here, computers enable the teachers to create a rich, stimulating environment that fosters collaboration, inquiry, and decision making.

How Are Educational Technologies Influencing Schools?

Carol Gilkinson's classroom looks like those of talented teachers everywhere—lively, filled with displays of students' work, photos of field trips, and information-filled posters. A closer look, however, reveals how computers have transformed teaching and learning in her classroom. Several computers in the room allow students to communicate via the Internet with other students in Germany, Holland, Russia, and Australia. Gilkinson's students also use child-oriented "search engines" like *Yahooli*gans! and KidsLink to search for information about whales, the Brazilian rain forest, or the planet Mars on the World Wide Web. They go to "chat rooms" or "newsgroups" for children, where they can "talk" to other children around the world or participate in various global networking projects for children.

Gilkerson's classroom and the James Madison High and Richmond Academy classrooms featured in this chapter's opening scenario are representative of how recently developed technologies have transformed the learning environments in thousands of schools around the country. Moreover, the pace of change shows no signs of letting up—as one technology expert said, "We may well assume that we haven't seen anything yet. [If] present trends continue, it seems not unreasonable to expect that digital technologies will have an impact on our classrooms proportionate to that of writing and the printing press" (Withrow 1997, 4). Similarly, one of the nation's foremost futurists, Marvin Cetron, has predicted that "Computers will free educators to adopt much more sophisticated, effective, and rewarding styles of teaching. Future teachers will be facilitators, monitors, and catalysts, rather than lecturers and taskmasters" (Cetron 1997, 19–20).

Technology and the Challenge to Schools

The Internet, the World Wide Web, and related telecommunications technologies have the potential to transform teaching and learning. However, one of the education issues for the twenty-first century is how committed are teachers, administrators, policy-makers, parents, and the general public to enabling students to realize the full impact that technology can have on their learning? As Howard Mehlinger (1996, 403) says, the future of schools may depend on their response to this challenge.

> The genie is out of the bottle. It is no longer necessary to learn about the American War of Independence by sitting in Mrs. Smith's classroom and hearing her version of it. There are more powerful and efficient ways to learn about the Revolutionary War, and they are all potentially under the control of the learner. Either schools will come to terms with this fact, or schools will be ignored.

Additionally, educators must develop new assessment techniques to evaluate students' learning that occurs through the use of advanced telecommunications like the Internet and the World Wide Web. The number of correct responses on homework, quizzes, and examinations will no longer suffice to measure students' learning. "If teachers want students to be able to use ditto masters, then they shouldn't spend thousands of dollars on systems that support computer-assisted instruction. If teachers want to reinforce their didactic role and their role as information providers, then they should also leave computers alone" (Morton 1996, 419).

In its *School Technology and Readiness Report,* the CEO Forum on Education and Technology (1999) called on teachers to incorporate technologies to create "new learning environments" that enable students to develop higher-order thinking skills to research, analyze, and creatively solve problems in the future. The following chart contrasts the "traditional" and "new" learning environments envisioned by the Forum.

Traditional Learning Environment	New Learning Environment
Teacher-centered instruction	Student-centered learning
Single-sense stimulation	Multisensory stimulation
Single-path progression	Multipath progression
Single medium	Multimedia
Isolated work	Collaborative work
Information delivery	Information exchange
Passive learning	Active/exploratory/inquiry-based learning
Factual, knowledge-based	Critical thinking and informed decision making
Reactive response	Proactive/planner action
Isolated, artificial context	Authentic, real-world context

When you think about your future as a teacher who will be expected to use technology to create a "new learning environment," you may find that future at once exciting and intimidating, enticing and threatening. You may ask, will I be ready to meet the challenge of integrating technologies into my teaching? In a very real sense, it is in the hands of people like you to develop new ways to use new technologies in the classrooms of tomorrow. The following "Professional Reflection" is designed to help you begin the process of planning for that future.

Professional Reflection   **How technically proficient are you?**

Following is a list of educational technologies and instructional strategies that are currently changing teaching and learning. For each, indicate with an X whether you are "proficient," "somewhat proficient," or "not proficient" with that technology or strategy. Then indicate whether you are "highly committed," "somewhat committed," "opposed," or "neutral" toward using that technology or strategy in your teaching. Space is provided for you to add technologies and strategies not on the list.

After responding to the items, reflect on those to which you are "highly committed" to integrating into your teaching. What steps will you take from this point on to ensure that those technologies and strategies will, in fact, be part of your teaching in the future?

Technology or Instructional Strategy	Proficiency Level			Commitment to Using			
	Proficient	Somewhat proficient	Not proficient	Highly committed	Somewhat committed	Opposed	Neutral
1. Student networking via computer							
2. Video teleconferencing							
3. Interactive multimedia/ hypermedia							
4. Web page authoring							
5. CD-ROMs/ videodiscs/digital video disks (DVD)							
6. Computer assisted instruction (CAI)							
7. Word processing							
8. Desktop publishing							
9. Presentation graphics							
10. Spreadsheets/graphing							
11. Databases							
12. e-mail							
13. Attaching files to e-mail							
14. Newsgroups							
15. Electronic gradebook							
16. Information retrieval on WWW							
17. Networking with file server							
18. Scanners							
19. Faxes							
20. Digital cameras							
21. Video cameras							
22. Other _____							
23. Other _____							

What Technologies Are Available for Teaching?

To enhance their classroom instruction, today's teachers can draw from a dazzling array of technological devices. Little more than a decade ago, the technology available to teachers who wished to use more than the chalkboard was limited to an overhead projector, a 16-mm movie projector, a tape recorder, and, in a few forward-looking school districts, television sets. Today, teachers and students use ever-more-powerful desktop and laptop computers with built-in modems, faxes, and CD-ROM players; videodisc players; camcorders; optical scanners; speech and music synthesizers; laser printers, digital cameras, and LCD projection panels. In addition, they use sophisticated software for web browsing, e-mail, word processing, desktop publishing, presentation graphics, spreadsheets, databases, and multimedia applications.

Although the array of currently available technology for the classroom is dazzling, Marvin Cetron predicts that future technologies will be even more impressive. He contends that by 2010 an "Information Appliance" (IA) "should be on the desks of most American students."

> The IA will be a computer, a fax machine, and a copier. Its 20 by 30 inch flat color screen will be half multimedia display and half picture-phone. Two buttons will set it to translate automatically among any of nine common languages, enabling users who don't speak the same language to communicate.
>
> This new one-box-does-all data center will handle all our information and communication needs. Radio, 500 television channels (many designed for the classroom), e-mail, Web access, and all forms of personal computing will come through the IA. Aimed at consumers, its controls will be simple enough for small children to use. And because it will contain more raw computing power than today's top-of-the-line PCs, it will run educational software as sophisticated as any now available for multi-user classroom systems (Cetron 1997, 21).

While the term *educational technology* is usually taken to mean computers in the classroom, many different forms of technology have influenced education in the United States. If we broadly define **educational technology** as inventions that enable teachers to reach their goals more effectively, it is clear that for some time teachers have been integrating into their classrooms many forms of educational technology, from the humble chalkboard to the overhead projector. One technology that has had a long and perhaps controversial history in education is television.

The Television Revolution

The television revolution in the United States began with great optimism. David Sarnoff, who founded NBC and introduced the first color television at the New York World's Fair in 1939, confidently predicted that television was "destined to provide greater knowledge to larger numbers of people, truer perception of the meaning of current events, more accurate appraisal of men in public life, and a broader understanding of the needs and aspirations of our fellow human beings" (Sarnoff 1940). Since that time, television has become an omnipresent feature of life in the United States, and its effects—both positive and negative—on all facets of American life are still being studied and debated, and for good cause. Children spend an estimated equivalent of two months of the year watching television. The typical child between six and eleven years of age watches about twenty-seven hours a week; and, by the time they graduate from high school, young people have watched an average of 22,000 hours of television (Shenk 1998)

Critics of television point out that it encourages passivity in the young, may be linked to increases in violence and crime, often reinforces sexual and ethnic stereotypes, retards growth and development, and may be linked to learning disorders. Psychologist Jerome Singers contends that "most [heavy-viewing] kids show lower information, lower reading recognition or readiness to reading, [and] lower reading levels; [and they] tend to show lower imaginativeness and less complex language usage" (quoted in Shenk 1998, 61). Some say that television robs children of the time they need to do homework, to read and reflect, and to build bonds with family members and others through interaction.

However, television can enhance students' learning. Excellent educational programs are aired by the Public Broadcasting Service and by some cable and other commercial networks. Television has also had a positive impact on how students are taught in schools. With the increased availability of video equipment, many schools have begun to have students produce their own television documentaries, news programs, oral histories, and dramas. Many schools have closed-circuit television systems that teachers use to prepare instructional materials for students in the district, and many districts have **distance learning networks** that use two-way, interactive telecommunications to provide enrichment instruction to students in remote areas or staff development to teachers.

Channel One   One of the most controversial uses of television in the schools is Channel One, started by Christopher Whittle in 1990. Watched daily by about eight million teenagers in more than 12,000 public and private schools in nearly every state, **Channel One** is a twelve-minute news broadcast, with two minutes of commercials for which advertisers pay as much as $200,000 per thirty-second time slot (Walsh, 1999a). On agreeing to show Channel One programs to most students on 90 percent of school days (students may opt out of viewing), schools receive the program free, including $25,000 worth of equipment (a satellite dish, two video cassette recorders, nineteen-inch color monitors mounted throughout the school, and internal wiring) that is regularly serviced at no charge. According to the Channel One Network, 99 percent of schools choose to renew their three-year contract to carry Channel One, and the Network has received numerous awards and aired more than $70 million worth of public service announcements. Moreover, the Network points out, schools are encouraged to use the equipment for other educational purposes such as viewing programs on the Learning Channel, CNN, the Discovery Channel, and C-Span; producing student news shows; conducting teacher in-service programs; and making daily announcements.

The Channel One contributions to education notwithstanding, professional associations such as the National Education Association, educational leaders, and politicians have maintained that advertisements have no place in the classroom. At a 1999 Senate committee hearing, consumer advocate Ralph Nader labeled Channel One "the most brazen marketing ploy in the history of the United States" and cited "parental neglect and the delinquency of school boards" as key reasons for the network's popularity (Walsh, 1999e). According to William Hoynes, a sociology professor at Vassar College, the primary goal of Channel One is not to inform students but to assemble a vast "teen market" and then sell high-priced advertising slots (Hoynes 1998). His analysis of Channel One programs led him to conclude that they were "fundamentally commercial" and their educational value "highly questionable."

The Computer Revolution

At Franklin Park Magnet School, a science-technology-environment-math magnet school in Lee County, Florida, students routinely experience learning via computer-based multimedia. Each morning students broadcast *FPM News* live from the school's television studio, which is controlled by a computer that allows students to produce professional-quality video shows with video fades, wipes, and special effects. Teachers have computer workstations with overhead projectors and LCD (liquid crystal display) projection panels, and their students work at individual computer workstations. According to teacher Sandi Agle, FPM students are learning essential computer skills: "In the future, these students will be using similar computer tools, not paper, to disseminate information" (Poole 1995, 354).

Although personal computers may not have transformed all schools so that all students have learning experiences like those at FPM, computers have had a significant impact on education. Like the dawn of the television era sixty years earlier, the widespread availability of personal computers has been heralded as a technological innovation that will change the teaching–learning process. As Bill Gates, founder of Microsoft, predicted in *The Road Ahead* (Gates, Myhrvold, and Rinearson 1996), "I expect education of all kinds to improve significantly within the next decade . . . information technology will empower people of all ages, both inside and outside the classroom, to learn more easily, enjoyably, and successfully than ever before."

Computers and Instruction   Since the early 1980s, the use of computers to enhance instruction has grown steadily. Two of the more common approaches are computer-

These students, like those at Franklin Park Magnet School in Lee County, Florida, are broadcasting a live program from their school's television studio. How have the television revolution and the computer revolution changed education for the better? For the worse?

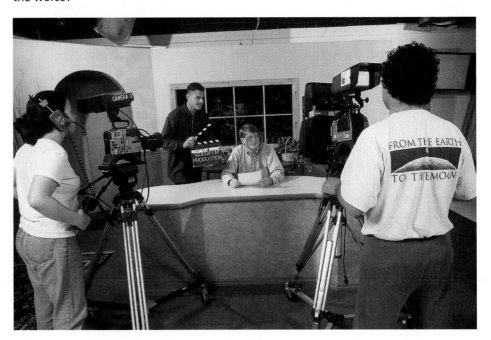

assisted instruction (CAI) (sometimes called computer-*aided* instruction) and computer-managed instruction (CMI). **Computer-assisted instruction (CAI)** relies on computer programs that provide students with highly structured drill-and-practice exercises or tutorials. Research has shown CAI to be effective with at-risk students and students with disabilities because it accommodates their special needs and instruction is appropriately paced (Bialo 1989; Jones 1994; Kozma et al. 1992; Norris 1994; Signer 1991). Moreover, CAI can provide students with a more positive, supportive environment for learning; students can avoid embarrassment since their inevitable mistakes while learning are not exposed to peers. Figure 11.1 presents several additional student-centered and technology-centered advantages of CAI.

Computer-managed instruction (CMI) relies on programs that evaluate and diagnose students' needs and then, based on that assessment, guide them through the next steps in their learning. CMI also records students' progress for teachers to monitor. This chapter's opening scenario, for example, began with a glimpse of how CMI is delivered at James Madison High School. CAI and CMI can result in reduced teacher–student interactions, if the teacher interprets his or her role as primarily that of record keeper or manager. On the other hand, CAI and CMI can enhance teacher–student interactions: "Freed from the necessity of conducting routine drills and performing many management duties, the teacher has more time to be the vital human link between student and knowledge. The computer does not supplant teachers; it supports them" (Bitter and Pierson 1999, 249).

An increasingly popular approach to computer-based instruction is computer-enhanced instruction (CEI). Unlike CAI and CMI, **computer-enhanced instruction (CEI)** is less structured and more inquiry-oriented. For example, the archeological inquiries conducted by Richmond Academy students in this chapter's opening scenario illustrate CEI. Unlike CAI or CMI, teachers in CEI play a critical role in facilitating inter-

Advantages of Computer-Assisted Instruction

Student-Centered Advantages

Students' self-tasking and self-pacing of their learning
Opportunities for individualized instruction
Low-risk learning context for learners what are less able
Multisensory modes of communication (voice, sound, text, graphic, art, animation)
Motivating, high-interest content
Enabling learning context for students with disabilities
Opportunities to learn for students with limited English proficiency
Likelihood of higher achievement (remediation or enrichment)

COMPUTER-ASSISTED INSTRUCTION

Technology-Centered Advantages

Efficiency and effectiveness
Savings in teachers' instructional time
Systematic response to users and high rates of reinforcement
Skill training in formal logic and technical skills
Consistent, reliable instruction independent of teacher, day/time, or place
Automatic record keeping and performance monitoring capabilities
Access to expanded knowledge base and global information resources
Enabling context for customizing or creating curricula, instructional materials, software

Figure 11.1

Advantages of Computer-Assisted Instruction (CAI)

actions between computer and student—teachers "are [essential] to the learning process, because simply seating students in front of their computers to surf the Net will not result in the same learning curve as when teachers assign well-designed projects in which students use the Net to gather information" (Kirkpatrick and Cuban 1998).

Some schools are using another inquiry-oriented approach to enhancing instruction with computers—the microcomputer-based laboratory (MBL), sometimes called CBL (computer-based laboratory). Through probes and sensors attached to computers, **microcomputer-based laboratories (MBL)** enable students to measure and graph data such as light, sound temperature, voltage, skin resistance, magnetic field, and heat flow. Students can gather data in the school laboratory or use a battery-operated interface to gather data in the field. For example, Concord Consortium, a nonprofit research and development organization dedicated to developing new ways to use technology in teaching, has developed MBL curriculum materials that enable students to learn about rain forests by using a sensor to gather local data for such variables as humidity, light, dissolved oxygen in rivers and streams, and acid rain. Students then compare local data with those obtained in an actual rain forest.

The "Magic" of Media

Personal computers have so revolutionized the instructional media available to teachers that today it is no exaggeration to refer to the "magic" of media. Carol Gilkerson, a Christa McAuliffe Educator, describes how instructional media have transformed her teaching:

> One of the chief strengths of using technology in the classroom is that it enables me to adapt my instruction to the individual needs and learning styles of the students. As computer activities can be tailored to student needs, the class becomes more student centered. CD-ROM, videodisc, and captioned instructional television present information visually and allow students to learn complex material more easily.

Some of the most exciting forms of media magic involve CD-ROMs, videodiscs, and interactive multimedia. Recent advances in computer technology have made it possible for students to become much more active in shaping their learning experiences. On a four-inch **CD-ROM,** they can access the equivalent of about 270,000 pages of text, about nine hundred 300-page books; or on a twelve-inch **videodisc** they can access the equivalent of about 54,000 photographic slides. Computer-supported **interactive multimedia** allow students to integrate information from huge text, audio, and video libraries.

Hypermedia   Systems consisting of computer, CD-ROM drive, videodisc player, video monitor, and speakers now allow students to control and present sound, video images, text, and graphics with an almost limitless array of possibilities. Students who use such hypermedia systems, the most familiar of which is the World Wide Web, can follow their curiosity, browse through enormous amounts of information, and develop creative solutions for multidimensional, real-life problem situations. On-line databases in many fields are changing the way students conduct library research, as more computerized reference works—such as directories, dictionaries, and encyclopedias—become available.

The term **hypermedia** refers to documents composed of text, audio, and visual information stored in a computer and accessed by the user in a nonlinear fashion. "Rather than reading an information space sequentially in a pre-determined order, a user of [hypermedia] explores the information space in his or her own order, usually based on his or her interests" (Schwartz and Beichner 1999, 56), with the computer used to "link" related segments of information into larger "webs" or networks. A hypermedia system is an effective learning tool because it allows students to actively construct their own learning experiences based on their interests, preferences, and learning styles.

Computer Simulations   For students, computer simulations can be engaging and very motivational. Simulations model complex, multidimensional events in the real world and can range from the lemonade stand that elementary school students plan and run vicariously, practicing basic arithmetic and problem-solving skills, to a mock trial, which Harvard Law students can participate in via videodisc and computer. As learners work their way through a simulation, they make decisions at critical points, enter their decisions into the computer, and then receive feedback on the consequences of those decisions.

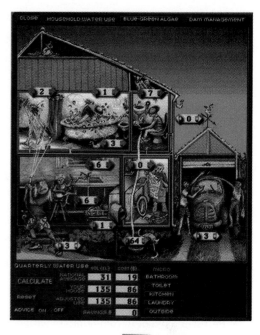

Figure 11.2

Household water use simulator from *Exploring the Nardoo*
Source: Interactive Multimedia Learning Laboratory, Faculty of Education, University of Wollongong, Wollongong, New South Wales, Australia. Used with permission.

Currently available **computer-based simulations** provide students with contextually rich learning experiences, from visiting the great museums of the world, to exploring the bottom of the Pacific Ocean, to experiencing what it was like to be a pioneer setting out in a wagon train from St. Louis to the coast of Oregon. Figure 11.2, for example, shows a household water use simulator from *Exploring the Nardoo*, a CD-ROM program that focuses on a range of water management investigations related to the Nardoo, an imaginary river in Australia. The Nardoo program, developed by the Interactive Multimedia Learning Laboratory at the University of Wollongong in Australia, requires students to solve problems, measure, synthesize data, and communicate findings as they "conduct" research at the Water Research Centre. After students enter the number of baths, showers, toilet flushes, dish washings, car washes, and so on a hypothetical family uses per day, the simulator calculates the family's water usage and compares it with national averages. Students then implement various water-saving strategies throughout the household and rerun the simulation to determine the amount of water saved.

Home–School Communication Systems   Computer-based home–school communication systems such as the Phone Master Notification System are helping busy teachers and parents exchange information. By interfacing a computer program with its computer-based student records, Georgetown Middle School in Georgetown, Kentucky, enables teachers to use a "Talking Gradebook" to communicate students' progress to parents. Or, by using a touchtone phone and entering a teacher's room number, Georgetown students and parents can access homework assignments, test scores, and current grades. Increasingly, schools are using sophisticated **home–school communication systems** to strengthen their educational programs. Some communication systems even include a "tip line" that uses voice disguising to provide students with an anonymous, safe way to provide tips to help reduce school violence. Schools are also using home–school communication systems to disseminate the following kinds of information:

absence and tardy parent notification

invitations to school events

PTA/PTO information

school cancellations, early dismissals

Kristi Rennebohm Franz
Technology and Multicultural Educator

". . . learning with the children."

First graders in Kristi Rennebohm Franz's class in Sunnyside Elementary School, Pullman, Washington, think that using the Internet to exchange drawings with children around the world and taking daily Spanish lessons from a teacher in Argentina are just part of going to school. The students also took in stride talking to their teacher while she attended an international conference in Budapest and participating in an hour-long live videoconference with twelve teachers from other countries. "Their communication skills are innate at that young age," Franz explains. "It's so natural for them to want to communicate with people, and technology becomes a natural way to do it."

What moved Franz most, as she watched from Budapest, was seeing her young students in Pullman form a huddle to figure out how to talk with one of the conference teachers who spoke only Spanish. After sharing their bits of knowledge, they said several sentences in Spanish to her. Franz was also pleased to have students discover that people in other countries were interested in learning about them, noting that "multicultural edu-

cation tends to focus only on learning about *other* people and places."

As an educator and life-long learner, Franz has developed a rich array of skills and talents, which serve her well as she designs motivating future-oriented curricula that tap students' varied learning modalities. In college she studied speech therapy and on graduation became a speech therapist in the public schools in Champaign, Illinois. She later earned a degree in music therapy so she could "use speech and music therapy together to help students with special needs." When she moved to Washington state with her husband, a university professor, she taught cello lessons and chamber music and played in the Washington Symphony. Traveling with her husband for a sabbatical in Nairobi, Kenya, she taught kindergarten at an international school.

Her rich storehouse of experiences contributes to

teacher reminders for assignments/activities
reminders to vote on bond issues
congratulatory calls

lunch menus
bus schedules
club information

The Internet

Observers estimate that the amount of information in the world doubles every 900 days (Bitter and Pierson 1999); the **Internet,** consisting of thousands of interconnected computers around the globe, and the **World Wide Web** (the most popular "entrance" to the Internet) make available to teachers and students much of this information. As Table 11.1 shows, the size of the World Wide Web has increased exponentially since 1995. In addition, newsgroups and chat rooms on the Internet enable teachers and students to communicate with people around the world.

Newsgroups Through **newsgroups,** students can create electronic bulletin boards of their own and discuss topics of mutual interest with students at other schools, in the same community, or around the world. Messages are "posted" on the bulletin board for others to read at their convenience. When students "surf" into a newsgroup, they

Franz's forward-looking perspective. The title of the project that Franz shared at the 1996 International Education and Resource Network conference in Budapest was "Reweaving the Global Tapestry of Education for Today's Students: Multicultural Education." Franz and her Internet colleague, Jane McLane Kimball, collaborated with teachers in twelve schools around the world, "on every continent except Antarctica," to exchange their young students' drawings of their families along with brief texts written by the children in their native languages explaining what they had drawn. Franz observes that including the brief texts, locally translated, helped the students "comprehend the multilingual aspect of our planet." The children then e-mailed their reactions to each others' drawings and discussed how families are different and alike in different countries. Franz's project was published as an article entitled "Toward a Critical Social Consciousness in Children: Multicultural Peace Education in a First Grade Classroom" in the journal *Theory into Practice* (1996, 264–70).

To teachers who want to begin using educational technology in their classrooms, Franz advises: "Choose what you feel are important curricular concepts and start by looking for ways software and telecommunications can enhance your teaching and learning with the chil-

dren." She suggests that teachers find two or three recommended websites to explore in depth, well enough to integrate them into their curriculum. "Partnering up with another school to develop a social context for learning" is the next step. Franz's students exchange e-mail daily with another class across their state, sometimes sending a letter with each line contributed by a different child. Her class has also built its own website.

Franz began using computers and telecommunication technology with her students when she realized that it was "a way to enhance their learning about the world." She learned along with the children, discovering a unique form of student–teacher collaborative learning—a process that "is making major changes in how we do our teaching and learning." Franz believes strongly in global awareness, multiculturalism, environmental education, and teaching to all learning modalities, as well as educational technology and telecommunications. As a Visiting Scholar at Harvard University's Graduate School of Education from January through August 1997, Franz assisted in the development of a summer institute on technology for teachers to help prepare students for the global future.

Table 11.1

Growth of the Internet and the World Wide Web (WWW)

	1995	1996	1997	1998	1999
Number of people online (worldwide)*	26,000,000	55,000,000	101,000,000	150,000,000	179,000,000
Number of WWW sites (worldwide)	23,500	299,403	1,681,868	3,689,227	4,389,131
Number of hosts (computers connected to Internet worldwide)	6,642,000	12,881,000	19,540,000	36,739,000	43,230,000
Number of WWW pages (worldwide)	18,000,000	—	—	—	829,000,000

*Figures include both adults and children
—Data not available.
Note: Numbers are estimates.

Sources: Data compiled from Nua Ltd, Internet Surveys, 1999; Internet Software Consortium (ISC), 1999; *Adobe Magazine, 10*(2), 100, Spring 1999; and Robert H. Zakon, Hobbes' Internet Timeline, 1999.

C an the Internet enhance school–
home communication and
parental involvement?

As the following table from the Fifth Phi Delta Kappa Poll of Teachers' Attitudes toward the Public Schools shows, both teachers and members of the public believe that traditional forms of communication such as newsletters and open houses are much more effective than Internet chat rooms. Why do you think the Internet is not seen as a more effective vehicle for school–home communication? Do parents who have the ability to communicate with schools and teachers via the Internet have an unfair advantage over parents who do not have access to the Internet? What suggestions do you have for how schools might use the Internet more effectively to foster communication with their constituencies?

Here are some ways In which public schools try to open lines of communication with citizens. In your opinion, how effective do you think each of the following would be?

	Very and Some-what Effective		Very effective	Somewhat effective	Not very effective	Not at all effective
	Teachers %	Public %	Teachers %	Teachers %	Teachers %	Teachers %
Public school newsletters	84	87 (2)	33	51	14	2
Public school open houses	81	89 (1)	35	46	15	3
Public school news hotlines	71	77 (5)	21	50	25	3
Neighborhood discussion groups	66	81 (4)	19	47	28	6
Open hearings	62	85 (3)	16	46	32	6
Televised school board meetings	60	74 (6)	16	45	33	7
Internet "chat rooms" set up by your local school	55	63 (7)	13	42	34	11

(Numbers in parentheses indicate where the item ranks with the public. Not all rows add to 100% because of rounding.)
Source: Carol A. Langdon, "The Fifth Phi Delta Kappa Poll of Teachers' Attitudes Toward the Public Schools," *Phi Delta Kappan,* April 1999, p. 618.

will find messages arranged by subject and author, with responses listed beneath the original message.

Chat rooms Students can also participate in "live" discussions held in a **chat room.** Chat rooms use Internet Relay Chat (IRC) technology and allow users to participate in live, on-line, typed discussions. In some chat rooms, students can talk to on-line experts in a wide array of fields and receive immediate responses to their questions.

KIDLINK, a well-known chat room for children ages 10 to 15, is carefully monitored and open only to registered users. The goal of KIDLINK is to promote global dialogue among young people, and students must answer four questions when they register: (1) "Who am I?" (2) "What do I want to be when I grow up?" (3) "How do I want the world to be better when I grow up?" and (4) "What can I do now to make this happen?" Teacher-leaders of KIDLINK organize and monitor numerous projects; for example, the ongoing Family History Project has the following goals:

- To bring history alive for students by assisting them in learning how their family participated in "real" history
- To learn how previous generations actually lived, values they had, customs they practiced, and so on
- To promote creative writing skills
- To develop research and note-taking skills by "digging" around in the family tree
- To learn about other cultures by sharing with each other on the Kidproj list (an e-mail list of participants)
- To increase computer skills by using word processors, perhaps drawing or graphics programs, e-mail, listserves, and the WWW
- To learn more about community resources in individual geographical areas (Schwartz and Beichner 1999, 119–120).

Videoconferencing   Video conferences can be held over the Internet if users have video cameras connected to their computers and C-U SeeMe, PictureTel, or similar software installed. For example, recall how students of first-grade teacher Kristi Rennebohm Franz (featured in this chapter's "Keepers of the Dream") participated in a video conference with their teacher while she attended an international conference in Budapest. As with any educational technology, care must be taken that **videoconferencing** is more than a "high tech" way for teachers to lecture to passive students at other locations. "Videoconferencing best supports meaningful learning by helping diverse learners to collaborate and converse with each other in order to solve problems and construct meaning" (Jonassen, Peck, and Wilson 1999, 82)

How Do Teachers Use Computers and the Internet?

As the preceding section illustrates, a dazzling array of technologies is available for teachers to use in the classroom. However, the availability and use of these tools for teaching and learning are two different matters. To what extent and how are teachers actually using new technologies? How useful do they find them? To answer these questions, the U.S. Department of Education sponsored the Teaching, Learning, and Computing (TLC) survey which gathered data from three groups: (1) a nationally representative sample of approximately 2,250 fourth- through twelfth-grade teachers at public and private schools throughout the country, (2) 1,800 teachers at "high-end" technology schools and schools participating in national or regional educational reform programs, and (3) 1,700 principals and school-level technology coordinators (Anderson and Ronnkvist 1999; Becker 1999; Ravitz, Wong, and Becker 1999).

Preparing Lessons

The Internet has been termed "the world's largest library," and, as such, it can be a remarkable resource for planning lessons. According to the TLC survey, 28 percent of teachers use the Internet weekly or more often to gather information and resources on

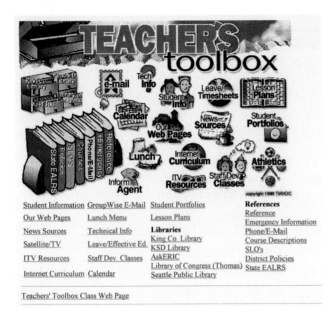

the Internet for their teaching, and 40 percent do so occasionally. Among teachers who have access to the Internet at school as well as at home, 46 percent report weekly or more frequent use. In Washington State's Kent School District, for instance, teachers learn to use the district's Teacher's Toolbox website (see Figure 11.3) where they share lesson plans and gather information on students' progress in other classes. Kent teachers also use the Toolbox to complete previously onerous paperwork online and to sign up for in-service training.

Communicating with Other Educators

Compared to their use of the Internet to prepare lessons and gather resources, teachers use the Internet less often to communicate with other educators, according to the TLC survey. Only 16 percent of teachers used e-mail to communicate with teachers in other schools, and 23 percent did so occasionally. However, "by far the most important variable in predicting teachers' Internet use is the teacher's level of classroom connectivity" (Becker 1999, 29). For example, a comparison of e-mail use between teachers who had Internet access at home and at school with teachers who had access only at home revealed that teachers with classroom access were *three times as likely* to e-mail teachers at other schools. Not surprisingly, if teachers don't have ready access to the Internet during their daily professional lives, their use of e-mail is less frequent.

Although efforts to integrate technology into schools require information about the extent of teachers' access to and use of the Internet, it is important to ask whether teachers believe the Internet is a valuable tool for teaching. In response to this question, TLC survey data revealed that 49 percent of teachers believe that having a computer with e-mail capabilities on their own desk is "essential," and, similarly, 47 percent believe having Web access in the classroom is "essential." In addition, another 38 percent believe e-mail access is "valuable," and 41 percent believe Web access is "valuable." These results seem to counter the observation that "a lot of teachers say, '[Technology] is one more thing on my plate and I don't know how it will help me'" (Ortiz 1999).

Posting Information and Student Work on the Web

In addition to using e-mail to communicate with other educators, 18 percent of teachers posted information, professional opinions, or student work at least once on the Web. For instance, as with the use of e-mail, the likelihood of teachers posting information, opinions, or student work was strongly related to connectivity in the classroom. As class-

Table 11.2

Percent of teachers having their students use different types of software by grade level

	Word Processing	CD-ROM Reference	World Wide Web	Games/ Drills	Simulations	Graphics	Spreadsheet/ Database	Multimedia Authoring	E-mail
Elementary	65%	54%	26%	63%	33%	26%	10%	14%	7%
Middle	44%	32%	26%	21%	18%	19%	16%	8%	6%
High	45%	29%	34%	11%	21%	20%	20%	8%	8%
All teachers	50%	36%	29%	28%	23%	21%	16%	9%	7%

Source: Henry Jay Becker, "Internet Use by Teachers: Conditions of Professional Use and Teacher-Directed Student Use." Report No. 1, Center for Research on Information Technology and Organizations, The University of California, Irvine, and The University of Minnesota, February 1999.

room access to the Internet continues to increase, teachers' use of the Internet to communicate with other educators and to post material will also increase. Many school districts have taken steps to increase teacher professional communications via the Internet. As part of a "Reinventing Education" grant program, teachers in the San Jose Unified School District keep journals of their progress at integrating technology into instruction, and they share these with other teachers online. To ensure that teachers use their training in technology, the principal of Philadelphia's Hill-Freedman Middle School accepts lesson plans only by e-mail and posts daily announcements exclusively on the Internet (CEO Forum on Education and Technology 1999).

Facilitating Students' Learning Via Computers and Cyberspace

In previous sections of this chapter, we have seen several examples of how teachers are using computers and the Internet to enhance students' learning. Table 11.2, based on TLC survey data, documents the extent of this usage and shows that a significant percentage of teachers are involving their students in an array of computer-based and online activities. After word processing and use of CD-ROM references, "research" on the Web is the most common teacher-directed use of computers by students. As with teachers' use of the Internet, student use is directly related to classroom connectivity; among teachers with modems in the classroom, almost half had students use Web search engines on at least three occasions. Moreover, teachers whose classrooms had direct high-speed connections instead of modem connections were 25 percent more likely to have students search the Web ten or more times.

Few teachers have students use the Internet to communicate with others, to collaborate on projects with classes at other schools, and to publish on the Web. The TLC survey revealed that about 5 percent of teachers have students involved in beyond-the-classroom projects and Web publishing, and by spring 1998, more than 70,000 teachers had helped students post their work on the Web (Ravitz, Wong, and Becker 1999). One example of a collaborative Web-based project is ThinkQuest at Lakeland High School in New York state. As their winning entry for a college scholarship contest, Lakeland students and a faculty sponsor developed a Web site to help others learn. Though she thought a computer teacher should oversee the project, the music teacher and band director who reluctantly agreed to be faculty sponsor found the project professionally energizing:

> At first I just wanted to give the team feedback. Then the kids' excitement and motivation got to me—they were doing extraordinary academic work and loving it. I discovered a whole new way to research, learn, and use technology. The kids taught me so much and as they did, they grew intellectually and socially. This has truly been one of the most rewarding and authentic professional development experiences of my career (CEO Forum on Education and Technology 1999).

What Are the Effects of Computer Technology on Learning?

The use of computers and other technologies in schools has grown enormously since the early 1980s, and, as a director of the North Central Regional Education Laboratory noted, "For policymakers, the honeymoon for technology is over. They are starting to say, 'Show us the results'" (Williams 1999). In addition to information about the effects of technology on learning, there is a realization that "no one knows for certain [h]ow it is used" or "how much it is used" (Mehlinger 1996, 403). Since educational technology is a tool to help teachers teach more effectively, how it is used is critical. For example, one science teacher might use computers primarily for student drills on science terminology, while another science teacher might have students use computer simulations to determine the impact of urbanization on animal populations. The lack of information about how technology is being used in the schools aside, research results are just now beginning to appear on the long-term effects of technology on learning.

Apple Classrooms of Tomorrow Project (ACOT)

One of the most informative research studies is based on the Apple Classrooms of Tomorrow (ACOT) project launched in seven K–12 classrooms in 1986. Participating students and teachers each received two computers—one for school and one for home. Eight years later, study results indicated that all ACOT students performed as well as they were expected without computers, and some performed better. More important, perhaps, "the ACOT students routinely and without prompting employed inquiry, collaboration, and technological and problem-solving skills" (Mehlinger 1996, 405). Also, 90 percent of ACOT students went on to college after graduating from high school, while only 15 percent of non-ACOT students did. Furthermore, the behavior of ACOT teachers also changed—they worked "more as mentors and less as presenters of information" (Mehlinger 1996, 404).

An additional positive finding of the ACOT study was how teachers gradually began to use the computers in new ways in the classroom. "When [ACOT] teachers were able to move past that pervasive teacher-centered view of education, students and teachers, as communities of learners, were able to benefit from the range of individual areas of expertise represented by the entire group" (Bitter and Pierson 1999, 43). Teachers rearranged their classrooms to enable students to work collaboratively on projects, and they frequently made arrangements for students who wished to stay after school to work on multimedia projects. Frequently, "Students and teachers collaborated together, with the students often in the role of expert or resource person" (Schwartz and Beichner 1999, 33–34).

Integrating Technology   Teacher participants in the ACOT study were volunteers, many of whom had little experience with educational technology. As with teachers learning any new instructional strategy, the ACOT teachers frequently struggled to adjust to their new computer-filled rooms. Researchers found that the teachers progressed through five distinct stages as they integrated the technology into their teaching (Sandholtz, Ringstaff, and Dwyer 1997).

1. *Entry stage*—For many teachers, this was a period of painful growth and discomfort; learning to use computers presented challenges similar to those faced by beginning teachers.
2. *Adoption stage*—Becoming more proactive toward the challenge of integrating computers, teachers began to teach students how to use the computers and software.
3. *Adaptation stage*—Teachers turned from teaching the technology to using the technology as a tool to teach content.
4. *Appropriation stage*—Teachers moved from merely accommodating computers in their daily routines to personally exploring new teaching possibilities afforded by the technology.
5. *Invention stage*—Eager to move beyond teacher-centered instruction, teachers began to collaborate with peers in developing authentic, inquiry-oriented learning activities.

As informative as the ACOT study has been, it is important to remember that the project was funded by a computer manufacturer; thus, the outcomes might have been influenced by commercial bias and/or the expectation that computers *could not* have had anything other than a significant positive influence on teaching and learning. In fact, Schwartz and Beichner (1999, 34) suggest that the ACOT project "epitomizes what might be termed the 'Emperor's New Clothes' perspective on technology in education. [To] take the ACOT reports at face value would be to accept the notion that technology is the panacea that education has been searching for for ages."

Findings from Other Research Studies

A powerful way to determine whether certain educational practices actually influence students' learning is to conduct *meta-analyses*, that is, to "take the findings from single studies and calculate a way to compare them with each other. The goal is to synthesize the findings statistically and determine what the studies reveal when examined all together" (Kirkpatrick and Cuban 1998). One such meta-analysis reviewed the results of 133 research studies on educational technology from 1990 through 1994. The results of that study follow:

- Educational technology has a significant positive impact on achievement in all subject areas, across all levels of school, and in regular classrooms as well as those for special-needs students.
- Educational technology has positive effects on student attitudes.
- The degree of effectiveness is influenced by the student population, the instructional design, the teacher's role, how students are grouped, and the levels of student access to technology.

- Technology makes instruction more student-centered, encourages cooperative learning, and stimulates increased teacher–student interaction.
- Positive changes in the learning environment evolve over time and do not occur quickly (Mehlinger 1996, 405).

Another meta-analysis conducted by Heather Kirkpatrick and Larry Cuban (1998) at Stanford University also addressed the complications and difficulties involved in determining the effects of computers on learning, particularly when much of the research in that area is methodologically flawed. Research studies, they pointed out, "are of little use unless they elaborate the children's ages, the subject, the software used, the kinds of outcomes that were sought, and how the study was done." With these limitations in mind, the following is a brief summary of Kirkpatrick and Cuban's findings:

1. Seven of the single studies of elementary and secondary students yielded positive findings related to achievement and attitude change, while seven studies yielded negative or mixed findings.
2. Ten of the single studies on the effectiveness of computers to teach in core areas such as mathematics, reading, science, and social studies yielded results ranging from very positive to "cautiously negative."
3. Ten meta-analyses found higher levels of student achievement in computer-using classrooms.
4. Five meta-analyses found that student attitudes improved and students learned more in less time in computer-using classrooms.

On the basis of their meta-analysis of the research, much of it considered methodologically flawed due to a lack of scientific controls, Kirkpatrick and Cuban conclude that "we are unable to ascertain whether computers in classrooms have in fact been or will be the boon they have promised to be."

The ambiguities of research on computer-based instruction aside, it is clear that educational technology *can* have positive effects on learning and teaching, and indications are that technology will influence all aspects of education even more in the twenty-first century. Thus the question to be asked about the effectiveness of educational technology is not, "Is it effective?" Instead, the question should be, . . . "How and under what circumstances does educational technology enhance students' learning?" As more funds are made available to purchase hardware and software, train teachers, and provide technical support, the benefits of classroom media magic will become even more widespread.

Should Technology Be at the Forefront of Efforts to Improve Schools in the United States?

Daily, the mass media feature stories on schools and classrooms that have been transformed through the use of computer-based modes of teaching and learning. Additional reports appear regularly describing the development of new technologies that hold further promise for the improvement of education in the United States. The advantages outlined in these reports include:

- Systematic, well-structured, and consistent lessons
- The ability of students to pace their learning
- The ability of teachers to accommodate their students' varied learning styles and preferred paces of learning

- Opportunities for students in rural and remote areas to interact with students and teachers in diversely populated urban and suburban areas
- Increased record-keeping efficiency, which allows teachers to spend more time with students
- Immediate feedback and reinforcement for students
- Improved student engagement and motivation that result from learning materials with color, music, video, and animated graphics
- More effective assessment of students' learning
- Cost effectiveness
- The acquisition of computer literacy skills needed for the twenty-first century workplace

These students receive immediate feedback and reinforcement, are more engaged and motivated, and are acquiring important twenty-first century workplace skills by using computers at school. Should computers and other technology be at the forefront of efforts to improve schools?

For several years, some people have been questioning the role of technology in improving schools in the United States. An *Atlantic Monthly* cover story titled "The Computer Delusion" even suggested that spending money on computers in the classroom was a form of "malpractice" (Oppenheimer 1997). Some critics, like Stanford professor Larry Cuban, believe it is misguided to assume that teaching will benefit from the use of computers, as have other forms of work:

> The essence of teaching is a knowledgeable, caring adult building a relationship with one or more students to help them learn what the teacher, community, and parents believe to be important. It is an intertwining of emotional and intellectual bonds that gives a tone and texture to teaching and learning unlike what occurs in other work environments. The lure of higher productivity in teaching and learning via computer technologies, however, has seduced reformers to treat teaching like other forms of labor that gained productivity after automation (Cuban 1999a).

Elsewhere, Cuban (1999b) suggests several seldom-considered factors that might account for why the increase in available educational technologies is not reflected in more effective use of technology in the classroom:

- *Contradictory advice from experts*—During the last two decades, Cuban points out, teachers have been presented with an "ever-shifting menu of advice" about what computer skills to teach students, ranging from how to program computers in the 1980s to how to do hypertext programming or HTML in the 1990s.
- *Intractable working conditions*—While technology has transformed most workplaces, conditions of teaching have changed little. As "people for whom rollerblades would be in order to meet the day's obligations," Cuban says, teachers are hard pressed to find time and energy to integrate new technologies into their teaching.
- *The inherent unreliability of the technology*—Software malfunctions, servers that

crash, and the continual need for computers with more memory and speed are among the problems Cuban notes.

- *Policymakers' disrespect for teachers' opinions*—Teachers are seldom consulted about which machines and software are most appropriate and reliable for their teaching.

Other critics, like *Chicago Tribune* columnist Bob Greene, are clear about the place of computers in the classroom: "The key to helping the next generation of American children be bright, literate, intellectually self-sufficient, steeped in the most important areas of knowledge? It all comes down to computers in the classroom. Get rid of them" (Greene 1999). Critics like Greene believe that computers can have a dampening effect on the intellectual development of children, not unlike television, and should not be used extensively in the classroom until the high school level. As Greene puts it: "We are not doing [children] any favors by plopping them in front of yet another set of screens and programming them to tap and stare away."

Lastly, many critics are concerned about what they view as tremendous pressure, much of it coming from technology-oriented corporations, for schools to "go online." As the daily fabric of our lives becomes increasingly shaped by sophisticated technologies and as a disconcerting number of politicians, business leaders, parents, and others continue to proclaim loudly that the United States is falling behind many other countries in educational attainment, technology is mistakenly touted as the "magic bullet," the panacea to turn the schools around.

Are schools falling prey to a tremendous computer-oriented "hype" encouraged by technology corporations, big business, and ambitious superintendents who want their districts to be ahead in the race for the latest technology, and politicians promoting the latest "quick fix" for education? What will be the consequences for the many schools that have cut art, music, and physical education classes to purchase computers? Will computer technology help the United States develop the kind of students and citizens the nation needs? Is there a "fit" between the undeniable power of computers and the educational goals we seek? Are there more cost-effective ways to achieve these educational goals? These are among the difficult questions that are being addressed as the role of technology in educational reform is being debated.

The Opposition:
Computers *Will Not* Improve Education

Among the first to question the role of technology in the classroom was Clifford Stoll, one of the pioneers of the Internet. In *Silicon Snake Oil: Second Thoughts on the Information Highway* (1996, 127), Stoll points out that "Our schools face serious problems, including overcrowded classrooms, teacher incompetence, and lack of security. Local education budgets hardly cover salaries, books, and paper. Computers address none of these problems. They're expensive, quickly become obsolete, and drain scarce capital budgets. Yet school administrators want them desperately." Similarly, David Shenk concludes his book, *Data Smog: Surviving the Information Glut* (1998, 220), with eight "Principles of Technorealism" endorsed by several of the nation's leading experts on technology; principle No. 5 states:

Wiring the schools will not save them.

The problems with America's public schools—disparate funding, social promotion, bloated class size, crumbling infrastructure, lack of standards—have almost nothing to do with technology. Consequently, no amount of technology will lead to the educational revolution prophesized by President Clinton and others. The art of teaching cannot be replicated by computers, the Net, or by "distance learning." These tools can, of course, augment an already high quality educational experience. But to rely on them as any sort of panacea would be a costly mistake.

Similarly, others critics have cautioned the public against pushing schools into the computer revolution. A sampling of their comments follow:

> Penetration of the education market with computer-based technology has depended more on effective conditioning of the market through a barrage of advertising and ideology than on the effectiveness of the technologies themselves (Noble 1996, 20).

> "Optimistic" is probably the kindest word to describe the current status of educational computing in the United States. The good examples [aren't] always easy to find and [are] far outnumbered by the bad ones (Healy 1998, 78).

> I do not go as far back as the radio and Victrola, but I am old enough to remember when 16-millimeter film was to be the sure-cure. Then closed-circuit television. Then 8-millimeter film. Then teacher-proof textbooks. Now computers. I know a false god when I see one (Postman, 1995).

The Advocates:
Computers *Will* Improve Education

Despite media stories and articles critical of the call for more computers in schools, enthusiasm for technology in schools remains strong. For example, in an MCI nationwide poll in 1998, almost 60 percent of the public answered "a great amount" when asked, "How much do you think computers have helped improve student learning?" (Trotter 1998, 6). Following are a few representative comments that rebut arguments against computers in the schools.

> It has become fashionable to say that computers in education are a bust. [However,] the new media can positively change the role of the teacher and student, shifting education from broadcast to interactive learning. When done effectively, [the] results are dramatic (Tapscott July 6, 1999).

> There are real dangers in looking to technology to be the savior of education. But it won't survive without the technology (Jane David, Apple consultant, quoted in Oppenheimer 1997).

> Industrial Age educators will fight Information Age education tooth and nail. [However], in the long run they will probably do no more than slow the implementation of an emerging and vastly improved educational system. Not only is the encroachment of information technology into children's lives inevitable, but it is critical to their future—and ours (Snider 1996).

What Barriers Limit the
Integration of Technology into Schools?

In his 1996 State of the Union address, President Clinton stated that "every classroom in America must be connected to the information superhighway with computers and good software and well-trained teachers." Toward that end, he launched the President's Educational Technology Initiative, which included "four pillars" of "The Technology

Is the use of technology in schools overemphasized?

According to futurist Marvin Cetron, most students in the United States will be using "Information Appliances"—a computer, fax machine, copier, and picture-phone in one unit—by 2010 (Cetron 1997). (See page 418.) Is this good news or bad? Many say that it is great news! They claim that failing to use such technological advances will shortchange children and prevent them from fully participating in the global village of the future. Others disagree and direct educators to ask *why, to what end,* and *what* regarding the uses of technology, not just *how* and *how soon.* They believe that educators are unthinkingly accepting technology without evaluating its impact on the curriculum, student learning, and the social settings for education.

Where do you stand on this issue? Do you think that the use of technology in schools is being overemphasized?

The use of technology in schools is not overemphasized.

Technology is not overemphasized in education today, and schools would be foolish to turn their backs on the world of information available to them through the Internet, CD-ROMs, and computer programs. In addition to making grading and record-keeping easier for teachers, educational technology can expand their instructional capabilities beyond what was imagined just a few years ago.

For instance, in *Curriculum Update* Larry Mann (1998) describes the benefits of using the website *GlobaLearn.* He reports the experiences of fans of the site such as Christy Harmon, a resource teacher in grades K–5, who uses *GlobaLearn* in her special education and English as a Second Language programs in Oklahoma. Through the multimedia site her students are able to interact with live remote expedition teams around the world in activities that develop the skills, awareness, and determination they will need to become responsible stewards of the Earth. Harmon's students research

their subjects online and then prepare and present their reports in PowerPoint productions. They also prefer to use Internet encyclopedias rather than those in their school libraries because they have more pictures and include videos. Her students are stretching their knowledge and perspectives, and Harmon observes, "I look forward to seeing what these kids can do with their lives. . . . They are so good at this at such a young age."

Interacting on the Internet is also equalizing. Upper- and lower-income students, those with and without special needs, classroom stars and shy students, even young and old, have equal voices and equal respect on the Internet. And for students at risk of dropping out of school, educational technology in alternative schools can be the life raft that keeps them afloat. Working with computers, they can learn at their own pace and make mistakes out of the sight of critical peers.

Educational technology is not an end in itself but a tool to use. To avoid using it, whatever the reason, is to limit learning possibilities. Motion pictures, videos, and television, once viewed as threats to education, have become generally accepted in classrooms. The advances in today's educational technology will do the same. Knowing how and when to use them will make the difference.

The use of technology in schools is overemphasized.

The use of technology in schools is overemphasized, distracting educators from what should be their focus—students, their learning, and their lives. Technology depersonalizes education, distancing students from each other and their teachers. Computers are not sensitive to students' needs. They don't notice when a student's work habits, communication, demeanor, grooming, or dress change abruptly, signaling trouble. They don't know when a student is discouraged, sad, lonely, fearful, or "stuck" in his or her learning. Computers are poor substitutes for true companions. They do not laugh, commiserate, or share warmly with their users. Clearly, they cannot provide the human dimension that is needed so greatly in today's society.

The utilitarian goals of technology are inadequate for students' education for life. We are told that students need technology to keep up in a competitive global economy. But is the purpose of education solely to prepare workers for the economy? In an article entitled "Visions of Sugarplums: The Future of Technology, Education, and the Schools," Stephen Kerr suggests four improved goals for education, all of them clustering around essential human concerns:

[F]irst, a focus on the acquisition of knowledge as a tool for self-discovery and liberation . . . second, self-esteem and a feeling of self-worth; third, respect for others with differing values and characteristics; and fourth . . . a "democratic world view," a willingness to participate in the affairs of democratic society (Kerr 1999).

Educational technology is not essential to achieve any of these goals.

Kerr joins Neil Postman (1995) and others in bemoaning the sleep-walking embrace of technology in the United States. Kerr points out that for various reasons, people in this country are blindly attracted to innovations, especially technological ones. He writes:

Americans . . . seem particularly susceptible to a set of related propositions: that technology is *good,* that it is *value-free,* that it *should* find application in many fields, disciplines, and aspects of our lives. Perhaps most troubling is the assumption that, if technology makes it possible to do something, then that thing *should* be done (Kerr 1995).

Failure to consider the ways that technology can shape or change the curriculum and the school culture can have serious consequences. When technology is approached this way, the tail begins to wag the dog. The available technology begins to determine what will be taught and what values will be stressed, rather than the reverse.

Even more serious are the dangers of students' exposure to knowledge we don't want them to have, like the listings on one webpage index reported by Daniel Okrent of *Time* a month after the Littleton, Colorado, incident: "'Counterfeit Money,' 'Hot-Wiring Cars,' 'Breaking into Houses,' 'Thermite Bombs,' and 'Tennis Ball Bombs.'" Okrent observes that communication with another on the Internet is actually interaction with the facsimile of a human being and explains:

I remember passing through the study in our house when my 13-year-old daughter was engaged in a chat with someone who said she was a 15-year-old Californian named Cheryl. It

occurred to me—and I suggested to my daughter—that her chatmate, with whom she was sharing the sort of intimacies a 13-year-old will indulge in, could just as likely be a 53-year-old backwoods hermit named Earl. It was a nauseating thought to both of us (Okrent 1999).

Finally, instruction by teachers cannot be replaced by technology. Brain research and the constructivist approach to learning confirm that live adults need to be present and ready to scaffold students' efforts when needed. Children and youths should have committed, dynamic adults to believe in them, to encourage them when they fail, and to celebrate with them when they succeed. Technology, no matter how advanced, cannot replace the direction and care of a good teacher.

Where do you stand on this issue?

1. Which side do you take, and which arguments do you prefer? Why?

2. What can you add to defend your position?

3. What are your experiences with educational technology?

4. What guidelines would you propose for a balanced, healthy, and beneficial use of educational technology and of the Internet in particular?

Recommended Sources

Cetron, M. (1997). Reform and tomorrow's schools. *TECHNOS Quarterly, 6*(1), 19–22.

Kerr, S. T. (1999). Visions of sugarplums: The future of technology, education, and the schools. In M. J. Early and K. J. Rehage (Eds.). *Issues in curriculum: A selection of chapters from past NSSE yearbooks, Part II.* Chicago, IL: The National Society for the Study of Education.

Mann. L. (1998, Summer). Getting global with technology. *Curriculum Update.*

Okrent, D. (1999, May 10). Raising kids online: What can parents do? *Time.*

Postman, N. (1995, October 9). Virtual students, digital classrooms. *The Nation.*

Withrow, F. B. (1997, June). Technology in education and the next twenty-five years. *T. H. E. Journal (Technological Horizons in Education),* 1–4.

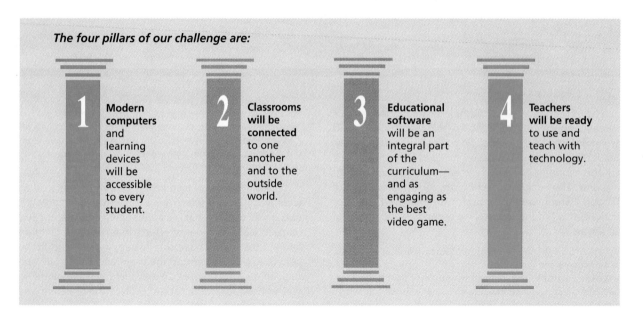

The four pillars of our challenge are:

1 Modern computers and learning devices will be accessible to every student.

2 Classrooms will be connected to one another and to the outside world.

3 Educational software will be an integral part of the curriculum—and as engaging as the best video game.

4 Teachers will be ready to use and teach with technology.

Figure 11.4

The Technology Literacy Challenge . . .
Source: U.S. Department of Education, Office of Educational Technology, *Getting America's Students Ready for the 21st Century: Meeting the Technology Literacy Challenge,* 1996.

Literacy Challenge" (see Figure 11.4). Today, the four pillars of that challenge provide an appropriate framework for examining the nation's progress toward its educational technology goals.

Pillar 1: Access to Technology for All Students

The Technology Literacy Challenge, U.S. Department of Education publication to promote the President's Educational Technology Initiative (1996a), was clear about the importance of access to technology: *"Computers become effective instructional tools only if they are readily accessible by students and teachers"* (italics in original). However, the CEO Forum on Education and Technology reported that by 1998 only 24 percent of schools had reached a "High Tech" or "Target (advanced) Tech" level of effectiveness at integrating technology, while more than half of 79,415 K–12 schools were "Low Tech" (see Figure 11.5). Access to technology in the six percent of schools at the "Target Tech" level fit the following profile.

- *Ubiquitous access to modern computers*—Student-to-computer ratio of 3:1. Student-to-multimedia capable computer ratio of 3:1.
- *New technology*—Eighty-one percent of all computers have processors equal to or greater than an Intel 386.
- *Ubiquitous Internet access*—Ninety-five percent of these schools have Internet access.
- *Prevalent networked computers*—Eighty-nine percent of these schools have access to one or more LANs (Local Area Networks).

Anderson and Ronnkvist (1999) reported the results of a survey by Quality Education Data to identify "high-end technology schools." Technology-intensive schools were defined as having all three of the following: (1) a student–computer ratio of 6:1 or less, (2) at least 25 percent of computers equipped with CD-ROM drives for multimedia, and (3) a moderate or high-speed Internet access. Using these criteria, Anderson and Ronnkvist found that only 25 percent of K–12 schools were "technology-intensive."

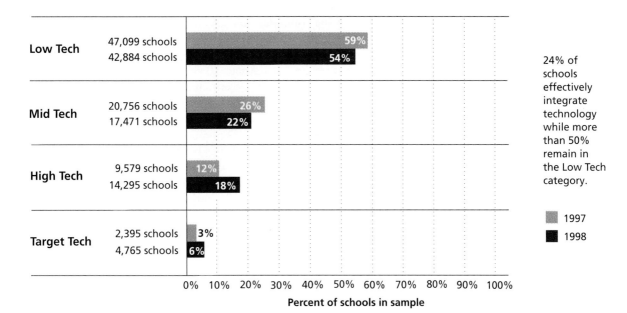

Low Tech	47,099 schools	59%
	42,884 schools	54%
Mid Tech	20,756 schools	26%
	17,471 schools	22%
High Tech	9,579 schools	12%
	14,295 schools	18%
Target Tech	2,395 schools	3%
	4,765 schools	6%

0% 10% 20% 30% 40% 50% 60% 70% 80% 90% 100%

Percent of schools in sample

24% of schools effectively integrate technology while more than 50% remain in the Low Tech category.

■ 1997
■ 1998

Figure 11.5

Level of school technology and readiness (STaR)
Source: CEO Forum on Education and Technology, *The CEO Forum StaR Chart: A Tool for Assessing School Technology and Readiness.* Washington, DC: CEO Forum on Education and Technology, 1999, p. 8. Used with permission.

High schools were more technology-intensive (31 percent), compared to middle schools (29 percent), and elementary schools (22 percent). The survey also revealed that about half of the nation's K–12 schools had outdated computers—as the survey report put it: "To run multimedia applications efficiently, a Pentium or Power Macintosh is needed, but only 45 percent of the school inventory consist[ed] of those computers. [So], using contemporary standards for home and office computers, over half of the computers[were] out of date" (Anderson and Ronnkvist 1999, 5).

On the positive side, Figure 11.5 shows that schools have made significant progress in their technological capabilities between 1997 and 1998, and this trend is continuing. In fact, Anderson and Ronnkvist (1999, 6) believe that schools overall are doing a good job of updating their computers. "[The] typical school acquires roughly 20 or more computers per year on the average. [Only] six years ago, the obsolete equipment made it seem doubtful that U.S. schools could keep up with the rapid pace of computing technology. The latest data suggest that schools are doing an impressive job of catching up."

The Appendix "The CEO Forum on Education and Technology's STaR Assessment of a School's Effectiveness at Integrating Technology into the Teaching and Learning Process" on this book's website, presents an assessment instrument developed by the CEO Forum that yields an approximate measure of a school's access to technology and its effectiveness at integrating technology into the teaching and learning process. The assessment score, ranging from "Low Tech" to "Target Tech," is based on five categories: hardware, connectivity to the Internet, quality of software programs, professional development for teachers, and integration and use of technology.

Funding for Computers and Technical Support To enable schools to participate more fully in the computer revolution, some school districts have passed bond measures to fund educational technology, and New Jersey and a few other states have adopted long-term budgets for computers and technical support. In Milwaukee, a comprehensive technology plan calls for all 156 buildings in the school system to be networked and for a mini-network, a printer, a television, and a multimedia teacher workstation in every classroom by 2002. In Cleveland, a state program has provided every primary grade classroom with three multimedia computers and each teacher with a laptop computer (Harrington-Lueker 1999).

Although schools are getting more computer hardware, most cannot afford to hire sufficient support staff for technology. About 30 percent of schools employ a full-time coordinator of technology, about 40 percent employ a part-time coordinator, and about 30 percent have no on-site technical support personnel (Furger 1999). As a result, most schools rely on central district personnel or computer-savvy teachers for support.

At urban schools, the ability to narrow what has been termed the **"digital divide"** between poor and more affluent schools is often limited by enormous obstacles, including "limited resources, low expectations, overwhelming poverty, teacher contracts, entrenched bureaucracies, political infighting, and the sheer size of these districts" (Williams 1999). *Barriers and Breakthroughs: Technology in Urban Schools,* a 1999 study by the Education Writers Association, revealed that, while most urban districts have "lighthouse" schools in which sophisticated technologies are fully integrated into the curriculum, they also have schools with woefully limited technologies. The national ratio of students to multimedia computers is about 8:1; however, in Chicago, the ratio is 16:1; Cleveland, 15:1; Detroit, 13:1; and Milwaukee 10:1 (Harrington-Lueker 1999).

Commercial Computer Labs   Confronted with limited budgets to purchase computers, many public and private schools are accepting "free" computer labs (complete with software, training, and maintenance) from companies such as California-based ZapMe. In exchange, schools agree that classes will use the labs at least four hours a day and that students will be exposed to on-screen advertisements that run continuously in a $2'' \times 4''$ box in a bottom corner of the screen, changing every fifteen seconds. In addition, schools agree to allow ZapMe and its for-profit partners to use the labs for computer training and related activities.

Each ZapMe lab consists of fifteen Pentium II PCs, seventeen-inch monitors, pre-installed software selected by ZapMe, a laser printer, and a high-speed satellite connection to the Internet. The PCs have no diskette drives or CD-ROM drives, thus preventing schools from using other software with the lab. The ZapMe labs, which the company predicted would number 2,000 at the end of 1999 (*PC World* 1999a), have led some critics to compare the labs to the controversial Channel One.

Unequal Access to Technology   Although schools are making substantial gains in making technology available to students, a significant "digital divide" is evident when access to computers is compared to minority-group status, family income, and gender. Table 11.3 shows that between 1984 and 1997 African American and Latino students were consistently less likely than their white peers to use a computer at school or at home. In addition, research by Quality Education Data revealed that schools with fewer than 1 percent minority students enroll an average of 6.8 students per computer, whereas schools with more than 90 percent minority students enrolled an average of 10.7 students per computer (Furger 1999). A study of computers in schools by Anderson and Ronnkvist (1999) also found a similar relationship between access to computers and minority-group membership; however, the pattern was found to be "uneven" and not as significant as the relationship between computer access and family income.

Table 11.3 also shows consistent disparities over the years between access to computers and family income. Similarly, the Anderson and Ronkvist (1999) study, which used federal Chapter 1 funding as a measure of the socioeconomic status of a school and ZIP codes as a measure of community income, found a connection between access to

Table 11.3

Percentage of students who used a computer at school and/or home, by current grade level, race-ethnicity, and family income: 1984, 1989, 1993, and 1997

Current grade level, race-ethnicity, and family income**	1984* Used a computer at:			1989* Used a computer at:			1993* Used a computer at:			1997 Used a computer at:		
	School	Home	Home or school	School	Home	Home or school	School	Home	Home or school	School	Home	Home or school
Total (Grades 1–12)	29.7	12.6	36.2	48.0	18.4	54.6	62.0	25.2	68.3	76.4	46.2	84.0
Grades 1–6												
Total	30.5	11.8	36.2	52.4	16.1	56.9	66.6	23.0	70.7	79.1	41.3	83.8
Race-ethnicity												
White	35.5	1.44	42.3	58.9	20.4	64.5	71.6	29.2	76.6	84.4	52.3	89.9
Black	15.1	5.1	18.3	34.3	6.0	36.2	54.1	8.3	56.5	70.1	19.3	72.9
Hispanic	16.4	3.5	18.5	41.1	5.1	42.3	55.1	6.8	56.8	67.7	17.9	70.5
Family Income												
Low income	18.5	2.5	20.0	39.4	5.7	39.0	57.4	3.9	58.1	70.9	12.4	71.9
Middle income	29.5	9.7	34.5	52.3	17.0	49.9	66.2	18.0	69.5	78.6	36.4	82.8
High Income	42.2	24.4	53.0	62.5	38.3	63.9	74.0	48.5	82A	86.5	74.6	95.0
Grades 7–12												
Total	28.9	13.4	36.2	43.0	21.1	52.1	57.0	27.7	65.6	75.5	60.9	89.0
Race-ethnicity												
White	31.9	16.2	40.8	45.5	25.6	56.7	59.6	34.7	70.2	75.5	60.9	89.0
Black	18.4	4.9	20.8	36.5	8.5	39.7	50.5	10.2	53.5	74.2	22.3	77.9
Hispanic	21.2	3.6	23.2	34.4	9.0	38.3	52.6	9.5	56.1	65.4	21.5	69.4
Family Income												
Low income	20.0	3.3	22.3	36.7	5.7	39.0	49.0	5.6	50.4	67.6	14.9	70.7
Middle income	28.4	10.1	33.6	42.6	17.0	49.9	57.3	22.2	64.1	74.1	44.2	83.5
High Income	34.1	24.8	48.1	47.2	38.3	63.9	60.7	51.2	77.0	75.4	78.6	93.3

*Data are revised from previously published figures.

Note: Data for 1984, 1989, and 1993 are revised from previously published figures.

**Low income is the bottom 20 percent of all family incomes; high income is the top 20 percent of all family incomes; and middle income is the 60 percent in between.

Source: U.S. Department of Commerce. Bureau of the Census, October Current Population Surveys. Taken from *The Condition of Education 1999,* p.38.

computers and family income; however, on several indicators the gap was rather small and uneven (e.g., students per computer, percent with high-speed access, and percent with an Internet server). Nevertheless, as *The Technology Literacy Challenge* stated, "It will take careful planning to make certain that, in our reach for technological literacy, schools in all types of communities—middle income, lower-income, and better-off communities—have access to up-to-date technology in their classrooms."

Discrepancies in access to computers are also related to gender. In *Does Jane Compute?: Preserving Our Daughter's Place in the Cyber Revolution,* Roberta Furger

(1998), a columnist and contributing editor at *PC World* magazine, estimates that only 16 percent of children and youth online are girls. In a chapter titled "Jane@Home," Furger suggests that boys get the largest share of family computing time. She also cites the lack of software based on girls' interests and even harassment in some male-dominated online forums. In "Jane@School," Furger contends that girls have less access to computers and receive less encouragement to pursue computer-related careers. Furger also suggests that boys tend to regard the computer as a toy, whereas girls regard it as a tool.

Some schools are taking steps to encourage girls to explore and learn with technology. Schools in Palos Park, Illinois, for example, developed a program called Girls and Technology: Skills, Computers, Awareness, and Peer Empowerment (GATSCAPE). Sixth-, seventh-, and eighth-grade girls at all levels of computer literacy get unrestricted access to technology during classes and after school. As they acquire new skills with technology, the girls are encouraged to pass on these skills to other girls formally and informally (CEO Forum on Education and Technology 1999).

Pillar 2: Internet Access for All Schools

Internet access, according to *The Technology Literacy Challenge*, is a vital part of a school's capacity to benefit from the vast resources found in cyberspace: "*Connections to networks, especially the Internet, multiply the power and usefulness of computers as learning tools by putting the best libraries, museums, and other research and cultural resources at our students' and teachers' fingertips*" (italics in original). In

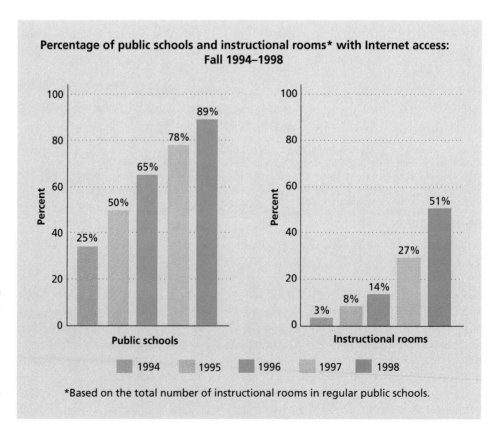

Figure 11.6

Internet access in public schools
Source: U.S. Department of Education, National Center for Education Statistics, "Internet Access in Public Schools," Issue Brief, February 1998, and "Internet Access in Public Schools, 1994–1998," Issue Brief, February 1999. Taken from *The Condition of Education 1999*, p. 37.

1995, President Clinton created the **National Information Infrastructure (NII)** to encourage all schools, libraries, hospitals, and law enforcement agencies to become connected to the "information superhighway." At that time, schools in the United States were hardly ready to "go online"; 50 percent of schools had Internet access, but only 8 percent of all classrooms had access (see Figure 11.6). Four years later, the percentage of schools with Internet access had risen to 89 percent, and the percentage of classrooms with access had risen to 51 percent. In 1998, to provide funds to help schools and libraries connect to the Internet, the federal government launched **E-Rate,** a controversial program that provides discounts on telecommunications services and wiring to schools and libraries. With increased purchasing power from the E-rate program, schools can purchase improved telephone service and greater bandwidth, thus allowing more data to travel across wires for Internet and e-mail use. Currently, E-rate discounts are financed by fees the Federal Communications Commission (FCC) collects from telecommunications companies. Since some companies pass these costs on to consumers, critics claim that the FCC has imposed an illegal tax on telephone users. By fall 1999, E-Rate had helped more than 30,000 schools and libraries connect to the Internet (*PC World* 1999b).

Though many schools continue to report barriers to either the acquisition or the use of advanced telecommunications, schools have made steady progress toward overcoming these barriers, as evidenced, perhaps, by *FamilyPC* magazine's launching in 1999 an annual list of the "Top 100 Wired High Schools" in the nation.

Pillar 3: Quality Educational Software

As *The Technology Literacy Challenge* made clear, for students and teachers to benefit from Information Age technology, high quality software, not just the latest hardware, must be readily available: *Software and on-line learning resources can increase students' learning opportunities, but they must be high quality, engaging, and directly related to the school's curriculum"* (italics in original). Since computers first began to be used extensively in education in the 1980s, inadequacy of software has been a common criticism. By the turn of the century, the situation had not changed much: "Though schools have increased their outlays for software, their choices are few and far between when it comes to superior programs designed specially for classroom use" (Furger 1999). Some programs tend to deemphasize humanistic, holistic, and open-ended fields of knowledge, which are not easily quantified. Others are merely electronic page-turners, known as "drill-and-kill" software, that simply transfer textbooks or workbooks to the computer monitor, as Clifford Stoll, author of *Silicon Snake Oil,* suggests in the following:

> I find plenty of educational software that teaches factoids in arithmetic and geography, almost nothing about electricity, plumbing, or chemistry. What's there is uninspired—they work remarkably like flash cards. Many other programs just dilute minor educational messages with nifty graphics and squiggly sounds. I can't understand why students put up with such stuff (Stoll 1996, 139).

Of the bestselling program for teaching arithmetic, Stoll says:

> A poorly animated green spaceman and little blue robot accompany a tedious drill-and-practice program. It's little more than a stack of arithmetic flash cards accompanied by bleeping sounds. Instead of teaching the meaning of numbers, the software rewards kids for answering questions like 5 + 4 =? Kids see it as an imitation PacMan. Arithmetic becomes an ersatz game (Stoll 1996, 139).

These negative appraisals of educational software aside, promising efforts are being made to upgrade the quality of educational software. For example, the International Society for Technology in Education, the largest teacher-based organization devoted to disseminating effective methods for using educational technology and developer of national "Technology Foundation Standards" for preK–12 students, is working with teachers around the country to identify high-quality software to meet their curriculum goals. Steadily, new, more powerful hypermedia learning software programs are appearing that present students with problems to solve that are interesting, multifaceted, and embedded in real-world contexts. For example, the *Astronomy Village: Investigating the Universe*, developed by the National Aeronautics and Space Administration (NASA) and available at a modest cost, promotes ninth and tenth grade students' learning within a virtual observatory community (see Figure 11.7) that includes extensive multimedia resources and sophisticated exploration tools. The *Astronomy Village* requires that teams of three students select one of the following ten investigations, develop a plan, and carry it out.

- *Search for a Supernova*—Uses neutrino data to locate a supernova
- *Looking for a Stellar Nursery*—Views Omega nebula using different wavelengths
- *Variable Stars*—Identifying a Cepheid variable star in another galaxy
- *Search for Nearby Stars*—Movement of stars' positions as Earth circles sun
- *Extragalactic Zoo*—Different galaxies and clusters
- *Wedges of the Universe*—Viewing depths of space in two wedges of sky
- *Search for a "Wobbler"*—Looking for stars that wobble in their motion
- *Search for Planetary Building Blocks*—Examines Orion nebula for proplanetary disks
- *Search for Earth-Crossing Objects*—Looks for asteroids that cross Earth's path
- *Observatory Site Selection*—Selects a site for an observatory (Jonassen, Peck, and Wilson 1999, 94–95).

Included as part of the *Astronomy Village* are a star life-cycle simulator, orbital simulator, and 3D star simulator. In addition, the student teams can use the program's digitized video clips, images from the Hubble space telescope and other instruments, audio clips of astronomers discussing their work, and book chapters, NASA publications, and articles from astronomy journals and magazines. To help you evaluate computer-based instructional materials, Appendix 11.1 presents "Criteria for Evaluating Software Programs," and Appendix 11.2 presents "Criteria for Evaluating World Wide Web Sites."

Pillar 4: Teacher Training in Technology

Using technology to enhance students' learning requires more than investing in the latest hardware, software, and connectivity to the Internet. In the words of *The Technology Literacy Challenge, "Upgrading teacher training is key to integrating technology into the classroom and to increasing student learning"* (italics in original). E-mailing students, parents, and peers; con-

Figure 11.7

The Astronomy Village: Investigating the Universe
Source: NASA Classroom of the Future, National Aeronautics and Space Administration (NASA) and Wheeling Jesuit University, Wheeling, WV. Copyright 1999 by Wheeling Jesuit University/NASA Classroom of the Future. All Rights Reserved.

ducting classroom demonstrations augmented with multimedia; using presentation graphics to address students' varied learning styles; and designing lessons that require students to use the Internet as a resource for inquiry should be second nature for teachers. Just as new technological skills are needed in the workplace—the number of jobs requiring a high level of information technology skills is expected to double between 1996 and 2006 (CEO Forum on Education and Technology 1999)—a high degree of technological literacy is needed in the classroom. Thus acquiring proficiency in the ever-evolving array of technologies should be an important part of professional development for new and veteran teachers. However, teachers frequently complain of a lack of training in how to use technology to reach their curriculum goals. Only 20 percent of teachers believe they are well prepared to integrate educational technology into the curriculum, and among the teachers who seek training in technology, 50 percent pay for their training with their own money (CEO Forum on Education and Technology 1999). On average, only 9 percent of a school district's technology budget is spent on teacher training, less than one-third of the U.S. Department of Education's recommendations (Furger 1999).

Although survey data indicate that about half of teachers have participated in technology-related staff development, those training sessions often tend to emphasize the basics of computer use rather than how to integrate technology with instruction in their subject matter (Ravitz, Wong, and Becker 1999). Moreover, 38 percent of teachers reported that at least once a month they needed help integrating computers into their lessons, but only 15 percent reported that they "always" get that help and only 12 percent more say such help is "mostly" available.

In addition, teachers have similar experiences related to technical support to keep computers working and software programs functioning properly. Forty-six percent of teachers say they need technical help at least once a month, and only 31 percent of these teachers say that such help is "always" or "mostly" available when they need it. After technical help is given, about one-third of teachers say the help was "excellent" or "very good," one-third say it was "good," and the remaining third say it was "fair" or "poor."

In response to the uneven quality of professional development and technical support, several state departments of education, school districts, and individual schools are taking steps to ensure that teachers have the help they need to fully integrate technology into their teaching.

By 1999, half of the states plus the District of Columbia required computer education for licensure (CEO Forum on Education and Technology 1999). In North Carolina, for example, all new teachers must take an examination to demonstrate their mastery of basic technology competencies in the following nine areas:

- Computer operation skills
- Setup, maintenance, and troubleshooting
- Word processing/introductory desktop publishing
- Spreadsheet/graphing
- Databases
- Networking
- Telecommunications
- Media communications (including image and audio processing)
- Multimedia integration

In addition, North Carolina is one of two states (along with Vermont) that require new teachers to develop a portfolio demonstrating mastery of "advanced" technology competencies, which is evaluated by public school and university faculty chosen by the new teacher's preservice program. The advanced competencies reflect the ability to use multiple forms of technology as they relate to the following four dimensions of learning:

- Curriculum
- Subject-specific knowledge
- Design and management of learning environments/resources
- Child development, learning, and diversity

In addition, teachers applying for five-year license renewal in North Carolina must have thirty to fifty hours of technology training.

At the school district level, creative approaches are extending teachers' technological literacy. For example, the board of education in Baldwin Park, California, leased 900 notebook computers and gave them to teachers and administrators in all of the district's 21 schools (Caterinicchia 1999).

Teacher-education programs also will play a key role in preparing technologically competent teachers to fill the roughly two million teaching vacancies the National Center for Education Statistics has projected between 1998 and 2008. However, as the CEO Forum on Education and Technology stated in its *School Technology and Readiness Report* released in 1999: "America's schools of education have only just begun to focus on preparing their students [to] understand, access, and bring technology-based experiences into the learning process." For example, according to the Milken Exchange on Education Technology's report *Will New Teachers Be Prepared to Teach in a Digital Age?*, less than half of student teachers routinely use technology during their field experience, and less than half of field experience supervisors or cooperating teachers can advise them on how to integrate technology into the curriculum (Milken Exchange on Education Technology 1999).

To ensure that preservice teachers possess the ability to integrate technology into the classroom, the National Council for the Accreditation of Teacher Education (NCATE) has developed technology-related guidelines that teacher-education programs must meet as a criterion for accreditation (National Council for the Accreditation of Teacher Education 1997a). Also, many teacher-education programs have taken innovative steps such as the following to ensure that their graduates possess the ability to integrate technology into the classroom.

- At Washington State University, identified as the nation's "most-wired" public university (Yahoo Internet Life 1999), students develop an online portfolio of literacy strategies that are critiqued by teachers around the state.
- At the University of Virginia, students use the Internet to link with students at eleven other universities to analyze case studies based on commonly occurring problems in classrooms; students also write their own cases and post them on the Web.
- At San Diego State University, student teachers, along with classroom teachers and school administrators, participate in a weekly "Multimedia Academy" taught by university staff and former student teachers.
- At the University of Northern Iowa, students learn from television-mediated observations of "live" classrooms at a P–12 laboratory school and conduct question-answer sessions with the laboratory school teachers.
- At Indiana University, students, as well as visitors from around the world, learn about educational technology at the Center for Excellence in Education, a new state-of-the-art facility with 700 computers, an "enhanced technology suite," a building-wide video distribution system, and a two-way video distance-learning classroom.

- At Boise State University, students complete a fifteen-hour technology fieldwork internship in a public school classroom with a teacher who effectively integrates technology into the curriculum.

In spite of considerable progress, much remains to be done before *The Technology Literacy Challenge* issued in 1996 will become a reality. "Current applications only scratch the surface of the capabilities that the world-wide digital communications infrastructure will eventually provide for teachers and their students" (Becker 1999, 32). Schools will need extensive support as they continue striving to establish the "four pillars" of technology. Teachers, professional associations, the private sector, state and federal governments, and local communities must continue to work together to enable classroom "media magic" to enhance every student's learning. (To assist you in contributing to this effort, see the Appendix "Selected Resources for Integrating Technology into Instruction" on this book's website.)

Fortunately, teachers, along with others who have an interest in education, are becoming more sophisticated in understanding the strengths and limitations of technology as a tool to promote learning. They know full well that "If [they] bring in these technologies and don't think ahead to how they'll be used to promote learning and the acquisition of skills, then the only thing that will change in school is the electric bill" (educational technology expert quoted in Goldberg 1998). They also know that, like another educational tool—the book—the computer *can* be a powerful, almost unlimited medium for instruction and learning, if they carefully reflect on *how* it will further the attainment of the goals and aspirations they have for their students.

SUMMARY

How Are Educational Technologies Influencing Schools?

- Technology is a tool teachers can use to achieve educational goals and to create particular kinds of learning environments.

- Technology can provide students with a structured, efficient instructional delivery system, or it can spark their interest in open-ended, inquiry-oriented learning.

- In many schools and classrooms, technology has already transformed teaching and learning; however, teachers, administrators, policymakers, and parents must realize that advanced telecommunications will require new approaches to teaching and assessing students' learning.

What Technologies Are Available for Teaching?

- Through technologies such as two-way interactive telecommunications, CD-ROM players, interactive multimedia, computer simulations, and hypermedia, teachers are creating learning environments that allow students to become more active in shaping their learning experiences.

- If *educational technology* is broadly defined as inventions that enable teachers to reach their goals more effectively, then it is clear that for some time all teachers have been using various forms of educational "technology."

- Though considerable evidence suggests that television retards children's growth and development, the medium, if properly used, can enhance students' learning.

- Channel One is a controversial use of commercial-based television in the schools, and many critics question its educational value.

- Three common uses of computers in instruction are computer-assisted instruction (CAI), computer-managed instruction (CMI), and computer-enhanced instruction (CEI).

- Some schools have microcomputer-based laboratories (MBL) that students use to gather and analyze various kinds of data.

- Newsgroups, chat rooms, and videoconferencing on the Internet enable teachers and students to communicate with people around the world.

How Do Teachers Use Computers and the Internet?

- Teachers most frequently use the Internet to gather information and resources for teaching.

- Teachers who have classroom access to the Internet are more likely than those without access to communicate via e-mail and to post information and student work on the World Wide Web.

- After word processing and using CD-ROM references, performing "research" on the Web is the most common teacher-directed use of computers by students.

What Are the Effects of Computer Technology on Learning?

- Although how and to what extent computers and other technologies are being used in schools is not known, research indicates that technology has a positive impact on students' achievement and attitudes.

- The Apple Classrooms of Tomorrow (ACOT) project showed that teachers progress through five stages as they integrate technology into teaching: entry, adoption, adaptation, appropriation, and invention.

- Single research studies and meta-analyses of large numbers of single studies indicate that the effects of computers on students' learning are varied—some report learning gains, some don't, and others report "mixed" outcomes.

- In spite of the ambiguities of research on computer-based instruction, it is clear that technology *can* have positive effects on learning.

Should Technology Be At the Forefront of Efforts to Improve Schools in the United States?

- From the need to acquire computer literacy skills for the twenty-first century to the importance of allowing students to pace their learning, the role that technology should play in improving schools has been widely publicized.

- Some critics believe that schools are under tremendous pressure, much of it coming from technology-oriented corporations, to integrate technology.

- According to some critics, technology has little to add to the art of teaching, and it will not help schools face critical problems such as overcrowding, limited funds, and school violence.

- Despite criticisms of technology in the schools, the public believes that computers have increased students' learning.

What Barriers Limit the Integration of Technology into Schools?

■ Access to technology for all students is uneven, and more than half of schools are at a low level of effectiveness at integrating technology.

■ Many schools report inadequate funding for computers and technical support.

■ A "digital divide" is evident when access to computers is compared to minority-group status, family income, and gender.

■ Since the National Information Infrastructure (NII) was developed to encourage all schools to use advanced telecommunications, nearly all schools and 50 percent of classrooms have access to the Internet.

■ Though the quality of many software programs is low, new hypermedia programs are being introduced that present students with multifaceted, engaging, and authentic learning experiences.

■ Only 20 percent of teachers believe they are well prepared to integrate technology into the curriculum.

■ Though school district spending on technology training for teachers is often inadequate and the quality of that training uneven, state departments of education, school districts, and individual schools are developing new approaches to providing teachers with support as they integrate technology.

■ Many teacher-education programs have developed innovative approaches to preparing technologically competent teachers.

KEY TERMS AND CONCEPTS

CD-ROM, 422
Channel One, 419
chat rooms, 426
computer-assisted instruction (CAI), 423
computer-based simulations, 423
computer-enhanced instruction (CEI), 421
computer-managed instruction (CMI), 421

"digital divide," 440
distance learning networks, 419
education technology, 418
E-rate, 443
home–school communication systems, 423
hypermedia, 422
interactive multimedia, 422

Internet, 424
microcomputer-based laboratories (MBL), 422
National Information Infrastructure (NII), 423
newsgroups, 424
videoconferencing, 427
videodisc, 422
World Wide Web, 424

APPLICATIONS AND ACTIVITIES

Teacher's Journal

1. In your opinion, what are the most important benefits of technology for education, and what are its most important drawbacks?

2. What impact has television had on your life? What steps might teachers take to increase the educational benefits of television in society?

3. A concern voiced by some is that the use of computers in education will lead to a depersonalization of the teacher–learner relationship. How valid is this concern?

4. Write a scenario forecasting how technology will change the teaching profession during the next two decades. During the next four decades.

Teacher's Database

1. With classmates, join or start an online discussion on one or more of the following topics or another topic in Chapter 11.

computer simulations	educational software
computer-assisted instruction (CAI)	educational technology
computer-managed instruction (CMI)	hypermedia
computer-enhanced instruction (CEI)	interactive multimedia

2. Find out more about educational newsgroups and distance learning networks. How might you use newsgroups or distance learning networks in your preparation as a teacher? As a teacher, how might you and your students use these two forms of educational technology? What knowledge and skills do you need to start or participate in an educational newsgroup or distance learning network? Using the Internet, develop a list of resources for both.

Observations and Interviews

1. Survey a local school district to determine the educational technologies used by teachers. How and how often are these technologies used for instruction? What is the availability of computers and software for student use?

2. Find an online chat room frequented by teachers and enter (or initiate) a discussion on educational technology. What are the teachers' views of integrating technology into the classroom? What technologies, software, and instructional activities have they found most effective?

Professional Portfolio

Prepare a catalog of interactive multimedia resources and materials that you will use as a teacher. For each entry, include an annotation that briefly describes the resource materials, how you will use them, and where they may be obtained. As with the selection of any curriculum materials, try to find evidence of effectiveness, such as results of field tests, published reviews of educational software, awards, or testimonials from educators. View and report on at least one program you have included in your personal catalog. Explain in your report how you will integrate this multimedia resource into your curriculum. For some ideas to get you started, ask your instructor for Handout master M11.6.

Appendix 11.1

Criteria for evaluating software programs

User friendliness	Poor	Fair	Excellent
How easy is it to start the program?	❏	❏	❏
Is there an overview or site map for the program?	❏	❏	❏
Can students easily control the pace of the program?	❏	❏	❏
Can students exit the program easily?	❏	❏	❏
Can students create their own paths through the program and develop their own links among elements?	❏	❏	❏
After first-time use, can students bypass introductory or orientation material?	❏	❏	❏
Does the program include useful hotlinks to Internet sites?	❏	❏	❏

Inclusiveness	Poor	Fair	Excellent
Can students with hearing or visual impairments make full use of the program?	❏	❏	❏
Can students navigate the program by making simple keystrokes with one hand?	❏	❏	❏
Does the material avoid stereotypes and reflect sensitivity to racial, cultural, and gender differences?	❏	❏	❏

Textual Material	Poor	Fair	Excellent
How accurate and thorough is the content?	❏	❏	❏
Is the content well organized and clearly presented?	❏	❏	❏
Is the textual content searchable?	❏	❏	❏
Can the content be integrated into the curriculum?	❏	❏	❏

Images	Poor	Fair	Excellent
Is the image resolution high quality?	❏	❏	❏
Is the layout attractive, "user friendly," and uncluttered?	❏	❏	❏
Do the graphics and colors enhance instruction?	❏	❏	❏
How true are the colors of the images?	❏	❏	❏
Are the images large enough?	❏	❏	❏
Does the program have a zoom feature that indicates the power of magnification?	❏	❏	❏
Does the program make effective use of video and animation?	❏	❏	❏

Audio	Poor	Fair	Excellent
Are the audio clips high quality?	❏	❏	❏
Does the audio enhance instruction?	❏	❏	❏

Technical	**Poor**	**Fair**	**Excellent**
Is installation of the program easy and trouble-free?	❏	❏	❏
Are instructions clear and easy to follow?	❏	❏	❏
Is user-friendly online help available?	❏	❏	❏
Are technical support people easy to reach, helpful, and courteous?	❏	❏	❏

Motivational			
Does the program capture and hold students' interest?	❏	❏	❏
Are students eager to use the program again?	❏	❏	❏
Does the program give appropriate, motivational feedback?	❏	❏	❏
Does the program provide prompts or cues to promote students' learning?	❏	❏	❏

Appendix 11.2

Criteria for evaluating World Wide Web sites

Authoritativeness	Poor	Fair	Excellent
The author(s) are respected authorities in the field.	❏	❏	❏
The author(s) are knowledgeable.	❏	❏	❏
The author(s) provide a list of credentials and/or educational background.	❏	❏	❏
The author(s) represent respected, credible institutions or organizations.	❏	❏	❏
Complete information on references (or sources) is provided.	❏	❏	❏
Information for contacting the author(s) and webmaster is provided.	❏	❏	❏

Comprehensiveness	Poor	Fair	Excellent
All facets of the subject are covered.	❏	❏	❏
Sufficient detail is provided at the site.	❏	❏	❏
Information provided is accurate.	❏	❏	❏
Political, ideological, and other biases are not evident.	❏	❏	❏

Presentation	Poor	Fair	Excellent
Graphics serve an educational, rather than decorative, purpose.	❏	❏	❏
Links are provided to related sites.	❏	❏	❏
What icons stand for is clear and unambiguous.	❏	❏	❏
The website loads quickly.	❏	❏	❏
The website is stable and seldom, if ever, nonfunctional.	❏	❏	❏

Timeliness	Poor	Fair	Excellent
The original website was produced recently.	❏	❏	❏
The website is updated and/or revised regularly.	❏	❏	❏
Links given at the website are up-to-date and reliable.	❏	❏	❏

part four

Your Teaching Future

dear mentor

**On Being Involved in
Your Educational Community**

Dear Mentor,

I am in the process of completing my degree and earning my teaching credential. I have always been active in the social issues of my community. How can I, as a teacher, be active in my school's decisions about education reform? What opportunities should I look for?

Sincerely,
Sara Waltmire

Dear Sara,

I, too, have been involved consistently in the social issues of my community. When I started teaching, I wanted to bring those issues into my school. I have come up with some pretty unusual math lessons on community, diversity, and other social issues. I also saw opportunities for students to be involved in serving others. We started a community service club and planned activities with a local food bank and a children's hospital. A few months after the club began, I learned a valuable lesson: One of the students who had taken the lead in organizing and supporting the club's activities was in much need of help herself. Her family was in financial and personal turmoil. Sometimes she had to look after herself. But still, she managed to be a good student.

Because my life had been sheltered from many of the realities of the world, I did not realize that the people who needed help weren't just "out there" somewhere but were also right inside my classroom. Problems at home are not left outside school on the steps; they travel with the student and impact everything that happens in that child's life and education. All children, whatever challenges life has put in their path, deserve a safe place to learn and construct their understanding of the world. I began to realize that changing what went on in my classroom alone was not enough. If I wanted to create real change, I had to become involved in reforming education on a wider plane.

First, I began participating on a district Pre-Algebra committee whose goal was to get input about what was working and what was not from as many teachers as possible. I was concerned that I did not have much to offer. However, on that committee I found other teachers who confront many of the same problems I did, and who wanted to make a change. We wrote a new curriculum to address the varied learning styles of our students. Participating in this project led to more projects and more people who are working to improve education.

Join in a committee, a project, or a seminar. Speak out at every chance you get. Be an advocate for kids. Sooner than you think, you will have more opportunities to serve and people asking you to help than you will have time for. One thing of which I am certain—that has been proven to me time and again—is that teachers are the most creative, devoted, and caring people you will meet. In my travels, I have met teachers from all over the United States, and I have been amazed by the different challenges we face. At the same time, if I talk with them at length, I discover that underneath it all, we are faced with many of the same challenges. We are a great community of educators working together on the critical assignment of educating children and youth.

Sincerely,

Diane Crim, Math Teacher
1999 Utah Teacher of the Year

12

Teachers as Educational Leaders

As a fledgling teacher I saw the principal come to the veteran teachers on an informal basis to get their opinions on administrative and curricular decisions. The principal knew the best way to determine how policy affects students was to ask the person who was most directly involved with students—the classroom teacher. I was very fortunate to have a forward-thinking principal who embraced the concept of site-based decision making.

—a North Carolina teacher
Teachers Leading the Way: Voices from the National Teacher Forum,
U.S. Department of Education, April 1998

focus questions

1. To what extent is teaching a full profession?

2. What is professionalism in teaching?

3. To what professional organizations do teachers belong?

4. How do teachers help shape education as a profession?

5. What new leadership roles for teachers are emerging?

6. How do teachers contribute to educational research?

7. How are teachers involved in school restructuring and curriculum reform?

It is November of your fifth year of teaching, and you are attending a meeting of the steering committee for a statewide teacher network launched that September. The state department of education divided the state into twelve regions, and you were elected by your peers to be the network leader for your region. The network is based on the premise that teachers should have opportunities to participate in, and to lead, professional development activities of their own choosing, such as curriculum workshops, leadership institutes, internships, and conferences.

The purpose of this two-day meeting at the state capitol is to begin the process of designing a series of two-week summer institutes for teachers. The institutes will be invitational; and institute "fellows" will be selected by the steering committee after an extensive application and interview process. One institute will be held in each region throughout the state, and teachers will receive a $600 stipend plus expenses for attending. To disseminate the knowledge and skills they acquire and to further develop their leadership abilities, the institute fellows will design and deliver staff development programs at their home schools.

The committee chair, a teacher from a school in the state's largest city, has just laid out the group's task for the next two days. "By the end of the day tomorrow, we need to have identified which institutes will be offered in each region. Also, we need to have a 'game plan' for how each of you will facilitate the development of the summer institute in your region."

"Well, the way I see it," says the teacher next to you, "the institutes should accomplish at least two major purposes. First, they should provide teachers with ways to increase their effectiveness in the classroom by acquiring new strategies and materials. Second, and just as important, the institutes should give teachers opportunities to play key leadership roles in school reform efforts around the state."

"That's right," says another teacher. "Teachers should recognize that the institutes give them a voice and meaningful opportunities to function as professionals."

"What I like about the institutes," says the teacher across the table from you, "is that they give teachers a chance to break out of the role of passively *receiving* in-service training. It's no different for teachers than it is for students —we learn best by actively shaping our learning environment and constructing meaning."

As several members of the group, including you, nod in agreement, you reflect on what you've just heard. What does it really mean to be a professional? What are the characteristics of a profession, and to what extent does teaching reflect those characteristics? What new leadership roles for teachers are emerging? What leadership roles will you play in educational reform?

Educational reform, as the preceding scenario illustrates, is continuing to change dramatically what it means to be a teacher. State-sponsored teacher networks, the professionalization of teaching, shared decision making, peer review, and mentor teacher programs are just a few of the changes that are providing unprecedented opportunities for teachers to assume new leadership roles beyond the classroom. In addition, as Joseph Murphy points out in "Reconnecting Teaching and School Administration: A Call for a Unified Profession," approaches to educational leadership are becoming more collaborative and participatory:

> The hierarchical, bureaucratic organizational structures that have defined schools over the past 80 years are giving way to more decentralized and more professionally controlled systems that create new designs for school management. In these new postindustrial educational organizations, there are important shifts in roles, relationships, and responsibilities: traditional patterns of relationships are altered, authority flows are less hierarchical, role definitions are both more general and

flexible, leadership is connected to competence for needed tasks rather than to formal position, and independence and isolation are replaced by cooperative work (Murphy, April 1999).

We have referred to teaching as a **profession** throughout this book; however, if we compare teaching with other professions—law and medicine, for example—we find some significant differences. As a result of these differences, current opinion is divided as to whether teaching actually is a full profession. Some have labeled teaching a *semi-* profession (Etzioni 1969), an *emerging* profession (Howsam et al. 1976), an *uncertain* profession (Powell 1980), an *imperiled* profession (Duke 1984; Sykes 1983; Freedman, Jackson, and Botes 1983; Boyer 1990), an *endangered* profession (Goodlad 1983b), and a *not-quite* profession (Goodlad 1990)!

To What Extent Is Teaching a Full Profession?

We use the terms *professional* and *profession* quite frequently, usually without thinking about their meanings. Professionals "possess a high degree of specialized *theoretical knowledge,* along with methods and techniques for applying this knowledge in their day-to-day work. . . . [and they] are united by a high degree of in-group solidarity, stemming from their common training and common adherence to certain doctrines and methods" (Abrahamsson 1971, 11–12).

From several sociologists and educators who have studied teaching come additional characteristics of occupations that are highly professionalized, summarized in Figure 12.1. Before reading further, reflect on each characteristic and decide whether it applies to teaching. Then, continue reading about the extent to which teaching satisfies each of these commonly agreed-upon characteristics of full professions. Do our perceptions agree with yours?

Institutional Monopoly of Services

On one hand, teachers do have a monopoly of services. As a rule, only those who are certified members of the profession may teach in public schools. On the other hand, the varied requirements we find for certification and for teaching in private schools weaken this monopoly. In addition, any claim teachers might have as exclusive providers of a service is further eroded by the practice of many state systems to approve temporary, or emergency, certification measures to deal with teacher shortages—a move that establishes teaching as the only profession that allows noncertified individuals to practice the profession. The National Commission on Teaching and America's Future (1996), for example, reported that more than 25 percent of the nation's teachers were not fully licensed, and about one-fourth of the high school teachers surveyed lacked a minor degree in their primary field of instruction. Furthermore, a decline of inadequately licensed teachers seems unlikely, given the U.S. Department of Education's projection that more than two million teachers would be needed between 1999 and 2009.

Perhaps the most significant argument against teachers claiming to be the exclusive providers of a service, however, is the fact that a great deal of teaching occurs in informal, nonschool settings and is done by people who are not teachers. Every day,

Yes	Uncertain	No	
○	○	○	1. Professionals are allowed to institutionalize a monopoly of essential knowledge and services. For example, only lawyers may practice law; only physicians may practice medicine.
○	○	○	2. Professionals are able to practice their occupation with a high degree of autonomy. They are not closely supervised, and they have frequent opportunities to make their own decisions about important aspects of their work. Professional autonomy also implies an obligation to perform responsibly, to self-supervise, and to be dedicated to providing a service rather than meeting minimum requirements of the job.
○	○	○	3. Professionals must typically undergo a lengthy period of education and/or training before they may enter professional practice. Furthermore, professionals usually must undergo a lengthy induction period following their formal education or training.
○	○	○	4. Professionals perform an essential service for their clients and are devoted to continuous development of their ability to deliver this service. This service emphasizes intellectual rather than physical techniques.
○	○	○	5. Professionals have control over their governance, their socialization into the occupation, and research connected with their occupation.
○	○	○	6. Members of a profession form their own vocational associations, which have control over admissions to the profession, educational standards, examinations and licensing, career development, ethical and performance standards, and professional discipline.
○	○	○	7. The knowledge and skills held by professionals are not usually available to nonprofessionals.
○	○	○	8. Professionals enjoy a high level of public trust and are able to deliver services that are clearly superior to those available elsewhere.
○	○	○	9. Professionals are granted a high level of prestige and higher-than-average financial rewards.

Figure 12.1

Does teaching meet the criteria for a profession?

thousands of people teach various kinds of how-to-do-it skills: how to water-ski, how to make dogs more obedient, how to make pasta from scratch, how to tune a car's engine, and how to meditate.

Teacher Autonomy

In one sense teachers have considerable autonomy. They usually work behind a closed classroom door, and only seldom is their work observed by another adult. In fact, one of the norms among teachers is that the classroom is a castle of sorts, and teacher privacy a closely guarded right. Although the performance of new teachers may be observed and evaluated on a regular basis by supervisors, veteran teachers are observed much less frequently, and they usually enjoy a high degree of autonomy.

Teachers also have extensive freedom regarding how they structure the classroom environment. They may emphasize discussions as opposed to lectures. They may set certain requirements for some students and not for others. They may delegate responsibilities to one class and not another. And, within the guidelines set by local and state authorities, teachers may determine much of the content they teach.

There are, however, constraints placed on teachers and their work. Teachers, unlike doctors and lawyers, must accept all the "clients" who are sent to them. Only infrequently does a teacher actually "reject" a student assigned to him or her.

Teachers must also agree to teach what state and local officials say they must. Moreover, the work of teachers is subject to a higher level of public scrutiny than that found in other professions. Because the public provides "clients" (students) and pays for schools, it has a significant say regarding the work of teachers. Nevertheless, it has been suggested that some "leveling" of professions will occur in the United States during the early twenty-first century: "More of the work of the traditional high-status professions, particularly medicine, will occur in bureaucratic or large organizational settings under the watchful eye of managers. [While] doctors are accepting more and more regulation, the school teachers . . . will slowly break out of long-established bureaucratic hierarchies and share more of the autonomy previously enjoyed by members of the high-status professions" (Grant and Murray 1999, 231–32).

Years of Education and Training

As sociologist Amitai Etzioni (1969) points out in his classic discussion of the "semi-professions," the training of teachers is less lengthy than that required for other professionals—lawyers and physicians, for example. The professional component of teacher education programs is the shortest of all the professions—only 15 percent of the average bachelor's degree program for a high school teacher is devoted to professional courses. However, as we learned in Chapter 2, several colleges and universities have begun five-year teacher education programs. Similarly, in its comprehensive report, *What Matters Most: Teaching for America's Future,* the National Commission on Teaching and America's Future (1996) recommended that teacher education be moved to the graduate level. If the trend toward five-year and graduate-level teacher education programs continues, the professional status of teaching will definitely be enhanced.

In most professions, new members must undergo a prescribed induction period. Physicians, for example, must serve an internship or residency before beginning practice, and most lawyers begin as clerks in law firms. In contrast, teachers usually do not go through a formal induction period before assuming full responsibility for their work. Practice teaching comes closest to serving as an induction period, but it is often relatively short, informal, and lacking in uniformity. As the National Commission on Teaching and America's Future (1996) noted, "Our society can no longer accept the [s]ink-or-swim induction [of teachers]."

Provision of Essential Service

Although it is generally acknowledged that teachers provide a service that is vital to the well-being of individuals and groups, the public does need to be reminded of this fact from time to time. This importance was driven home on a large scale during the early 1980s when several reports calling for school reform linked the strength of our country to the quality of its schools. In a sense, it is no exaggeration to say that teaching is a matter of life and death:

> every moment in the lives of teachers and pupils brings critical decisions of motivation, reinforcement, reward, ego enhancement and goal direction. Proper professional decisions enhance learning and life; improper decisions send the learner towards incremental death in openness to experience and in ability to learn and contribute. Doctors and lawyers probably have neither more nor less to do with life, death, and freedom than do teachers (Howsam et al. 1976, 15).

Table 12.1

Percentages of teachers and principals who report that teachers have a "good deal of influence" or "control" over school and classroom decisions, by control of school

	Public School		Private School	
	Teachers	Principals	Teachers	Principals
Setting discipline policy	34.9	74.6	59.2	75.3
Determining the content of in-service programs	30.6	70.6	35.3	61.6
Establishing curriculum	34.3	61.5	55.7	72.1
Selecting textbooks and other instructional materials	55.2	—	68.8	—
Selecting content, topics, and skills to be taught	60.5	—	74.9	—
Selecting teaching techniques	86.5	—	91.7	—

— data not available

Notes: Respondents were asked about influence and control on a scale of 0+–5, with 0 meaning "no influence" or "no control," and 5 meaning a "great deal of influence" or "complete control." Responses 4 and 5 were combined in this analysis. Data are revised from previously published figures.

Source: National Center for Education Statistics, *The Condition of Education 1998.* Washington, DC: National Center for Education Statistics, 1998.

Degree of Self-Governance

The limited freedom of teachers to govern themselves has detracted from the overall status of the profession. In many states, licensing guidelines are set by government officials who may or may not be educators; and at the local level, decision-making power usually resides with local boards of education, largely made up of people who have never taught. As a result, teachers have had little or no say over what they teach, when they teach, whom they teach, and, in extreme instances, *how* they teach.

However, recent efforts to empower teachers and to professionalize teaching are creating new roles for teachers and expanded opportunities to govern important aspects of their work. At schools throughout the country, teachers are having a greater voice in decisions related to curriculum development, staffing, budget, and the day-to-day operation of schools. Table 12.1, for example, compares public- and private-school teachers' and principals' perceptions of teacher influence or control over discipline policies, in-service programs, curricula, textbook selection, selection of content, and teaching techniques. Although teachers and principals differ significantly in the amount of influence or control they believe teachers have, teachers should experience greater degrees of self-governance as principals respond to increasing pressure to become more effective at facilitating collaborative, emergent approaches to leadership (Parkay, Shindler, and Oaks 1997). As Gerald Grant and Christine Murray point out in *Teaching in America: The Slow Revolution* (1999, 217), "schoolteachers can assert that they have genuine expertise in their subject matter and that there is a body of pedagogical content knowledge that is specific to their work. Most important, they are no longer willing to let the administrators define themselves as the exclusive class of experts controlling either the content of the curriculum or decisions about who is fit to teach it."

Professional Associations

Teachers, like other professionals, have formed a number of vocational associations that are vitally concerned with issues such as admission to the profession, educational standards, examinations and licensing, career development, ethical and performance standards, and professional discipline. It is clear, though, that the more than 500 national teacher organizations have not progressed as far as other professions have in gaining control of these areas.

Professional Knowledge and Skills

Professionals are granted a certain status because they possess knowledge and skills not normally held by the general public. Within the profession of teaching, however, the requirements for membership are less precise. In spite of the ongoing efforts of educational researchers, there is less than unanimous agreement on the knowledge and skills considered necessary to teach. This lack of agreement is reflected in the varied programs at the 1,300 or so colleges and universities that train teachers.

During the last ten years, the National Board for Professional Teaching Standards (NBPTS) has made significant progress toward clarifying the knowledge base for teaching. As you learned in Chapter 2, the NBPTS (the majority of whose members are teachers) offers board certification to teachers who possess a high level of NBPTS-identified knowledge and skills. By the start of 2000, the NBPTS had granted national certification to about 2,000 teachers, and the Board planned to certify 100,000 teachers by 2006.

Level of Public Trust

The level of trust the public extends to teachers as professionals varies greatly. On the one hand, the public appears to have great confidence in the work that teachers do. Because of its faith in the teaching profession, the public invests teachers with considerable power over its children. For the most part, parents willingly allow their children to be molded and influenced by teachers, and this willingness must be based on a high degree of trust. In addition, most parents expect their children to obey and respect teachers.

Though all professions have some members who might be described as unprofessional, teaching is especially vulnerable to such charges. The sheer size of the teaching force makes it difficult to maintain consistently high professional standards. Moreover, teaching is subject to a level of public scrutiny and control that other, more established, professions traditionally have not tolerated. However, the era of widespread public trust may be running out for these other professions as well. Mushrooming malpractice suits against doctors, for example, may be a sign that here, too, public confidence has significantly eroded.

Prestige, Benefits, and Pay

As mentioned in Chapter 1, teachers are viewed as having higher social status than most of the population; however, this higher status is based on level of education attained rather than wealth. Thus teachers have not received salaries in keeping with other professions requiring approximately the same amount of schooling. Nevertheless, there is significant support for reducing the salary gap—on the 1999 Phi Delta Kappa/

Gallup Poll, 62 percent of the respondents favored increased pay for *all* teachers; 90 percent favored increased pay for teachers who "demonstrate high performance"; and 63 percent favored tax credits for high-performing teachers (Rose and Gallup 1999).

What Is Professionalism in Teaching?

The current goal among teachers, teacher educators, policymakers, and the general public is to make teaching a full profession. Toward this end, teachers are willing to take risks and learn new roles as they press for greater self-governance, better working conditions, and increased financial rewards. In addition, teachers are acquiring the analytical skills needed to understand and provide leadership for the complex processes of educational reform. The following sections look at the three key dimensions of professionalism in teaching presented in Figure 12.2: professional behavior, life-long learning, and involvement in the profession.

Professional Behavior

The professional teacher is guided by a specific set of values. He or she has made a deep and lasting commitment to professional practice. He or she has adopted a high standard of professional ethics and models behaviors that are in accord with that code of ethics. The professional teacher also engages in serious, reflective thought about how to teach more effectively. Moreover, he or she does this while teaching, continually examining experiences to improve practice.

Reflection-in-Action Donald Schön (1983, 1987, and 1991) has described this professional behavior as **reflection-in-action,** and he describes how a teacher might use it to solve a problem in the classroom:

> An artful teacher sees a child's difficulty in learning to read not as a defect in the child but as a defect "of his own instruction." And because the child's difficulties may be unique, the teacher cannot assume that his repertoire of explanations will suffice, even though they are "at the tongue's end." He must be ready to invent new methods and must "endeavor to develop in himself the ability of discovering them" (1983, 66).

The professional teacher Schön describes makes careful, sensitive observations of classroom events, reflects on the meaning of those observations, and then decides to act in a certain way. Steven Lacy, selected by the Walt Disney Company as the Outstanding General Elementary Teacher for 1994–95, describes the reflective decision-making process this way:

> Our effectiveness as teachers is not reflected in the materials and structures of our pedagogy as

Figure 12.2

Professionalism in teaching

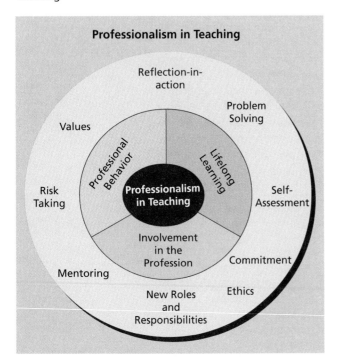

Professionalism in Teaching

Reflection-in-action

Problem Solving

Values

Professional Behavior

Lifelong Learning

Professionalism in Teaching

Risk Taking

Self-Assessment

Involvement in the Profession

Commitment

Mentoring

New Roles and Responsibilities

Ethics

much as it is in the countless decisions we make every day, decisions that are made in an instant. [D]o I help him with that problem or let him struggle? Do I pursue her question or stick with the lesson? Does this behavior need to be punished or ignored? Does this composition need to be criticized or praised (Levey 1996, 2–3)?

Becoming a Mentor   Because of their positions and their encounters with young people, teachers may find opportunities to become mentors to some of their students. Accepting this responsibility is another example of professional behavior. The role of **mentor** is unique in several ways. First, mentorship develops naturally and is not an automatic part of teaching, nor can it be assigned to anyone. True mentorships grow from teaching relationships and cannot be artificially promoted. Second, the role of mentor is a *comprehensive* one: Mentors express broad interest in those whom they mentor. Third, the role of mentor is *mutually* recognized by student and teacher; both realize that their relationship has a special "depth." Fourth, the role of mentor is significant and has the potential to change the quality and direction of students' lives. And fifth, the opportunity to work with a mentor is free, what Gehrke (1988) terms the mentor's "gift of care."

The longer you teach, the more you will encounter opportunities for mentorships to develop, discovering that you can mentor less experienced teachers and student teachers as well as students. The rewards that come from the unique role of mentor are among the most satisfying.

What characteristics distinguish teaching as a profession? What characteristics might distinguish this teacher as a professional?

Lifelong Learning

The professional teacher is dedicated to continuous learning—both about the teaching-learning process and about the subject taught. No longer is it sufficient for career teachers to obtain only a bachelor's degree and a teaching certificate. Rather, teachers are lifelong members of learning communities.

Several states have mandated continuing education for teachers. The content of the curriculum as well as methods and materials for teaching that content are changing so rapidly that teachers must be involved in continuous learning to maintain their professional effectiveness. In addition, we feel that teachers must practice what they preach. A teacher who is not continuously learning raises serious questions for students: If it's not important for our teachers to learn, why should we? The attitude toward learning that teachers model for students may be as important as the content they teach.

Many opportunities are available for teachers to learn new knowledge and skills. Nearly every school district makes provisions for in-service training or staff development. Topics can range from classroom-focused issues such as authentic assessment, using the Internet, classroom management, integrated curricula, or learning styles to schoolwide management issues such as restructuring, shared governance, or school–community partnerships. Beyond these in-service opportunities, professional teachers actively seek additional avenues for growth, as this teacher observes during her fourth

Martha's Leadership

The following case is based on several interviews in a research study by the second author of this book. "Martha Townsend" is a pseudonym for a woman who had taught music in urban elementary schools for twenty-five years. She was selected for the study because of her enthusiasm for teaching and her perseverance in the profession.

Martha Townsend smiled and nodded slightly to Teresa, the small child who stood quietly in the doorway of her music classroom, waiting to be invited in. When the girl did not move, Martha bent further in a second nod, smiled more broadly, and added in an expressive whisper, "Come in, come in. Please!" Teresa beamed and entered quickly, finding her seat among the chairs and tables grouped into a semicircle around Martha. Close behind Teresa were twenty other Mexican American children, all around her age. They smiled shyly at Martha and whispered to each other as they hurried single-file to their places.

"Probably third graders," the visitor guessed. "I wonder why they're so excited." The children remained enthusiastic throughout the music class. Always intent on Martha, they answered each of her questions eagerly. They smiled often, sat tall, sang with enthusiasm, and seemed to love music, Ms. Townsend, or both. The visitor, a researcher studying exceptional veteran teachers, was glad she could see Martha in action.

After the children left, Martha and the researcher began the interview with open-ended questions about why Martha had persevered in teaching so long and with such enthusiasm. In her lengthy, thoughtful answers, some patterns began to emerge. The clearest was that this soft-spoken Texan was a determined leader who had battled against odds to develop the school's music program. Recalling coming to the school eleven years earlier, Martha explained:

> I faced a situation where I was told that I was not Mexican so therefore, I could not teach Mexican students. I went into the school and nobody showed up for the instrumental tryouts. They [the adults] spoke in rapid Spanish to me when I came to the door. I am bilingual, but it was too fast for me to pick up. "I don't understand," I responded, and then they said, "You're not Latino." I said (speaking in Spanish), "My heart is Latino." The leader of the group looked at me and shook his head. And they left.

Persistent in her desire to develop a music program for the children, Martha arranged a music assembly for the school and community. The visiting 118-piece orchestra had won awards six years in a row. Their superb performance was well received. After the applause, Martha explained to the audience that the orchestra was not a special group of gifted musicians but instead one that she had developed in her previous school. She invited the parents to let her do the same for their children. A steady focus on her goal and her creative leadership over the years has resulted today in an impressive music program that includes a large orchestra and the participation of every class in school.

Several times a year, under Martha's leadership, over a hundred children performed to capacity crowds of appreciative parents, friends, and relatives. Several weeks after the interview, Martha single-handedly directed a musical with an extensive cast and repertoire of songs and skits—some that made the crowd burst out in laughter. The audience packed the gymnasium, filling all the seats, spilling into the side aisles, and crowding the space across the back of the gym. Parents stretched to catch sight of their children when they performed and applauded with enthusiasm for each set in the program. Martha could rightly regard her program as a success.

Martha also demonstrated leadership in her guidance of student teachers, her lobbying of state legislators, her trust-earning relationships with her principals, the workshops she presented in professional conferences, the writing she did for the state department of education, and the college teaching she did as an adjunct professor. But of all her leadership opportunities, Martha believed that guiding her students and getting to know their families were most important. "If we really want to affect change in our society, we have to get our best minds working where it counts, and that's with the kids who don't have opportunities otherwise."

In her advice for new teachers Martha emphasized the importance of being active in the community and a resource for parents:

> It's very important that teachers not be a people who just come to the neighborhood during school hours. I think they have to make a connection with the people who live there. And I strongly recommend that they do some volunteer work in the community. Attending things that are meaningful in the community says a lot. For instance, I just went to a Harvest Parade. . . . Our school is in a port town, so a lot of people who are just coming into the community might not have met me yet, but there I was. When the children started yelling out my name and waving, their families realized that I was there. On Monday three of the mothers came in to tell me about problems they were having. That happened because I was at the parade. They felt differently about me because they saw me in the community.

From Martha's perspective, to be a teacher is to be a leader, and the position is permanent. She tells her elementary school children and her college students, "I'm your teacher, I am always your teacher, forever, no matter how old and gray you get. I am still your teacher. If you want to come to me later and ask me something, come." And they do.

Questions:

1. How did Martha handle the parents who didn't think she should teach in their children's school? What other approaches could she have tried?

2. Describe Martha's leadership style and compare it to your own.

3. How else could Martha be a leader in her school? What areas did she overlook?

4. How do you envision using your leadership skills?

year of teaching: "After realizing what it could mean to work with colleagues and support colleagues in their work, I began arranging my own 'in-service' opportunities in my building and in the professional community. Even though I am a young teacher, I learned that I too am responsible for continuing my own learning in my profession" (Visconti 1996, 154).

Many teachers have attained National Board Certification, a professional growth experience several Board-certified teachers describe this way:

- "One of the best professional development experiences—it gave me lots of self-confidence."
- "The certification process was a real eye-opener. I realized I've done an awful lot—the process helps document your accomplishments."
- "It was like the final stages of a major graduate course or a cumulative comprehensive exam or thesis."
- "The certification process far exceeds everything I've ever done, including my M.A."
- "The certification process was more focused than a master's program and more valuable because it was what I was really doing in the classroom" (Rotberg, Futrell, and Lieberman, 1998, 463).

Learning to Become a Leader   For professional teachers, an important goal of life-long learning is to acquire leadership skills. Successful educational reform in the twenty-first century will require teacher participation in leadership. In fact, it is quite possible that "schools of the [twenty-first] century will be run by teams of teachers who [have] the tools, incentives, and leadership they need to accomplish their jobs" (Gerstner et al. 1994, 169). One such school is Anzar High School in California, which operates under a team leadership model, *without* a principal. According to Anzar High teachers, after the school opened in 1994, they "had to develop personal and interpersonal sensibilities in order not to re-create the same kind of hierarchical system with which we were familiar and comfortable" (Barnett, McKowen, and Bloom 1998, 48). The success of the team leadership model is the result of teachers' commitment to the "Anzar Communication Guidelines":

- I commit to practice these guidelines.
- We are all part of the same team; we collectively own the problems, and we collectively solve them.
- We will allow conflict/differing ideas to exist.
- We will help and support others.
- I will be honest (Barnett, McKowen, and Bloom 1998, 48–49).

Involvement in the Profession

Today's teachers realize that they have the most important role in the educational enterprise and that, previously, they have not had the power they needed to improve the profession. Therefore, they are taking an increasingly broader view of the decisions that, as professionals, they have the right to make, as this elementary teacher points out:

> One of the problems is legislative people deciding what the education reforms should be and how they should be handled. I think it entails a lack of trust in the teachers by these authorities, and I think it's passed on to the public by the authorities. . . . Every time they start reforming education, they start reforming the teachers. For example, there's all the talk about competency testing and we're going to get rid of all the bad teachers. Teachers have the feeling that they're talking about

all of us. We sometimes are used as public relations by authorities. And then often they take credit for what we do (Godar 1990, 264).

Across the country, professional teachers are deeply involved with their colleagues, professional organizations, teacher educators, legislators, policy makers, and others in a push to make teaching more fully a profession. Through their behaviors and accomplishments, they are demonstrating that they are professionals, that the professional identity of teachers is becoming stronger. During the last decade, for example, teachers have become more involved in teacher education reform, teacher certification, and professional governance. And, through the efforts of scores of teacher organizations, teachers have also made gains in working conditions, salaries, and benefits.

To What Professional Organizations Do Teachers Belong?

The expanding leadership role of teachers has been supported through the activities of more than 500 national teacher organizations (*National Trade and Professional Associations of the United States* 1999). These organizations and the scores of hardworking teachers who run them support a variety of activities to improve teaching and schools. Through lobbying in Washington and at state capitols, for example, teacher associations acquaint legislators, policymakers, and politicians with critical issues and problems in the teaching profession. Many associations have staffs of teachers, researchers, and consultants who produce professional publications, hold conferences, prepare grant proposals, engage in school improvement activities, and promote a positive image of teaching to the public. In the quest to improve the professional lives of all teachers, two national organizations have led the way: the National Education Association (NEA) and the American Federation of Teachers (AFT). These two groups have had a long history of competition for the allegiance of teachers.

The National Education Association

Membership in the **National Education Association (NEA),** the oldest and largest of the two organizations, includes both teachers and administrators. Originally called the National Teachers Association when it was founded in 1857, the group was started by forty-three educators from a dozen states and the District of Columbia (West 1980, 1).

The NEA has affiliates in every state plus Puerto Rico and the District of Columbia, and its local affiliates number more than 13,000. About two-thirds of the teachers in this country belong to the NEA. More than 78 percent of NEA's 2.4 million members are teachers; about 12 percent are guidance counselors, librarians, and administrators; almost 3 percent are university professors; about 2 percent are college and university students; about 3 percent are support staff (teacher aides, secretaries, cafeteria workers, bus drivers, and custodians); and about 2 percent are retired members.

To improve education in this country, the NEA has standing committees in the following areas: affiliate relationships, higher education, human relations, political action, teacher benefits, and teacher rights. These committees engage in a wide range of activities, among them preparing reports on important educational issues, disseminating the results of educational research, conducting conferences, working with federal agencies on behalf of children, pressing for more rigorous standards for the teaching profession, helping school districts resolve salary disputes, developing ways to improve personnel practices, and enhancing the relationship between the profession and the public.

Currently, more than two-thirds of states have passed some type of collective bargaining laws that apply to teachers. There is little uniformity among these laws, with most of the thirty-one states permitting strikes only if certain conditions have been met. The NEA has gone on record as supporting a federal statute that would set up uniform procedures for teachers to bargain with their employers.

The NEA continues today to focus on issues of concern to teachers, primarily in the area of professional governance. Efforts are being made to broaden teachers' decision-making powers related to curriculum, extracurricular responsibilities, staff development, and supervision. To promote the status of the profession, the NEA conducts annual research studies and opinion surveys in various areas and publishes *NEA Today*, the *NEA Research Bulletin*, and its major publication, *Today's Education*.

The American Federation of Teachers

The **American Federation of Teachers (AFT)** was founded in 1916. Three teachers' unions in Chicago issued a call for teachers to form a national organization affiliated with organized labor. Teacher unions in Gary, Indiana; New York City; Oklahoma; Scranton, Pennsylvania; and Washington, D.C., joined the three Chicago unions to form the AFT.

The AFT differs from the NEA in that it is open only to teachers and nonsupervisory school personnel. The AFT is active today in organizing teachers, collective bargaining, public relations, and developing policies related to various educational issues. In addition, the organization conducts research in areas such as educational reform, bilingual education, teacher certification, and evaluation, and also represents members' concerns through legislative action and technical assistance.

The AFT has more than one million members who are organized through 2,265 local affiliates. The AFT is affiliated with the American Federation of Labor–Congress of Industrial Organizations (AFL-CIO), which has over thirteen million members. To promote the idea that teachers should have the right to speak for themselves on important issues, the AFT does not allow superintendents, principals, and other administrators to join. As an informational brochure on the AFT states, "Because the AFT believes in action—in 'getting things done' rather than issuing reports, letting someone else do the 'doing'—a powerful, cohesive structure is necessary."

Unlike the NEA, the AFT has been steadfastly involved throughout its history in securing economic gains and improving working conditions for teachers. Though the AFT has been criticized for being unprofessional and too concerned with bread-and-butter issues, none other than the great educator and philosopher John Dewey took out the first AFT membership card in 1916. After twelve years as a union member, Dewey made his stance on economic issues clear:

> It is said that the Teachers Union, as distinct from the more academic organizations, overemphasizes the economic aspect of teaching. Well, I never had that contempt for the economic aspect of teaching, especially not on the first of the month when I get my salary check. I find that teachers have to pay their grocery and meat bills and house rent just the same as everybody else (Dewey 1955, 60–61).

Traditionally, the AFT has been strongest in urban areas. Today, the AFT represents teachers not only in Chicago and New York but in Philadelphia, Washington, D.C., Kansas City, Detroit, Boston, Cleveland, and Pittsburgh. NEA membership has tended to be suburban and rural. The NEA has always been the larger of the two organizations, and it is presently more than twice the size of its rival.

A Merger between the NEA and AFT?

Over the years, the differences between the NEA and the AFT have become less apparent. Collective bargaining and the use of strikes, long opposed by the NEA, are now used by both organizations. The major difference between the two groups now is the AFT's affiliation with organized labor, a relationship that has led to public disaffection in some areas.

Many people within both the NEA and the AFT believe that the interests of teachers and students could best be served through a merger of the two organizations. One national teachers' union with enormous political strength is the goal. In 1968, Charles Cogen, president of the AFT, proposed a merger with the NEA. In the AFT's publication, *The American Teacher,* Cogen wrote:

> There is no use denying that the AFT and the NEA are engaged in dire competition for the membership of the teachers of America. But we must do this without giving aid and power to the governmental authorities, boards of education, and superintendents with whom we are contending. And then, let us keep the door open; let us look forward to the day when AFT-NEA unity may become a reality. Heaven knows, we fully need a strong, unified, militant, and labor-oriented teachers' union to fight the great battles that lie ahead.

The NEA, however, declined the AFT's invitation to explore that possibility and proposed instead that the AFT drop its AFL-CIO affiliation and join the NEA. A few local affiliates, however, did go on to merge.

Another attempt was made to merge in 1973–74. After several months of talks, however, the possibility of a merger was abandoned. Once again, the NEA cited the AFT's insistence on AFL-CIO affiliation as the major stumbling block.

In early 1998, a "conceptual agreement" to merge the organizations was announced by the presidents of the NEA and the AFT. The presidents cited an "assault" on public education in the form of voucher plans, charter schools, and other approaches to school privatization as a primary reason to merge (Bradley 1998a). The proposal to merge was ultimately rejected that summer in a vote by NEA and AFT members; however, in Minnesota, the AFT and NEA affiliates merged to become the nation's only state organization made up of members of both national teachers' unions.

Other Professional Organizations

In addition to the NEA and AFT, teachers' professional interests are represented by more than 500 other national organizations. Several of these are concerned with improving the quality of education at all levels and in all subject areas. **Phi Delta Kappa (PDK)**, for example, is a professional and honorary fraternity of educators concerned with enhancing quality education through research and leadership activities. Founded in 1906, Phi Delta Kappa now has a membership of 166,000. Members, who are graduate students, teachers, and administrators, belong to one of more than 666 chapters. To be initiated into Phi Delta Kappa, one must have demonstrated high academic achievement, have completed at least fifteen semester hours of graduate work in education, and have made a commitment to a career of educational service. Phi Delta

Do teachers' unions have a positive effect on education?

The public seems to be divided over whether teachers' unions such as the National Education Association (NEA) and the American Federation of Teachers (AFT) have a positive effect on education. According to a Phi Delta Kappa/Gallup Poll, "27 percent believed that unions have improved the quality of the public schools, 26 percent believe that unions have hurt the public schools, and 37 percent believe that unions have made no difference" (Rose and Gallup 1998).

Opponents object to unions as being too focused on increasing teachers' salaries, improving their working conditions, and protecting their jobs. Such concerns make teachers resist educational reform efforts such as the voucher system and a longer school year. Those in favor of unions believe that the unions' interests are not self-centered and that improving the quality of education for children and youth is their ultimate goal. By uniting teachers, the unions can advocate for the rights and needs of children and influence legislation on their behalf.

What do you think? Do teachers' unions have a positive effect on education?

Yes, teachers' unions have a positive effect on education.

Yes, teachers' unions do have a positive effect on education. They "protect against efforts to dismantle public education and lobby for increased funding to strengthen schools" (Noll 1999, p. 355). They bring about specific changes that increase students' opportunities to learn. For instance, in California the NEA helped lobby the state to approve a "$177 million dollar program to reduce kindergarten through third-grade [class] sizes to 20 pupils, down from current class sizes that reach as high as 40," according to Bob Chase, the organization's president (Chase 1999, p. 358).

When he began his NEA presidency, Chase proposed a new unionism. "We aim not so much to redirect NEA as to reinvent it." His goal for the organization was to be proactive in reforming education:

Instead of just protecting our members from dysfunctional systems, it is time for us to challenge and change those systems —both for the sake of our members and for the sake of the children.

The NEA has showed vigorous support of the charter-school movement and in the late 1990s sponsored six charter schools in various locations around the United States.

The internet websites of the NEA and the AFT reveal the groups' contrasting but equally effective approaches to helping teachers, the profession, and education. The NEA website provides a variety of news sources, including an e-mail newsletter that reports "what NEA members are doing to make things better for children and public schools," a code of ethics, and a list of ten categories of resolutions for the year. In the 1999 list several resolutions focused on improving the quality of teaching and accessibility to learning in schools:

weblink

Advance the Cause of Education for All Individuals
Promote the Health and Welfare of Children and/or Students
Promote Professional Excellence Among Educators

The wide range of books, videos, and services provided in the NEA website store are also directed toward assisting teachers in their work and improving education.

The AFT website appears more political, featuring a book, *Educators' Guide to School Reform,* a lengthy report entitled "Fresh Arguments to Fight against Vouchers," and press releases updating readers on the AFT's law suits challenging voucher programs. Together the two groups are doing a great deal to improve education in the United States.

No, teachers' unions do not have a positive effect on education.

Those who oppose teachers' unions believe that the unions' successes in increasing salaries have come at the cost of improvements to education. Myron Lieberman, author of *The Teachers Unions: How the NEA and AFT Sabotage Reform and Hold Students, Parents, Teachers, and Taxpayers Hostage to Bureaucracy* (1997), writes "unionization has increased costs of public education but not improved outcomes."

One way that opponents say unions have hurt schools is through their insistence that all teachers be paid according to the same scale. In teaching-shortage areas such as math and science, where pay in fields outside the classroom is higher, the only way to meet the demand for teachers is to pay more. Union resistance to doing so shows more caring about teachers than about the education of children and youth.

Opponents also object to teacher strikes. They believe that teachers are professionals working with human services and that they should not strike under any circumstance. "Professionals owe their primary responsibility to the needs of clients; this ethical commitment should override secondary imperatives, such as personal gain, political exigencies, or simple expedience," Linda Darling-Hammond explained in a discussion of professionalism in teaching (1993).

The NEA and the AFT appear to be working against education reforms in order to protect their own interests. For instance, they resist school choice, opponents say, because they would lose union memberships who would be harder to recruit after they move into privately run schools. Former Senator Bob Dole of Kansas strongly criticized unions at the 1996 Republican National Convention in his presidential nomination acceptance speech:

I say this not to the teachers, but to their unions: If education were a war, you would be losing it. If it were a business, you would be driving it into bankruptcy. . . . When I am president I will disregard your political power for the sake of the children, the schools, and the nation. I plan to enrich your vocabulary with those words you fear— school choice, competition, and opportunity scholarships—so that you will join the rest of us in accountability. . . .

Where do you stand on this issue?

1. What are the strongest points in each position?

2. What do you believe? Do teachers' unions have a positive effect on education?

3. What illustrations can you add to defend your position?

4. Investigate the NEA and AFT websites and make your own evaluation of them. What underlying messages does each site convey?

5. If you were to join a teacher's union, which one would you join and why?

Recommended Sources

Chase, B. (1999). Unions lead the fight for innovation and investment in public education. In J. W. Noll (Ed.). *Clashing views on controversial educational issues,* 10th ed. Guilford, CT: Dushkin/McGraw-Hill.

Chase, B. (1997, October 15). Restoring the impulse to dream: the right to a quality public education. *Vital speeches of the day.* City News Publishing Company.

Darling-Hammond, L. (1993). Progress toward professionalism in teaching. In Gordon Cawelti (Ed.).*Challenges and achievements of American education: The 1993 Yearbook of the Association for Supervision and Curriculum Development.* Washington, DC: Association for Supervision and Curriculum Development.

Lieberman, M. (1997). *The teachers' unions: How the NEA and AFT sabotage reform and hold students, parents, teachers, and taxpayers hostage to bureaucracy.* New York: The Free Press.

Noll, J. W. (1999). *Taking sides: Clashing views on controversial issues,* 10th ed. Guilford, CT: Dushkin/McGraw-Hill.

Rose, L. C. and Gallup, A. M. (1998, September). The 30th annual Phi Delta Kappa/Gallup poll of the public's attitudes toward the public schools. *Phi Delta Kappan,* 41–56.

Kappa members receive *Phi Delta Kappan,* a journal of education published ten times a year.

Another example is the **Association for Supervision and Curriculum Development (ASCD),** a professional organization of teachers, supervisors, curriculum coordinators, education professors, administrators, and others. The ASCD is interested in school improvement at all levels of education. Founded in 1921, the association has a membership of 150,000. ASCD provides professional development experiences in curriculum and supervision, disseminates information on educational issues, and encourages research, evaluation, and theory development. ASCD also conducts several National Curriculum Study Institutes around the country each year and provides a free research information service to members. Members receive *Educational Leadership*, a well-respected journal printed eight times a year. ASCD also publishes a yearbook, each one devoted to a particular educational issue, and occasional books in the area of curriculum and supervision.

In addition, as you will see in Appendix 12.1 many professional associations exist for teachers of specific subject-areas, such as mathematics, English, social studies, music, physical education, and so on, as well as for teachers of specific student populations, such as exceptional learners, young children, and students with limited English proficiency.

What New Leadership Roles for Teachers Are Emerging?

Teachers' roles are changing in fundamental and positive ways at the beginning of the twenty-first century. Greater autonomy and an expanded role in educational policy-making has led to "unprecedented opportunities for today's teachers to extend their leadership roles beyond the classroom" (Gmelch and Parkay 1995, 48). To prepare for this future, today's teachers will need to develop leadership skills to a degree not needed in the past.

Teacher Involvement in Teacher Education, Certification, and Staff Development

Teacher input into key decisions about teacher preparation, certification, and staff development is on the rise. Through their involvement with professional development schools and the National Board for Professional Teaching Standards (see Chapter 2), state professional standards boards (see Chapter 2), and scores of local, state, and national education committees, teachers are changing the character of pre- and in-service education. For example, in 1992, the National Board for Professional Teaching Standards (NBPTS) established a network designed to allow nearly 7 percent of the nation's 2.5 million teachers to participate in field-testing various components of the NBPTS certification system. The NBPTS allocated $1 million to teachers, in the form of honoraria, for helping to field-test the NBPTS assessment materials. In commenting on the teachers' role in the field-test network, the NBPTS vice-president for assessment and research said, "Teachers are indispensable for the development of these assessments. We need their real-world perspective" (National Board for Professional Teaching Standards 1992, 3).

Teachers who have received National Board Certification are recognized as professionals not only in their schools, but also in their districts and beyond. For example, after receiving Board Certification, these teachers had the following professional opportunities:

■ Helene Alolouf (Early Adolescence/English Language Arts certificate) of Yonkers, New York, was invited to teach at the Manhattanville Graduate School of Education as an adjunct professor.

- Sandra Blackman (Early Adolescence/English Language Arts certificate) of San Diego, California, was promoted to resource teacher for the Humanities Departments for fifty-five schools, where she provides staff development for a standards-based system.
- Edward William Clark Jr. (Early Childhood/Generalist certificate) of Valley, Alabama, helped the State Department of Education and the Alabama Education Association develop National Board Certification training modules to assist Alabama teachers with National Board Certification.
- Linda Lilja (Middle Childhood/Generalist certificate) of Scranton, Kansas, was invited to serve as a member of the task force for the National Teachers Hall of Fame.
- Donna W. Parrish (Early Adolescence/Generalist certificate) of Shelby, North Carolina, was appointed curriculum specialist at a middle school.

Teacher-Leaders

As the titles of the following books published during the 1990s suggest, the term **teacher-leader** has become part of the vocabulary of educational reform:

- *Awakening the Sleeping Giant: Leadership Development for Teachers* (Katzenmeyer and Moller 1996).
- *Collaborative Leadership and Shared Decision Making: Teachers, Principals, and University Professors* (Clift et al. 1995).
- *Educating Teachers for Leadership and Change* (O'Hair and Odell 1995).
- *A Handbook for Teacher Leaders* (Pellicer and Anderson 1995).
- *Teachers as Leaders: Evolving Roles* (Livingston 1992).
- *Teachers as Leaders: Perspectives on the Professional Development of Teachers* (Walling 1994).
- *Who Will Save Our Schools?: Teachers as Constructivist Leaders* (Lambert et al 1996).

"In their new leadership roles, teachers are being called upon to form new partnerships with business and industry; institutions of higher education; social service agencies; professional associations; and local, state, and federal governmental agencies. In this new role, teachers will be the key to promoting widespread improvement of our educational system" (Gmelch and Parkay 1995, 50–51). A brief look at the professional activities of Sandra MacQuinn, a teacher-leader who worked with the first author and a colleague on a major restructuring effort at Rogers High School in Spokane, Washington, illustrates the wide-ranging roles of a teacher-leader. In addition to teaching, here are just a few of MacQuinn's leadership activities while serving as liaison and on-site coordinator of a school-university partnership between Rogers High School and Washington State University's College of Education:

- Writing grant proposals for teacher-developed projects
- Helping other teachers write grant proposals
- Facilitating the development of an integrated school-to-work curriculum
- Preparing newsletters to keep faculty up-to-date on restructuring
- Organizing and facilitating staff development training
- Developing connections with area businesses and arranging "job shadowing" sites for students
- Working with a community college to create an alternative school for Rogers High students at the college

highlights

Bobcats

Kristin Hatcher

How are teachers playing a leadership role in the development and dissemination of multimedia software?

As pointed out in Chapter 11, a key to the effective use of technology to enhance students' learning is the availability of high-quality educational software. Since computer-enhanced instruction (CEI) first began to be used widely in the schools during the early 1990s, there has been a consistent call for higher-quality educational software and a realization that teachers, with their deep understanding of students' learning needs, would need to play a central role in the development of that software. As a software publisher stated in the U.S. Department of Education's publication *Getting America's Students Ready for the 21st Century: Meeting the Technology Literacy Challenge* (1996a): "We definitely need teachers to help identify good software—to put some models out there that producers can emulate. Teachers need to be involved in separating the wheat from the chaff."

In response to that call, scores of teachers have become directly involved in developing and disseminating innovative, cutting-edge educational software. Perhaps the best known teacher-developed software is Roger Wagner's *HyperStudio®,* with more than two million users in the United States alone. As a science and mathematics teacher in California, Wagner launched *HyperStudio®* in 1978. According to Wagner, "We wanted to make multimedia authoring a reality for students on the humble Apple IIGS. [The] world at large sets the stage for what is happening in classrooms now. As students increasingly use electronic sources of information for their research, and see the pervasion of multimedia around them, they expect to create their own projects in the same manner" (Davitt, 1997). Currently, dozens of teachers provide Wagner with input as he continues to develop newer versions of *HyperStudio®.*

weblink

Many other teachers around the country are working with instructional technology laboratories to develop and field test multimedia software. For example, scores of teachers have collaborated with researchers at Wheeling Jesuit University's Center for Educational Technologies (CET), also home of NASA's Classroom of the Future program, to develop *Astronomy Village* and *Investigating the Solar System,* two of the most innovative computer simulations currently available.

Still other teachers are providing leadership for the integration of technology into teaching and learning environments. For example, dozens of teachers have attended the CET's Teacher-Leader Institutes, where they acquire strategies for integrating technology into education. Similarly, other teachers have completed the Teacher2Teacher Technology Leadership programs in San Jose, California, where they can earn Teacher Technology Integration Certification (TTIC), Train the Trainer Certification (TTC), or Technology Leadership (TL) Certification.

Clearly, teachers will play three vital leadership roles in the development of multimedia software for classrooms of the twenty-first century:

- Developing and disseminating increasingly powerful versions of multimedia software
- Developing strategies for the most effective ways to use that software in the classroom
- Training other teachers to use that software

- Scheduling substitute teachers to provide Rogers teachers with release-time to work on restructuring
- Making presentations on the Rogers High restructuring at state and regional conferences
- Arranging for Rogers students to visit Washington State University (WSU)

- Meeting with the principal, assistant principals, WSU professors, and others to develop short- and long-range plans for implementing site-based management; chairing meetings of the site-based council, the restructuring steering committee, and other restructuring-related committees.

At West Forest Intermediate School in Opelika, Alabama, which has several schools within a school, teachers have the following roles: coordinator of special education services and lead teacher, coordinator of the media center responsible for schoolwide implementation of technology, and director of the school's whole-language program (Gerstner et al. 1994). At a Florida elementary school with a shared decision making (SDM) form of governance, teachers work on committees that make hiring, budget, and school policy decisions. In the words of one teacher at that school: "I'm not just a teacher in a classroom, I am a member of an organization, a company that helps to run the school. I'm not just alone in my room" (Ross and Webb 1995, 76).

Dimensions of Teacher Leadership Beyond the Classroom

Figure 12.3 illustrates ten dimensions of teacher leadership beyond the classroom. The many teachers whom we have assisted on school restructuring projects during the last few years have used these skills to reach an array of educational goals. Clearly, these teachers have modeled what Rallis (1990, 193) terms "an elevated conception of teaching."

At schools around the country, teachers and principals are using a "collaborative, emergent" approach to leadership; that is, the person who provides leadership for a particular schoolwide project or activity may or may not be the principal or a member of

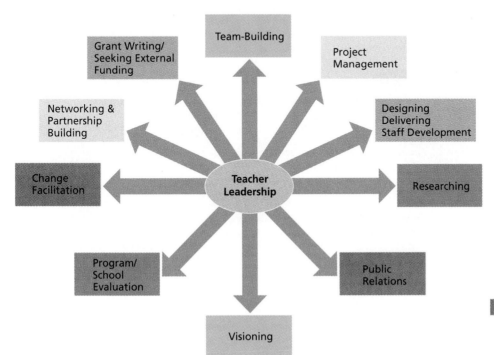

Figure 12.3

Ten dimensions of teacher leadership beyond the classroom

the administrative team (Parkay, Schindler and Oaks, 1997). Such schools are characterized by a "higher level of professional community" (Newmann and Wehlage 1995). They are similar to the schools Wohlstetter (1995, 24) identified as having successfully implemented school-based management (SBM): "[They] had principals who played a key role in dispersing power. [T]he principals were often described as facilitators and managers of change." In addition, teachers who accept the challenge of becoming teacher-leaders and redefining their roles to include responsibilities beyond the classroom recognize the importance of five principles Michael Fullan and Andy Hargreaves present in their book, *What's Worth Fighting for in Your School?* (1996); they use these principles to guide their professional actions (see Figure 12.4).

Five Principles That Guide the Actions of Teacher-Leaders

PRINCIPLE 1

Teacher-leaders accept their responsibility to increase the degree and quality of daily interactions with other teachers, administrators, and staff members. They know that "even if done on a small scale regularly, this can make a very significant difference for other individual teachers and for oneself."

PRINCIPLE 2

Teacher-leaders recognize that they have a responsibility to understand and to improve the culture of the school. "Every teacher must be concerned about the health of the school as an organization. This does not mean getting obsessively involved in every aspect of school life, but it does mean taking some responsibility for the welfare of one's colleagues and the wider life of the school."

PRINCIPLE 3

Teacher-leaders recognize that every teacher is a leader, and that a teacher's leadership role will vary according to the stage of the teacher's life and career. However, "all teachers have a leadership contribution to make beyond their own classrooms and should take action accordingly."

PRINCIPLE 4

Teacher-leaders recognize that they have a responsibility to become informed about the development of educational policies as well as professional and research issues. "This does not mean having a second career as an academic. But it does mean connecting with the knowlege base for improving teaching and schools. The more knowledgeable a teacher is about global educational and professional issues, the more resourceful he or she will be for students as well as for other teachers."

PRINCIPLE 5

Teacher-leaders recognize that all teachers have a responsibility for helping to shape the quality of the next generation of teachers. Teachers can make a contribution by working with student teachers, mentoring new teachers, and supporting and praising other teachers who assume those roles.

Figure 12.4

Five principles that guide the actions of teacher-leaders
Source: Adapted from Michael Fullan and Andy Hargreaves, *What's Worth Fighting for in Your School?* New York: Teachers College Press, 1996.

The new calls to leadership for teachers suggest that teachers' essential knowledge and skills may not differ much from those traditionally required for educational administrators. The National Commission for the Principalship has identified the following "performance domains" for the Principalship. Which of these domains also apply to teacher-leaders? To what extent are the knowledge and skills required of teacher-leaders and of principals becoming similar?

I. Functional Domains
1. *Leadership*
2. *Information Collection*
3. *Problem Analysis*
4. *Judgment*
5. *Organizational Oversight*
6. *Implementation*
7. *Delegation*

II. Programmatic Domains
8. *Instructional Program*
9. *Curriculum Design*
10. *Student Guidance and Development*
11. *Staff Development*
12. *Measurement and Evaluation*
13. *Resource Allocation*

III. Interpersonal Domains
14. *Motivating Others*
15. *Sensitivity*
16. *Oral Expression*
17. *Written Expression*

IV. Contextual Domains
18. *Philosophical and Cultural Values*
19. *Legal and Regulatory Applications*
20. *Policy and Political Influences*
21. *Public and Media Relationships (National Commission for the Principalship)*

How Do Teachers Contribute to Educational Research?

Today's teachers play an increasingly important role in educational research. By applying research to solve practical, classroom-based problems, teachers validate the accuracy and usefulness of educational research and help researchers identify additional areas to investigate. As consumers of educational research, teachers improve their teaching, contribute to educational reform, and enhance the professional status of teaching.

In addition, increasing numbers of teachers are becoming competent researchers in their own right and making important contributions to our understanding of teaching and learning. Prior to the mid 1980s, teachers were the missing "voice" in educational research. However, as teachers and staff developers Holly and McLoughlin (1989, 309) noted more than a decade ago, "We've moved from research on teachers to research with teachers and lately to research by teachers." Since their observation, we have seen the emergence of the **teacher-researcher**, the professional teacher who conducts classroom research to improve his or her teaching.

Part of being a professional is the ability to decide *how* and *when* to use research to guide one's actions. For example, Emmerich Koller, a teacher of German at a suburban high school, describes in an article he wrote for the book *Teachers Doing Research: Practical Possibilities* (Burnaford, Fischer, and Hobson 1996) how he experimented with new teaching methods based on the latest findings from brain research

and "accelerated learning," a strategy for optimizing learning by integrating conscious and unconscious mental processes. After determining how and when to put that research into practice, he commented, "At age 50, after 27 years of teaching, I have found something that has made teaching very exciting again" (Koller 1996, 180).

Sources of Educational Research

Research findings are reported in scores of educational research journals (see Appendix 12.2). In addition, there are several excellent reviews of research with which you should become familiar during your professional preparation, such as the third edition of the *Handbook of Research on Teaching* (published by Macmillan, 1986), a project sponsored by the American Educational Research Association. Its more than 1,000 pages synthesize research in several areas, including research on teaching at various grade levels and in various subject areas. Other comprehensive, authoritative reviews of research you might wish to consult include the following:

This teacher is conducting classroom research on the ways students come to understand a problem and to apply appropriate problem-solving skills. What are several ways the teacher might use this research as a professional?

- *Encyclopedia of Educational Research,* 6th ed., four volumes (Macmillan, 1992)
- *Handbook of Research on the Education of Young Children* (Macmillan, 1993)
- *Handbook of Research on Mathematics Teaching and Learning* (Macmillan, 1992), sponsored by the National Council of Teachers of Mathematics
- *Handbook of Research on Multicultural Education* (Macmillian, 1995)
- *Handbook of Research on Music Teaching and Learning* (Macmillan, 1992), sponsored by the Music Educators National Conference
- *Handbook of Research on Science Teaching and Learning* (Macmillan, 1994), sponsored by the National Science Teachers Association
- *Handbook of Research on Social Studies Teaching and Learning* (Macmillan, 1991), sponsored by the National Council for the Social Studieshool Mathematics, and High School Mathematics (Macmillan, 1993), three volumes
- *Handbook of Research on Teaching the English Language Arts* (Macmillan, 1991), sponsored by the International Reading Association and the National Council of Teachers of English
- *Handbook of Research on Teaching Literacy through the Communicative and Visual Arts (Macmillan, 1997)*
- *Research Ideas for the Classroom: Early Childhood Mathematics, Middle School Mathematics, and High School Mathematics* (Macmillan, 1993), three volumes sponsored by the National Council of Teachers of Mathematics

Government Resources for Research Application

The federal government supports several efforts designed to help teachers improve their practice through the application of research findings. In 1966, three agencies were created to support and disseminate research: **Educational Resources Information Center (ERIC)**, **Research and Development Centers**, and **Regional Educational Laboratories.**

ERIC is a national information system made up of sixteen **ERIC Clearinghouses** and several adjunct clearinghouses—all coordinated by the central ERIC agency in Washington, D.C. (see the Appendix "Educational Resources Information Center (ERIC) Clearlinghouses" on this book's website). The ERIC system, available in most college and university libraries, contains descriptions of exemplary programs, the results of research and development efforts, and related information that can be used by teachers, administrators, and the public to improve education. Each Clearinghouse specializes in one area of education and searches out relevant documents or journal articles that are screened according to ERIC selection criteria, abstracted, and indexed.

Within the **Office of Educational Research and Improvement (OERI)** in Washington, D.C., the Office of Research (formerly the National Institute of Education) maintains fourteen research centers at universities around the country (see the Appendix "Selected National Educational Research and Improvement [OERI] Centers"on this book's website). The centers are devoted to high-quality, fundamental research at every level of education, with most of the research done by scholars at the host university. Among the areas these centers focus on are the processes of teaching and learning, school organization and improvement, the content of education, and factors that contribute to (or detract from) excellence in education.

OERI also houses Programs for the Improvement of Practice (PIP), which support exemplary projects at the state and local levels. PIP also maintains nine regional educational laboratories and sponsors a number of Assistance Centers (see the Appendix "Department of Education Regional Assistance Centers" on this book's website). Each laboratory serves a geographic region and is a nonprofit corporation not affiliated with a university. Laboratory staff work directly with school systems, state educational agencies, and other organizations to improve education through the application of research findings.

Conducting Classroom Action Research

More than three decades ago, Robert Schaefer (1967, 5) posed the following questions in *The School as the Center of Inquiry:*

> Why should our schools not be staffed, gradually if you will, by scholar-teachers in command of the conceptual tools and methods of inquiry requisite to investigating the learning process as it operates in their own classroom? Why should our schools not nurture the continuing wisdom and power of such scholar-teachers?

Schaefer's vision for teaching has become a reality. Today, thousands of teachers are involved in action research to improve their teaching. Using their classrooms as "laboratories," these teacher-researchers are systematically studying the outcomes of their teaching through the application of various research methods. In addition, they are disseminating the results of their research at professional conferences and through publications, including *Teacher as Researcher,* a journal edited, written, and published by teachers.

Simply put, **action research** is the classroom-based study by teachers, individually or collaboratively, of how to improve instruction. As in the *reflection-in-action* approach described earlier in this chapter, action research begins with a teacher-identified question, issue, or problem. How can I more effectively motivate a group of students? How do students experience the climate in my classroom? What factors limit parental participation in our school? How can our department (or teacher team) become more collegial? How does computer use in the foreign language classroom affect students' oral communication? Identification of the question to be investigated via action research is a critical step, as the staff development coordinator at an urban elementary school points out:

> As a member of the school leadership team responsible for staff development, I helped guide the process of designing and carrying out the [action research] projects. One of the major challenges in conducting action research projects for this particular group of teachers was the first step: defining the question or problem to be studied. The delicate part of the facilitator's role for this part of action research is to guide teachers toward questions that accurately represent their real concerns and to help them articulate questions in ways that clarify the important elements. If action research is to be useful and engaging, then questions must focus on significant issues related to the success of students within the classroom (Mills 2000, 130).

Action research is also "a natural part of teaching. [T]o be a teacher means to observe students and study classroom interactions, to explore a variety of effective ways of teaching and learning, and to build conceptual frameworks that can guide one's work. This is a personal as well as a professional quest, a journey toward making sense out of and finding satisfaction in one's teaching. It is the work of teacher-researchers" (Fischer 1996, 33).

Action research can be used to study almost any dimension of teaching and learning. At the beginning of the action research cycle, Mills (2000, 41) suggests developing an "action plan" consisting of these steps:

- Write an area-of-focus statement.
- Define the variables.
- Develop research questions.
- Describe the intervention or innovation.

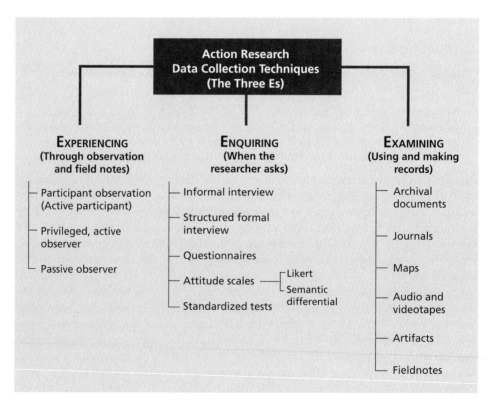

Figure 12.5

Action research data collection techniques (The Three Es)

Source: Geoffrey E. Mills, *Action Research: A Guide for the Teacher Researcher.* Upper Saddle River, NJ: Merrill, 2000, p. 66. © 2000. Reprinted by permission of Prentice Hall, Inc., Upper Saddle River, NJ.

- Describe the membership of the action research group.
- Describe negotiations that need to be undertaken.
- Develop a timeline.
- Develop a statement of resources.
- Develop data collection ideas.

Figure 12.5 presents a "taxonomy" of data collection techniques for action research.

Not surprisingly, becoming a teacher-researcher is hard work, given the daily demands of teaching itself. However, more schools are redefining the teacher's role to include doing action research. These schools realize that action research can provide data on the effectiveness of educational programs, enhance student learning, and energize teachers for professional growth. Four teachers who are members of the Action Research Laboratory at Highland Park High School near Chicago comment on the benefits of action research:

> By far the most rewarding part of working on an action research team was the opportunity to learn and grow with a small group of teacher colleagues. This experience of mutual commitment provided a wonderful staff development experience; by working with these colleagues consistently throughout the year, we were able to explore new ideas and take risks in the classroom with a type of "safety net" in place. For that reason alone, as well as our desire to explore the new questions and challenges raised by our research, we will continue to conduct action research into the effectiveness of our teaching and grading practices (Mills 2000, 97).

How Are Teachers Providing Leadership for School Restructuring and Curriculum Reform?

Today's teachers welcome opportunities to provide leadership for school restructuring and curriculum reform. Although teachers may have played a limited role in school governance in the past, there are currently many opportunities for teachers to become educational leaders beyond the classroom. Figure 12.6 presents five clusters of educational reform, each of which will offer teachers opportunities to shape policies during the twenty-first century.

Leadership and Collaboration for School Reform

The key to successful school restructuring and curriculum reform is teacher leadership and collaboration. At the 1998 National Teacher Forum on Leadership, sponsored by the U.S. Department of Education, participating teachers identified the following ways in which teachers can lead and collaborate for school reform. To illustrate each form of leadership, we provide one example from among the thousands of teachers exercising similar leadership.

Participating in professional teacher organizations—As President of the Wisconsin Science Teachers' Association, Sharon Nelson worked with the National Science Teachers Association, Goals 2000, to disseminate national science education standards in her state.

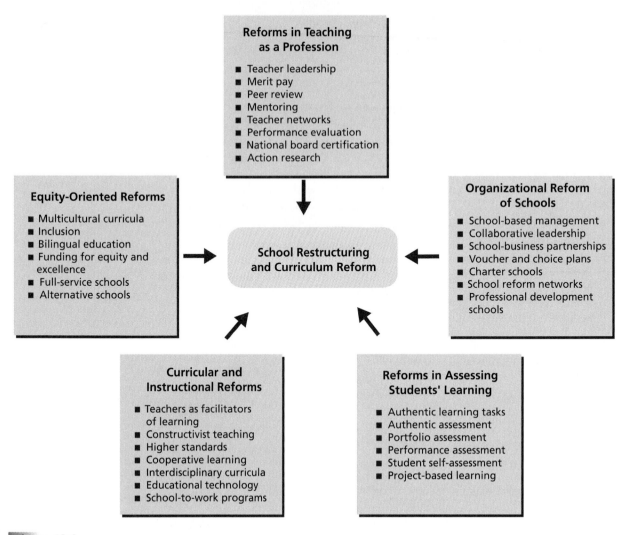

Figure 12.6

Opportunities for teacher leadership in school restructuring and curriculum reform

Taking part in school decisions—Melisa Hancock, an elementary school teacher in Kansas, became a clinical instructor at Kansas State University and played a key role in engineering a partnership with the university that led to her school becoming a professional development school.

Defining what students need to know and be able to do—Delaware teacher Jan Parsons was one of several teachers who took leadership roles on Delaware commissions that wrote standards for mathematics, science, social studies, and language arts; teachers also wrote and piloted new statewide assessments in line with the new standards.

Sharing ideas with colleagues—Tom Howe and other Wisconsin teachers developed a "Share Net Program" which allows teachers to make formal presentations to their peers on effective instructional practices.

Being a mentor to new teachers—Science teacher Fie Budzinsky serves as a Teacher Mentor for the State of Connecticut; Budzinsky had, in turn, been mentored earlier in her career by Dick Reagan, another science teacher.

Helping to make personnel decisions—North Carolina teacher Mary Ostwalt served on a selection committee formed to replace a teacher who resigned; other teachers in her district serve on selection committees for the hiring of new principals.

Improving facilities and technology—Ray Hasart and other teachers were the driving force behind the creation of a new $3.5 million technology facility at a Redmond, Oregon, high school; the facility is visited regularly by people throughout the West Coast.

Working with parents—Martina Marquez and a team of colleagues in New Mexico visit Native American villages and surrounding communities to disseminate math and reading activities parents can do with their children.

Creating partnerships with the community—North Carolina teacher Scott Griffin became a member of his community's volunteer fire department and spearheaded the redesign of the fire safety curriculum presented at schools in the community.

Creating partnerships with businesses and organizations—Georgia teacher Stephanie Blakney took the lead in developing a systemwide Partnership with Education program that led to the creation of a food bank and the Atlanta Coca-Cola Bottling Company "adopting" her school.

Creating partnerships with colleges and universities to prepare future teachers—Former Kansas Teacher of the Year Christy McNally and other award-winning teachers organized a partnership with teacher education programs throughout Kansas.

Becoming leaders in the community—Teacher Jacqueline Omland is President of the Legion auxiliary in Aberdeen, South Dakota, and a colleague is Chairman of the Legion.

Becoming politically involved—Washington State teacher Ivy Chan served as treasurer for a person who ran for State Superintendent of Public Instruction.

Leading efforts to make teachers more visible and communicate positive information—High school teacher Larry Torres started a weekly news column in his New Mexico community paper that focuses on positive articles about education; the column has now expanded to a full page.

Collaborative School Reform Networks

Many teachers are involved in restructuring and curriculum change through their schools' participation in collaborative networks for reform. Networks provide teachers with training and resources for restructuring, and they create opportunities for teachers at network schools to help teachers at nonnetwork schools with their restructuring efforts. Among the many collaborative reform networks are the Coalition of Essential Schools, the National Network for Educational Renewal, Accelerated Schools, and state-based networks, such as the League of Professional Schools.

Coalition of Essential Schools   The **Coalition of Essential Schools (CES)**, started in 1984 by Theodore R. Sizer at Brown University, is a network of more than 1,000 schools and 24 regional support centers. The regional centers, with the support of CES National, coach schools through a systematic process of change at the school site. No two Coalition schools are alike; each develops an approach to restructuring suited to its students, faculty, and community. However, the efforts of Coalition schools to restructure are guided by ten Common Principles (see Appendix 12.3) extrapolated from Sizer's (1997a, 1997b, 1997c; Sizer and Sizer 1999) books on redesigning U.S. schools and the beliefs that top-down, standardized solutions to school problems don't work and that teachers must play a key role in the operation of their schools. Recently, the Coalition organized resource centers so teachers at Coalition schools can provide non-Coalition schools with restructuring assistance.

National Network for Educational Renewal   The Center for Educational Renewal at the University of Washington created the **National Network for Educational Renewal (NNER)** to encourage new opportunities for teachers to become involved in school restructuring, curriculum reform, and the preparation of teachers. Members of the NNER include 33 colleges and universities that collaborate with more than 100 school districts and nearly 500 partner schools. The NNER is based on 19 postulates for reforming teacher education that John Goodlad presented in *Educational Renewal: Better Teachers, Better Schools* (1994). For a school to become a member of the NNER, its teachers must demonstrate that they "understand their appropriate role in site-based management and school renewal" (Goodlad 1994, 89).

Accelerated Schools   Stanford economist Henry M. Levin has developed a nationwide network of **accelerated schools** that provide enriched, rigorous curricula to "speed up" the learning of students at risk. Instead of placing at-risk students into remedial classes, accelerated schools provide students with challenging learning activities traditionally reserved for gifted and talented students. Accelerated Schools are based on the belief that teachers—in collaboration with administrators, parents, and community members—must be able to make important educational decisions, take responsibility for implementing those decisions, and take responsibility for the outcomes of those decisions. The National Center for the Accelerated Schools Project at Stanford operates twelve regional Accelerated Schools Satellite Centers across the country. The satellite centers provide assistance to teachers and administrators who wish to restructure their schools according to the accelerated schools model.

State-Based Educational Partnerships   Many states have established state-based partnerships between a state university or college and a coalition of public schools. Several of these partnerships are patterned after the League of Professional Schools started by Carl Glickman at the University of Georgia. The overall goal of the League is to improve student learning by using shared governance and action research to focus on instructional and curricular issues. Following guidelines Glickman has outlined in *Renewing America's Schools: A Guide for School-Based Action* (1993) and *Revolutionizing America's Schools* (1998), League schools usually begin the restructuring process by developing a *covenant,* a set of mutually agreed on beliefs about how students learn best, and a *charter,* a set of democratically developed guidelines for how shared governance will operate at the school. Presently, nearly 100 League schools exchange resources and ideas and support one another in their restructuring efforts.

SUMMARY

To What Extent Is Teaching a Full Profession?

- Teachers are assuming new leadership roles beyond the classroom as educational systems become more decentralized and approaches to school leadership become more collaborative and participatory.

- For an occupation to be considered a profession, it must satisfy several criteria. Of the following nine criteria for a profession, teaching meets some more fully than others: (1) institutional monopoly of services, (2) teacher autonomy, (3) years of education and training, (4) provision of essential service, (5) degree of self-governance, (6) professional associations, (7) professional knowledge and skills, (8) level of public trust, and (9) prestige, benefits, and pay.

■ Although teaching does not currently satisfy all criteria for a profession, the collaborative efforts of individuals and groups such as the National Commission on Teaching and America's Future and the National Board for Professional Teaching Standards are rapidly professionalizing teaching.

What Is Professionalism in Teaching?

■ The most potent force for enhancing the professional status of teaching is for teachers to see that their actions are professional and to commit themselves to life-long learning and active involvement in the profession.

■ Professional behavior as a teacher is characterized by reflection-in-action (the ability to observe sensitively in classrooms, reflect on those observations, and then act accordingly) and a willingness to serve as a mentor to those entering the profession.

■ As life-long learners, professional teachers actively seek opportunities for growth —from participating in training provided by a school district to arranging one's own "in-service" activities, to acquiring new leadership skills.

To What Professional Organizations Do Teachers Belong?

■ Teachers help shape education as a profession through their leadership roles in more than 500 national teacher organizations.

■ As the oldest and largest professional organization for educators, the National Education Association has played a key role in addressing issues of concern to the 78 percent of its members who are teachers.

■ Affiliated with organized labor and open only to teachers and nonsupervisory personnel, the American Federation of Teachers has done much to secure greater financial rewards and improved working conditions for teachers.

■ Teachers are members of professional associations for specific subject areas and student populations.

What New Leadership Roles for Teachers Are Emerging?

■ Through their involvement with professional development schools, the National Board for Professional Teaching Standards, and local, state, and national education committees, teachers participate in making key decisions about teacher preparation, certification, and staff development.

■ In their new role as teacher-leaders, many teachers are playing a key role beyond the classroom as they form partnerships that focus on the transformation of schools in the United States.

■ Teachers who work collaboratively with principals on school improvement use ten dimensions of teacher leadership beyond the classroom: team-building, project management, designing and delivering staff development, researching, public relations, visioning, program/school evaluation, change facilitation, networking and partnership building, and grant writing/seeking external funding.

How Do Teachers Contribute to Educational Research?

■ Teachers validate the accuracy and usefulness of educational research and identify additional areas to research when they put "research into practice."

■ In the role of teacher-researcher, many teachers conduct action research and systematically study the outcomes of their teaching. Teachers use a five-step action research cycle to study their classrooms and improve their teaching: problem identification, planning, organization, evaluation, and action.

How Are Teachers Providing Leadership for School Restructuring and Curriculum Reform?

■ Five "clusters" of educational reform provide teachers with many opportunities to provide leadership for school restructuring and curriculum reform: reforms in teaching as a profession, equity-oriented reforms, organizational reform of schools, reforms in assessing students' learning, and curricular and instructional reforms.

■ Through collaborative school reform networks such as the Coalition of Essential Schools, the National Network for Educational Renewal, Accelerated Schools, and the League of Professional Schools, teachers provide leadership for restructuring their schools and help other teachers promote school reform at nonnetwork schools.

KEY TERMS AND CONCEPTS

accelerated schools, 486
action research, 481
American Federation of
  Teachers (AFT), 470
Association for
  Supervision and
  Curriculum Development
  (ASCD), 473
Coalition of Essential
  Schools, 485
Educational Resources
  Information Center
  (ERIC), 480

ERIC Clearinghouses, 481
mentor, 465
National Education
  Association
  (NEA), 469
National Network
  for Educational
  Renewal, 486
Office of Educational
  Research and
  Improvement
  (OERI), 481

Phi Delta Kappa (PDK),
  471
profession, 459
reflection-in-action, 464
Regional Educational
  Laboratories, 480
Research and
  Development
  Centers, 480
teacher-leader, 475
teacher-researcher, 479

APPLICATIONS AND ACTIVITIES

Teacher's Journal

1. In your opinion, what accounts for public trust and lack of trust in the teaching profession? What might be the best way to increase that trust?
2. Review several recent issues of the NEA publication, *Today's Education*, and the AFT publication, *The American Teacher*. Compare and contrast concerns or issues that

each publication addresses. What overall differences do you find between the NEA and AFT publications?

3. Do you plan to join a teacher's association such as the NEA or AFT? What are your reasons? What advantages and disadvantages are most important to you?

Teacher's Database

1. With classmates, join or start an online discussion on one or more of the following topics or another topic in Chapter 12 of this text.

action research	school restructuring
educational reform	teacher leadership
grant writing	teacher strikes
mentoring	teacher unions
National Board for Professional Teaching Standards (NBPTS)	teacher–principal collaboration

2. Using your favorite search engine, gather online information and resources about school networking and teacher networking. How might online networking contribute to your preparation as a teacher? As a teacher, how might you and your students use networking in connection with your curriculum? What knowledge and skills do you need to start to participate in a school-based networking project?

Observations and Interviews

1. Survey adults who are not involved in education to get their views on teaching as a profession. What images of teachers and teaching emerge? How do you account for these views?
2. Interview teachers about their involvement in professional associations and the teachers' union. What benefits do teachers obtain from their professional involvement?
3. Find out if teacher strikes are legal in your state. What risks do striking teachers face? How are disputes between teachers and school districts settled?
4. Collaborate with classmates to study a school that is involved in restructuring and participants' roles in the change process. Compare teachers' activities with the new leadership roles for teachers discussed in this chapter. Are any of the teachers involved in action research in the classroom? How does teacher research contribute to restructuring efforts?
5. Visit a school that has developed a partnership with one or more community agencies, schools of higher education, businesses, parent groups, or neighborhood associations. Arrange to observe a planning meeting between the school and the community representatives. Write a narrative account of the meeting followed by an evaluation of the effectiveness of this partnership. To help you with this activity, ask your instructor for Handouts M12.1, "Observing a School-Community Partnership," and M12.2, "Evaluating the Effectiveness of a School-University Partnership."

Professional Portfolio

Focusing on the grade level and subject area for which you are preparing to teach, consult several of the sources of educational research listed in this chapter and prepare a set of research findings to guide your teaching. For each entry, include a bibliographic citation and an annotation that briefly describes the research and the results of that research.

Appendix 12.1

Sampler of Professional Organizations for Teachers

American Alliance for Health, Physical Education, Recreation and Dance (AAHPERD)
1900 Association Drive
Reston, VA 22091
(703) 476-3400
Fax (703) 476-9527
info@aahperd.org

Students and educators in physical education, dance, health, athletics, safety education, recreation, and outdoor education. Purpose is to improve its fields of education at all levels through such services as consultation, periodicals and special publications, leadership development, determination of standards, and research. Publications: *AAHPERD Update: Health Education: Journal of Physical Education; Recreation and Dance; Leisure Today; News Kit on Programs for the Aging; Research Quarterly.*

American Alliance of Teachers of French (AATF)
57 E. Armory Avenue
Champaign, IL 61820
(217) 333-2842
Fax (217) 333-2842

Teachers of French in public and private elementary and secondary schools, colleges, and universities. Maintains Pedagogical Aids Bureau, conducts annual French contest in elementary and secondary schools, awards scholarships to teachers for study in France, maintains placement bureau and a pen pal agency. Publications: *AATF National Bulletin, French Review.*

American Association of Teachers of German (AATG)
112 Haddontowne Court, No. 104
Cherry Hill, NJ 08034
(609) 795-5553
Fax (609) 795-9398
73740.3231@compuserve.com

Teachers of German at all levels. Offers in-service teacher-training workshops and awards and scholarships to outstanding high school students and teachers of German. Publications: *American Association of Teachers of German—Newsletter, Die Unterrichtspraxis: For the Teaching of German, German Quarterly,*

American Association of Teachers of Spanish and Portuguese (Hispanic) (AATSP)
University of Northern Colorado

Gunter Hall
Greeley, CO 80636 (970) 351-1090
lsandste@bentley.univnorthco.edu

Teachers of Spanish and Portuguese languages and literatures and others interested in Hispanic culture. Operates placement bureau and maintains pen pal registry. Sponsors honor society, Sociedad Honoraria Hispanica and National Spanish Examinations for secondary school students. Publication: *Hispania.*

American Classical League (Language) (ACL)
Miami University
Oxford, OH 45056
(513) 529-7741
Fax (513) 529-7742
americanclassicalleague@muohio.edu

Teachers of classical languages in high schools and colleges. To promote the teaching of Latin and other classical languages. Maintains placement service, teaching materials, and resource center. Publications: *Classical Outlook, Prima* (handbook for elementary school teachers).

American Council on the Teaching of Foreign Languages (ACTEL)
6 Executive Plaza
Yonkers, NY 10701-6801
(914) 963-8830
Fax (914) 963-1275

Individuals interested in the teaching of classical and modern foreign languages in schools and colleges. Operates materials center, conducts seminars and workshops, and presents awards. Publications: *ACTFL Newsletter, Foreign Language Annals* (professional journal covering teaching methods and educational research).

American Federation of Teachers (Education) (AFT)
555 New Jersey Avenue NW
Washington, DC 20001
(202) 879-4400
(800) 242-5465

Works with teachers and other educational employees at the state and local level in organizing, collective bargaining, research, educational issues, and public relations. Conducts research in areas such as educational reform, bilingual education, teacher certification, and evaluation. Represents members' concerns through legislative action; offers technical assistance. Operates Education for Democracy Project. Publications: *American Educator, American Teacher, On Campus, Public Service Reporter,* and others.

Appendix 12.1 *(continued)*

Association for Childhood Education International (ACEI)
11501 Georgia Avenue, Suite 315
Wheaton, MD 20902
(301) 942-2443
(800) 423-3563
aceihq@aol.com

Teachers, parents, and other caregivers in thirty-one countries interested in promoting good educational practices for children from infancy through early adolescence. Conducts workshops and travel/study tours abroad, bestows awards, conducts research and educational programs, maintains speakers bureau. Publications: *ACEI Exchange, Childhood Education, Journal of Research in Childhood Education.*

Association for Supervision and Curriculum Development (ASCD)
1250 N. Pitt Street
Alexandria, VA 22314-1403 (703) 549-9110
Fax (703) 549-3891
member@ascd.org

Professional organization of supervisors, curriculum coordinators and directors, consultants, professors of education, classroom teachers, principals, superintendents, parents, and others interested in school improvement at all levels of education. Provides professional development experiences and training in curriculum and supervision; provides Research formation Service. Publications: *ASCD Update, Curriculum and Supervision.*

Association of American Educators (AAE)
26012 Marguerite Pkwy #333
Mission Viejo, CA 92692
(800) 704-7799
(949) 595-7979

A nonpartisan, nonprofit professional association designed to provide an "alternative to the partisan politics and social agendas of the national teacher unions." Membership open to any employee of an educational entity. According to the AAE, "the 'values-neutral' teaching experiment has been a monumental failure and has led to much of the public's negative opinion of our profession. We believe our schools must once again integrate academics, character, and citizenship."

Council for Exceptional Children (Special Education) (CEC)
1920 Association Drive
Reston, VA 22091-1589
(703) 620-3660

cec@sped.org
www.cec.sped.org

Teachers, school administrators, teacher educators, and others with a direct or indirect concern for the education of the disabled and gifted. Provides information to teachers, parents, and others concerning the education of exceptional children. Maintains 63,000 volume library. Operates the ERIC Clearinghouse on Handicapped and Gifted Children. Publications: *Exceptional Child Education Resources, Exceptional Children, Teaching Exceptional Children.*

Education International (EI)
Boulevard Emile Jacqmain 155 (8th floor)
1210 Brussels, Belgium
32-2-224-06-80
Fax 32-2-224-06-06

World's largest educators' federation, representing 23 million members in more than 150 countries. EI's 294 member organizations include the NEA.

Foundation for Exceptional Children (Special Education) (FEC)
1 920 Association Drive
Reston, VA 22091
(703) 620-1054

Institutions, agencies, educators, parents, and persons concerned with the education and personal welfare of gifted or disabled children. Established to further the educational, vocational, social, and personal needs of the disabled child or youth and the neglected educational needs of the gifted. Publication: *Foundation for Exceptional Children—Focus.*

International Reading Association (IRA)
800 Barksdale Road
P.O. Box 8139
Newark, DE 1971 4-8139
(302) 731-1600
Fax (302) 731-1057
73314.1411@compuserve.com

Teachers, reading specialists, consultants, administrators, supervisors, researchers, psychologists, librarians, and parents interested in promoting literacy. Seeks to improve the quality of reading instruction at all educational levels; stimulate and promote the life-time reading habit and an awareness of the impact of reading; encourage the development of every reader's proficiency to the highest possible level. Disseminates information pertaining to research on reading. Publications: *Desktop Reference to* the International Reading Association, *Journal of Reading Reading Teacher, Reading Today.*

Music Teachers National Association (MTNA)

617 Vine Street, Suite 1432
Cincinnati, OH 45202
(513) 421-1420
Fax (513) 421-2503
mtnaadmin@aol.com

Professional society of music teachers in studios conservatories, music schools, and public and private schools, colleges, and universities; undergraduate and graduate music students. Seeks to raise the level of musical performance, understanding, and instruction. Publications: *American Music Teacher Magazine, Music Teachers National Association—Directory of Nationally Certified Teachers.*

National Art Education Association (Arts) (NAEA)

1916 Association Drive
Reston, VA 22091-1590
(703) 860-8000
Fax (703) 860-2960
naea@dgs.dgsys com

Teachers of art at elementary, secondary, and college levels; colleges, libraries, museums, and other educational institutions. Studies problems of teaching art; encourages research and experimentation. Serves as clearinghouse for information on art education programs, materials, and methods of instruction. Maintains placement services and library on art education. Publications: *Art Education, Studies in Art Education.*

National Association for Bilingual Education (Bilingualism) (NABE)

1220 L Street NW
Suite 605
Washington, DC 20005-4018
(202) 898-1829
Fax (202) 789-2866

Educators, administrators, paraprofessionals, community and laypeople, and students. Purposes are to recognize, promote, publicize bilingual education. Seeks to increase public understanding of the importance of language and culture. Utilizes and develops student proficiency and ensures equal opportunities in bilingual education for language-minority students. Works to preserve and expand the nation's linguistic resources. Educates language-minority parents in public policy decisions. Promotes research in language education, linguistics, and multicultural education. Coordinates development of professional standards. Publications: *Annual Conference Journal, Journal, Newsletter.*

National Association of Biology Teachers (NABT)

11250 Roger Bacon Drive, No. 19
Reston, VA 22090
(703) 471-1134
nabter@aol com

Professional society of biology and life science teachers and teacher educators at all educational levels. Works to achieve scientific literacy among citizens. Promotes professional growth and development; fosters regional activities for biology teachers; confronts issues involving biology, society, and the future; provides a national voice for the profession. Publications: *American Biology Teacher National Association of Biology Teachers—News and Views,* and others.

National Association for the Education of Young Children (Childhood Education) (NAEYC)

1509 16th Street NW Washington. DC 20036
(202) 232-8777
(800) 424-2460
Fax (202) 328-1846 naeyc@org/naeyc

Teachers and directors of preschool and primary schools, kindergartens, childcare centers, cooperatives, church schools, and groups having similar programs for young children. Open to all individuals interested in serving and acting on behalf of the needs and rights of young children, with primary focus on the provision of educational services and resources. Offers voluntary accreditation for early childhood schools and centers through the National Academy of Early Childhood Programs. Publications: *Early Childhood Research Quarterly, Young Children.*

National Association for Gifted Children (NAGC)

1707 L Street NW
Suite 550
Washington, DC 20036
(202) 785-4268

Teachers, university personnel, administrators, and parents. To advance interest in programs for the gifted. Seeks to further education of the gifted and to enhance their potential creativity. Distributes information to teachers and parents on the development of the gifted child; sponsors annual convention to provide training in curriculum planning, program evaluation, and parenting and guidance relevant to gifted children. Maintains speakers' bureau. Publication: *Gifted Child Quarterly*

National Association for Trade and Industrial Education (NATIE)

P.O. Box 1665
Leesburg, VA 22075
(703) 777-1740

Educators in trade and industrial education. Works for the promotion, development, and improvement of trade and industrial education. Supports instructional programs for members to prepare for job instruction, apprentice training, adult retraining, and special training for industry. Publications: *NATIE News Notes, State Supervisors/Consultants of Trade and Industrial Education*, and others.

National Business Education Association (NBEA)
1914 Association Drive
Reston, VA 22091
(703) 860-8300

Teachers of business subjects in secondary and postsecondary schools and colleges; administrators and research workers in business education; businesspeople interested in business education; teachers in educational institutions training business teachers. Publication: *Business Education Forum.*

National Council for the Social Studies (NCSS)
3501 Newark Street, NW
Washington, DC 20016
(202) 966-7840
Fax (202) 966-2061
ncss@ncss.org

Teachers of elementary and secondary social studies, including instructors of civics, geography, history, economics, political science, psychology, sociology, and anthropology. Publications: *Social Education, The Social Studies Professional, Social Studies and the Young Learner, Theory and Research in Social Education.*

National Council of Teachers of English (NCTE)
1111 West Kenyon Road
Urbana, IL 61801
(217) 328-3870
Fax (217) 328-9645

Teachers of English at all school levels. Works to increase the effectiveness of instruction in English language and literature. Presents achievement awards for writing to high school juniors and students in the eighth grade, and awards for high school literary magazines. Provides information and aids for teachers involved in formulating objectives, writing and evaluating curriculum guides, and planning in-service programs for teacher education. Publications: *English Education, English Journal, Language Arts, Research in the Teaching of English*, and others.

National Council of Teachers of Mathematics (NCTM)
1906 Association Drive
Reston, VA 22091-1 593

(703) 620-9840
Fax (703) 476-2970
infocentra@nctm.org

Teachers of mathematics in grades K–12, two-year colleges, and teacher educators. Publications: *Arithmetic Teacher, Journal for Research in Mathematics Education, Mathematics Teacher, National Council of Teachers of Mathematics—Yearbook*, and others.

National Education Association (NEA)
1201 16th Street, NW
Washington, DC 20036
(202) 833-4000

Professional organization and union of elementary and secondary school teachers, college and university professors, administrators, principals, counselors and others concerned with education. Publications: *NEA Today, Thought and Action*, and others.

National Middle School Association (NMSA)
4151 Executive Parkway, Suite 300
Westerville, OH 43081
(800) 528-NMSA (6672)
info@NMSA.org

Professional organization for teachers, administrators, parents, and others interested in the education of young adolescents (10–15 years of age). The only national organization devoted to improving the education of young adolescents, NMSA has more than 20,000 members worldwide. State, provincial, and international affiliates work to provide support for middle-level education at the local level. Publications: *Middle School Journal, Middle Ground*, and others.

National Science Teachers Association (NSTA)
1840 Wilson Blvd.
Arlington, VA 22201-3000
(703) 243-7100
Fax (703) 243-71 77

Teachers seeking to foster excellence in science teaching. Studies students and how they learn, the curriculum of science, the teacher and his or her preparation, the procedures used in classroom and laboratory, the facilities for teaching science, and the evaluation procedures used. Affiliated with: American Association for the Advancement of Science. Publications: *Journal of College Science Teaching, Quantum, Science and Children, Science Scope, The Science Teacher*

Phi Delta Kappa (Education)
8th and Union
P.O. Box 789
Bloomington, IN 47402-0789

Appendix 12.1 *(continued)*

(812) 339-1156
(800) 766-1156
Fax (812) 339-0018
headquarters@pdkintl.org

Professional, honorary, and recognition fraternity—education. To enhance quality education through research and leadership activities. Conducts seminars and workshops. Publications: *Phi Delta Kappan,* and others.

Pi Lambda Theta (Education)
4101 E. 3rd Street
P.O. Box 6626
Bloomington, IN 47407-6626
(812) 339-3411
members@pilambda.org

Honor and professional association—education. Presents biennial awards. Sponsors comparative education tours and educational conferences. Publication: *Educational Horizons.*

Reading Is Fundamental (RIF)
600 Maryland Avenue, SW, Suite 800
Washington, DC 20024
(202) 287-3220
Fax (202) 287-3196

Volunteer groups composed of community leaders, educators, librarians, parents, and service club members who sponsor local grass roots reading motivation programs serving 3,000,000 children nationwide. Purpose is to involve youngsters, preschool to high school age, in reading activities aimed at showing that reading is fun. Provides services to parents to help them encourage reading in the home. Publication: *RIF Newsletter.*

Speech Communication Association (SCA)
5105 Backlick Road, Bldg. E

Annandale, VA 22003
(703) 750-0533
Fax (703) 914-9471

Elementary, secondary, college, and university teachers, speech clinicians, media specialists, communication consultants, students, theater directors, and others. To promote study, criticism, research, teaching, and application of the artistic, humanistic, and scientific principles of communication, particularly speech communication. Sponsors the publication of scholarly volumes in speech. Conducts international debate tours in the United States and abroad. Maintains placement service. Publications: *Communication Education, Speech Communication Teacher, Text and Performance Quarterly*, and others.

Teachers of English to Speakers of Other Languages (TESOL)
1600 Cameron Street, Suite 300
Alexandria, VA 22314-2751
(703) 836-0774
Fax (703) 836-7864
tesol@tesol.edu

School, college, and adult education teachers who teach English as a second or foreign language. Aims to improve the teaching of English as a second or foreign language by promoting research, disseminating information, developing guidelines and promoting certification, and serving as a clearinghouse for the field. Offers placement service. Publications: *Directory of Professional Preparation, TESOL Journal, TESOL Quarterl,y* and others.

For complete information on professional organizations, see *Encyclopedia of Associations,* (2000) Gale Research, Inc.

Appendix 12.2

Selected Education Journals

Academic Computing
Action in Teacher Education
Adolescence
American Biology Teacher
American Educational Research Journal
American Educator: The Professional Journal of the American Federation of Teachers
American Journal of Education
American School Board Journal
Arithmetic Teacher
Art Education
Bilingual Review
Black Scholar
Business Education Forum
Career Development for Exceptional Individuals
Career Development Quarterly
Child Abuse and Neglect: The International Journal
Child Development
Child Study Journal
Child Welfare
Childhood Education
Children Today
Children's Literature in Education
Classroom Computer Learning
Clearing House
Communication Education
Comparative Education
Computers and Education
Computers and the Humanities
Computers in the Schools
Computing Teacher
Contemporary Education
Curriculum and Teaching
Early Childhood Research Quarterly
Education and Computing
Education and Urban Society
Educational Forum
Educational Horizons
Educational Leadership
Educational Record
Educational Research
Educational Research Quarterly
Educational Researcher

Educational Review
Educational Technology
Educational Theory
Electronic Learning
Elementary School Journal
English Education
English Journal
English Language Teaching Journal (ETL Journal)
Equity and Choice
Equity and Excellence
Exceptional Children
Focus on Exceptional Children
Focus on Learning Problems in Mathematics
Forum for Reading
Geographical Education
Gifted Child Quarterly
Gifted Child Today
Gifted Education International
Harvard Educational Review
Health Education
Health Education Quarterly
High School Journal
History and Social Science Teacher
History Teacher
Home Economic Research Journal
Horace
Industrial Education
Instructor
International Journal of Early Childhood
International Journal of Educational Research
Journal for Research in Mathematics Education
Journal for Vocational Special Needs Education
Journal of Adolescence
Journal of Alcohol and Drug Education
Journal of American Indian Education
Journal of Black Studies
Journal of Classroom Interaction
Journal of Computer-Assisted Learning

Journal of Computer-Based Instruction
Journal of Computers in Mathematics and Science Teaching
Journal of Curriculum and Supervision
Journal of Curriculum Studies
Journal of Developmental Education
Journal of Drug Education
Journal of Early Intervention
Journal of Education
Journal of Educational Computing Research
Journal of Educational Research
Journal of Environmental Education
Journal of Home Economics
Journal of Humanistic Education and Development
Journal of Learning Disabilities
Journal of Negro Education
Journal of Physical Education, Recreation, and Dance
Journal of Reading
Journal of Reading Behavior
Journal of Research in Childhood Education
Journal of Research in Computing in Education
Journal of Research in Music Education
Journal of Research in Reading
Journal of Research in Science Teaching
Journal of Rural and Small Schools
Journal of Social Studies Research
Journal of Special Education
Journal of Teacher Education
Journal of Teaching in Physical Education
Journal of Youth and Adolescence
Kappa Delta Pi Record
Language Arts
Language, Speech, and Hearing Services in Schools
Learning

Learning Disabilities Focus
Learning Disabilities Research
Learning Disability Quarterly
Mathematics and Computer
    Education
Mathematics Teacher
Middle Ground
Middle School Journal
Music Educators Journal
NABE: The Journal for the
    National Association for
    Bilingual Education
NASSP Bulletin
Negro Educational Review
New Directions for Child
    Development
New Directions for Teaching and
    Learning
Peabody Journal of Education
Phi Delta Kappan
Physical Educator
Physics Teacher

Preventing School Failure
Programmed Learning and
    Educational Technology
Psychology in the Schools
PTA Today
Reading Horizons
Reading Improvement
Reading Research and
    Instruction
Reading Research Quarterly
Reading Teacher
Remedial and Special Education
Research in Rural Education
Research in the Teaching of
    English
Review of Educational Research
Rural Educator
School Arts
School Science and Mathematics
Science and Children
Science Education
Science Teacher

Social Studies and the Young
    Learner
Social Studies Journal
Social Studies Professional
Sociology of Education
Studies in Art Education
Teacher Magazine
Teachers College Record
Teaching Exceptional Children
TESOL Quarterly
T.H.E. Journal (Technological
    Horizons in Education)
Theory and Research in Social
    Education
Theory into Practice
Topics in Early Childhood Special
    Education
Urban Education
Vocational Education Journal
Young Children
Youth and Society

Appendix 12.3

Principle One

The school should focus on helping young people develop the habit of using their minds well. Schools should not attempt to be comprehensive if such a claim is made at the expense of the school's central intellectual purpose. Schools should be learner centered, addressing students' social and emotional development, as well as their academic progress.

Principle Two

The school's academic goal should be simple: that each student master a limited number of essential skills and areas of knowledge. The aphorism "Less Is More" should dominate. Curricular decisions should be guided by student interest, developmentally appropriate practice, and the aim of thorough student mastery and achievement.

Principle Three

The school's goals should apply to all students, while the means to these goals will vary as those students themselves vary.

Principle Four

Teaching and learning should be personalized to the maximum feasible extent. To capitalize on this personalization, decisions about the details of the course of study, the use of students' and teachers' time and the choice of teaching materials and specific pedagogies must be unreservedly placed in the hands of the principal and staff.

Principle Five

The governing practical metaphor of the school should be student-as-worker, rather than the more familiar metaphor of teacher-as-deliverer-of-instructional-services.

Principle Six

Teaching and learning should be documented and assessed with tools based on student performance of real tasks. The final diploma should be awarded upon a successful final demonstration of mastery for graduation—an "Exhibition." As the diploma is awarded when earned, the school's program proceeds with no strict age grading and with no system of credits earned by "time spent" in class. The emphasis is on the students' demonstration that they can do important things.

Principle Seven

Families should be vital members of the school community. Close collaboration between home and school yields respect and understanding. Correspondingly, the tone of the school should explicitly and self-consciously stress values of unanxious expectation ("I won't threaten you and I expect much of you") of trust (until abused) and of decency (the values of fairness, generosity and tolerance).

Principle Eight

The principal and teachers should perceive themselves as generalists first (teachers and scholars in general education) and specialists second (experts in but one particular discipline). Staff should expect multiple obligations (teacher-counselor-manager) and a sense of commitment to the entire school.

Principle Nine

Ultimate administrative and budget targets should include substantial time for collective planning by teachers, competitive salaries for staff and an ultimate per pupil cost not to exceed that at traditional schools by more than 10 percent.

Principle Ten

The school should demonstrate nondiscriminatory and inclusive policies, practices, and pedagogies. It should model democratic practices that involve all who are directly affected by the school.

Source: Excerpted from *Ten Common Principles.* Oakland, CA: Coalition of Essential Schools, National Office 1999.

13

Your First Teaching Position

What I've found very helpful is to get in touch with all my kids' parents right after the first day. I tell them a bit about how I run my class, what we're going to do that year, and how pleased I am to have their child in my room. I keep it upbeat, very positive. We're going to have a great year!

— A first-grade teacher

focus questions

1. How will you become certified or licensed to teach?

2. Where will you teach?

3. How will you find your first teaching job?

4. What can you expect as a beginning teacher?

5. How can you become a part of your learning community?

6. How can you participate in teacher collaboration?

7. How will your performance as a teacher be evaluated?

Y our spring student teaching seminar ended minutes ago; now you and three other students are seated in the faculty–student lounge enjoying sodas and talking about finding a job.

"What was the interview like?" you ask one of your classmates, upon learning that he interviewed yesterday for a position at an urban school.

"Yeah, tell us," another student adds. "I'm really anxious about interviewing. I don't know what to expect. There're so many things they could ask."

"Well, I was interviewed by the principal and two people from the district office—I think they were in personnel. At first, they asked questions like the ones we used in our seminar role plays: 'Why do you want to teach? What are your weaknesses? Use five adjectives to describe yourself.'"

"What else?" you ask, anxious to complete a mental image of the interview process so you'll be ready for your first interview next week.

"They asked me to describe a student teaching lesson that went well," he continues. "After I did that, one of them asked 'How could the lesson have been better—either for the entire class or for a certain student?' That one took some thinking."

As he goes on to reconstruct his response, you imagine how you would answer the same question.

Moments later, he says, "Then, one that really surprised me came when I was asked 'What would you do if your principal told you to discontinue a classroom activity because it was too noisy and left a mess for the custodians to clean up? But, the activity really involved the kids and they learned a lot.'"

He pauses for a sip of soda and then continues, "Another one was, 'Give us an example of a principle that guides your teaching.'"

Impressed with the district's ability to pose challenging questions, you again imagine how you would respond.

A few minutes later, another student asks, "What about portfolios? Did they spend much time looking at yours?"

"Did they ever!" your classmate exclaims. "With my application materials I included a portfolio on CD-ROM; plus I gave them the web address for my portfolio. They were pretty impressed. It was obvious that they had looked at just about everything in the portfolio. They asked all kinds of questions. Half the questions were about how to make a digital portfolio. But they also really wanted to see things that were related to how much my students learned while I was student teaching."

With the mention of portfolios, you're reminded of tomorrow's computer lab workshop on how to create an electronic portfolio. Hopefully, you'll have a portfolio on CD-ROM that you can take to your first job interview next week. In addition, you wonder what else you should do to prepare for the interview and what steps you can follow to increase your chances of finding the best possible teaching position.

On completion of your teacher education program, you will still have several important steps to take before securing your first teaching position. Preparing well for these steps will go a long way toward helping you begin teaching with confidence.

It is natural that you feel both excited and a bit fearful when thinking about your first job. While taking the courses required in your teacher education program, you probably feel secure in your role as a student; you know what is expected of you. As a teacher, however, you will assume an entirely new role—a role that requires some time before it becomes comfortable. The aim of this chapter, then, is to help make the transition from student to professional teacher a positive, pleasant one. We first look at the steps you can take to become certified or licensed to teach and to identify current trends related to teacher supply and demand.

How Will You Become Certified or Licensed to Teach?

State certification is required for teaching in the public schools, and in many private schools as well. In some cases, large cities (e.g., Chicago, New York, Buffalo) have their own certification requirements that must be met. And certain local school districts have additional requirements, such as a written examination, before one can teach in those districts.

A **teaching certificate** is actually a license to teach. The department of education for each of the fifty states and the District of Columbia sets the requirements for certification. A certificate usually indicates at what level and in what content areas one may teach. One might, for example, be certified for all-level (K–12) physical education or art, secondary English, elementary education, or middle-level education. In 1999, thirty-two states offered certification for teaching at the middle school or junior high level—an increase from 1987, when twenty-six states offered such certification. In addition, a certificate may list other areas of specialization, such as driver's training, coaching, or journalism. If you plan to go into nonteaching areas such as counseling, librarianship, or administration, special certificates are usually required.

State Certification Requirements

In order for a person to receive a teaching certificate, all states require successful completion of an approved teacher education program that culminates with at least a bachelor's degree. To be approved, programs must pass a review by the state department of education approximately every five years. In addition to approval at the state level, most of the nearly 1,300 programs in the nation have regional accreditation, and more than 500 voluntarily seek accreditation by the **National Council for Accreditation of Teacher Education (NCATE)** (1999). Currently, all states require an average of six to eight semester credits of supervised student teaching. Alabama, Colorado, Idaho, Indiana, Nevada, New York, and Virginia require a master's degree for advanced certification; and Arizona, Maryland, Montana, Oregon, and Washington require either a master's degree or a specified number of semester credits after certification (Tryneski 1999). Additional requirements may also include U.S. citizenship, an oath of loyalty, fingerprinting, or a health examination.

A few states, including Iowa, North Carolina, New Mexico, and Oklahoma, waive state licensing requirements for teachers certified by the National Board for Professional Teaching Standards (NBPTS). Other states, including Massachusetts and Ohio, accept NBPTS certification as an alternative to their own requirements. For a current listing of state and local action supporting NBPTS certification, call the NBPTS at (800)-22TEACH.

Nearly all states now require testing of teachers for initial certification. States use either a standardized test (usually the National Teacher Examination [NTE] or Praxis) or a test developed by outside consultants. Areas covered by the states' tests usually include basic skills, professional knowledge, and general knowledge. Many states also require an on-the-job performance evaluation for certification (see Table 13.1).

There is a trend away from granting teaching certificates for life. Some states, for example, issue three- to five-year certificates, which may be renewed only with proof of coursework completed beyond the bachelor's degree. And, amid considerable controversy, Arkansas, Georgia, and Texas have enacted testing for **recertification** of experienced teachers.

Table 13.1

States requiring testing for initial certification of teachers, by authorization, year enacted, year effective, and test used: 1990 and 1998

State	Assessment for certification 1990				Assessment for certification 1998				
	Basic skills exam	Knowledge of teaching exam	Subject matter exam	Assessment of teaching performance	Basic skills exam	Subject matter exam	General knowledge exam	Knowledge of teaching exam	Assessment of teaching performance
1	2	3	4	5	6	7	8	9	10
Alabama					(1)	✓		✓	✓
Alaska									
Arizona	✓	✓			✓				
Arkansas		✓	✓		✓	✓		✓	
California	✓		✓		✓	✓			✓
Colorado	✓			✓	✓	✓	✓	✓	
Connecticut	✓		✓	✓	✓	✓			
Delaware	✓				✓				
District of Columbia	✓		✓		✓	✓			
Florida		✓	✓	✓	✓	✓	✓	✓	✓
Georgia			✓	✓	✓	✓			
Hawaii	✓	✓	✓		✓	✓		✓	✓
Idaho		✓	✓						
Illinois		✓	✓		✓	✓			
Indiana	✓	✓	✓		✓	✓	✓	✓	
Iowa	✓	✓	✓	✓					
Kansas	✓	✓			✓			✓	
Kentucky				✓	✓	✓	✓	✓	✓
Louisiana	✓	✓	✓		✓	✓	✓	✓	✓
Maine	✓	✓	✓	✓			✓	✓	
Maryland	✓	✓	✓		✓	✓	✓	✓	
Massachusetts	(2)				(1)				
Michigan					✓	✓	(3)		
Minnesota	✓				✓				
Mississippi		✓	✓	✓	✓	✓	✓	✓	
Missouri			✓		(1)	✓			
Montana	✓	✓			✓				
Nebraska	✓				✓				
Nevada	✓	✓	✓		✓	✓		✓	
New Hampshire	✓				✓				

Certification requirements differ from state to state, and they are frequently modified. To remain up-to-date on the requirements for the state in which you plan to teach, it is important that you keep in touch with your teacher placement office or certification officer at your college or university. You may also wish to refer to *Requirements for Certification for Elementary and Secondary Schools* (The University of Chicago Press), an annual publication that lists state-by-state certification requirements for teachers, counselors, librarians, and administrators. Or, you may contact the teacher certification office in the state where you plan to teach (see Appendix 13.1, for a "Directory of State Teacher Certification Offices in the United States").

Table 13.1 continued

State	Assessment for certification 1990				Assessment for certification 1998				
	Basic skills exam	Knowledge of teaching exam	Subject matter exam	Assessment of teaching performance	Basic skills exam	Subject matter exam	General knowledge exam	Knowledge of teaching exam	Assessment of teaching performance
1	2	3	4	5	6	7	8	9	10
New Jersey			✓			✓	(4)		
New Mexico	✓	✓		✓	✓		✓		
New York	✓	✓							
North Carolina				✓	(1)	✓			
North Dakota					(1)	✓	✓		
Ohio[5]		✓	✓		✓	✓	✓	✓	
Oklahoma				✓	✓	✓			✓
Oregon	✓	✓	✓	✓	✓	(6)	✓	✓	(7)
Pennsylvania	✓	✓	✓		✓	✓	✓	✓	
Rhode Island	✓	✓		✓	✓		✓	✓	
South Carolina		✓		✓	✓	✓		✓	
South Dakota					✓	✓			✓
Tennessee				✓	✓	✓	✓	✓	✓
Texas		✓	✓		✓	✓		✓	
Utah			✓						
Vermont									
Virginia	✓	✓	✓	✓	✓	✓	✓	✓	
Washington				✓	(1)				
West Virginia[8]	✓		✓	✓	✓	✓			✓
Wisconsin	✓				✓				
Wyoming									

[1]For admission to program.
[2]Test required for foreign language, bilingual, and English as a Second Language.
[3]Elementary certificate exam (subject-area exam).
[4]For elementary education.
[5]Test requirements set by local school districts.
[6]Specialty area exams.
[7]For Oregon graduates.
[8]Required for individuals entering West Virginia-approved education programs as of fall 1985.

Source: Council of Chief State School Officers, "State Education Indicators, 1990;" and National Association of State Directors of Teacher Education and Certification, "The NASDTEC Manual, 1996–1997 and 1998–1999: Manual on Certification & Preparation of Educational Personnel in the United States & Canada." (This table was prepared November 1998.) Taken from Digest of Education Statistics 1998. Washington, DC, National Center for Education Statistics, 1999, p. 168.

Currently, forty-four states are members of the **Interstate Certification Agreement Contract,** a reciprocity agreement whereby a certificate obtained in one state will be honored in another (see Appendix 13.2). If you plan to teach in a state other than the one in which you are currently studying, you should find out whether both states share a reciprocity agreement.

About 362,000 teachers, many of whom are noncertified, teach in America's growing system of private, parochial, for-profit, and charter schools (National Center for Education Statistics, 1998b). Private and parochial schools supported largely by tuition and gifts, and for-profit schools operated by private educational

What are some alternatives for becoming certified or licensed to teach? What are some current trends in certification and what conditions might account for those trends?

corporations, usually have no certification requirements for teachers. Also, teacher-created and teacher-operated charter schools, though they are public, are often free of state certification requirements. A school's **charter** (an agreement between the school's founders and its sponsor—usually a local school board) may waive certification requirements if the school guarantees that students will attain a specified level of achievement.

Alternative Certification

Despite the national movement to make certification requirements more stringent, concern about meeting the demand for 2.2 million new teachers during the first decade of the twenty-first century and attracting minority-group members into the teaching profession has resulted in increasing use of alternative teacher certification programs. In 1983, only eight states offered alternatives; by 1998, forty-one states had alternative routes to certification (Feistritzer 1999).

Alternative certification programs are designed for people who already have at least a bachelor's degree in a field other than education and want to become licensed to teach. It is estimated that about 80,000 people have been licensed through alternative certification programs since 1983 (Feistritzer 1999). Most alternative certification programs are collaborative efforts among state departments of education, teacher education programs in colleges and universities, and school districts. For example, Washington State University, in collaboration with area school districts, has a federally funded program to prepare paraprofessional educators (teachers' aides, for example) in southwest Washington to become bilingual/ESL teachers. According to the National Center for Education Information, which has studied alternative certification trends since the 1980s, effective alternative teacher certification programs include the following components:

- [Candidates demonstrate a] strong academic coursework component.
- The [programs] are field-based, . . . individuals get into classrooms early in their training.
- Teacher candidates work with a qualified mentor teacher.
- Candidates usually go through their programs in cohorts, not as isolated individuals (Feistritzer 1999).

All but two states may grant certification to those who do not meet current requirements. About half of the states may even give a substandard credential to those who hold less than a bachelor's degree. In response to occasional shortages of teachers in particular subject and grade-level areas, many state systems approve temporary measures such as **emergency certification**. Nationwide, more than 12 percent of newly hired teachers enter the profession without any training at all, and another 15 percent enter without having fully met state standards, according to the National Commission on Teaching and America's Future.

Emergency certification is strongly resisted by professional teacher organizations and several state departments of education. New York, for example, decreed that underperforming schools in the state would not be allowed to hire teachers with temporary licenses as of fall 1999, and the practice would be eliminated altogether by fall 2003 (Bradley 1999). Teachers on provisional certificates in Maryland, the majority of whom teach poor and minority children, no longer can continue teaching indefinitely on a provisional certificate; they must pass the state's teacher test within two years and complete academic coursework within four years (Bradley 1999). Though strongly resisted by professional teacher organizations, alternative certification is likely to become even more widespread in the event of a teacher shortage.

The Praxis Series

Thirty-five of the forty-three states that include tests as part of their certification process require completion of the **Praxis Series: Professional Assessments for Beginning Teachers** developed by Educational Testing Service (ETS) in consultation with teachers, educational researchers, the National Education Association, and the American Federation of Teachers. The Praxis Series (*praxis* means putting theory into practice) enables states to create a system of tests that meet their specific licensing requirements.

The Praxis Series, which replaced the National Teacher Examination in the mid-1990s, consists of three components:

Praxis I: Academic skills assessments—Praxis I covers the "enabling skills" in reading, writing, and mathematics that all teachers need, regardless of grade or subject taught. Two formats, computer-based and pencil-and-paper, are available for the Praxis I assessment, which is given early in a student's teacher education program. To help students pass Praxis I, ETS offers online practice test items and, for students who need help in improving basic academic skills, LearningPlus, an interactive computer software program that provides instruction and diagnostic placement tests in reading, writing, and mathematics.

Praxis II: Subject assessments—Praxis II measures teacher education students' knowledge of the subjects they will teach. In most cases, Praxis II tests are taken on completion of an undergraduate program. The tests, available in more than seventy subject areas, have a core content module required by every state, with the remaining modules selected on an individual basis by the states. Each state can base its assessment on multiple-choice items or on candidate-constructed-response modules. In addition, Praxis II includes the Principles of Learning and Teaching (PLT) test and the Professional Knowledge test; each is a two-hour test to assess teachers' professional knowledge. The PLT is available in three versions: K–6, 5–9, and 7–12.

Praxis III: Classroom performance assessments—Praxis III is a performance-based assessment system, not a test. Developed after extensive job analyses, reviews of research, and input from educators, Praxis III involves the assessment of actual teaching skills of the beginning teacher. The assessments focus on the four domains of the Praxis Framework for Teaching as presented in Chapter 9 (see Figure 9.5, page 357): planning and preparation, the classroom environment, instruction, and professional responsibilities. In addition, Praxis III assesses the teacher's sensitivity to developmental levels and cultural differences among students. In-class assessments and pre- and post-observation interviews conducted by trained state and local personnel are the main components of Praxis III. The observations are supplemented by work samples—for example, lesson plans. Following Praxis III assessments, which normally are completed by the end of the first year of teaching, the state makes a decision about whether to grant a license to teach.

Where Will You Teach?

When you think ahead to a career in teaching, two questions you are likely to ask yourself are, How hard will it be to find a job? And, Where will I teach? From time to time, **teacher supply and demand** figures have painted a rather bleak picture for those entering the teaching profession. At other times, finding a position in a preferred location has been relatively easy.

After the U.S. Department of Education announced in 1999 that more than two million teachers would be needed during the next decade, a debate ensued about whether, in fact, the nation would soon face a critical teacher shortage. Citing statistics related to higher student enrollments resulting from the "baby boom echo" (a 1980s increase in births similar to the "baby boom" that occurred after World War II), increased immigration, teacher retirements, fewer college students going into teaching, and increased employment opportunities for women and minorities in other fields, some observers predicted a teacher shortage "crisis." Others, however, predicted that a teacher shortage would not develop. They pointed to a leveling off, and then slight decline, of school enrollments during the first decade of the new century and the fact that many "new" teachers would actually be former teachers coming back into the profession.

Despite the difficulty of predicting trends in teacher supply and demand, it is clear that even during times of teacher surplus, talented, qualified teachers are able to find jobs. Teaching is one of the largest professions in the United States; out of a national population of about 273 million, more than 53 million attended public and private elementary and secondary schools in fall 1999, where they were taught by approximately 3.2 million teachers (National Center for Education Statistics 1999). By 2009, enrollments are expected to total approximately 54.5 million students, who will be taught by approximately 3.5 million teachers (National Center for Education Statistics 1999). Within such a large profession, annual openings resulting from retirements and career changes alone are sizable.

A Favorable Job Market

Although the need for new teachers is difficult to determine, most analysts predict a favorable job market for teachers in all regions of the country during the early twenty-first century. Enrollments in public and private elementary and secondary schools are expected to continue to increase into the next century and surpass the previous high set in 1971. Elementary school enrollment is expected to reach 38 million by the year 2008, while secondary school enrollment is expected to reach 16.2 million. However, as Figure 13.1 shows, not all sections of the country will experience equivalent growth

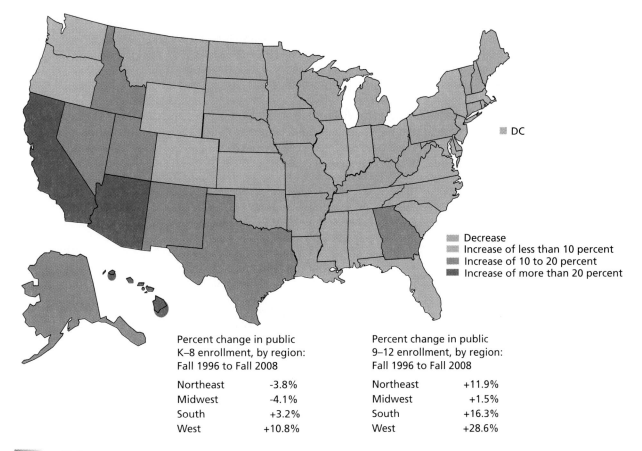

Percent change in public
K–8 enrollment, by region:
Fall 1996 to Fall 2008

Northeast	-3.8%
Midwest	-4.1%
South	+3.2%
West	+10.8%

Percent change in public
9–12 enrollment, by region:
Fall 1996 to Fall 2008

Northeast	+11.9%
Midwest	+1.5%
South	+16.3%
West	+28.6%

Figure 13.1

Percent change in grades K–12 enrollment in public schools, by state: Fall 1996 to Fall 2008.
Source: Adapted from *Projection of Education Statistics to 2008.* National Center for Education statistics, Washington, DC, June 1998, pp. 101–03.

in public school K–12 enrollments during this period, and the greatest enrollment increases will be at the high school level.

Demand by Speciality Area and Geographic Region

The ease with which you will find your first teaching position is also related to your area of specialization and to the part of the country where you wish to locate. In 1999, for example, job seekers able to teach bilingual education or special education were in an especially favorable position. Also, the West had the greatest overall demand for teachers, followed by Alaska, the Great Plains/Midwest, and the South Central Region. For current employment opportunities according to speciality area and geographic region and for other job-search resources, check the following publications by the American Association for Employment in Education (820 Davis Street, Suite 222, Evanston, IL 60201-4445, (847) 864-1999). Be aware, however, that the Association does not provide placement services nor does it maintain lists of vacancies.

- *AAEE Annual: The Job Search Handbook for Educators* (Supply-demand data, interview techniques, résumé advice, and other job-search suggestions, $8.00).
- *Guide to Services and Activities for Teacher Employment* (Employment assistance services, career fair dates, contacts, teacher certification reciprocity among states, vacancy listing information, candidates' computer data banks, and other resources, $8.00).
- *AAEE Directory of Public School Systems in the United States* (Names, addresses, and phone numbers of contact persons, district size, school grade levels, and other information, $70.00 for complete directory; from no charge to $12.00 for individual state directories).

When considering supply and demand estimates, remember that jobs are to be had in oversupplied areas. Job hunting will be more competitive, though, and you may have to relocate to another region of the country.

Other Career Opportunities for Teachers

There are also a great many nonteaching jobs in education and education-related fields, such as principal, assistant principal, librarian, and counselor. In addition, there are many jobs that, although removed from the world of the classroom, would nevertheless enable you to use your teaching skills.

The following outline lists several places other than schools where individuals with teaching backgrounds are often employed. The number of education-related careers is likely to increase in the coming decades.

Industry
- Publishers
- Educational materials and equipment suppliers
- Specialized educational service firms
- Communications industries
- Research and development firms
- Management consulting firms
- Education and training consultants
- Educational divisions of large corporations—Xerox, IBM, CBS, General Electric, Westinghouse, etc.

Government
- Federal agencies—U.S. Office of Education, Bureau of Prisons, Department of Labor, Office of Economic Opportunity, Department of Justice, Department of Health, Education and Welfare, etc.
- Federal programs—Bureau of Indian Affairs Schools, Bureau of Prisons Schools, Job Corps, Overseas Dependent Schools, Peace Corps, Teacher Corps, Upward Bound, VISTA, etc.
- Regional educational networks—Research and development centers, regional educational laboratories, sixteen clearinghouses of the Educational Resources Information Center (ERIC), etc.
- Jobs in state departments of education

Education-Related Associations
- Research centers and foundations
- Professional associations—National Council of Teachers of English, National Association of Mathematics Teachers, National Education Association, American

Federation of Teachers, Phi Delta Kappa, Kappa Delta Pi, Educational Testing Service, etc.

Community Organizations

■ Community action programs—Upward Bound, neighborhood health centers, legal services, aid to migrant workers, etc.
■ Social service agencies—United Fund agencies, Boy Scouts, Girl Scouts, YMCAs and YWCAs, settlement houses, boys' and girls' clubs, etc.
■ Adult education centers
■ Museums
■ Hospitals

How Will You Find Your First Teaching Job?

During the last year of your teacher education program, you will probably become increasingly concerned about finding a teaching position. The "Job Search Timetable Checklist" presented in Appendix 13.3 may help you plan your job search. Also, Figure 13.2 presents an overview of the data and impressions that more than 200 school hiring officials consider most important when they are considering first-time teachers for employment. In the remainder of this section we discuss five critical steps in that sequence: finding out about teaching vacancies, preparing a résumé, writing letters of inquiry and letters of application, being interviewed, and selecting a position.

Finding Out about Teaching Vacancies

Your college or university probably has a **placement service** designed to help graduates find jobs. On a regular basis, placement offices usually publish lists of vacancies, which are posted and, in many cases, mailed to students who have registered with the office and set up a credentials file. In addition, you can use the Internet to connect with other universities that have accessible online placement services.

A **credentials file** (known as placement papers at some institutions) usually includes the following: background information on the applicant, the type of position sought, a list of courses taken, performance evaluations by the applicant's cooperative teacher, and three or more letters of recommendation. With each job application, the candidate requests that his or her credentials be sent to the appropriate person at the school district, or the school district itself may request the applicant's papers. Placement offices usually charge a small fee for each time a candidate's papers are sent out.

A job announcement describes the position and its requirements and provides the name and address of the individual to contact at the school district. For each position you are interested in, send a letter of application to the appropriate person along with your résumé. In addition, you may have your placement office send your credentials file. Placement offices also frequently set up on-campus interviews between candidates and representatives of school district personnel departments.

State department of education employment offices help teachers locate positions. Like college and university placement offices, states publish lists of job openings, which are then distributed to registered candidates. Because most of these states will assist out-of-state candidates, you can register in more than one state.

Personal networking will play an important role in landing the right job. Let people know you are looking for a job—friends, teachers at schools you've attended, faculty at the school where you student teach, and people you meet at workshops and

CANDIDATE

Employers evaluate first-time teachers' job applications for:

(a) Letters of recommendation from public school personnel
(b) A mentoring teacher's evaluation
(c) Examples of teaching skills and classroom management skill
(d) Experience with specific programs used in the school district
(e) Number of certifications which the candidate holds
   (e.g. elementary *and* special education).

Employers evaluate first-time teachers' academic preparation for:

(a) Knowledge of subject matter
(b) Success in student teaching
(c) Computer knowledge and skill

Important factors about candidates' work experience in paid employment not related to teaching include:

(a) A positive work ethic   (c) Good quality work
(b) Punctuality   (d) Low absenteeism

The following factors influence the decision to invite an applicant for an interview:

(a) Correct spelling, punctuation, and English usage of the candidate's application
(b) Letters of recommendation from those who have seen the candidate work with students
(c) Neatness of the applicant's materials
(d) Evaluation from the mentoring teacher

Employers use interview questions to assess the ways in which first-time teachers respond to:

(a) "Real life" and "what if" situations
(b) Classroom management issues
(c) Enthusiasm about teaching
(d) Demonstrating their knowledge of subject matter
(e) Describing and evaluating their own strengths
(f) Structured questions that range from impersonal to personal

In evaluating interviews, employers look for the following:

(a) The candidate's commitment to teaching
(b) Knowledge of the teaching field
(c) Interpersonal skills
(d) The candidate's understanding of the role of a teacher
(e) Professional judgment

TEACHER

Figure 13.2

Moving from "candidate" to "teacher"

Note: Items arranged in order of importance.

Source: Adapted from Judy McEnany and Patricia Reuss, "Fascinating Facts for First-Time Teachers," *1999 Job Search Handbook for Educators,* American Association for Employment in Education, p. 31. Used with permission.

conferences. Also, with access to the Internet, you can conduct a global job search and even make your résumé available to millions of people. The following noncommercial Internet sites can be helpful in your job search efforts:

- School district websites
- State departments of education websites
- *Project Connect:*—After obtaining a free user name and password, you can search teaching vacancies on the Web and post information about yourself, sponsored in part by the American Association for Employment in Education.
- *America's Job Bank:*—A comprehensive, free job-search service linked to 2,000 state employment offices.

Preparing Your Résumé

A **résumé** presents a concise summary of an individual's professional experiences, education, and skills. Résumés must be typed and preferably no longer than one page, two pages at most. Though there is no right way to prepare a résumé, it should present—in a neat, systematic way—key information that will help an employer determine your suitability for a particular position. Because your résumé will most likely be your first contact with an employer, it must make a good impression.

Ordinarily, a résumé contains the following information:

- Personal data
- Education
- Certificates held
- Experience
- Activities and interests
- Honors and offices held
- Professional memberships
- References

Figure 13.3 on page 512 is a résumé prepared by Linda M. Rodriguez that you can use as a model. To prepare an effective résumé, read "Résumé Advice for Educators" in Appendix 13.4.

Writing Letters of Inquiry and Applications

As a job seeker, you will most likely have occasion to write two kinds of letters: letters of inquiry and letters of application. A **letter of inquiry** is used to determine if a school district has, or anticipates, any teaching vacancies. This type of letter states your general qualifications and requests procedures to be followed in making a formal application (see Figure 13.4 on page 513). A letter of inquiry should also include your résumé as well as a self-addressed, stamped envelope for the school district's convenience. Be prepared not to receive a reply for each letter of inquiry you send out. Many school districts are unable to respond to all inquiries.

A **letter of application** (often called a cover letter) indicates your interest in a particular position and outlines your qualifications for that job. As most districts have several vacancies at any given time, it is important that the first sentence of your letter refer to the specific position for which you are applying. The body of the letter should then highlight why you would be an excellent choice to fill that position. Also, inform the reader that your credentials file will be sent on request or is being sent by your placement office. Close the letter by expressing your availability for an interview (see Figure 13.5 on page 514).

Linda M. Rodriguez

Personal Data

Born: October 16, 1980

Address and Phone: 948 W. Third
Spokane, WA 99206
(509) 924-1234
lmrodrig@abc.com

Education

B.A., Elementary Education, Washington State University, June 2001.

Certificates Held

Major Area: Elementary Education, K–8

Minor Area: Bilingual Education

Experience

Student Teaching, Garden Springs Elementary, W. 5116 Garden Springs Road, Spokane, WA 99204, Spring 2001. Cooperating teacher: Mrs. Becky Jones. Observed, assisted, and taught regular and accelerated 3rd grade classes in a multilingual setting. Organized after-school tutoring program and developed a unit on using the World Wide Web in the classroom. Attended site-based council meetings with Mrs. Jones and assisted in the development of community-based partnerships.

Camp Counselor and Recreation Director, YWCA Summer Camp, Spokane, WA.
Directed summer recreation program comprised of 10 counselors and 140 elementary aged girls.

Volunteer Telephone Counselor, Spokane County Crisis Hotline, June 1999–June 2001.

Activities and Interests

Spokane County Historical Society, Secretary, 2001.

Member, Washington State University Community Service Learning Center.

Hobbies: Jogging, Aerobics, Piano, Water Skiing.

Honors

B.A. with Honors, Washington State University, June 2001.

Washington State Scholarship, 1999–2001.

Professional Memberships

Washington Association for Supervision and Curriculum Development.

Kappa Delta Pi.

Instructional Technology Skills

Word processing, Internet and World Wide Web, optical scanner, interactive electronic whiteboard,

LCD computer projection panel, NovaNET (computer-based learning system).

Career Objective

Seeking K–8 position in multicultural/multilingual setting.

References

References and credentials file available upon request.

Figure 13.3

Résumé

Linda M. Rodriguez
948 W. Third
Spokane, Washington 99206

April 5, 2001

Dr. Lawrence Walker
Office of Personnel Services
City School District
100 Post Oak Boulevard
Houston, Texas 77056

Dear Dr. Walker:

This letter is to express my interest in a teaching position in the Houston City School District. Specifically, I would like to know if you anticipate any vacancies at the elementary level for fall of 2001. This June I will receive my B.A. (with honors) in elementary education from Washington State University. My supporting endorsement will be in bilingual education.

As a student teacher this spring semester, I taught regular and accelerated 3rd grade classes at Garden Springs Elementary School in Spokane, Washington. One class had 25 students, 3 of whom were diagnosed as having learning disabilities. At Garden Springs, I introduced students to science resources on the World Wide Web, and each student learned how to send e-mail messages to students in other countries.

My education at Washington State University, I believe, has prepared me well to teach in today's classrooms. I have had a course that focuses on meeting the needs of at-risk learners, and my supporting endorsement in bilingual education has prepared me to meet the challenges of working with students from diverse linguistic backgrounds. If possible, I would like a position that would allow me to develop programs for students with non–English backgrounds.

Enclosed you will find my resume, which provides additional information about my experiences and activities. If there are any positions for which you think I might be suited, please send application materials in the enclosed stamped, self-addressed envelope. I appreciate your consideration, and I look forward to hearing from you.

Sincerely,

Linda M. Rodriguez
Linda M. Rodriguez

Participating in a Job Interview

Figure 13.4

Letter of inquiry

The interview is one of the most important steps in your search for an appropriate position. As the dialogue in the scenario at the beginning of this chapter suggests, school district representatives may ask a wide range of questions, both structured and open-ended.

In some districts, you might be interviewed by the principal only; in others, the superintendent, the principal, and the department chairperson might interview you; and in still others, classroom teachers might interview you. Regardless of format, the interview enables the district to obtain more specific information regarding your probable

Linda M. Rodriguez
948 W. Third
Spokane, Washington 99206

May 5, 2001

Dr. Mary Lamb
Associate Superintendent for Personnel
Metropolitan School District
Wacker Office Building
773 Ranier Avenue
Seattle, Washington 98504

Dear Dr. Lamb:

This letter is in support of my application for the position of 4th grade teacher at City Elementary School. This June I will receive my B.A. (with honors) in elementary education from Washington State University. My supporting endorsement will be in bilingual education.

As my enclosed resume indicates, I just completed my student teaching at Garden Springs Elementary School in Spokane. During that 16-week period, I taught regular and accelerated 3rd grade classes. One class had 25 students, 3 of whom were diagnosed as having learning disabilities. I also organized an after-school tutoring program and assisted my cooperating teacher in developing community-based partnerships.

A major interest of mine is using technology in the classroom. I am familiar with various hypermedia programs and NovaNET, a computer-based learning system. At Garden Springs, I introduced students to science resources on the World Wide Web, and each student learned how to send e-mail messages to students in other countries.

As a result of my rewarding experiences at Garden Springs Elementary and in light of my preparation in bilingual education, I believe I could make a significant contribution to the educational program at City Elementary.

I have arranged for my credentials to be forwarded from Washington State University's placement office. If you require additional information of any sort, please feel free to contact me. At your convenience, I am available for an interview in Seattle. I thank you in advance for your consideration.

Sincerely,

Linda M. Rodriguez

Linda M. Rodriguez

Figure 13.5

Letter of Application

success as an employee, and it gives you an opportunity to ask questions about what it is like to teach in the district. By asking questions yourself, you demonstrate your interest in working in the district. The Appendix "Sample Interview Questions for Candidates to Ask,"on this book's website, presents seventeen questions you can ask, and Appendix 13.5 presents "Critical Information to Know about School Districts," which can be used to formulate questions. In addition, at some point in the interview process you may wish to present brief highlights from your professional portfolio. Or, if you have created Internet and/or CD-ROM versions of your portfolio, you could give the hiring offical(s) the URL for the portfolio or a copy of the CD-ROM itself.

Accepting an Offer

One day you are notified that a school district would like to hire you. Your job search efforts have paid off! In the competition for positions, you have been successful. However, accepting your first teaching position is a major personal and professional step. Before signing a contract with a district, you should carefully consider job-related questions such as the following:

■ In regard to my abilities and education, am I suited to this position?
■ Would I like to work with this school's students, administrative staff, and teachers?
■ Is the salary I am being offered sufficient?
■ Will this position likely be permanent?
■ Would I like to live in or near this community?
■ Would the cost of living in this community enable me to live comfortably?
■ Are opportunities for continuing education readily available?

What questions might you be asked in an interview for a teaching position? What questions should you have about the teaching position? about the school?

If you accept the offer, you will need to return a signed contract to the district along with a short letter confirming your acceptance. As a professional courtesy, you should notify other districts to which you have applied that you have accepted a position elsewhere. The following Professional Reflection can help you identify the type of school that would be most satisfying for your first teaching position.

 **Professional Reflection** **What elements are essential for your job satisfaction?**

Job satisfaction as a teacher depends on many factors: the size and location of a school; the backgrounds of students; the surrounding community; and the climate, or culture, of the school itself, to name a few. The following sentence completion items can help you determine what conditions are essential for your job satisfaction. Write your responses on a separate sheet or in your teacher's journal. For each item, write at least a few additional sentences to elaborate on how you completed the sentence.

1. Ideally, my first position would be teaching students who had the following backgrounds and characteristics:
2. For me, an ideal work setting would be a school that
3. My fellow teachers would help me during my first year of teaching by
4. When not in school, my colleagues and I would enjoy
5. My principal and/or supervisor would appreciate the way I

How can you create an electronic professional portfolio?

As this chapter's opening scenario suggested, job candidates can use technology to create Internet-accessible and CD-ROM versions of a professional portfolio. The possibilities for creating a digital portfolio that uses a computer to record information are endless. Although it is beyond the scope of this Technology Highlights feature to present in detail all the steps involved in preparing an electronic portfolio, what follows is a broad outline of how to prepare Internet-accessible and CD-ROM versions of your portfolio. A helpful article on how to prepare an electronic portfolio is Helen Barrett's "Create Your Own Electronic Portfolio (Using Off-the-Shelf Software)" in the April 2000 *Learning & Leading with Technology.* In addition, your university's computer lab probably provides training in hypermedia techniques necessary to create an electronic portfolio.

The first step in compiling an electronic portfolio is the same as that for a traditional portfolio—identify and organize the materials to include in the portfolio. In the case of an electronic portfolio, however, the contents will be in the form of text, sound, graphics, and video data that a computer can access and manipulate.

To create an Internet-accessible version of an electronic portfolio, you must use an HTML (hypertext markup language) web editor such as Adobe PageMill, Claris Home Page, or Microsoft FrontPage. If you want to include video and/or audio clips, you also need a video input device. Today's HTML editors function much like word processing programs, and, unlike early editors, they don't require knowledge of complex HTML programming. HTML editors are based on WYSIWYG—"what you see is what you get"—which means you don't see a myriad of formatting "tags"; the program inserts the tags automatically. To create Internet-accessible material with an editor, the user formats desired material and saves it as an HTML file. To add hyperlinks, the user highlights the desired material, clicks on a "link" button, and then types in the URL (Internet address).

6. In his or her feedback on my teaching, my principal and/or supervisor would be most impressed with
7. During my first year at the school I would volunteer to
8. Five years after I began teaching at this school, I would like to be

What Can You Expect as a Beginning Teacher?

Once you accept the professional challenge of teaching, it is important to prepare well in advance of the first day of school. In addition to reviewing the material you will teach, you should use this time to find out all you can about the school's students, the surrounding community, and the way the school operates. Also reflect on your expectations.

The First Day

The first day of school can be both exciting and frightening, as the following veteran teacher acknowledges; however, if the teacher is well prepared, he or she can use anxiety to set a positive tone for the rest of the school year:

Another approach to making an Internet-accessible portfolio is to "print" your data to PDF (portable document format) files using Adobe Acrobat. Once the files are placed on the Internet, they are accessible by using the Acrobat Reader plug-in available for free on the Internet. Remember that you will need access to a server on which to "publish" your Internet-accessible electronic portfolio. Check with your college or university, or with your Internet service provider, to see whether they make any server space available to you for personal websites such as this.

You can use any of several different software tools to create an electronic portfolio in CD-ROM format. Each CD-ROM can store up to 650 megabytes of data and costs about $2.00 if purchased by the hundred. The most common approach to making a CD-ROM is to use a hypermedia "card" program, or "authoring" tool, such as HyperStudio. A hypermedia program allows you to integrate different forms of media into a single file and then,

using a CD-ROM burner, place the data on a CD-ROM. HTML files (Web documents) can also be "burned" onto a CD-ROM and then be accessed using a web browser.

By creating digital versions of items that appear in a traditional portfolio and skillfully using video and audio clips, you can enhance the presentation of your professional portfolio. For example, you can include voice-over explanations of your performance while teaching, or you can include scanned images of certificates, awards, photographs, or completed projects. Clearly, "digital portfolios are more than just electronic file cabinets. The technological enhancements add markedly to the value of a portfolio" (Weidmer 1998, 586).

To see a good example of an electronic portfolio, got to the website for this book and follow the link there to seventh-grade teacher Kelly Mandia's electronic teaching portfolio.

The anxiety level for both teachers and students about [the] first day is high. Taking advantage of these feelings can make for a good beginning.

Students like to have guidelines on how the class will be run as well as what is expected of them academically. I always begin by welcoming the students into my class and immediately giving them something to do. I hand them their textbook and an index card. On the card, they write their name, address, telephone number, and book number.

While the students are filling out their cards and looking at the textbook, I set up my seating chart and verify attendance. Within ten minutes of meeting the students, I begin my first lesson. By keeping clerical chores to a minimum, I try to have more time on task. After a closure activity, somewhere in the middle of the class period I take a few minutes to explain how their grade will be determined, the rules of the class, and when extra help sessions are available.

Next, we deal with some curriculum content, and then I make a homework assignment. I tell the students that any homework assignment will be written on the chalkboard every day in the same location.

Setting high standards on the first day makes the following days easier. We will always need to monitor and adjust, but this will be within the framework set on the first day (Burden and Byrd 1999, 177).

Creating a pleasant, learning-oriented climate on the first day, as this teacher has done, will contribute greatly to your success during the first year. On the first day, students are eager to learn and are hopeful that the year will be a productive one. In addition, nearly all students will be naturally receptive to what you have to say. To them, you are a new, unknown quantity, and one of their initial concerns is to find out what kind of a teacher you will be. It is therefore critical that you be well organized and ready to take charge.

Advice from Experienced Teachers

In our work with schools and teachers, we have gathered recommendations on preparing for the first day from experienced K–12 teachers in urban, suburban, and rural schools. Teachers' recommendations focus on planning, establishing effective management practices, and following through on decisions.

> There are little things you can do, such as having a personal note attached to a pencil welcoming each child. You may want to do a few little tricks in science class or read them your favorite children's story. But, don't put all your energy into the first day and have that day be the highlight of the year. Be well prepared and have plenty of things to do. Don't worry if you don't get everything done. Remember, you have all year.
>
> —Middle school science teacher

> It really helps on the first day to have plenty of material to cover and things to do. I'd recommend taking the material you plan to cover that day and doubling it. It's better to have too much than to run out. What you don't use the first day, you use the next. It takes a while to get a feeling for how fast the kids are going to go.
>
> —Third-grade teacher

> The first day is a good time to go over rules and procedures for the year. But don't overdo it. Be very clear and specific about your expectations for classroom behavior.
>
> —Sixth-grade teacher

> From the beginning, it's important to do what you're there to do—that's teach. Teach the class something, maybe review material they learned last year. That lets them know that you're in charge, you expect them to learn. They'll look to you for direction—as long as you give it to them, you're fine.
>
> —Junior high language arts teacher

How Can You Become a Part of Your Learning Community?

Your success in your first year of teaching will be determined by the relationships you develop with the pupils, their families, your colleagues, school administrators, and other members of the school community. All of these groups contribute to your effectiveness as a teacher, but the relationships you establish with students will be the most important (and complex) you will have as a teacher.

Relationships with Students

The quality of your relationships with students will depend in large measure on your knowledge of students and commitment to improving your interactions with them. As one teacher put it:

Students respond to praise, compliments, and encouragement. I must know the subject matter, but also have a lot of patience, mental energy, and selflessness. I have found that you have to be encouraging even to the most negative students, or they can make your life miserable. Even though you might know the subject matter, you will not be a successful teacher if you can't motivate your students by talking with them, not at them (Burden and Byrd 1999, 290).

Your relationships with students will have many dimensions. Principally, you must see that each student learns as much as possible; this is your primary responsibility as a professional teacher. You will need to establish relationships with a great diversity of students based on mutual respect, caring, and concern. Without attention to this personal realm, your effectiveness as a teacher will be limited. In addition, teachers are significant models for students' attitudes and behaviors.

Relationships with Colleagues and Staff

Each working day, you will be in close contact with other teachers and staff members. As the experience of the following teacher suggests, it will definitely be to your advantage to establish friendly, professional relationships with them:

> I was on a staff with a group of teachers who really supported me. They made it a part of their day to come into my room and see how I was doing and to share things. They made it easy to ask questions and work with them. They started me on the track of cooperating with other teachers and sharing my successes and failures with them.

> They did such a good job of taking care of each other that my needs were always met. I had plenty of supplies, counseling help, administrative help. The school was a community. Anything I needed to be successful was provided.

During your first few months at the school, it would be wise to communicate to colleagues that you are willing to learn all you can about your new job and to be a team player. In most schools it is common practice to give junior faculty members less desirable assignments, reserving the more desirable ones for senior faculty. By demonstrating your willingness to take on these responsibilities with good humor and to give them your best effort, you will do much to establish yourself as a valuable faculty member. Appendix 13.6, "Negotiating a School's Culture: A Political Roadmap for the First-Year Teacher," provides additional suggestions for developing collaborative relationships with colleagues and staff.

Your colleagues may also appreciate learning from you about new approaches and materials—if you share in a manner that doesn't make others feel inferior. The following comments by a high school department chair, for example, illustrate a first-year Spanish teacher's positive influence on others:

> She won the respect of all her colleagues in the school who have dealt with her almost immediately, not because she's so competent in Spanish and not because she's so competent as a teacher, but because she handles everything with such sensitivity and sensibleness.

> Because of the way she operates—which is quietly but effectively—she has raised the whole tenor of expectations in the department. We have some very fine faculty in Spanish, but I would speculate they don't see their group self-image as intellectuals but rather as "people people." Because of what Elizabeth has brought to the school: the knowledge about how to use computers, her knowledge of foreign language oral proficiency, her knowledge of Spanish film and Spanish authors,

she has kind of lifted everybody up and helped her colleagues see themselves in a little bit different light and to improve professionally (Dollase 1992, 49).

It is important that you get along with your colleagues and contribute to a spirit of professional cooperation or **collegiality** in the school. Some you will enjoy being around; others you may wish to avoid. Some will express obvious enthusiasm for teaching; others may be bitter and pessimistic about their work. Be pleasant and friendly with both types. Accept their advice with a smile, and then act on what you believe is worthwhile.

Relationships with Administrators

Pay particular attention to the relationships you develop with administrators, department heads, and supervisors. Though your contacts with them will not be as frequent as with other teachers, they can do much to ensure your initial success. They are well aware of the difficulties you might encounter as a first-year teacher, and they are there to help you succeed.

The principal of your new school will, most likely, be the one to introduce you to other teachers, members of the administrative team, and staff. He or she should inform you if there are assistant principals or department heads who can help you enforce school rules, keep accurate records, and obtain supplies, for example. The principal may also assign an experienced teacher to serve as a mentor during your first year. In addition, your principal will indicate his or her availability to discuss issues of concern, and you should not hesitate to do so if the need arises.

Relationships with Parents

Developing positive connections with your students' parents can contribute significantly to students' success and to your success as a teacher. In reality, teachers and parents are partners—both concerned with the learning and growth of the children in their care. As U.S. Secretary of Education Richard Riley pointed out, "Parents, teachers and school officials working closely together are proven ingredients for success in our nation's schools" (Riley 1999). Unfortunately, research indicates that mothers typically spend less than Riley's recommended 30 minutes per day talking with or reading to their children, and fathers spend less than 15 minutes. The time parents spend interacting with their children differs as much as five times from family to family (Sadker and Sadker 1994).

It is important that you become acquainted with parents at school functions, at meetings of the Parent–Teacher Association or Organization (PTA or PTO), at various community events, and in other social situations. To develop good communication with parents, you will need to be sensitive to their needs, such as their work schedules and the language spoken at home.

By maintaining contact with parents and encouraging them to become involved in their children's education, you can significantly enhance the achievement of your students. Figure 13.6, based on interviews with the parents and guardians of almost 17,000 K–12 students, shows that parental involvement is associated with higher levels of student achievement, more positive attitudes toward school, greater participation in extracurricular activities, fewer suspensions and expulsions, and fewer grade repetitions. In light of such significant findings, it is important that you be willing to take the extra time and energy to pursue strategies such as the following for involving parents:

- Ask parents to read aloud to the child, to listen to the child read, and to sign homework papers.
- Encourage parents to drill students on math and spelling and to help with homework lessons.
- Encourage parents to discuss school activities with their children and suggest ways parents can help teach their children at home. For example, a simple home activity might be alphabetizing books; a more complex one would be using kitchen supplies in an elementary science experiment.
- Send home suggestions for games or group activities related to the child's schoolwork that parent and child can play together.

Figure 13.6

Source: U.S. Department of Education, National Center for Education Statistics. *Fathers' Involvement in Their Children's School,* NCES 98-091, by Christine Winquist Nord, DeeAnn Brimhall, and Jerry West, Washington, DC, 1997, p. 55.

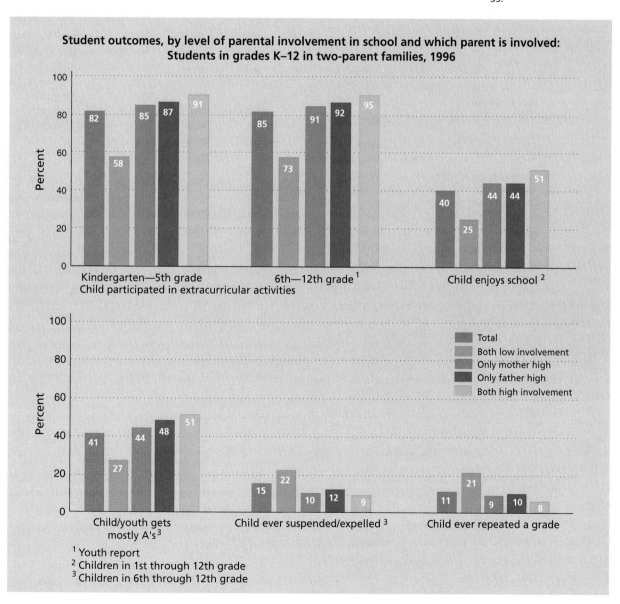

Student outcomes, by level of parental involvement in school and which parent is involved: Students in grades K–12 in two-parent families, 1996

[1] Youth report
[2] Children in 1st through 12th grade
[3] Children in 6th through 12th grade

Should teachers be required to make home visits?

Home visits by teachers were a common practice in the past, but more recently, teachers have limited their communication with parents to their own classrooms. From earlier days of schooling in the United States, when families had their children's teachers over for Sunday dinner, to the 1970s, when teachers in many districts were required to have conferences with every parent, even if that meant catching them at home or on a tractor plowing the fields, teachers connected with families outside of their classrooms. By the 1990s, the situation had changed significantly. Parent conferences were still required, but teachers' home visits were a rarity.

Why would this happen? What caused the change? Has anything been lost because teachers no longer visit their students and parents in their homes?

Many articles in education journals emphasize the importance of parent involvement in children's education and teacher–parent partnerships. However, they rarely mention that teachers should make home visits to strengthen connections with parents. Instead, the suggested settings for launching parent programs are the classroom, school, or a "neutral" location.

According to Anne Lewis, author of "Helping Young Urban Parents Educate Themselves and Their Children," an *ERIC/CUE Digest,* the literature on parent involvement describes parent–school communications as formal, one-way transactions, from the school to the parent. She notes that "parents complain that their most personal communication with schools usually only occurs because of a problem or crisis" (Lewis, 1992).

Perhaps home visits are returning, however. In addition to traditional strategies for involving parents, such as "open houses, fund-raising fairs, parent conferences, volunteers, intergenerational literacy programs, and advisory and policy councils," Lewis adds new ideas, including "parent centers, family support programs, such as home visits and parenting workshops, and school and community organization partnerships with universities, businesses, civic groups and such" (Lewis 1992).

What do you think? Is it time to revive the practice of requiring teachers to make home visits?

Yes, teachers should be required to make home visits.

Home visits can be informative, helpful, and a good way to connect with parents. A thirty-year veteran third-grade teacher in Azusa, California, Joseph Rocha, explained that his twice-a-year home visits are invaluable. For years, in August before the school year begins and in December, at the middle of the school year, he has made it a practice to visit each of his students' homes. In the summer he tells the parents how pleased he is that their child will be in his class and explains his goals for the coming school year. In December he returns to update them and learn about their interests and concerns. "It's time consuming," he admits, "but it is well worth the effort."

Home visits can help teachers better understand their students. One Los Angeles teacher, concerned about a child's inattentiveness, made a home visit that, she says, turned out to be an "eye opener. They didn't have a door. Somehow the door had been removed and they just had a blanket up." The teacher then understood the cause of the student's problem. "I realized he probably couldn't sleep because there was this traffic going by. And he didn't have a bed, he was on a pallet. Those kinds of things are important to know." She returned from the visit feeling a connection with the family and closer to the child.

Making such connections is the most important reason for home visits. However, teachers must conduct them in the right spirit. They should not appear to be inspecting the home, checking up on family members' activities, or judging the parents. Instead they should genuinely respect parents and family members and seek to learn from them if the visits are to be beneficial. In an article on "Forging Partnerships between Mexican American Parents and the Schools," Nancy Feyl Chavkin and Dora Lara Gonzalez (1995) caution:

There is a big difference between the rhetoric of partnerships and the activity of partnerships. Educators must truly believe and act on the belief that parents are their children's first teacher and the only teacher that remains with a child for a long period of time.

In an often-cited article entitled "School/Family/Community Partnerships: Caring for the Children We Share," Joyce Epstein (1995) recommends that home visits be conducted "at transition points to preschool, elementary, middle, and high school." She also recommends holding "neighborhood meetings to help families understand schools and to help schools understand families."

No, teachers should not be required to make home visits.

Requiring teachers to make home visits would be a mistake for several reasons. First, if teachers are less sensitive and respectful, such visits would be counterproductive. Also, teachers who prefer not to visit in their students' homes but do so because they are required to may show their discomfort or conduct their visits in a perfunctory manner, thus defeating the purpose of such visits.

Secondly, depending on the neighborhood, the teacher's familiarity with it, and the teacher's professional experience, home visits could actually be dangerous for the teacher. An inexperienced teacher visiting in an unfamiliar, violence-prone neighborhood at the wrong time would be taking a risk making home visits.

Third, depending on the teacher's experience and sensitivity, home visits could embarrass or even anger parents. If parents felt they were being judged as inadequate or believed that the teacher was investigating them, the home visit would be a failure.

Finally, teachers do not need to make home visits in order to connect with parents. They can make parents feel welcome and valued through phone calls, personal notes, afterschool visits, and meetings in their classrooms. There is no need to impose on parents at home.

It is one thing for teachers to make home visits at the invitation of parents and quite another to be *required* to. Because of all these potential problems, administrators should not require teachers to make home visits.

Where do you stand on this issue?

1. Are you in favor of teachers making home visits? Why or why not?

2. What have your home visit experiences been as a student or parent? How would you feel as a novice teacher about making home visits?

3. How could an inexperienced teacher learn about making home visits?

4. How could teachers protect their safety in making home visits into dangerous neighborhoods?

5. What other means can you recommend for better understanding a student's home situation? For connecting with parents?

Recommended Sources

Chavkin, N. F. and Gonzalez, D. L. (1995). Forging partnerships between Mexican American parents and the schools. *ERIC Digest.*

Epstein, J. (1995, May). School/family/community partnerships: Caring for the children we share. *Phi Delta Kappan, 76* (9), 701–712.

Lewis, A. (1992). Helping young urban parents educate themselves and their children. *ERIC/CUE Digest,* No. 85.

■ Encourage parents to participate in school activities such as a sports booster club, career day, and music and drama events.

■ Involve parents in their children's learning by having them co-sign learning contracts and serve as guest speakers.

The Goals 2000: Educate America Act funded parent resource centers in twenty-eight states (see the Appendix "Parent Information and Resource Centers" on this book's website). To help families get involved in their children's learning, these centers offer training for parents, hotlines, mobile training teams, resource and lending libraries, support groups, and referral networks. The U.S. Department of Education also sponsors the Partnership for Family Involvement in Education, designed to help students act as a link

weblink

between their teachers and schools and their families and communities. (For information, call 1-800-USA-LEARN.)

Family involvement resources are also available on the Internet through the National Parent Information Network (NPIN), a project sponsored by the ERIC system. (For information, call (800) 583-4135.) NPIN resources include information for parents on child development, testing, working with teachers, and home learning activities. AskERIC Question & Answer Service provides forums for parents and teachers to address mutual concerns, listings of useful and inexpensive learning materials, and descriptions of model parent involvement programs. Other online resources for parental involvement in schools can be obtained from the Consortium for School Networking.

Community Relations

Communities provide significant support for the education of their young people and determine the character of their schools. In addition, communities often help their schools by recruiting volunteers, providing financial support for special projects, and operating homework hotline programs. For example, school–community partnerships have been formed through "The Employer's Promise," a national effort to involve communities in supporting the family's central role in children's learning:

- John Hancock Financial Services sponsors "Kids-to-Go," a program of day-long supervised activities for employees' school-age children during school holidays in Boston.
- Southern California Edison supports the Parent Institute for Quality Education, which has trained 7,500 parents from East Los Angeles to participate actively in their children's education.
- Hewlett-Packard staggers start times for employees who volunteer at the corporation's on-site elementary school and accommodates the schedules of employees with school-age children.
- American College Testing's "Realize the Dream" program provides workshops and resources to involve parents in their children's education.

How Can You Participate in Teacher Collaboration?

The relationships that build a learning community involve **collaboration**—working together, sharing decision making, and solving problems. As a member of a dynamic, changing profession, your efforts to collaborate will result in an increased understanding of the teaching–learning process and improved learning for all students. By working with others on school governance, curriculum development, school–community partnerships, and educational reform, you will play an important role in enhancing the professional status of teachers.

The heart of collaboration is meaningful, authentic relationships among professionals. Such relationships, of course, do not occur naturally; they require commitment and hard work. Friend and Bursuck (1999, 72–74) have identified seven characteristics of collaboration which are summarized in the following:

- Collaboration is voluntary; teachers make a personal choice to collaborate.
- Collaboration is based on parity; all individuals' contributions are valued equally.

- Collaboration requires a shared goal.
- Collaboration includes shared responsibility for key decisions.
- Collaboration includes shared accountability for outcomes.
- Collaboration is based on shared resources; each teacher contributes something—time, expertise, space, equipment, or other resource.
- Collaboration is emergent; as teachers work together, the degree of shared decision making, trust, and respect increases.

Schools that support the essential elements of collaboration are collegial schools "characterized by purposeful adult interactions about improving schoolwide teaching and learning" (Glickman, Gordon, and Ross-Gordon 1998, 5–6). In the following, we examine four expressions of teacher collaboration: peer coaching, staff development, team teaching, and co-teaching.

Peer Coaching

Experienced teachers traditionally help novice teachers, but more formal peer coaching programs extend the benefits of collaboration to more teachers. **Peer coaching** is an arrangement whereby teachers grow professionally by observing one another's teaching and providing constructive feedback. The practice encourages teachers to learn together in an emotionally safe environment. According to Bruce Joyce and Marsha Weil (2000, 440), peer coaching is an effective way to create communities of professional educators, and all teachers should be members of coaching teams:

> If we had our way, *all* school faculties would be divided into coaching teams—that is, teams who regularly observe one another's teaching and learn from watching one another and the students. In short, we recommend the development of a "coaching environment" in which all personnel see themselves as coaches.

Through teacher-to-teacher support and collaboration, peer coaching programs improve teacher morale and teaching effectiveness.

Staff Development

Increasingly, teachers are contributing to the design of staff development programs that encourage collaboration, risk-taking, and experimentation. Some programs, for example, give teachers the opportunity to meet with other teachers at similar grade levels or in similar content areas for the purpose of sharing ideas, strategies, and solutions to problems. A day or part of a day may be devoted to this kind of workshop or idea exchange. Teachers are frequently given released time from regular duties to visit other schools and observe exemplary programs in action.

One example of a collaborative staff development program is Project MASTER (Mathematics and Science Teachers Education Renewal), developed by the Chicago public schools. Groups of eight teachers (four in mathematics and four in science) from ten high schools form collegial support groups or professional cadres at their schools. A department chair or lead teacher heads the mathematics and science cadres at each school. Participants read and discuss educational research, attend workshops, and form peer coaching groups. The groups also receive training in conferencing skills, classroom observation and data collection, and analysis of instruction. Participants visit other Project MASTER schools to exchange ideas and to practice coaching

and instructional analysis skills. As the following comments by participants indicate, collaboration is a powerful catalyst for professional growth and change:

> The project strengthened my understanding of instructional leadership and my own instructional leadership skills. The focus was on improving instruction, and I became more aware of certain aspects of teaching through observation (Ponticell, Olson, and Charlier 1995, 104).

> We have a chance to share, to get together with each other as a staff; this helped us become a team and help each other (103).

Team Teaching

In **team teaching** arrangements, teachers share the responsibility for two or more classes, dividing up the subject areas between them, with one preparing lessons in mathematics, science, and health, for instance, while the other plans instruction in reading and language arts. The division of responsibility may also be made in terms of the performance levels of the children, so that, for example, one teacher may teach the lowest- and highest-ability reading groups and the middle math group, while the other teaches the middle-ability reading groups and the lowest and highest mathematics group. In many schools, team teaching arrangements are so extensive that children move from classroom to classroom for forty- to fifty-minute periods just as students do at the high school level.

The practice of team teaching is often limited by student enrollments and budget constraints. As integrated curricula and the need for special knowledge and skills increase, however, the use of collegial support teams (CSTs) will become more common. A **collegial support team (CST)** provides teachers with a "safe zone" for professional growth, as one teacher commented:

> [The CST] allows me much discretion as to the areas I'd like to strengthen. Therefore, I am truly growing with no fear of being labeled or singled out as the "teacher who is having problems." I am aware of problem spheres and I work to correct these with the aid of my colleagues (Johnson and Brown 1998, 89).

The members of a team make wide-ranging decisions about the instruction of students assigned to the team, such as when to use large-group instruction or small-group instruction, how teaching tasks will be divided, and how time, materials, and other resources will be allocated.

Co-Teaching

In **co-teaching** arrangements, two or more teachers, such as a classroom teacher and a special education teacher or other specialist, teach together in the same classroom.

What are some forms of professional collaboration in which you will participate as a teacher? In what types of co-teaching arrangements might these teachers cooperate?

Co-teaching builds on the strengths of two teachers and provides increased learning opportunities for all students (Friend and Bursuck 1999). Typically, co-teaching arrangements occur during a set period of time each day or on certain days of the week. Among the several possible co-teaching variations, Friend and Bursuck (1999) have identified the following:

- *One teach, one support*—one teacher leads the lesson; the other assists.
- *Station teaching*—the lesson is divided into two parts; one teacher teaches one part to half of the students while the other teaches the other part to the rest. The groups then switch and the teachers repeat their part of the lesson. If students can work independently, a third group may be formed, or a volunteer may teach at a third station.
- *Parallel teaching*—a class is divided in half, and each teacher instructs half the class individually.
- *Alternative teaching*—a class is divided into one large group and one small group. For example, one teacher may provide remediation or enrichment to the small group, while the other teacher instructs the large group.

How Will Your Performance as a Teacher Be Evaluated?

Most teachers are evaluated on a regular basis to determine whether their performance measures up to acceptable standards, if they are able to create and sustain effective learning environments for students. Performance criteria used to evaluate teachers vary and are usually determined by the school principal, district office, the school board, or a state education agency. In most schools, the principal or a member of the leadership team evaluates teachers.

Teacher evaluations serve many purposes: to determine whether teachers should be retained, receive tenure, or be given merit pay. Evaluations also help teachers assess their effectiveness and develop strategies for self-improvement. National studies indicate that "teachers want to be observed more, they want more feedback, and they want to talk more with other professionals about improving learning for their students" (Glickman, Gordon, and Ross-Gordon 1998, 313).

Quantitative and Qualitative Evaluation

Typically, supervisors use quantitative or qualitative approaches (or a combination) to evaluate teachers' classroom performance. **Quantitative evaluation** includes pencil-and-paper rating forms the supervisor uses to record classroom events and behaviors objectively in terms of their number or frequency. For example, a supervisor might focus on the teacher's verbal behaviors—questioning, answering, praising, giving directions, and critiquing. The Florida Performance Measurement System (FPMS) discussed in Chapter 2 is an example of a quantitative approach to teacher evaluation; (see Appendix 2.1 for the "Screening/Summative Observation Instrument" used by the FPMS).

Qualitative evaluation, in contrast, includes written, open-ended narrative descriptions of classroom events in terms of their qualities. These more subjective measures are equally valuable in identifying teachers' weaknesses and strengths. In addition, quali-

Mary Lynn Peacher
The Teacher with Heart
1999 National Teacher of the Year Finalist

". . . all children are special."

Mary Lynn Peacher, 1999 Oklahoma Teacher of the Year and one of four finalists for National Teacher of the Year, exudes creativity, good will, and a love of students and learning. The fourth grade teacher challenges her students with "math problems in proportional reasoning, with scientific studies of the geometric properties of soap film, and correspondence with pen pals through poetry," according to the Web page on the 1999 finalists. In addition, Peacher's profile on the web page notes the passion she shares for serving others in need:

When the fourth grade students of Jenks East Elementary School mentor younger students, and make flowers for the homebound quilts for the Ronald McDonald House, the students know they are making a difference in their community. . . .

Her volunteer commitments are many and include the Cerebral Palsy Infant Therapy Unit, Big Brothers and Sisters of Tulsa, and the Little Lighthouse for the Blind and Physically Limited. Her love of music led to singing for the elderly in nursing homes and working with professional artists to bring the arts to her students.

[According to Peacher,] "Teachers must reach beyond their classrooms to become the impetus behind desperately needed change."

Peacher's spirit and heart are what make her different —hard things to capture in words. A fifth grade boy, Simon Plohocky, does it well. In a writing assignment to describe the person he admired the most, he chose his former teacher, Mrs. Peacher. His essay became part of an important letter:

Dear Teacher of the Year Selection Committee:

It was August 15th, the first day of school. The sun was just grasping the breath of dawn when children started to flow into the classrooms of their new teachers. Not known to me yet was that this teacher was special, someone unique.

I sat down at my assigned seat and waited. Then after a moment a woman with blond hair and the biggest, happiest smile I've ever seen walked in the door. She

---

tative evaluation can capture the complexities and subtleties of classroom life that might not be reflected in a quantitative approach to evaluation.

Clinical Supervision

Many supervisors follow the four-step **clinical supervision** model in which the supervisor first holds a preconference with the teacher, then observes in the classroom, analyzes and interprets observation data, and finally holds a postconference with the teacher (Anderson and Snyder 1993; Goldhammer, Anderson, and Krajewski 1993; Pajak 1993; Smyth 1995; Acheson and Gall 1997). During the preconference, the teacher and supervisor schedule a classroom observation and determine its purpose and focus and the method of observation to be used. At the postconference, the teacher and supervisor discuss the analysis of observation data and jointly develop a plan for instructional improvement.

Fulfilling the clinical supervision model is difficult and time-consuming, and time-pressed administrators must often modify the approach. For example, Kim Marshall,

greeted us and asked us our names. Then she addressed the rules. "I will always try to make work fun" is the one rule I distinctly remember. I found out that it was definitely true.

Simon continued describing the "fun" things his class did that year, from "testing how much sugar was in different types of gum," to marbleizing book covers, making candles, creating "coat hanger inventions," holding celebrations like a Mexican fiesta, a U.S.A. fest, and "a world's fair," and constructing a bridge lab "where we built bridges out of toothpicks, glue, and string, [and] then tested how much weight they could handle." All were fun learning experiences, but it was Mrs. Peacher's heart that mattered to him the most:

> The biggest reason I think she should get the award is because she thinks with her heart, not just any heart, literally the biggest heart I've ever seen.

> To prove this is true I'll tell you something that has touched my life forever.

> On April 2nd 1996, I went to the doctor because I was extremely pale and not eating.

> The next day I had to go to the hospital. That night I was diagnosed with leukemia. The next day, just out of surgery, I received a pile of cards literally two feet high and word that Mrs. Peacher had stopped by but

I was still asleep. Every day in the hospital and on the outpatient service she either came to see me or called me on the telephone. Since I was in the hospital during Easter the whole class and she sent me tons of candy, baskets, presents, and cards. If something happened in class, or we were doing something special and I couldn't make it because of chemo, she'd come over to my house and talk to me. Once we went on a field trip and she offered to take me in her car so in case I got sick she could take me home.

She is such a dear friend and so compassionate. Any one that knows her will say this is true.

Her colleagues agree. The teacher whose classroom has been next to hers for eight years explains that Peacher's work with students with special needs is especially sensitive. "Her love of students is visible. . . . They *always* receive her best." That colleague recalled, "At one point, when inclusion in her room was distressing to a child [with special needs], she used *reverse* inclusion and brought her whole class to *his* [resource] classroom. Lynn has encouraged a generation of students to understand that all children are special." Over the years, Peacher has taught many intellectually stretching and "fun" lessons, but her ongoing lessons of the heart are the most important.

principal at a Boston elementary school with thirty-nine teachers, makes four random, unannounced five-minute visits to classrooms each day. This schedule allows him to observe every teacher during a two-week period, and each teacher about 19 times during a year. To make the most of his five-minute classroom visits, he follows these guidelines:

- Be a perceptive observer in order to capture something interesting and helpful to say during the feedback session.
- Give teachers a mixture of praise, affirmation, suggestions, and criticism.
- When sharing critical observations with teachers, be tactful and nonthreatening but totally honest.
- Use good judgment about when to deliver criticism and when to hold off (Marshall 1996, 344).

Regardless of the approach a school district will use to evaluate your performance as a beginning teacher, remember that evaluation will assist your professional growth and development. Experienced teachers report that periodic feedback and assistance from knowledgeable, sensitive supervisors is very beneficial; such evaluation results in "improved teacher reflection and higher-order thought, more collegiality, openness, and communication, greater teacher retention, less anxiety and burnout, greater teacher autonomy and efficacy, improved attitudes, improved teaching behaviors, and better student achievement and attitudes" (Glickman, Gordon, and Ross-Gordon, 1998, 317).

SUMMARY

How Will You Become Certified or Licensed to Teach?

- State certification is required for teaching in public schools and in many private schools. Some large cities and local school districts have additional criteria for certification. Certification requirements for teachers vary from state to state and are frequently modified. Some states waive licensing requirements for teachers certified by the National Board for Professional Teaching Standards (NBPTS).

- Most states require testing of teachers for initial certification, and some require recertification after a three- to five-year period.

- States that are members of the Interstate Certification Agreement Contract honor teaching certificates granted by certain other states.

- Private, parochial, for-profit, and charter schools employ about 362,000 noncertified teachers. Many states offer alternative and emergency certification programs.

- The Praxis Series: Professional Assessments for Beginning Teachers is required in most states for initial certification. The Praxis Series includes assessments of academic (basic) skills, subject matter knowledge, and classroom performance.

Where Will You Teach?

- Teacher supply and demand in content areas and geographic regions influences finding a teaching position.

- Teaching is a large profession, involving more than 53 million students in public and private K–12 schools and more than 3 million teachers.

- Job vacancies result from retirements, relocation, and career changes. Elementary and secondary enrollments and the demand for new teachers will increase through 2009.

- Education-related career opportunities for teachers include principal, assistant principal, librarian, counselor, and teaching roles in government and the private sector.

How Will You Find Your First Teaching Job?

- Information about teaching vacancies may be obtained through placement services, state departments of education, and personal networking on the Internet.

- A résumé is a concise summary of an individual's experiences, education, and skills. A letter of inquiry is used to find out if a school district has any teaching vacancies, and a letter of application (or cover letter) indicates an individual's interest in and qualifications for a teaching position.

What Can You Expect as a Beginning Teacher?

■ Beginning teachers should prepare instructional strategies and materials and learn about their students and the community well in advance of the first day of school.

■ Experienced teachers' recommendations for beginning teachers focus on planning, organizing, and following through.

How Can You Become a Part of Your Learning Community?

■ The learning community includes students, their families, colleagues, and members of the community.

■ Research indicates that parental involvement is a key factor in children's academic achievement.

■ Training programs, hotlines, referral networks, and partnership programs are among the resources teachers can use to involve parents and members of the community.

How Can You Participate in Teacher Collaboration?

■ Teachers collaborate through participation in school governance, curriculum development, school-community partnerships, and educational reform.

■ Four approaches to teacher collaboration are peer coaching, staff development, team teaching, and co-teaching.

How Will Your Performance as a Teacher Be Evaluated?

■ Performance criteria for evaluating teachers are developed by school principals, districts, school boards, or states.

■ Quantitative approaches to teacher evaluation focus on the incidence, frequency, or amount of teacher or student behavior in various categories.

■ Qualitative approaches to teacher evaluation are usually written narratives focusing on the qualities of classrooms and events, such as classroom climate and teaching style.

KEY TERMS AND CONCEPTS

alternative
  certification, 504
charter, 504
clinical supervision, 528
collaboration, 524
colliegal support team
  (CST), 526
collegiality, 520
co-teaching, 526
credentials file, 509
emergency
  certification, 504

Interstate Certification
  Agreement Contract, 503
letter of application, 511
letter of inquiry, 511
National Council for
  Accreditation of
  Teacher Education
  (NCATE), 501
peer coaching, 525
placement service, 509
Praxis Series: Professional
  Assessments for

Beginning Teachers, 505
qualitative evaluation, 527
quantitative
  evaluation, 527
recertification, 501
résumé, 511
teacher supply and
  demand, 504
teaching certificate, 501
team teaching, 526

APPLICATIONS AND ACTIVITIES

Teacher's Journal

1. Record in your journal your plan for becoming certified or licensed to teach.

2. Develop answers to possible interview questions and brainstorm questions to ask.

3. Envision your first day as a teacher and describe what you see.

4. When you become a teacher, in what collaborations and partnerships will you participate? How might these activities contribute to your effectiveness as a teacher? How might your involvement enhance students' learning and your relationships with them?

Teacher's Database

1. Explore and compare teacher proficiencies and teaching standards according to state boards of education, national standards organizations, and teacher and subject area organizations. Begin by locating the following organizations online and information about your school's education program in relation to state and national standards.

   National Association for State Boards of Education (NASBE)

   National Association of State Directors for Teacher Education and Certification (NASDTEC)

   National Board for Professional Teaching Standards (NBPTS)

   National Council for Accreditation of Teacher Education (NCATE)

   Continue your search by accessing the government or education department of a locality, region, or state where you plan to teach and gathering information about becoming a teacher there.

2. Formulate a research question concerning demographic aspects of teachers and schools in the United States. Then go online to gather current national and state statistics on your question. For example, your question might relate to one or more of the following topics.

teacher recruitment	information about school districts
teacher shortages	public schools compared to private schools
teaching salaries and benefits	independent and private schools
characteristics of the teaching force	characteristics of parochial schools
attitudes of teachers	

   Begin your data search in the U.S. Department of Education's National Center for Education Statistics (NCES).

Observations and Interviews

1. If you can arrange it, observe the first day of classes at a local school. What strategies did the teachers use to begin the year on a positive, task-oriented note? What

evidence did you see that the teachers followed the advice given by the experienced teachers in this chapter? Record your qualitative observations on Handout Master M13.3 (Qualitative Observation Log) and share them with your classmates. What common themes do you detect in the data?

2. Survey teachers at a local school to get information about how they prepare for the first day of school. To help you develop questions for your survey, ask your instructor for the handout master that supports this activity (M13.1, Developing and Conducting a Survey 1).

3. Prepare a questionnaire and then survey a group of experienced teachers for their recollections about the triumphs and defeats they experienced as beginning teachers. What lessons are evident in their responses to your questionnaire? Are there common themes that characterize the triumphs they recall? The defeats? For help in developing the items for your questionnaire, ask your instructor for Handout Master M13.2, Developing and Conducting a Survey 2.

4. Interview teachers and administrators about their experiences with professional collaboration and parental involvement. What examples do they provide, and how do these reflect the seven characteristics of collaboration presented in this chapter? How do students benefit from collaboration and parental involvement? What suggestions do the teachers and administrators have for improving collaboration and parental involvement?

Professional Portfolio

1. Draft a preliminary professional résumé. Review the section in this chapter titled "Preparing Your Résumé" and "Résumé Advice for Educators" in Appendix 13.4. In addition, examine the résumé prepared by Linda M. Rodriguez (Figure 13.3).

   In your résumé, under "Personal Data," provide a current address and a permanent address. Also, under "Education," specify an anticipated graduation date. Under "Experience," include work experience that indicates your ability to work with people. Begin with your most recent experiences and present information in reverse chronological order.

   When you have finished your preliminary résumé, critique it against "Résumé Advice for Educators."

2. Draft an essay describing what you will bring to your first year of teaching. It may help to review the essay you wrote for the Chapter 1 portfolio entry on what has drawn you to teaching.

Appendix 13.1

Alabama
Teacher Education and Certification
State Department of Education
P.O. Box 302101
Montgomery, AL 36130-2101
(334) 242-9560
Fax: (334) 242-0498

Alaska
Department of Education
Teacher Education & Certification
801 West 10th Street, Suite 200
Juneau, AK 99801–1894
(907) 465-2831 or 2026

Arizona
Arizona Dept. of Education
Certification Unit
P.O. Box 6490
Phoenix, AZ 85005-6490
(602) 542-4367

Arkansas
Teacher Education & Licensure
State Dept. of Education
4 State Capitol Mall
Little Rock, AR 72201-1071
(501) 682-4342
(501) 682-4898

California
Commission on Teacher
  Credentialing
Box 944270
Sacramento, CA 94244-2700
(916) 445-7254
Fax: (916) 327-3166
credentials@ctc.ca.gov

Colorado
Educator Licensing
State Dept. of Education
201 E. Colfax Avenue
Denver, CO 80203
(303) 866-6628

Connecticut
Bureau of Certification and Teacher
  Preparation
State Dept. of Education
P.O. Box 150471
Hartford, CT 06115-0471

(860) 566-5201
Fax: (860) 566-8929 (fax)

Delaware
Teacher Certification
Dept. of Public Instruction
P.O. Box 1402
Dover, DE 19903
(302) 739-4686

District of Columbia
Educational Credentialing &
  Standards
825 N. Capitol Street, N.E.
6th Floor Washington, DC 20002
(202) 442-5377
Fax: (202) 442-5311

Florida
Bureau of Teacher Certification
Florida Education Center
325 W Gaines, Rm. 201
Tallahassee, FL 32399-0400
(850) 488-2317 (out of state)
(800) 445-6739 (in state)

Georgia
Professional Standards Commission
Certification Section
1454 Twin Towers East
Atlanta, GA 30334
(404) 657-9000
mail@gapsc.com

Hawaii
Office of Personnel Services
Teacher Recruitment Unit
P.O. Box 2360
Honolulu, HI 96804
(808) 586-3420
(800) 305-5104
Fax: (808) 586-3419

Idaho
Teacher Certification
State Dept. of Education
P.O. Box 83720
Boise, ID 83720-0027
(208) 332-6880

Illinois
Illinois State Board of Education

Certification & Placement Section
100 N. First Street
Springfield, IL 62777-0001
(217) 782-4321

Indiana
Indiana Professional Standards
  Board
Teacher Licensing
251 East Ohio Street, Suite 201
Indianapolis, IN 46204-2133
(317) 232-9010
Fax: (317) 232-9023

Iowa
Board of Educational Examiners
Grimes State Office Building
Des Moines, IA 50319-0147
(515) 281-3245

Kansas
Certification Section
Kansas State Dept. of Education
Kansas State Education Building
120 SE 10th Ave.
Topeka, KS 66612-1182
(785) 296-2288

Kentucky
Kentucky Dept. of Education
Division of Certification
1024 Capital Center Drive
Frankfort, KY 40601-1972
(502) 573-4606

Louisiana
Louisiana Dept. of Education
Teacher Certification, Room 700
P.O. Box 94064
Baton Rouge, LA 70804-9064
(225) 342-3490
(225) 342-3499

Maine
Division of Certification
Department of Education
State House Station 23
Augusta, ME 04333
(207) 287-5944

Maryland
Division of Certification 18100

Appendix 13.1 *(continued)*

State Dept. of Education
200 West Baltimore St.
Baltimore, MD 21201
(410) 767-0412

Massachusetts
Massachusetts Dept. of Education
Office of Teacher Certification and
    Credentialling
350 Main Street
Malden, MA 02148
(781) 388-3300, X665
Fax: (781) 388-3475

Michigan
Office of Professional Preparation &
    Certification
Michigan Dept. of Education
P.O. Box 30008
Lansing, MI 48909
(517) 373-3310

Minnesota
Teacher Licensing
State Dept. of Children, Families
    and Learning
1500 Highway 36 West
Roseville MN 55113
(651) 582-8691

Mississippi
Teacher Certification
State Dept. of Education
Box 771
Jackson, MS 39205-0771
(601) 359-3483
Fax: (601) 359-2778

Missouri
Teacher Certification
Dept. of Elementary and Secondary
    Education
P.O. Box 480
Jefferson City, MO 65102
(573) 751-3486

Montana
Teacher Certification
Office of Public Instruction
P.O. Box 202501
Helena, MT 59620-2501
(406) 444-3150

Nebraska
Teacher Certification

State Dept. of Education
301 Centennial Mall South
Box 94987
Lincoln, NE 68509-4987
(800) 371-4642

Nevada
Licensure and Certification
Nevada Dept. of Education
700 East 5th St.
Carson City, NV 89701
(702) 687-3115

New Hampshire
Bureau of Credentialing
State Dept. of Education
101 Pleasant St.
Concord, NH 03301
(603) 271-2407
Fax: (603) 271-4134

New Jersey
Office of Licensing and Credentials
P.O. Box 500
Trenton, NJ 08625-0500
(609) 292-2070

New Mexico
Director
Professional Licensure Unit
Education Building
300 Don Gaspar
Santa Fe, NM 87501-2786
(505) 827-6587

New York
Office of Teaching
State Education Department
Albany, NY 12234
(518) 474-3901/2/3/4

North Carolina
North Carolina Dept. of Public
    Instruction
Licensure Section
301 N. Wilmington Street
Raleigh, NC 27601-2825
(919) 733-4125
(800) 577-7994

North Dakota
Education Standards and Practice
    Board
Teacher Certification
600 E. Boulevard Ave.

Bismarck, ND 58505-0880
(701) 328-2264

Ohio
Professional Development and
    Licensure
State Dept. of Education
65 South Front St., Rm. 412
Columbus, OH 43215-4183
(614) 466-3593
Fax: (614) 466-1999

Oklahoma
Professional Standards
State Dept. of Education
2500 N. Lincoln Blvd.
Rm. 211
Oklahoma City, OK 73105-4599
(405) 521-3301
Fax: (405) 521-6205

Oregon
Teacher Standards and Practices
    Commission
Public Service Bldg.
255 Capitol Street, N. E.
Suite 105
Salem, OR 97310-1332
(503) 378-3586

Pennsylvania
Bureau of Teacher Certification &
    Preparation
Dept. of Education
333 Market Street
Harrisburg, PA 17126-0333
(717) 787-3356
00certifica@psupen.psu.edu

Rhode Island
Office of Teacher Certification
State Dept. of Education
Shepard Building
255 Westminster St.
Providence, RI 02903-3400
(401) 222-4600

South Carolina
Office of Teacher Education,
    Certification, & Evaluation
1600 Gervais St.
Columbia, SC 29201
(803) 734-8466

Appendix 13.1 *(continued)*

Fax: (803) 734-2873
licensure@sde.state.sc.us

South Dakota
Teacher Certification
Office of Policy and Accountability
700 Governors Drive
Pierre, SD 57501-2291
(605) 773-3553
Fax: (605) 773-6139

Tennessee
Office of Teacher Licensing
State Dept. of Education
5th Floor, Andrew Johnson Tower
710 James Robertson Parkway
Nashville, TN 37243-0377
(615) 533-4885
Fax: (615) 532-7860

Texas
State Board for Educator
   Certification
1001 Trinity
Austin, TX 78701
(512) 469-3001

Utah
Certification and Professional
   Development Section

State Board of Education
250 East 500 South Street
Salt Lake City, UT 84111
(801) 538-7740
Fax: (801) 538-7973

Vermont
Licensing Office
Dept. of Education
120 State Street
Montpelier, VT 05620-2501
(802) 828-2445
Fax: (802) 828-3140

Virginia
Office of Professional Licensure
Department of Education
P.O. Box 2120
Richmond, VA 23216-2120
(804) 225-2022

Washington
Office of Professional Education
Superintendent of Public Instruction
Old Capitol Building
P.O. Box 47200
Olympia, WA 98504-7200
(360) 753-6773

West Virginia
State Dept. of Education
Building 6, Room 337
1900 Kanawha Blvd., East
Charleston, WV 25305-0330
(800) 982-2378

Wisconsin
Teacher Education, Licensing and
Placement
Box 7841
Madison, WI 53707-7841
(608) 266-1028 (direct line)
(608) 266-1027 (voice mail)
Fax: (608) 264-9558

Wyoming
Professional Teaching Standards
   Board
2300 Capitol Avenue
Hathaway Building, 2nd Floor
Cheyenne, WY 82002
Fax: (307) 777-6234
PTSB@www.k12.wy.us

Note: Many state offices have websites; use a search engine to determine whether an office has a website and its current URL.

Appendix 13.2

Parties to the Interstate Certification Agreement Contract

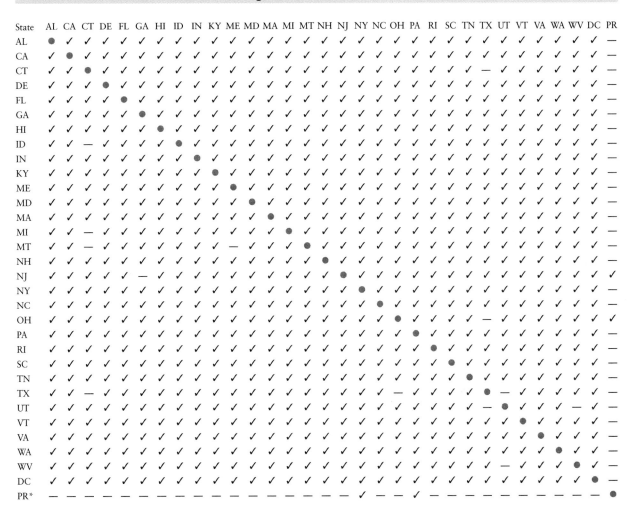

State	AL	CA	CT	DE	FL	GA	HI	ID	IN	KY	ME	MD	MA	MI	MT	NH	NJ	NY	NC	OH	PA	RI	SC	TN	TX	UT	VT	VA	WA	WV	DC	PR
AL	●	✓	✓	✓	✓	✓	✓	✓	✓	✓	✓	✓	✓	✓	✓	✓	✓	✓	✓	✓	✓	✓	✓	✓	✓	✓	✓	✓	✓	✓	✓	—
CA	✓	●	✓	✓	✓	✓	✓	✓	✓	✓	✓	✓	✓	✓	✓	✓	✓	✓	✓	✓	✓	✓	✓	✓	✓	✓	✓	✓	✓	✓	✓	—
CT	✓	✓	●	✓	✓	✓	✓	—	✓	✓	✓	✓	✓	—	—	✓	✓	✓	✓	✓	✓	✓	✓	✓	—	✓	✓	✓	✓	✓	✓	—
DE	✓	✓	✓	●	✓	✓	✓	✓	✓	✓	✓	✓	✓	✓	✓	✓	✓	✓	✓	✓	✓	✓	✓	✓	✓	✓	✓	✓	✓	✓	✓	—
FL	✓	✓	✓	✓	●	✓	✓	✓	✓	✓	✓	✓	✓	✓	✓	✓	✓	✓	✓	✓	✓	✓	✓	✓	✓	✓	✓	✓	✓	✓	✓	—
GA	✓	✓	✓	✓	✓	●	✓	✓	✓	✓	✓	✓	✓	✓	✓	✓	—	✓	✓	✓	✓	✓	✓	✓	✓	✓	✓	✓	✓	✓	✓	—
HI	✓	✓	✓	✓	✓	✓	●	✓	✓	✓	✓	✓	✓	✓	✓	✓	✓	✓	✓	✓	✓	✓	✓	✓	✓	✓	✓	✓	✓	✓	✓	—
ID	✓	✓	—	✓	✓	✓	✓	●	✓	✓	✓	✓	✓	✓	✓	✓	✓	✓	✓	✓	✓	✓	✓	✓	✓	✓	✓	✓	✓	✓	✓	—
IN	✓	✓	✓	✓	✓	✓	✓	✓	●	✓	✓	✓	✓	✓	✓	✓	✓	✓	✓	✓	✓	✓	✓	✓	✓	✓	✓	✓	✓	✓	✓	—
KY	✓	✓	✓	✓	✓	✓	✓	✓	✓	●	✓	✓	✓	✓	✓	✓	✓	✓	✓	✓	✓	✓	✓	✓	✓	✓	✓	✓	✓	✓	✓	—
ME	✓	✓	✓	✓	✓	✓	✓	✓	✓	✓	●	✓	✓	✓	—	✓	✓	✓	✓	✓	✓	✓	✓	✓	✓	✓	✓	✓	✓	✓	✓	—
MD	✓	✓	✓	✓	✓	✓	✓	✓	✓	✓	✓	●	✓	✓	✓	✓	✓	✓	✓	✓	✓	✓	✓	✓	✓	✓	✓	✓	✓	✓	✓	—
MA	✓	✓	✓	✓	✓	✓	✓	✓	✓	✓	✓	✓	●	✓	✓	✓	✓	✓	✓	✓	✓	✓	✓	✓	✓	✓	✓	✓	✓	✓	✓	—
MI	✓	✓	—	✓	✓	✓	✓	✓	✓	✓	✓	✓	✓	●	✓	✓	✓	✓	✓	✓	✓	✓	✓	✓	✓	✓	✓	✓	✓	✓	✓	—
MT	✓	✓	—	✓	✓	✓	✓	✓	✓	✓	—	✓	✓	✓	●	✓	✓	✓	✓	✓	✓	✓	✓	✓	✓	✓	✓	✓	✓	✓	✓	—
NH	✓	✓	✓	✓	✓	✓	✓	✓	✓	✓	✓	✓	✓	✓	✓	●	✓	✓	✓	✓	✓	✓	✓	✓	✓	✓	✓	✓	✓	✓	✓	—
NJ	✓	✓	✓	✓	✓	—	✓	✓	✓	✓	✓	✓	✓	✓	✓	✓	●	✓	✓	✓	✓	✓	✓	✓	✓	✓	✓	✓	✓	✓	✓	✓
NY	✓	✓	✓	✓	✓	✓	✓	✓	✓	✓	✓	✓	✓	✓	✓	✓	✓	●	✓	✓	✓	✓	✓	✓	✓	✓	✓	✓	✓	✓	✓	—
NC	✓	✓	✓	✓	✓	✓	✓	✓	✓	✓	✓	✓	✓	✓	✓	✓	✓	✓	●	✓	✓	✓	✓	✓	✓	✓	✓	✓	✓	✓	✓	—
OH	✓	✓	✓	✓	✓	✓	✓	✓	✓	✓	✓	✓	✓	✓	✓	✓	✓	✓	✓	●	✓	✓	✓	✓	—	✓	✓	✓	✓	✓	✓	✓
PA	✓	✓	✓	✓	✓	✓	✓	✓	✓	✓	✓	✓	✓	✓	✓	✓	✓	✓	✓	✓	●	✓	✓	✓	✓	✓	✓	✓	✓	✓	✓	—
RI	✓	✓	✓	✓	✓	✓	✓	✓	✓	✓	✓	✓	✓	✓	✓	✓	✓	✓	✓	✓	✓	●	✓	✓	✓	✓	✓	✓	✓	✓	✓	—
SC	✓	✓	✓	✓	✓	✓	✓	✓	✓	✓	✓	✓	✓	✓	✓	✓	✓	✓	✓	✓	✓	✓	●	✓	✓	✓	✓	✓	✓	—	✓	—
TN	✓	✓	✓	✓	✓	✓	✓	✓	✓	✓	✓	✓	✓	✓	✓	✓	✓	✓	✓	✓	✓	✓	✓	●	✓	✓	✓	✓	✓	✓	✓	—
TX	✓	✓	—	✓	✓	✓	✓	✓	✓	✓	✓	✓	✓	✓	✓	✓	✓	✓	✓	—	✓	✓	✓	✓	●	—	✓	✓	✓	✓	✓	—
UT	✓	✓	✓	✓	✓	✓	✓	✓	✓	✓	✓	✓	✓	✓	✓	✓	✓	✓	✓	✓	✓	✓	✓	✓	—	●	✓	✓	—	✓	✓	—
VT	✓	✓	✓	✓	✓	✓	✓	✓	✓	✓	✓	✓	✓	✓	✓	✓	✓	✓	✓	✓	✓	✓	✓	✓	✓	✓	●	✓	✓	✓	✓	—
VA	✓	✓	✓	✓	✓	✓	✓	✓	✓	✓	✓	✓	✓	✓	✓	✓	✓	✓	✓	✓	✓	✓	✓	✓	✓	✓	✓	●	✓	✓	✓	—
WA	✓	✓	✓	✓	✓	✓	✓	✓	✓	✓	✓	✓	✓	✓	✓	✓	✓	✓	✓	✓	✓	✓	✓	✓	✓	—	✓	✓	●	✓	✓	—
WV	✓	✓	✓	✓	✓	✓	✓	✓	✓	✓	✓	✓	✓	✓	✓	✓	✓	✓	✓	✓	✓	✓	—	✓	✓	✓	✓	✓	✓	●	✓	—
DC	✓	✓	✓	✓	✓	✓	✓	✓	✓	✓	✓	✓	✓	✓	✓	✓	✓	✓	✓	✓	✓	✓	✓	✓	✓	✓	✓	✓	✓	✓	●	—
PR*	—	—	—	—	—	—	—	—	—	—	—	—	—	—	—	—	✓	—	—	✓	—	—	—	—	—	—	—	—	—	—	—	●

*Commonwealth of Puerto Rico

Note: Parties to the contract through September 30, 2000. A fully certified teacher in a contract state may be issued a certificate for a minimum of one year by another contract state.

Appendix 13.3

Job Search Timetable Checklist

This checklist is designed to help graduating students who are seeking teaching positions make the best use of their time as they conduct job searches. We encourage you to use this checklist in conjunction with the services and resources available from your college or university career planning and placement office.

August/September
(12 months prior to employment)
- _____ Attend any applicable orientations/workshops offered by your college placement office.
- _____ Register with your college placement office and inquire about career services.
- _____ Begin to define career goals by determining the types, sizes and geographic locations of school systems in which you have an interest

October
(11 months prior to employment)
- _____ Begin to identify references and ask them to prepare letters of recommendation for your credential or placement files.
- _____ See a counselor at your college placement office to discuss your job-search plan.

November
(10 months prior to employment)
- _____ Check to see that you are properly registered at your college placement office.
- _____ Begin developing a résumé and a basic cover letter.
- _____ Begin networking by contacting friends, faculty members, etc., to inform them of your career plans. If possible, give them a copy of your résumé.

December/January
(8–9 months prior to employment)
- _____ Finalize your résumé and make arrangements for it to be reproduced. You may want to get some tips on résumé reproduction from your college placement office.
- _____ Attend any career planning and placement workshops designed for education majors.
- _____ Use the directories available at your college placement office to develop a list of school systems in which you have an interest
- _____ Contact school systems to request application materials.
- _____ If applying to out-of-state school systems, contact the appropriate State Departments of Education to determine testing requirements.

February
(7 months prior to employment)
- _____ Check the status of your credential or placement file at your college placement office.
- _____ Send completed applications to school systems, with a résumé and cover letter.
- _____ Inquire about school systems which will be recruiting at your college placement office, and about the procedures for interviewing with them.

March/April
(5–6 months prior to employment)
- _____ Research school systems with which you will be interviewing.
- _____ Interview on campus and follow up with thank you letters.
- _____ Continue to follow up by phone with school systems of interest.
- _____ Begin monitoring the job vacancy listings available at your college placement office.

May/August
(1–4 months prior to employment)
- _____ Just before graduation, check to be sure you are completely registered with your college placement office, and that your credential or placement file is in good order.
- _____ Maintain communication with your network of contacts.
- _____ Subscribe to your college placement office's job vacancy bulletin.
- _____ Revise your résumé and cover letter if necessary.
- _____ Interview off campus and follow up with thank you letters.
- _____ If relocating away from campus, contact a college placement office in the area to which you are moving and inquire about available services.
- _____ Continue to monitor job vacancy listings and apply when qualified and interested.
- _____ Begin considering job offers. Ask for more time to consider offers, if necessary.
- _____ Accept the best job offer. Inform those associated with your search of your acceptance.

—Adapted from material originally prepared at Miami University of Ohio.

Source: American Association for Employment in Education (AAEE), _1999 Job Search Handbook for Educators._ Evanston, IL: American Association for Employment in Education, p. 10. The Handbook is available for $8.00 from AAEE.

Appendix 13.4

Résumé Advice for Educators

A modern-day résumé, is a written advertisement focused toward a prospective employer. In a résumé, however, the "product" being advertised is you, the candidate.

Many job applicants become confused about what to include on a résumé. This article covers the most common informational categories, but you should strive to include any information that you feel will enhance your chances of being selected for an interview.

Seeking the "Perfect" Résumé   Just as every individual is different, each résumé presents a distinct combination of skills, abilities, and qualifications about its author. This is why it is impossible to find a perfect sample résumé and simply copy it. Your background is unique, and cannot be found in a book. However, reviewing other résumés will certainly be helpful because they will provide a rich supply of ideas and perspectives for your document.

While the perfect résumé may be an elusive concept, excellent résumés have many characteristics in common. An excellent résumé is one to two pages in length. It is free of typographical errors, produced on high-quality bond paper, accentuates your most salient qualities and qualifications, is organized and easy to read, and conveys a sense of who you are to the reader. This is easier said than done!

You need to remember that in today's job market, school principals are inundated with résumés. One or two pages is about the maximum they are willing to read about each candidate. As a prospective teacher, a résumé with any typographical error is a signal that you are poorly prepared to instruct others, so be sure to have your final document read by others, until all errors are eliminated.

Résumés for teaching and résumés for business have both similarities and differences. Organization, style, appearance, neatness, and punctuation issues apply to both. (If you need help with these issues, you will find useful books on the topic in your institution's career planning and placement office or at local bookstores.) However, educators' résumés typically include additional categories: student teaching, clinical experience, and certification information.

As you work to write the "perfect" résumé you will undoubtedly receive a variety of well-intentioned advice, and some of it will be conflicting. Everyone will have an opinion to offer. One of your most difficult tasks will be to evaluate what you hear. Pursue different opinions, and then decide what makes sense for you.

Statement of Teaching Objective   It is appropriate to include a "Career Objective" or "Teaching Objective" statement on your résumé. While optional, this statement is highly recommended because it helps identify the specific areas in which you wish to teach. Consider the advantages and disadvantages of the following three sample objectives, then develop your own to fit your requirements.

1. Elementary Teaching Position, K–6.
2. Seeking a classroom position in the upper elementary grades that provides an opportunity to facilitate academic, social, and personal growth of students.
3. Secondary or middle school position in science/math, in a suburban location. Qualified and interested in coaching track, volleyball, or swimming.

Objective "A" is descriptive and to the point. However, additional elements are incorporated into examples "B" and "C." Objective "C" is well thought out and developed, although unless you intend to decline all offers other than those in suburban locations, you should avoid using a phrase which defines location too tightly. The reader will assume that you mean what you say.

Student Teaching Information   It is important that beginning teachers provide information about their student teaching experiences. Do not assume that all student teaching experiences are alike, and therefore need not be described. Some principals remain interested in your student teaching experience even after you have several years of professional experience.

Review the two examples below, and then develop a section that accurately portrays your own experience.

1. Northwestern High School
   Rolling Hills, Illinois
   Student Teacher
   Taught 11th grade chemistry and math courses in an open classroom format. Coordinated field study trips, and a "Careers in Science" day.

2. MacKenzie Elementary School
   Chicago, Illinois
   Student Teacher
   September–December, 1995
   Observed, assisted, and taught regular and accelerated classes. Developed daily lesson and unit plans. Assisted in after-school tutoring program. Coordinated a revised parent conference format that increased teacher–parent interaction.
   Refined an existing computer database for classroom record keeping.

Note how the examples include pertinent details of student teaching experiences beyond the routine aspects. it is this information that demonstrates ways in which you made yourself valuable. In your narrative, try to focus on how your presence made something better to make your experience stand out from those who merely developed lesson plans and assisted teachers.

Past Employment Information   Normally, an employer wants to know about your last ten years of professional experience. As a prospective teacher, you should include any experiences in which you worked with K–12-age individuals. Examples of pertinent positions would include camp counselor, teacher's aide, tutor, Scout troop leader, and so forth.

Many candidates dismiss nonteaching experiences as unrelated, and fail to include them on their résumés. However, principals and school administrators can draw valuable inferences regarding your work habits from this information. Dependability, responsibility, and leadership potential are just a few of the desirable traits you can document with information about jobs you have held.

Related Activities and Interests   Information about activities and interests helps you present the image of a well-rounded and versatile teacher. The following categories represent just a few of the areas you may want to include.

- Volunteer activities
- Professional memberships
- Special interests
- Honors and awards
- Committee work
- Training
- Study abroad
- Community involvement
- Fluency in languages other than English

- Computer skills
- Leadership activities
- Professional development activities
- Class projects
- Scholarships

Remember, the more areas of knowledge and expertise that you demonstrate, the more likely you are to become a desirable candidate in the eyes of school administrators. School districts actively seek candidates who are flexible and willing to take on a variety of tasks in the school.

A Few Final Do's and Don't's   Make sure that your résumé is not a jig saw puzzle of unrelated odds and ends, expecting that the principal will be able to piece them together. If those who receive your résumé have to work hard to figure it out, it is likely that they will just move on to the next résumé!

When your résumé is complete, print your final copy on a laser-jet printer, and have copies made at a printing service on high-quality, bond paper. Conservative paper—white, off-white or ivory—is always suitable. Your printing service can help you select a paper which has matching envelopes to enhance you presentation. Be sure to purchase blank paper that matches your résumé so your cover letters will also match your presentation package.

Writing your résumé should be an introspective, exhilarating, positive, pat-yourself-on-the-back experience. If you approach it with this spirit, your résumé will be one of which you are justifiably proud.

Source: Lorn B. Coleman, *1999 Job Search Handbook for Educators.* Evanston, IL: American Association for Employment Education, pp. 16–17. Used with permission.

Appendix 13.5

In your interviews with K–12 school district administrators, it is very important that you know as much as possible about the school, district, and community in which you might be employed. You might want to visit the district while classes are in session to visit the department and building in which you might be working. If at all possible, try to meet the department head and/or building principal by whom you would be supervised. Also, you should be prepared to ask about concerns and issues related to your employment that are of interest to you.

The following are topics about which job applicants typically have questions:

District

- Type of district (elementary, high school, or unit)
- History and development of the district
- Characteristics of the student population and community
- Size of the district (number of elementary, junior high/middle, and high schools)
- Central office administrators and their roles
- Grades included at each level of education

Curriculum

- Courses in the curriculum in your discipline and their content, sequence, prerequisites, and status as electives or required courses
- Typical schedule of courses in the curriculum (first and/or second semester courses)
- Textbook and supplementary materials, the recency of their adoption, and district adoption procedures
- Availability of AV materials and equipment for classroom use
- New and/or innovative curriculum developments in your discipline in recent years
- Curriculum developments currently being planned

Students

- Type and size of student body in which a position is available
- Typical class size
- Procedures for student placement
- Characteristics of entering and exiting students (i.e., number or percentage who are enrolled in vocational and college preparatory curricula and the number or percentage who enroll in college on graduation)

Instructional Assignment

- Reasons why the position is available (enrollment increase, retirement, resignation, etc.)
- Number and type of teaching preparations (i.e., self-contained classes or team-taught classes)
- Other instructional assignments
- Methods and frequency of teacher evaluation
- Availability of summer employment
- Assignments on department, school, or district committees
- Duties in the supervision/sponsorship of student activities
- Starting and ending dates of employment
- Contract length

Faculty

- Number of administrators in the building and their responsibilities
- Size of the faculty within departments and the building
- Number of new teachers hired each year
- Special interests and/or expertise of faculty

Student Services

- Student clubs, organizations, and sports
- Counselling and guidance personnel and services
- Social worker, school nurse, librarian, and other support staff and their roles

Community

- Community support for education
- Involvement of parents and other community members in the school program
- Recreational and other facilities in the community
- Demographic information about community residents
- Cost of living and housing in the community

Salary And Fringe Benefits

- District salary schedule
- Pay for extracurricular responsibilities
- Reimbursement policies for graduate study
- District requirements for continuing professional education

- Vacation and sick leave, personal leave, and other leave policies
- Substitute teacher procedures
- Payroll schedule
- Medical insurance

Selection Procedures

- Number and type of interviews that job candidates can expect
- Individuals involved in the preliminary screening of candidates, interviews, and the final selection

- District requirements for residency of staff

Final Suggestions

- Be certain to read your employment contract carefully before signing it.

Source: Jan E. Kilby, *The ASCUS Annual 1988: A Job Search Handbook for Educators.* Addison, IL: Association for School, College and University Staffing, p. 16. Used with permission.

Appendix 13.6

Congratulations! You've completed your teacher education training program, become certified, and been offered a teaching position! As you begin your assignment, it is essential to keep in mind that successful teachers possess skills in many areas: teaching ability, content knowledge, interpersonal relations and communications, and those nebulous areas—"etiquette, politics and culture."

Etiquette, Politics and Culture What do those words—*etiquette, politics, and culture*—mean, and what impact do they have on first-year teachers? Some refer to these as the "informal structure" of schools, the "rites of passage" that new teachers must experience.

- Every school has formal and informal cultures and political structures. Learn about these structures as soon as possible. Become acquainted with the informal leaders. The sooner you understand the established culture at the school—whether it is participating in football pools, sitting at a particular table at lunch, or joining in after school activities—the sooner you will be considered effective and involved.

- Watch, listen, learn to ask questions! Know who to ask! Frequently, colleagues are available for assistance during those first days of school, but once classes begin, you may be left on your own. Ask for help, watch what others do, and be an intuitive observer.

- Seek a mentor. New teachers all need someone to turn to for guidance and support. Identify another teacher you respect and like, and ask that teacher to provide information, counselling, and encouragement.

- Volunteer! Join the PTA, work at the school carnival, chaperone a school dance. Become involved with curriculum committees. You'll get to meet many people this way, and your fellow teachers will respect your involvement.

- Volunteer, but don't be "pushy," and don't intrude. Be available as others invite you into the group.

- Distinguish between the "good guys" and the "bad guys." Identify the positive staff members and join their team. Avoid the complaining, negative teachers. When you walk into the teacher's lounge and hear a teaching colleague criticizing the principal or ridiculing a student, walk the other way!

- Be a role model for students. Yes, students may need friends, but you're more than that— you're their teacher. Have well-prepared lessons, be fair and consistent, and provide a positive learning environment.

- Be professional—look the part and act the part. Work on your wardrobe. Weed out the casual, informal clothes that make you look like a college—or high school—student. Exude an aura of dependability and professionalism.

- Accept the fact that you're the expert! Remember, you are the teacher. Parents and students look to you as the one with all the answers. Don't let them down!

- Be open, yet sensitive, in dealing with parents. Whenever you talk to a mom or a dad about one of their children, you are talking about an extension of their very beings. Understand that they may be very sensitive and may react emotionally about little Johnny or Susie. Be clear and concise, but tactful and kind.

- Watch what you say and where you say it. Be honest and open, but sensitive to the informal culture of the school. Don't criticize the school secretary to an aide who may be her best friend. Don't complain about a student in the faculty lounge. Don't talk about school problems in the grocery store.

Meet the Challenge New teachers face the challenges of discipline and classroom management, motivation of students, assessment of students' needs and abilities, heavy teaching loads, insufficient preparation time, and building appropriate relationships with fellow teachers, administrators, and parents. However, beginning teachers often have the most difficulty adjusting to the emotional rigors—the politics and etiquette—of the job. Remember:

- Focus on the positive; avoid the negative.
- Teaching can be lonely; find a friend.
- Be patient—wisdom takes time to acquire.
- Learn to love teaching!
- Be the best you can be!

The job of teaching is an incredibly challenging one. You will need to give a total commitment to your role as a teacher. But don't confuse something that's difficult with something that's negative. The excitement of teaching is embodied in hard work, meeting challenges, and accomplishing goals.

As time passes (and with help from others), you will learn to work more efficiently and figure out easier and better ways to do those things that at first seemed so difficult. You will have mastered the school's formal and informal structures!

Accept the challenge—be your best—and you'll find that you will be appreciated, respected, and perhaps even loved! You are a teacher—there is no better or more rewarding career!

Source: Mary Lee Howe in American Association for Employment in Education, *1995 Job Search Handbook for Educators*, Evanston, IL: Association for School, College and University Staffing, Inc., p. 31. Used with permission.

14

Education Issues for the Twenty-First Century

At the turn of the century, more and more educators are working in a world of intensifying and rapid change. . . . New technologies, greater cultural diversity, the skills called for in a changing economy, restructured approaches to administration and management, and a more sophisticated knowledge-base about teaching and learning, are all pulling students and their teachers in new directions.

— Mission Statement excerpt
International Centre for Educational Change
Ontario Institute for Studies in Education
University of Toronto

focus questions

1. What knowledge and skills will prepare students for a global information age?

2. How can schools and teachers provide an outstanding education for all learners?

3. How can community-based partnerships address social problems that hinder students' learning?

4. How will the privatization movement affect equity and excellence in education?

5. What can teachers and schools learn from international education?

6. What is our vision for the future of education?

How will education change during the twenty-first century? What new school–community linkages will help schools meet the needs of all learners? In what ways will teachers' professional lives become more collaborative and oriented toward systemwide reform? How likely is it that, as a teacher, you will have experiences similar to the following?

After a short drive through early-morning traffic less heavy than usual, you arrive at school in time for a 7:30 A.M. meeting of your school's Teacher Leadership Team (TLT), a group that makes curricular and instructional decisions for the school. The TLT also works directly with the school's Site-Based Council (SBC), which makes budget, personnel, and other policy decisions. SBC members include three teachers, the principal, five community members, and two professors from a nearby university.

Like most schools around the country, the changing demographics of the nation are reflected in an increasingly diverse student population at your school. About 15 percent of students are from families who live below the poverty line, and one in eight students is identified as limited-English speaking. According to a district survey, students represent eighteen different languages. Overall, students at your school score in the top percentiles on state and national standardized tests; 80 percent of students go on to college, and 15 percent enroll in other forms of postsecondary programs. Within the last five years, the school has been designated twice by the state as a Blue Ribbon school.

With a few minutes before the meeting begins, you enter the classroom of another TLT member. Both of you were selected to be part of a nationwide network of teachers who will field test an interactive computer simulation developed by an instructional technology laboratory at a major university. Last week you both received the beta-test (trial) software, field-test guidelines, and registration materials for a four-day preparatory workshop to be held at the university. The university is paying for travel plus expenses, as well as providing a stipend.

"Well, did you have a chance to try out the software?" you ask upon entering the room. "I did last night, and it looks pretty impressive. I'm anxious to see what the kids think."

"I haven't had a chance yet; I've been preparing for this morning's TLT meeting," your friend says, pausing momentarily as she staples handouts arranged in neat stacks on top of her desk. Last spring she was elected to be one of the school's two curriculum coordinators. At today's TLT meeting, she and the other coordinator are presenting a model for schoolwide curriculum integration. "What do we have to do as field testers?" she asks, continuing with her stapling task. "I just glanced at the field-test guidelines."

"Well, actually quite a lot, but I think it'll be interesting," you say. "The lab wants us to use the software every day for three weeks. Also, collect student performance data on a regular basis and samples of students' work. Plus, students will complete a survey at the beginning and at the end of the field test. That's about it . . . oh, I forgot, they want us to do some student interviews . . . there's a set of constructivist-oriented questions we're supposed to use. Basically, the lab wants us to develop a picture of students' problem-solving strategies as they work through the simulation."

"That does sound interesting," your friend says.

"Right. Well, I better get out of here and let you finish getting ready for the TLT meeting," you say.

Walking down the hallway to the conference room, you think about how satisfying it is to teach at your school. Teachers are hard-working and share a strong commitment to good teaching and to building a collegial professional community. Ample leadership opportunities, common planning periods, stimulating colleagues who are professionally involved, and solid support from the district and community are just a few of the factors that make working conditions at your school very positive.

Though no one has an educational crystal ball that can give a totally accurate glimpse of how the profession of teaching will evolve during the twenty-first century and how students will be taught, powerful forces are shaping schools and teaching in the directions just outlined. Moreover, thousands of teachers are collaborating and playing key leadership roles in shaping that future; and, today, hundreds of schools have professional communities identical to that described in the preceding scenario. We believe that the conditions under which teachers will work in this century will provide a dramatic contrast to those that many teachers experienced throughout much of the previous century. Isolation, lack of autonomy and self-governance, and few chances for professional growth are being replaced by collaboration, empowerment, stronger professionalism, and opportunities to provide leadership for educational change.

What Knowledge and Skills Will Prepare Students for a Global Information Age?

What knowledge and skills will students need to succeed in a global information age? Teachers in every generation have asked that question. At the beginning of the twenty-first century, the answer is confounded by conflicting theories, expectations, and values. One thing everyone agrees on, however, is that increasing cultural diversity in the United States and other countries and increasing global economic interdependence will call for communication and cooperation skills. People will need to be able to live together well and use environmental resources wisely. To equip students to do this, teachers will need to dedicate themselves to ensuring that all students develop knowledge, skills, attitudes, and values in nine key areas (see Figure 14.1). Though these nine areas of learning will not be all that students will need, learning in these areas will best enable them to meet the challenges of the future.

Literacy in Language, Mathematics, and Science

To solve the problems of the future, students will need to be able to write and speak clearly and succinctly. To access critical information from enormous data banks, they will need to be able to read complex material with a high degree of comprehension. Moreover, the continued development of "user-friendly" technologies such as voice-activated computers and reading machines will not reduce the need for high-level language arts literacy. As Sue Walters, a junior high school

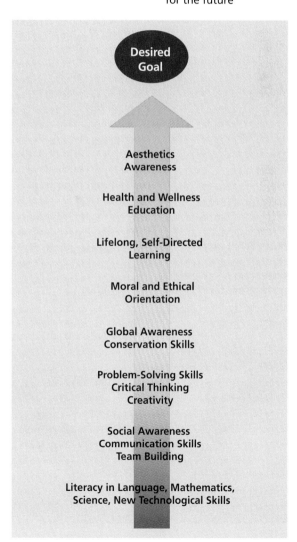

Figure 14.1

Educational priorities for the future

Desired Goal

Aesthetics Awareness

Health and Wellness Education

Lifelong, Self-Directed Learning

Moral and Ethical Orientation

Global Awareness Conservation Skills

Problem-Solving Skills Critical Thinking Creativity

Social Awareness Communication Skills Team Building

Literacy in Language, Mathematics, Science, New Technological Skills teacher in Kennebunk, Maine, told the prestigious Council of 21, a group of leaders in business, government, and education chaired by Senator John Glenn: "Reading, writing, and math are needed for continued learning and should not be lost in our race toward the future" (American Association of School Administrators 1999, 29). Students will also need to be able to apply mathematical and scientific concepts to solve new problems. For example, they will need to be able to analyze unfamiliar situations, pose appropriate questions, use trial-and-error methods to gather and evaluate relevant data, and summarize results.

New Technological Skills

Students of the future will also need to attain high levels of skill in computer-based technologies. To teach students skills in accessing the vast stores of information that computers routinely handle today, our nation's schools will become more technologically rich and teachers more technologically sophisticated. No longer able to resist the "irresistible force" of Information Age technology (Mehlinger 1996), schools will join the larger society where "the computer is a symbol of the future and all that is good about it" (Morton 1996, 417). In such an environment, students will not only learn to use computers as "tools" to access information—they will use computers to communicate worldwide and to generate creative solutions to real-world problems.

Problem Solving, Critical Thinking, and Creativity

What knowledge and skills for the twenty-first century does this learning activity support? What else will students need to know and be able to do in the future?

Students of the future will need to be able to think rather than to remember. Although the information that students learn in schools may become outdated or useless, the thinking processes they acquire will not. These processes focus on the ability to find, obtain, and use information resources for solving problems or taking advantage of opportunities. Students will need to learn how to cope with change, how to anticipate alternative future developments, how to think critically, and how to analyze and synthesize large amounts of complex data.

Forecasts about the future share one thing in common—they place a priority on creative thinking to solve future problems. The acquisition of structured bodies of knowledge, while important, is not sufficient preparation for the future. Students must learn to think creatively to solve unforeseen problems. Students who are stretched to develop their creativity today will become the adults who invent ways to solve tomorrow's problems.

Can creative thinking be taught? William J. J. Gordon (1968, 1971a, 1971b, 1975), who has devoted his career to the study of creativity, believes it can. Gordon developed synectics, a teaching method based on the thinking process that is designed to "teach" creativity through the use of metaphor and analogy. **Synectics** is based on the assumptions that (1) creativity is important; (2) creativity is not mysterious; (3) in all fields, creative invention draws from the same underlying intellectual processes; and (4) the creativity of individuals and groups is similar (Joyce, Weil, and Calhoun 2000).

Social Awareness, Communication Skills, and Team Building

Tomorrow's students must be able to communicate with people from diverse cultures. The ability to create a better world in the future, then, will surely depend on our willingness to celebrate our rich diversity through the kind of communication that leads to understanding, friendly social relations, and the building of cohesive teams. "[T]he classroom should be a laboratory for collaborative decision making and team building" (Uchida, Cetron, and McKenzie 1996, 8).

An important lesson for students will be to learn that poverty, discrimination, violence, crime, and unequal opportunities, wherever they occur, affect us all. To solve these and other social problems, students will need to become socially aware, politically active, and skilled in conflict resolution strategies.

Global Awareness and Conservation Skills

Tomorrow's students will need to recognize the interconnectedness they share with all countries and with all people. Our survival may depend on being able to participate intelligently in a global economy and respond intelligently to global threats to security, health, environmental quality, and other factors affecting the quality of human life. The curriculum of the future must emphasize cultural diversity, interdependence, respect for the views and values held by others, an orientation toward international cooperation for resolving global issues, and practical knowledge and skills on, for example, the conservation of natural energy resources.

Health and Wellness Education

With ever-increasing health care costs, the spread of diseases such as AIDS, increased risks of cancer, and longer life spans, it is imperative that students of the future acquire appropriate knowledge, skills, and attitudes in the area of health education. To live healthy lives, then, students of tomorrow will need consumer education to select from among an increasingly complex array of health care services. In addition, they will need to be able to make informed choices among alternatives for the prevention or treatment of problems relating to substance abuse, nutrition, fitness, and mental health. Sex education, still a matter for debate in some communities, seems more critical today than at any time in the past.

Moral and Ethical Orientation

The school culture and the curriculum reflect both national and community values. The traditional practice of using values-clarification activities in the classroom, however, has been criticized by some for promoting relativism at the expense of family values or religious doctrines. Yet, as we witness the effects of violence in schools, gang warfare, racial violence, sexual exploitation of children, drunk driving, white-collar crime, false advertising, unethical business practices, excessive litigation, and so on, many citizens are calling for schools to pay more attention to issues of public morality and ethical behavior. "[T]o survive and prosper in the twenty-first century, students will need self-discipline, which entails an ethical code and the ability to set and assess progress toward their own goals" (Uchida, Cetron, and McKenzie 1996, 17). In response to harassment and intimidation that can lead to violence in the hallways, for example, many schools have implemented anger management programs similar to the Second Step program created by the Seattle-Based Committee for Children. According to a teacher at a school that begins the year with Second Step lessons for all students, "We have created a culture in our school that says we all recognize that some things just aren't accepted" (Gutloff 1999).

Aesthetics Awareness

Another challenge for teachers and schools is to encourage creativity and greater appreciation for the arts. Many observers of U.S. education point out that emotional, spiritual, aesthetic, and reflective, or meditative, dimensions of life receive less emphasis than analytical thinking and practical life skills. Although literature and drama are standard fare in curricula, most students know little, for example, about music, painting, and sculpture. Public school students are rarely taught art history or principles of design or other criteria for evaluating creative works. As a result, students may lack the concepts and experiences that lead to an appreciation of beauty and the development of aesthetic judgment.

Lifelong, Self-Directed Learning

The key educational priority that should guide teachers of the future is to create within each student the ability, and the desire, to continue self-directed learning throughout his or her life.

It has often been said that one of the primary purposes of schooling is for students to learn how to learn. In a world characterized by rapid social, technological, economic, and political changes, all persons must take responsibility for their own learning. Career changes will be the norm, and continuing education over a lifetime will be necessary.

How Can Schools and Teachers Provide an Outstanding Education for All Learners?

Although we don't know exactly how teaching will change during the twenty-first century, we do know that teachers will continue to have a professional and moral obligation to reach all learners, many of whom will be from environments that provide little support for education. Imagine, for example, that one of your students is Dolores, described in the following scenario.

> Fifteen-year-old Dolores and her twin brother, Frank, live with their mother in a housing project in a poor section of the city. Their mother divorced her third husband two years ago, after she learned that he had been sexually abusing Dolores. Since then, Dolores' mother has been struggling to make ends meet with her job as a custodian at a hospital. Two evenings a week, she goes to a neighborhood center to learn English. She hopes to become proficient enough in English to get a job as a secretary.

Dolores wishes her mother and Frank didn't fight so much. The fights usually revolve around Frank missing school and his drinking. Just last night, for example, Frank came home drunk and he and his mother got into another big fight. When she accused him of being involved in a street gang, Frank stormed out and went to spend the night at his cousin's apartment two blocks away.

At 6:30 that morning, Dolores awoke just as her mother left for work. The hinges on the apartment door, painted over by a careless maintenance worker, creaked loudly as she closed the door behind her. Dolores felt reassured by the sound of her mother locking the dead bolt—the apartment beneath them had been burglarized last week. Like Frank, she wasn't getting along well with her mother lately, so it would be nice to have the apartment to herself while she got ready for school.

Dolores got up slowly, stretched, and looked around the cluttered livingroom of the one-bedroom apartment. Her mother slept in the bedroom, and Frank, when he wasn't out all night or at his cousin's, slept on the other couch in the living room.

She had trouble sleeping last night. Now that it was winter, the radiator next to the beige couch on which she slept clanked and hissed most of the night. Also, she was worried—two weeks ago a doctor at the neighborhood clinic confirmed that she was pregnant. Yesterday, she finally got up enough courage to tell her boyfriend. He got angry at her and said he "wasn't gonna be no father."

Dolores knew she ought to be seeing a doctor, but she dreaded going to the clinic alone. Her mother took a day off from work—without pay—when she went two weeks ago. Right after that, her mother complained about missing work and said, "Don't expect me to take off from work every time you go to the clinic. You should have thought about that before you got in trouble."

Later that morning, Dolores is in your class, sitting in her usual spot in the middle of the back row. While your students work on an in-class writing assignment, you glance at Dolores and wonder why she hasn't been paying attention during the last few weeks like she usually does. At that moment, Dolores, wearing the same clothes she wore yesterday, stifles a yawn.

As you continue to move about the room, checking on students' progress and answering an occasional question, you wonder if you should talk with Dolores after class. You don't want to pry into her life outside of school, but you're worried about what might be causing her to act differently.

Although the family will continue to remain a prominent part of our culture, evidence indicates that many children, like Dolores and Frank, live in families that are under acute stress. Soaring numbers of runaway children and cases of child abuse suggest that the family is in trouble. In addition, teachers will continue to find that more and more of their students are from families that are smaller, have working mothers, have a single parent present, or have unrelated adults living in the home.

Equity for All Students

A dominant political force in the twenty-first century will be continued demands for equity in all sectors of U.S. life, particularly education. For example, the constitutionality of school funding laws will be challenged where inequities are perceived, and tax reform measures will be adopted to promote equitable school funding. Classroom teachers will continue to be held accountable for treating all students equitably.

In Chapter 7, you learned about the importance of preparing multicultural instructional materials and strategies to meet the learning needs of students from diverse cul-

An Exemplary School

The following case describes a prototypical exemplary urban elementary school, "Paul Robeson Elementary School," as compiled by Gloria Ladson-Billings, award-winning researcher and author of *Dreamkeepers: Successful Teachers of African American Children.* Not a futuristic school, the school is an example for today—incorporating the best practices and perspectives that Ladson-Billings observed in eight classrooms that she studied over a two-year period. Consider Ladson-Billings' Robeson School as presented and then project it twenty years into the future. How might it be different and even better?

Paul Robeson Elementary School is located in a low-income predominantly African American community. More than merely a school, Robeson is a neighborhood center and gathering place that is open from 6:00 A.M. to 10:00 P.M. It includes a daycare center, a preschool, a health clinic, and a job training center. Local civic and church groups use the school as a meeting place. If one needs information about the community, the school is the likely place to locate it.

The banner across the main hallway of the school reads, "It takes a whole village to educate a child." Robeson's teaching staff is multicultural. There are African American, Latino, Asian American, and white teachers. However, every credentialed adult at Robeson, not just the teachers, teaches a class—the principal, the counselor, the special teachers. This means that classes are relatively small—twelve to fifteen students. There are no "pull out" programs, such as those used by many federally funded programs that require students to be taken out of their regular classrooms to receive remedial instruction while simultaneously depriving them of the instruction that is occurring in the regular class. There is no separate "special day" class for students evaluated as learning-disabled. Instead, students with learning disabilities are integrated into the regular classrooms and receive additional attention with the help of teachers' aides, the classroom teacher, and more advanced peers.

Robeson has one requirement—that its students be successful. The curriculum is rigorous and exciting. The student learning is organized around problems and issues. For example, one fourth-grade class is studying how cities develop. The students have studied cities in ancient African kingdoms, Europe, and Asia. They are studying their own city. They have taken trips to City Hall and have seen the City council in action. The mayor visited their classroom. In current events they read about the city news. Groups of students are working on solutions to problems specific to their city. The problems include the city's budget deficit, homelessness, the poor conditions of roads, and crime—particularly drug-related crime.

The students have read Carl Sandburg's poetry about his beloved Chicago. They have studied architecture—buildings and bridges. They have studied geography and urban planning. They have written letters to the editor of a city newspaper about conditions in the city and in their neighborhood. Each student is an "expert" in some aspect of cities. Together they are planning an exhibition that will be shown in the evening so that their parents and other community members can attend.

All students at Robeson Elementary participate in a community service program. The students in the primary grades usually participate as a class group. Community service activities include visiting a local nursing home, where students participate in the Adopt-a-Grandparent program. They also participate in neighborhood cleanup days and recycling drives. The older students develop their own community service projects, which are approved by their teachers. They usually work in small groups or in pairs. Occasionally, an intermediate class will take on a project such as becoming readers at the local library, volunteering in the pediatric ward of the hospital, and planting and maintaining a community garden.

Parents play an important role at Robeson. Each household is assessed twenty hours of volunteer service to the school. Some volunteer one hour a week in the classroom. Others participate in the school's Artists and Scholars in Residence program. Parents who participate in the local church choir offer their musical skills. Others share their cooking, sewing, knitting, woodworking, or athletic talents.

School governance at Robeson involves the principal, the teachers, the parents, and the students. The school council meets once a month to discuss the curriculum, instruction, personnel, and finances. The council members determine school policy and hiring and firing issues, and they constitute the school's disciplinary board.

One of Robeson's unique qualities is its residence program. By working with local social-service agencies Robeson obtained use of a renovated small apartment building nearby to house students whose family lives are in turmoil. Under the best circumstances students spend only a short time at the residence; in some unfortunate cases they spend the entire year there. By living in a center in their own community, they do not have to leave Robeson or the neighborhood they know. The residence is not for students with disciplinary problems. It is designed simply to alleviate family stresses.

As a testament to the success of Robeson Elementary School, its students score above the national norm on standardized tests, but Robeson does not make a fuss over its test score performance. The school community knows that in a caring, supportive environment where all of the children are made to feel special, test scores are but one of the marks of accomplishment that can be expected.

Questions

1. What features of this school are exemplary?

2. What societal problems are addressed by the school? How?

3. Do you agree with the school's perspective on test scores? Why or why not?

4. How would you add to this exemplary school to make it an ideal school for the year 2020?

5. Design your own ideal school, making it a rural, urban, suburban, or virtual school in the year 2020.

Source: Reprinted with permission from Gloria Ladson-Billings, *The Dreamkeepers: Successful Teachers of African American Children.* San Francisco, Jossey-Bass, 1994. Selection from pp. 140–42.

tural, ethnic, and linguistic backgrounds. In Chapter 8, you learned how to create an inclusive classroom to meet the needs of all students, regardless of their developmental levels, intelligences, abilities, or disabilities. In addition, you should create a learning environment in which high-achieving and low-achieving students are treated the same. Thomas Good and Jere Brophy (2000) reviewed the research in this area and found that several teacher behaviors indicated unequal treatment of students. The behaviors identified include waiting less time for them to answer questions, interacting with them less frequently, giving less feedback, calling on them less often, seating them farther way, failing to accept and use their ideas, smiling at them less often, making less eye contact, praising them less, demanding less, grading their tests differently, and rewarding inappropriate behaviors.

Effective teachers establish respectful relationships with *all* students; they listen to them; they give frequent feedback and opportunities to ask questions; and they demand higher-level performance. In their assessment of student's learning, they give special attention to the questions they ask of students. Research indicates that most questions teachers ask are **lower-order questions,** those that assess students' abilities to recall specific information. Effective teachers, however, also ask **higher-order questions** that demand more critical thinking and answers to questions such as, Why? What if . . . ? In addition, to reach all learners and prepare them for the future, effective teachers provide students with active, authentic learning experiences.

Active, Authentic Learning

Since the 1970s, educational researchers have increased our understanding of the learning process. Though learning theorists and researchers disagree about a definition for *learning,* most agree that **learning** "occurs when experience causes a relatively permanent change in an individual's knowledge or behavior" (Woolfolk 1998, 204). Research into multiple intelligences and multicultural learning modes has broadened our understanding of this definition of learning. In addition, research in the fields of neurophysiology, neuropsychology, and cognitive science will continue to expand our understanding of how people think and learn.

Our growing understanding of learning indicates that all students learn best when they are actively involved in authentic activities that connect with the "real world." Small-group activities, cooperative learning arrangements, field trips, experiments, and integrated curricula are among the instructional methods you should incorporate into your professional repertoire.

How Can Community-Based Partnerships Address Social Problems That Hinder Students' Learning?

Earlier in this book, we examined social problems that affect schools and place students at risk of dropping out: poverty, family stress, substance abuse, violence and crime, teen pregnancy, HIV/AIDS, and suicide (see Chapter 4). We also looked at intervention programs schools have developed to ensure the optimum behavioral, social, and academic adjustment of at-risk children and adolescents to their school experiences: peer counseling, full-service schools, school-based interprofessional case management, compensatory education, and alternative schools and curricula. Here, we describe innovative, community-based partnerships that some schools have developed recently to prevent social problems from hindering students' learning.

The range of school-community partnerships found in today's schools is extensive. For example, as the "Interactive Organizational Model" in Figure 14.2 illustrates, Exeter High School in suburban Toronto has developed partnerships with 13 community organizations and more than 100 employers. Through Exeter's Partners in Learning program, business, industry, service clubs, and social service agencies make significant contributions to students' learning.

The Community as a Resource for Schools

To assist schools in addressing the social problems that impact students, many communities are acting in the spirit of a recommendation made by Ernest Boyer: "Perhaps the time has come to organize, in every community, not just a *school* board, but a *children's* board. The goal would be to integrate children's services and build, in every community, a friendly, supportive environment for children" (Boyer 1995, 169). In partnerships between communities and schools, individuals, civic organizations, or businesses select a school or are selected by a school to work together for the good of students. The ultimate goals of such projects are to provide students with better school experiences and to assist students at risk.

Civic Organizations   To develop additional sources of funding, many local school districts have established partnerships with community groups interested in improving educational opportunities in the schools. Some groups raise money for schools. The American Jewish Committee and the Urban League raised funds for schools in Pittsburgh, for example. Other partners adopt or sponsor schools and enrich their educational programs by providing funding, resources, or services.

Volunteer Mentor Programs   Mentorship is a trend in community-based partnerships today, especially with students at risk. Parents, business leaders, professionals, and peers volunteer to work with students in neighborhood schools. Goals might include dropout prevention, high achievement, improved self-esteem, and healthy decision making. Troubleshooting on lifestyle issues often plays a role, especially in communities plagued by drug dealing, gang rivalry, casual violence, and crime. Mentors also model success.

Some mentor programs target particular groups. For instance, the Concerned Black Men (CBM), a Washington, DC–based organization with fifteen chapters around the country, targets inner-city African American male youth. More than 500 African American men in diverse fields and from all walks of life participate as CBM mentors to students in area schools. Their goal is to serve as positive adult male role models for youth, many of whom live only with their mothers or grandmothers and lack male teachers in school. To date, CBM has given cash awards and scholarships to more than 4,000 youth selected on the basis of high academic achievement, motivation, leadership in academic and nonacademic settings, and community involvement.

Corporate-Education Partnerships   Business involvement in schools has taken many forms, including, for example, contributions of funds or materials needed by a school, release time for employees to visit classrooms, adopt-a-school programs, cash grants for pilot projects and teacher development, educational use of corporate facilities and expertise, employee participation, student scholarship programs, and political lobbying for school reform. Extending beyond advocacy, private sector efforts include job ini-

Student Activities and Clubs

- Ambassadors
- Art
- Band/Choir/Chamber
- Band/Stage Band
- Bowling
- Chess
- Culinary
- Design
- Drama
- Fish-On
- Interact (Junior Rotarians)
- Math Clinic
- OSAID
- Outers
- Sign Language
- Ski
- Squash
- Technology
- Weight Training
- Welding
- Woodworking
- Youth Alive

Support Staff

- Secretarial
- LAN Administrator
- Custodial

Departments

- Art
- Business
- English
- Family Studies
- Geography
- History
- Library Media
- Mathematics
- Modems
- Music
- Physical & Health Education
- Science
- Technology
- Special Education
- Student Services
- Work Education

Community Groups

- Exeter Citizenship
- Exeter Intergenerational
- Tech Advisory
- Music Advisory
- OISE/U of T
- Ontario Hydro
- Durham Regional Police
- C.A.M.C.
- McDonalds
- Durham Health and the Youth Council
- Rogers Cablesystem
- School Town
- Library
- Bell Canada
- Pioneers
- Over 100 employers for Work Education Program

MISSION STATEMENT

Exeter High School is committed to excellence through innovative academic and technological programming within a culture of mutual respect, community involvement, and partnerships.

School Growth Team

Administration Team

Department Heads

Student Council

School Community Council

Student Athletic Associations

- Alpine Skiing
- Archery
- Badminton
- Baseball
- Cross Country Running
- GoH
- Field Hockey
- Hockey
- Soccer
- Softball
- Swimming
- Tennis
- Track & Field
- Volleyball
- Wrestling

Task Forces

- Integrated Curriculum
- Curriculum Focus Day
- Exam Scheduling
- Staff Supervision

Committees

- Ethnocultural
- P.D.
- Beautification
- Safe Schools
- Wellness
- Evaluation
- Specialization Years
- Public Relations
- Site Management Team
- Schoolwide Action Research
- Health & Safety
- New Teachers
- Computers

Activity Groups

- Breakfast Club
- Food and Toy Drive
- Graduation/Junior Awards
- Open House
- Picture Day
- Sunshine Club
- Transition Years
- United Way
- School Profile
- Citizenship
- Intergenerational
- Yearbook

Liason Groups

- Group 1
- Group 2
- Group 3
- Group 4
- Group 5
- Group 6
- Group 7
- Group 8

Figure 14.2

Exeter High School interactive organizational model

Source: Gordon Cawelti, *Portraits of Six Benchmark Schools: Diverse Approaches to Improving Student Achievement.* Arlington, VA: Educational Research Service, 1999, p. 32. Used with permission.

tiatives for disadvantaged youths, inservice programs for teachers, management training for school administrators, minority education and faculty development, and even construction of school buildings.

Business-sponsored school experiments focus on creating model schools, laboratory schools, or alternative schools that address particular local needs. In Minneapolis, for example, the General Mills Foundation has provided major funding to create the Minneapolis Federation of Alternative Schools (MFAS), a group of several schools designed to serve students who have not been successful in regular school programs. The goals for students who attend MFAS schools include returning to regular school when appropriate, graduating from high school, and/or preparing for postsecondary education or employment.

In addition to contributing more resources to education, chief executive officers and their employees are donating more time; 83 percent of the top managers surveyed by a recent *Fortune* poll said they "participate actively" in educational reform, versus 70 percent in 1990. At Eastman Kodak's Rochester, New York, plant, for example, hundreds of employees serve as tutors or mentors in local schools. In some dropout prevention programs, businessmen and businesswomen adopt individual students, visiting them at school, eating lunch with them once a week, meeting their families, and taking them on personal field trips.

Schools as Resources for Communities

A shift from the more traditional perspective of schools needing support from the community to meet the needs of students whose lives are impacted by social problems is the view that schools should serve as multipurpose resources *for* the community. By focusing not only on the development of children and youth, but on their families as well, schools ultimately enhance the ability of students to learn. As Ernest Boyer (1995, 168) put it, "No arbitrary line can be drawn between the school and life outside. Every [school] should take the lead in organizing a *referral service*—a community safety net for children that links students and their families to support agencies in the region—to clinics, family support and counseling centers, and religious institutions."

Beyond the School Day   Many schools and school districts are serving their communities by providing educational and recreational programs before and after the traditional school day and during the summers. Increasingly, educational policymakers recognize that the traditional school year of approximately 180 days is not the best arrangement to meet students' learning needs. As the RCM Research Corporation, a nonprofit group that studies issues in educational change, points out: "Historically, time has been the glue that has bonded the traditions of our public school system—i.e., the Carnegie units, equal class periods, no school during summer months, 12 years of schooling, etc.—and, as a result, the use of time has become sacrosanct, 'We have always done it this way!' How time is used by schools often has more to do with administrative convenience than it does with what is best educationally for the student" (RCM Research Corporation 1998).

Proposals for year-round schools and educationally oriented weekend and after-school programs address the educational and developmental needs of students impacted by social problems. According to the San Diego–based National Association for Year-Round Education, more than 2,800 public schools now extend their calendars into the summer, and more than two million students go to school year-round. In Austin, Texas, for example, schools can participate in an Optional Extended Year (OEY) program that allows them to provide additional instruction in reading and mathematics to students at risk of being retained a grade. Schools participating in OEY can choose from among four school day options: (1) extended day, (2) extended week, (3) intersession of year-round schools, and (4) summer school (Idol 1998; Washington 1998). Futurist Marvin Cetron predicts that, soon, "schools will educate and train both children and adults around the clock: the academic day will stretch to seven hours for children; adults will work a 32-hour week and prepare for their next job in the remaining time" (Uchida, Cetron, and McKenzie 1996, 35).

Programs that extend beyond the traditional school day also address the needs of parents and the requirements of the work world. More than two million elementary-age, "latchkey" children come home to an empty home every afternoon, according to Census Bureau figures. As an elementary teacher in Missouri said, "Many of my students just hang around at the end of every day. They ask what they can do to help me. Often there's no one at home, and they're afraid to go home or spend time on the streets" (Boyer 1995, 165).

After-school educational and recreational programs are designed to (1) provide children with supervision at times when they might become involved in antisocial activities, (2) provide enrichment experiences to widen children's perspectives and increase their socialization, and (3) improve the academic achievement of children not achieving at their potential during regular school hours (Fashola 1999). Ernest Boyer argued that schools should adapt their schedules to those of the workplace so that parents could become more involved in their children's education, and that businesses, too, should give parents more flexible work schedules. Drawing on the model of Japan, Boyer suggested that the beginning of the school year could be a holiday to free parents to attend opening day ceremonies and celebrate the launching and continuation of education in the same way that we celebrate its ending.

For several years, the After-School Plus (A+) Program in Hawaii has operated afternoon enrichment programs from 2:00 to 5:00 for children in kindergarten through sixth grade. The children, who are free to do art, sports, drama, or homework, develop a sense of *ohana*, or feeling of belonging (Cohen 1990, 1). Since the mid-1970s, schools in Buena Vista, Virginia, have operated according to a Four Seasons Calendar that includes an optional summer enrichment program. Buena Vista's superintendent estimates that the district saves more than $100,000 a year on retention costs; though some students take more time, they are promoted to the next grade (Boyer 1995).

Although some research indicates that extended school days and school calendars have a positive influence on achievement (Gandara and Fish 1994; Center for Research on Effective Schooling for Disadvantaged Students 1992), the Center for Research on the Education of Students Placed at Risk (CRESPAR) at Johns Hopkins University concluded that "there is no straightforward answer to the question of what works best in after-school programs" (Fashola 1999). According to CRESPAR, few studies of the effects of after-school programs on measures such as achievement or reduction of antisocial behavior meet minimal standards for research design. Nevertheless, CRESPAR found that after-school programs with stronger evidence of effectiveness had four elements: training for staff, program structure, evaluation of program effectiveness, and planning that includes families and children (Fashola 1999).

Social Services In response to the increasing number of at-risk and violence-prone children and youth, many schools are also providing an array of social services to students, their families, and their communities. The following comments by three female students highlight the acute need for support services for at-risk youth who can turn to aggression and violence in a futile attempt to bolster their fragile self-esteem and to cope with the pain in their lives. All three girls have been involved in violent altercations in and around their schools, and all three frequently use alcohol and illegal drugs.

Fifteen-year-old "Mary" has been physically abused by both her father and mother, and she was raped when she was fourteen. "Linda," also fifteen years old, was sexually molested during a four-year period by a family acquaintance, and she endures constant physical and psychological abuse from her father. Fourteen-year-old "Jenny" is obsessed with death and suicide, and she aspires to join a gang.

> When you're smoking dope, you just break out laughing, you don't feel like punching people because it's just too hard. It takes too much. . . . You're mellow. . . . You just want to sit there and trip out on everybody. . . . It's even good for school work. When I used to get stoned all the time last year, I remember, I used to sit in class and do my work because I didn't want the teacher to catch me, and this year I'm getting failing marks 'cause I'm not doing my work 'cause I'm never stoned (Mary).

> I just know I got a lot of hatred. . . . And there's this one person [Jenny], and it just kinda happened after she mouthed me off, I was just like totally freaked with her and now I just want to slam her head into something. I wanna shoot her with a gun or something. I wanna kill her. . . . If I could get away with it I'd kill her. I wouldn't necessarily kill her, but I'd get her good. I just want to teach her a lesson. I'd beat the crap out of her. She's pissed me off so badly. I just want to give her two black eyes. Then I'd be fine. I'd have gotten the last word in (Linda).

> I like fighting. It's exciting. I like the power of being able to beat up people. Like, if I fight them, and I'm winning, I feel good about myself, and I think of myself as tough. . . . I'm not scared of anybody, so that feels good. My friends are scared of a lot of people, and I go "Oh yeah, but I'm not scared of them. . . . All these people in grade eight at that junior high are scared of me, they don't even know me, and they're scared of me. It makes me feel powerful (Jenny) (Artz 1999, 127, 136, 157).

In Chapter 4, we looked at how full-service schools provide educational, medical, social and/or human services, and how the school-based interprofessional case management model uses case managers to deliver services to at-risk students and their families. Although many believe that schools should not provide such services, an increase in the number of at-risk students like Mary, Linda, and Jenny suggest that the trend is likely to continue, with more schools following the lead of schools in Charlotte-Mecklenburg, North Carolina; Seattle; and Palm Beach County, Florida. Charlotte-Mecklenburg schools organized a Children's Services Network, "which brings together all of the community agencies concerned with children, coordinates the services, increases support, and prepares a report card on progress" (Boyer 1995, 169). In Seattle, a recent referendum required that a percentage of taxes be set aside to provide services to elementary-age children. And Palm Beach County officials created the Children's Services Council to address sixteen areas, from reducing the dropout rate to better child care. From parent support groups, to infant nurseries, to programs for students with special needs, the council has initiated scores of projects to benefit the community and its children.

How Will the Privatization Movement Affect Equity and Excellence in Education?

One of the most dramatic reforms in American education during the last decade has been the development of charter schools and for-profit schools, both of which were developed to provide an alternative to the perceived inadequacies of the public schools. On many different levels—governance, staffing, curricula, funding, and accountability—the **privatization movement** is a radical departure from schools as most people have known them.

Charter Schools

In 1991, Minnesota passed the nation's first charter school legislation calling for up to eight teacher-created and -operated, outcome-based schools that would be free of most state and local rules and regulations. When the St. Paul City Academy opened its doors in September 1992, it became the nation's first charter school.

Charter schools are independent, innovative, outcome-based, public schools. "The charter school concept allows a group of teachers, parents, or others who share similar interests and views about education to organize and operate a school. Charters can be granted by a local school district, by the state, or by the national government. In effect, charter schools offer a model for restructuring that gives greater autonomy to individual schools and promotes school choice by increasing the range of options available to parents and students within the public schools system" (Wohlstetter and Anderson 1994, 486). As of late 1999, thirty-six states, Puerto Rico, and the District of Columbia had adopted charter school legislation; and 1,700 charter schools were open (White House Press Release 1999). Charter schools in Arizona range from those focusing on the fine arts to charter schools in remote regions of the state that serve Native American communities.

To open a charter school, an original charter (or agreement) is signed by the school's founders and a sponsor (usually the local school board). The charter specifies the learning outcomes that students will master before they continue their studies. Charter schools, which usually operate in the manner of autonomous school districts (a feature that distinguishes them from the alternative schools that many school districts operate), are public schools and must teach all students. If admission requests for a charter school exceed the number of available openings, students are selected by drawing.

Because charter schools are designed to promote the development of new teaching strategies that can be used at other public schools, they can prove to be an effective tool for promoting educational reform and the professionalization of teaching in the future. Moreover, as Milo Cutter, one of the two teachers who founded St. Paul City Academy points out, charter schools give teachers unprecedented leadership opportunities and the ability to respond quickly to students' needs:

> [We had] the chance to create a school that takes into account the approaches we know will work. We listen to what the students want and need, because we ask them. And each day we ask ourselves if we are doing things the best way we can. We also have the flexibility to respond. We can change the curriculum to meet these needs as soon as we see them. Anywhere else it would take a year to change. It is much better than anything we have known in the traditional setting (North Central Regional Education Laboratory 1993, 3).

Murnane and Levy (1996) suggest that charter schools are "too new to have a track record," and they should not be seen as a "magic bullet" that will dramatically, and with little effort, improve students' achievement. In addition, they suggest four questions that observers should pose to determine whether individual charter schools promote both equity and excellence.

- Does the charter school commit itself to a goal, such as mastery of critical skills for all its students, or will it emphasize other goals?
- Does the charter school commit itself to serve a fair share of the most difficult-to-

educate children, and does it have a strategy for attracting such children—or will it discourage applications from such children?

■ Does the charter school's contract with the school district provide enough time and enough financial support for the school to persevere and learn from the mistakes that are inevitable in any ambitious new venture?

■ Does the charter school commit itself to providing information about student achievement that will allow parents to make sound judgments about the quality of the education their children are receiving (Murnane and Levy 1996, 113)?

For-Profit Schools

One of the most controversial educational issues for the twenty-first century is the practice of turning the operation of public schools over to private, for-profit companies. Advocates of **privatization** believe privately operated schools are more efficient; they reduce costs and maximize "production"—that is, student achievement. Opponents, however, are concerned that profit, rather than increasing student achievement, is the real driving force behind **for-profit schools.** Figure 14.3, for example, shows that for-profit education companies had revenues of $82 billion in 1998, a 25 percent increase over 1997; and revenues were projected to reach $99 billion in 1999 and $123 billion in 2000. Critics of for-profit schools are also concerned that school districts may not be vigilant enough in monitoring the performance of private education companies.

Concerned about the slow pace of educational reform in the United States, Christopher Whittle, the originator of Channel One, launched the $3 billion Edison Project in 1992—an ambitious plan to develop a national network of more than 1,000 for-profit secondary schools by 2010. As of 1999, the Edison Project, now named Edison Schools, Inc., had become the largest company involved in the for-profit management of schools, and it managed seventy-seven public schools attended by 37,000 students nationwide (Walsh 1999b).

In 1999, Edison Schools, Inc. reported that achievement was steadily moving upward at the "vast majority" of Edison schools. At seventeen of the Edison schools that had been able to establish achievement trends, fourteen had records the company labeled "positive" or "strongly positive," and three had records that were labeled "weak" (Walsh 1999b). However, in a report analyzing the results reported by Edison the previous year, the American Federation of Teachers claimed that the company exaggerated achievement gains at many schools and downplayed negative results at others. "On the whole, Edison results were mediocre," the report claimed (American Federation of Teachers 1998a).

Another approach to for-profit schools was developed by Education Alternatives, Inc. (EAI), a company that negotiates with school districts to operate their public schools. Participating school districts give the company the same per-pupil funding to operate the school that the district would have used. The company, using its own curricula and cost-saving techniques, agrees to improve student performance and atten-

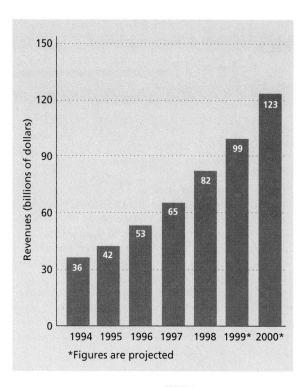

Figure 14.3

Big business—revenues for the education industry
Source: The Education Industry: Markets & Opportunities. Boston: EduVentures, Spring 1999. Used with permission.

Is privatization an effective way to improve education in the United States?

Would businesses do a better job running public schools in the United States than the government-based system? Should businesses make a profit from schools? Should taxpayers contribute funds to schools that in turn give businesses profits? With the rise of privatization of education in the late 1990s, people were beginning to ask such questions.

A portion of the United States education system is being referred to as an "education industry," and stock market and consulting firms are tracking its progress. *The Economist,* a London publication, reported on privatization of U.S. education (1999b), noting that

. . . the government says that the country spends a total of $625 billion a year on education—more than it devotes to pensions or defence [sic]—and predicts that spending per pupil will rise by 40% over the next decade. Private companies currently have only 13% of the market. . . . But International Data Corporation, a consultancy, reckons that this share will expand to 25% over the next two decades.

U.S. businesses engage in privatizing schools in three ways: establishing for-profit charter schools, placing public schools under corporate management (for example, the Edison Schools), and providing supplementary services such as testing and coaching (for example, the Sylvan Learning Systems). The "education industry" covers schooling from preschool through college, with the former in particular regarded as a "boom area."

Teachers' unions and education scholars and writers expressed alarm over the expansion of privatization. Henry Giroux criticized its advocates:

They view education primarily as a commercial venture in which the only form of citizenship offered to young people is consumerism. Yet reducing public education to the ideological imperatives of corporate culture works against the critical social demands of educating citizens who can sustain and develop inclusive democratic identities, relations, and public spheres. (Giroux 1999)

Education researchers questioned the merit and ethics of commercializing education. In a study of eleven for-profit schools in western Michigan, Christy Lancaster Dykgraaf and Shirley Kane Lewis concluded that the emergence of such schools was "cause for concern," adding, "Issues related to cost-cutting strategies, communication, and public ownership of the public schools deserve serious attention if these charter schools are to match the expectations and meet the needs of the constituencies they are intended to serve" (1998).

In April 1999, Henry Levin, Stanford education professor and leader of the Accelerated Schools Project, moved to Columbia University to head the new National Center for the Study of Privatization in Education. According to an *Education Week* issue paper (1999, July 29), Levin "hopes to conduct neutral research, without any political pull from conservatives or liberals, on the impact of privatization to advance the debate about vouchers, charter schools, and private companies in education."

While the experts are evaluating the matter, what do you think about the move toward privatization? Is this an effective way to improve education in the United States?

Yes, privatization is an effective way to improve education in the United States.

The country's poor record in student achievement compared to that in other countries makes it imperative to do something different. U.S. businesses and colleges complain about the inadequate skills and limited knowledge of high school graduates. What the country has been doing has not been working. Now the problem is too great to ignore. As the world news journal, *The Economist* (1999b), observes:

America spends more of its GDP on education than most countries, yet it gets mediocre results. Children in Asia and Europe often trounce their American counterparts in standardised [sic] scholastic tests. More than 40% of American ten-year-olds cannot pass a basic reading test; as many as 42m. adults are functionally illiterate. Part of the reason for this dismal performance is that close to half of the $6,500 spent on each child is eaten up by "non-instructional services"—mostly administration.

The best solution is to combine business expertise with government regulation to spend education money more effectively. "Government's oversight function and its responsiveness to the needs of citizens can be retained while taking advantage of private enterprise's ability to be more efficient, reduce costs, and maximize production—in this case, student achievement," *Education Week* observed (1999, July 29).

Many believe that the competition that free enterprise provides will motivate schools to improve. Others believe privatization will bring fresh ideas to a weary education system. Michael R. Sandler, the chief executive officer for EduVentures, is quoted in a May 1999 *Education Week* article saying, "The true agents of change for education reform in the 21st century are going to be the innovative for-profit enterprises built by education entrepreneurs" (Walsh 1999). And *The Economist* (1999, Jan. 16) reported that "Such schemes free education from the stifling grip of teaching unions and bureaucrats." With the freedom to innovate and the unique perspectives and know-how of business, for-profit charter schools and corporate management of public schools may breathe new life into education in the U.S.

No, privatization is not an effective way to improve education in the United States.

Most of the arguments against privatization fall into two broad areas—reductionism of education and alteration of the purpose of schools.

Privatization reduces education by narrowing the curriculum, standardizing the way it is taught, and devaluing the gifts of teachers. Because for-profit schools and management corporations need to demonstrate that they are effective, they must specify exactly what will be learned and then be able to prove that students have learned it. Accountability is the prime focus; and the narrower and more standardized the curriculum, the easier it is to assess. Curricula also become limited to that which can be tested. Lessons regarding attitudes, values, correct behavior, creative expression, leadership, art, music, sports, speech, and drama all are difficult to assess. As a consequence they tend to be set aside or given limited focus so that teachers and students can prepare for tests on core curricula. Similarly, instruction teachers provide is strictly prescribed to maximize the likelihood that test scores rise. Teachers' abilities to enrich school experiences and make learning meaningful are squelched by the standardization process and assessment focus.

More serious is privatization's impact on the direction and purpose of schools. Its focus on profit, integration of commercialism in curricula, and preparation of students as consumers is a far cry from the original purposes of schools—to prepare students to lead morally good lives and be good and informed citizens able to participate in a democratic government. Henry Giroux, a passionate voice against the corporatizing of U.S. education, writes that advocates of privatization are attempting to "transform public education from a public good, benefiting all students, to a private good designed to expand the profits of investors, educate students as consumers, and train young people for the low-paying jobs of the new global marketplace" (Giroux 1999). He observes that these advo-cates critique U.S. education by viewing it separate from the social conditions in society:

Stripped of a language of social responsibility advocates of privatization reject the assumption that school failure might be better understood within the political, economic, and social dynamics of poverty, joblessness, sexism, race and class discrimination, unequal funding, or a diminished tax base.

Privatization of education serves the profit interests of businesses, not the good of students and the country. Citizens need to be wary.

Where do you stand on this issue?

1. Which are the best arguments on each side of this issue?

2. What are your experiences with privatization of education?

3. Where do you stand on this issue? Why do you hold this position?

4. What are the potential costs if either side has complete control of education?

5. Update yourself on this issue by following it on the web through Ebscohost or First Search. In First Search choose "all data bases" and then explore Wilson Select and PerAbs for full text articles.

Recommended Sources

AFT on the Issues (1999, July). Vouchers and the accountability dilemma.

Kane, S. and Dykgraaf, C. L. (1998, October). For-profit charter schools: What the public needs to know. *Educational Leadership, v. 56*(2), 51–53.

The Economist (1999a, January 16). A contract on schools: Why handing education over to companies can make sense.

The Economist (1999, January 16). Reading, writing and enrichment: Private money is pouring into American education—and transforming it.

Education Week on the Web (1999, July 29). Issue Paper: Privatization of public education.

Giroux, H. A. (1999, Winter). Schools for sale: public education, corporate culture, and the citizen-consumer. *The Educational Forum, 63*(2), 140–49.

Nathan, J. (1998, March). Heat and light in the charter school movement. *Phi Delta Kappan 79*(7), 499–505.

Pipho, C. (1999, February). The profit side of education. *Phi Delta Kappan, 80*(6), 421–22.

Walsh, M. (1999, May). Two reports offer bright outlook for education industry. *Education Week, 18*(36), 5.

highlights

How does the United States compare to other countries regarding the importance of information technology in the curriculum?

Students leaving school today, both in the United States and around the world, will compete for jobs in a global economy that is powerfully influenced by information technology. In many respects, the "coin of the realm" for the global economy of the twenty-first century will be neither raw materials nor labor but information. As a result, the place of information technology in the school curriculum is critical.

Figure 14.4 shows the percentage of the public in eleven OECD (Organization for Economic Co-operation and Development) countries who gave information technology and technical studies a rating of either "essential" or "very important" in the school curriculum. Information technology (e.g., computing and database management) was viewed as relatively more important than

technical studies (e.g., metal shop and drafting) in all countries except Spain, where they were viewed as nearly the same. It is noteworthy that the U.S. public, more than the public in the other countries, views information technology as especially important. To what extent do you believe the *actual* emphasis on information technology in school curricula reflects the importance the U.S. public attaches to instruction in information technology? As a teacher, what role can you play in ensuring that your students acquire the information technology skills they will need for their future in a global economy?

dance in return for the opportunity to operate schools at a profit. Education Alternatives, Inc., which began operating its first for-profit school in Dade County, Florida, in 1991, became the first private company to run an entire school district when the Duluth, Minnesota, School Board awarded the company a three-month contract in 1992 to serve as interim superintendent for the district. In Baltimore and Hartford, Connecticut, where EAI operated several schools in the mid-1990s, critics challenged the achievement gains the company reported and accused the company of mismanaging finances. After numerous disputes over the management of schools, both school systems eventually terminated their contracts with the company. In 1999, EAI moved its headquarters from Bloomington, Minnesota, to Scottsdale, Arizona, and became the Tesseract Group, Inc. At that time, the company operated forty schools serving more than 6,000 students.

What Can Teachers and Schools Learn from International Education?

The world has truly become smaller and more interconnected as telecommunications, cyberspace, and travel by jet bring diverse people and countries together. As we continue to move closer together, it is clear that education is crucial to the well-being of every country and to the world as a whole. "For teachers, on whom the quality of education ultimately depends, the challenges and opportunities the twenty-first century will bring are remarkably similar worldwide, and there is much the U.S. can learn from other countries about the conditions that promote the ability of teachers and students to deal with that future" (Parkay and Oaks 1998). For example, an observation in a *Bangkok Post* editorial on the need to prepare Thai youth for a changing world echoes calls for educational reform in the United States: "The country's policy plan-

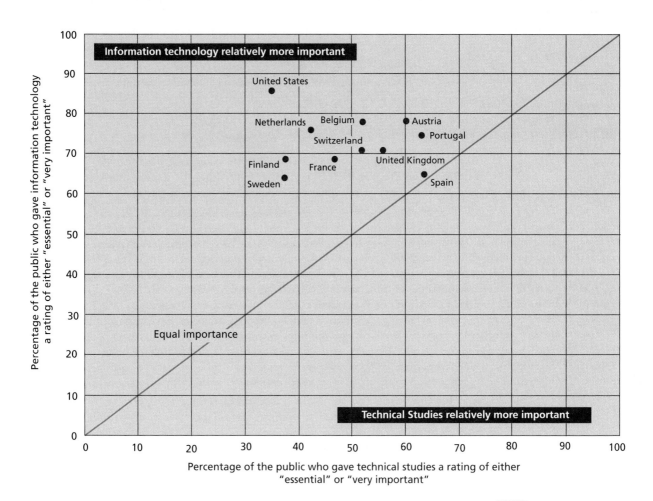

The chart shows axes labeled: Y-axis "Percentage of the public who gave information technology a rating of either "essential" or "very important"" and X-axis "Percentage of the public who gave technical studies a rating of either "essential" or "very important""

Information technology relatively more important

United States

Netherlands   Belgium   Austria
Switzerland   Portugal

Finland   France   United Kingdom
Sweden   Spain

Equal importance

Technical Studies relatively more important

Figure 14.4

The importance of information technology and technical studies: An international perspective.
Source: Public Attitudes Toward Secondary Education: The United States in an International Context. Washington, DC: U.S. Department of Education, 1997.

ners [s]hould seriously review and revamp the national education system to effectively prepare our youths [for] the next century" (Sricharatchanya 1996, 15). Similarly, a community leader's comments about educating young substance abusers in Bangkok's Ban Don Muslim community could apply to youth in scores of American communities: "We are in an age of cultural instability. Children are exposed to both good and bad things. [I]t's hard to resist the influences and attitudes from the outside world that are pulling at the children's feelings" (Rithdee 1996, 11). Lastly, the curriculum goals at Shiose Junior High School in Nishinomiya, Japan, are based on Japan's fifteenth Council for Education and would "fit" American junior high schools as well; according to principal Akio Inoue (1996, 1), "Students will acquire the ability to survive in a changing society, that is, students will study, think and make judgments on their own initiative. It is also important that we provide a proper balance of knowledge, morality, and physical health, and that we nurture humanity and physical strength for that purpose." As a result of the universal challenges that confront educators, we are entering an era of increasing cross-national exchanges that focus on sharing resources, ideas, and expertise for the improvement of education worldwide.

Comparative Education

As the nations of the world continue to become more interdependent, policies for educational reform in the United States will be influenced increasingly by **comparative**

education, the study of educational practices in other countries. Comparative education studies show how school systems in other countries work and how American students compare with students in other countries on certain measures of schooling and achievement. In addition, research in comparative education enables professionals to share information about successful innovations internationally. Teachers can collaborate on global education projects and test change models that other countries have used to help match educational and societal needs and goals.

International Comparisons of Achievement   The first **International Assessment of Educational Progress (IAEP)** in 1991 revealed that the achievement levels of U.S. students were often below those of students from other countries. Subsequent IAEP comparisons have shown some improvement in the rankings of American students in mathematics and science. Figure 14.5(a), for example, based on the **Third International Mathematics and Science Study (TIMSS)** sponsored by the International Association for the Evaluation of Educational Achievement (1997a, 1997b), shows how the mathematics and science achievement levels of fourth-grade U.S. students compare with those of students from several other countries. However, as Figure 14.5 (b) shows, the relative standing of U.S. students in these subject areas was significantly lower by the final year of secondary school. Gains in literacy, however, have been more significant; for example, *A First Look—Findings from the National Assessment of Educational Progress* reported that U.S. fourth-graders ranked second in 1995 on a thirty-two-nation survey of reading skills.

Since the publication of *A Nation at Risk* in 1983, there has been an unbroken trend for the media and some observers of U.S. education to decry the perceived poor performance of U.S. students on international comparisons of achievement. A closer examination of international comparisons, however, reveals the seldom-reported fact that the United States's position in country-by-country rankings is based on *aggregate* achievement scores—in other words, achievement scores of all students are used to make the comparisons. Not taken into account is the United States's commitment to educating all students (not just the academically able or those from home environments that encourage education), the widely varying quality of U.S. schools, and differences in students' *opportunity to learn* the content covered in achievement tests. That is, when only the top students of each country are compared, the rankings of U.S. students improve dramatically. As David Berliner and Bruce Biddle point out in *The Manufactured Crisis: Myths, Fraud, and the Attack on America's Public Schools* (1995, 52), "If one actually looks at and thinks about the comparative evidence, [o]ne discovers that it does not confirm the myth of American educational failure. Indeed, it suggests that in many ways American education stands head and shoulders above education in other countries."

To illustrate their point, Berliner and Biddle summarize Ian Westbury's (1992) analysis of data from the International Association for the Evaluation of Educational Achievements' (IEA) Second International Mathematics Study, which purported to show U.S. eighth-graders significantly behind their Japanese peers in mathematics achievement. Westbury noted that Japanese eighth-grade students were *required* to take courses that covered algebra, while U.S. students typically take such courses a year or two later. When Westbury compared the achievement of U.S. and Japanese students who had taken prealgebra and algebra, the achievement of U.S. students matched or exceeded that of Japanese students (see Figure 14.6).

Berliner and Biddle (1995, 63) go on to offer these cautions about interpreting cross-national studies of educational achievement.

■ Few of those studies have yet focused on the unique values and strengths of American education.

- Many of the studies' results have obviously been affected by sampling biases and inconsistent methods for gathering data.
- Many, perhaps most, of the studies' results were generated by differences in curricula—in opportunities to learn—in the countries studied.

(a)

Nations' Average Mathematics and Science Performance Compared with the United States — Grade 4

MATHEMATICS		SCIENCE	
Nation	**Average**	**Nation**	**Average**
Singapore	625	↑ Korea	597
Korea	611		
↑ Japan	597	Japan	574
Hong Kong	587	United States	565
(Netherlands)	577	= (Austria)	565
(Czech Republic)	567	(Australia)	562
(Austria)	559	(Netherlands)	557
		Czech Republic	557
(Slovenia)	552		
Ireland	550	England	551
(Hungary)	548	Canada	549
= (Australia)	546	Singapore	547
United States	545	(Slovenia)	546
Canada	532	Ireland	539
(Israel)	531	Scotland	536
		Hong Kong	533
(Latvia LSS)	525	(Hungary)	532
Scotland	520	↓ New Zealand	531
England	513	Norway	530
Cyprus	502	(Latvia LSS)	512
Norway	502	(Israel)	505
↓ New Zealand	499	Iceland	505
Greece	492	Greece	497
(Thailand)	490	Portugal	480
Portugal	475	Cyprus	475
Iceland	474	(Thailand)	473
Iran, Islamic Republic	429	Iran, Islamic Republic	416
(Kuwait)	400	(Kuwait)	401
International Average = 529		**International Average = 524**	

(b)

Nations' Average Mathematics and Science General Knowledge Performance Compared with the United States — Final Year of Secondary School

MATHEMATICS		SCIENCE	
Nation	**Average**	**Nation**	**Average**
(Netherlands)	560	↑ Sweden	559
Sweden	552	(Netherlands)	558
(Denmark)	547	(Iceland)	549
Switzerland	540	(Norway)	544
(Iceland)	534	(Canada)	532
(Norway)	528	New Zealand	529
↑ (France)	523	(Australia)	527
New Zealand	522	Switzerland	523
(Australia)	522	(Austria)	520
(Canada)	519	(Slovenia)	517
(Austria)	518	(Denmark)	509
(Slovenia)	512		
(Germany)	495		
Hungary	483	(Germany)	497
		(France)	487
		Czech Republic	487
(Italy)	476	= (Russian Fed)	481
(Russian Fed)	471	(United States)	480
= (Lithuania)	469	(Italy)	475
Czech Republic	466	Hungary	471
(United States)	461	(Lithuania)	461
↓ Cyprus	446		
(South Africa)	356	↓ (Cyprus)	448
		(South Africa)	349
International Average = 500		**International Average = 500**	

Notes:
1) Nations not meeting international guidelines are shown in parentheses.
2) The international average is the average of the national averages of the 21 nations.

↑ Nations with average scores significantly higher than the U.S.

= Nations with average scores not significantly different from the U.S.

↓ Nations with average scores significantly lower than the U.S.

Figure 14.5

Nation's average mathematics and science performance compared with the United States.
Source: National Center for Education Statistics. *Pursuing Excellence: A Study of U.S. Fourth-Grade Mathematics and Science Achievement in International Context,* Figures 1 & 2. Washington, DC, NCES, 1997.

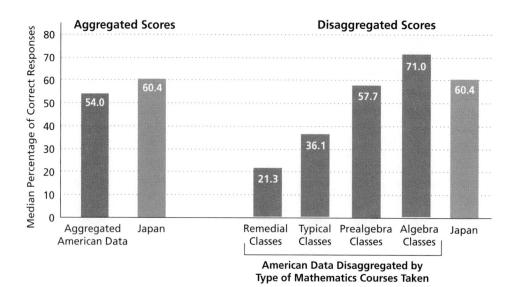

Figure 14.6

Japanese and American achievement scores for students age 13—from The Second International Mathematics Study of the IEA

Source: Ian Westbury. "Comparing American and Japanese Acheivement: Is the United States Really a Low-Achiever?" *Educational Researcher, 21*(5), 1992, pp. 18–24. Taken from David C. Berliner and Bruce J. Biddle, *The Manufactured Crisis: Myths, Fraud, and the Attack on America's Public Schools.* Reading, MA: Addison-Wesley Publishing Company, 1995, p. 57.

- Aggregate results for American schools are misleading because of the huge range of school quality in this country—ranging from marvelous to terrible.
- The press has managed to ignore most comparative studies in which the United States has done well.

A National Curriculum? Decisions about the operation of schools in the United States are made largely at the district or individual school level. However, in some countries (Japan, Korea, and England, for example) education is centralized and teachers follow a standardized national curriculum. Since the first International Assessment of Educational Progress (IAEP) in 1991 revealed that the achievement levels of U.S. students are often below that of students from other countries (many of which have national curricula), some have proposed a **national curriculum** for the United States. Proposals for a national curriculum are also supported by the public. On the last Gallup Poll of the Public's Attitudes toward the Public Schools that asked for opinions about a national curriculum and national examinations, 46 percent believed they were "very important" and 27 percent "quite important" (Elam and Rose 1995, 48).

Although there is widespread support for national examinations and a national curriculum, there is also widespread opposition to such a system. For example, in his comparative study of U.S. and Japanese education, Harry Wray (1999, 137) concluded that Japan's system of national examinations "reinforce[s] excessive conformity, passivity, standardization, anxiety, group consciousness, and controlled education." Furthermore, Wray goes on to say, "Excessive emphasis on passing entrance examinations plays a contributing role in killing most students' interest in studying and scholarship after entering a university, especially for those outside the science, engineering, and medical areas. Students exhausted by the dehumanizing methodology lose motivation and curiosity" (Wray 1999, 138). Additionally, national examinations have been criticized because they encourage students to take a narrow view of learning and they tend to emphasize lower-order thinking skills that can be assessed easily by pencil-and-paper measures. As one Japanese university student confided to Wray: "In elementary school we had many occasions to give our opinions; however, after we entered junior high school, we did not get such opportunities because all the studies are for high school entrance examinations, and all the studies in high school are for university entrance examinations. One who is considered 'intelligent' is one who can get good grades, not those who have their own opinions" (Wray 1999, 137).

Lessons from Other Countries

The previous comments about Japanese education aside, U.S. educators can learn a great deal from their colleagues around the world regarding what works and what doesn't work in other countries. When considering the possibility of adopting practices from other countries, however, it is important to remember that educational practices reflect the surrounding culture. When one country tries to adopt a method used elsewhere, a lack of support from the larger society may doom the new practice to failure. In addition, it is important to realize that the successes of another country's educational system may require sacrifices that are unacceptable to our way of life. Nevertheless, there are many practices in other countries that American educators and policymakers should consider.

Support for Teachers and Teaching   In many other countries, teachers and the profession of teaching receive a level of societal support that surpasses that experienced by teachers in the United States. For example, teachers in many countries are accorded greater respect than their U.S. counterparts; and, as Figure 14.7 shows, the salary range (as a ratio of per-capita Gross Domestic Product) for teachers in Japan, the UK, Italy, and Germany is significantly greater than it is for U.S. teachers.

Figure 14.7

Ratio of teacher salaries (starting and maximum) per-capita GDP, by education level and career point
Source: Organization for Economic Co-operation and Development, Center for Educational Research and Innovation, International Indicators Project, 1995.

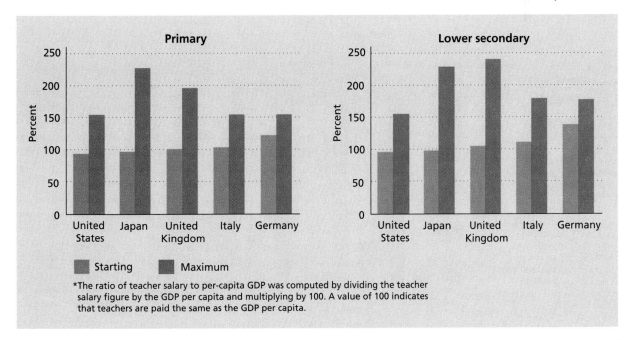

*The ratio of teacher salary to per-capita GDP was computed by dividing the teacher salary figure by the GDP per capita and multiplying by 100. A value of 100 indicates that teachers are paid the same as the GDP per capita.

In addition, most U.S. teachers have about one hour or less per day for planning, and U.S. high school teachers teach about thirty classes a week, compared with twenty by teachers in Germany and fewer than twenty by Japanese teachers (U.S. Department of Education and International Institute on Education 1996). "[T]his leaves them with almost no regular time to consult together or learn about new teaching strategies, unlike their peers in many European and Asian countries where teachers spend between 15 and 20 hours per week working jointly on refining lessons, coaching one another, and learning about new methods" (National Commission on Teaching and America's Future 1996, 14).

The National Commission on Teaching and America's Future (1996) also found that other countries invest their resources in hiring more teachers, who comprise about 60 to 80 percent of total staff compared to only 43 percent in the United States (see Figure 14.8). In the United States, the Commission (1996, 15) noted that in U.S. schools "too many people and resources are allocated to activities outside of classrooms, sitting on the sidelines rather than the front lines of teaching and learning." Many other countries also invest more resources in staff development and beginning teacher support programs than U.S. schools. A joint report by the U.S. Department of Education and the Education Forum of APEC (Asia-Pacific Economic Cooperation) nations indicated that the experiences of beginning teachers in other countries are more positive than those of their U.S. counterparts for the following reasons:

1. New teachers are viewed as professionals on a continuum, with increasing levels of experience and responsibility; novice teachers are not expected to do the same job as experienced teachers without significant support.
2. New teachers are nurtured and not left to "flounder on their own"; interaction with other teachers is maximized.
3. Teacher induction is a purposive and valued activity.
4. Schools possess a culture of shared responsibility and support, in which all or most of the school's staff contributes to the development and nurturing of the new teacher.
5. Assessment of new teachers is downplayed (U.S. Department of Education 1997).

Figure 14.8

Comparisons of educational staff by function

Source: Organization for Economic Cooperation and Development (OECD), *Education at a Glance: OECD Indicators.* Paris, OECD, 1995, table, p. 31, pp. 176–77. Taken from National Commission on Teaching and America's Future, *What Matters Most: Teaching for America's Future.* New York, National Commission on Teaching and America's Future, p. 15.

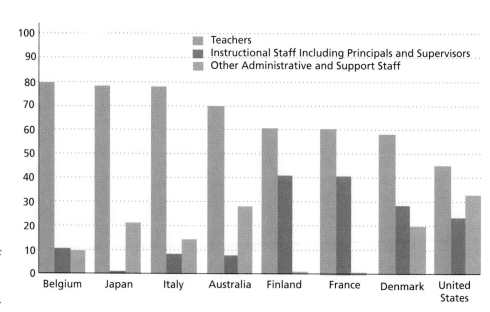

Parental Involvement   The powerful influence of parental involvement on students' achievement is well documented (Booth and Dunn 1996; Buzzell 1996; ERIC Clearinghouse 1993; Epstein 1992). Japan probably leads the world when it comes to parental involvement in education. Japanese mothers frequently go to great lengths to ensure that their children get the most out of the school's curriculum. The *kyoiku mama* (literally, education mother) will tutor her child, wait for hours in lines to register her child for periodic national exams, prepare healthy snacks for the child to eat while studying, forego television so her child can study in quiet, and ensure that her child arrives on time for calligraphy, piano, swimming, or martial arts lessons. Though few U.S. parents might wish to assume the role of the *kyoiku parent*, it seems clear that U.S. students would benefit from greater parental involvement.

Pressure to Excel   There have been many calls to make U.S. schooling more rigorous—a longer school calendar, longer school days, more homework, and harder examinations, for example, have all been proposed. These changes, it is assumed, would increase student achievement and find favor with the majority of the public that wants greater academic rigor in the schools. More often than not, Japan, Korea, and other Asian countries are held up as models for the direction U.S. education should take.

But should U.S. schools be patterned after schools in these countries? Several of those who have studied and experienced Asian schools are beginning to think not. For example, Paul George (1995), who studied the Japanese public school his son attended for two years, reports in *The Japanese Secondary School: A Closer Look* that large numbers of students, deprived of sleep from having attended *jukus* (cram schools) to do well on college entrance exams, waste time in school, having been told by their *juku* instructors not to pay attention to their teachers. Additionally, a teacher of English in rural Japan reports that 70 percent of students at her school attend *jukus* and frequently are awake past midnight (Bracy 1996). According to Gerald Bracey (1996, 128), if U.S. parents want their children to achieve at the level of Asian students, which is often only a few percentage points higher on standardized examinations, they must understand the sacrifices made by Asian students and their parents and be prepared to adhere to these guidelines:

1. [W]hen their children come home from public school, they should feed them and then ship them off to a private school or tutor until 10 P.M.; most youngsters, both elementary and secondary, will need to go to school all day on Sunday, too.
2. [They should] spend 20 to 30 percent of their income on [a]fter-school schools.
3. [W]hen their children turn four, they should take them on their knees and tell them, "You are big boys and girls now, so you need to start practicing for college entrance examinations" (Bracey 1996, 128).

In addition, U.S. students would need to realize that "if they sleep four hours a night, they will get into college, but if they sleep five hours a night, they won't; they must study instead" (Bracey 1996, 128).

What Is Our Vision for the Future of Education?

Imagine that it is the year 2020, and we are visiting Westside Elementary school, a school in a medium-sized city in a midwestern state. All of the teachers at Westside have been certified by the National Board for Professional Teaching Standards (NBPTS). The salaries of the board-certified teachers are on a par with those of other professionals with comparable education and training. About half of the fifty-five teachers at Westside have also earned the advanced professional certificate now offered by the NBPTS. These teachers are known as lead teachers and may earn as much as $125,000 per year. Westside has no principal; the school is run by an executive committee of five lead teachers elected by all teachers at the school. One of these lead teachers is elected to serve as committee chair for a two-year period. In addition, the school has several paid interns and residents who are assigned to lead teachers as part of their graduate-level teacher-preparation program. Finally, teachers are assisted by a diagnostician; hypermedia specialist; computer specialist; video specialist; social worker; school psychologist; four counselors; special remediation teachers in reading, writing, mathematics, and oral communication; bilingual and ESL teachers; and special-needs teachers.

Westside Elementary operates many programs that illustrate the close ties the school has developed with parents, community agencies, and businesses. The school houses a daycare center that provides after-school employment for several students from the nearby high school. On weekends and on Monday, Wednesday, and Friday evenings the school is used for adult education and for various community group activities. Executives from three local businesses spend one day a month at the school visiting with classes and telling students about their work. Students from a nearby college participate in a tutoring program at Westside, and the college has several on-campus summer enrichment programs for Westside students.

Westside has a school-based health clinic that offers health care services and a counseling center that provides individual and family counseling. In addition, from time to time Westside teachers and students participate in service-learning activities in the community. At the present time, for example, the fifth-grade classes are helping the city develop a new recycling program.

All the facilities at Westside—classrooms, library, multimedia learning center, gymnasium, the cafeteria, and private offices for teachers—have been designed to create a teaching/learning environment free of all health and safety hazards. The cafeteria, for example, serves meals based on findings from nutrition research about the best foods and methods of cooking. The school is carpeted, and classrooms are soundproofed and well lit. Throughout, the walls are painted in soft pastels tastefully accented with potted plants, paintings, wall hangings, and large murals depicting life in different cultures.

The dress, language, and behaviors of teacher, students, and support personnel at Westside reflect a rich array of cultural backgrounds. In the cafeteria, for example, it is impossible not to hear several languages being spoken and to see at least a few students and teachers wearing non-Western clothing. From the displays of students' work on bulletin boards in hallways and in classrooms, to the international menu offered in the

What vision of the school of the future does this photograph suggest? What might you add to the image to achieve a broader perspective on tomorrow's teachers and learners?

cafeteria, there is ample evidence that Westside is truly a multicultural school and that gender, race, and class biases have been eliminated.

Each teacher at Westside is a member of a teaching team and spends at least part of his or her teaching time working with other members of the team. Furthermore, teachers determine their schedules, and every effort is made to assign teachers according to their particular teaching expertise. Students attend Westside by choice for its excellent teachers; its curricular emphasis on problem solving, human relations, creative thinking, and critical thinking; and its programs for helping at-risk students achieve academic success.

Instruction at Westside is supplemented by the latest technologies. The school subscribes to several computer databases and cable television services, which teachers and students use regularly. The hypermedia learning center has an extensive collection of CD-ROMs and computer software, much of it written by Westside teachers. The center also has virtual-reality interactive videodisc systems, workstations equipped with the latest robotics, and an extensive lab with voice-activated computers. The computer-supported interactive multimedia in the center use the CD-ROM format and the more advanced Integrated Services Digital Network (ISDN) delivery system based on the optical fiber.

Every classroom has a video camera, fax machine, hypermedia system, and telephone that, in addition to everyday use, are used frequently during satellite video teleconferences with business executives, artists, scientists, scholars, and students at schools in other states and countries. Westside Elementary's technological capabilities permit students to move their education beyond the classroom walls, as they determine much of how, when, where, and what they learn.

Tomorrow's Teacher

Teaching and the conditions under which teachers work may change in some fundamental and positive ways during the next two decades. Teaching will become increasingly professionalized, for example, through such changes as more lengthy and rigorous preprofessional training programs, salary increases that put teaching on a par with other professions requiring similar education, and greater teacher autonomy and an expanded role for teachers in educational policy making. There will be more male teachers who are African Americans, Hispanic and Latino, or members of other minority groups. There will be greater recognition for high-performing teachers and schools through such mechanisms as merit pay plans, master teacher programs, and career ladders. Tomorrow's teachers will achieve new and higher levels of specialization. The traditional teaching job will be divided into parts. Some of the new jobs may be the following:

- Learning diagnostician
- Researcher for software programs
- Courseware writer
- Curriculum designer
- Mental health diagnostician
- Evaluator of learning performances
- Evaluator of social skills
- Small-group learning facilitator
- Large-group learning facilitator
- Media-instruction producer
- Home-based instruction designer
- Home-based instruction monitor

Though we cannot claim to have handed you an educational crystal ball so that you can ready yourself for the future, we hope you have gained both knowledge and inspiration from our observations in this chapter. Certainly, visions of the future, such as the one of Westside Elementary, will not become a reality without a lot of dedication and hard work. The creation of schools like Westside will require commitment and vision on the part of professional teachers like you.

Professional Reflection

What does the future hold for education in your state?

Predict the future of education in your state in terms of the following list of innovations and trends. Rate each development according to whether it already exists in your state or when you think it will become common practice in the schools—within the next five or the next fifteen years. If you don't know the status of a particular development in your state, find out. Add at least one new item representing a trend in your state that does not appear on the list. When you have finished rating the items, share your results with your classmates. What reasons or evidence will you give for your predictions?

Innovation//Trend	Now	Within 5 years	Within 15 years	Not likely
1. Alternative/authentic assessment of students' learning	___	___	___	___
2. Cross-age tutoring/mentoring	___	___	___	___
3. Peer counseling/peer coaching	___	___	___	___
4. Faculty teams/team teaching	___	___	___	___
5. Business–school partnerships	___	___	___	___
6. Community–school teaming	___	___	___	___
7. School-based clinics/counseling centers	___	___	___	___
8. Organized after-school programs	___	___	___	___
9. Year-round schools	___	___	___	___
10. School restructuring	___	___	___	___
11. Equity in school funding	___	___	___	___
12. Open enrollment/school choice	___	___	___	___
13. Telephones in the classroom	___	___	___	___
14. Student computer networking	___	___	___	___
15. Video teleconferencing	___	___	___	___
16. Interactive multimedia/hypermedia	___	___	___	___
17. Multimedia distance learning	___	___	___	___
18. Sex education	___	___	___	___
19. AIDS education	___	___	___	___
20. Moral orientation on curricula	___	___	___	___
21. Globalism/multiculturalism	___	___	___	___
22. Aesthetics orientation	___	___	___	___
23. Alcohol and drug intervention	___	___	___	___
24. Reduction of gender bias	___	___	___	___
25. Reduction of racial/ethnic prejudice	___	___	___	___

26. Full inclusion of students with special needs ____ ____ ____ ____
27. Teacher empowerment ____ ____ ____ ____
28. Constructivist approaches to teaching ____ ____ ____ ____
29. Charter schools ____ ____ ____ ____
30. Corporate-education partnerships ____ ____ ____ ____
31. For-profit schools ____ ____ ____ ____
32. _____ ____ ____ ____ ____
33. _____ ____ ____ ____ ____

SUMMARY

What Knowledge and Skills Will Prepare Students for a Global Information Age?

■ Conflicting theories, expectations, and values make it difficult to answer what students need to know and be able to do in the future; however, increasing cultural diversity and global economic interdependence call for communication and cooperation skills and wise use of environmental resources.

■ To meet the challenges of the future, students will need knowledge, skills, attitudes, and values in nine key areas: literacy in language, mathematics, and science; new technological skills; problem solving, critical thinking, and creativity; social awareness, communication skills, and team building; global awareness and conservation skills; health and wellness education; moral and ethical orientation; aesthetics awareness; and life-long, self-directed learning.

How Can Schools and Teachers Provide an Outstanding Education for All Learners?

■ To reach all learners, teachers must understand how some families are under acute stress, how crime and violence impact students' lives, and how to develop multicultural curricula and instructional repertoires that develop the potentialities of students from varied backgrounds.

■ In addition to preparing multicultural instructional materials and strategies for students from diverse cultural, ethnic, and linguistic backgrounds, teachers treat students equitably when they treat high- and low-achieving students the same. Research has identified several teacher behaviors that reflect inequitable treatment of low-achieving students: waiting less time for them to answer questions, interacting with them less frequently, giving them less feedback, calling on them less often, seating them farther away, failing to accept and use their ideas, smiling at them less often, making less eye contact, praising them less, demanding less, grading their tests differently, and rewarding inappropriate behaviors.

■ Effective teachers establish positive relationships with all students by listening to them, giving frequent feedback and opportunities to ask questions, and demanding higher-level performance by asking higher-order questions that require more critical thinking.

■ To reach all learners, teachers should provide them with active, authentic learning experiences.

How Can Community-Based Partnerships Address Social Problems That Hinder Students' Learning?

■ Communities help schools address social problems that hinder students' learning by providing various kinds of support.

■ Civic organizations raise money for schools, sponsor teams, recognize student achievement, award scholarships, sponsor volunteer mentor programs, and provide other resources and services to enrich students' learning.

■ Corporate–education partnerships provide schools with resources, release time for employees to visit schools, scholarships, job initiatives for disadvantaged youth, in-service programs for teachers, and management training for school administrators.

■ Schools serve as resources for their communities by providing educational and recreational programs before and after the school day, and by providing health and social services.

How Will the Privatization Movement Affect Equity and Excellence in Education?

■ Charter schools and for-profit schools, both part of the privatization movement, were developed in response to perceived inadequacies of the public schools.

■ Charter schools are independent, innovative, outcome-based public schools started by a group of teachers, parents, or others who obtain a charter from a local school district, a state, or the federal government.

■ Edison Schools, Inc. (formerly the Edison Project) and the Tesseract Group, Inc. (formerly Education Alternatives, Inc.) are examples of for-profit schools operated by private corporations.

What Can Teachers and Schools Learn from International Education?

■ The challenges and opportunities for teachers in the twenty-first century are remarkably similar worldwide, and teachers in different countries can learn much from one another. Comparative education, the study of educational practices in other countries, enables educators to collaborate internationally.

■ The International Assessment of Educational Progress (IAEP) has revealed that the achievement levels of U.S. students are lower than those of students in other countries; however, these results reflect America's commitment to educating all students and differences in opportunity to learn among countries.

■ Education in many other countries is centralized and teachers follow a national curriculum. While some people support a national curriculum and national examinations for America's educational system, there are several disadvantages to such a system.

- Many other countries tend to provide greater support for teachers and teaching and have greater parental involvement, two practices that would benefit U.S. education. However, pressure for students in other countries to excel is often extreme.

- The International Assessment of Educational Progress (IAEP) and the Third International Mathematics and Science Study (TIMSS) have revealed that the achievement levels of U.S. students are often lower than those of students in other countries.

- Disparities in achievement between U.S. students and students in other countries reflect the United States's commitment to educating *all* students and differences in *opportunity to learn* among countries.

- Many other countries provide greater support for teachers and the teaching profession, have greater parental involvement, and take more steps to nurture beginning teachers.

What Is Our Vision for the Future of Education?

- It is not unrealistic to imagine that teachers in schools during the year 2020 will be well-paid, NBPTS-certified, self-governing professionals who have developed specialized areas of expertise. This vision becomes more possible with each teacher who makes a commitment to its realization.

KEY TERMS AND CONCEPTS

charter schools, 560
comparative education, 565
for-profit schools, 561
higher-order questions, 554
International Assessment of Educational Progress

(IAEP), 566
learning, 554
lower-order questions, 554
national curriculum, 568
privatization movement, 561

synectics, 548
Third International Mathematics and Science Study (TIMSS), 566

APPLICATIONS AND ACTIVITIES

Teacher's Journal

1. Write a scenario forecasting how the teaching profession will change during the next two decades.

2. Select one of the following areas and develop several forecasts for changes that will occur during the next two decades: energy, environment, food, the economy, governance, family structure, demographics, global relations, media, and technology. On what current data are your forecasts based? How might these changes affect teaching and learning?

3. Think about two children you know and project them into the future, twenty years from now. What skills are they likely to need? Which talents should help them? How can schools better promote the development of these skills and talents?

Teacher's Database

1. Begin at the web home pages for the U.S. Department of Education and the National Center for Education Statistics and gather data on the International Assessment of Educational Progress (IAEP), the Third International Mathematics and Science Study (TIMSS), and other federally sponsored comparative education studies. In what areas of the curriculum and at what levels is the achievement of U.S. students at or above the international average? What conclusions about the strengths and weaknesses of U.S. schools can you draw from your analysis of these data?

2. Explore the field of international education or comparative education and talk to teaching professionals in other countries online. For example, you might ask them what they see as the greatest challenge facing educators in their respective countries. Or, you might ask them about working conditions for teachers—that is, number of students taught, time for planning, professional responsibilities beyond the classroom, and so on.

Observations and Interviews

1. Interview the principal at a local or nearby school and ask him or her to describe what the school will be like in ten years. Now interview several teachers at the school. Compare the forecasts of the principal with those of the teachers. What might account for any differences you find?

2. Search for examples of school–community partnership arrangements in the local school district. Find out how these partnerships are progressing and propose a specific new one based on your knowledge of the community.

Professional Portfolio

Prepare a portfolio entry of instructional resources—curriculum guides, teaching tips, assessment strategies, relevant professional associations, books and articles, software, and online resources—related to one of the nine areas of learning students will need to meet the challenges of the future (i.e., literacy in language, mathematics, and science; new technological skills; problem solving, critical thinking, and creativity; social awareness, communication skills, and team building; global awareness and conservation skills; health and wellness education; moral and ethical orientation; aesthetics awareness; and life-long, self-directed learning). For each entry include a brief annotation describing the materials, how you will use them, and where they may be obtained. After you have prepared this portfolio entry, meet with your classmates and exchange information.

References

Abrahamsson, B. (1971). *Military professionalization and political power*. Stockholm: Allmanna Forlagret.

Acheson, A. A., and Gall, M. D. (1997). *Techniques in the clinical supervision of teachers: Preservice and inservice applications*, 4th ed. New York: Longman.

*Ackerman, R. H., Moller, G., and Katzenmeyer, M. (eds.). (1996). *Every teacher as a leader: Realizing the potential of teacher leadership*. San Francisco: Jossey-Bass.

Acton v. Vernonia School District, 66 F.3d 217 (9th Cir. 1995); 115 S. Ct. 2386 (1995).

*Adler, M. (1982). *The paideia proposal: An educational manifesto*. New York: Macmillan.

*Adler, M. (1984). *The paideia program: An educational syllabus*. New York: Macmillan.

Aiken, W. M. (1942). *The story of the Eight-Year Study*. New York: Harper and Row.

Alali, A. A. (ed.). (1995). *HIV and AIDs in the public schools: A handbook for curriculum development, teacher education, and the placement of affected students, with a directory of resources*. Jefferson, NC: McFarland.

Alan Guttmacher Institute. (1999). *Teenage pregnancy: Overall trends and state-by-state information*. New York: Alan Guttmacher Institute.

*Alexander, C. J. (1998). Studying the experiences of gay and lesbian youth. *Journal of Gay and Lesbian Social Services, 8.*

Alfonso v. Fernandez, 606 N. Y. S.2d 259 (N. Y. App. Div. 1993).

Alvin Independent School District v. Cooper, 404 S. W.2d 76 (Tex. Civ. App. 1966).

*American Association for the Advancement of Science. (1999). *Middle grades mathematics textbooks: a benchmark-based evaluation*. New York: Oxford University Press, 1999.

*American Association for the Advancement of Science. (2000). *Atlas of science literacy goals: mapping K–12 learning goals*. New York: Oxford University Press.

*American Association of School Administrators. (1999). *Preparing schools and school systems for the 21st century*. Arlington, VA: American Association of School Administrators.

American Association of University Women (AAUW). (1991). *Shortchanging girls, shortchanging America*. Washington, DC: American Association of University Women.

American Association of University Women (AAUW). (1992). *How schools shortchange girls: The AAUW report*. Researched by The Wellesley College Center for Research on Women. Washington, DC: AAUW Educational Foundation.

American Association of University Women (AAUW). (1993). *Hostile hallways: The AAUW survey on sexual harassment in America's schools*. New York: Louis Harris and Associates.

American Council on the Teaching of Foreign Languages. (1996). *Standards for foreign language learning: Preparing for the 21st century*. Lawrence, KS: American Council on the Teaching of Foreign Languages.

*American Federation of Teachers. (1998a). *Student achievement in Edison schools: Mixed results in an ongoing experiment*. Washington, DC: American Federation of Teachers.

*American Federation of Teachers. (1998b). *Teacher salaries in the 100 largest cities, 1996–97*. Washington, DC: American Federation of Teachers.

*American Federation of Teachers. (1999a). [Online]. AFT on the issues: Vouchers and the accountability dilemma. http://www. aft.org [1999, July]

*American Federation of Teachers. (1999b). *Teaching as a career: From the American Federation of Teachers*. Washington, DC: American Federation of Teachers. http://www.aft.org/pr/teaching.htm

American School Board Journal. (1998, December). School leaders focus on standards and achievement, A13–A15.

*Anderson, J. D. (1997). Supporting the invisible minority. *Educational Leadership, 54*. 65–68.

*Anderson, J. P., Floisand, B., Martinez, D., and Robinson, D. P. (1997). Horizonte—where students come first. *Educational Leadership, 54*(7), 50–52.

*Anderson, R. E., and Ronnkvist, A. (1999). The presence of computers in American schools. The University of California, Irvine, and the University of Minnesota, Center for Research on Information Technology and Organizations.

*Anderson, R. H., and Snyder, K. J. (eds.). (1993). *Clinical supervision: Coaching for higher performance*. Lancaster, PA: Technomic.

*Anderson, R. J., Keller, C. E., and Karp, J. M. (eds.) (1998). *Enhancing diversity: Educators with disabilities*. Washington, DC: Gallaudet University Press.

*Annie E. Casey Foundation. (1999). *Kids count data book, 1999*. Baltimore, MD: Annie E. Casey Foundation.

Anyon, J. (1996). Social class and the hidden curriculum of work. In E. Hollins (ed.). *Transforming curriculum for a culturally diverse society*. Mahwah, NJ: Lawrence Erlbaum, 179–203.

Application of Bay v. State Board of Education, 233 Ore. 609, 378 P.2d 558 (1963).

Aristotle. (1941). *Politics* (Book VIII). In Richard McKoen (ed.). *The basic works of Aristotle*. New York: Random House.

Aronson, E., and Gonzalez, A. (1988). Desegregation, jigsaw, and the Mexican-American experience. In P. A. Katz, and D. A. Taylor (eds.). *Eliminating racism: Profiles in controversy*. New York: Plenum Press.

*Artz, S. (1999). *Sex, power, and the violent school girl*. New York: Teachers College Press.

Ashton-Warner, S. (1963). *Teacher*. New York: Simon and Schuster.

*Asian Americans/Pacific Islanders in Philanthropy. (1997). *An invisible crisis: The educational needs of Asian Pacific American youth*. New York: Asian Americans/Pacific Islanders in Philanthropy.

Astuto, T. (ed.). (1993). *When teachers lead*. University Park, PA: University Council for Educational Administration.

Baker, K. A. (1991). *Bilingual Education*. Bloomington, IN: Phi Delta Kappa.

*Ballantine, J. H. (1997). *The sociology of education: A systematic analysis, 4th ed*. Upper Saddle River, NJ: Prentice Hall.

Banks, C. A. M. (1997, Spring). The challenges of national standards in a multicultural society. *Educational Horizons*, 126–32.

*Banks, J. A. (1993, September). Multicultural education: Development, dimensions, and challenges. *Phi Delta Kappan*, 22–28.

Banks, J. A. (1997). *Teaching strategies for ethnic studies*, 6th ed. Boston, Allyn and Bacon.

*Banks, J. A. (1999). *An introduction to multicultural Education*, 2nd ed. Boston: Allyn and Bacon.

Banks, J. A., and Banks, C. A. (eds.). (1997). *Multicultural education: Issues and perspectives,* 3rd ed. Boston: Allyn and Bacon.

Barbin v. State, 506 So. 2d 88 (1st Cir. 1987).

*Barnett, D., McKowen, C., and Bloom, G. (1998). A school without a principal. *Educational Leadership, 55*(7), 48–49.

*Barrett, H. (2000, April). Create your own electronic portfolio (using off-the-shelf software). *Learning and Leading with Technology.*

Barth v. Board of Education, 490 N.E. 2d 77 (Ill.app. 186 Dist. 1986).

Battles v. Anne Arundel County Board of Education, 904 F. Supp. 471 (Md. 1995), aff'd, 95 F.3d 41 (4th Cir. 1996).

Beard, C. (1938). *The nature of the social sciences*. New York: Charles Scribner.

*Becker, H. J. (1999). *Internet use by teachers: Conditions of professional use and teacher-directed student use*. The University of California, Irvine, and The University of Minnesota, Center for Research on Information Technology and Organizations.

Bell, T. H. (1986, March). Education policy

References marked with asterisks are new to this edition.

development in the Reagan administration. *Phi Delta Kappan*, 487–93.

*Bennett, C. I. (1999). *Comprehensive multicultural education: Theory and practice*, 4th ed. Boston: Allyn and Bacon.

*Bennett, L. (1997). Break the silence: Gay and straight students in Massachusetts team up to make a difference. *Teaching Tolerance*, 6, 24–31.

Bennett, W. (1987). *James Madison High School: A curriculum for American students*. Washington, DC: U.S. Department of Education.

Berliner, D. C., and Biddle, B. J. (1995). *The manufactured crisis: Myths, fraud, and the attack on America's public schools*. Reading, MA: Addison-Wesley Publishing Company.

*Bernstein, B. B. (1996). *Pedagogy, symbolic control and identity: Theory, research, critique (critical perspectives on literacy and education)*. New York: Taylor and Francis.

Besner, H. F., and Spungin, C. I. (1995). *Gay and lesbian students: Understanding their needs*. Washington, DC: Taylor and Francis.

*Bialo, E. (1989). Computers and at-risk youth: A partial solution to a complex problem. *Classroom Computer Learning*, 9(4), 48–55

*Bielaska v. Town of Waterford, 491 A. 2d 1071 (Conn. 1985).

*Bitter, G. G., and Pierson, M. E. (1999). *Using technology in the classroom*. Boston: Allyn and Bacon.

Bloom, B. S. (1981). *All our children learning: A primer for parents, teachers, and other educators*. New York: McGraw-Hill.

Board of Education, Sacramento City Unified School District v. Holland, 786 F. Supp. 874 (ED Cal. 1992).

Board of Education of Oklahoma City Public Schools v. Dowell, 498 U.S. 237, 249–50 (1991).

Boleman, L. G., and Deal, T. E. (1994). *Becoming a teacher leader: From isolation to collaboration*. Thousand Oaks, CA: Corwin Press.

Booth, A., and Dunn, J. F. (eds.). (1996). *Family–school links: How do they affect educational outcomes?* Mahwah, NJ: Lawrence Erlbaum Associates, Publishers.

Borich, G. D. (1996). *Effective teaching methods*, 3rd ed. Englewood Cliffs, NJ: Merrill.

Boyer, E. (1990). Teaching in America. In M. Kysilka (ed.). *Honor in Teaching: Reflections*. West Lafayette, ID: Kappa Delta Pi.

Boyer, E. (1995). *The basic school: A community for learning*. Princeton, NJ: The Carnegie Foundation for the Advancement of Teaching.

Boyer, E. L. (1983). *High school: A report on secondary education in America*. New York: Harper.

Bracy, G. W. (1993). "Now then, Mr.

Kohlberg, about moral development in women . . . " In G. Hass, and F. W. Parkay. (eds.). *Curriculum planning: A new approach*, 6th ed. Boston: Allyn and Bacon, 165–66.

Bracey, G. W. (1996, October). The sixth Bracey report on the condition of public education. *Phi Delta Kappan*, 127–38.

*Bracey, G. W. (1999, March). Getting along without national standards. *Phi Delta Kappan*, 80(7), 548–50.

*Bradley, A. (1997, April 30). Staying in the game. *Education Week on the Web*.

*Bradley, A. (1998a, February 4). Unions agree on blueprint for merging. *Education Week on the Web*.

*Bradley, A. (1998b, September 9). New teachers are hot commodity. *Education Week on the Web*.

*Bradley, A. (1999, April 2). Crackdown on emergency licenses begin as teacher shortage looms. *Education Week on the Web*.

Brameld, T. (1956). *Toward a reconstructed philosophy of education*. New York: Holt, Rinehart and Winston.

Brameld, T. (1959). Imperatives for a reconstructed philosophy of education. *School and Society*, 87.

Brown, F. B., Kohrs, D., and Lanzarro, C. (1991). The academic costs and consequences of extracurricular participation in high school. Paper presented at the Annual Meeting of Educational Research Association.

Brown, M. E. (1994). *Computer simulation: Improving case study methods for preservice and inservice teacher education*. ERIC Document Reproduction Services No. ED371–730.

Brown v. Board of Education of Topeka, Kansas, 347, U.S. 483, 74 S. Ct. 686 (1954).

Brown v. Board of Education of Topeka, Kansas, 349, U.S. 294, 75 S. Ct. 753 (1955).

Brown v. Hot, Sexy and Safer Productions, Inc., 68 F. 3d 525 (1st Cir. 1995), cert. denied, 116 S. Ct. 1044 (1996).

*Bruner, C., and Bennett, D. (1997). Technology and gender: Differences in masculine and feminine views. *NASSP Bulletin*, 81, 46–51.

Bruner, J. S. (1960). *The process of education*. New York: Random House.

*Brunwer, C. and Tally, W. (1999). *The new media literacy handbook: An educator's guide to bringing new media into the classroom*. New York: Anchor Books.

*Bryk, A. S., Sebring, P. B., Kerbow, D., Rollow, S., and Easton, J. Q. (1998). *Charting Chicago school reform: Democratic localism as a lever for change*. Boulder, CO: Westview Press.

*Bucky, P. A. (1992). *The private Albert Einstein*. Kansas City: Andrews and McMeel.

Burch v. Barker, 651 F. Supp. 1149 (W. D. Wash. 1987)

Burch v. Barker, 861 F. 2d 1149 (9th Cir. 1988).

*Burden, P. R., and Byrd, D. M. (1999). *Methods for effective teaching*, 2nd ed. Boston: Allyn and Bacon.

Burnaford, G., Fischer, J., and Hobson, D. (1996). *Teachers doing research: Practical possibilities*. Mahwah, NJ: Lawrence Erlbaum Associates.

Burton v. Cascade School Dist. Union High School No. 5, 512 F.2d 850 (9th Cir. 1975).

*Button, H. W., and Provenzo, E. G. (1989). *History of education and culture in America*, 2nd ed. Englewood Cliffs, NJ: Prentice Hall.

Buzzell, J. B. (1996). *School and family partnerships: Case studies for regular and special educators*. Albany, NY: Delmar Publishers.

*Calkins, L. (1991). *Listening between the lines*. Portsmouth, NH: Heinemann.

Campbell, D. M., Cignetti, P. B., Molenyzer, B. J., Nettles, D. H., and Wyman, Jr., W. M. (1996). *How to develop a professional portfolio: A manual for teachers*. Boston: Allyn and Bacon.

Cantor, L. (1989). Assertive Discipline— more than names on the board and marbles in a jar. *Phi Delta Kappan*, 71(1), 57 –61.

Carmichael, L. B. (1981). *McDonogh 15: The making of a school*. New York: Avon Books.

*Carnegie Council on Adolescent Development. (1989). *Turning points: Preparing American youth for the 21st century*. New York: Carnegie Council on Adolescent Development.

Carnegie Council on Adolescent Development. (1995). *Great transitions: Preparing adolescents for a new century*. New York: Carnegie Council on Adolescent Development.

Carroll, J. (1963). A model of school learning. *Teachers College Record*, 64.

*Caterinicchia, D. (1999, June 18). Teachers' limited tech know-how prompts laptop lease. *CNN Interactive*.

*Catri, D. B. (1999). *Vocational education's image for the 21st century*. Columbus, OH: Center on Education and Training for Employment, Ohio State University.

*Cawelti, G. (1999). *Portraits of six benchmark schools: Diverse approaches to improving student achievement*. Arlington, VA: Educational Research Service.

Center for Research on Effective Schooling for Disadvantaged Students. (1992). Helping students who fall behind, Report No. 22. Baltimore, MD: The Johns Hopkins University.

*Center for the Study and Prevention of Violence, University of Colorado at Boulder. (1998). [Online]. Response to the Columbine school incident. http://www.colorado.edu/cspv [1999, April 21].

*Centers for Disease Control and Prevention. (1998a). Characteristics of health education among secondary schools—school health education profiles, 1996. Atlanta, GA: Centers for Disease Control and Prevention.

*Centers for Disease Control and Prevention. (1998b). *Youth risk behavior surveillance—United States, 1997*. Atlanta, GA: Centers for Disease Control and Prevention.

*CEO Forum on Education and Technology. (1999). *School Technology and Readiness Report*. Washington, DC: CEO Forum on Education and Technology.

*Cetron, M. (1997). Reform and tomorrow's schools. *TECHNOS*, 61, 19–22.

*Chase, B. (1997, October 15). Restoring the impulse to dream: The right to a quality public education. *Vital Speeches of the Day*, 20–23.

*Chase, B. (1999). Teachers lead the fight for innovation and investment in public education. In J. W. Noll (ed.). *Taking sides: Clashing views on controversial issues* 10th ed. Guilford, CT: McGraw–Hill.

Chaskin, R. J., and Rauner, D. M. (1995, May). Youth and caring: An introduction. *Phi Delta Kappan*.

*Chavkin, N. F., and Gonzalez, D. L. (1995). Forging partnerships between Mexican American parents and schools. *ERIC Digest*.

Cheeks, E. H., Flippo, R. F., and Lindsey, J. D. (1997). *Reading for success in elementary schools*. Madison, WI: Brown and Benchmark.

*Child Care Bureau. (1997). *Out-of-school time: School–age care*. Washington, DC: U.S. Department of Health and Human Services, Child Care Bureau.

Chubb, J. E., and Moe, T. (1990). *Politics, markets and America's schools*. Washington, DC: Brookings Institution.

*Clift, R. T., et al. (1995). *Collaborative leadership and shared decision making: Teachers, principals, and university professors*. New York: Teachers College Press.

*Clinton, B. (1999, May 19). White House press briefing.

*Codell, E. R. (1999). *Educating Esmé*. Chapel Hill, NC: Algonquin Books.

Cohen, D. (1990, March 14). Hawaii program for after–school care irks private firms. *Education Week*.

Cohen, S. (ed.) (1974). *Massachusetts School Law of 1648. Education in the United States*. New York: Random House.

Cohn, M. M., and Kottkamp, R. B. (1993). *Teachers: The missing voice in education*. Albany, NY: State University of New York Press.

*Coladarci, T., and Cobb, C. D. (1996). Extracurricular participation, school size, and achievement and self-esteem among high school students: A national look. *Journal of Research in Rural Education*,12(2), 92–103.

Coleman, J. S., Campbell, E. Q., Hobson, C. J., McPartland, J., Mood, A. L., Weinfeld, F. D., and York, R. L. (1966). *Equality of educational opportunity*. Washington, DC: U.S. Government Printing Office.

*Comber, C., et al. (1997). The effects of age, gender and computer experience upon computer attitudes. *Educational Research*, 39, 123–33.

Combs, A. (1979). *Myths in education: Beliefs that hinder progress and their alternatives*. Boston: Allyn and Bacon.

*Comer, J. P. (1997). *Waiting for a miracle: Why schools can't solve our problems—and how we can*. New York: Dutton.

*Committee for Economic Development. (1994). *Putting learning first: Governing and managing schools for high achievement*. New York: Research and Policy Committee, Committee for Economic Development.

*Cookson, P. W., Jr., and Shroff, S. M. (1997). Recent experience with urban school choice plans. *ERIC/CUE Digest*, 127.

Cornbleth, C. (1990). *Curriculum in context*. London: the Falmer Press.

Cornfield v. Connsolidated High School District No 230, F.2d 1316 (7th Cir. 1993).

Costa, A. L. (1984). A reaction to Hunter's knowing, teaching, and supervising. In P. L. Hosford (ed.). *Using what we know about teaching*. Alexandria, VA: Association for Supervision and Curriculum Development.

Coughlin, E. K. (1993, March 24). Sociologists examine the complexities of racial and ethnic identity in America. *Chronicle of Higher Education*.

Counts, G. (1932). *Dare the school build a new social order?* New York: The John Day Company.

Csikszentmihalyi, M., and McCormack, J. (1986, February). The influence of teachers. *Phi Delta Kappan*, 415–19.

*Cuban, L. (1997, August 10). Unless teachers get involved, wiring schools just enriches computer makers. *The Los Angeles Times*.

*Cuban, L. (1999a, January). High-tech schools, low-teach teaching. *The Education Digest*.

*Cuban, L. (1999b, August 4). The technology puzzle: Why is greater access not translating into better classroom use? *Education Week*, 47, 68.

Curtis v. School Committee of Falmouth, 652 N.E. 2d 580 (Mass. 1995), *cert.* denied, 116 S. Ct. 753 (1996).

*Curwin, R., and Mendler, A. (1989, March). We repeat, let the buyer beware: A response to Canter. *Educational Leadership*, 46(6), 83.

Curwin, R. and Mendler, A. (1988, October) Packaged discipline programs: Let the buyer beware. *Educational Leadership, 46(6), 68–71.

Cziko, G. A. (1992, March). The evaluation of bilingual education: From neces-

sity and probability to possibility. *Educational Researcher*, 10–15.

Daniels, C. B. (1984). Quality of educational materials: A marketing perspective. In F. W. Parkay, S. Obrien, and M. Hennesey, (Eds). *Quest for quality: Improving basic skills instruction in the 1980s*. Lanham, MD: University Press of America.

*Danzberger, J. P. (1994a, January). Governing the nation's schools: The case for restructuring local school boards. *Phi Delta Kappan*, 67–73.

*Danzberger, J. P. (1994b, January). School board reform in West Virginia. *Phi Delta Kappan*.

*Darling-Hammond, L. (1993). Progress toward professionalism in teaching. In G. Cawelti (ed.). *Challenges and achievements of American education: The 1993 yearbook of the Association for Supervision and Curriculum Development*. Washington, DC: Association for Supervision and Curriculum Development.

*Darling-Hammond, L. (1999). Educating teachers for the next century: Rethinking practice and policy. In G. A. Griffin (ed.). *The education of teachers: Ninety–eighth yearbook of the National Society for the Study of Education*. Chicago: University of Chicago Press.

*Darling-Hammond, L., Wise, A. E., and Klein, S. P. (1995). *A license to teach: Building a profession for 21st–century schools*. Boulder, CO: Westview Press.

*Davis, G. A., and Rimm, S. B. (1998). *Education of the gifted and talented, 4th ed..* Boston: Allyn and Bacon.

Davis v. Meek, 344 F. Supp. 298 N.D. Ohio (1972).

Davis v. Monroe County Board of Education, Supp. 97–843. Georgia (1999).

*Davitt, J. (1997, January 3). The ultimate good shepherd. *Times Educational Supplement*.

*Deal, T. E., and Peterson, K. D. (1999). *Shaping school culture: The heart of leadership*. San Francisco: Jossey–Bass Publishers.

Dean v. Board of Education, 523 A. 2d 1059 (Md. App. 1987).

*Department of Health and Human Services. (1999). *Profile of homelessness in America*. Washington, DC: Department of Health and Human Services.

Dewey, J. (1900). *The school and society*. Chicago: University of Chicago Press.

Dewey, J. (1902). *The child and the curriculum*. Chicago: University of Chicago Press.

Dewey, J. (1916). *Democracy and education: An introduction to the philosophy of education*. New York: Macmillan.

Dewey, J. (1955). Quoted in *Organizing the teaching profession: The story of the American Federation of Teachers*. Glencoe, IL: The Commission on Educational Reconstruction.

*Dobbs, S. M. (1998). *Learning in and

through arts: A guide to discipline-based art education. Los Angeles: Getty Education Institute for the Arts.

Doe v. Renfrow, 635F.2d 582 (7th Cir. 1980), cert. denied, 451 U.S. 1022, rehearing denied, 101 S. Ct. 3015 (1981).

Dollase, R. H. (1992). Voices of beginning teachers: Visions and realities. New York: Teachers College Press.

Doyle, W. (1986). Classroom organization and management. In M. Wittrock (ed.). Handbook of research on teaching, 3rd ed. New York: Macmillan.

Dryfoos, J. G.(1994). Full-service schools: A revolution in health and social services for children, youth, and families. San Francisco: Jossey-Bass.

*Dryfoos, J. G. (1998). Safe passage: Making it through adolescence in a risky society. New York: Oxford University Press.

Duffy, G., and Roehler, L. (1989). The tension between information-giving and mediation: Perspectives on instructional explanation and teacher change. In J. Brophy (Ed.). Advances in research on teaching, Vol. 1. Greenwich, CT: JAI Press.

Duke, D. L. (1984). Teaching—the imperiled profession. Albany, NY: State University of New York Press.

Durlak, J. A. (1995). School-based prevention programs for children and adolescents. Thousand Oaks, CA: Sage Publications.

*Dykgraaf, C. L., and Kane, S. (1998, October). For-profit charter schools: What the public needs to know. Educational Leadership, 56(2), 51–53.

*Economist. (1999a, January 16). A contract on schools: Why handing education over to companies can make sense.

*Economist. (1999b, January 16). Reading, writing, and enrichment: Private money is pouring into American education—and transforming it.

Edelman, M. W. (1993). The measure of our success: A letter to my children. New York: Harper Perennial.

*Edelman, M. W. (1997, November 9). Young families shut out of the American dream. Seattle Times, B5.

Education Week (1996a, January 10). Studies seek to adjust for pay variables.

Education Week. (1996b, April 24). Virginia governor victorious in rejecting Goals 2000.

Education Week. (1997). Staying in the game.

*Education Week. (1998, September 9). New teachers are hot commodity.

*Education Week. (1999a, March 31). N.M. governor digs in his heels on vouchers.

*Education Week. (1999b, April 14). States increasingly flexing their policy muscle.

Education Week. (1999c, May 5). Battle over principals in Chicago: Administration vs. local councils.

*Education Week. (1999d, May 26). Clinton ESEA plan targets accountability.

*Education Week. (1999e, June 2). Substituting the privilege of choice for the right to equality.

*Education Week on the Web. (1999, July 29). Issue paper: Privatization of public education.

Educational Testing Service. (1995, Spring). Bringing volunteers into teacher education programs. ETS Policy Notes, 8–9.

*Edwards, A. T. (1997). Let's stop ignoring our gay and lesbian youth. Educational Leadership, 54.

Edwards, P., and Young, L. (1992). Beyond parents: family, community, and school involvement. Phi Delta Kappan, 74(1), 72, 74, 76, 78, 80.

Edwards v. Aguillard, 482 U.S. 578(1987).

*Ehrenreich, B. 1989. Fear of falling: The inner life of the middle class. New York: Harper Perennials.

Eisner, E. (1994). The educational imagination: On the design and evaluation of school programs, 3rd ed. New York: Macmillan.

*Eisner, E. W. (1998). The kind of schools we need: Personal essays. Portsmouth, NH: Heinemann.

Elam, S. M., and Rose, L. C. (1995, September). The 27th annual Gallup poll of the public's attitudes toward the public schools. Phi Delta Kappan, 41–56.

Elam, S. M., Rose, L. C., and Gallup, A. (October 1993). The 25th annual Phi Delta Kappa Gallup Poll of the public's attitudes toward the public schools. Phi Delta Kappan, 137–52.

Elam, S. M., Rose, L. C., and Gallup, A. (1994, September). The 26th annual Phi Delta Kappan/Gallup Poll of the public's attitudes toward the public schools. Phi Delta Kappan, 41–56.

*Emerson, R., Fretz, R., and Shaw, L. (1995). Writing ethnographic field notes. Chicago: University of Chicago Press.

Engel v. Vitale, 370 U.S. 421 (1962).

*Epstein, J. (1995, May). School/family/community partnerships: Caring for the children we share. Phi Delta Kappan, 76(9), 701–12.

Epstein, J. L. (1992). School and family partnerships. In M. C. Alkin (Ed.). Encyclopedia of educational research, 6th ed. New York: Macmillan.

ERIC Clearinghouse. (1993). Value search: Parent involvement in the educational process. Eugene, OR: ERIC Clearinghouse on Educational Management.

Erikson, E. H. (1963). Childhood and society. New York: W. W. Norton.

*Erikson, E. H. (1997). The life cycle completed: Extended version with new chapters on the ninth stage of development by Joan M. Erikson. New York: W.W. Norton and Company.

*Esbensen, F., and Osgood, D.W. (1997). National evaluation of G.R.E.A.T. research in brief. Washington, DC: U.S. Department of Justice, Office of Justice Programs, National Institute of Justice, NCJ 167264.

*Essex, N. L. (1999). School law and the public schools: A practical guide for educational leaders. Boston: Allyn and Bacon.

Etzioni, A. (1969). The semi-professions and their organization: Teachers, nurses, social workers. New York: Free Press.

Etzioni, A. (1999, June 9). The truths we must face to curb youth violence. Education Week on the Web.

Evertson, C. M., Emmer, E. T., Clements, R. S., and Worsham, M. E. (1997). Classroom management for elementary teachers, 4th ed. Boston: Allyn and Bacon.

Fagen v. Summers, 498 P.2d 1227 (Wyo. 1972).

*Fashola, O. (1999). Review of extended-day and after-school programs and their effectiveness. Johns Hopkins University: Center for Research on the Education of Students Placed at Risk.

*Feistritzer, E. (1999, May 13). Teacher quality and alternative certification programs. Testimony before the House Committee on Education and the Workforce. Washington, DC.

*Feldhusen, J.F. (1997). Educating teachers for work with talented youth. In N. Colangelo and G. A. Davis (Eds). Handbook of gifted education. Boston: Allyn and Bacon.

Felsenthal, H. (1982, March). Factors influencing school effectiveness: An ecological analysis of an "effective" school. Paper presented at the Annual Meeting of the American Educational Research Association, New York.

*Ferguson, A., Barovick, H., et al. (1999, May 24). Character goes back to school. Time, 153, 68–69.

Fischer, J. C. (1996). Open to ideas: Developing a framework for your research. In G. Burnaford, J. Fischer, and D. Hobson, (Eds.). Teachers doing research: Practical possibilities. Mahwah, NJ: Lawrence Erlbaum Associates, Publishers.

Fischer, L., and Sorenson, G. P. (1996). School law for counselors, psychologists, and social workers, 3rd ed. White Plains, NY: Longman.

Franklin, B. (1931). Proposals relating to the education of youth in Pennsylvania. In Thomas Woody (Ed.), Educational views of Benjamin Franklin. New York: McGraw–Hill.

Franklin v. Gwinnett County Public Schools, 112 S. Ct. 1028 (1992).

Franz, K. R. (1996, Autumn). Toward a critical social consciousness in children: multicultural peace education in a first grade classroom. Theory into Practice, 35(4), 264–70.

Freedman, S., Jackson, J., and Botes, K. (1983). Teaching: An imperiled profession. In L. Shulman, and G. Sykes, (Eds.). (1983). Handbook of teaching and policy. New York: Longman.

*Freeman v. Pitts, 503 U.S. 467 (1992).

*Friend, M., and Bursuck, W. D. (1999).

Including students with special needs: A practical guide for classroom teachers, 2nd ed. Boston: Allyn and Bacon.

*Frost, D. (1997). *Reflective action planning for teachers: A guide to teacher-led school and professional development.* London: D. Fulton Publishers.

Fuligni, A. J., and Stevenson, H. W. (1995). Home environment and school learning. In Lorin W. Anderson (Ed.), *International encyclopedia of teaching and teacher education,* 2nd ed. Oxford: Pergamon, 378–82.

*Fullan, M., and Hargreaves, A. (1996). *What's worth fighting for in your school?* New York: Teachers College Press.

*Fuller, B., Burr, E., Huerta, L., Puryear, S., and Wexler, E. (1999). *School choice: Abundant hopes, scarce evidence on results.* University of California–Berkeley and Stanford University: Policy Analysis for California Education.

*Furger, R. (1998). *Does Jane compute? Preserving our daughters' place in the cyber revolution.* New York: Warner Books.

*Furger, R. (1999, September). Are wired schools failing our kids? *PC World.*

*Gaddy, B. B., Hall, W. W., and Marzano, R. J. (1996). *School wars: Resolving our conflicts over religion and values.* San Francisco: Jossey-Bass Publishers.

*Gagné, R. M. (1974). *Essentials of learning for instruction.* Hinsdale, IL: Dryden.

*Gagné, R. M. (1977). *The conditions of learning,* 3rd ed. New York: Holt, Rinehart and Winston.

Gallup, G. H. (1975, September). The 7th annual Gallup poll of the public's attitudes toward the public schools. *Phi Delta Kappan,* 227–41.

Gandara, P., and Fish, J. (Spring 1994). Year-round schooling as an avenue to major structural reform. *Educational Evaluation and Policy Analysis, 16.*

*Garbarino, J. (1999). *Lost boys: Why our sons turn violent and how we can save them.* New York: Free Press.

Gardner, H. (1983). *Frames of mind.* New York: Basic Books.

Gardner, H. (1995, November). Reflections on multiple intelligences: Myths and messages. *Phi Delta Kappan,* 200–03, 206–09.

*Gardner, H. (1999). *The disciplined mind: What all students should understand.* New York: Simon and Schuster.

*Gates, B., Myhrvold, N., and Rinearson, P. M. (1996). *The road ahead.* New York: Penguin.

Gaylord v. Tacoma School District No. 10, 88 Wa. 2d 286, 599 P.2d 1340 (1977).

Gehrke, N. (1988, Summer). Toward a definition of mentoring. *Theory Into Practice,* 190–94

*Gehrke, N. J., and Romerdahl, N. S. (1997). *Teacher leaders: Making a difference in schools.* West Lafayette, IN: Kappa Delta Pi.

George, P. (1995). *The Japanese secondary school: A closer look.* Columbus, OH: National Middle School Association; and Reston, VA: National Association of Secondary School Principals.

*Gerber, S. B. (1996). Extracurricular activities and academic achievement. *Journal of Research and Development in Education, 30*(1), 42–50.

Gerstner, L. V., Semerad, R. D., Doyle, D. P., and Johnston, W. B. (1994). *Reinventing education: Entrepreneurship in America's public schools.* New York: Dutton.

Gilligan, C. (1993). *In a different voice: Psychological theory and women's development.* Cambridge, MA: Harvard University Press.

Gipp, G. (1979, August-September). Help for Dana Fast Horse and friends. *American Education, 15.*

*Giroux, H. A. (1999, Winter). Schools for sale: Public education, corporate culture, and the citizen-consumer. *The Educational Forum, 63*(2), 140–49.

*Glasser, W. R. (1997, April). A new look at school failure and school success. *Phi Delta Kappan,* 596–602.

*Glasser, W. R. (1998a). *Quality school,* 3rd ed. New York: Harper Perennial.

*Glasser, W. R. (1998b). *The quality school teacher: Specific suggestions for teachers who are trying to implement the lead-management ideas of the quality school.* New York: Harper Perennial.

*Glasser, W. R. (1998c). *Choice theory: A new psychology of personal freedom.* New York: HarperCollins.

*Glasser, W. R., and Dotson, K. L. (1998). *Choice theory in the classroom.* New York: Harper Perennial.

*Glickman, C. D. (1993). *Renewing America's schools: A guide for school-based action.* San Francisco: Jossey-Bass.

*Glickman, C. D. (1998). *Revolutionizing America's schools.* San Francisco: Jossey-Bass.

*Glickman, C., Gordon, S. P., and Ross-Gordon, J. M. (1998). *Supervision of instruction: A developmental approach,* 4th ed. Boston: Allyn and Bacon.

Gmelch, W. H., and Parkay, F. W. (1995). Changing roles and occupational stress in the teaching profession. In M. J. O'Hair, and S. J. Odell (Eds.). *Educating teachers for leadership and change: Teacher education yearbook III.* Thousand Oaks, CA: Corwin Press, 46–65.

Godar, J. (1990). *Teachers talk.* Macomb, IL: Glenbridge Publishing.

*Goldberg, D. (1998). Does technology make the grade? *Family Circle PC World.*

Goldhammer, R., Anderson, R. H., and Krajewski, R. J. (1993). *Clinical supervision: Special methods for the supervision of teachers,* 3rd ed. Fort Worth, TX: Harcourt Brace Jovanovich.

Goleman, D. (1997). *Emotional intelligence.* New York: Bantam Books.

*Goleman, D. (1998). *Working with emotional intelligence.* New York: Bantam Books.

*Good, T. E., and Brophy, J. E. (1997). *Looking in classrooms,* 7th ed. New York: Longman.

*Good, T. E., and Brophy, J. E. (2000). *Looking in classrooms,* 8th ed. Boston: Pearson Publishing.

*Good, T. E., and Grouws, D. (1979). The Missouri mathematics effectiveness project: An experimental study in fourth-grade classrooms. *Journal of Educational Psychology, 71,* 355–62.

Goodlad, J. I. (1983a, April). What some schools and classrooms teach. *Educational Leadership,* 8–19.

Goodlad, J. (1983b, Spring). Teaching: An endangered profession. *Teachers College Record,* 575–78.

Goodlad, J. (1990). *Teachers for our nation's schools.* San Francisco: Jossey-Bass.

Goodlad, J. (1994). *Educational renewal: Better teachers, better schools.* San Francisco: Jossey-Bass.

Gordon, W. J. J. (1968). *Making it strange,* Books 1 and 2. Evanston, IL: Harper and Row.

Gordon, W. J. J. (1971a). *Invent-o-rama.* Cambridge, MA: Porpoise Books.

Gordon, W. J. J. (1971b). *What color is sleep?* Cambridge, MA: Porpoise Books.

Gordon, W. J. J. (1975). *Strange and familiar,* Book 1. Cambrdige, MA: Porpoise Books.

Goss v. Lopez, 419 U.S. 565 (1975).

*Grant, C. A. (1978). Education that is multicultural: Isn't that what we mean? *Journal of Teacher Education, 29*(5), 45–58.

Grant, C. A. (1994, Winter). Challenging the myths about multicultural education. *Multicultural Education,* 4–9.

*Grant, G., and Murray, C. E. (1999). *Teaching in America: The slow revolution.* Cambridge, MA: Harvard University Press.

Grant, P. G., Richard, K. J., and Parkay, F. W. (1996, April). *Using video cases to promote reflection among preservice teachers: A qualitative inquiry.* Paper presented at the Annual Meeting of the American Educational Research Association, New York.

*Greene, B. (1999, July 7). A 21st century idea for schools: Log off and learn. *Chicago Tribune,* Sec. 2, p. 1.

Greene, M. (1995). What counts as philosophy of education? In Wendy Kohli (Ed.). *Critical conversations in philosophy of education.* New York: Routledge.

Griego-Jones, T. (1996). Reconstructing bilingual education from a multicultural perspective. In C. A. Grant, and M. L. Gomez (Eds.), *Making schooling multicultural: Campus and classroom.* Englewood Cliffs, NJ: Merrill.

*Griffin, G. A. (1999). Changes in teacher education: Looking to the future. In G. A. Griffin (Ed.). *The education of teachers: Ninety–eighth yearbook of the National*

Society for the Study of Education (pp. 1–28). Chicago: University of Chicago Press.

*Grossman, D., and Siddle, P. (1999). Combat. In L. Kurtz (ed.). *The encyclopedia of violence, peace, and conflict.* San Diego: Academic Press.

*Guskey, D. (1996, March). "Uniform" improvement? *Education Digest.*

*Gutloff, K. (1999, October). Anger in the halls. *NEA Today,* 8–9.

Haberman, M. (1995, June). Selecting "star" teachers for children and youth in urban poverty. *Phi Delta Kappan,* 777–81.

*Haberman, M. (1996). Selecting and preparing urban teachers. In J. Sikula (Ed.). *The second handbook of research on teacher education* (pp. 747–60). New York: Macmillan.

*Hadderman, M. (1998). Charter schools. *ERIC Digest,* 118.

*Hale-Benson, J. E. (1986). *Black children: Their roots, culture, and learning styles.* Baltimore, MD: Johns Hopkins University Press.

*Hallahan, D. P., and Kauffman, J. M. (2000). *Exceptional children: Introduction to special education,* 8th ed. Boston: Allyn and Bacon.

*Hamburg, D. A. (1997). Toward a strategy for healthy adolescent development. *American Journal of Psychiatry, 154*(6), 6–12.

*Hammett, R. F. (1997). Computers in schools: White boys only? *English Quarterly 28,*1.

*Hankins, K. H. (1998). Cacophony to Symphony: Memoirs in Teacher Research. *Harvard Educational Review, 68*(1), 80–95.

Hansen, D. T. (1995). *The call to teach.* New York: Teachers College Press.

*Hardman, M. L., Drew, C. J., and Egan, M. W. (1999). *Human exceptionality: Society, School, and family,* 6th ed. Boston: Allyn and Bacon.

*Harrington-Lueker (ed.). (1999). *Barriers and breakthroughs: Technology in urban schools.* Washington, DC: Education Writers Association.

Hazelwood School District v. Kuhlmeier, 56 U.S.L.W. 4079, 4082 (1988); 484 U.S. 260, 108 S. Ct. 562 (1988).

Health. (June 1999). New York: Family Media, Inc.

*Healy, J. M. (1998). *Failure to connect: How computers affect our children's minds—for better and worse.* New York: Simon and Schuster.

*Heath, S. B. (1983). *Ways with words.* Cambridge: Cambridge University Press.

Hedges, L. V. (1996). Quoted in Hedges finds boys and girls both disadvantaged in school. *Education News.* The Department of Education, University of Chicago.

Heinich, R., Molenda, M., and Russell, J. D. (1993). *Instructional media and the new technologies of instruction,* 4th ed. New York: Macmillan.

*Hendrie, C. (1999, May 5). Battle over principals in Chicago: Administration vs. local councils. *Education Week on the Web.*

*Henriques, M. E. (1997, May). Increasing literacy among kindergartners through cross-age training. *Young Children,* 42–47.

Henry, E., Huntley, J., McKamey, C., and Harper, L. (1995). *To be a teacher: Voices from the classroom.* Thousand Oaks, CA: Corwin Press.

Henry, M. (1993). *School cultures: Universes of meaning in private schools.* Norwood, NJ: Ablex.

Henry, M. E. (1996). *Parent–school collaboration: Feminist organizational structures and school leadership.* Albany, NY: State University of New York Press.

Herbert, B. (1993, June 27). Listen to the children. *New York Times,* OP–ED.

*Herndon, J. (1969). *The way it spozed to be.* New York: Bantam Books.

Hess, G. A., Jr. (1995). *Restructuring urban schools: A Chicago perspective.* New York: Teachers College Press.

Hirshfelder, A. B. (1986). *Happily may I walk: American Indians and Alaska Natives today.* New York: Charles Scribner.

*Hoff, D. (1999, January 13). With 2000 looming, chances of meeting national goals iffy. *Education Week on the web.*

*Hole, S. (1998). Teacher as rain dancer. *Harvard Educational Review, 68*(3), 413 –21.

Holland, A., and Andre, T. (1987, Winter). Participation in extracurricular activities in secondary schools. *Review of Educational Research,* 437–466.

Holly, M. L., and McLoughlin, C. (eds.). (1989). *Perspectives on teacher professional development.* New York: Falmer Press.

The Holmes Group. (n.d.). *Tomorrow's schools: Principles for the design of professional development schools.* East Lansing, MI: Holmes Group.

Holmes, M., and Weiss, B. J. (1995). *Lives of women public schoolteachers: Scenes from American educational history.* New York: Garland.

*Holmes Partnership. (1999). *Origins of the Holmes Partnership (1987–1997).* Auburn, AL: Holmes Partnership.

*Holt, J. (1964). *How children fail.* New York: Delta.

Holt v. Shelton, 341 F. Supp. 821 (M.D. Tenn. 1972).

*Holt–Reynolds, D. (1999). Good readers, good teachers? Subject matter expertise as a challenge in learning to teach. *Harvard Educational Review, 69*(1), 29–50.

*Hopkins, B. J., and Wendel, F. C. (1997).

Creating school-community-business partnerships. Bloomington, IN: Phi Delta Kappa Educational Foundation.

Hortonville Joint School District No. 1 v. Hortonville Education Association, 426 U.S. 482, 96 S. Ct. 2308 (1976).

Howsam, R. B., Corrigan, D. C., Denemark, G. W., and Nash, R. J. (1976). *Educating a profession.* Washington, DC: American Association of Colleges for Teacher Education.

*Hoynes, W. (1998, Summer). News for a teen market: The lessons of Channel One. *Journal of Curriculum and Supervision,* 339–56.

*Hoyt, W. H. (1999). An evaluation of the Kentucky Education Reform Act. In *Kentucky Annual Economic Report 1999.* Lexington, KY: University of Kentucky, Center for Business and Economic Research, 21–36.

Huling-Austin, L. (1990). Teacher induction programs and internships, In W. R. Houston (ed.), *Handbook of research on teaching.* New York: Macmillan.

Hun-Choe. (1996, November 15). Bringing the cane down on school bullies. *Bangkok Post,* 8.

*Hunter, M. (1994). *Enhancing teaching.* New York: Macmillan.

*Hurwitz, S. (1999, April). New York: Can Rudy Crew hang tough on vouchers and pull off a turnaround in the nation's biggest school system? *The American School Board Journal,* 36–40.

Hutchins, R. M. (1963). *A conversation on education.* Santa Barbara, CA: Fund for the Republic.

Hyman v. Green, 403 N.W. 2d 597 (Mich. App. 1987).

*Idol, L. (1998). Optional extended year program, Feedback, Publ. No. 97.20. Austin Independent School District, TX, Office of Program Evaluation.

Igoa, C. (1995). *The inner world of the immigrant child.* New York: Lawrence Erlbaum Associates, Publishers.

Imber, M., and van Geel, T. (1993). *Education law.* New York: McGraw–Hill, Inc.

Immediato v. Rye Neck School Dist., 73 F.3d 454 (2d Cir. 1996).

*Indiana University. (1999, February). *IU school of education programs offer life-changing experiences.* Bloomington, IN: Indiana University, Office of Communication and Marketing.

*Inger, M. (1991). Improving urban education with magnet schools. ERIC/CUE Digest, 76.

Ingraham v. Wright, 430 U.S. 651 (1977).

Inoue, A. (1996, October 10). *Creating schools with special characteristics.* Paper presented at the eighth Washington State University College of Education/Nishinomiya Education Board Education Seminar. Washington State University, Pullman.

*International Association for the Evaluation of Educational Achievement. (1997a). *Mathematics achievement in the primary school years: IEA's third international mathematics and science study.* Amsterdam, Netherlands: International Association for the Evaluation of Educational Achievement.

*International Association for the Evaluation of Educational Achievement. (1997b). *Science achievement in the primary school years: IEA's third international mathematics and science study.* Amsterdam, Netherlands: Author International Association for the Evaluation of Educational Achievement.

*International Reading Association. (1999, April). *Using multiple methods of beginning reading instruction.* Newark, DE: International Reading Association.

Jackson, P. (1990). *Life in classrooms.* New York: Teachers College Press.

*Jacobson, L. (1996, November 22). Gay student to get nearly $1 million in settlement. *Education Week on the Web.*

Jeglin v. San Jacinto Unified School District, 827 F. Supp. 1459 (Cal. 1993).

*Jencks, C., and Phillips, M. (eds.). (1998). *The black–white test score gap.* Washington, DC: Brookings Institution Press.

*Jencks, C., et al. (1972). *Inequality: A reassessment of the effect of family and schooling in America.* New York: Basic Books.

*Jenkinson, E. B. (1995). Myths and misunderstandings surround the schoolbook protest movement. *Contemporary Education,* 66(2), 70–73.

*Jensen, E. (1998). *Teaching with the brain in mind.* Alexandria, VA: Association for Supervision and Curriculum Development.

Jersild, A. (1955). *When teachers face themselves.* New York: Teachers College Press.

*Johnson, D. W., and Johnson, R. T. (1999). *Learning together and alone: Cooperative, competitive, and individualistic learning,* 5th ed. Boston: Allyn and Bacon.

Johnson, J., and Immerwahr, J. (1994). *First things first: What Americans expect from the public schools, a report from Public Agenda.* New York: Public Agenda.

Johnson, J., and Yates, J. (1982). *A national survey of student teaching programs.* DeKalb, IL: Northern Illinois University, Teaching Programs. Eric Document Reproduction Services No. ED 232–963.

Johnson, M. (1926). The educational principles of the School of Organic Education, Fairhope, Alabama. In G. M. Whipple, (Ed.). *The twenty–sixth yearbook of the National Society for the Study of Education.* Bloomington, IL: Public School Publishing Company.

*Johnson, M. J., and Brown, L. (1998). Collegial support teams. In D. J. McIntyre, and D. M. Byrd (Eds). *Strategies for career-long teacher education: Teacher education yearbook VI.* Thousand Oaks, CA: Corwin Press.

*Jonassen, D. H., Peck, K. L., and Wilson, B. G. (1999). *Learning with technology: A constructivist perspective.* Upper Saddle River, NJ: Merrill.

*Jones, J. (1994). Integrated learning systems for diverse learners. *Media and Methods* 31(3).

*Jones, J. M. (1981). The concept of racism and its changing reality. In B. D. Bowser and R. G. Hunt (eds.). *Impacts of racism on white Americans.* Beverly Hills, CA: Sage.

*Jordan, K. M., Vaughan, J.S., and Woodworth, K. J. (1997). I will survive: Lesbian, gay, and bisexual youths' experience of high school. *Journal of Gay and Lesbian Social Services,* 7, 17–33.

*Jordan, W. J., and Nettles, S. M. (1999). *How students invest their time out of school: Effects on school engagement, perceptions of life chances, and achievement.* Baltimore, MD: Center for Research on the Education of Students Placed at Risk.

*Joyce, B., Weil, M., and Calhoun, E. (2000). *Models of teaching,* 6th ed. Boston: Allyn and Bacon.

*Karp, J. M., and Keller, C. E. (1998). Preparation and employment experiences of educators with disabilities. In R. J. Anderson, C. E. Keller, and J. M. Karp, (Eds.). *Enhancing diversity: Educators with disabilities.* Washington, DC: Gallaudet University Press.

Karr v. Schmidt, 401 U.S. 1201, 91 S. Ct. 592, 27 L. Ed.2d 797 (1972).

*Katzenmeyer, G. M., and Moller, G. (1996). *Awakening the sleeping giant: Leadership development for teachers.* Thousand Oaks, CA: Corwin Press.

*Kavarsky, M. (1994). Salome Urena Middle Academies. *Journal of Emotional and Behavioral Problems,* 3(3), 37–40.

*Keller, C. E., Anderson, R. J., and Karp, J. M. (1998). Introduction in R. J. Anderson, C. E. Keller, J. M. and Karp, (Eds.). *Enhancing diversity: Educators with disabilities.* Washington, DC: Gallaudet University Press.

*Keresty, B., O'Leary, S., and Wortley, D. (1998). *You can make a difference: A teacher's guide to political action.* Portsmouth, NH: Heinemann.

*Kerr, S. T. (1999). Visions of sugarplums: The future of technology, education, and the schools. In *Issues in curriculum: A selection of chapters from past NSSE yearbooks: Ninety–eighth yearbook of the National Society for the Study of Education, Part II.* Chicago: University of Chicago Press.

King, S. H. (1993, Summer). The limited presence of African-American teachers. *Review of Educational Research.*

*Kirkpatrick, H., and Cuban, L. (1998). Computers make kids smarter—right? *TECHNOS Quarterly* 7(2), 26–31.

*Kleinfeld, J. (1998). *The myth that schools shortchange girls: Social science in the service of deception.* Washington, DC: Women's Freedom Network.

Knezevich, S. J. (1984). *Administration of public education: A source book for the leadership and management of educational institutions,* 4th ed. New York: Harper and Row.

*Knupfer, N. N. (1998). Gender divisions across technology advertisements and the WWW: Implications for educational equity. *Theory into Practice* 37, 1, 54–63.

*Kohl, H. R. (1967). *36 children.* New York: Signet.

Kohlberg, L. (2000). The cognitive-developmental approach to moral education. In F. W. Parkay, and G. Hass, (Eds.). *Curriculum planning: A contemporary approach,* 7th ed. Boston: Allyn and Bacon, 136–48.

*Kohn, A. (1997, February). How not to teach values: A critical look at character education. *Phi Delta Kappan,* 428–39.

Koller, E. (1996). Overcoming paradigm paralysis: A high school teacher revists foreign language education. In G. Burnaford, J. Fischer, and D. Hobson, (Eds.). *Teachers doing research: Practical possibilities.* Mahwah, NJ: Lawrence Erlbaum Associates.

*Kotlowitz, A. (1991). *There are no children here: The story of two boys growing up in the other America.* New York: Doubleday.

Kounin, J. (1970). *Discipline and group management in classrooms.* New York: Holt, Rinehart and Winston.

*Kozma, R., et al. (1992). Technology and the fate of at-risk students. *Education and Urban Society* 24(4), 440–53..

*Kozol, J. (1967). *Death at an early age.* Boston: Houghton Mifflin.

Kozol, J. (1991). *Savage inequalities: Children in America's schools.* New York: Crown Publishers.

Krizek v. Cicero–Stickney Township High School District No. 201, 713 F. Supp. 1131 (1989).

*Krogh, S. L. (2000). Weaving the web. In F. W. Parkay, and G. Hass, (Eds.). *Curriculum planning: A contemporary approach,* 7th ed. Boston: Allyn and Bacon, 338–41.

*Ladson-Billings, G. (1994). *The dreamkeepers: Successful teachers of African American children.* San Francisco: Jossey-Bass.

*Lambert, L., et al. (1996). *Who will save our schools?: Teachers as constructivist leaders.* Thousand Oaks, CA: Corwin Press.

*LaMorte, M. W. (1999). *School law: Cases and Concepts,* 6th ed. Boston: Allyn and Bacon.

Larry, P. v. Riles, 793 F.2d 969 (9th Cir. 1984).

Lau v. Nichols, 414 U.S. 563 (1974).

Lee, V. E., Chen, X., and Smerdon, B. A. (1996). *The influence of school climate on gender differences in the achievement and engagement of young adolescents.* American Association of University Women.

Lemon v. Kurtzman, 403 U.S. 602, 91 S. Ct. 2105, 291 L. Ed.2d 745 (1971).

Levey, S. (1996). *Starting from scratch: One classroom builds its own curriculum.* Portsmouth, NH: Heinemann.

Levine, D. U., and Levine, R. F. (1996). *Society and education,* 9th ed. Boston: Allyn and Bacon.

Levy, F. (1996, October). What General Motors can teach U.S. schools about the proper role of markets in education reform. *Phi Delta Kappan,* 108–14.

*Lewis, A. (1992). Helping young urban parents educate themselves and their children. *ERIC/CUE Digest,* 85.

*Lewis, J. F. (1995, September). Saying no to vouchers: What is the price of democracy? *NASSP Bulletin,* 45–51.

*Lewis, R. B., and Doorlag, D. H. (1999). *Teaching special students in general education classrooms,* 5th ed. Upper Saddle River, NJ: Merrill.

*Lickona, T. (1993). The return of character education. *Educational Leadership, 51*(3), 6–11.

Lickona, T. (1998, February). A more complex analysis is needed. *Phi Delta Kappan,* 449–54.

Lieberman, A. (1990). Foreword. In S. Mei –ling Yee, (Eds.).*Careers in the classroom: When teaching is more than a job.* New York: Teachers College Press.

*Lieberman, M. (1997). *The teachers unions: How the NEA and AFT sabotage reform and hold students, parents, teachers, and taxpayers hostage to bureaucracy.* New York: Free Press.

*Lightfoot, S. L. (1982). *The good high school: Portraits of character and culture.* New York: Basic Books.

Lindsay, D. (1996, March 13). N.Y. bills give teachers power to oust pupils. *Education Week.*

Livingston, C. (ed.). (1992). *Teachers as leaders: Evolving roles.* Washington, DC: National Education Association.

Locilento v. John A. Coleman Catholic High School, 523 N.Y.S. 2d 198 (A.D. 3d Dept. 1987).

Louis Harris and Associates. (1990). *The Metropolitan Life survey of the American teacher 1990: New teachers: Expectations and ideals.* New York: Louis Harris and Associates.

Louis Harris and Associates. (1991). *The Metropolitan Life survey of the American teacher, 1991: Coming to terms—teachers' views on current issues in education.* New York: Louis Harris and Associates.

Louis Harris and Associates. (1995). *The Metropolitan Life survey of the American teacher, 1984–1995: Old problems, new challenges.* New York: Louis Harris and Associates.

*Louis Harris and Associates. (1997). *The Metropolitan Life survey of the American teacher, 1997: Examining gender issues in public schools.* New York: Louis Harris and Associates.

*Macías, R. F., et al. (1998). *Summary report of the survey of the states limited English proficient students and available educational programs and services, 1996–97.* Washington, DC: National Clearinghouse for Bilingual Education.

*MacLeod, J. (1995). *Ain't no makin' it: Aspirations and attainment in a low–income neighborhood.* Boulder, CO: Westview Press.

MacNaughton, R. H., and Johns, F. A. (1991, September). Developing a successful schoolwide discipline program. *NASSP Bulletin,* 47–57.

*Madaus, G. F. (1999). The influence of testing on the curriculum. In M. J. Early and K. J. Rehage (eds.). *Issues in curriculum: A selection of chapters from past NSSE yearbooks: Ninety-eighth yearbook of the National Society for the Study of Education, Part II* (pp. 73–111). Chicago: University of Chicago Press.

*Mahoney, J., and Cairns, R. B. (1997). Do extracurricular activities protect against early school dropout? *Developmental Psychology, 33*(2), 241–53.

Mailloux v. Kiley, 323 F., 448 F.2d 1242 Supp. 1387, 1393 (1st Cir. 1971).

Mann, H. (1868). Annual reports on education. In Mary Mann (Ed.). *The life and works of Horace Mann,* vol. 3. Boston: Horace B. Fuller.

Mann, H. (1957). *Twelfth annual report.* In Lawrence A. Cremin (Ed.). *The republic and the school: Horace Mann on the education of free men.* New York: Teachers College Press.

*Mann, L. (1998, Summer). Getting global with technology. *Curriculum Update.*

Manning, M. L., and Baruth, L. G. (1996). *Multicultural education of children and adolescents.* Boston: Allyn and Bacon.

*Manzo, K. K. (1999, June 2). States setting strategies to reduce mistakes in textbooks. *Education Week on the Web..*

Marcus v. Rowley 695 F.2d 1171 (9th Cir. 1983).

*Marks, H. M., Newmann, F. M., and Gamoran, A. (1996). Does authentic pedagogy increase student achievement? In F. M. Newmann, et al. (Eds). *Authentic achievement: Restructuring schools for intellectual quality.* San Francisco: Jossey-Bass Publishers, 49–76.

Marshall, K. (1996, January). How I confronted HSPS (hyperactive superficial principal syndrome) and began to deal with the heart of the matter. *Phi Delta Kappan,* 336–45.

Maslow, A. (1954). *Motivation and personality.* New York: Basic Books.

Maslow, A. (1962). *Toward a psychology of being.* New York: Basic Books.

*McCarthy, M. M., Cambron-McCabe, N. H., and Thomas, S. B. (1998). *Public school law: Teachers' and students' rights,* 4th ed. Boston: Allyn and Bacon.

*McGhan, B. (1997, Winter). Compulsory school attendance: An idea past its prime? *The Educational Forum,* 134–39.

Mehlinger, H. D. (1996, February). School reform in the Information Age. *Phi Delta Kappan,* 400–07.

*Mental Health in Schools Center. (1998). *Restructuring boards of education to enhance effectiveness in addressing barriers to student learning: A Center report.* University of California–Los Angeles: Mental Health in Schools Center. Eric Document No. ED423–479.

*Miami Herald. (1999, April 26). It's clear sailing for school vouchers: Legislators agree on tuition plan.

*Milken Exchange on Education Technology. (1999). *Will new teachers be prepared to teach in a digital age? A national survey on information technology in teacher education.* Santa Monica, CA: Milken Exchange on Education Technology.

*Mills, G. E. (2000). *Action research: A guide for the teacher researcher.* Upper Saddle River, NJ: Merrill.

Missouri v. Jenkins, 515 U.S. 70 (1995).

*Modi, M., Konstantopoulos, S., and Hedges, L. V. (1998). Predictors of academic giftedness among U.S. high school students: Evidence from a nationally representative multivariate analysis. Paper presented at the Annual Meeting of the American Educational Research Association, San Diego. Eric Document No. ED422-356.

*Molino, F. (1999). My students, my children. In M. K. Rand, and S. Shelton-Colangelo, (Eds.). *Voices of student teachers: Cases from the field.* (pp. 55–56). Upper Saddle River: Merrill.

Montagu, A. (1974). *Man's most dangerous myth: The fallacy of race,* 5th ed. New York: Oxford University Press.

Moore, D. R. (1992). Voice and choice in Chicago. In W. H. Clune, and J. F. Witte (eds.). *Choice and control in American education: Volume II. The practice of choice, decentralization and school restructuring.* Philadelphia: Falmer Press.

*Moore, J. P., and Terrett, C. P. (1999). *Highlights of the 1997 national youth gang survey. Fact sheet.* Washington, DC: U.S. Department of Justice, Office of Justice Programs, Office of Juvenile Justice and Delinquency Prevention.

Moran v. School District No. 7, 350 F. Supp. 1180 (DC Mont. 1972).

*Moreno, N. P. (1999, July). K–12 science education reform—A primer for scientists. *Bioscience, 49*(7), 569–577.

Morris, J. E., and Curtis, K. E. (1983, March/April). Legal issues relating to field-based experiences in teacher education. *Journal of Teacher Education,* 2–6.

Morris, V. C., and Pai, Y. (1994). *Philosophy and the American school: An introduction to the philosophy of education.* Lanham, MD: University Press of America.

Morrison v. State Board of Education, 82 Cal. Rptr. 175, 461 P.2d 375 (Cal. 1969).

Morton, C. (1996, February). The modern land of Laputa: Where computers are used in education. *Phi Delta Kappan,* 416–19.

Moyers, B. D. (1989). *A world of ideas: Conversations with thoughtful men and women.* New York: Doubleday.

Mozert v. Hawkins County Board of Education, 827 F.2d 1058 (6th Cir. 1987), cert. denied, 484 U.S. 1066 (1988).

*Murphy, J. (1999, April). Reconnecting teaching and school administration: A call for a unified profession. Paper presented at the Annual Meeting of the American Educational Research Association, Montreal.

Murray v. Pittsburgh Board of Public Education, 919 F. Supp. 838 (Pa. 1996).

*Nash, R. J. (1997). *Answering the "virtuecrats": A moral conversation on character education.* New York: Teachers College Press.

*Nathan, J. (1998, March). Heat and light in the charter school movement. *Phi Delta Kappan,* 79(7), 499–505.

National Assessment of Educational Progress (NAEP). (1996). *Measuring essential learning in science.* Washington, DC: National Assessment Governing Board, U.S. Department of Education.

*National Assessment of Educational Progress (NAEP). (1999). *The nation's report card.* Washington, DC: Office of Educational Research and Improvement.

*National Association for Sport and Physical Education. (1999). *National standards for physical education.* Reston, VA: National Association for Sport and Physical Education.

*National Association for Year–Round Education. (1999). History of year–round education. San Diego, CA: National Association for Year–Round Education. http://www.nayre.org.

National Board for Professional Teaching Standards. (1992, June 22). Press release. Detroit: National Board for Professional Teaching Standards.

*National Board for Professional Teaching Standards. (1994). *Toward high and rigorous standards for the teaching profession.* National Board for Professional Teaching Standards.

National Board for Professional Teaching Standards. (1995). *An invitation to national board certification.* Detroit: National Board for Professional Teaching Standards.

National Center for Education Statistics. (1980). *High school and beyond study.* Washington, DC: National Center for Education Statistics.

National Center for Education Statistics (1995). *Public school teacher cost differences across the United States.* Washington, DC: National Center for Education Statistics.

*National Center for Education Statistics (1998a). *The condition of education 1998.* Washington, DC: National Center for Education Statistics.

*National Center for Education Statistics (1998b). *Private school universe survey, 1995–96.* Washington, DC: National Center for Education Statistics.

*National Center for Education Statistics. (1999). *Digest of education statistics 1998.* Washington, DC: U.S. Department of Education, Office of Educational Research and Improvement.

*National Clearinghouse on Child Abuse and Neglect. (1998). *Child maltreatment 1996: Reports from the states to the National Child Abuse and Neglect data system.* Washington, DC: U.S. Government Printing Office.

*National Commission on Civic Renewal. (1998). *A Nation of Spectators.* College Park, MD: National Commission on Civic Renewal.

*National Commission on Excellence and Education. (1983). *A nation at risk: The imperative for educational reform.* Washington, DC: U. S. Government Printing Office.

National Commission on Teaching and America's Future. (1996). *What matters most: Teaching for America's future.* New York: National Commission on Teaching and America's Future.

*National Council for Accreditation of Teacher Education (NCATE). (1997a). *Standards for accreditation of teacher education.* Washington, DC: National Council for Accreditation of Teacher Education (NCATE).

*National Council for Accreditation of Teacher Education (NCATE). (1997b). *Standards, procedures, and policies for the accreditation of professional education units.* Washington, DC: National Council for Accreditation of Teacher Education (NCATE).

*National Council for Accreditation of Teacher Education (NCATE). (1999). *NCATE: Did you know?* Washington, DC: National Council for Accreditation of Teacher Education (NCATE).

National Council for the Social Studies. (1994). *Expect excellence: Curriculum standards for the social studies.* Washington, DC: National Council for the Social Studies.

*National Council of Teachers of Mathematics. (1998). *Principles and standards for school mathematics: Discussion draft.* Reston, VA: National Council of Teachers of Mathematics.

*National Education Association. (1997). *NEA Research: Status of the American public school teacher, 1995–96: Highlights.* Washington, DC: National Education Association.

*National Education Goals Panel. (1998). *The national education goals report: Building a nation of learners, 1998.* Washington, DC: U.S. Government Printing Office.

*National Education Goals Panel. (1999). National Education Goals Panel recommends that goals be renamed "America's Education Goals" and continue beyond the year 2000. Press Release, National Education Goals Panel.

*National Governors' Association. (1998, November 4). Press release.

*National Institute for Mental Health. (1999). *Suicide fact sheet.* Washington, DC: National Institute for Mental Health.

*National Joint Committee on Learning Disabilities. (1997). *Operationalizing the NJCLD definition of learning disabilities for ongoing assessment in schools.* Rockville, MD: National Joint Committee on Learning Disabilities.

National Trade and Professional Associations of the United States, 34th ed. (1999). B. Downs, S. E. White, and A. G. Wood, (Eds.). New York: Columbia Books, Inc.

*Neill, A. S. (1960). *Summerhill: A radical approach to child rearing.* New York: Hart.

*Nelson, J. L., Carlson, K., and Palonsky, S. B. (2000). *Critical issues in education: A dialectic approach,* 4th ed. New York: McGraw–Hill.

New Jersey v. Massa, 231 A.2d 252, N.J. Sup. Ct. (1967).

New Jersey v. T.L.O., 221 Cal. Rptr. 118, 105 S. Ct. 733 (1985).

*Newmann, F. M., et al.(eds). (1996). *Authentic achievement: Restructuring schools for intellectual quality.* San Francisco: Jossey-Bass.

Newmann, F. M., and Wehlage, G. G. (1995). *Successful school restructuring: A report to the public and educators by the Center on Organization and Restructuring of Schools.* Madison, WI: University of Wisconsin, Center on Organization and Restructuring of Schools.

Nieto, S. (1992). *Affirming diversity: The sociopolitical context of multicultural education.* White Plains, NY: Longman.

*Noble, D. (1996, November). Mad rushes into the future: The overselling of educational technology. *Educational Leadership,* 18–23.

Noddings, N. (1992). *The challenge to care in schools: An alternative approach to education.* New York: Teacher's College Press.

Noddings, N. (1995, May). Teaching themes of care. *Phi Delta Kappan, 76*(9), 675–79

*Noll, J. W. (ed.). (1999). *Taking sides: Clashing views on controversial educational issues,* 10th ed. Guilford, CT: McGraw–Hill.

*Norris, C. (1994). Computing and the classroom: Teaching the at–risk student. *Computing Teacher 21*(5), 12, 14.

North Central Regional Educational Laboratory. (1993). *Policy briefs, report 1, 1993.* Elmhurst, IL: Author.

*Northwest Regional Educational Laboratory. (1999). *Arts education: Basic to learning.* Portland: Northwest Regional Educational Laboratory.

Null v. Board of Education, 815 F. Supp. 937 (W. Va. 1993).

Oberti v. Board of Education of the Borough of Clementon School District, 789 E. Supp. 1322 (D. N.J. 1992)

*Odden, A., and Busch, C. (1998). *Financing schools for high performance: Strategies for improving the use of educational resources.* San Francisco: Jossey–Bass.

O'Hair, M. J., and Odell, S. J. (eds.). (1995). *Educating Teachers for Leadership and Change: Teacher education yearbook III.* Thousand Oaks, CA: Corwin Press, Inc.

Ohman v. Board of Education, 301 N.Y. 662, 93 N.E. 2d 927 (1950).

*Okrent, D. (1999, May 10). Raising kids online: What can parents do? *Time,* 38–43.

*Olsen, L. (1997). *Made in America: Immigrant students in our public schools.* New York: New Press.

*Oppenheimer, T. (1997, July). The computer delusion. *The Atlantic Monthly,* 45–62.

O'Reilly, R. C., and Green, E. T. (1983). *School law for the practitioner.* Westport, CN: Greenwood Press.

*Orfield, G. and Yun, J. T. (1999). *Resegregation in American schools.* Cambridge, MA: Harvard University, the Civil Rights Project.

*Ortiz, M. G. (1999, April 19,). Urban schools lag in technology. *Detroit Free Press.*

*Ozmon, H. W., and Craver, S. M. (1999). *Philosophical foundations of education,* 6th ed. Upper Saddle River, NJ: Merrill.

Pajak, E. (1993). *Approaches to clinical supervision: Alternatives for improving instruction.* Norwood, MA: Christopher-Gordon.

*Paliokas, K. L., and Rist, R. C. (1996, April 3). School Uniforms: Do they reduce violence—or just make us feel better? *Education Week, 61*(7), 46–49.

Pang, V. O. (1994, December). Why do we need this class: Multicultural education for teachers. *Phi Delta Kappan.*

Parkay, F. W. (Summer 1988). Reflections of a protégé. *Theory into Practice,* 195–200.

*Parkay, F. W., and Hass, G. (2000). *Curriculum planning: A contemporary approach,* 7th ed. Boston: Allyn and Bacon.

*Parkay, F. W., and Oaks, M. M. (1998, April 15). *Promoting the professional development of teachers: What the U.S. can learn from other countries.* Paper presented at the Annual Meeting of the American Educational Research Association, San Diego.

Parkay, F. W., Shindler, J., and Oaks, M. M. (1997, January). Creating a climate for collaborative, emergent leadership at an urban high school: Exploring the stressors, role changes, and paradoxes of restructuring. *International Journal of Educational Reform,* 64–74.

*Parkay, F. W., Potisook, P., Chantharasakul, A., and Chunsakorn, P. (1999). *New roles and responsibilities in educational reform: A study of Thai and U.S. principals' attitudes toward teacher leadership.* Kasetsart University, Bangkok: Center for Research on Teaching and Teacher Education.

*Parker, L., and Shapiro, J. P. (1993). The context of educational administration and social class. In C. A. Capper (Ed.). *Educational administration in a pluralistic society* (pp.36–65). Albany, NY: State University of New York Press.

PASE (Parents in Action on Special Education) v. Hannon, No. 74C3586, U.S. District Court for the Northern District of Illinois, Eastern Division, 506 F. Supp. 831; 1980 U.S. Dist.

Patchogue–Medford Congress of Teachers v. Board of Education of Patchogue–Medford Union Free School District, 70 N.Y. 2d 57, 510 N.E. 2d 325 (1987).

PC World. (1999a, September). "Free" computer labs saddle kids with on–screen commercials.

PC World. (1999b, September). Schools may lose cheap Internet access.

*Pellicer, L.O., and Anderson, L. W. (1995). *A handbook for teacher leaders.* Thousand Oaks, CA: Corwin Press.

Peter Doe v. San Francisco Unified School District, 131 Cal. Rptr. 854 (1976).

*Piirto, J. (1999). *Talented children and adults: Their development and education.* Upper Saddle River, NJ: Merrill.

*Pipho, C. (1999, February). The profit side of education. *Phi Delta Kappan, 80*(6), 421–22.

*Pitton, D. E. (1998). *Stories of student teaching: A case approach to the student teaching experience.* Upper Saddle River, NJ: Merrill.

Ponticell, J. A., Olson, G. E., and Charlier, P. S. (1995). Project MASTER: Peer coaching and collaboration as catalysts for professional growth in urban high schools. In M. J. O'Hair, and S. J. Odell, (Eds.). *Educating teachers for leadership and change: Teacher education yearbook III.* Thousand Oaks, CA: Corwin Press, 96–116.

Poole, B. J. (1995). *Education for an information age: Teaching in the computerized classroom.* Madison, WI: Brown and Benchmark.

*Popham, W. J. (1999, May 12). Commentary: Assessment apathy. *Education Week on the Web.*

Portner, J. (1999, May 12). Schools ratchet up the rules on student clothing, threats. *Education Week on the Web.*

Posner, G. J. (1993). *Field experience: A guide to reflective teaching,* 3rd ed. New York: Longman.

*Postman, N. (1995, October 9). Virtual students, digital classrom. *The Nation.*

Powell, A. G. (1980). *The uncertain profession: Harvard and the search for educational authority.* Cambridge, MA: Harvard University Press.

Power, E. J. (1982). *Philosophy of education: Studies in philosophies, schooling, and educational policies.* Englewood Cliffs, NJ: Prentice Hall.

Public Agenda. (1994). *First things first: What Americans expect from the public schools.* New York: Public Agenda.

*Public Agenda. (1998). *A lot to be thankful for: What parents want children to learn about America.* New York: Public Agenda.

*Public Agenda. (1999). *Reality check: The status of standards reform..* New York: Public Agenda.

Rallis, S. F. (1990). Professional teachers and restructured schools: Leadership challenges. In B. Mitchell, and L. L. Cunningham, (Eds.). *Educational leadership and changing contexts of families, communities, and schools* (89th NSSE yearbook). Chicago: University of Chicago Press.

*Rand, M. K., and Shelton–Colangelo, S. (1999). *Voices of Student Teachers: Cases from the Field.* Upper Saddle River, NJ: Merrill.

Ravitch, D. (1983). *The troubled crusade: American education, 1945–1980.* New York: Basic Books.

*Ravitch, D. (1990). Multiculturalism: E pluribus plures. *American Scholar, 59*(3), 337–55.

*Ravitch, D. (1997, December). The fight for standards. *Forbes, 160*(13), 106.

*Ravitz, J. L., Wong, Y. T., and Becker, H. J. (1999). Report to participants. The University of California, Irvine, and The University of Minnesota: Center for Research on Information Technology and Organizations.

Ray v. School District of DeSoto County, 666 F. Supp. 1524 (M. D. Fla. 1987).

*RCM Research Corporation. (1998). *Time: Critical issues in educational change.* Portsmouth, NH: RCM Research Corporation.

*Renzulli, J. S. (1998). The three–ring conception of giftedness. In S. M. Baum, S. M. Reis, and L. R. Maxfield, (Eds.). *Nurturing the gifts and talents of primary grade students.* Mansfield Center, CT: Creative Learning Press.

Rice, R., and Walsh, C. E. (1996). Equity at risk: The problem with state and federal education reform efforts. In C. Walsh (Ed.). *Education reform and social change: Multicultural voices, struggles, and visions.* Mahwah, NJ: Lawrence Erlbaum Associates, Publishers.

Rickover, H. G. (1959). *Education and freedom.* New York: E. P. Dutton.

Rickover, H. G. (1983, February 3). Educating for excellence. *Houston Chronicle.*

*Ries, E. (1997). To "V" or not to "V": For many the word "vocational" doesn't work. *Techniques* 72(8), 32–36.

*Riley, R. W. (1998, August 19). Research shows teachers, schools work hard on parental involvement; parents want even more partnerships. Press release. Washington, DC.

*Rippa, S. A. (1997). *Education in a free society: An American history,* 8th ed. New York: Longman.

*Ripple, R. E., and Rockcastle, V. E. (Eds.). (1964). *Piaget rediscovered: A report of the conference on cognitive studies and curriculum development.* Ithaca, NY: Cornell University, School of Education.

Rithdee, K. (1996, November 3–9). Fighting drugs with faith. *The Bangkok Post Sunday Magazine.*

Roberts v. City of Boston, 59 Mass. (5 Cush.) 198 (1850).

Robinson, G. E., and Protheroe, N. (1994, September). Local school budget profiles study. *School Business Affairs,* 31–32, 34–40.

Rogers, C. (1961). *On becoming a person.* Boston: Houghton Mifflin.

Rogers, C. (1974). *Freedom to learn.* Columbus, OH: Merrill.

Rogers, C. (1982). *Freedom to learn in the eighties.* Columbus, OH: Merrill.

*Rogers, K. (1991). *The relationship of grouping practices to the education of the gifted and talented learner.* Storrs, CT: University of Connecticut, National Research Center on the Gifted and Talented.

Romans v. Crenshaw, 354 F. Supp. 868 (S.D. Tex. 1972).

*Romer, R. (2000). Today standards—tomorrow success. In F. W. Parkay, and G. Hass, (Eds.). *Curriculum planning: A contemporary approach,* 7th ed. Boston: Allyn and Bacon, 314–17.

*Rose, L. C., and Gallup, A. M. (1998, September). The 30th annual Phi Delta Kappa/Gallup poll of the public's attitudes toward the public schools. *Phi Delta Kappan,* 41–56.

*Rose, L. C., and Gallup, A. M. (1999). The 31st annual Phi Delta Kappa/Gallup poll of the public's attitudes toward the public schools. *Phi Delta Kappan,* 81(1), 41–56.

*Rose, L. C., Gallup, A. M., and Elam, S. M. (1997, September). The 29th annual Phi Delta Kappa/Gallup poll of the public's attitudes toward the public schools. *Phi Delta Kappan,* 41–56.

Rosenshine, B. (1988). Explicit teaching. In D. Berliner and B. Rosenshine (eds.), *Talks to teachers.* New York: Random House.

*Rosenshine, B. (1995). Advances in research on instruction. *The Journal of Educational Research,* 88(5), 262–268.

Rosenshine, B., and Stevens, R. (1986). Teaching functions. In Merlin C. Wittrock (Ed.). *Handbook of research on teaching,* 3rd ed. New York: Macmillan.

*Rosenshine, B., Meister, C., and Chapman, S. (1996). Teaching students to generate questions: A review of the intervention studies. *Review of Educational Research,* 66(2), 181–221.

Ross, D. D., and Webb, R. B. (1995). Implementing shared decision making at Brooksville Elementary School. In A. Lieberman (Ed.). *The work of restructuring schools: Building from the ground up.* New York: Teachers College Press.

Rossell, C. H. (1990, Winter). The research on bilingual education. *Equity and Choice,* 29–36.

*Rotberg, I. C., Futrell, M. H., and Lieberman, J. M. (1998). National board certification: Increasing participation and assessing impacts. *Phi Delta Kappan,* 79(6), 462–466..

*Rothstein, R. (1998, May). Bilingual education: The controversy. *Phi Delta Kappan,* 672, 674–678.

*Ruenzel, D. (1999, April). Pride and prejudice. *Teacher Magazine on the Web.*

Sadker, M., and Sadker, D. (1994). *Failing at fairness: How our schools cheat girls.* New York: Touchstone.

Sallie Mae Corporation. (1995). *A report from the 1994 Sallie Mae symposium on quality education.* Washington, DC: Sallie Mae Corporation.

*Salovey, P., and Sluyter, D. J. (eds.). (1997). *Emotional development and emotional intelligence: Educational implications.* New York: Basic Books.

*Sandholtz, J. J., Ringstaff, C., and Dwyer, D. C. (1997). *Teaching with technology: Creating student-centered classrooms.* New York: Teachers College Press.

*Sarason, S. B. (1997). *How schools might be governed and why.* New York: Teachers College Press.

*Sarnoff, D. (1940). Foreword to L. R. Lohr. *Television broadcasting.* New York: McGraw-Hill.

Sartre, Jean-Paul. (1972). Existentialism. In John Martin Rich (ed.). *Readings in the philosophy of education.* Belmont, CA: Wadsworth.

Schaefer, R. (1967). *The school as the center of inquiry.* New York: Harper and Row.

Schaill v. Tippecanoe School Corporation, 864 F.2d 1309 (7th Cir. 1988).

*Schifter, D. (ed.). (1996). *What's happening in math class? Envisioning new practices through teacher narratives, vol. 1.* New York: Teachers College Press.

Schmidt, P. (1991, February 20). Three types of bilingual education effective, E. D. study concludes. *Education Week on the Web.*

Schmuck, R. A., and Schmuck, P. A. (1997). *Group processes in the classroom,* 7th ed. Madison, WI: Brown and Benchmark.

Schnaiberg, L. (1995, November 1). Record increase in special-education students reported. *Education Week on the Web.*

Schnaiberg, L. (1996, June 12). Staying home from school. *Education Week on the Web.*

*Schneider, R. B. and Barone, D. (1997, spring). Cross-age tutoring. *Childhood Education,* 136–143.

Schön, D. (1983). *The reflective practitioner: How professionals think in action.* New York: Basic Books.

Schön, D. (1987). *Educating the reflective practitioner: Toward a new design for teaching and learning in the professions.* San Francisco: Jossey-Bass.

Schön, D. (1991). *The reflective turn: Case studies in an educational practice.* New York: Teachers College Press.

School District of Abington Township v. Schempp, 374 U.S. 203, 83 S. Ct. 1560, 10 L.Ed. 2d 844 (1963).

*Schwartz, J. E., and Beichner, R. J. (1999). *Essentials of educational technology.* Boston: Allyn and Bacon.

*Schwartz, W. (1995, December). Opportunity to learn standards: Their impact on urban education. *ERIC/CUE Digest,* 110.

*Schwebel, A. J., et al. (1996). *The student teacher's handbook,* 3rd ed. Mahwah, NJ: Lawrence Erlbaum Associates.

Scopes, J. (1966). *Center of the storm.* New York: Holt, Rinehart, and Winston.

Scoville v. Board of Education of Joliet Township High School District 204, cert. denied, 400 U.S. 826, 91 S. Ct. 51 (1970); 425 F.2d 10 (7th Cir. 1971).

Sears, J. T. (1991). Educators, homosexuality and homosexual students: Are personal feelings related to professional beliefs? *Journal of Homosexuality,* 22.

*Shade, B. J. (1982). Afro-American cognitive style: A variable in school success? *Review of Educational Research* 52,2, 219–238.

Shanley v. Northeast Independent School District, 462 F.2d 960 (5th Cir. 1972).

Sharan, Y., and Sharan, S. (1989/1990, December/January). Group investigation expands cooperative learning. *Educational Leadership,* 17–21.

*Shenk, D. (1998). *Data smog: Surviving the information age.* New York: HarperEdge.

Sheuerer, D., and Parkay, F. W. (1992). The new Christian right and the public school curriculum: A Florida report. In J. B. Smith, and J. G. Coleman, Jr. (Eds.). *School library media annual:*

1992, vol. 10. Englewood, CO: Libraries Unlimited.

Shoop, R. J., and Dunklee, D. R. (1992). *School law for the principal: A handbook for practitioners.* Boston: Allyn and Bacon.

*Sigalit, U., and Van Lehn, K. (1995). STEPS: A simulated, tutorable physics student. *Journal of Artificial Intelligence in Education,* 6(4), 405–37.

*Signer, B. (1991). CAI and at–risk minority urban high school students. *Journal of Research on Computing in Education,* 24(2).

Simonetti v. School District of Philadelphia, 308 Pa Super. 555, 454 A. 2d 1038 (Pa. Super. 1982).

Singer, A. (1994, December). Reflections on multiculturalism. *Phi Delta Kappan,* 284–88.

*Sizer, T. (1997a). *Horace's compromise: The dilemma of the American high school,* 3rd ed. Boston: Houghton Mifflin.

*Sizer, T. (1997b). *Horace's school: Redesigning the American high school.* Boston: Houghton Mifflin.

*Sizer, T. (1997c). *Horace's hope: What works for the American high school.* Boston: Houghton Mifflin.

*Sizer, T. and Sizer, N. (1999). *The students are watching: Schools and the moral contract.* Boston: Beacon Press.

Skinner, B. F. (1972). Utopia through the control of human behavior. In J. M. Rich (Ed.). *Readings in the philosophy of education.* Belmont, CA: Wadsworth.

*Slavin, R. E. (2000). *Educational psychology: Theory and practice,* 6th ed. Boston: Allyn and Bacon.

*Slavit, D. (1998). Above and beyond AAA: The similarity and congruence of polygons. *Mathematics Teaching in the Middle School,* 3(4), 276–280.

*Sleeter, C. E. (1999). Curriculum controversies in multicultural education. In M. J. Early and K. J. Rehage (eds.). *Issues in curriculum: A selection of chapters from past NSSE yearbooks: Ninety-eighth yearbook of the National Society for the Study of Education* (pp. 257–280). Chicago: University of Chicago Press.

*Smith, D. D. (1998). *Introduction to special education: Teaching in an age of challenge,* 2nd ed. Boston: Allyn and Bacon.

Smith, K. B., and Meier, K. K. (1995). *The case against school choice: Politics, markets, and fools.* Armonk, NY: M.E. Sharpe.

*Smith, M. S., Stevenson, D. L., and Li, C. P. (1998, November). Voluntary national tests: Helping schools improve instruction and learning in reading and math. *Phi Delta Kappan,* 41–56.

Smith v. Archbishop of St. Louis, 632, S.W. 2d 516 (Mo. app. 1982).

Smith v. Board of School Commissioners of Mobile County, 655 F. Supp. 939 (S. D.

Ala.), *rev'd,* 827 F.2d 684 (11th Cir. 1987).

*Smolkin, R. (1999, February 27–28). The reading debate rages. *Moscow-Pullman Daily News,* 1A, 10A.

*Smyth, J. W. (1995). *Clinical supervision: Collaborative learning about teaching.* New York: State Mutual Book and Periodical Service.

*Snider, J. H. (1996, May–June). Education wars: The battle over information-age technology. *The Futurist,* 24–29.

Sommers, C. H. (1994). *Who stole feminism?: How women have betrayed women.* New York: Simon and Schuster.

Sommers, C. H. (1996, June 12). Where the boys are. *Education Week on the Web.*

*Sosniak, L. A. (1999). Professional and subject matter knowledge for teacher education. In G. A. Griffin (ed.). *The education of teachers: Ninety-eighth yearbook of the National Society for the Study of Education.* Chicago: University of Chicago Press.

Sowell, E. J. (1996). *Curriculum: An integrative introduction.* Boston: Allyn and Bacon.

Splintered vision (A): An investigation of U.S. science and mathematics education. (1996). Washington, DC: U.S. Department of Education and Internation al Institute on Education.

Spokesman Review. (1993, June 4). Harassment claims vex teachers.

*Spring, J. (1997). *The American school 1642–1996,* 4th ed. New York: McGraw Hill.

*Spring, J. (1998). *Conflict of interests: The politics of American education,* 3rd ed. Boston: McGraw Hill.

Spring, J. (1999). *American education,* 8th ed. New York: McGraw–Hill.

Sricharatchanya, P. (1996, November 5). Education reforms are also crucial. *Bangkok Post.*

St. Michel, T. (1995). *Effective substitute teachers: Myth, mayhem, or magic?* Thousand Oaks, CA: Corwin Press.

Stahl v. Cocalico School District, 534 A. 2d 1141 (Pa. Cmwlth. 1987).

Stanford, B. H. (1992). Gender equity in the classroom. In D. A. Byrnes and G. Kiger (Eds.), *Common bonds: Anti–bias teaching in a diverse society.* Wheaton, MD: Association for Childhood Education International.

State v. Rivera, 497 N. W.2d 878 (Iowa 1993).

Station v. Travelers Insurance Co., 292 So.2d 289 (La. Ct. App. 1974).

*Steinberg, A. (1999, March/April). The human cost of over-reliance on tests. *Harvard Education Letter.*

Steinberg, L., Dornbusch, S., and Brown, B. (1996) *Beyond the classroom: Why school reform has failed and what parents need to do.* New York: Simon and Schuster.

Sternberg, R. J. (1996, March). Myths,

countermyths, and truths about intelligence. *Educational Researcher,* 11–16.

*Stoll, C. (1996). *Silicon snake oil: Second thoughts on the information highway.* New York: Anchor.

Stover, D. (1992, March). The at-risk kids schools ignore. *The Executive Educator,* 28–31.

*Sue, D. W., and Sue, D. (1999). *Counseling the culturally different: Theory and practice,* 3rd ed. New York: Wiley.

Sullivan v. Houston Independent School District, 475 F.2d 1071 (5th Cir. 1969), *cert. denied* 414 U.S. 1032 (1969).

*Swisher, K., and Deyhle, D. (1987). Styles of learning and learning styles: Educational conflicts for American Indian/ Alaskan Native youth. *Journal of Multilingual and Multicultural Development,* 8(4).

Sykes, G. (1983, October). Contradictions, ironies, and promises unfulfilled: A contemporary account of the status of teaching. *Phi Delta Kappan,* 87–93.

*Tapscott, D. (1999, July 6,). Kids, technology and the schools. *Computerworld.*

Teach for America. (1999). About us. New York: Teach for America. http://www.teachforamerica.org

Teacher Centers of New York State. (1999) What is a teacher center? http://www.tier.net/tcenters/class. htm.

Tellijohann, S. K., and Price, J. H. (1993). A qualitative examination of adolescent homosexuals' life experiences: Ramifications for secondary school personnel. *Journal of Homosexuality,* 26.

Terman, L. M., and Oden, M. H. (1947). The gifted child grows up. In L. M. Terman (Ed.). *Genetic studies of genius,* vol. 4. Stanford, CA: Stanford University Press.

Terman, L. M., and Oden, M. H. (1959). The gifted group in mid–life. In L. M. Terman (Ed.). *Genetic studies of genius,* vol. 5. Stanford, CA: Stanford University Press.

Terry, W. (1993, February). Make things better for somebody. *Parade Magazine.*

Terman, L. M., Baldwin, B. T., and Bronson, E. (1925). Mental and physical traits of a thousand gifted children. In L. M. Terman (ed.). *Genetic studies of genius,* vol. 1. Stanford, CA: Stanford University Press.

Thelen, H. A. (1960). *Education and the human quest.* New York: Harper and Row.

Thelen, H. A. (1981). *The classroom society: The construction of educational experience.* London: Croom Helm.

Tinker v. Des Moines Independent Community School District, 393 U.S. 503 (1969).

*Tombari, M. L., and Borich, G. D. (1999). *Authentic assessment in the classroom: Applications and practice..* Upper Saddle River, NJ: Merrill.

Tozer, S. E., Violas, P. C., and Senese, G.

(1993). *School and society: Educational practice as social expression.* New York: McGraw-Hill.

*Trotter, A. (1998, October 1). A question of effectiveness. *Education Week on the Web.*

Trueba, H. T., Cheng, L. R. L., and Kenji, I. (1993). *Myth or reality: Adaptive strategies of Asian Americans in California.* Washington, DC: Falmer Press.

*Tryneski, J. (Ed.). (1999). *Requirements for certification of teachers, counselors, librarians, administrators for elementary and secondary schools: Sixty–fourth ed., 1999–2000.* Chicago: University of Chicago Press.

Tyler, R. (1949). *Basic principles of curriculum and instruction.* Chicago: University of Chicago.

U.S. Census Bureau. (1993, September). *We the . . . first Americans.* Washington, DC: U.S. Census Bureau.

*U.S. Census Bureau. (1998). *Statistical abstract of the United States 1998.* Washington, DC: U.S. Census Bureau.

*U.S. Census Bureau. (1999). *The Asian and Pacific Islander population in the United States: March 1997.* Washington, DC: U.S. Census Bureau.

*U.S. Department of Education. (1996a). *Getting America's students ready for the 21st century: Meeting the technology literacy challenge.* Washington, DC: U.S. Department of Education.

*U.S. Department of Education. (1996b). *Manual on school uniforms.* Washington, DC: U. S. Department of Education.

*U.S. Department of Education. (1996c). *The technology literacy challenge.* Washington, DC: U.S. Department of Education.

*U.S. Department of Education. (1997). *From students of teaching to teachers of students.* Washington, DC: U.S. Department of Education.

*U.S. Department of Education (1998). *Twentieth annual report to Congress on the implementation of the Individuals with Disabilities Education Act: To assure the free appropriate public education of all children with disabilities.* Washington, DC: U.S. Department of Education.

*U.S. Department of Education. (1999a). [Online]. Safe schools, healthy schools: Remarks as prepared for delivery by U.S. Secretary of Education Richard W. Riley. http://www.ed.gov/Speeches/04–1999/990430.html [1999, April 30].

*U.S. Department of Education. (1999b). *Schools with IDEAs that work.* Washington, DC: U.S. Department of Education.

U.S. Department of Education and International Institute on Education. (1996). *A splintered vision: An investigation of U.S. science and mathematics education.* Washington, DC.

*U.S. Department of Health and Human Services. (1998, October 27). *Improving Head Start: A success story.* Washington, DC: U.S. Department of Health and Human Services.

U.S. Department of Justice. (1996). *1995 national youth gang survey.* Washington, DC: U.S. Department of Justice.

U.S. Government Printing Office. (1990). *Who's Minding the Kids?.* Washington, DC: U.S. Government Printing Office.

Uchida, D., Cetron, M., and McKenzie, F. (1996). *Preparing students for the 21st century.* Arlington, VA: American Association of School Administrators.

Unified School Dist. No 241 v. Swanson, 717 P.2d 526 (Kan.App.1986).

*United Press International. (1998, November 15). Teachers may soon make $100,000.

The University of Memphis. (1994/95, Winter). Technology provides field experiences. *Perspectives.* Memphis: University of Memphis, College of Education.

Uribe, V., and Harbeck, K. M. (1991). Addressing the needs of lesbian, gay and bisexual youth. *Journal of Homosexuality, 22.*

Utay, C., and Utay, J. (1997). Peer–assisted learning: The effects of cooperative learning and cross–age peer tutoring with word processing on writing skills of students with learning disabilities. *Journal of Computing in Childhood Education, 8.*

*Valenza, J. K. (1997). Girls + technology = turnoff? *Technology Connections, 3.*

Van Lehn, K. (1994). Applications of simulated students: An exploration. *Journal of Artificial Intelligence in Education, 5*(2).

van Manen, M. (1991) *The tact of teaching: The meaning of pedagogical thoughtfulness.* Albany, NY: State University of New York Press.

*Vaughn, S., Bos, C. S., and Schumm, J. S. (1997). *Teaching mainstreamed, diverse, and at-risk students in the general education classroom.* Boston: Allyn and Bacon.

Venezky, R. L. (1992). Textbooks in school and society. In P. W. Jackson (Ed.). *Handbook of research on curriculum.* New York: Macmillan.

Viadero, D. (1996, May 8). Math texts are multiplying. *Education Week.*

*Viadero, D. (1999, January). [Untitled article]. *Education Week, 10*(4), 23.

Visconti, K. (1996). Stay in or get out? A "twenty–something" teacher looks at the profession. In G. Burnaford, J. Fischer, and D. Hobson, (Eds.). *Teachers doing research: Practical possibilities.* Mahwah, NJ: Lawrence Erlbaum Associates.

*Vygotsky, L. S. (1978). *Mind in society: The development of higher mental process.* Cambridge, MA: Harvard University Press.

*Vygotsky, L. S. (1986). *Thought and language.* Cambridge, MA: MIT Press.

*Walberg, H. J., and Greenberg, R. C. (1997, May). Using the learning environment inventory. *Educational Leadership,* 45–47.

Walberg, H. J., and Niemiec, R. P. (1994, May). Is Chicago school reform working? *Phi Delta Kappan,* 713–715.

Walberg, H. J., and Niemiec, R. P. (1996, May 22). Can the Chicago reforms work? *Education Week on the Web.*

Waller, W. (1932). *The sociology of teaching.* New York: Wiley.

Walling, D. R. (ed.). (1994). *Teachers as leaders: Perspectives on the professional development of teachers.* Bloomington, IN: Phi Delta Kappa Educational Foundation.

*Walsh, M. (1999a, April 2). Conservatives join effort to pull the plug on Channel One. *Education Week on the Web.*

*Walsh, M. (1999b, April 14). Most Edison schools report rise in test scores. *Education Week on the Web.*

*Walsh, M. (1999c, May). Two reports offer bright outlook for education industry. *Education Week, 18*(36), 5.

*Walsh, M. (1999d, May 5).Shootings raise host of legal questions. *Education Week on the Web.*

*Walsh, M. (1999e, May 26). Nader, Schlafly lambaste Channel One at Senate hearing. *Education Week on the Web.*

*Walsh, M. (1999f, September 8). Edison Project, now Edison Schools Inc., plans to go public. *Education Week on the Web.*

*Walters, L. S. (1999, January/February). What makes a good school violence prevention program? *Harvard Education Letter.*

*Walthers, K. (1995, September). Saying yes to vouchers: Perception, choice, and the educational response. *NAASP Bulletin,* 52–61.

*Washington State Department of Health, Non–Infectious Disease and Conditions Epidemiology Section. (1994). *Youth violence and associated risk factors: An epidemiological view of the literature.* Olympia, WA: Washington State Department of Health, Non–Infectious Disease and Conditions Epidemiology Section.

*Washington, W. (1998). Optional extended year program feedback. Austin Independent School District, TX, Department of Accountability, Student Services, and Research.

Wasserman, S. (1994, April). Using cases to study teaching. *Phi Delta Kappan,* 602–11.

*Webb, L. D., Metha, A., and Jordan, K. F. (1999). *Foundations of American education,* 3rd ed. Englewood Cliffs, NJ: Prentice Hall.

Wechsler, D. (1958). *The Measurement and appraisal of adult intelligence,* 4th ed. Baltimore: Williams and Wilkins.

*Weidmer, T. L. (1998). Digital portfolios: Capturing and demonstrating skills and levels of performance. *Phi Delta Kappan, 79*(8), 586–589.

West, A. M. (1980). *The National Education*

Association: The power base for education. New York: Free Press.

West v. Board of Education of City of New York, 187 N. Y. S.2d 88 8 A.D. 2d 291 (N.Y. App. 1959).

*White House Press Release. (1999). President Clinton releases $100 million in grants to support public charter schools. Washington, DC: White House.

*White, K. A. (1997). A matter of policy. *Education Week on the Web.* http://www.edweek.org/sreports/tc/policy/po–n.htm

*Whitely, B. E. (1997). Gender differences in computer–related attitudes and behavior: A meta–analysis. *Computers in Human Behavior, 13.*

*William Randolph Hearst Foundation. (1999). *United States Senate Youth Program Survey.* San Francisco: William Randolph Hearst Foundation.

*Williams, J. (1999, April 18). Urban schools' obstacles hindering technology. *Milwaukee Journal Sentinel.*

Willig, A. C. (1987, Fall). Examining bilingual education research. *Review of Educational Research,* 363–376.

*Willingham, W. W., and Cole, N. S. (1997). *Gender and fair assessment.* Mahwah, NJ: Lawrence Erlbaum Associates.

*Wirt, F. M., and Kirst, M. W. (1997). *The political dynamics of American education.* Berkeley: McCutchan Publishing Corporation.

*Withrow, F. B. (1997). Technology in education and the next twenty-five years. *T.H.E. Journal,* 2411, 59–61.

Wohlstetter, P. (1995, September). Getting school-based management right: What works and what doesn't. *Phi Delta Kappan,* 22–24, 26.

Wohlstetter, P., and Anderson, L. (1994, February). What can U.S. charter schools learn from England's grant-maintained schools? *Phi Delta Kappan,* 486–491.

*Wolfe, D. T., and Antinarella, J. (1997). *Deciding to lead: The English teacher as reformer.* Portsmouth, NH: Boynton Cook Publishers.

*Wolfgang, C. H. (1999). *Solving discipline problems: Methods and models for today's teachers,* 4th ed. Boston: Allyn and Bacon.

*Woolfolk, A. E. (1998). *Educational psychology,* 7th ed. Boston: Allyn and Bacon.

Woolfolk, A. E. (1995). *Educational psychology,* 6th ed. Boston: Allyn and Bacon.

*Wray, H. (1999). *Japanese and American education: Attitudes and practices.* Westport, CT: Bergin and Garvey.

*Yahoo Internet Life. (1999). America's 100 most wired colleges.

Yamamoto, K., Davis, O. L. Jr., Dylak, S., Whittaker, J., Marsh, C., and van der Westhuizen, P C. (Spring 1996). Across six nations: Stressful events in the lives of children. *Child Psychiatry and Human Development,* 139–150.

*Young, C. (1999). *Ceasefire! Why women and men must join forces to achieve true equality.* New York: Free Press.

Zehm, S. J., and Kottler, J. A. (1993). *On being a teacher: The human dimension.* Newbury Park, CA: Corwin Press.

Zucker v. Panitz, 299 F. Supp. 102 (DCS.D. N.Y. 1969).

*Zukowski, V. (1997, Fall). Teeter–totters and tandem bikes: A glimpse into the world of cross–age tutors. *Teaching and change,* 71–91.

Glossary

A

Academic freedom (p. 211): the right of teachers to teach, free from external constraint, censorship, or interference.

Academic learning time (p. 345): the amount of time students spend working on academic tasks with a high level of success (80 percent or higher).

Academies (p. 100): early secondary schools with broader and more practical curricula than those found in grammar schools of the previous era.

Accelerated schools (p.486): a national network of schools that provide enriched, rigorous curricula to "speed up" the learning of students at risk.

Accountability (p. 114): the practice of holding teachers responsible for adhering to high professional and moral standards and creating effective learning environments for all students.

Action research (p. 481): classroom-based study, by teachers, of how to improve their instruction.

Aesthetics (p. 88): the branch of axiology concerned with values related to beauty and art.

Afrocentric schools (p. 263): schools that focus on African American history and cultures for African American pupils.

Aims of education (p. 125): what a society believes the broad, general purposes of education should be—for example, socialization, achievement, personal growth, and social improvement.

Allocated time (p. 345): the amount of time teachers allocate for instruction in various areas of the curriculum.

Alternative certification (p. 504): a provision allowing people who have completed college but not a teacher education program to become certified teachers.

Alternative school (p. 156): a small, highly individualized school separate from a regular school; designed to meet the needs of students at risk.

Amendments to the Individuals with Disabilities Education Act (IDEA 97) (p. 313): amendments to IDEA that emphasize educational outcomes for students with disabilities and provide greater access through changes in eligibility requirements, IEP guidelines, public and private placements, student discipline guidelines, and procedural safeguards.

American Federation of Teachers (AFT) (p. 470): a national professional association for teachers, affiliated with the AFL-CIO.

Assertive discipline (p. 350): an approach to classroom discipline requiring that teachers establish firm, clear guidelines for student behavior and follow through with consequences for misbehavior.

Assessment (p. 358): the process of gathering information related to how much students have learned.

Assistive technology (p. 315): technological advances (usually computer-based) that help exceptional students learn and communicate.

Association for Supervision and Curriculum Development (ASCD) (p. 473): a professional organization for educators interested in school improvement at all levels.

Attention deficit disorder (ADD) (p. 309): a learning disability characterized by difficulty in concentrating on learning.

Attention deficit hyperactivity disorder (ADHD) (p. 309): a learning disability characterized by difficulty in remaining still so that one can concentrate on learning.

Authentic assessments (p. 358): an approach to assessing students' learning that requires them to solve problems or work on tasks that approximate as much as possible those they will encounter beyond the classroom.

Authentic learning tasks (p. 343): learning activities that enable students to see the connections between classroom learning and the world beyond the classroom.

Axiology (p. 87): the study of values, including the identification of criteria for determining what is valuable.

B

Back-to-basics movement (p. 114): a movement begun in the mid-1970s to establish the "basic skills" of reading, writing, speaking, and computation as the core of the school curriculum.

Behaviorism (p. 93): a philosophical orientation based on behavioristic psychology that maintains that environmental factors shape people's behavior.

Between-class ability grouping (p. 341): the practice of grouping students at the middle and high school levels for instruction on the basis of ability or achievement, often called *tracking*.

Bicultural (p. 268): the ability to function effectively in two or more linguistic and cultural groups.

Bilingual education (pp. 253): a curriculum for non-English-speaking and English-speaking students in which two languages are used for instruction and biculturalism is emphasized.

Block grants (p. 187): a form of federal aid given directly to the states, which a state or local education agency may spend as it wishes with few limitations.

Block scheduling (p. 346): a high school scheduling arrangement that provides longer blocks of time each class period, with fewer periods each day.

***Brown v. Board of Education of Topeka* (p. 111):** a 1954 landmark court case rejecting the "separate but equal" doctrine used to prevent African Americans from attending schools with whites.

Buckley Amendment (p. 230): a 1974 law, the Family Educational Rights and Privacy Act, granting parents of students under eighteen and students over eighteen the right to examine their school records.

Burnout (p. 19): an acute level of stress resulting in job dissatisfaction, emotional and physical exhaustion, and an inability to cope effectively.

C

Caring classroom (p. 338): a classroom in which the teacher communicates clearly an attitude of caring about students' learning and their overall well-being.

Categorical aid (p. 189): state-appropriated funds to cover the costs of educating students with special needs.

CD-ROM (p. 422): a small plastic disk (usually 4.72 or 5.25 inches in diameter) that holds 600 or more megabytes of information that can be read by a computer.

Censorship (p. 223): the act of removing from circulation printed material judged to be libelous, vulgar, or obscene.

Channel One (p. 419): a controversial twelve-minute news broadcast, including two minutes of commercials, aired daily in more than 12,000 public and private schools; schools receive Channel One programs, equipment, and service free of charge upon agreeing to show the programs to students.

Character education (p. 295): an approach to education that emphasizes the teaching of values, moral reasoning, and the development of "good" character.

Charter (p. 504): an agreement between a charter school's founders and its sponsors specifying how the school will operate and what learning outcomes students will master.

Charter schools (p. 560): independent schools, often founded by teachers, that are given a charter to operate by a school district, state, or national government, with the provision that students must demonstrate mastery of predetermined outcomes.

Chat rooms (p. 426): Internet sites where students can participate in on-line discussions by typing in their comments and questions.

Chief state school officer (p. 179): the chief administrator of a state department of education and head of the state board of education, often called the commissioner of education or superintendent of public instruction.

Choice theory (p. 347): an approach to classroom management, developed by psychiatrist William Glasser, based on a belief that students will usually make good choices (i.e., behave in an acceptable manner) if they experience success in the classroom and know that teachers care about them.

Classroom climate (p. 335): the atmosphere or quality of life in a classroom, determined by how individuals interact with one another.

Classroom culture (p. 136): the "way of life"

characteristic of a classroom group; determined by the social dimensions of the group and the physical characteristics of the setting.

Classroom management (p. 346): day-to-day teacher control of student behavior and learning, including discipline.

Classroom organization (p. 341): how teachers and students in a school are grouped for instruction and how time is allocated in classrooms.

Clinical supervision (p. 528): a four-step model supervisors follow in making teacher performance evaluations.

Coalition of Essential Schools (p. 485): a national network of public and private high schools that have restructured according to nine common principles.

Code of ethics (p. 203): a set of guidelines that defines appropriate behavior for professionals.

Cognitive development (p. 291): the process of acquiring the intellectual ability to learn from interaction with one's environment.

Cognitive science (p. 94): the study of the learning process that focuses on how individuals manipulate symbols and process information.

Collaboration (p. 524): the practice of working together, sharing decision making, and solving problems among professionals.

Collaborative consultation (p. 317): an approach in which a classroom teacher meets with one or more other professionals (such as a special educator, school psychologist, or resource teacher) to focus on the learning needs of one or more students.

Collective bargaining (p. 210): a process followed by employers and employees in negotiating salaries, hours, and working conditions; in most states, school boards must negotiate contracts with teacher organizations.

Collegial support team (CST) (p. 526): a team of teachers—created according to subject area, grade level, or teacher interests and expertise—who support one another's professional growth.

Collegiality (p. 520): a spirit of cooperation and mutual helpfulness among professionals.

Committee of Fifteen (p. 385): an NEA committee that recommended an academically oriented elementary curriculum (1895).

Committee of Ten (p. 384): an NEA committee that recommended an academically rigorous curriculum for high school students (1893).

Common schools (p. 101): free state-supported schools that provide education for all students.

Comparative education (p. 365): the comparative study of educational practices in different countries.

Compensatory education programs (p. 155): federally funded educational programs designed to meet the needs of low-ability students from low-income families.

Computer-assisted instruction (CAI) (p. 421): the use of computers to provide individualized drill-and-practice exercises or tutorials to students.

Computer-based simulations (p. 423): computer programs that present the user with multifaceted problem situations similar to those they will encounter in real life.

Computer-enhanced instruction (CEI) (p. 421): the use of computers to provide students with inquiry-oriented learning experiences such as simulations and problem-solving activities.

Computer-managed instruction (CMI) (p. 421): the use of computers to evaluate and diagnose students' learning needs and record students' progress for teachers to monitor.

Concrete operations stage (p. 291): the stage of cognitive development (seven to eleven years of age) proposed by Jean Piaget in which the individual develops the ability to use logical thought to solve concrete problems.

Constructivism (p. 94): a psychological orientation that views learning as an active process in which learners *construct* understanding of the material they learn—in contrast to the view that teachers transmit academic content to students in small segments.

Constructivist teaching (p. 354): a method of teaching based on students' prior knowledge of the topic and the processes they use to *construct* meaning.

Cooperative learning (p. 341): an approach to education in which students work in small groups, or teams, sharing the work and helping one another complete assignments.

Copyright laws (p. 220): laws limiting the use of photocopies, videotapes, and computer software programs.

Core curriculum (p. 390): a set of fundamental courses or learning experiences that are part of the curriculum for all students at a school.

Corporal punishment (p. 232): physical punishment applied to a student by a school employee as a disciplinary measure.

Cost of living (p. 11): the amount of money needed, on average, for housing, food, transportation, utilities, and other living expenses in a given locale.

Co-teaching (p. 526): an arrangement whereby two or more teachers teach together in the same classroom.

Credentials file (p. 509): a file set up for students registered in a teacher placement office at a college or university, which includes background information on the applicant, the type of position desired, transcripts, performance evaluations, and letters of recommendation.

Cross-age tutoring (p. 356): a tutoring arrangement in which older students tutor younger students; evidence indicates that cross-age tutoring has positive effects on the attitudes and achievement of tutee and tutor.

Cultural identity (p. 252): an overall sense of oneself, derived from the extent of one's participation in various subcultures within the national macroculture.

Cultural pluralism (p. 252): the preservation of cultural differences among groups of people within one society. This view is in contrast to the melting-pot theory, which says that ethnic cultures should melt into one.

Culture (p. 252): the way of life common to a group of people; includes knowledge deemed important, shared meanings, norms, values, attitudes, ideals, and view of the world.

Curriculum (p. 370): the school experiences, both planned and unplanned, that enhance (and sometimes impede) the education and growth of students.

D

Dame schools (p. 97): colonial schools, usually held in the homes of widows or housewives, for teaching children basic reading, writing, and mathematical skills.

Democratic classroom (p. 346): a classroom in which the teacher's leadership style encourages students to take more power and responsibility for their learning.

Departmentalization (p. 135): an organizational arrangement for schools in which students move from classroom to classroom for instruction in different subject areas.

Desegregation (p. 111): the process of eliminating schooling practices based on the separation of racial groups.

"Digital divide" (p. 440): inequities in access to computer technology that are related to minority-group status, family income, and gender.

Direct instruction (p. 353): a systematic instructional method focusing on the transmission of knowledge and skills from the teacher to the students.

Discipline-based art programs (p. 402): art education in which students learn art production, art criticism, art history, and aesthetics.

Discovery learning (p. 355): an approach to teaching that gives students opportunities to inquire into subjects so that they "discover" knowledge for themselves.

Dismissal (p. 209): the involuntary termination of a teacher's employment; termination must be made for a legally defensible reason with the protection of due process.

Distance learning (p. 54): the use of technology such as video transmissions that enables students to receive instruction at multiple, often remote, sites.

Distance learning networks (p. 419): two-way, interactive telecommunications systems used to deliver instruction to students at various locations.

Diversity (p. 251): differences among people in regard to gender, race, ethnicity, culture, and socioeconomic status.

Due process (p. 206): a set of specific guidelines that must be followed to protect individuals from arbitrary, capricious treatment by those in authority.

E

Education Consolidation and Improvement Act (ECIA) (p. 187): a 1981 federal law giving the states a broad range of choices for spending federal aid to education.

Education for All Handicapped Children Act (Public Law 94-142) (pp. 115, 312): a 1975 federal act that guarantees a free and appropriate education to all handicapped children (often referred to as the mainstreaming law or Public Law 94-142).

Educational malpractice (p. 217): liability for injury that results from the failure of a teacher, school, or school district to provide a student with adequate instruction, guidance, counseling, and/or supervision.

Educational philosophy (p. 83): a set of ideas and beliefs about education that guide the professional behavior of educators.

Educational reform movement (p. 51): a comprehensive effort made during the 1980s and into the 1990s to improve schools and the preparation of teachers.

Educational Resources Information Center (ERIC) (p. 480): a national information system made up of sixteen clearinghouses that disseminate descriptions of exemplary programs, results of research and development efforts, and related information.

Educational technology (p. 418): computers, software, multimedia systems, and advanced telecommunications systems used to enhance the teaching-learning process.

Eight-Year Study (p. 386): an experiment in which thirty high schools were allowed to develop curricula that did not meet college entrance requirements (1932-1940).

Elementary and Secondary Education Act (p. 113): part of President Lyndon B. Johnson's Great Society Program, this act allocated federal funds on the basis of the number of poor children in school districts.

Emergency certification (p. 504): temporary, substandard certification requirements set by a state in response to a shortage of teachers.

Emotional intelligence (p. 128): a level of awareness and understanding of one's emotions that allows the person to achieve personal growth and self-actualization.

Entitlements (p. 187): federal programs to meet the educational needs of special populations.

Epistemology (p. 87): a branch of philosophy concerned with the nature of knowledge and what it means to know something.

E-rate (p. 443): a controversial program that uses fees from telecommunications companies to provide discounts on telecommunications services and wiring to schools and libraries.

ERIC Clearinghouses (p. 481): sixteen Educational Resources Information Center Clearinghouses that disseminate descriptions of exemplary educational programs, the results of research and development efforts, and related information.

Essentialism (p. 90): formulated in part as a response to progressivism, this philosophical orientation holds that a core of common knowledge about the real world should be transmitted to students in a systematic, disciplined way.

Ethical dilemmas (p. 206): problem situations in which an ethical response is difficult to determine; that is, no single response can be called "right" or "wrong."

Ethics (p. 88): a branch of philosophy concerned with principles of conduct and determining what is good and evil, right and wrong, in human behavior.

Ethnic group (p. 252): individuals within a larger culture who share a racial or cultural identity and a set of beliefs, values, and attitudes and who consider themselves members of a distinct group or subculture.

Ethnicity (p. 256): a shared feeling of common identity that derives, in part, from a common ancestry, common values, and common experiences.

Evaluation (p. 358): making judgments about, or assigning a value to, measurements of students' learning.

Exceptional learners (p. 306): students whose growth and development deviate from the norm to the extent that their educational needs can be met more effectively through a modification of regular school programs.

Existentialism (p. 91): a philosophical orientation that emphasizes the individual's experiences and maintains that each individual must determine his or her own meaning of existence.

Expenditure per pupil (p. 183): the amount of money spent on each pupil in a school, school district, state, or nation; usually computed according to average daily attendance.

Explicit curriculum (p. 371): the behavior, attitudes, and knowledge that a school intends to teach students.

Extracurricular/cocurricular programs (p. 373): school-sponsored activities students may pursue outside of, or in addition to, academic study.

F

Fair use (p. 220): the right of an individual to use copyrighted material in a reasonable manner without the copyright holder's consent, provided that use meets certain criteria.

Female seminaries (p. 100): schools established in the early nineteenth century to train women for higher education and public service outside the home.

Field experiences (p. 53): opportunities for teachers-in-training to experience firsthand the world of the teacher, by observing, tutoring, and instructing small groups.

For-profit schools (p. 561): schools that are operated, for profit, by private educational corporations.

Formal operations stage (p. 291): the stage of cognitive development (eleven to fifteen years of age) proposed by Jean Piaget in which cognitive abilities reach their highest level of development.

Formative evaluation (p. 358): an assessment, or diagnosis, of students' learning for the purpose of planning instruction.

Freedom of expression (p. 223): freedom, granted by the First Amendment to the Constitution, to express one's beliefs.

Fringe benefits (p. 13): benefits (i.e., medical insurance, retirement, and tax-deferred investment opportunities) that are given to teachers in addition to base salary.

Full inclusion (p. 315): the policy and process of including exceptional learners in general education classrooms.

Full-funding programs (p. 188): state programs to ensure statewide financial equity by setting the same per-pupil expenditure level for all schools and districts.

Full-service schools (p. 154): schools that provide students and their families with medical, social, and human services in addition to their regular educational programs.

G

Gender bias (p. 281): subtle bias or discrimination on the basis of gender; reduces the likelihood that the target of the bias will develop to the full extent of his or her capabilities.

Gender-fair classroom (p. 281): education that is free of bias or discrimination on the basis of gender.

G.I. Bill of Rights (p. 180): a 1944 federal law that provides veterans with payments for tuition and room and board at colleges and universities and special schools; formally known as the Servicemen's Readjustment Act.

Gifted and talented (p. 310): exceptional learners who demonstrate high intelligence, high creativity, high achievement, or special talent(s).

Goals 2000: Educate America Act (p. 125): a comprehensive funding program to help schools achieve a set of eight national goals emphasizing student achievement, effective learning environments, professional development for teachers, and parental involvement.

Grievance (p. 210): a formal complaint filed by an employee against his or her employer or supervisor.

Group investigation (p. 356): an approach to teaching in which the teacher facilitates learning by creating an environment that allows students to determine what they will study and how.

H

Hidden curriculum (p. 371): the behaviors, attitudes, and knowledge the school culture unintentionally teaches students.

Hierarchy of needs (p. 298): a set of seven needs, from the basic needs for survival and safety to the need for self-actualization, that motivate human behavior.

Higher-order questions (p. 554): questions that require the ability to engage in complex modes of thought (synthesis, analysis, and evaluation, for example).

Holmes Group (p. 51): a group of ninety-six colleges of education that prepared *Tomorrow's Teachers*, a 1986 report calling for all teachers to have a bachelor's degree in an academic field and a master's degree in education.

Holmes Partnership (p. 52): a consortium of professional organizations—including the Holmes Group, the National Board for Professional Teaching Standards, the National Education Association, and the American Federation of Teachers—committed to the reform of teacher education.

Home-school communication systems (p. 423): computer-based systems that allow schools to disseminate information to parents and, in turn, enable parents to communicate directly with school personnel.

Horn book (p. 97): a copy of the alphabet covered by a thin transparent sheet made from a cow's horn.

Humanism (p. 93): a philosophy based on the belief that individuals control their own destinies through the application of their intelligence and learning.

Humanistic psychology (p. 93): an orientation to human behavior that emphasizes personal freedom, choice, awareness, and personal responsibility.

Hypermedia (p. 422): an interactive instructional system consisting of a computer, CD-ROM drive, videodisc player, video monitor, and speakers. Hypermedia systems allow students to control and present sound, video images, text, and graphics in an almost limitless array of possibilities.

I

Inclusion (p. 315): the practice of integrating all students with disabilities into general education classes.

Indian Education Act of 1972 and 1974 Amendments (p. 267): a federal law and subsequent amendment designed to provide direct educational assistance to Native American tribes and nations.

Individual racism (p. 259): the prejudicial belief that one's ethnic or racial group is superior to others.

Individualized education plan (IEP) (p. 313): a plan for meeting an exceptional learner's educational needs, specifying goals, objectives, services, and procedures for evaluating progress.

Individuals with Disabilities Education Act (IDEA) (p. 312): a 1990 federal act providing a free, appropriate education to disabled youth between three and twenty-one years of age. IDEA superseded the earlier Education for all Handicapped Children Act (Public Law 94-142).

Induction programs (p. 60): programs of support for beginning teachers, usually during their first year of teaching.

Information processing (p. 355): a branch of cognitive science concerned with how individuals use long- and short-term memory to acquire information and solve problems.

Inquiry-based curriculum (p. 387): a curriculum that teaches not only the content but also the thought processes of a discipline.

Inquiry learning (p. 355): an approach to teaching that gives students opportunities to explore, or *inquire* into, subjects so that they develop their own answers to problem situations.

Inservice workshops (p. 67): on-site professional development programs in which teachers meet to learn new techniques, develop curricular materials, share ideas, or solve problems.

Institution (p. 131): any organization a society establishes to maintain, and improve, its way of life.

Institutional racism (p. 259): institutional policies and practices, intentional or not, that result in racial inequities.

Instructional goals (p. 357): general statements of purpose that guide schools and teachers as they develop instructional programs.

Integrated curriculum (p. 376): a school curriculum that draws from two or more subject areas and focuses on a theme or concept rather than on a single subject.

Intelligence (p. 302): the ability to learn; the cognitive capacity for thinking.

Interactive multimedia (p. 422): computer-supported media that allow the user to interact with a vast, nonlinear, multimedia database to combine textual, audio, and video information.

Interactive teaching (p. 26): teaching characterized by face-to-face interactions between teachers and students in contrast to preactive teaching.

Internet (p. 68, 424): a set of more than 10,68, 424 interconnected computer networks created for the rapid dissemination of vast amounts of information around the world.

International Assessment of Educational Progress (IAEP) (p. 566): a program established in 1991 for comparing the achievement of students in the United States with that of students from other countries.

Internship programs (p. 60): programs of assistance and training for beginning teachers, usually for those who have not gone through a teacher education program.

Interstate Certification Agreement Contract (p. 503): a reciprocity agreement among approximately thirty states whereby a teaching certificate obtained in one state will be honored in another.

Interstate New Teacher Assessment and Support Consortium (INTASC) (p. 50): an organization of states established in 1987 to develop performance-based standards for what beginning teachers should know and be able to do.

J

Job analysis (p. 48): a procedure for determining the knowledge and skills needed for a job.

K

Kentucky Education Reform Act (KERA) (p. 177): comprehensive school-reform legislation requiring all Kentucky schools to form school-based management councils with authority to set policies in eight areas.

Kindergarten (p. 106): a school for children before they begin formal schooling at the elementary level; based on the ideas of German educator Friedrick Fröebel, *kindergarten* means "garden where children grow."

Knowledge base (p. 46): the body of knowledge that represents what teachers need to know and be able to do.

L

Language-minority students (p. 258): students whose language of the home is a language other than English.

Latchkey children (p. 144): children who, because of family circumstances, must spend part of each day unsupervised by a parent or guardian.

Latin grammar school (p. 98): colonial schools established to provide male students a precollege education; comparable to today's high schools.

Learning (p. 554): changes in behavior the individual makes in response to environmental stimuli; the acquisition and organization of knowledge and skills.

Learning disability (LD) (p. 308): a limitation in one's ability to take in, organize, remember, and express information.

Learning objectives (p. 358): specific, measurable outcomes of learning that students are to demonstrate.

Learning styles (p. 305): cognitive, affective, and physiological behaviors through which an individual learns most effectively; determined by a combination of hereditary and environmental influences.

Least restrictive environment (p. 313): an educational program that meets a disabled student's special needs in a manner that is identical, insofar as possible, to that provided to students in general education classrooms.

Lemon test (p. 236): a three-part test, based on *Lemon v. Kurtzman,* to determine whether a state has violated the separation of church and state principle.

Letter of application (p. 511): a letter written in application for a specific teaching vacancy in a school district.

Letter of inquiry (p. 511): a letter written to a school district inquiring about teaching vacancies.

Limited English proficiency (LEP) (p. 253): a designation for students with limited ability to understand, read, or speak English and who have a first language other than English.

Local school council (p. 174): a group of community members that is empowered to develop policies for the operation of local schools.

Local school district (p. 169): an agency at the local level that has the authority to operate schools in the district.

Logic (p. 89): a branch of philosophy concerned with the processes of reasoning and the identification of rules that will enable thinkers to reach valid conclusions.

Lower-order questions (p. 554): questions that require students to recall specific information.

M

Magnet school (p. 130): a school offering a curriculum that focuses on a specific area such as the performing arts, mathematics, science, international studies, or technology. Magnet schools, which often draw students from a larger attendance area than regular schools, are frequently developed to promote voluntary desegration.

Mainstreaming (pp. 115, 314): the policy and process of integrating disabled or otherwise exceptional learners into regular classrooms with nonexceptional students.

Massachusetts Act of 1642 (p. 98): a law requiring each town to determine whether its young people could read and write.

Massachusetts Act of 1647 (p. 98): a law mandating the establishment and support of schools; often referred to as the Old Deluder Satan Act because education was seen as the best protection against the wiles of the devil.

Mastery learning (p. 353): an approach to instruction based on the assumptions that (1) virtually all students can learn material if given enough time and taught appropriately and (2) learning is enhanced if students can progress in small, sequenced steps.

McGuffey readers (p. 105): an immensely popular series of reading books for students in grades one through six, written in the 1830s by Reverend William Holmes McGuffey.

Measurement (p. 358): the gathering of data that indicate how much students have learned.

Mentor (pp. 64): a wise, knowledgeable individual who provides guidance and encouragement to someone.

Mentoring (p. 64): an intensive form of teaching in which a wise and experienced teacher (the mentor) inducts a student (the protégé) into a professional way of life.

Metaphysics (p. 86): a branch of philosophy concerned with the nature of reality.

Microcomputer-based laboratories (MBL) (p. 422): the use of computers to gather and then analyze data that students have collected in a school laboratory or in the field.

Microteaching (p. 37): a brief, single-concept lesson taught by a teacher education student to a small group of students; usually designed to give the education student an opportunity to practice a specific teaching skill.

Minorities (p. 257): groups of people who share certain characteristics and are smaller in number than the majority of a population.

Modeling (p. 354): the process of "thinking out loud" which teachers use to make students aware of the reasoning involved in learning new material.

Modes of teaching (p. 30): different aspects of the teaching function—for example, teaching as a way of being, as a creative endeavor, as a live performance, and so on.

Montesorri Method (p. 109): a method of teaching, developed by Maria Montessori, based on a prescribed set of materials and physical exercises to develop children's knowledge and skills.

Moonlight (p. 12): to hold a second job to increase one's income.

Moral reasoning (p. 291): the reasoning process people follow to decide what is right or wrong.

Morrill Land-Grant Act (p. 105): an 1862 act that provided federal land that states could sell or rent to raise funds to establish colleges of agriculture and mechanical arts.

Multicultural curriculum (p. 275): a school curriculum that addresses the needs and backgrounds of all students regardless of their cultural identity and includes the cultural perspectives, or "voices," of people who have previously been silent or marginalized.

Multicultural education (p. 272): education that provides equal educational opportunities to all students—regardless of socioeconomic status; gender; or ethnic, racial, or cultural backgrounds—and is dedicated to reducing prejudice and celebrating the rich diversity of American life.

Multiculturalism (p. 256): a set of beliefs based on the importance of seeing the world from different cultural frames of reference and valuing the diversity of cultures in the global community.

Multiple intelligences (p. 303): a perspective on intellectual ability, proposed by Howard Gardner, suggesting that there are at least seven types of human intelligence.

N

A Nation at Risk **(p. 28):** a 1983 national report critical of American education.

National Assessment of Educational Progress (NAEP), (p. 284): an ongoing, large-scale national testing program to assess the effectiveness of education in the United States.

National Board for Professional Teaching Standards (NBPTS) (p. 50): a board established in 1987 that began issuing professional certificates in 1994-95 to teachers who possess extensive professional knowledge and the ability to perform at a high level.

National Council for Accreditation of Teacher Education (NCATE) (p. 501): an agency that accredits, on a voluntary basis, almost half of the nation's teacher education programs.

National curriculum (p. 568): a standardized curriculum set at the national level and delivered to students at all schools throughout the country. Usually, countries with national curricula have nationwide testing to assess students' mastery of the curriculum.

National Defense Education Act (p. 111): a 1958 federally sponsored program to promote research and innovation in science, mathematics, modern foreign languages, and guidance.

National Education Association (NEA) (p. 469): the oldest and largest professional association for teachers and administrators.

National Governor's Association (p. 178): an association of state governors that influences policies in several areas, including teacher education and school reform.

National Information Infrastructure (NII) (p. 443): a federal plan to create a telecommunications infrastructure linking all schools, libraries, hospitals, and law enforcement agencies to the Internet and the World Wide Web.

National Network for Educational Renewal (p. 486): a national network of colleges and universities that collaborate with school districts and partner schools to reform education according to nineteen postulates in John Goodlad's *Teachers for Our Nation's Schools.*

Negligence (p. 217): failure to exercise reasonable, prudent care in providing for the safety of others.

Newsgroups (p. 424): Internet sites where students can post and exchange information on electronic bulletin boards.

Nondiscrimination (p. 208): conditions characterized by the absence of discrimination; for example, employees receive compensation, privileges, and opportunities for advancement without regard for race, color, religion, sex, or national origin.

Normal schools (p. 104): schools that focus on the preparation of teachers.

Null curriculum (p. 372): the intellectual processes and subject content that schools do not teach.

O

Observations (p. 55): field experiences wherein a teacher education student observes a specific aspect of classroom life such as the students, the teacher, the interactions between the two, the structure of the lesson, or the setting.

Office of Educational Research and Improvement (OERI) (p. 481): a federal agency that promotes educational research and improving schools through the application of research results.

Open-space schools (p. 135): schools that have large instructional areas with movable walls and furniture that can be rearranged easily.

Opportunity to learn (OTL) (p. 345): the time during which a teacher provides students with challenging content and appropriate instructional strategies to learn that content.

Outcome-based education (p. 390): an educational reform that focuses on developing students' ability to demonstrate mastery of certain desired outcomes or performances.

Outcome-based teacher education (p. 48): an approach to teacher education emphasizing outcomes (what teachers should be able to do, think, and feel) rather than the courses they should take.

P

Parochial schools (p. 97): schools founded on religious beliefs.

Pedagogical content knowledge (p. 43): the knowledge accomplished teachers possess regarding how to present subject matter to students though the use of analogies, metaphors, experiments, demonstrations, illustrations, and other instructional strategies.

Peer coaching (p. 525): an arrangement whereby teachers grow professionally by observing one another's teaching and providing constructive feedback.

Peer counseling (p. 153): an arrangement whereby students, monitored by a school counselor or teacher, counsel one another in such areas as low achievement, inter-

personal problems, substance abuse, and career planning.

Peer-mediated instruction (p. 356): approaches to teaching, such as cooperative learning and group investigation, that utilize the social relationships among students to promote their learning.

Peer-tutoring (p. 356): an arrangement whereby students tutor other students in the same classroom or at the same grade level.

Perennialism (p. 89): a philosophical orientation that emphasizes the ideas contained in the Great Books and maintains that the true purpose of education is the discovery of the universal, or perennial, truths of life.

Performance assessment (p. 358): the process of determining what students can *do* as well as what they know.

Performance-based education (p. 390): an educational reform that focuses on developing students' ability to demonstrate mastery of certain desired performances or outcomes.

Performance-based teacher education (p. 48): an approach to teacher education emphasizing performances (what teachers should be able to do, think, and feel) rather than the courses they should take.

Personal-development view (p. 47): the belief that teachers become more effective by increasing their self-knowledge and developing themselves as persons.

Phi Delta Kappa (p. 471): a professional and honorary fraternity of educators with 650 chapters and 130,000 members.

Placement service (p. 509): a school, government, or commercial service that matches job applicants with job openings and arranges contacts between employers and prospective employees.

Portfolio assessment (p. 358): the process of determining how much students have learned by examining collections of work that document their learning over time.

Practicum (p. 58): a short field-based experience during which teacher education students spend time observing and assisting in classrooms.

Praxis Series: Professional Assessments for Beginning Teachers (p. 505): a battery of tests available to states for the initial certification of teachers. Consists of assessments in three areas: academic skills, knowledge of subject, and classroom performance.

Preactive teaching (p. 26): the stage of teaching when a teacher prepares to teach or reflects on previous teaching experiences in contrast with interactive teaching.

Preoperational stage (p. 291): the stage of cognitive development (two to seven years of age), proposed by Jean Piaget, in which the individual begins to use language and symbols to think of objects and people outside of the immediate environment.

Primer (p. 97): a book with very explicit reli-

gious and moral messages about the proper conduct of life that colonial children used to learn to read.

Privatization movement (p. 561): Umbrella term for reform initiatives that seek to run public schools as private enterprises.

Problem-centered learning (p. 394): an approach to instruction in which students work in small groups on problems that have many or open-ended solutions.

Problem-solving orientation (p. 50): an approach to teaching that places primary emphasis on the teacher's role as a decision maker and problem solver.

Profession (p. 459): an occupation that requires a high level of expertise, including advanced study in a specialized field, adherence to a code of ethics, and the ability to work without close supervision.

Professional development schools (PDS) (p. 52): schools that have formed partnerships with a college or university for the purpose of improving the schools and contributing to the improvement of teacher preparation programs. Activities at a PDS may include collaborative research, team teaching, demonstration lessons by teacher education faculty, and various professional growth opportunities for teachers and teacher educators.

Professional empowerment (p. 19): a trend for teachers to have expanded opportunities to make decisions that affect their professional lives.

Professional portfolio (p. 37, 62): a collection of various kinds of evidence (e.g., projects, written work, and video demonstrations of skills) documenting the achievement and performance of individuals in an area of professional practice.

Professional standards boards (p. 53): state agencies to regulate and improve the professional practice of teachers, administrators, and other education personnel.

Progressive movement (p. 108): a movement during the 1920s and 1930s to create schools that emphasized democracy, children's interests and needs, and closer connections between school and community.

Progressivism (p. 91): a philosophical orientation based on the belief that life is evolving in a positive direction, that people may be trusted to act in their own best interests, and that education should focus on the needs and interests of students.

Property taxes (p. 186): local taxes assessed against real estate and, in some areas, against personal property such as cars, household furniture and appliances, and stocks and bonds.

Prosocial values (p. 126): values such as honesty, patriotism, fairness, and civility that promote the well-being of a society.

Psychosocial crisis (p. 291): a life crisis at one of eight different stages of growth and development. According to psychologist Erik Erikson, individuals must resolve each crisis to reach the next stage.

Psychosocial development (p. 291): the progression of an individual through various stages of psychological and social development.

Q

Qualitative evaluation (p. 527): the appraisal of teacher performance through the use of written, open-ended descriptions of classroom events in terms of their qualities.

Quantitative evaluation (p. 527): the appraisal of teacher performance by recording classroom events in terms of their number or frequency; for example, teacher verbal behaviors such as questioning, praising, or critiquing.

R

Race (p. 256): a concept of human variation used to distinguish people on the basis of biological traits and characteristics.

Reading and writing schools (p. 97): colonial schools, supported by public funds and fees paid by parents, that used a religiously oriented curriculum to teach boys reading and writing skills and, to a lesser degree, mathematics.

Realities of teaching (p. 21): actual conditions teachers face in the classroom; the demands as well as the rewards.

Recertification (p. 501): the practice in some states of requiring experienced teachers to undergo periodic testing to maintain their teaching certificates.

Redistricting (p. 189): the practice of redrawing district boundaries to equalize educational funding by reducing the range of variation in the ability of school districts to finance education.

Reflection (p. 50): the process of thinking carefully and deliberately about the outcomes of one's teaching.

Reflection-in-action (p. 464): the process of engaging in serious, reflective thought about improving one's professional practice while one is engaged in that practice.

Reflective teaching log (p. 59): a journal of classroom observations in which the teacher education student systematically analyzes specific episodes of teaching.

Regional Educational Laboratories (p. 480): nine federally supported, nonprofit agencies that serve a region of the country and work directly with educators to improve schools.

Regional Educational Service Agency (RESA) (p. 180): a state educational agency that provides supportive services to two or more school districts; known in some states as education service centers, intermediate school districts, multicounty education service units, board of cooperative educational services, or educational service regions.

Relevancy-based curriculum (p. 387): a curriculum that is relevant to students' needs, interests, and concerns about social issues.

Reorganization of Secondary Education (p. 385): an NEA commission that recommended a high-school curriculum based on individual differences (1913).

Research and Development Centers (p. 480): fourteen federally supported, university-based centers, each conducting research and development activities in a different area of education.

Research-based competencies (p. 47): specific behaviors that educational research has identified as characteristic of effective teachers.

Restructuring (p. 173): reorganizing how schools are controlled at the local level so that teachers, principals, parents, and community members have greater authority.

Résumé (p. 511): a concise summary of an individual's professional experiences and education.

S

Scaffolding (p. 354): an approach to teaching based on the student's current level of understanding and ability; the teacher varies the amount of help given (e.g., clues, encouragement, or suggestions) to students based on their moment-to-moment understanding of the material being learned.

School-based interprofessional case management (p. 155): an approach to education in which professionally trained case managers work directly with teachers, the community, and families to coordinate and deliver appropriate services to at-risk students and their families.

School-based management (p. 174): various approaches to school improvement in which teachers, principals, students, parents, and community members manage individual schools and share in the decision-making processes.

School-based teacher education (p. 61): a model of teacher preparation through which professional coursework is presented on-site at a school, usually to students who have a bachelor's degree.

School board (p. 170): the primary governing body of a local school district.

School choice (p. 189): various proposals that would allow parents to choose the schools their children attend.

School culture (p. 134): the collective "way of life" characteristic of a school; a set of beliefs, values, traditions, and ways of thinking and behaving that distinguish it from other schools.

School restructuring (p. 138): approaches to school improvement that change the way students are grouped for instruction, uses of classroom time and space, instructional methods, and procedures for decision making and governance.

School-to-work programs (p. 404): educational programs, often developed collaboratively by schools and industry, that emphasize the transfer of knowledge and skills learned at school to the job setting.

School traditions (p. 136): those elements of a school's culture that are handed down from year to year.

School-within-a-school (p. 156): an alternative school (within a regular school) designed to meet the needs of students at risk.

Scientific management (p. 106): the application of management principles and techniques to the operation of big business and large school districts.

Search and seizure (p. 228): the process of searching an individual and/or his or her property if that person is suspected of an illegal act; reasonable or probable cause to suspect the individual must be present.

Self-assessment (p. 66): the process of measuring one's growth in regard to the knowledge, skills, and attitudes possessed by professional teachers.

Self-contained classroom (p. 138): an organizational structure for schools in which one teacher instructs a group of students (typically, twenty to thirty) in a single classroom.

Service learning (p. 128): an approach to teaching in which students participate in community-based service activities and then reflect on the meaning of those experiences.

Sex-role socialization (p. 278): socially expected behavior patterns conveyed to individuals on the basis of gender.

Sex-role stereotyping (p. 278): beliefs that subtly encourage males and females to conform to certain behavioral norms regardless of abilities and interests.

Sexual harassment (p. 223): unwanted and unwelcome sexual behavior directed toward another person, whether of the same or opposite sex.

Social reconstructionism (p. 92): a philosophical orientation based on the belief that social problems can be solved by changing, or *reconstructing,* society.

Socratic questioning (p. 89): a method of questioning designed to lead students to see errors and inconsistencies in their thinking, based on questioning strategies used by Socrates.

Special education (p. 312): a teaching specialty for meeting the special educational needs of exceptional learners.

Stages of development (p. 290): predictable stages through which individuals pass as they progress through life.

State aid (p. 186): money given by a state to its cities and towns to provide essential services, including the operation of public schools.

State board of education (p. 178): the highest educational agency in a state, charged with regulating the state's system of education.

State department of education (p. 179): the branch of state government, headed by the chief state school officer, charged with implementing the state's educational policies.

Stereotyping (p. 259): the process of attributing behavioral characteristics to all members of a group; formulated on the basis of limited experiences with and information about the group, coupled with an unwillingness to examine prejudices.

Student-centered curriculum (p. 376): curricula that are organized around students' needs and interests.

Student diversity (p. 6): differences among students in regard to gender, race, ethnicity, culture, and socioeconomic status.

Student-mobility rates (p. 7): the proportion of students within a school or district who move during an academic year.

Student variability (p. 6): differences among students in regard to their developmental needs, interests, abilities, and disabilities.

Students at risk (p. 139): students whose living conditions and backgrounds place them at risk for dropping out of school.

Students with disabilities (p. 307): students who need special education services because they possess one or more of the following disabilities: learning disabilities, speech or language impairments, mental retardation, serious emotional disturbance, hearing impairments, orthopedic impairments, visual impairments, or other health impairments.

Subject-centered curriculum (p. 376): a curriculum that emphasizes learning an academic discipline.

Substitute teaching (p. 61): Temporary teachers who replace regular teachers absent due to illness, family responsibilities, personal reasons, or professional workshops and conferences.

Successful schools (p. 137): schools characterized by a high degree of student learning, results that surpass those expected from comparable schools, and steady improvement rather than decline.

Summative evaluation (p. 358): an assessment of student learning made for the purpose of assigning grades at the end of a unit, semester, or year and deciding whether students are ready to proceed to the next phase of their education.

Superintendent (p. 170): the chief administrator of a school district.

Synectics (p. 548): a method for "teaching" creativity through the use of metaphors and analogies.

T

Teach for America (p. 10): a program that enables recent college graduates without a teaching certificate to teach in districts with critical shortages of teachers and, after taking professional development courses and supervision by state and school authorities, earn a teaching certificate.

Teacher accountability (p. 30): society's expectations that teachers will adhere to high professional and moral standards and create effective learning environments for all students.

Teacher centers (p. 67): centers where teachers provide other teachers with instructional materials and new methods and where teachers can exchange ideas.

Teacher-leader (p. 475): a teacher who assumes a key leadership role in the improvement and/or day-to-day operation of a school.

Teacher-researcher (p. 479): a teacher who regularly conducts classroom research to improve his or her teaching.

Teacher-student ratio (p. 16): a ratio that expresses the number of students taught by a teacher.

Teacher supply and demand (p. 504): the number of school-age students compared to the number of available teachers; may also be projected based on estimated numbers of students and teachers.

Teachers' thought processes (p. 26): the thoughts that guide teachers' actions in classrooms. These thoughts typically consist of thoughts related to planning, theories and beliefs, and interactive thoughts and decisions.

Teaching certificate (p. 501): a license to teach issued by a state or, in a few cases, a large city.

Teaching contract (p. 208): an agreement between a teacher and a board of education that the teacher will provide specific services in return for a certain salary, benefits, and privileges.

Teaching simulations (p. 57): an activity in which teacher education students participate in role-plays designed to create situations comparable to those actually encountered by teachers.

Team teaching (p. 526): an arrangement whereby a team of teachers teaches a group of students equal in number to what the teachers would have in their self-contained classrooms.

Tech-prep programs (p. 404): an arrangement that enables students to prepare for the world of work by spending time at local businesses and industries during their last two years in high school; students learn to transfer knowledge and skills learned at school to the job setting.

Tenure (pp. 13, 209): an employment policy in which teachers, after serving a probationary period, retain their positions indefinitely and can be dismissed only on legally defensible grounds.

Third International Mathematics and Science Study (TIMSS) (p. 566): an international assessment of mathematics and science achievement among fourth-,

eighth-, and twelfth-grade students in forty-one nations.

Time on task (p. 345): the amount of time students are actively and directly engaged in learning tasks.

Title IX (p. 115): a provision of the 1972 Education Amendments Act prohibiting sex discrimination in educational programs.

Tort liability (p. 215): conditions that would permit the filing of legal charges against a professional for breach of duty and/or behaving in a negligent manner.

Tyler rationale (p. 375): a four-step model for curriculum development in which teachers identify purposes, select learning experiences, organize experiences, and evaluate.

V

Vertical equity (p. 189): an effort to provide equal educational opportunity within a state by providing different levels of funding based on economic needs within school districts.

Videoconferencing (p. 427): the use of computer-mounted video cameras to conduct two-way interactive conferences over the Internet.

Videodisc (p. 422): a twelve-inch plastic disk, each side of which holds about thirty minutes of motion video, or 54,000 frames of video; each frame can be frozen with a high degree of clarity.

Vocational-technical education (p. 403): schooling that prepares students for particular jobs or provides them with the basic skills and career awareness needed to enter the world of work.

Voucher system (p. 192): funds allocated to parents that they may use to purchase education for their children from public or private schools in the area.

W

Whole-language approach (p. 392): the practice of teaching language skills (listening, reading, and writing) as part of students' everyday experiences rather than as isolated experiences.

Within-class ability grouping (p. 341): the practice of creating small, homogeneous groups of students within a single classroom for the purpose of instruction, usually in reading or mathematics, at the elementary level.

Women's Educational Equity Act (WEEA) (p. 279): a 1974 federal law that guarantees equal educational opportunity for females.

World Wide Web (WWW) (p. 424): the most popular connection to the Internet; composed of home pages which users access through browser programs such as Netscape Communicator, Microsoft Internet Explorer, or America Online.

Name Index

Subject Index

Head Start Act Amendments (1994), 188
Health and wellness education, 152, 549
Health care services, 572
Hearing impairment, 307, 308
Hewlett-Packard, 524
Hidden curriculum, 296, 371–372
Hierarchy of needs, 316, 318
High authentic pedagogy, 344–345
Higher-order questions, 554
High School: A Report on Secondary Education in America (Boyer), 115
High school exit exams, 176
High-tech schools, percentage of, 181
Hispanic Americans, education and, 251, 263–264
Historical development of education, 96–116
  colonial era (1620–1750), 96–99
  compulsory education, effects of (1865–1920), 105–108
  general patterns of trends, 111
  postwar era (1945–2000), 110–116
  progressive era (1920–1945), 108–110
  revolutionary period (1750–1820), 99–101
  state-supported common schools (1820–1865), 101–105
History of Education Site, 84–85
HIV/AIDS, 152, 231–232
HIV education programs, 152
Holmes Group, 51–52, 67
Holmes Partnership, 52
Holt v. Sheldon, 231
Home education movement, 114
Homeless children, 144
Home-school communication systems, 423–424
Home schooling, 237–238
Home visits by teacher, debate over, 522–523
Homosexuality
  discrimination on basis of, 281–282
  due process in tenure and dismissal involving, 209
  revocation of certificate on basis of, 207
  same-sex harassment and, 235
Horn book, 97
Hortonville Joint School District No. 1 v. Hortonville Education Association, 211, 237
How Schools Shortchange Girls (AAUW), 279, 280
How to Develop a Professional Portfolio: A Manual for Teachers (Campbell et al), 63–64
HTML editors, 516
Hull House, 108
Human immunodeficiency virus/acquired immune deficiency syndrome (HIV/AIDS), 152, 231–232

Humanism, 93, 212
Humanistic psychology, 93
Hyman v. Green, 216
Hypermedia, 422–423, 517
HyperStudio (software), 476
IDEA, 307–309, 312–314, 320
  Amendments to (IDEA 97), 313
Identity, cultural, 252–253, 259–260
Identity vs. role diffusion stage, 300–301
IEP (Individualized education plan), 313–314, 328–330
Immediacy of teaching, 25
Immersion programs, 269
Immigrants, education of, 110, 388
Immigration Act (1882), 265
Immigration Act (1924), 265
In a Different Voice: Psychological Theory and Women's Development (Gilligan), 294
Inclusion, 317–322
  assistive technology and, 320–322
  collaborative consultation for, 317–320
  debate over, 315–316
  full, 315
  instructional strategies for, 331
  working with parents for, 320
Income, family
  access to computers and, 440–441
  dropout rate and, 139, 140
  early childhood program enrollment and, 129
Income taxes, 186
Independent study, 311
Indiana University, 256, 446
Indian Education Acts (1972, 1974), 115, 187, 267
Individualized education plan (IEP), 313–314, 328–330
  for gifted students, 311–312
Individual needs, learners' (*see* Learning needs)
Individual racism, 259
Individuals with Disabilities Education Act (IDEA), 307–309, 312–314, 320
  Amendments to (IDEA 97), 313
Indochina Migration and Refugee Assistance Act (1975), 115
Induction period, lack of, 461
Induction programs, 60–61
Inductive reasoning, 89
Industry, career opportunities in, 508
Inequities in school funding, correcting, 188–193
Influence of teachers, 7–9
Information processing, 355–356
"Information superhighway," 443
Information technology, importance in curriculum of, 564, 565
Ingraham v. Wright, 232
In My Own Voice: Multicultural Poets on Identity (software), 396–397

Inquiry-based curriculum, 387
Inquiry learning, 355–356
Inservice workshops/training, 67, 465
Institutional monopoly of services, 459–460
Institutional racism, 259
Institutions, schools as social, 131–137
Instruction
  computers and, 420–422
  linked with assessment, 358–359
  organizing and planning for, 348
  in Praxis framework for teaching, 357
  Instructional goals, 357–358
  Instructional materials and strategies for inclusion, 331
  multicultural, 276–277
Instructional methods, 351–356
  based on child development, 353–355
  based on learning new behaviors, 353
  based on peer-mediated instruction, 356
  based on thinking process, 355–356
Instructional reforms, 484
Integrated curriculum, 376–377
Integration of technology into teaching, 431
Integrative accelerative learning, 311
Intellectual ability, variation in, 319–323
Intellectual property, copyright laws on use of, 220–223
Intelligence(s), 302
  emotional, 128
  multiple, 303–305
  sensorimotor, 292
Intelligence testing, 302–303
Interactions, teacher-student, 337–338
Interactive compressed video technology, 53–54
Interactive multimedia, 422
Interactive teaching, 25–26
Interdependence, 336
"Interdistrict" transfer, 192
International Assessment on Educational Progress (IAEP), 566, 568
International Association for the Evaluation of Educational Achievement, 566
International education, 464–471, 564–571
  comparative education, 565–569
  lessons from other countries, 569–571
International Institute of Education, 393–394
International Institute on Education, 570
International Reading Association (IRA), 391, 392–393, 491
International Society for Technology in Education, 444
Internet, 424–427
  access to, for all schools, 442–443
  chat rooms on, 426–427
  copyright laws and, 222

doctrine of fair use and use of, 220
equalizing effect of using, 436
family involvement resources on, 524
growth of, 424, 425
job search on, 509–511
newsgroups on, 424–426
publishing on, 222–223
study on, 68
teachers uses of, 427–430
technology-related special education resources and curriculum materials on, 322
videoconferencing, 427
Internet-accessible electronic portfolio, 516–517
Internet Relay Chat (IRC) technology, 426
Internship programs, 60–61
Interpersonal domains, 479
Interpersonal intelligence, 304
Interpersonal skills, cooperative learning to strengthen, 343
Interprofessional case management, school-based, 155
Interstate Certification Agreement Contract, 503, 537
Interstate New Teacher Assessment and Support Consortium (INTASC), 50, 76
Intervention programs and resources, 153–155, 162–163, 302
Interview
admission, 8
job, 513–515
Intrapersonal intelligence, 304
Intrinsic motivation, 56
Intuition, knowing based on, 87
Inventorying your knowledge of children and youth, 42–43
Invisible Crisis: The Educational Needs of Asian Pacific American Youth, An, 266
IQ, 331
IQ tests, 303
Islam, African Americans practicing, 263
Isolation, professional and psychological, 41–42
James Madison High School: A Curriculum for American Students (Bennett), 115, 390
James Madison High School (New York), 413–414, 421
Japanese education, 568–569, 571
Japanese immigrants, 265
Japanese Secondary School: A Closer Look, The 571
Jeglin v. San Jacinto Unified School District, 225
Job-analysis approach, 48–50
Job Corps, 113
Job interview, 513–515
Job market, favorable, 506–507
Job opportunities, 13–16 (*see also* Teaching positions)

Job satisfaction, factors in, 515–516
Job search, 509–516
timetable checklist, 538
Job security, 13
Job stress, 16, 19
John Hancock Financial Services, 524
Jonesboro, Arkansas shootings, 225
Joplin Plan, 341
Journals, education, 495–496 (*see also specific journals*)
Journal writing, 39–40, 58–59
Junior high school, acceleration options in, 311
Justice, ethics of, 294
Juvenile vigilantism, 149
Karr v. Schmidt, 224
Keepers of the dream, teachers as, 33
Kennedy administration, 112
Kentucky Education Reform Act (KERA, 1990), 177
Kentucky Supreme Court, 177
KIDLINK, 426–427
Kids Count Data Book, 141
Kindergarten, 106–107
Knowledge
beliefs about, 85–86
epistemology and focus on, 87
essential, 41–46, 51, 277
of methods for applying educational theory and research, 43–46
to prepare students for global information age, 547–550
professional, 44–45, 463
self-knowledge, 41–42, 47, 95
of students, 42–43
of subject, 43, 44
Knowledge base, ways of viewing, 46–51
Knowledge construction in multicultural education, 273
Krizek v. Cicero-Stickney Township High School District No. 201, 212, 237
Kyoiku mama, 571
Labeling, 316–317, 331
Laboratory School, 109
Lab Pack, 222
Land-grant colleges, 105
Language(s)
culture embedded in, 253–256
foreign, 400–401, 410
with greatest number of speakers in U.S. after English, 254
literacy in, 547–548
Native American, 267, 268
Language arts, current trends in, 391–393
Language impairment, 307, 308
Language minority students, 258–259
Language patterns from culture, 254–256
Lanham Act (1941), 180
Larry P. v. Riles, 303
Latchkey children, 144, 300, 558

Latina women, teen pregnancy among, 151
Latin grammar schools, 96, 102
Latinos, education and, 139, 251, 263–264
Lau v. Nichols, 269
Law(s)
antidiscrimination, 207
compulsory school attendance, 384
copyright, 220–223
on educator's rights and responsibilities, 237, 238
English-only, 263
related to education, state legislature and, 177
special education, 312–314
Leaders, teachers as educational, 20, 115–116, 456–497
in charter schools, 560
contributions to educational research, 479–483
example of, 466–467
new leadership roles emerging, 474–479
professionalism in teaching and, 464–469
professional organizations for teachers and, 469–474, 483, 490–494
school effectiveness and, 138
for school restructuring and curriculum reform, 483–486
teaching as full profession, extent of, 459–464
Leadership in student interaction, 338
League of Professional Schools, 486
Learnball approach, 211
Learning, 554
accelerated, 480
action, 274
assessing students', difficulty of, 23–24
to become leader, 468
behaviorist conception of, 94
beliefs about, 83–84
computers and, 429–432
constructivist focus on processes of, 94–95
cooperative, 341–343, 352, 356
discovery, 355–356
distance, 54, 419
focus on student, 138
humanistic view of, 93
inquiry, 355–356
integrated curriculum for natural, 377
lifelong, 125, 465–468, 550
mastery, 353
as measure of school success, 137
problem-centered, 394–395
service, 128, 274–275
television and, 419
Learning centers, 340
Learning Channel, 28